CHEVROLET TRUCK SHOP MANUAL 1948-51 MODELS

●

FOREWORD

This manual is designed to provide the service man with complete information on the construction, operation, maintenance and repair of various units of the 1948-51 model Chevrolet trucks.

An effort has been made to produce a manual that will not only serve as a ready reference book for the experienced service man but also cover step-by-step procedure for the guidance of the less experienced man.

The Section Index on the title page enables the user to quickly locate any desired section. At the beginning of each section is a Table of Contents followed by an index listing the page on which each main subject begins. In those sections that cover more than one major subject, the Table of Contents gives the page number on which the coverage of the subject begins, and the detailed index of that subject appears on this page. This arrangement, we believe, will make it easy for the service man to locate the desired information.

Provision is made to enter references to any supplementary information received by the dealer in the form of *Service News* and *Service Bulletins*.

The Special Service Tools shown in this manual, or their equivalent, are necessary for the efficient servicing of Chevrolet trucks. All tools listed are available through Kent-Moore Organization, Inc., General Motors Building, Detroit 2, Michigan.

This manual should be kept in a handy place for ready reference. If properly used, it will enable the mechanic to better serve the owners of Chevrolet trucks and thereby build or maintain a reputation for reliable service.

●

CHEVROLET MOTOR DIVISION

General Motors Corporation
DETROIT, MICHIGAN

COPYRIGHT—1950
CHEVROLET MOTOR DIVISION
GENERAL MOTORS CORPORATION

Printed in U.S.A.

Reprinted with Permission of General Motors Corporation

SECTION	NAME	PAGE
0	UNIT SERIAL NUMBERS LOAD CAPACITY LUBRICATION	0-1
1	BODY	1-1
2	FRAME SHOCK ABSORBERS	2-1 2-3
3	FRONT SUSPENSION	3-1
4	REAR AXLE UNIVERSAL JOINTS REAR SPRINGS	4-1 4-50 4-59
5	BRAKES HYDROVAC	5-1 5-29
6	ENGINE FUEL SYSTEM COOLING SYSTEM CLUTCH	6-1 6-49 6-81 6-88
7	TRANSMISSION	7-1
8	FUEL AND EXHAUST	8-1
9	STEERING GEAR	9-1
10	WHEELS AND TIRES	10-1
11	CHASSIS SHEET METAL	11-1
12	ELECTRICAL SYSTEM	12-1

MODEL DESIGNATIONS

Throughout this book the different models are described as ½ ton, ¾ ton, 1 ton, 1½ ton and 2 ton, or as Cab-Over-Engine (C.O.E.), Forward Control and School Bus Chassis, but these descriptions do not appear on the vehicle. However, the model series number is affixed to each side of the engine hood of the (1949-51) trucks, while on 1948 models only, the model name designation appears. So that you will know what information in this book applies to the particular vehicle, the following list is given showing the model number appearing on the engine hood and the corresponding description in the book.

1948 Model Designation	1949-51 Model Number on Engine Hood	Description in Book
Thriftmaster	3100	½ ton
Thriftmaster	3600	¾ ton
Thriftmaster	3742	¾ ton Forward Control
Thriftmaster	3800	1 ton
Thriftmaster	3802	1 ton School Bus Chassis
None	3942	1 ton Forward Control
Loadmaster	4100, 4400	1½ ton
Loadmaster	4502	1½ ton School Bus Chassis
Loadmaster	5100, 5400, 5700	2 ton Cab-Over-Engine (C.O.E.)
Loadmaster	6100, 6400, 6500	2 ton
Loadmaster	6702	2 ton School Bus Chassis

UNIT SERIAL NUMBER LOCATIONS

For the convenience of servicemen when writing up certain business papers such as Application for Policy Adjustment, Product Information Reports, or reporting product failures in any way, we are showing below the location of the various unit numbers. These unit numbers and their prefixes are necessary on these papers for various reasons—such as, accounting, follow-up on production, etc.

The prefixes on certain units identify the plant in which the unit was manufactured, and thereby permits proper follow-up of the plant involved to get corrections made when necessary.

Always include the prefix in the serial number.

Radiator code and number located on the left rear of the top tank (fig. 1).

Generator serial and model number are located on a metal plate staked on the generator body just forward of armature terminal (fig. 2).

Ignition distributor serial and model number are located on the distributor breaker plate which is under distributor cap (fig. 3).

Engine serial number located on right side of engine on a boss just to the rear of the ignition distributor (fig. 4).

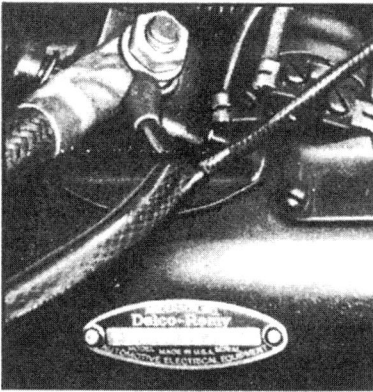

Starting motor serial and model number are located on starting motor body just below starter switch (fig. 5).

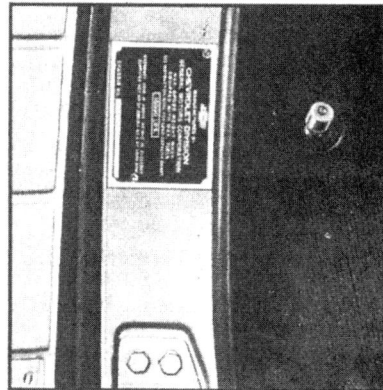

Vehicle serial number except F.F. cowl and Forward Control is located on left front body pillar between door hinges and is exposed when door is opened (fig. 6). F.F. cowl located on left cowl inner panel. Forward Control located on left side of instrument support.

Transmission serial number (three-speed) located on side of case at rear edge of cover (fig. 7).

Transmission serial number (four-speed) located on the rear right hand side of case (fig. 8).

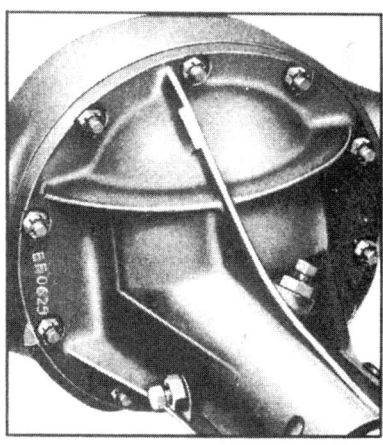

On ½ ton truck models the rear axle serial number is located on the right front of differential carrier flange (fig. 9).

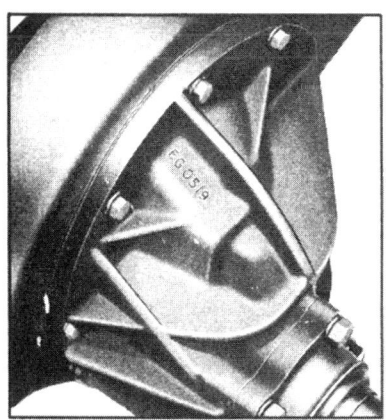

On the ¾ and 1 ton truck models the rear axle serial number is located on the front upper surface of the differential carrier to the right of the vertical rib (fig. 10).

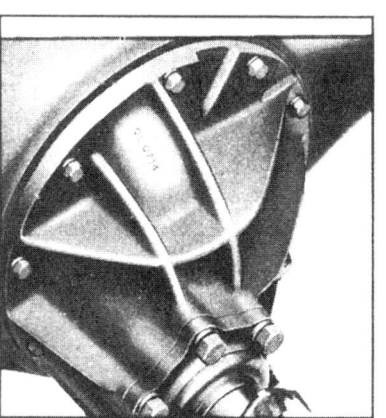

On 1½ ton C.O.E. and 2 Ton models the rear axle serial number is located on the top of the differential carrier, on right side between the two vertical ribs (fig. 11).

The serial number on the two-speed rear axle is located on top of the differential carrier to the rear of the pinion cage and toward the right side (fig. 12).

1948
LOAD CAPACITY CHART

MODEL			NOMINAL RATING	GROSS VEHICLE WEIGHT	TIRE SIZE AND PLY RATING		REQUIRED EQUIPMENT		REAR AXLE
TYPE	SERIES	WHEEL-BASE			FRONT	REAR	REAR SPRINGS	GOVERNED SPEED	
SEDAN DELIVERY	1508 FJ	116	— —	4000	6.00-16-4	6.00-16-4	8 leaf	—	4.11 or 3.73
					6.70-15-4	6.70-15-4			
				4100	6.70-15-6	6.70-15-6			
					6.00-16-6	6.00-16-6			
LIGHT DUTY	3100 FP	116	½ Ton	4200	6.00-16-6	6.00-16-6	8 leaf	—	4.11
					6.70-15-6	6.70-15-6			
				4500	6.50-16-6	6.50-16-6			
				*4600	15-6 or 8	15-6 or 8			
MEDIUM DUTY	3600 FR	125¼	¾ Ton	5200	15-6	15-6	2-stage, 7 leaf	—	4.57
					7.00-17-6	7.00-17-6	2-stage, 8 leaf		
				5400	15-8	15-8	2-stage, 7 leaf		
				*5800	7.00-17-8	7.00-17-8	2-stage, 8 leaf		
					7.50-17-8	7.50-17-8			
	3742 FT	125¼	¾ Ton	6200	15-6	15-6	8 leaf	—	
				6400	15-8	15-8			
				6600	7.00-17-6	7.00-17-6			
				*7000	7.00-17-8	7.00-17-8			
					7.50-17-8	7.50-17-8			
→	3800 FS	137	1 Ton	5700	7.00-17-6	7.00-17-6	2-stage, 8 leaf	—	5.14
				6100	7.00-17-8	7.00-17-8			
				6700	7.50-17-8	7.50-17-8			
				*8800	7.00-17-6	7.00-18-8 Dual	11 leaf		
	3942 FU	137	1 Ton	6700	7.00-17-6	7.00-17-6	8 leaf	—	
				7100	7.00-17-8	7.00-17-8*			
				7500	7.50-17-8	7.50-17-8†			
				*10000	7.00-18-8	7.00-18-8 Dual†	11 leaf		
HEAVY DUTY	4100 RJ	137	1½ Ton	7500	7.00-20-8	7.00-20-8	Heavy 11 leaf	—	6.17 or 5.43
				9500	6.50-20-6	6.50-20-6 Dual			
	4400 RK	161		*11000	7.00-20-8	7.00-20-8 Dual			
				*12500	7.50-20-8	7.50-20-8 Dual			6.17
	6100S RVS	137	1½ Ton Special Conventional	13000	7.50-20-8	7.50-20-8 Dual	Heavy 11 leaf and auxiliary, brake booster, and heavy duty frame.	•48 MPH	6.17 HD or 2 speed 6.13 & 8.10
	6400S RWS	161		*15000	7.50-20-8‡	8.25-20-10 Dual		•49 MPH	
					8.25-20-10	9.00-20-10 Dual		•52 MPH	
	6100 RV	137	2 Ton Conventional	13000	7.50-20-8	7.50-20-8 Dual		•48 MPH	
	6400 RW	161		*16000	8.25-20-10	8.25-20-10 Dual		•49 MPH	
					8.25-20-10	9.00-20-10 Dual		•52 MPH	
	5100S RPS	110	1½ Ton Special Cab-Over-Engine	13000	7.50-20-8	7.50-20-8 Dual		•48 MPH	
	5400S RRS	134		*15000	7.50-20-8‡	8.25-20-10 Dual		•49 MPH	
	5700S RSS	158			8.25-20-10	9.00-20-10 Dual		•52 MPH	
	5100 RP	110	2 Ton Cab-Over-Engine	13000	7.50-20-8	7.50-20-8 Dual		•48 MPH	
	5400 RR	134		*16000	8.25-20-10	8.25-20-10 Dual		•49 MPH	
	5700 RS	158			8.25-20-10	9.00-20-10 Dual		•52 MPH	
SCHOOL BUS CHASSIS	6702 RX	199	42 Pupils	13000	7.50-20-8	7.50-20-8 Dual	2-stage, heavy 11 leaf with brake booster and heavy duty frame.	35 MPH	
			48-52 Pupils	*15000	8.25-20-10	8.25-20-10 Dual			
	4502 RL	161	30 Pupils	10500	6.50-20-6	6.50-20-6 Dual	2-stage, heavy 11 leaf and heavy duty frame.		6.17 or 5.43
			36 Pupils	*12000	7.00-20-8	7.00-20-8 Dual			

*A plate is supplied with each vehicle showing chassis number and maximum Gross Vehicle Weight (GVW). These GVW ratings are reduced per above table when tires of a lesser capacity are used. Series FJ plate shows no GVW.

†Requires double-acting shock absorber and rear stabilizer equipment.

‡On 1½ Ton Special RPS, RRS, RSS, RVS and RWS Series, 8.25-20-10 ply rating tires are released as a Regular Production Option for the front with no allowable increase in the 15000 lb. GVW.

•Governed speed at 2800 RPM of engine.

*Requires double-acting shock absorber equipment.

The following extra ply rating tires are released as Regular Production Options for Front and Rear but with no allowable increase in GVW: 6.50-20-8, 7.00-20-10, 7.50-20-10, 8.25-20-12. These tires mount on the same wheels as the regular ply rating balloons of the corresponding sizes.

Never use an extra ply rating (high pressure) front with a balloon rear.

1949
LOAD CAPACITY CHART

MODEL			NOMINAL RATING	GROSS VEHICLE WEIGHT	TIRE SIZE AND PLY RATING		REQUIRED EQUIPMENT		REAR AXLE
TYPE	SERIES	WHEEL-BASE			FRONT	REAR	REAR SPRINGS	GOVERNED SPEED	
SEDAN DELIVERY	1508	GJ	115		4000	6.70-15-4	6.70-15-4	8 leaf		4.11 or 3.73
					4100	6.70-15-6	6.70-15-6			
LIGHT DUTY	3100	GP	116	½ Ton	4200	6.00-16-6	6.00-16-6	8 leaf		4.11
						6.70-15-6	6.70-15-6			
					4500	6.50-16-6	6.50-16-6			
					*4600	15-6 or 8	15-6 or 8			
MEDIUM DUTY	3600	GR	125¼	¾ Ton	5200	15-6	15-6	2 stage, 7 leaf		4.57 or 5.14
						7.00-17-6	7.00-17-6	2-stage, 8 leaf		
					5400	15-8	15-8	2-stage, 7 leaf		
					*5800	7.00-17-8	7.00-17-8	2-stage, 8 leaf		
						7.50-17-8	7.50-17-8			
	3742	GT	125¼	¾ Ton	6200	15-6	15-6	8 leaf		
					6400	15-8	15-8			
					6600	7.00-17-6	7.00-17-6			
					*7000	7.00-17-8	7.00-17-8			
						7.50-17-8	7.50-17-8			
	3800	GS	137	1 Ton	5700	7.00-17-6	7.00-17-6	2-stage, 8 leaf		5.14
					6100	7.00-17-8	7.00-17-8			
					6700	7.50-17-8	7.50-17-8			
					*8800	7.00-18-8	7.00-18-8 Dual	11 leaf		
	3942	GU	137	1 Ton	6700	7.00-17-6	7.00-17-6	8 leaf		
					7100	7.00-17-8	7.00-17-8★			
					7500	7.50-17-8	7.50-17-8†			
					*10000	7.00-18-8	7.00-18-8 Dual†	11 leaf		
HEAVY DUTY	4100	SJ	137	1½ Ton	7500	7.00-20-8	7.00-20-8	Heavy 11 leaf		6.17 or 5.43
					9500	6.50-20-6	6.50-20-6 Dual			
	4400	SK	161		*11000	7.00-20-8	7.00-20-8 Dual			
					*12500	7.50-20-8	7.50-20-8 Dual			6.17
	6100S	SVS	137	1½ Ton Special Conventional	13000	7.50-20-8	7.50-20-8 Dual		•48 MPH	
	6400S	SWS	161		*15000	7.50-20-8‡	8.25-20-10 Dual		•49 MPH	
						8.25-20-10	9.00-20-10 Dual		•52 MPH	
	6100	SV	137	2 Ton Conventional	13000	7.50-20-8	7.50-20-8 Dual	Heavy 11 leaf and auxiliary, brake booster, and heavy duty frame.	•48 MPH	6.17 HD or 2 speed 6.13 & 8.10
	6400	SW	161		*16000	8.25-20-10	8.25-20-10 Dual		•49 MPH	
						8.25-20-10	9.00-20-10 Dual		•52 MPH	
	5100S	SPS	110	1½ Ton Special Cab-Over-Engine	13000	7.50-20-8	7.50-20-8 Dual		•48 MPH	
	5400S	SRS	134		*15000	7.50-20-8‡	8.25-20-10 Dual		•49 MPH	
	5700S	SSS	158			8.25-20-10	9.00-20-10 Dual		•52 MPH	
	5100	SP	110	2 Ton Cab-Over-Engine	13000	7.50-20-8	7.50-20-8 Dual		•48 MPH	
	5400	SR	134		*16000	8.25-20-10	8.25-20-10 Dual		•49 MPH	
	5700	SS	158			8.25-20-10	9.00-20-10 Dual		•52 MPH	
SCHOOL BUS CHASSIS	6702	SX	199	42 Pupils	13500	7.50-20-8	7.50-20-8 Dual	2-stage, heavy 11 leaf with brake booster and heavy duty frame.	35 MPH	
				48-54 Pupils	*15000	8.25-20-10	8.25-20-10 Dual			
	4502	SL	161	30 Pupils	10500	6.50-20-6	6.50-20-6 Dual	2-stage, heavy 11 leaf and heavy duty frame.		6.17 or 5.43
				36 Pupils	*12000	7.00-20-8	7.00-20-8 Dual			
	3802	GS	137	16 Pupils	7600	7.50-17-10	7.50-17-10	9 leaf		5.14

*A plate is supplied with each vehicle showing chassis number and maximum Gross Vehicle Weight (GVW). The maximum GVW Rating as warranted by the chassis manufacturer shall include the truck chassis with lubricants, water and full tank or tanks of fuel, plus the weight of the cab or driver's compartment, body, special chassis and body equipment, and payload. These GVW Ratings are reduced per above table when tires of a lesser capacity are used. Series GJ plate shows no GVW.

‡On 1½ Ton Special SPS, SRS, SSS, SVS and SWS Series, 8.25-20-10 ply rating tires are released as a regular Production Option for the front with no allowable increase in the 15000 lb. GVW.

†Requires double-acting shock absorber and rear stabilizer equipment.

•Governed speed at 2800 RPM of engine.

★Requires double-acting shock absorber equipment.

The following extra ply rating tires are released as Regular Production Options for front and rear but with no allowable increase in GVW: 6.50-20-8, 7.00-20-10, 7.50-20-10, 8.25-20-12. These tires mount on the same wheels as the regular ply rating balloons of the corresponding sizes.

Never use an extra ply rating (high pressure) front with a balloon rear.

1950 LOAD CAPACITY CHART

MODEL			NOMINAL RATING	GROSS VEHICLE WEIGHT	TIRE SIZE AND PLY RATING		REQUIRED EQUIPMENT		REAR AXLE
TYPE	SERIES	WHEEL-BASE			FRONT	REAR	REAR SPRINGS	GOVERNED SPEED	
SEDAN DELIVERY	1508 HJ	115		4000	6.70-15-4	6.70-15-4	8 leaf		
				4100	6.70-15-6	6.70-15-6			
LIGHT DUTY	3100 HP	116	½ Ton	4200	6.00-16-6	6.00-16-6	8 leaf		4.11
					6.70-15-6	6.70-15-6			
				4500	6.50-16-6	6.50-16-6			
				*4600	15-6 or 8	15-6 or 8			
MEDIUM DUTY	3600 HR	125¼	¾ Ton	5200	15-6	15-6	2-stage, 7 leaf		4.57 or 5.14
					7.00-17-6	7.00-17-6			
				5400	15-8	15-8			
				*5800	7.00-17-8	7.00-17-8	2-stage, 8 leaf		
					7.50-17-8	7.50-17-8			
	3742 HT	125¼	¾ Ton	6200	15-6	15-6	8 leaf		5.14
				6400	15-8	15-8			
				6600	7.00-17-6	7.00-17-6			
				*7000	7.00-17-8	7.00-17-8			
					7.50-17-8	7.50-17-8			
	3800 HS	137	1 Ton	5700	7.00-17-6	7.00-17-6	2-stage, 8 leaf		5.14
				6100	7.00-17-8	7.00-17-8			
				6700	7.50-17-8	7.50-17-8			
				*8800	7.00-18-8	7.00-18-8 Dual	2-stage, 8 leaf & aux.▲		
	3942 HU	137	1 Ton	6700	7.00-17-6	7.00-17-6	8 leaf		
				7100	7.00-17-8	7.00-17-8★			
				7500	7.50-17-8	7.50-17-8†			
				*10000	7.00-18-8	7.00-18-8 Dual†	2-stage, 8 leaf & aux.▲		
HEAVY DUTY	4100 TJ	137	1½ Ton	7500	7.00-20-8	7.00-20-8	Heavy 11 leaf		6.17 or 5.43
				9500	6.50-20-6	6.50-20-6 Dual			
				*11000	7.00-20-8	7.00-20-8 Dual			
	4400 TK	161		*12500	7.00-20-8	7.00-20-10 Dual			6.17
					7.50-20-8	7.50-20-8 Dual			
	6100S TVS	137	1½ Ton Special Conventional	13000	7.50-20-8	7.50-20-8 Dual	Heavy 11 leaf and auxiliary, brake booster, and heavy duty frame.	•54 MPH	6.17 HD or 2 speed 6.13 & 8.10
	6400S TWS	161		*15000	7.50-20-8‡	8.25-20-10 Dual		•56 MPH	
					8.25-20-10	9.00-20-10 Dual		•59 MPH	
	6100 TV	137	2 Ton Conventional	13000	7.50-20-8	7.50-20-8 Dual		•54 MPH	
	6400 TW	161		*16000	7.50-20-8‡	8.25-20-10 Dual		•56 MPH	
					8.25-20-10	9.00-20-10 Dual		•59 MPH	
	5100S TPS	110	1½ Ton Special Cab-Over-Engine	13000	7.50-20-8	7.50-20-8 Dual		•54 MPH	
	5400S TRS	134		*15000	7.50-20-8‡	8.25-20-10 Dual		•56 MPH	
	5700S TSS	158			8.25-20-10	9.00-20-10 Dual		•59 MPH	
	5100 TP	110	2 Ton Cab-Over-Engine	13000	7.50-20-8	7.50-20-8 Dual		•54 MPH	
	5400 TR	134		*16000	7.50-20-8‡	8.25-20-10 Dual		•56 MPH	
	5700 TS	158			8.25-20-10	9.00-20-10 Dual		•59 MPH	
SCHOOL BUS CHASSIS	6702 TX	199	42 Pupils	13500	7.50-20-8	7.50-20-8 Dual	2-stage, heavy 11 leaf with brake booster and heavy duty frame	35 MPH unless specified otherwise on order	
			48-54 Pupils	*15000	8.25-20-10	8.25-20-10 Dual			
	4502 TL	161	30 Pupils	10500	6.50-20-6	6.50-20-6 Dual	2-stage, heavy 11 leaf and heavy duty frame.		6.17 or 5.43
			36 Pupils	*12000	7.00-20-8	7.00-20-8 Dual			
	3802 HS	137	16 Pupils	7600	7.50-17-10	7.50-17-10	9-leaf & brake booster		5.14

*A plate is supplied with each vehicle showing chassis number and maximum Gross Vehicle Weight (GVW). The maximum GVW rating as warranted by the chassis manufacturer shall include the truck chassis with lubricants, water and full tank or tanks of fuel, plus the weight of the cab or driver's compartment, body, special chassis and body equipment, and payload. These GVW ratings are reduced per above table when tires of a lesser capacity are used. Series HJ plate shows no GVW.

‡On 1½ Ton Special and 2 Ton Series 8.25-20-10 ply rating tires are released as a Regular Production Option for the front with no allowable increase in the GVW.

†Requires double-acting shock absorber and rear stabilizer equipment.

•Governed speed at 3200 RPM of engine, 6.17:1 axle.

★Requires double-acting shock absorber equipment.

▲Brake booster equipment mandatory.

The following extra ply rating tires are released as Regular Production Options for front and rear but with no allowable increase in GVW: 6.50-20-8, 7.00-20-10, 7.50-20-10, 8.25-20-12. These tires mount on the same wheels as the regular ply rating balloons of the corresponding sizes.

Never use an extra ply rating (high pressure) front with a balloon rear.

1951
LOAD CAPACITY CHART

TYPE	SERIES	WHEEL-BASE	NOMINAL RATING	GROSS VEHICLE WEIGHT	MINIMUM TIRES - FRONT	MINIMUM TIRES - REAR	REQUIRED R.P.O. EQUIPMENT
SEDAN DELIVERY	1508 JJ	115		§ 4000	6.70-15-4	6.70-15-4	
				4100	6.70-15-6	6.70-15-6	
LIGHT DUTY	3100 JP	116	½ Ton	§ 4200	6.00-16-6	6.00-16-6	
				* 4800	6.00-16-6	6.50-16-6	
MEDIUM DUTY	3600 JR	125¼	¾ Ton	§ 5400	15-6	15-6	
				* 5800	7.00-17-6	7.00-17-8	2-stage, 8-leaf rear spring
	3742 JT	125¼	¾ Ton	§ 6200	15-6	15-6	
				6600	7.00-17-6	7.00-17-6	
				* 7000	7.00-17-6	7.00-17-8	
	3800 JS	137	1 Ton	§ 6200	7.00-17-6	7.00-17-8	
				7000	7.00-17-6	7.50-17-8	
				* 8800	7.00-18-8	7.00-18-8 Dual	2-stage, 8-leaf rear spring and auxiliary, and hydrovac
	3942 JU	137	1 Ton	§ 6700	7.00-17-6	7.00-17-6	
				7100	7.00-17-6	7.00-17-8	Double acting rear shock absorbers
				7500	7.00-17-6	7.50-17-8	Above plus stabilizer
				*10000	7.00-18-8	7.00-18-8 Dual	Above plus 2-stage, 8-leaf rear spring and auxiliary, and hydrovac
HEAVY DUTY	4100 UJ	137	1½ Ton	§10000	6.50-20-6	6.50-20-6 Dual	
				11000	6.50-20-6	7.00-20-8 Dual	
	4400 UK	161		12500	6.50-20-6	7.00-20-10 Dual	11-leaf rear spring & aux., hydrovac, and on 4100, heavy duty frame
				14000	7.00-20-8	7.50-20-8 Dual	Above plus 8-leaf front spring
	5100S UPS	110	1½ Ton Special Cab-Over-Engine	§14000	7.50-20-8	7.50-20-8 Dual	
	5400S URS	134		*15000	7.50-20-8	8.25-20-10 Dual	
	5700S USS	158					
	6100S UVS	137	1½ Ton Special Conventional				
	6400S UWS	161					
	6500S UYS	179					
	5100 UP	110	2 Ton Cab-Over-Engine	§14000	7.50-20-8	7.50-20-8 Dual	
	5400 UR	134		*16000	7.50-20-8	8.25-20-10 Dual	
	5700 US	158					
	6100 UV	137	2 Ton Conventional				
	6400 UW	161					
	6500 UY	179					
SCHOOL BUS CHASSIS	3802 Plus RPO 329A	JS 137	16 Pupils	*§7600	7.50-17-8	7.50-17-10	9-leaf rear spring and hydrovac
	4502 UL	161	30 Pupils	§10500	6.50-20-6	6.50-20-6 Dual	
			36 Pupils	*12000	6.50-20-6	7.00-20-8 Dual	
	6702 UX	199	42 Pupils	§13500	7.50-20-8	7.50-20-8 Dual	
			48-54 Pupils	*15000	7.50-20-8	8.25-20-10 Dual	

*A plate is supplied with each vehicle showing chassis number and maximum Gross Vehicle Weight (GVW). The maximum GVW rating includes the truck chassis with lubricants, water and full tank or tanks of fuel, plus the weight of the cab or driver's compartment, body, and special chassis and body equipment, and payload. These GVW ratings are reduced per above table when tires of a lesser capacity are used. Series JJ plate shows no GVW.

§Base trucks, tires shown included in base price.

Extra ply rating and/or oversize tires and equipment are available with no increase in gross vehicle weight rating.

SECTION 0

GENERAL LUBRICATION

CONTENTS OF THIS SECTION

	Page
General Lubrication	0-1
Service News Reference	0-12

INDEX

	Page		Page
Engine Lubrication	0-1	Distributor	0-4
Oil Gauge	0-1	Rear Axle and Transmission	0-5
Lubrication	0-2	Recommended Lubricants	0-5
First 500 Miles	0-2	Multi-Purpose Gear Lubricants	0-5
After 500 Miles	0-2	Lubricant Additions	0-5
Fall—Winter—Spring—Summer	0-2	Lubricant Changes	0-5
Maintaining Oil Level	0-2	Universal Joint	0-5
When to Change Crankcase Oil	0-2	Front Wheel Bearings	0-5
Crankcase Dilution	0-3	Rear Wheel Bearings	0-6
Abnormal Conditions	0-3	Spring Shackles	0-6
Water in Crankcase	0-4	Brake and Clutch Pedals	0-6
Corrosion	0-4	Steering Gear	0-6
S.A.E. Viscosity Number	0-4	Gear Shift Control Housing	0-6
Viscosity Grades	0-4	Shock Absorber	0-6
Water Pump	0-4	Hydrovac	0-6
Carburetor Accelerating Pump	0-4	General Note	0-6
Starting Motor	0-4	Chassis Lubrication	0-6
Generator	0-4	Body Lubrication	0-7
		Lubrication Charts	0-8

GENERAL LUBRICATION

The selection of the proper lubricant and its correct application at regular intervals does much to increase the life and operation of all moving parts of the vehicle. Consequently, it is important that the correct grade of oil or grease, as noted in the following pages, be used.

ENGINE LUBRICATION

Proper selection of the oil to be used will add much to the performance, reliability, economy and long life of the engine.

It is imperative that the recommended light oils be used in the engine during the break-in period. Light oils assure a better breaking in of the engine as they assure ease of starting, prompt flow of a sufficient quantity of oil to the bearings, less friction between moving parts, less wear of moving parts, etc.

Oil Gauge

When starting a cold engine, it will be noted that the oil gauge on the instrument panel registers a high oil pressure. As the engine warms up, the pressure will drop until it reaches a point where changes to higher speeds will raise the pressure very little, if at all.

If the oil pressure registers abnormally high after the engine is thoroughly warmed up, an inspection should be made to ascertain if the oil lines and passages are plugged up.

Lubrication First 500 Miles

The engine crankcase of all new trucks is filled with a light body breaking-in oil and it is recommended that this oil be used only during the first 500 miles.

At the end of the first 500 miles, the crankcase should be drained — when hot — and refilled to the proper level with the recommended oil.

Lubrication After 500 Miles

After the first 500 miles the crankcase oil should be selected to give the best performance under the climatic and driving conditions in the territory in which the vehicle is driven.

Fall-Winter-Spring

During the colder months of the year, an oil which will permit easy starting at the lowest atmospheric temperature likely to be encountered, should be used.

When the crankcase is drained and refilled, the crankcase oil should be selected, not on the basis of the existing temperature at the time of the change, but on the lowest temperature anticipated for the period during which the oil is to be used.

Unless the crankcase oil is selected on the basis of viscosity or fluidity at the anticipated temperature, difficulty in starting will be experienced at each sudden drop in temperature.

The viscosity grade of crankcase oil will, therefore, depend upon the climatic conditions under which the vehicle will operate. The grades best suited for use in an engine at the various temperatures are shown in the following table.

If you anticipate that the lowest atmospheric temperature will be	Use the grade indicated
Not lower than 32°F.	S.A.E. 20W or S.A.E. 20
As low as 10°F.	S.A.E. 20W
As low as minus 10°F.	S.A.E. 10W
Below minus 10°F	S.A.E. 10W plus 10% kerosene

S.A.E. 10W oil plus 10% kerosene is recommended only for those territories where the temperature falls below 10 degrees below zero for protracted periods.

Figure 1 shows the data in the above table as it would appear on a thermometer—the lowest temperature at which the indicated grades of oil will permit easy starting.

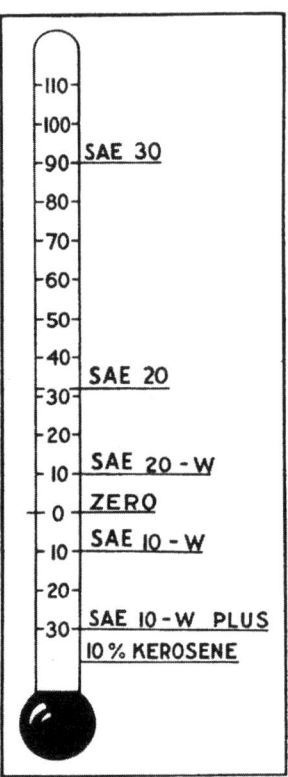

Fig. 1—Lowest Starting Temperature for Oils Indicated

NOTE: When in doubt use the lighter grade of oil. The use of S.A.E. 20W is recommended rather than S.A.E. 20 if temperatures are anticipated to drop to freezing.

Summer

The use of S.A.E. 20W or S.A.E. 20 during the summer months will permit better all around performance of the engine than will the heavier body oils, with no appreciable increase in oil consumption.

If S.A.E. 20 or S.A.E. 20W oil is not available, S.A.E. 30 oil may be used if it is expected that temperatures will be consistently above 90 degrees F.

Maintaining Oil Level

The oil gauge rod (fig. 2) is marked "Full" and "Add Oil." These notations have broad arrows pointing to the level lines. The oil level should be maintained between the two lines, neither going above the "Full" line nor under the "Add Oil" line.

Check the oil level frequently and add oil when necessary. Always be sure the crankcase is full before starting on a long drive.

When To Change Crankcase Oil

Oils have been greatly improved, driving conditions have changed and improvements in engines, such as the crankcase ventilating system,

GENERAL LUBRICATION 0-3

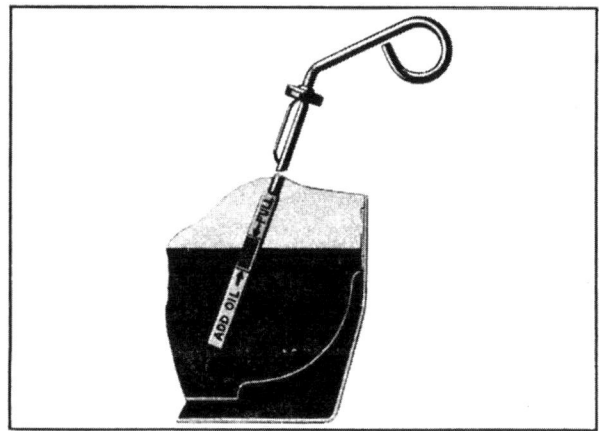

Fig. 2—Oil Gauge Rod

have greatly lengthened the life of good lubricating oils. However, to insure continuation of best performance, low maintenance cost and long engine life, it is necessary to change the crankcase oil whenever it becomes contaminated with harmful foreign materials. Under normal driving conditions draining the crankcase and refilling with fresh oil every 2000 to 3000 miles is recommended.

Under the driving conditions described in the following paragraphs, it may become necessary to drain the crankcase oil more frequently.

Frequent long runs at high speed, or continuous driving with heavy loads, with the resultant high engine operating temperatures, may oxidize the oil and may result in the formation of sludge and varnish. While no definite drain periods can be recommended under these conditions, they should be more frequent than under normal driving conditions.

Driving over dusty roads or through dust storms introduces abrasive material into the engine. Carburetor air cleaners decrease the amount of dust that may enter the crankcase. The frequency of draining depends on severity of dust conditions and no definite draining periods can be recommended, but should be more frequent than under normal driving conditions.

Short runs in cold weather, such as city driving and excessive idling, does not permit thorough warming up of the engine and water may accumulate in the crankcase from condensation of moisture produced by the burning of the fuel. Water in the crankcase may freeze and interfere with proper oil circulation. It also promotes rusting and may cause clogging of oil screens and passages. Under normal driving conditions this water is removed in the form of vapor by the crankcase ventilator. However, if water accumulates, it should be removed by draining the crankcase as frequently as may be required.

It is always advisable to drain the crankcase only after the engine has become thoroughly warmed up or reached normal operating temperature. The benefit of draining is, to a large extent, lost if the crankcase is drained when the engine is cold, as some of the suspended foreign material will cling to the sides of the oil pan and will not drain out readily with the cold, slower moving oil.

Crankcase Dilution

Probably the most serious phase of engine oil deterioration is that of crankcase dilution which is the thinning of the oil by fuel vapor leaking by pistons and rings and mixing with the oil.

Leakage of fuel, or fuel vapors, into the oil pan mostly occurs during the "warming up" period when the fuel is not thoroughly vaporized and burned.

Automatic Control Devices to Minimize Crankcase Dilution

The Chevrolet engine is equipped with automatic devices which aid greatly in minimizing the danger of crankcase dilution.

Rapid warming up of the engine is aided by the thermostatic water temperature control which automatically prevents circulation of water in the cooling system until it reaches a pre-determined temperature.

Thermostatic heat control on the exhaust manifold which, during the warming up period, automatically directs the hot exhaust gases against the center of the intake manifold, greatly aids in proper vaporization of the fuel.

Sparing use of the choke reduces danger of raw or unvaporized fuel entering the combustion chamber and leaking into the oil pan.

An efficient crankcase ventilating system drives off fuel vapors and aids in the evaporation of the raw fuel and water which may find its way into the oil pan.

Control By Truck Owners Under Abnormal Conditions

Ordinarily the above automatic control devices will minimize or eliminate the danger of crankcase dilution. However, there are abnormal conditions of service when the truck owners must aid in the control of crankcase dilution.

Short runs in cold weather, such as city driving and excessive idling do not permit the thorough warming up of the engine nor the efficient operation of automatic control devices. It is recommended that the oil be changed more often when the truck is subjected to this type of operation.

Poor mechanical condition of the engine, such as scored cylinders, poor ring fit, sloppy or loose pistons, faulty valves and poor ignition will increase crankcase dilution.

Poor fuels which contain portions hard to ignite and slow to burn will increase crankcase dilution.

WATER IN CRANKCASE

Serious lubrication troubles may result in cold weather by an accumulation of water in the oil pan. This condition is, as a rule, little understood by the truck owner. To demonstrate the chief cause of water in the oil pan, hold a piece of cold metal near the end of the exhaust pipe of the engine and note the rapid condensation and collection of drops of water on it. The exhaust gases are charged with water vapor and the moment these gases strike a cold surface, they will condense, forming drops of water.

A slight amount of these gases pass the pistons and rings, even under the most favorable conditions, and cause the formation of water in the oil pan, in a greater or lesser degree, until, the engine becomes thoroughly warm, the crankcase will no longer act as a condenser and all of these gases will pass out through the crankcase ventilator system.

Short runs in cold weather, such as city driving, will aggravate this water forming condition.

CORROSION

Practically all present day gasolines contain a small amount of sulphur which, in its natural form, is harmless. This sulphur, however, when it burns, forms a gas, a small portion of which is likely to leak past pistons and rings and reacting with water when present in the oil pan forms a very corrosive acid. The more sulphur in the gasoline the greater the danger from this type of corrosion. This is a condition which cannot be wholly corrected, but it may be reduced to a minimum by proper care of the engine.

As long as the gases and internal walls of the crankcase are hot enough to keep water vapor from condensing, no harm will result. However, when the engine is run in low temperatures, moisture will collect and unite with the gases formed by combustion resulting in an acid formation. The acid thus formed is likely to cause serious etching or pitting which will manifest itself in excessively rapid wear on piston pins, camshaft bearings and other moving parts of the engine, oftentimes causing the owner to blame the car manufacturer or the lubricating oil when in reality the trouble may be traced back to the character of fuel used, or a condition of the engine such as excessive blowby or improper carburetor adjustment.

S.A.E. VISCOSITY NUMBERS

The viscosity of a lubricant is simply a measure of its body or fluidity. The oils with the lower S.A.E. numbers are lighter and flow more readily than do oils with the higher numbers.

The S.A.E. numbers constitute a classification of lubricants in terms of viscosity or fluidity, but with no reference to any other characteristic or property.

These S.A.E. numbers have been adopted by practically all oil companies and no difficulty should be experienced in obtaining the proper grade of lubricant to meet seasonal requirements.

VISCOSITY GRADES OF OIL

The S.A.E. Viscosity Numbers constitute a classification for crankcase lubricating oils in terms of viscosity only. Viscosity numbers without an additional symbol are based on the viscosity at 210°F. Viscosity numbers with the additional "W" are based on the viscosity at 0°F. The viscosity of oils included in this classification for use in crankcases shall not be less than 39 SUS at 210°F. Other factors of oil character or quality are not considered.

SAE Viscosity Number	Viscosity Range, Saybolt Univ. Sec.			
	At 0° F		At 210° F	
	Minimum	Maximum	Min.	Max.
10-W	6000 (Note A)	Less than 12000	—	—
20-W	12000 (Note B)	Less than 48000	—	—
20	—	—	45	Less than 58
30	—	—	58	Less than 70
40	—	—	70	Less than 85
50	—	—	85	Less than 110

Note A: Minimum Viscosity at 0° F. can be waived provided viscosity at 210° F. is not below 40 Saybolt Seconds Universal.

Note B: Minimum Viscosity at 0° F. can be waived provided viscosity at 210° F. is not below 45 Saybolt Seconds Universal.

WATER PUMP

The water pump is of the ball bearing type, lubricated at the time of manufacture and is permanently sealed. This type pump requires no further or additional lubrication.

CARBURETOR ACCELERATING PUMP
(1948-49) Except C.O.E. and Forward Control

Every 5000 miles, remove the dust cover and saturate the felt ring on the carburetor pump lever shaft with light oil or engine oil.

STARTING MOTOR

On 1948 models with oil cup, lubricate every 1000 miles with a few drops of light oil, or engine oil. Starting motors on (1949-51) and some 1948 models have an aluminum end frame with an oilless bearing and do not require lubrication.

GENERATOR

Every 1000 miles put a few drops of a light oil, or engine oil, in the 2 oil cups.

DISTRIBUTOR

Lubricant cup located on side of housing is filled with chassis lubricant. Turn cup down one turn every 1,000 miles. Distributor cap should be removed every 5,000 miles, then remove rotor and place a few drops of SAE 10 engine oil on felt wicking in top of cam. Apply a small amount of petroleum jelly on distributor cam surface by holding a clean cloth which has been soaked in jelly against it while cranking starter.

REAR AXLE AND TRANSMISSION

The lubrication requirements for heavy duty hypoid truck axles differs somewhat from the passenger car hypoid axle. The truck operates under the most severe lubrication conditions in low gear under heavy load, while the passenger car operates under the most severe lubrication conditions at high speed.

Recommended Lubricants

Rear Axles—S.A.E. 90 "Multi-Purpose" gear lubricant.

Two-Speed Rear Axles—S.A.E. 90 "Multi-Purpose" gear lubricant.

Transmissions—S.A.E. 90 Straight Mineral Oil gear lubricant.
S.A.E. 90 "Multi-Purpose gear lubricant.

CAUTION: Straight Mineral Oil gear lubricants must not be used in Hypoid rear axles or two-speed rear axles.

The S.A.E. 90 viscosity grade is recommended for year round use. However, when extremely low temperatures are encountered for protracted periods during the winter months, the S.A.E. 80 viscosity grade may be used.

"Multi-Purpose" Gear Lubricants

Gear lubricants that will satisfactorily lubricate truck hypoid rear axles have been developed and are commonly referred to as "Multi-Purpose" gear lubricants.

These lubricants can also be satisfactorily used in truck transmissions, steering gears, and universal joints requiring a fluid lubricant.

"Multi-Purpose" gear lubricants must be manufactured under carefully controlled conditions and the lubricant manufacturer must be responsible for the satisfactory performance of his product. His reputation is the best indication of quality.

Lubricant Additions

The lubricant level in the axle and transmission housings should be checked periodically.

It is recommended that any additions required to bring up the lubricant level be made using the same type lubricant already in the housing.

When checking lubricant level in transmission or rear axle the unit being checked should be at operating temperature. With unit at operating temperature the lubricant should be level with bottom of the filler plug hole. If the lubricant level is checked with the unit cold the lubricant level should be ½ inch below the filler plug hole.

Lubricant Changes

Seasonal changes of the lubricant are not required. When refilling is necessary, refill with lubricants recommended above.

UNIVERSAL JOINT

Universal joints are of two types—the enclosed type which uses bushings in place of needle bearings and receives lubrication from the transmission. Additional lubrication is not necessary. This type is used on ½ and ¾ ton vehicles. The universal joint housing should be filled through the pipe plug hole for initial lubrication after a repair operation.

The second type is of needle bearing construction, equipped with lubrication fittings and should be lubricated with the same type of lubricant used in the transmission. This type universal joint is used on the rear propeller shaft of the ¾ ton vehicle and on front and rear of all other truck models.

CAUTION: Under no circumstances should any of the soap type lubricants such as chassis lubricant, fibrous universal joint lubricants, etc., be used in lubricating either the enclosed bushing type universal or the needle bearing type.

Propeller shaft slip joints are also fitted with a lubrication fitting and should be lubricated with chassis lubricant.

FRONT WHEEL BEARINGS

It is necessary to remove the wheels to lubricate the bearings. The bearing assemblies should be cleaned before repacking with lubricant. Do not pack the hub between the inner and outer bearing assemblies or the hub caps, as this excessive lubrication results in the lubricant working out into the brake drums and linings.

Front wheels of all truck models except the Cab-Over-Engine, the 1½ ton school bus and the 2 ton heavy duty trucks are equipped with ball bearings and should be packed with a high melting point front wheel bearing lubricant.

Front wheels of Cab-Over-Engine, 1½ ton school bus and 2 ton heavy duty trucks are equipped with "Barrel" type roller bearings and should be packed with a soft smooth lubricant. Fibrous or viscous type lubricants must not be used.

The proper adjustment of front wheel bearings is one of the important service operations that has a definite bearing on safety. Improperly adjusted front wheel bearings cause increased tire wear, lack of steering stability, and a tendency of the truck to wander or shimmy. Therefore, it is important that the wheel and tire assembly be removed from the hub when making front wheel bearing adjustments. This eliminates the heavy drag of wheel and tire and enables the workman to perform a much more accurate adjustment. For adjustment procedure see Front Wheel Bearings—Adjust, Sec. 3.

REAR WHEEL BEARINGS

The rear wheel bearings receive their lubrication from the rear axle.

SPRING SHACKLES

The spring shackles are equipped with pressure gun lubrication fittings and should be lubricated with lubricant recommended under "Chassis Lubrication."

BRAKE AND CLUTCH PEDALS

The brake and clutch pedals on the C.O.E. and Forward Control are equipped with pressure gun lubrication fittings. On the other truck models, only the brake pedal is equipped with a pressure gun lubrication fitting; the lubricant so applied lubricates both the brake pedal and the clutch pedal.

The brake idler lever on the C.O.E. and Forward Control is equipped with a pressure gun lubrication fitting. Lubricate with chassis lubricant every 1,000 miles.

STEERING GEAR

The steering gear is filled at the factory with a special all-season gear lubricant. Seasonal change of this lubricant is unnecessary and the housing should not be drained. Whenever required, additions should be made using a lubricant which, at low temperatures, is fluid and will not "channel" or cause "hard steering" and which will provide satisfactory lubrication under extreme summer conditions. Steering gear lubricants are marketed by many oil companies and either "Multi-Purpose" or "Universal" gear lubricants are satisfactory to use.

The pipe plug is installed in its particular location in the steering gear housing to prevent over-lubrication, generally occasioned by the use of a pressure gun. Over-lubrication of this unit might result in forcing lubricant up the steering gear tube to the horn button and steering wheel.

GEARSHIFT CONTROL HOUSING

This mechanism, lubricated at the factory, is well protected and should not require further lubrication. However, should the shifting effort become noticeably greater, remove the cap on the gearshift control housing cover and fill housing with soft, smooth grease.

SHOCK ABSORBER

The shock absorbers used on 1948-49 models should be kept filled with a low viscosity (light body) shock absorber fluid that has a pour test not higher than 30° below zero.

The same fluid is used both summer and winter and will have similar operating characteristics the year round.

The shock insulation fluid recommended should have a viscosity of from 70 to 80 seconds at 100°F (Saybolt Universal) and should not exceed 975 to 1000 seconds at 20° F. This type of fluid is carried by all Chevrolet dealers.

NOTE: Do not, under any circumstances, use a shock insulation fluid heavier in viscosity or body than that recommended above. Heavy body fluids are detrimental to the proper functioning of the unit.

On 1950-51 models, shock absorbers are standard equipment on front and rear of 3100, 3600 and 3700 series and on front only on 3800 and 3900 series. These shock absorbers are non-adjustable direct acting bayonet type, consisting of three concentric tubes known as the pressure tube, reservoir tube and dust shield or outer tube. These shock absorbers are permanently sealed and require no maintenance other than replacement if necessary.

HYDROVAC

The Hydrovac unit is equipped with a lubrication plug in the closed end of the shell approximately ½" from the bottom of the cylinder. One ounce of Bendix Vacuum Cylinder Oil should be added at 10,000 mile intervals or each six month period especially prior to the start of cold weather.

This oil is necessary to facilitate oiling of the vacuum piston leather. Oiling of the leather is necessary to prevent piston drag and possible bending of the piston rod.

GENERAL NOTE

Cab-Over-Engine trucks are provided with removable floor pans for easy access to the engine compartment.

To lubricate the steering gear and generator front and rear bearings, stand pipes are provided which are readily accessible after raising the upper half of the front cowling.

CHASSIS LUBRICATION

For chassis lubrication, consult the lubrication charts. Figures 3, 4, 5 and 6 show the points to be lubricated and how often the lubricant should be applied.

The term "chassis lubricant" as used in this manual, describes a semi-fluid lubricant designed for application by commercial pressure gun equipment. It is composed of mineral oil (300 to 500 seconds Saybolt Universal viscosity at 100° F) combined with approximately 8% soap, or soaps, which are insoluble in water.

BODY LUBRICATION

Normal use of a truck causes metal-to-metal movement at certain points in the cab or panel body. Noise, wear and improper operation at these points will result when a protective film of lubricant is not provided.

Many service stations do not consider body lubrication a part of a normal lubrication job; therefore, body lubrication is often neglected.

The following points should be lubricated occasionally:

Door Hinges (Oil Hole)..............Engine Oil
Door Hold Open Spring........Graphite Grease
Door Latch........................Engine Oil
Panel Model L. H. Rear Door Lock
    Rod Handle Shaft and Catches......Engine Oil
Panel Model Rear Door Check.......Engine Oil
Seat Adjuster Slides...........Graphite Grease
Seat Regulator Pulleys..............Engine Oil
Cowl Ventilator Linkage and Hinges..Engine Oil
Hood Hinge and Support............Engine Oil

GENERAL LUBRICATION 0-8

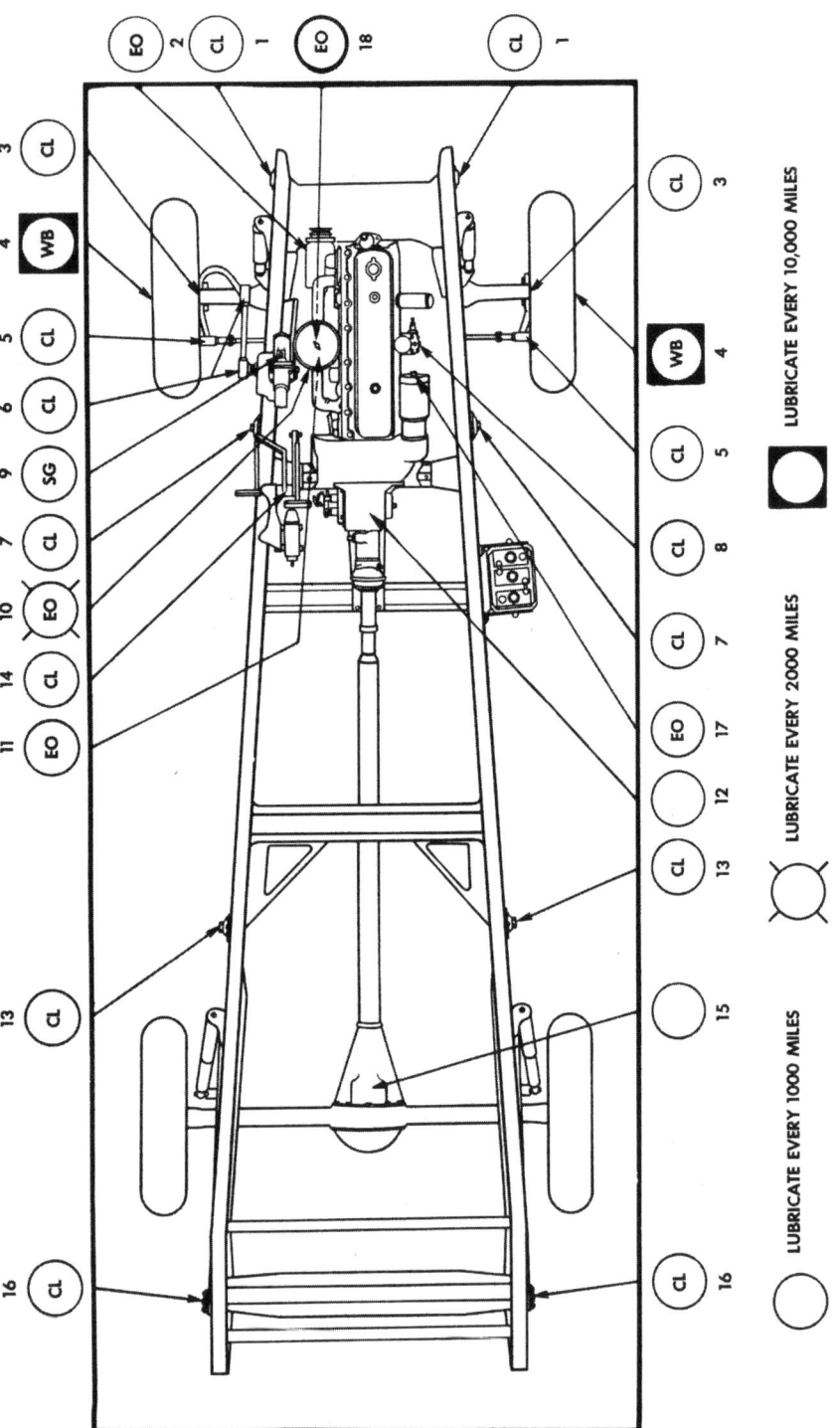

Fig. 3—½ Ton Lubrication Chart

Points of Lubrication

1. Front Spring Shackle (2 each side)............ 1,000 miles
2. Generator (2 oil cups)............................. 1,000 miles
3. King Pin (2 each side)............................. 1,000 miles
4. Front Wheel Bearings............................. 10,000 miles
5. Tie Rod (1 each side).............................. 1,000 miles
6. Steering Connecting Rod (1 each end)...... 1,000 miles
7. Front Spring Bolt (1 each side)................. 1,000 miles
8. Distributor (1 cup).................................. 1,000 miles
9. Steering Gear... 1,000 miles
10. Air Cleaner.. 2,000 miles
11. Throttle Bell Crank................................. 1,000 miles
12. Transmission... 1,000 miles
13. Rear Spring Bolt (1 each side)................. 1,000 miles
14. Brake Pedal Shaft................................... 1,000 miles
15. Rear Axle.. 1,000 miles
16. Rear Spring Shackle (2 each side) (1948).. 1,000 miles
17. Starting Motor (1 oil cup) (1948).............. 1,000 miles
18. Carburetor Accelerating Pump Shaft (1948-49).. 5,000 miles

Lubricant Key

CL Chassis Lubricant
EO Light Engine Oil
WB Wheel Bearing Lubricant
SG Steering Gear Lubricant

GENERAL LUBRICATION 0-9

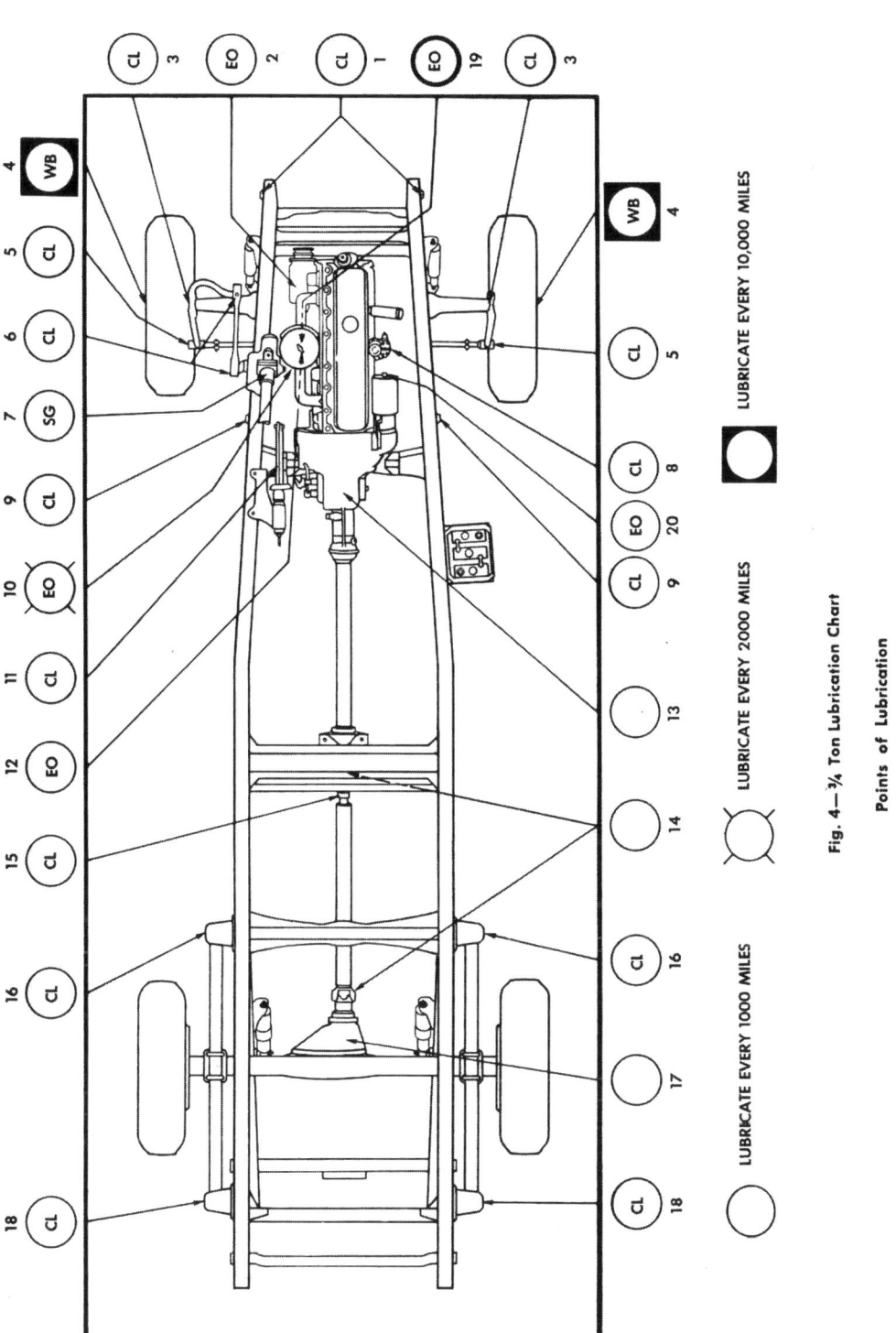

Fig. 4—¾ Ton Lubrication Chart

Points of Lubrication

1. Front Spring Shackle (2 each side)	1,000 miles	
2. Generator (2 oil cups)	1,000 miles	
3. King Pin (2 each side)	1,000 miles	
4. Front Wheel Bearings	10,000 miles	
5. Tie Rod (1 each side)	1,000 miles	
6. Steering Connecting Rod (1 each end)	1,000 miles	
7. Steering Gear	1,000 miles	
8. Distributor (1 cup)	1,000 miles	
9. Front Spring Bolt (1 each side)	1,000 miles	
10. Air Cleaner	2,000 miles	
11. Brake Pedal	1,000 miles	
12. Throttle Bell Crank	1,000 miles	
13. Transmission	1,000 miles	
14. Universal Joints (1 each)	1,000 miles	
15. Universal Joint Sleeve Yoke	1,000 miles	
16. Rear Spring Bolt (1 each side)	1,000 miles	
17. Rear Axle	1,000 miles	
18. Rear Spring Shackle (2 each side)	1,000 miles	
19. Carburetor Accelerating Pump Shaft (1948-49)	5,000 miles	
20. Starting Motor (1 oil cup) (1948)	1,000 miles	

Lubricant Key

CL   Chassis Lubricant   WB   Wheel Bearing Lubricant
EO   Light Engine Oil   SG   Steering Gear Lubricant

GENERAL LUBRICATION 0-10

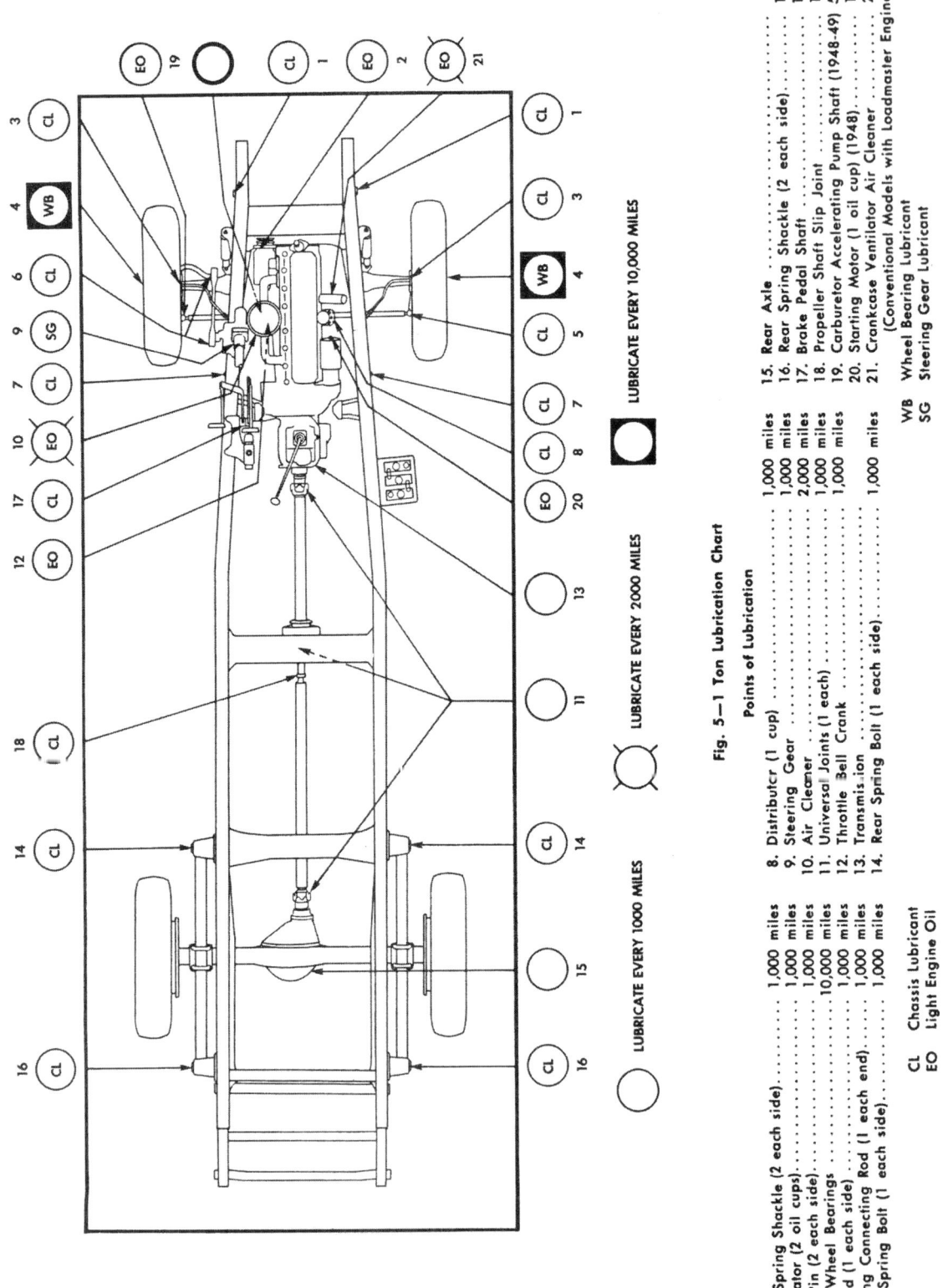

Fig. 5—1 Ton Lubrication Chart

Points of Lubrication

1. Front Spring Shackle (2 each side) .... 1,000 miles
2. Generator (2 oil cups) .... 1,000 miles
3. King Pin (2 each side) .... 1,000 miles
4. Front Wheel Bearings .... 10,000 miles
5. Tie Rod (1 each side) .... 1,000 miles
6. Steering Connecting Rod (1 each end) .... 1,000 miles
7. Front Spring Bolt (1 each side) .... 1,000 miles
8. Distributor (1 cup) .... 1,000 miles
9. Steering Gear .... 1,000 miles
10. Air Cleaner .... 2,000 miles
11. Universal Joints (1 each) .... 1,000 miles
12. Throttle Bell Crank .... 1,000 miles
13. Transmission .... 1,000 miles
14. Rear Spring Bolt (1 each side) .... 1,000 miles
15. Rear Axle .... 1,000 miles
16. Rear Spring Shackle (2 each side) .... 1,000 miles
17. Brake Pedal Shaft .... 1,000 miles
18. Propeller Shaft Slip Joint .... 1,000 miles
19. Carburetor Accelerating Pump Shaft (1948-49) .. 5,000 miles
20. Starting Motor (1 oil cup) (1948) .... 1,000 miles
21. Crankcase Ventilator Air Cleaner .... 2,000 miles
(Conventional Models with Loadmaster Engine)

CL Chassis Lubricant
EO Light Engine Oil
WB Wheel Bearing Lubricant
SG Steering Gear Lubricant

GENERAL LUBRICATION 0-11

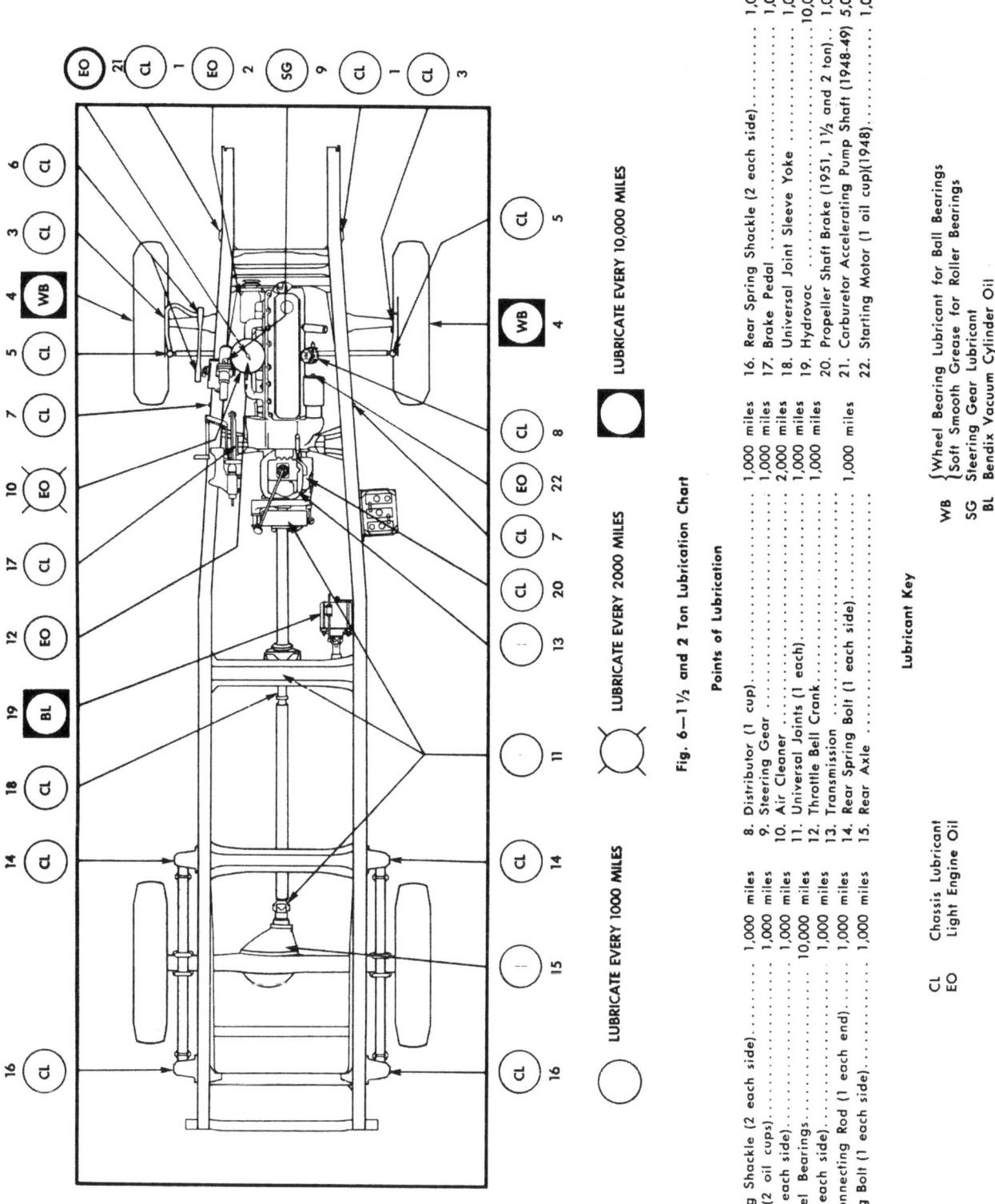

Fig. 6—1½ and 2 Ton Lubrication Chart

Points of Lubrication

1. Front Spring Shackle (2 each side).......... 1,000 miles
2. Generator (2 oil cups).......... 1,000 miles
3. King Pin (2 each side).......... 1,000 miles
4. Front Wheel Bearings.......... 10,000 miles
5. Tie Rod (1 each side).......... 1,000 miles
6. Steering Connecting Rod (1 each end).......... 1,000 miles
7. Front Spring Bolt (1 each side).......... 1,000 miles
8. Distributor (1 cup).......... 1,000 miles
9. Steering Gear.......... 1,000 miles
10. Air Cleaner.......... 2,000 miles
11. Universal Joints (1 each).......... 1,000 miles
12. Throttle Bell Crank.......... 1,000 miles
13. Transmission
14. Rear Spring Bolt (1 each side).......... 1,000 miles
15. Rear Axle
16. Rear Spring Shackle (2 each side).......... 1,000 miles
17. Brake Pedal.......... 1,000 miles
18. Universal Joint Sleeve Yoke.......... 1,000 miles
19. Hydrovac.......... 10,000 miles
20. Propeller Shaft Brake (1951, 1½ and 2 ton).......... 1,000 miles
21. Carburetor Accelerating Pump Shaft (1948-49).......... 5,000 miles
22. Starting Motor (1 oil cup)(1948).......... 1,000 miles

Lubricant Key

CL   Chassis Lubricant
EO   Light Engine Oil
WB   {Wheel Bearing Lubricant for Ball Bearings / Soft Smooth Grease for Roller Bearings}
SG   Steering Gear Lubricant
BL   Bendix Vacuum Cylinder Oil

SERVICE NEWS REFERENCE

Month	Page No.	Subject

# SECTION 1

CAB AND BODY

CONTENTS OF THIS SECTION

	Page
Cab and Body	1- 1
Service News Reference	1-23

INDEX

	Page		Page
Cab	1- 1	Lock Cylinder—Replace	1-13
General Description	1- 1	Lock Assembly—Replace	1-13
Mounting	1- 1	Checks and Adjustment	1-14
Replacement	1- 2	Lock Operation	1-14
Body Glass	1- 3	Handle Operation	1-14
Windshield	1- 3	Striker Plate	1-14
Rear Window	1- 5	Remote Control	1-15
Doors	1- 5	Seats	1-15
Removal	1- 5	Cleaning	1-15
Adjustment	1- 6	Cushion and Seat Back	1-15
Hold Open Device	1- 6	Seat Frame—Replace	1-15
Opening Weatherstrip	1- 7	Seat Adjusters	1-16
Door Ventilator Assembly	1- 8	Cowl Ventilator	1-17
Adjustment	1- 8	Windshield Wipers	1-17
Replacement	1- 9	Motor—Replace	1-18
Glass Replacement	1- 9	Adjustment	1-18
Door Window Glass—Replace	1-10	Water Leaks	1-18
Glass Run Channel—Replace	1-11	Panel Bodies	1-19
Window Regulator—Replace	1-11	Rear Door Lock	1-19
Rain Deflector—Replace	1-12	Suburban Carryall	1-20
Outer Reveal Moulding—Replace	1-12	Side Window Replacement	1-20
Handle and Lock	1-12	End Gate Assembly Hinge	1-20
Outside Handle—Replace	1-12	End Gate Assembly Lock	1-21
		End Gate Assembly Cable	1-22

GENERAL DESCRIPTION

CAB

A UNISTEEL cab, the most durable type of all automotive body structures, is used. In this UNISTEEL cab, the four major panels (the cowl, the back, the top, and the floor), with numerous reinforcing panels and braces, are all welded into one permanently rigid, integral unit.

Mounting

The 1948 cab is flexibly mounted at three points (fig. 1). The front corners just ahead of the door hinge pillar, are bolted through rubber shims "A" to mounting brackets projecting outward from the frame side rails. At the rear it is supported by a shackle type mount. In this rear mount a wide faced bracket "B" bolts to the bottom of the cab immediately below the back panel center strainer and carries the lower pin of the shackle. An inverted "U" shaped bracket "C" which contains the eye for the upper shackle pin is bolted to the frame cross member "D" that spans the frame. Two shackle bars "E" connect the two brackets and rubber bushings are used on the shackle pins for insulation. With the cab mounted in this manner, stresses resulting from frame deflection while driving over rough roads are transmitted to the shackle bars and there absorbed. To prevent excessive freedom in the mountings, there are soft rubber stabilizer bumpers "F" attached to the rear corners of the cab directly over the frame side rails. Lightly compressed between the cab and the rail, they prevent any possibility of side sway or rocking motion in the cab.

The 1949-51 cab is flexibly mounted at four

CAB AND BODY 1-2

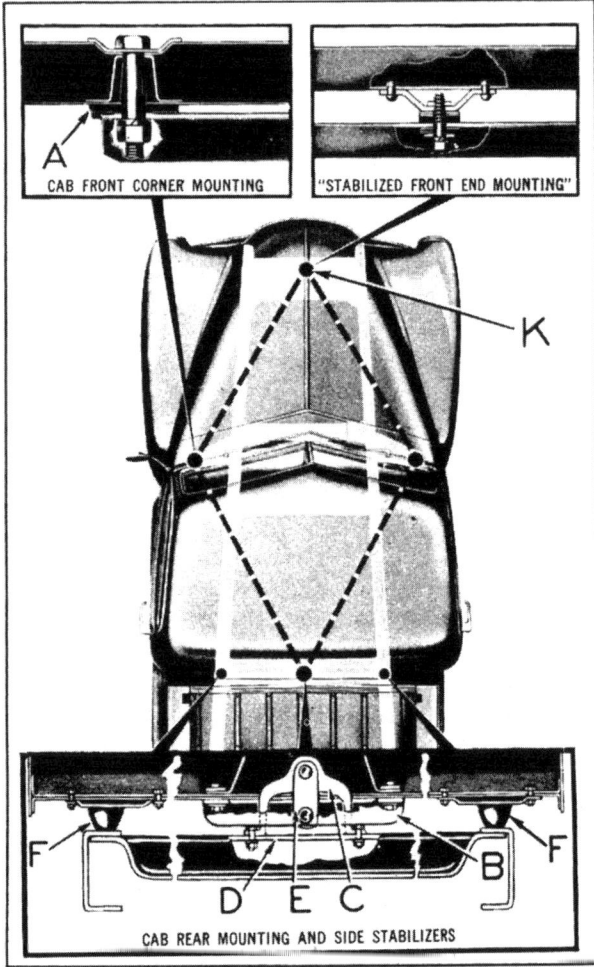

Fig. 1—Cab Mounting (1948) Models

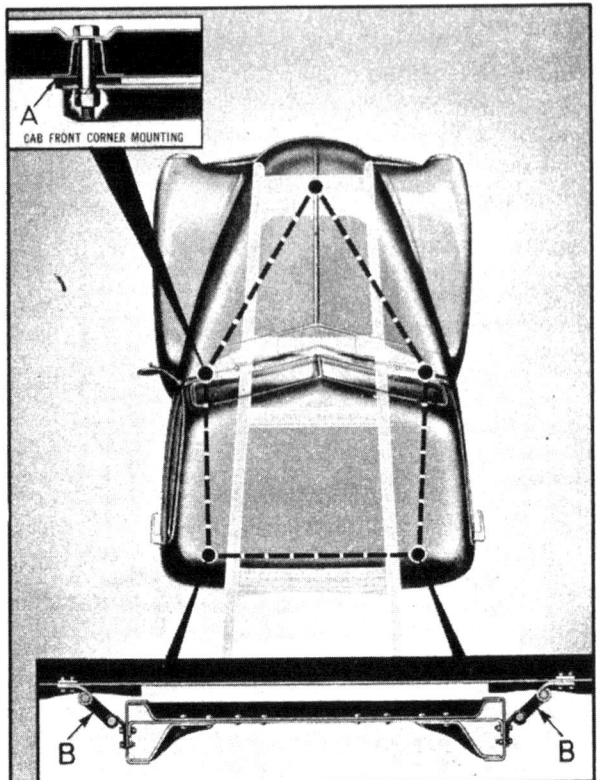

Fig. 2—Cab Mounting (1949-51) Models

points (fig. 2). The front corners just ahead of the door hinge pillars are bolted through rubber shims "A" to mounting brackets projecting outward from the frame side rails. At each rear corner, the cab is supported by a shackle type mount "B." Eye-shaped brackets are bolted to both the frame and the cab underbody near the door lock pillar. Shackles, similar to those used in spring suspension, connect the eye brackets. The shackle studs are mounted in rubber bushings at the eyes.

Mounting Replacement (1948 Models)

1. Remove the hex head nuts attaching front of cab to the frame side rail mounting brackets "A" (fig. 1).
2. Remove two hex head bolts attaching rear cab mounting to frame cross member.
3. Raise the rear of the cab body up approximately 1½" for clearance to remove mounting.
4. Remove the four hex head cap screws attaching rear cab mounting to the cab.
5. Remove rear cab mounting.
6. Inspect shackle rubber bushings and if necessary replace.
7. Remove the two hex head nuts attaching the shackle bars to the brackets.
8. Slide the wide base bracket and the shackle pin out of the shackle bar.
9. Slide the upper shackle pin out of the "U" shaped bracket.
10. Slide bushings off the shackle pins and out of the brackets as necessary.
11. Assemble the mounting and tighten the shackle bar to bracket nuts securely
12. Place mounting in position under cab and install mounting to cab cap screws and tighten securely.
13. Lower rear of cab and install mounting to cross member bolts and tighten securely.
14. Replace cab front mounting bolts and tighten securely.

Mounting—Replacement (1949-51 Models)

1. Remove the hex head nuts, washers and bolts attaching front of cab to frame side rail mounting brackets. Heads of bolts are inside the cab.
2. Raise the rear of cab body far enough to take the rear mounts out of compression.
3. Remove the rear mount or mounts that are to be replaced. This is accomplished by removing the two bolts with lockwashers attaching the mounting bracket to the cab underbody,

and then removing the two nuts, lockwashers and bolts attaching the rear mounting bracket to the frame.

4. Remove the nuts from the shackle studs and remove shackle link and the brackets from the studs.
5. Press the bushings out of the brackets and replace as necessary.
6. Assemble the shackle mounting and tighten the nuts on the studs securely.
7. Place mount in position under cab and install mounting to cab bolts, with lockwashers, and mounting to frame bolts, lockwashers, and nuts.
8. Lower the cab.
9. Check the clearance between the floor panel cross support and the frame at the rear mount. This distance should be $4\tfrac{9}{64}''$ to $5\tfrac{3}{64}''$ for all models except C.O.E. On C.O.E. models, this distance is measured from the floor panel cross support to the top of the subframe and should be $\tfrac{3}{4}''$ to $1\tfrac{3}{16}''$.

NOTE: If necessary, shim between the cab underbody and the mounting bracket, using shim No. 3690031, to bring this dimension within limits.

10. Replace cab front mounting bolts and tighten securely.
11. Check the clearance between the bottom of floor and top of frame at front mounting locations. This distance should be $1\tfrac{53}{64}''$ to $1\tfrac{57}{64}''$ for all models except C.O.E. On C.O.E. models, this distance is measured from bottom of floor to top of subframe front support bracket and should be $1\tfrac{43}{64}''$ to $1\tfrac{47}{64}''$. If necessary, shim between mounting support spacer and subframe support bracket.

BODY GLASS

Windshield Glass

The windshield is the divided type and is retained in the windshield opening by a moulded rubber weatherstrip. This weatherstrip is sealed in the windshield opening and sealed to the windshield glass.

When replacing a cracked windshield glass, it is very important that the cause of the glass breakage be determined and the condition corrected before a new glass is installed. Otherwise, it is highly possible that a small obstruction or high spot somewhere around the windshield opening will continue to crack or break the newly installed windshield; especially when the strain on the glass caused by this obstruction is increased by such conditions as wind pressures, extremes of temperature, motion of the vehicle, etc.

The procedure for replacing the windshield applies to only half of the windshield assembly. This may be either side or, when necessary, the complete windshield assembly.

1. Before removing the windshield, protect the paint finish inside of the cab. Mask around the windshield opening and outside, lay a suitable covering across the hood and fender.
2. Remove the garnish moulding from the windshield side being replaced; then, remove the center division moulding.

NOTE: The garnish moulding is made in three pieces; right hand, left hand, and center. The windshield glass rubber weatherstrip is one piece which includes both sides and center. The glass is held in a channel within the weatherstrip (fig. 3).

3. Run a putty knife around the rubber weatherstrip on the outside and inside to break the seal. Use care in this operation.
4. With the palm of the hand against the inside surface of the glass, carefully force the assembly outward until the lip of the rubber channel has been removed from the pinchweld flanges of the opening. Hand pressures should be applied alternately at the upper and lower corners at the outer or pillar edge.

Fig. 3—Cross Section—Windshield Weatherstrip

NOTE: It may be necessary to raise inner lip of weatherstrip and break seal between outer edge of pinchweld and weatherstrip.

5. Next, loosen the seal of weatherstrip cement between the glass and rubber weatherstrip. Disengage the weatherstrip from the glass and lift glass out of opening (fig. 4).

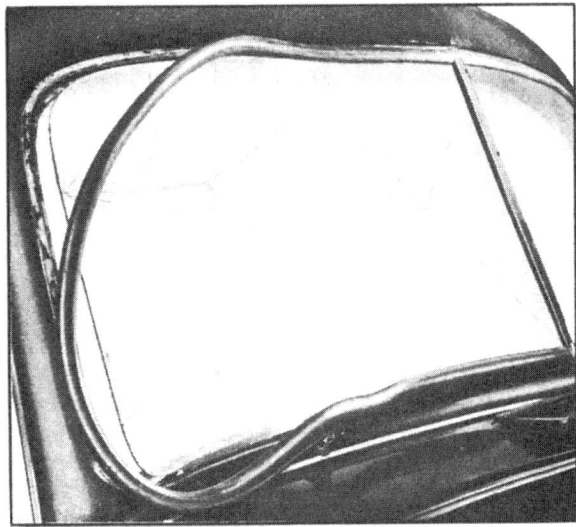

Fig. 4—Removing Glass from Weatherstrip

6. Using a scraper and oleum spirits, remove all old cement and dry thoroughly. Also clean rubber weatherstrip.
7. Inspect the contour of the windshield opening, especially at the point where the glass cracked, for any obstructions or irregularities. The cause, whatever it may be, of the windshield glass cracking should be corrected before a new glass is installed.
8. Apply a continuous $3/16''$ bead of 3-M "Weatherstrip Adhesive" along the outside rabbet pinchweld, completely around the windshield opening (fig. 5).
9. Install windshield glass into windshield rubber weatherstrip, working the rubber channel over the edge of the glass.
10. Lay a piece of cord in pinchweld slot of rubber weatherstrip to facilitate pulling this lip over the pinchweld during installation.
11. While applying pressure against outside of glass, pull inner lip of weatherstrip over pinchweld by pulling in on end of cord (fig. 6).
12. After assembly is in position, seal the weatherstrip to the glass and in the opening using 3-M "Weatherstrip Adhesive" in a sealing gun.
    a. Seal between outer lip of rubber weatherstrip and windshield glass completely around the opening.

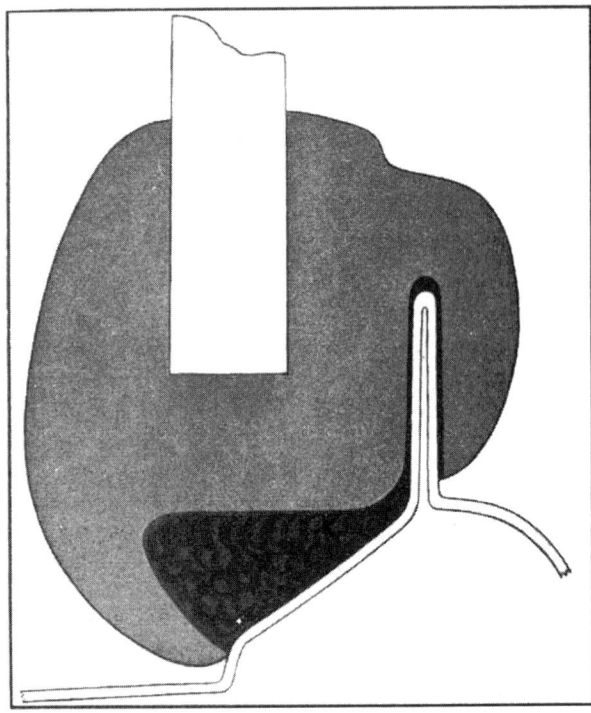

Fig. 5—Cross Section Showing Sealer Application

   b. Seal under the outer lip of rubber weatherstrip where it rests on the body metal completely around the opening.
   c. Seal under inner pinchweld lip of rubber channel completely around the opening.
   d. Remove any excess "adhesive" by using oleum spirits sparingly.
13. Re-install garnish mouldings and draw all screws up securely. Remove the masking tape.

Fig. 6—Installing Windshield

Rear Window

The moulded rubber weatherstrip around the rear window is one piece and has three channels or grooves. A cross section of this weatherstrip out of the window is shown at "A" (fig. 7).

The outside channel of the weatherstrip fits over the edges of the body panel around the rear window opening. The inside channel fits the outer edge of the rear window glass. The third channel, which is at the rear, is for a special moulded rubber weatherstrip retainer of triangular cross section. This retainer is installed after the weatherstrip and glass have been assembled in the opening. "B," figure 7, shows a cross section of the weatherstrip assembled.

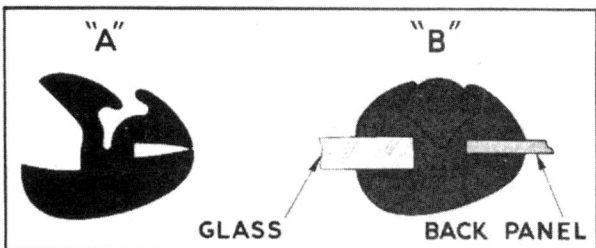

Fig. 7—Cross Section—Cab Rear Window Weatherstrip

No sealing compound or cement of any type is used at any point in the installation of a rear window glass.

To replace a cab rear window, proceed as follows:

1. Using a pointed tool, raise one end of the weatherstrip retainer until it is far enough out to take hold of by hand. Then pull retainer out of its channel all around the window.

2. From inside the cab, carefully push the window glass out through the rear of the opening.

   NOTE: The weatherstrip may remain in the window opening during removal of glass. To remove weatherstrip, merely pull it off the edges of the body panels.

3. Inspect the cab inner and outer flanges making sure they are true and that there are no irregularities around the opening. Any irregularities must be corrected.

4. Assemble the weatherstrip to the opening making sure the outer channel of weatherstrip is firmly seated on the edges of the body panel all around the opening.

5. Start one end of the glass into its channel in the weatherstrip. Using a pointed tool, follow around the rear lip of the glass channel so it bears against the rear surface of the glass (fig. 8).

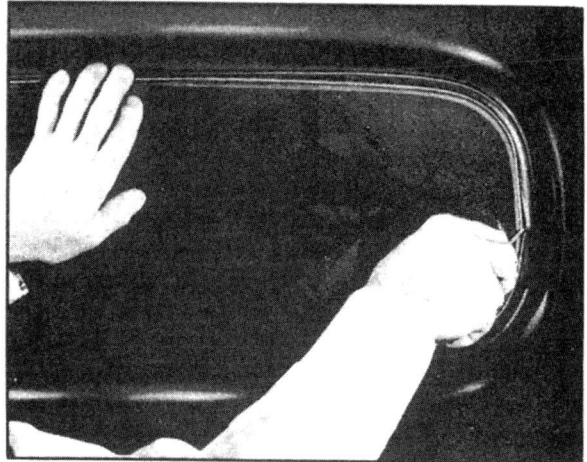

Fig. 8—Installing Cab Rear Glass

NOTE: Care should be used in this operation not to chip the edge of the glass. A pointed wooden tool, if available, should be used.

6. Feed one end of the weatherstrip retainer into the handle of special tool J-2189 (fig. 9) and out through the end which spreads the weatherstrip channel.

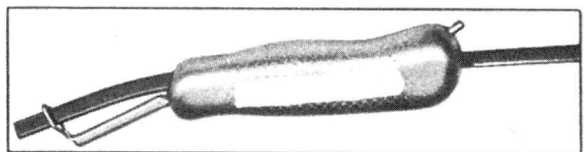

Fig. 9—Weatherstrip Retainer Tool

7. Starting at the bottom center, insert the end of the tool and end of retainer in channel, tapered part of the retainer toward the glass.

8. While holding the tool firmly, with spreading end in channel, follow around the channel spreading it open and feeding retainer into the opening until the full length of the retainer has been fed into the channel (fig. 10). The ends of the retainer should join at the bottom center.

NOTE: Care must be used when installing the weatherstrip retainer to prevent stretching it since this may result in the ends drawing apart after assembly.

DOORS

Removal

Component sub-assemblies of cab doors, such as door glass, ventilator assembly, regulator, lock, etc., can be replaced without removing doors from cab. However, the doors can be removed, if neces-

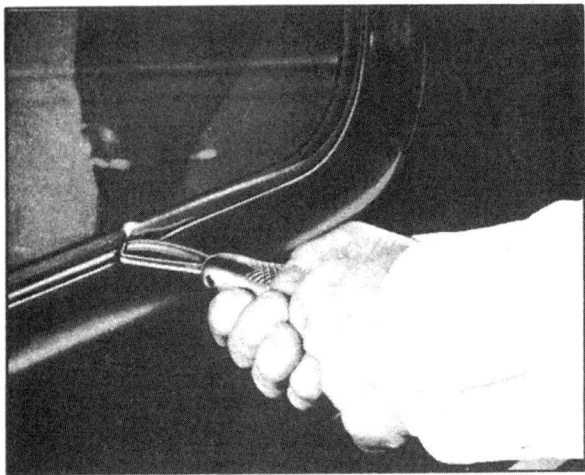

Fig. 10—Installing Cab Rear Glass Weatherstrip Retainer

sary, without prior removal of the above components.

To remove a door assembly proceed as follows:
1. Remove trim panel and lower hinge cover.
2. Remove the three-hinge strap to door bolts "A" (fig. 11) at each hinge and remove the door assembly.
3. Replace the door assembly by installing in position and replacing the hinge strap to door bolts loosely. Close the door for alignment and from inside tighten bolts securely.
4. Replace trim panel and lower hinge cover.

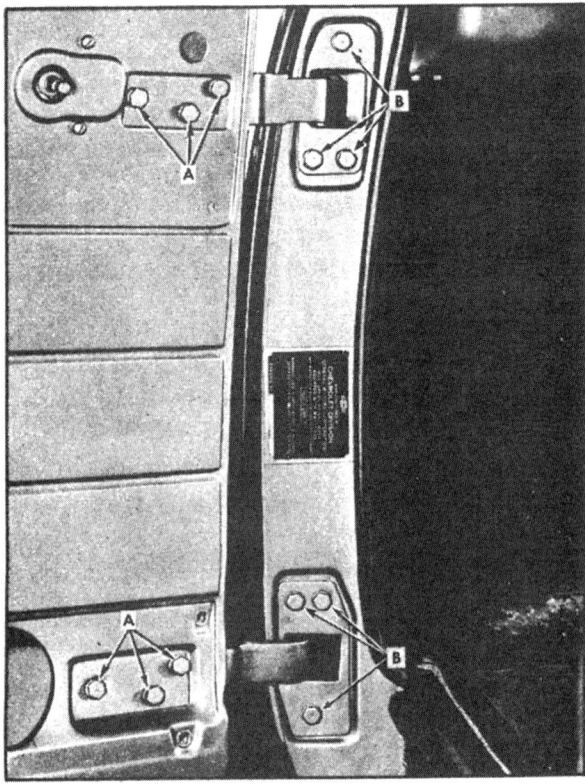

Fig. 11—Door Hinges

Adjustment

Door adjustment may be accomplished at two places; at the hinge straps to door panel and at the hinge bodies to cowl pillar. Before adjustment is made at either place, however, the striker plate should be removed.

To move the door up or down at the hinge pillar, loosen the hinge body to cowl bolts "B" (fig. 11) at both top and bottom hinge and move door up or down as required and tighten bolts. Check relationship of door to cowl panel. The door should be flush to 1/16" outside of cowl (fig. 12) to prevent wiping weatherstrip off door. Adjustment can be made by bending hinges.

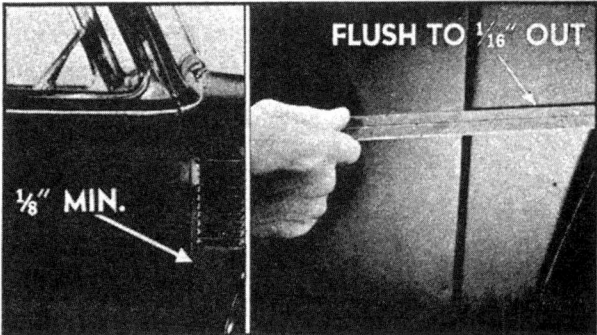

Fig. 12—Door Clearances

To move the door closer to or farther away from the hinge pillar, remove trim panel and lower hinge cover and loosen the hinge strap to door bolts "A" (fig. 11). Close door and move as required to obtain 1/8" to 3/16" between the door and cowl (fig. 12) when the door is fully closed. The door should be adjusted in the opening so that the edge of the door across the top and also at the lock side is parallel with the body opening as nearly as possible. Tighten bolts securely.

Replace the door striker plate and adjust as outlined under "Door Locks—Check and Adjust."

Hold Open Device

The hold open device is built into the upper hinge body and to replace the hold open device, the hinge assembly must be removed.

1. Remove door assembly by removing trim panel and lower hinge cover and disconnecting door assembly from hinge straps.
2. Scribe the location of the upper hinge on the cowl pillar and then remove upper hinge assembly by removing the hinge body to cowl pillar bolts "A" (fig. 13).
3. Place the hinge assembly in a bench vise and remove hinge pin.
4. Rotate hinge strap out of hinge box and remove hold open device.

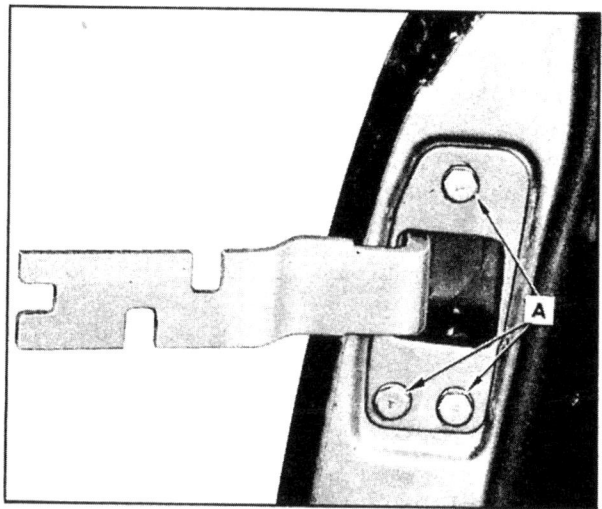

Fig. 13—Upper Door Hinge

5. Install new hold open device, rotate hinge strap into the hinge body and install hinge pin.
6. Replace hinge assembly into cowl pillar and realign using scribe marks made in step 2 above. Install hinge body to cowl pillar bolts and tighten securely.
7. Replace the door assembly and install the hinge straps to door bolts loosely. Close the door for alignment and from inside tighten bolts securely.
8. Replace trim panel and lower hinge cover.

Door Opening Weatherstrip

The door opening weatherstrip is installed around the inner edge of the body door opening. This weatherstrip serves as an additional protection against wind and drafts entering the body around the door.

The door opening weatherstrip is held firmly in position by a flat retainer held by sheet metal screws on 1948 models and by grooved retainers spotwelded along the front, top, and rear of the door opening on 1949-51 models (fig. 14). This weatherstrip is then joined at the floor by the door sill weatherstrip, which is held in place by a weatherstrip retainer and sheet metal screws.

To remove or replace this weatherstrip on 1948 models, remove the weatherstrip retainer screws including two screws at each end at the bottom of each pillar.

To remove the door opening weatherstrip on 1949-51 models, merely pry out a portion from the grooved retainers and grasping this portion, pull out the one complete weatherstrip which extends along the front, top and rear of door opening.

Bend up the flanges of the grooved retainers at those locations where they were crimped over at the time the weatherstrip was installed. Use care

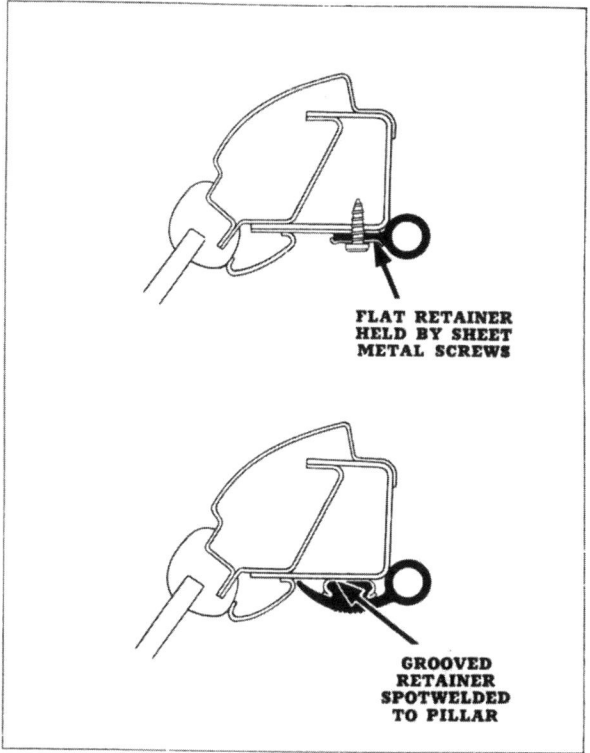

Fig. 14—Comparison of Door Opening Weatherstrip

not to leave any sharp edges or burrs as these would cut or tear the new weatherstrip.

To install a new door opening weatherstrip, proceed as follows:

1. Brush a rubber lubricant, No. 3692455, in the grooves of the weatherstrip retainers and on the matching portion of the weatherstrip.
2. Starting with the second notch on the weatherstrip, feed weatherstrip into upper retainer from lock pillar end until notch extends 6⅞ inches beyond front end of upper retainer (fig. 15).
3. Crimp upper retainer to weatherstrip; start at a point 4¾ inches forward of the rear end of the upper retainer and work forward for 2 inches.

NOTE: All crimping operations should be for a distance of approximately 2 inches.

4. Stretch weatherstrip slightly toward front end of retainer and crimp the front end of the upper retainer to weatherstrip.
5. Stretch weatherstrip around rear upper corner of door opening and crimp the rear end of the upper retainer to weatherstrip.
6. Feed weatherstrip into hinge pillar retainer starting with end notch (fig. 16) and pull down until notch will allow rubber to be inserted from lower end of retainer.
7. Stretch weatherstrip around front upper corner to eliminate any buckling of tubular por-

CAB AND BODY 1-8

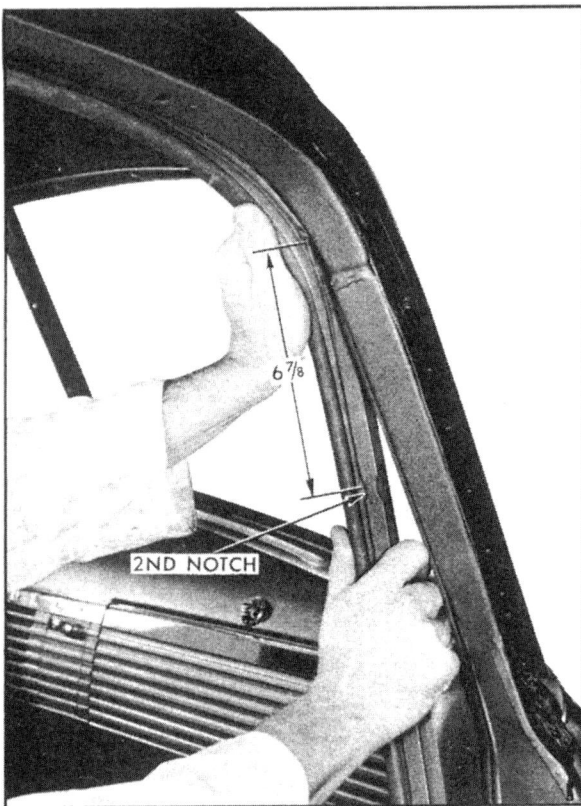

Fig. 15—Positioning Weatherstrip in Upper Retainer

tion and crimp the upper end of the hinge pillar retainer.

8. Back weatherstrip up into lower end of retainer, leaving sufficient weatherstrip extending to butt against body sill weatherstrip retainer, and crimp lower end of retainer.

Fig. 16—Starting Weatherstrip in Hinge Pillar Retainer

9. Feed weatherstrip into lock pillar retainer starting with end notch and pull down on weatherstrip until notch will allow rubber to be inserted from lower end of retainer.

10. Stretch weatherstrip tightly around rear upper corner of door opening to eliminate any buckling of tubular portion and crimp the upper end of lock pillar retainer.

11. Back weatherstrip up in lower end of retainer, leaving sufficient weatherstrip extending to butt against body sill weatherstrip retainer, and crimp the lower end of retainer to weatherstrip.

DOOR VENTILATOR ASSEMBLY
(1951 Models)

The side door ventilators on 1951 models are "Friction-Type" ventilators. The friction mechanism consists primarily of a coil spring, which is mounted on the ventilator lower pivot, exerting frictional force against the mounting support.

Adjustment

The tension of the spring on the ventilator lower pivot "A" (fig. 17) may be either too tight or too loose, resulting in a binding, hard to open ventilator or a loose ventilator that "flutters" or has a tendency to swing closed with wind pressure.

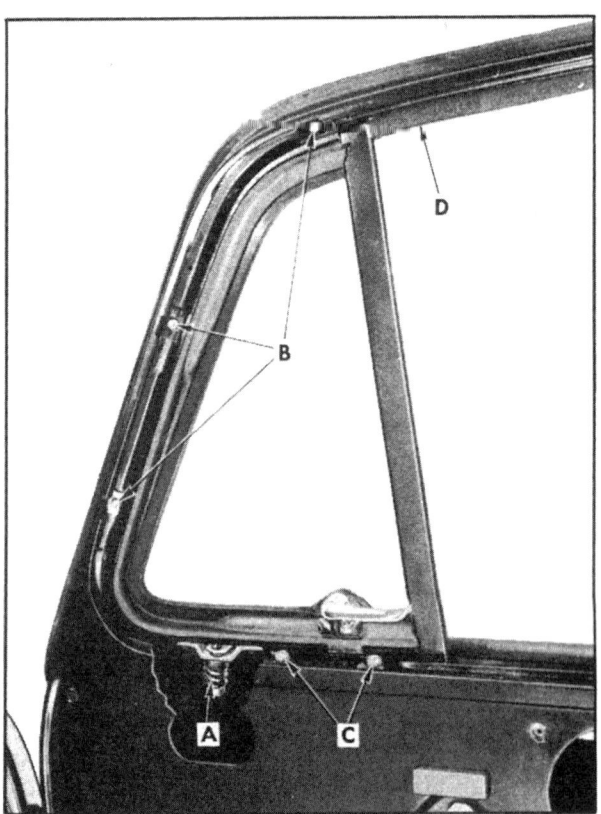

Fig. 17—Door Ventilator Mounting

To increase or decrease the ventilator torque:
1. Remove the inner door and window regulator handles and remove the door trim panel.
2. Accessible through an opening in the door inner panel is the nut which controls the tension on the ventilator lower pivot spring (fig. 17). Adjust this nut until proper torque is attained. This torque may be checked by getting the "feel" from another ventilator.
3. Replace trim panel and inside handles.

Replacement

The door ventilator assembly includes the door division channel.
1. Remove window garnish moulding.
2. Remove lower hinge cover.
3. Remove division channel lower attaching bolt "A" (fig. 18).

Fig. 18—Division Channel Lower Attaching Bolt

4. Remove the three screws "B" attaching the ventilator frame to door hinge pillar and the two ventilator lower support attaching bolts "C" (fig. 17).
5. Lower the door window.
6. Remove the door glass run channel screw at "D" (fig. 17).
7. Push the run channel out of the way and rotate ventilator assembly up and out of door (fig. 19).
8. To install, place the ventilator assembly in position in door and install bolt at lower end of division channel loosely.
9. Center vent assembly in reveal moulding opening to equalize seal of rubber lip and add washers as required to maintain vertical position of vent assembly.
10. Install the two ventilator lower support attaching bolts.

Fig. 19—Removing Ventilator Assembly

11. Install three ventilator frame to hinge pillar attaching screws and tighten securely while holding vent assembly forward.
12. Tighten bolt at lower end of division channel and ventilator lower support attaching bolts.
13. Install upper glass run channel screw.

Ventilator Glass Replacement

1. Using an oil can or similar means, squirt gasoline on the glass filler all around the glass channel or frame to soften the old seal. When the seal has softened, remove the glass from the channel.
2. Thoroughly clean the inside of the glass channel with sandpaper, removing all rust, etc.
3. Using new glass channel filler, cut the piece to be installed two inches longer than necessary for the channel. Place this piece of filler (soapstoned side of filler away from glass) evenly over the edge of the glass which will fit in the channel. The extra filler extending beyond the rear edge of the glass should be pinched together to hold it in place during glass installation.

NOTE: One side of this filler (the outside of the roll) is soapstoned. This is the side which goes into the metal channel. This glass channel filler is serviced in two thicknesses—.032" and .047"—to permit selection of the proper thickness so the glass may be installed without the use of special tools.

4. Brush the inside of the metal glass channel freely with ordinary SAE No. 10 engine oil. This will enable the glass and filler to slide freely into the channel. Push the glass with the filler around it into the channel until it is firmly seated. After the glass is firmly in place, the oil softens the filler, causing it to swell, thereby making a perfect, watertight seal. Trim off the excess filler material around the channel and at the ends of the channel.

It takes 24 hours for the oil to fully affect the filler, therefore, water-leak tests should not be made before this period has elapsed.

DOOR WINDOW GLASS—REPLACE

(1948-50 Models)

1. Remove window garnish moulding.
2. Remove inner door and window regulator handles and fibre washers.

   NOTE: These handles are retained to the shafts by set screws over which a finish head screw is installed.

3. Remove trim panel and sponge spacer washers.
4. Remove four regulator arm channel to window lower frame screws (fig. 20).

Fig. 20—Regulator Arm to Window Lower Frame Screws

5. Raise window and at the same time tip glass up on one end and remove assembly from door.
6. Disconnect lower channel of glass frame from "U" shaped frame after removing screw and sleeve nut from each end.
7. Remove glass and filler strip and clean frame channels thoroughly.
8. Position a length of filler strip over the edge of the glass, then press lower channel squarely onto the glass.

   NOTE: Do not attempt to press glass into channels—always press channel on glass.

9 Install "U" shaped metal frame over glass and filler strip, using a rubber hammer to tap into place.
10. Install screws and sleeve nuts, tightening firmly.
11. Install window assembly into door opening, engage lower frame with regulator arm channel and install four attaching screws tightening them securely.
12. Install window garnish moulding.
13. Place sponge rubber spacer washers over window regulator and inside door handle shafts and install trim panel.
14. Install window regulator and inside door handle fibre washers and install handles. Lock them in place with set screws and finish head screws.

(1951 Models)

1. Remove window garnish moulding.
2. Remove inner door and window regulator handles and fibre washers.

   NOTE: These handles are retained to the shafts by set screws over which a finish head screw is installed.

3. Remove trim panel and sponge spacer washers.
4. Remove the ventilator assembly, which includes the door division channel. See "Ventilator Assembly."
5. Install window regulator handle temporarily and raise the window to an almost closed position, then by tilting in at the top and rotating the window, disengage the regulator arm from the lower sash channel and remove the window (fig. 21).

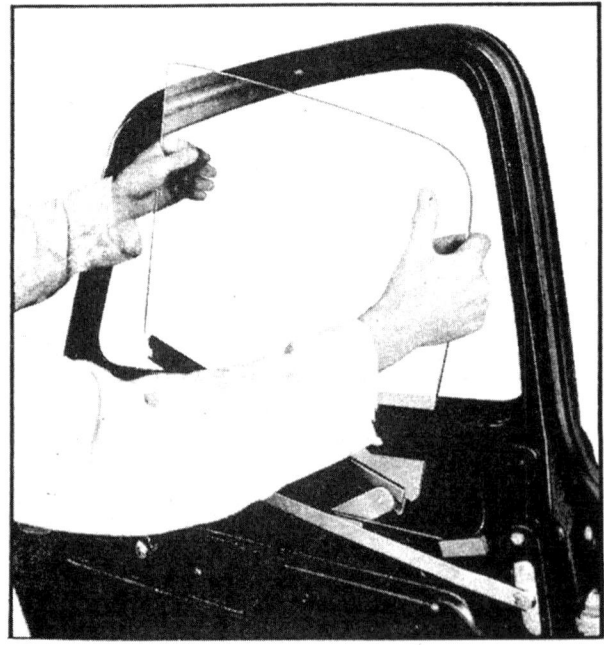

Fig. 21—Removing Door Glass

6. Squirt gasoline on the glass filler along the lower channel to soften the seal. When the seal has softened, remove the glass from the channel.
7. Thoroughly clean the inside of the lower sash channel with sandpaper, removing all rust, etc.
8. Using new glass channel filler, cut the piece to be installed two inches longer than the lower edge of the door glass. Place this piece of filler (soapstoned side of filler away from glass) evenly along the edge of the glass which will fit in the channel. The extra filler extending beyond the edges of glass should be pinched together to hold the filler in place during glass installation.
9. Brush the inside of the metal channel freely with SAE No. 10 engine oil. Push the glass, with the filler, into the channel until it is firmly seated.
10. After the glass is firmly in place, the oil softens the filler causing it to swell, thereby making a perfect watertight seal. Trim off the excess filler material along the channel and at the ends.
11. Install window glass assembly engaging regulator arm with window glass lower sash channel (fig. 21).
12. Install ventilator assembly in door and adjust door division channel as outlined under "Ventilator Assembly."
13. Place sponge spacer washers on shafts of door and window regulator handles and install trim panel and door and window regulator handles.
14. Install window garnish moulding.

DOOR GLASS RUN CHANNEL—REPLACE

1. Remove window garnish moulding.
2. Lower the window.
3. Remove inner door and window regulator handles and remove trim panel.
4. Remove the upper glass run channel screws, then pull the channel straight up to remove it from the door. On 1951 models, there is only one run channel screw located at "D" (fig. 17).

NOTE: The run channel is secured by a metal spring clip to the run channel guide.

5. Install the new run channel making sure the spring clip on the run channel engages the opening in the guide and the lip on the guide extends over the lower end of the run channel.
6. Install the upper glass run channel screws.
7. Install trim panel and door and window regulating handles.
8. Install window garnish moulding.

WINDOW REGULATOR—REPLACE

(1948-50 Models)

1. Remove inside door handle and window regulator handle.
2. Remove window garnish moulding, trim panel and lower hinge cover.
3. Remove door glass assembly as outlined under glass replacement.
4. Remove door window regulator screws "A" (fig. 22) and regulator arm pivot screws "B" and remove regulator assembly through bottom door opening.

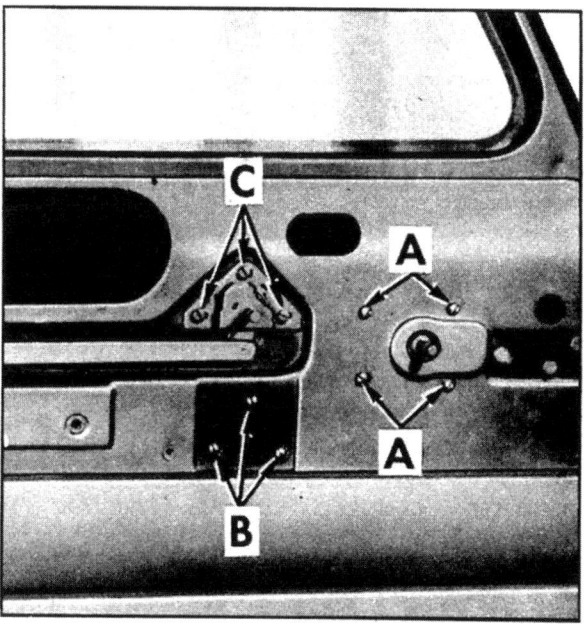

Fig. 22—Window Regulator and Door Lock Remote Control Retainer Screws

5. Install regulator assembly, less sliding regulator arm, up through bottom door opening (fig. 23).
6. Engage left arm pivot in roller track on inside of door and install attaching screws "A" and "B" (fig. 22) loosely.
7. Install sliding regulator arm on regulator arm pivots and install window glass assembly attaching lower window frame to sliding regulator arm.
8. Install upper glass run channel—raise window to closed position and tighten regulator attaching screws "A" and "B" securely.
9. Install window garnish moulding.
10. Install sponge spacer washers over shafts, trim panel, fibre spacer washers and operating handles.
11. Replace lower hinge cover.

(1951 Models)

1. Remove the ventilator assembly and door win-

CAB AND BODY 1-12

Fig. 23—Installing Regulator Assembly

dow glass as outlined under, "Ventilator Assembly" and "Door Window Glass."

2. Remove the four regulator bracket to inner panel attaching bolts "A" (fig. 24) and remove the regulator assembly through upper opening in door inner panel.
3. Install regulator assembly through upper opening in door inner panel and install the four regulator bracket to inner panel attaching bolts "A" (fig. 24) loosely.
4. Install door window glass and the ventilator assembly.

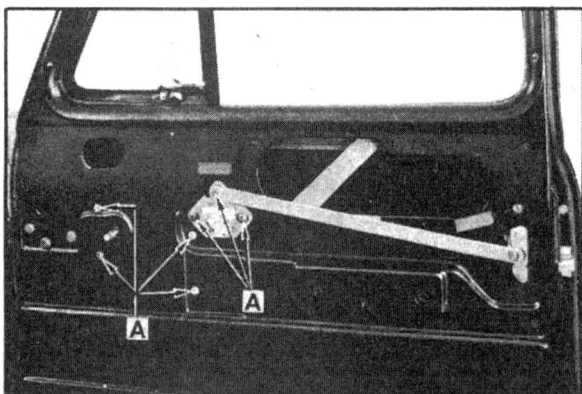

Fig. 24—Regulator Attaching Bolts

RAIN DEFLECTOR—REPLACE (1951 Models)

1. Remove the door ventilator assembly as outlined under "Ventilator Assembly."
2. Remove the three screws and remove rain deflector.
3. Clean old sealing cement from door surface.
4. Install the new rain deflector, install and securely tighten the attaching screws, and install the door ventilator assembly.
5. Carefully apply a 1/8" bead of sealing compound along entire length of rain deflector at junction with door.

OUTER REVEAL MOULDING—REPLACE

1. Remove door window glass as outlined under "Window Glass." This includes the removal of the door ventilator assembly on 1951 models.
2. Remove the upper glass run channel.
3. Remove the screws around the opening attaching the reveal moulding to the door reinforcement panel.
4. Bend back the metal tabs (2 places at bottom) where tabs on the reveal moulding are crimped through slots in the glass outer weatherstrip retainer.
5. Remove the reveal moulding.
6. Place new reveal moulding in position, install the moulding to reinforcement panel screws and crimp two lower tabs into openings in the weatherstrip retainer.
7. Replace the door glass run channel.
8. Install the door window glass and on 1951 models, install ventilator assembly.

HANDLES AND LOCKS—REPLACE

Outside Handle

1. Remove the two door handle retaining screws. One screw "A" (fig. 25) is accessible on the door inner flange and the other by turning down the outside handle.

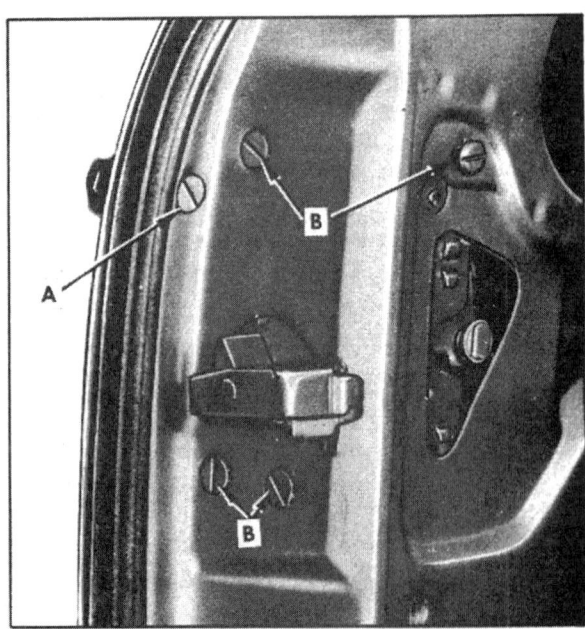

Fig. 25—Door Lock Retaining Screws

2. Pull handle, shaft and mounting plate straight out from door.
3. To replace, install handle, shaft and mounting plate, then install attaching screws.

Lock Cylinder

The left hand door of the cab is locked from inside by moving the inside door handle forward. The right hand door may also be locked from the inside in the same manner or it may be locked from the outside by a key operated cylinder lock.

To remove the lock cylinder assembly proceed as follows:

1. Release the door weatherstrip on the door lock pillar facing, at a point in line with the door lock rotor housing.
2. Insert the blade of putty knife or similar tool between the door outer flange and the lock retainer spring. At the same time pry the retainer out about ½" using another putty knife or thin screwdriver (fig. 26).
3. The lock cylinder assembly is now disengaged and may be removed from the door panel.
4. To install the lock cylinder when the retainer spring has not been removed from the door entirely, it is only necessary to guide the lock through opening in spring. Make sure the spring properly engages the recess immediately under the head of the lock and then push the spring into the locked position in the door lock pillar.
5. If the spring has been taken out of the lock pillar, (fig. 27), it must be inserted to within ½" of the locked position in its slot before attempting to install the lock.
6. Re-cement the door rubber weatherstrip securely.

Lock Assembly

1. Remove door lock cylinder (right door only) and door outside handle.
2. Remove inside control handles, trim panel and garnish moulding.
3. Remove door glass upper run channel and then raise door window to closed position.
4. Remove the screws which secure the run channel guide to the door pillar. Lift out the guide.
5. Remove screws "C" (fig. 22) and swing the remote control downward to free the connecting link from the rectangular tang of the door lock.
6. Remove the four screws "B" (fig. 25) which secure the lock to the door. Lift out the lock assembly through the access hole in the inner door panel.
7. Inspect the lock for sticking or other signs of faulty operation. If dry, lubricate with Lubri-Plate or equivalent. If lubricating does not correct the trouble replace the lock.
8. Make sure the new door lock assembly is lubricated properly and install it in the door. Install and tighten attaching screws securely.
9. Connect the remote control connecting link to the door lock, place the remote control in posi-

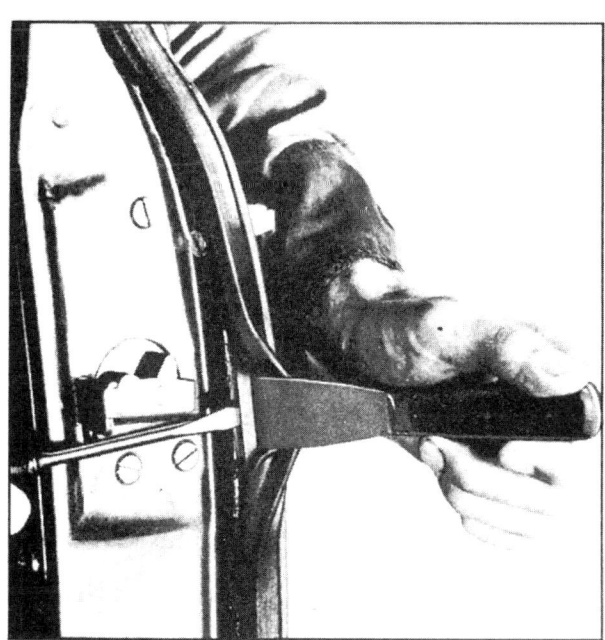

Fig. 26—Removal of Front Door Safety Lock

Fig. 27—Installing Front Door Safety Lock

tion on the door and install the three attaching screws loosely, adjust the remote control to provide full travel, then tighten screws securely.

NOTE: To adjust remote control to provide full travel; place the remote control handle in the fully locked position. Then move remote control toward lock (fig. 28) to remove all play and tighten screws securely.

10. Replace door lock outside handle.
11. Replace the run channel guide and then the door glass upper run channel making sure to engage the spring clip.
12. Install trim panel, inside control handles and garnish moulding.

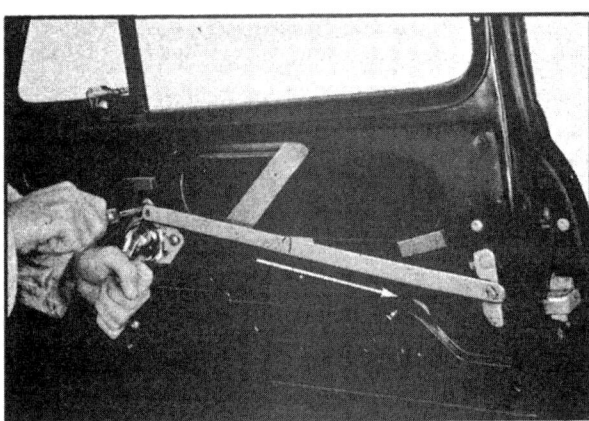

Fig. 28—Adjusting Remote Control

CHECKS AND ADJUSTMENTS

Lock Operation

One of the biggest contributing factors to improper door lock operation on truck models, is door misalignment. It is recommended, therefore, that door alignment be checked and corrected, as necessary, before corrections are attempted at the door lock or striker plate.

Operation of the door locks may be checked as follows:

1. Door must stay closed securely in safety catch position or in fully closed position. Check effectiveness in both positions by jerking on door. If lock does not hold, replace the lock.
2. Lock door while in open position with the inside handle. Check effectiveness of locking mechanism by trying to turn the outside handle after locking. The lock must release to unlocked position when the door is closed. If turning outside handle unlocks lock or lock does not release when door is closed, the door lock assembly must be replaced.
3. With door closed, check operation of key locking mechanism. Do not press down on handle while checking, or binding of lock mechanism will result. Key must turn freely to locked and unlocked position. With door in closed position and locked with key, check effectiveness of locking mechanism by trying to turn outside handle. If door unlocks, the lock assembly is defective and must be replaced.

Handle Operation

Check operation of handle. The ball joint of the handle is spring loaded and if operation is sticky, pry handle away from door mounting plate with a screwdriver at the lower side of the handle and lubricate ball.

Striker Plate

Measure the opening in the striker plate "A" (fig. 29). This opening should be $25/32'' + 1/64'' - 0$. If the opening is not within these limits, or if the striker plate is worn excessively or damaged, use a new striker.

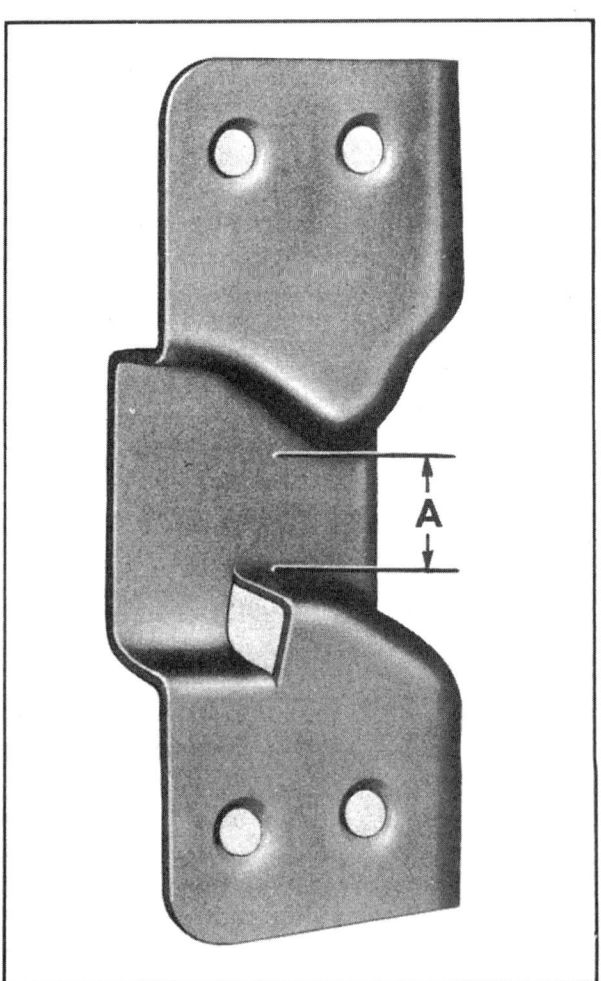

Fig. 29—Striker Plate

Correct striker plate adjustment is essential to proper door lock operation. The following clearances must be maintained.

1. With door closed, the clearance between the rear face of the rotor housing and the depression in the striker must not exceed 3/16". This clearance can be checked with a piece of 3/16" strip stock bent as shown (fig. 30). Correct, as necessary, using door lock striker shim, part #3689312.

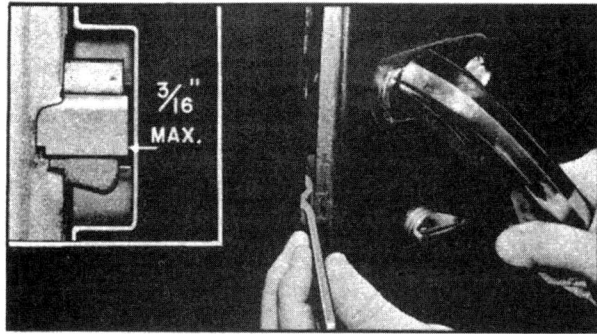

Fig. 30—Striker Plate Clearance

2. The bottom of the rotor housing should just clear the striker. Adjust by loosening the striker plate screws and raising or lowering the striker plate as required.

Remote Control

The remote control should be checked for proper positioning and operation. Sticking of the remote control handle (1) may be caused by binding of the control link on the door inner panel (2) or the safety catch lever in the lock sticking (3) (fig. 31).

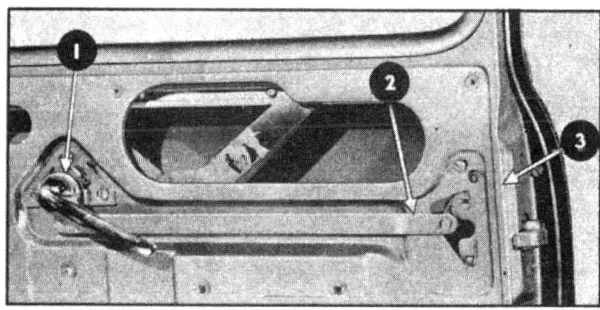

Fig. 31—Interference Points

1. Free up the remote control by bending the link or inner door panel to provide clearance. If lubricating lock does not free up lever, it will be necessary to replace the lock.

2. Check and adjust, if necessary, positioning of the remote control as follows. Loosen remote control to door inner panel screws and with door lock remote control in locked position, remove all play in slotted hole in remote control link by moving remote control toward lock (fig. 28). Tighten screws securely.

SEATS

Cleaning

Care of the upholstery is a relatively simple but important matter. Accumulation of dirt on the surface eventually turns into a hard, gritty substance which cuts into the surface of the upholstery.

To clean the seats, use luke warm, not hot or cold water, and any mild soap, such as castile. Work up thin suds on a piece of cheesecloth and rub upholstery briskly. Remove suds with a damp cheesecloth, using no soap, and finish by rubbing with a dry soft cloth. Do not use furniture polishes, oils, varnishes or ammonia.

Cushion and Seat Back

The cushion seat may be removed by lifting the cushion at the front edge and pulling forward. Cushion can then be removed through the door.

To install seat cushion, position seat in vehicle and push back into seat frame and down at the front to engage seat clips.

To remove seat back, remove three metal screws attaching seat back brackets to top of seat frame. Pull top of seat back forward, and lift up to disengage lower extensions from retaining brackets.

To install seat back, position seat back in seat frame with lower extensions engaged in retaining brackets. Push top of seat back against top of seat frame and install metal retaining screws.

Seat Frame—Replace (1948-50 Models)

1. Remove seat cushion.
2. Disconnect seat assist springs "F" (each side) (fig. 32).

    NOTE: When removing springs, seat must be all the way forward.

3. Remove cable connector "B" (each side).

    NOTE: Move seat all the way to rear when removing cable connector.

4. Remove seat frame to track retaining nuts "E" (each side).
5. Raise seat frame assembly to clear studs, move to the left to clear control handle and remove frame assembly through door opening.
6. Replace frame assembly, adjust cable as in step 8 under "Seat Adjuster Cable-Replacement" and install cable connectors.
7. Replace seat assist springs and seat cushion.

CAB AND BODY 1-16

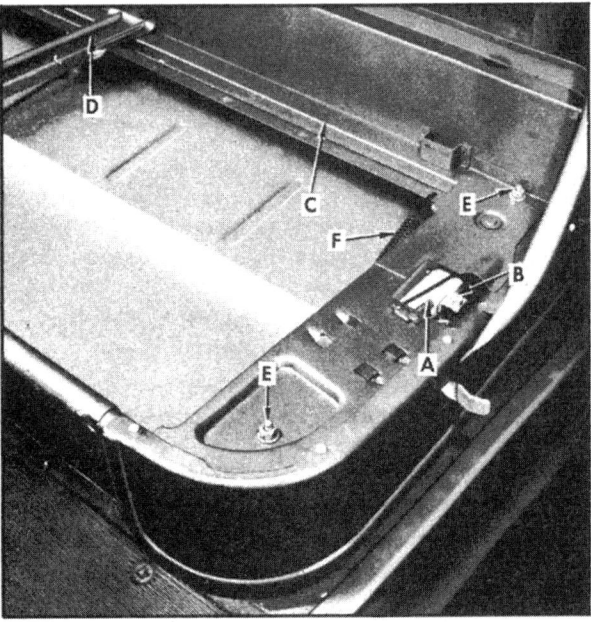

Fig. 32—Seat Frame and Cable Attachment

Seat Adjuster Cable—Replace (1948-50 Models)

1. Remove seat cushion.
2. Move seat fully forward and remove seat regulator springs.
3. Move seat all way to rear and loosen cable adjusting screw "A" (fig. 32) and remove cable connector "B" (each side).
4. Remove old cable.
5. Feed new cable through cable trough "C" and connect to non-adjustable pulley on right side of seat frame.
6. Feed other end of cable through cable trough under seat frame center brace "D" and connect to adjustable pulley on left side of seat frame.

   NOTE: Cable must be crossed where it lays in cable trough "C" in order to be operative.

7. Make sure cable is engaged properly in pulleys.
8. Tighten adjusting screw until cable tension measured with a scale results in a 1/8" deflection of cable when a pull of 3½ to 4 pounds is applied to the cable (fig. 33).
9. Push seat to full rear position and replace cable connectors "B" and tighten clamp bolt securely.
10. Move seat to full forward position and install seat regulator springs.
11. Replace seat cushion.

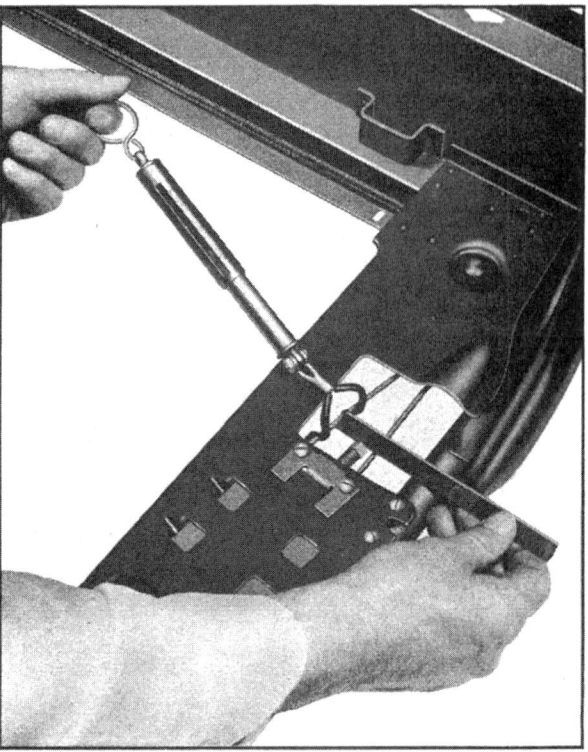

Fig. 33—Checking Cable Tension

Seat Frame—Replace (1951 Models)

1. Remove seat cushion.
2. Disconnect seat assist springs "A" (fig. 34) each side.

   NOTE: When removing springs, seat must be all the way forward.

3. Remove seat frame to adjuster retaining nuts "B" (fig. 34) each side, and remove seat adjuster rod support from hole in center retainer.
4. Raise seat frame assembly to clear studs, move to the left to clear control handle and remove seat frame assembly through door opening.
5. To install, replace and secure frame assembly to seat adjusters, replace assist springs and install seat cushion.

Seat Adjusters (1951 Models)

The seat adjusters are designed with ball and roller assemblies between the upper and lower channels of the seat adjuster mechanism. The control handle is located on the left side and a locking rod extends from the hand release of the left adjuster to the release of the right adjuster. Either adjuster may be removed separately and at least one must be removed when it is necessary to remove the locking rod which connects the two adjusters.

1. Remove seat cushion.

CAB AND BODY 1-17

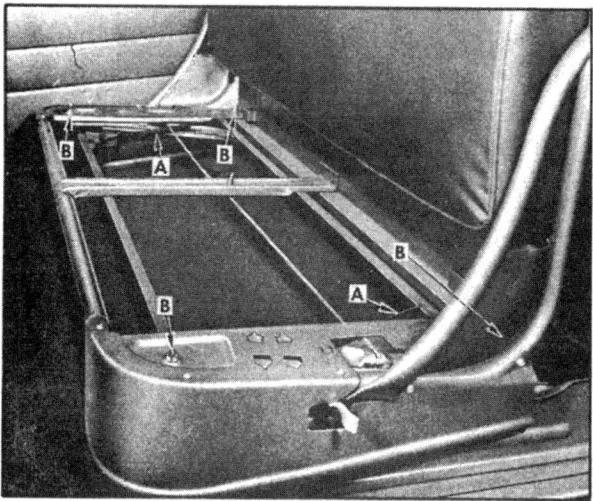

Fig. 34—Seat Frame Attachment

2. Move seat forward and remove assist springs.
3. Remove the seat frame to adjuster retaining nuts, remove seat adjuster locking rod support from hole in center strainer, and remove the seat frame assembly.
4. On either or both adjusters, remove the four adjuster to body floor retaining nuts "A" (fig. 35), lift the adjuster to detach the locking rod, and remove the adjuster from the vehicle.

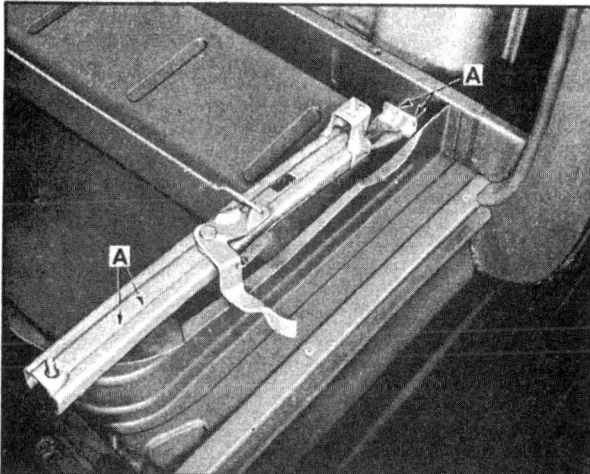

Fig. 35—Seat Adjuster Attachment

COWL VENTILATOR

To remove the cowl ventilator, open ventilator part way to release tension on the linkage and then proceed as follows:

1. From under the instrument panel, remove the bolt attaching the cowl ventilator control arm to the ventilator cover operating arm.
2. Remove the ventilator cover hinge bracket bolts to the cowl hinge.
3. Remove the ventilator cover from the outside by shifting it to the right in the opening to free the right end, then to the left to free the left end.

When replacing, it is necessary for one person to hold the ventilator cover firmly in the closed position while another installs and tightens the cover hinge bracket bolts to the hinges. Make sure the lid is properly centered before tightening bolts.

It is also necessary that the ventilator cover be fully closed and the control handle be backed down to the first notch when assembling the bolt holding the control arm to the operating arm.

The cowl ventilator rubber weatherstrip is securely cemented into the channel around the ventilator opening. The bottom flange of the ventilator cover seals against this weatherstrip to prevent water leakage.

To replace the cowl ventilator weatherstrip, first remove the old weatherstrip and clean out the channel. Remove all hardened cement and sandpaper any traces of rust. Make sure the cowl ventilator drain is open.

Cover the entire surface of the channel with 3-M "Weatherstrip Adhesive," allow to dry for four or five minutes and then install the new weatherstrip, flash side down, pressing it firmly down into channel.

Close ventilator cover and check to see that it fits tightly against rubber weatherstrip.

If the cover does not fit tightly against the weatherstrip, the closing tension should be adjusted as follows:

1. Open ventilator part way.
2. Loosen the bolt attaching the control arm to the operating arm.
3. Overlap the control and operating arms an additional serration, then tighten the bolt securely.
4. Close the ventilator and recheck the closing tension of the ventilator cover. If necessary, repeat adjustment procedure.

WINDSHIELD WIPER

Windshield wipers to be operating efficiently, must not only wipe the glass clean, but the sweep or stroke of the blades must be so adjusted that maximum visibility is maintained.

The wiper motor position is adjustable in the mounting brackets and when the motor is in the correct position, the sweep of the wiper blades should be equal.

The positioning of the sweep of each blade is adjustable in that the wiper arm may be placed on the transmission shaft in any one of several positions, all at intervals of one serration (fig. 36).

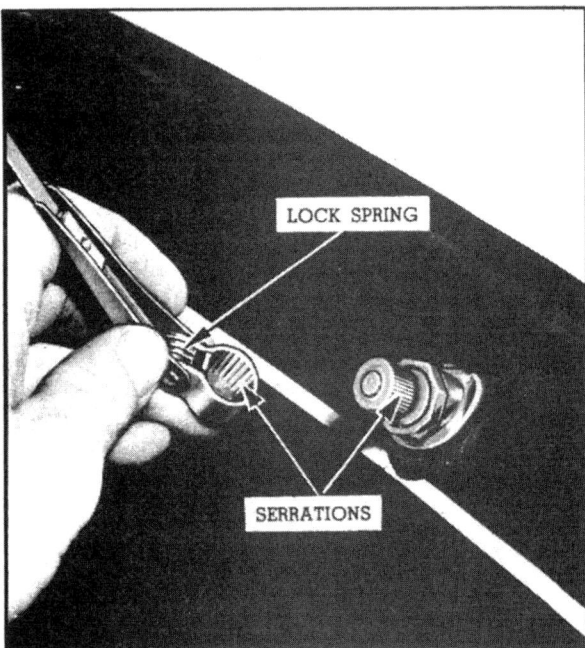

Fig. 36—Windshield Wiper Arm Mounting

A lock spring is used to lock the arm to the serrated shaft. To remove the arm it is only necessary to trip the lock spring to free it from the recess at the bottom of the serrated section of the shaft and pull outward on the cap section of the arm.

The windshield wiper motor is the vacuum type with the vacuum furnished by the engine intake manifold through hoses between the manifold fitting and the wiper motor. These motors require no special maintenance and should not be disturbed unless the wipers fail to function. If the wiper fails to operate, first check connections for leaks or plugging, before removing motor.

Wiper Motor—Replace

1. Disconnect vacuum line from motor under dash.
2. Remove hair pin retainer holding valve link to valve arm on motor.
3. Remove hair pin retainers attaching wiper arms to motor.
4. Remove attaching screws and remove motor assembly.
5. Replace motor assembly and install mounting screws loosely.
6. Attach wiper arms and valve link to motor and connect vacuum line to motor.
7. Adjust windshield wipers as outlined below.

Windshield Wipers—Adjust

1. Loosen the two wiper motor mounting screws. Then, with the motor operating arm vertical, shift the motor so both wiper arm operating levers are vertical. Tighten the motor mounting screws.
2. When the operating levers are vertical, the wiper blades should also be vertical. If not, shift the position of the blade arms on their serrated shafts as required (fig. 36).
3. If further adjustment of the sweep of the blades is desired, wet the windshield, then turn the wiper on to run about half speed and note the sweep at the arm. Then remove one or both wiper arms and change to whatever position may be necessary on the shaft to provide the desired sweep.

WATER LEAKS

Checking for water leaks and then applying the right correction are two operations that often require considerable skill or ingenuity on the part of the service man. Water which shows up at a certain place inside the cab may actually be entering at a point other than where the water is found. In locating and correcting a water leak, it is only by a thorough knowledge of the cab construction, the use of proper sealing compounds, and the knack of locating points at which a potential leak may occur, that enables the service man to make a successful correction.

Test windshield for leakage by spraying water under medium pressure against face of windshield. Direct a heavy stream along weatherstrip while an assistant inside cab marks points of leakage, paying particular attention to whether leakage occurs between glass and weatherstrip or between weatherstrip and cab.

After location of leak has been determined, apply 3-M "Weatherstrip Adhesive" using cement gun B-182-A, between lip of weatherstrip and glass and between lip of weatherstrip and body. Both applications on the outside should correct the leak condition. Allow cement to set and then retest with a water spray.

Testing of cab rear windows may be accomplished in the same manner.

In checking for water leaks at the cowl ventilator, first determine whether the ventilator cover fits tight against the rubber weatherstrip. Adjust if necessary. If leak still occurs, replace the weatherstrip making sure it is seated and cemented in place thoroughly.

If water leaks occur around door opening check to make sure door seats on rubber weatherstrip. If door does not rest firmly against weatherstrip door alignment *should be corrected*.

PANEL BODIES

Body operations on ½ and 1 ton panel bodies may be accomplished in the same manner that operations are performed on other truck bodies as already outlined in this section, with the exception of the rear doors.

The rear doors feature two positions of door opening; first, to approximately 90° (fig. 37) and

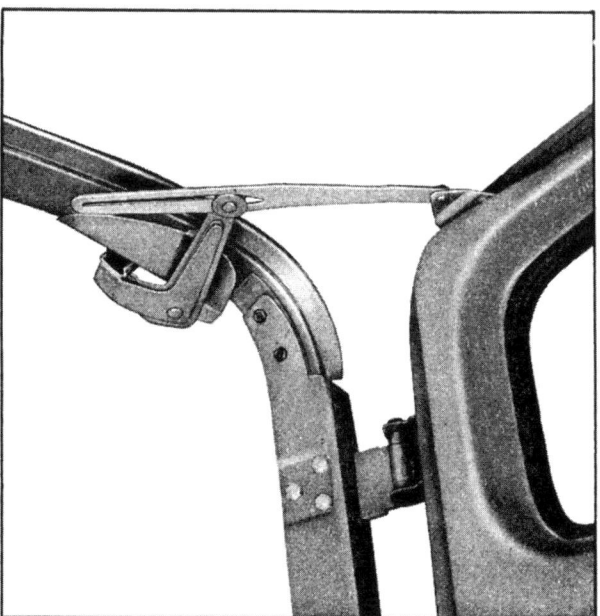

Fig. 37—Hinge Position 90°

second, fully open (fig. 38). With both doors opened to their full extent (at right angles to the body sides), the truck can be backed right up to a loading dock, eliminating the need for gangplank loading.

Door checks are slotted lever arrangements of a conventional design that are located at the top of each door where they are out of the way while the truck is being loaded. When the doors are

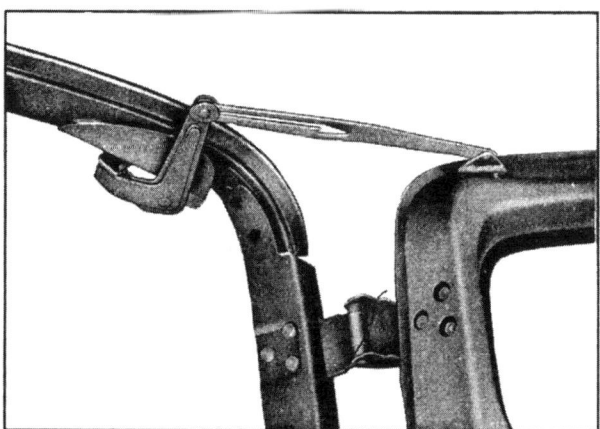

Fig. 38—Hinge Position—Fully Open

opened, catches in the slots stop and hold them in their first position (parallel to the body sides). When it is necessary to open the doors to their full extent, the catches can be unlatched by hand and the doors pushed into the extreme position.

Rear Door Locks

The rear left door lock is equipped with an inside door handle which is squeezed in the direction of pull to open the door (fig. 39). Lock rods extend from the lock which is bolted to a bracket welded within the door and are adjustable to allow for wear in the upper and lower catches "A" (fig. 39). Adjustment of upper or lower catches is accomplished as follows:

Fig. 39—Rear Left Door Lock—Panel Bodies

1. Remove door lock cover "B" (fig. 39).
2. Loosen set screws in trunnions of door lock lever and shaft assembly.
3. Use a screwdriver to adjust door lock rods which have screwdriver heads on exposed ends at upper and lower catch assemblies.

NOTE: Rods are to be adjusted so that the upper and lower catches will clear the strikers a minimum of ⅛ inch when the door handle is fully opened.

4. After desired adjustment of catch is made, tighten set screws on trunnions and replace door lock cover.
5. To adjust upper or lower strikers, loosen screws which are attached through slotted holes in top rear rail and platform rear panel and move striker in or out as desired and then tighten screws securely.

SUBURBAN CARRYALL

Body operations on the ½ ton Suburban Carryall are performed in the same manner that operations are performed on other truck bodies as already outlined in this section with the following additional operations necessary due to body design.

Side Window Replacement

1. Remove window garnish moulding and trim panel.
2. Remove two screws which retain sliding window lock to body inner panel and remove lock.
3. Remove two run channel screws "A" (fig. 40).
4. Using a putty knife break seal between run channel and window opening (fig. 40). Also break seal between outside face of run channel and sealing strip.

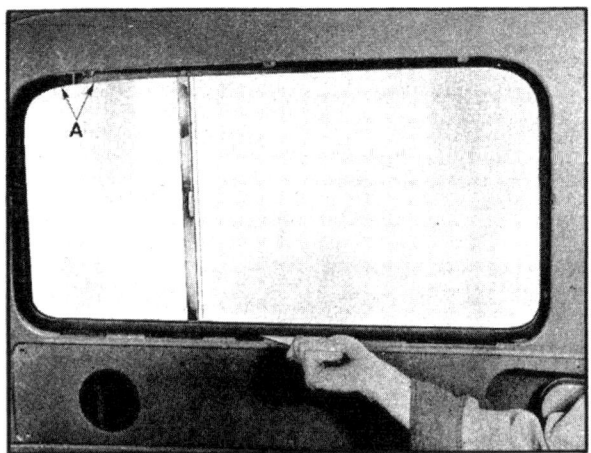

Fig. 40—Side Window Removal

5. From outside vehicle, carefully push window and run channel from window opening.
6. Remove glass from run channel.
7. If necessary, break seal around stationary window and from outside carefully push window from window opening.
8. Clean out all the old sealing compound from the window opening in the body and from the glass run channel.
9. If stationary window was removed, place a 5/32" bead of 3-M "Weatherstrip Adhesive" around that section of window opening against which stationary window is installed.
10. Install stationary glass pressing into place firmly. Remove excessive "adhesive" from outside of window by using oleum spirits sparingly.
11. Apply a 5/32" bead of 3-M "Weatherstrip Adhesive" around entire window opening including inside surface of stationary glass channel and also along moulding filler.
12. Install sliding glass in run channel and install run channel and sliding glass assembly into window opening pressing assembly firmly into place to seat run channel.
13. Install two run channel screws "A" (fig. 40).
14. Replace sliding window lock.
15. Install window garnish moulding and trim panel.

End Gate Assembly (upper half) Hinge—Replace

The upper end gate assembly (upper half) hinge is attached through elongated holes "A" (fig. 41) to the end gate and to a hinge box welded into the end gate body header, by three screws and nuts "B." To remove hinge assembly it is necessary to remove top lining panels to gain access to the mounting screws and nuts "B."

1. Remove sun visors.
2. Remove dome light assembly.
3. Remove windshield garnish moulding upper

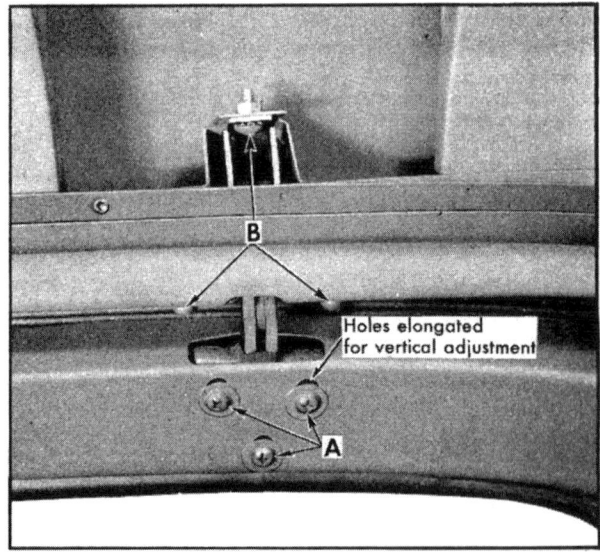

Fig. 41—End Gate Upper Hinge

screws and windshield post garnish moulding screws.

4. Remove top screw from windshield center division and remove garnish moulding retainer.
5. Remove front front half of top lining by pulling down at windshield header and sliding forward to disengage panel from panel retainer at rear.
6. Remove panel retainer.
7. Remove front rear half of top lining panel by sliding forward to disengage panel from panel retainer at rear.
8. Remove panel retainer.
9. Remove center front half of top lining panel by sliding forward and disengaging panel from panel retainer at rear and from side retainers.
10. Remove panel retainer.
11. Remove center rear half of top lining panel by sliding forward and disengaging panel from panel retainer at rear and from side retainers.
12. Remove panel retainer.
13. Remove rear top lining panel by sliding forward and disengaging panel from panel retainer at rear and from side retainers.
14. Remove screws and nuts "B" (fig. 41) retaining upper half of end gate hinge to the hinge box.
15. Remove three screws "A" which retain lower half of end gate hinge to the end gate and remove hinge assembly.
16. To replace hinge, reverse the preceding instructions and adjust end gate as outlined under "End Gate (upper half)—Adjust."

End Gate (upper half) Hinge—Adjust

Hinge screw holes in end gate are elongated for up and down adjustment of end gate (upper half) (fig. 41).

1. With upper half of end gate closed, loosen end gate to hinge screws.
2. Position end gate up or down to provide proper alignment.
3. Tighten end gate to hinge screws securely.

End Gate (lower half) Hinge—Adjust

Provision is made for adjustment of lower half of end gate horizontally through elongated holes at hinge attachment to end gate.

1. Remove end gate (lower half) hinge cover plate (fig. 42) and loosen three end gate to hinge screws.
2. With lower half of end gate closed, position gate horizontally to provide proper alignment.
3. Tighten end gate to hinge screws securely and replace hinge cover plate.

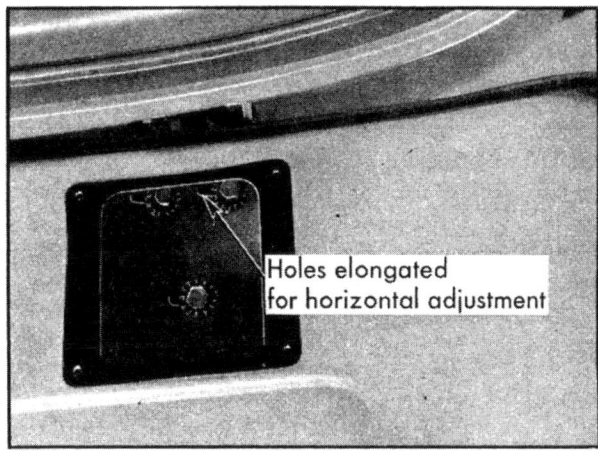

Fig. 42—End Gate Lower Hinge

End Gate (upper half) Lock—Replacement

1. Remove lock assembly cover plate.
2. Remove nut and lockwasher "B" (fig. 43) and remove outside lock handle.
3. Remove lock retaining screws "A" and remove lock assembly.
4. To replace, reverse foregoing instructions.
5. Adjust end gate (upper half) lock striker plate located on top edge of end gate (lower half) by loosening retaining screws, moving striker plate in or out as desired and then tightening screws securely.

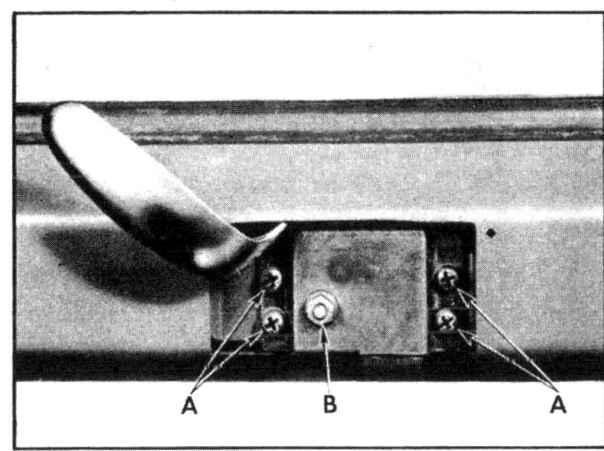

Fig. 43—End Gate Upper Lock

End Gate (lower half) Lock Catch and/or Spring—Replace

1. Remove end gate catch cover plate.
2. Hold down end gate inside handle and remove lock catch retaining screw "A" (fig. 44).
3. Pull inside handle and shaft from end gate and remove lock catch and spring from end gate.
4. To remove inside handle from shaft, remove retaining screw "D" and remove handle from shaft.

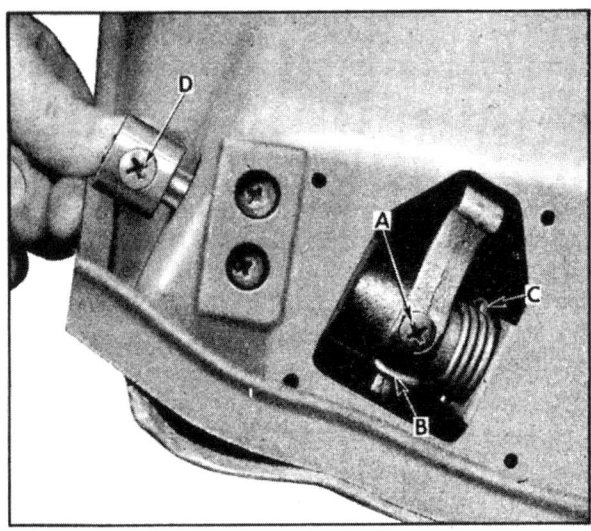

Fig. 44—End Gate Lower Lock Catch

Fig. 45—End Gate Cable and Cable Tape

5. Replace handle on shaft and tighten screw "D" securely.
6. Position lock catch spring on lock catch so one end of spring hooks over projection on lock catch at "B."
7. Insert lock catch and spring in catch opening in end gate making sure hooked end of spring hooks over catch support bracket at "C."
8. Insert inside handle and shaft and secure lock catch to handle shaft with set screw "A."
9. Install end gate catch cover plate, close end gate and adjust catch striker as required.

End Gate (lower half) Cable or Cable Tape Reel—Replace

1. Remove trim panel beneath rear side window.
2. Disconnect cable from tape reel at "A" (fig. 45) by removing cotter pin, clevis and two flat washers.
3. Disconnect cable from end gate (lower half) by removing cable end retainer from end gate.
4. If end gate cable tape reel assembly requires replacement, remove retaining bolt, lockwasher and nut at "B" and remove reel from mounting bracket.
5. Replace tape reel assembly to mounting bracket and install retaining bolt, lockwasher and nut.
6. Attach end of new cable to cable end retainer and mount retainer plate to end gate.
7. Thread cable into body, close end gate and then pull end of tape reel out and connect cable to tape reel with clevis, two flat washers and cotter pin.
8. Replace trim panel beneath rear side window.

CAB AND BODY 1-23

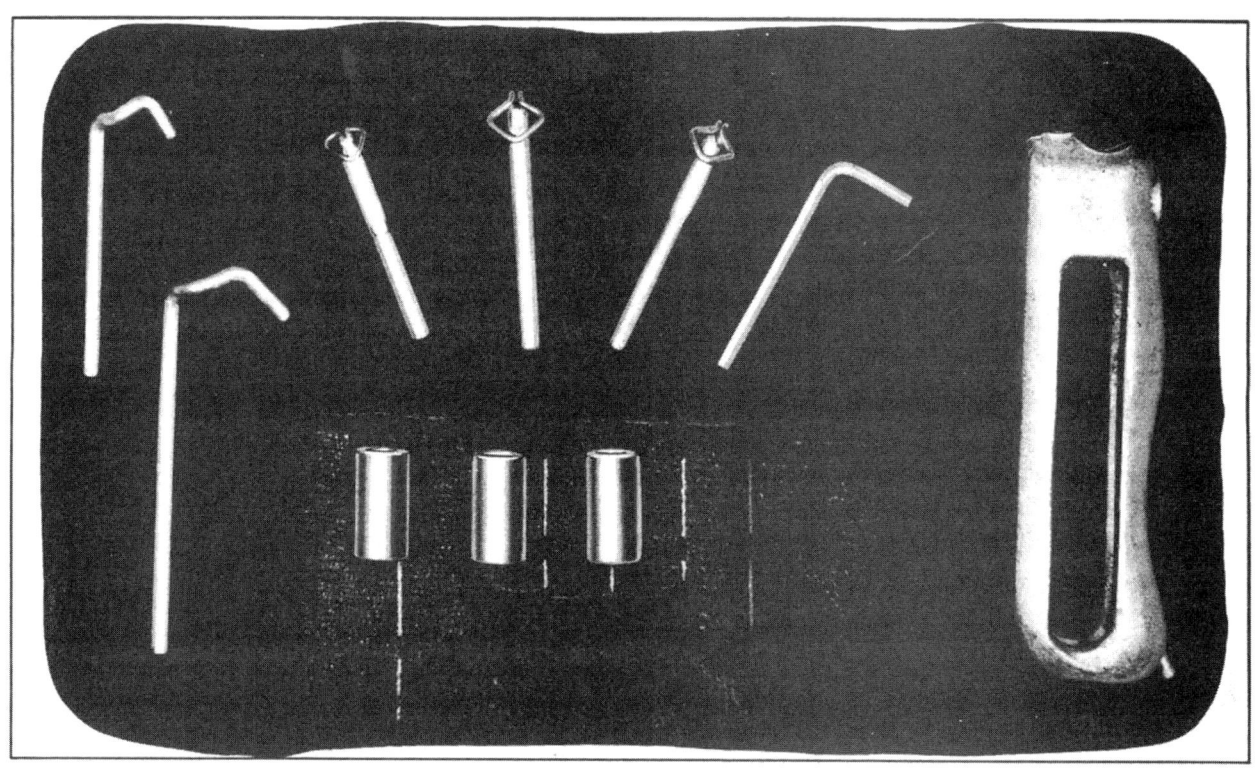

Fig. 46—Body Weatherstrip Tool Set (J-2189)

SERVICE NEWS REFERENCE

Month	Page No.	Subject

SERVICE NEWS REFERENCE

Month	Page No.	Subject

SECTION 2

FRAME AND SHOCK ABSORBERS

CONTENTS OF THIS SECTION

	Page
Frame	2-1
Frame Specifications	2-2
Shock Absorbers—	
Single Acting	2-3
Direct Double Acting	2-6
Double Acting—Cam and Lever Type	2-8
Shock Absorber Troubles and Remedies	2-14
Shock Absorber Special Tools	2-15
Service News References	2-15

FRAME

INDEX

	Page		Page
General Description	2-1	Straightening Frame	2-2
Checking Frame Alignment	2-1	Cross Members and Brackets	2-2

GENERAL DESCRIPTION

The frame is the structural center of a vehicle as it furnishes support to the body, power train and other units, and maintains their correct relationship in order that they may operate free from stress and strain and wear that may be caused by operating in a misaligned condition.

Frame side members are formed in a deep channel section and cross members are of a flanged "U" and box section construction for increased rigidity.

Strong braces and brackets are used to maintain proper longitudinal position of the side members relative to each other and at the same time providing additional resistance to twisting.

Cross member construction and number used will depend on the respective wheelbase.

A heavy sub-frame is used at the front end of C. O. E. models to provide proper clearance for the cab mounted over the engine. Illustration of frame used in this section is typical of all models; however, no attempt has been made to show gussets, angle or channel reinforcements peculiar to certain models. Axle and spring suspensions shown in this illustration are not necessarily representative of all models, but frame alignment checking is accomplished in the same manner regardless of these items.

CHECKING FRAME ALIGNMENT

Vehicles which have been in a collision, upset or an accident of any nature which might result in a "twisted" or "sprung" frame, should always be carefully checked for proper frame alignment in addition to steering geometry and wheel alignment.

When checking a frame for alignment in case of damage, the most efficient method is "X" checking with a tram from given points on each side member.

In Figure 1 reference points are indicated "A," "B," "C," "D" on each frame side member.

Frame alignment checks on all truck models should be made with the tram points set at the center of the lubrication fittings and the crossbar level to insure accuracy.

When "X" checking any section of the frame, the measurements should agree within 3/16". If the measurements do not agree within the above

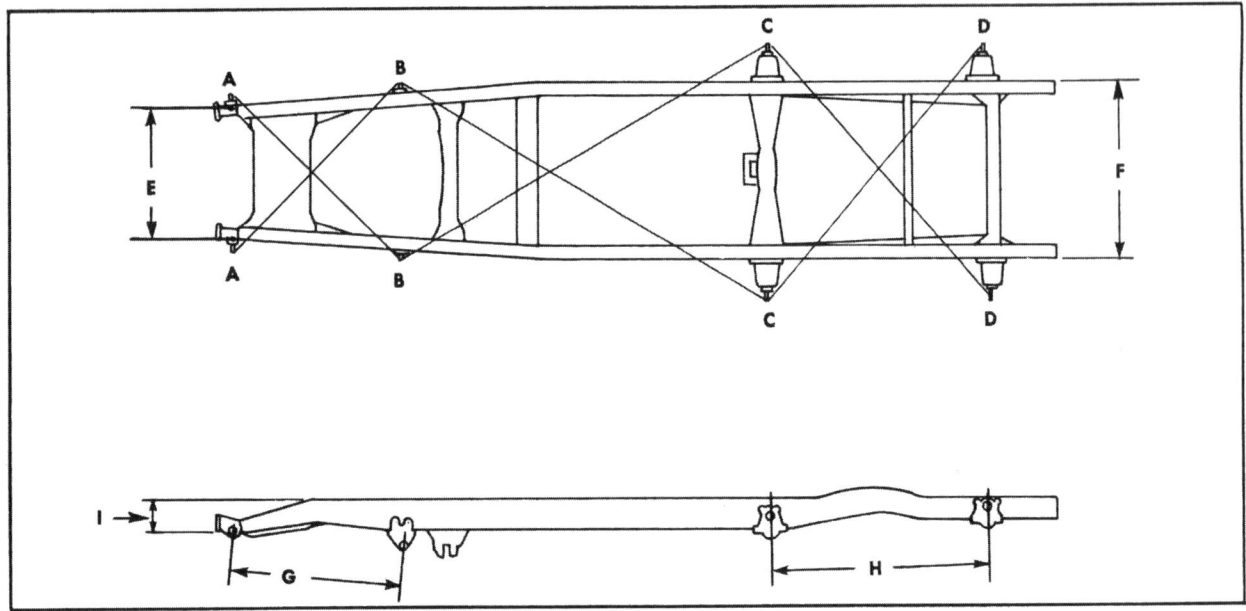

Fig. 1—Frame

limit, it means that corrections will have to be made between those measurement points that are not equal.

The minimum dimensions between spring hangers, both front and rear, are listed in the specifications table. In addition, the spread at the front and rear of the side members and the height of the front spring horns with reference to the top of the frame side members is also shown.

If a tram gauge is not available, the "plumb bob" method of checking may be used and to insure any degree of accuracy, the vehicle should be on a level floor when dimensions are checked.

By using this method, it is only necessary to have a piece of cord attached to an ordinary surveyor's plumb bob. When measuring the distance between two points, the free end of the cord should be placed on the reference point allowing the plumb bob to hang just off the floor. A checkmark should be made on the floor just under the tip of the plumb bob at each of the reference points. With these points located on the floor, the distances may be easily measured with a rule.

STRAIGHTENING FRAME

In the case of a collision or accident when the bending or twisting of a frame is not excessive, it is permissible to straighten the frame. Use of heat is not recommended when straightening

FRAME SPECIFICATIONS TABLE					
Series	E	F	G	H	I
½ Ton	25½"	46 1/32"	37¼"	52 5/16"	5 35/64"
¾ Ton	25½"	36"	37¼"	44 41/64"	5 35/64"
¾ Ton Forward Control	25"	36"	39 11/32"	44 41/64"	8⅛"
1 and 1½ Ton Short Wheelbase	25"	36"	39"	44 39/64"	5 13/16"
1 Ton Forward Control	25"	36"	39 3/16"	44 39/64"	8⅞"
1½ Ton Long Wheelbase and 2 Ton Conventional	25"	36"	38 25/32"	44 41/64"	5 23/32"
1½ Ton Schoolbus	25"	36"	38 25/32"	44 39/64"	5 23/32"
2 Ton C.O.E.	25"	36"	39 7/32"	44 41/64"	9"
2 Ton Schoolbus	25 1/16"	36 1/16"	38 25/32"	44⅝"	5¾"

frames as heat weakens the structural characteristics of frame members. Therefore, any straightening of frame members should be done cold. Frame members which are bent or buckled sufficiently to show strains or cracks after straightening should be reinforced or replaced.

CROSS MEMBERS AND BRACKETS

All cross members, brackets or gussets that are damaged or broken may be replaced. Cut off all rivets holding part to be replaced by first drilling the heads and then cutting them off using a sharp cold chisel. Care should be exercised to prevent distorting rivet holes. In permanently attaching a new piece, it is recommended that hot rivets be used to secure in place.

SHOCK ABSORBERS

INDEX

	Page		Page
SINGLE ACTING (1948-49)	2-3	Rear Shock Absorber	2-7
General Description	2-3	Removal	2-7
Operation	2-3	Installation	2-8
Minor Service Operations	2-4	DOUBLE ACTING—CAM AND LEVER	
Fluid Requirement Checks	2-4	TYPE (1948-51)	2-8
Filling Shock Absorber (on vehicle)	2-4	General Description	2-8
Replacement of Shock Absorber Parts	2-4	Operation	2-10
Relief Valve Removal	2-4	Minor Service Operations	2-10
Disassembly	2-5	Fluid Requirement Checks	2-10
Inspection	2-5	Filling Shock Absorbers	2-10
Assembly	2-6	Shock Absorber Links	2-10
DIRECT DOUBLE ACTING (1950-51)	2-6	Link and Clevis Type	2-10
General Description	2-6	Rod and Taper Stud Type	2-11
Operation	2-7	Replacement of Shock Absorber Parts	2-11
Minor Service Operations	2-7	Relief Valve Removal	2-12
Front Shock Absorber	2-7	Disassembly	2-13
Removal	2-7	Inspection	2-13
Installation	2-7	Assembly	2-13

SINGLE-ACTING

General Description

Single-acting shock absorbers are used as standard equipment on all ½ ton and ¾ ton trucks, both front and rear, and on the front of all 1 ton trucks. These trucks, as well as all other truck models, may use as special equipment, the double-action type shock absorbers.

The single-acting shock absorber is the most simple in construction of any used. A cutaway view of the external relief valve single-acting

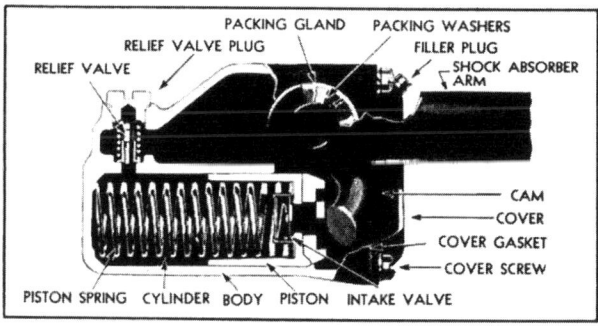

Fig. 2—Single-Action Shock Absorber

shock absorber is shown in Figure 2. The body is of cast iron and houses the various parts, as shown. A steel arm is securely attached to the shaft and a packing gland and washers are used around this shaft with a suitable seal provided. Inside the body and pressed on the same shaft is the cam which actuates the piston when the arm is moved. Since the piston must be returned to its normal position after a displacement, a spring is provided under the piston for this purpose.

An intake valve is mounted in the piston and its function is to replenish fluid in the cylinder as the piston returns to its normal position. The reservoir consists of all the space in the shock absorber body outside of the cylinder which holds the piston and piston spring. A relief valve is located between the cylinder and reservoir to relieve any excess pressure which may be created by sudden or rapid movement of the piston. This valve is easily accessible by removing the relief valve plug or nut. The open end of the shock absorber is covered by a stamped steel cover plate and gasket held in position by cap screws. Removing either the filler plug or relief valve permits filling or adding fluid.

The shock absorber body is mounted rigidly to the vehicle frame side member while the arm is connected through a shock absorber link to a fitting or plate on the vehicle axle.

Operation

When the wheels strike a bump, the springs compress and the frame moves downward carrying the shock absorber with it. This causes the shock absorber arm to move upward, relieving the cam pressure on the piston. Relieving this pressure allows the piston spring to force the piston outward creating a partial vacuum behind the piston. The partial vacuum causes the intake valve under the head of the piston to open, permitting the fluid to flow under the piston head and fill the piston chamber (fig. 3).

FRAME AND SHOCK ABSORBERS 2-4

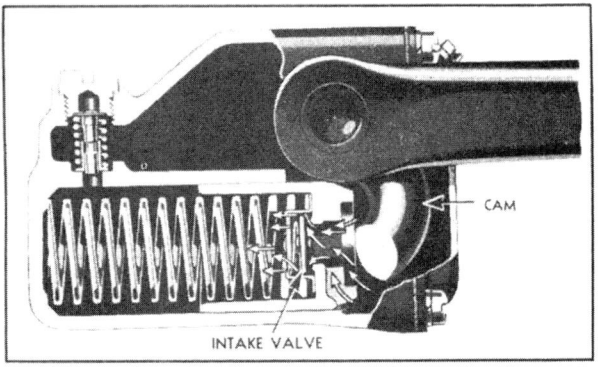

Fig. 3—Shock Absorber Action when Vehicle Strikes A Bump

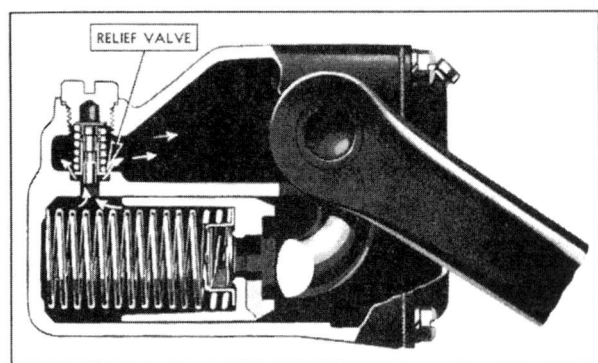

Fig. 4—Shock Absorber Action in Controlling Rebound of Vehicle Spring

As the wheels pass over the bump, the springs rebound and the frame moves up carrying the shock absorber with it. This causes the shock absorber arm to move down, applying cam pressure on the piston. The cam forces the piston into the cylinder, closing the intake valve. The oil trapped in the cylinder forces the relief valve off its seat and passes through a restricted orifice into the reservoir. This action (fig. 4) slows up the rebound of the springs.

MINOR SERVICE OPERATIONS

Shock absorber service operations, because of special equipment needed for complete disassembly, are minor operations consisting of lubrication, correction of fluid leaks at end caps, valve plugs or filler caps, replacement of damaged or worn linkage and replacement of valves.

FLUID REQUIREMENT CHECKS

1. Disconnect shock absorber link from axle bracket.
2. Pull shock absorber arm down. If shock absorber is functioning properly a resistance should be felt.

   NOTE: If arm comes down easily part way and then comes to a stop and moves down slowly the rest of the way, there is not enough fluid in the shock absorber.

FILLING SHOCK ABSORBERS
(on the vehicle)

1. Clean the shock absorber thoroughly with a suitable cleaning solvent.
2. Remove shock absorber cover and install new cover having a filler plug.
3. Remove filler plug and disconnect link at axle bracket.
4. Fill shock absorber to capacity, using fluid injector J-1026. Work shock absorber arm slowly up and down while filling.
5. Fill to level of filler plug hole. Air space above is sufficient to allow for expansion of fluid.
6. Replace filler plug and attach link to shock absorber axle bracket.

REPLACEMENT OF SHOCK ABSORBER PARTS

Because of special equipment needed for complete disassembly and assembly of shock absorbers, the body, arm, packing glands, camshaft and cam are not serviceable. Other parts may be serviced as follows:

1. Disconnect shock absorber link from axle bracket.
2. Remove mounting bolts and shock absorber from vehicle.

   NOTE: On ½ ton trucks it will be necessary to remove gas tank.

3. Clean shock absorber thoroughly with cleaning solvent and drain fluid.
4. Mount shock absorber on holding fixture J 895.

Relief Valve Removal

1. Remove valve nut using offset screwdriver J 900 (fig. 5).

FRAME AND SHOCK ABSORBERS 2-5

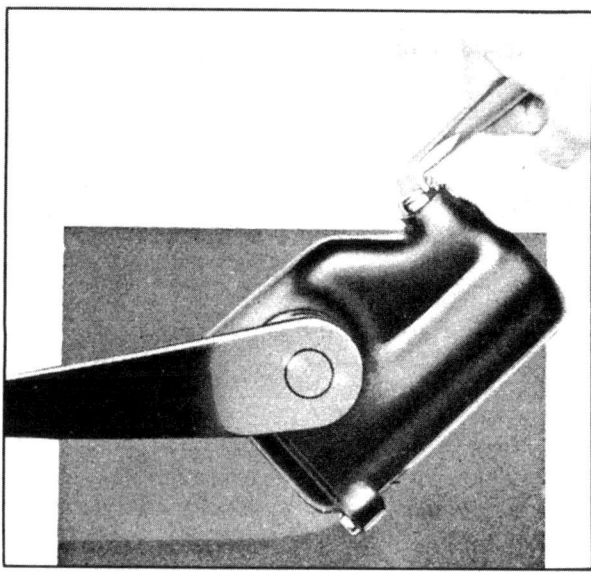

Fig. 5—Removing Shock Absorber Filler Plug

2. Remove relief valve, using a small hooked tool or bent wire (fig. 6).
3. Insert new relief valve and replace valve nut, using a new gasket.

Disassembly

1. Mount shock absorber on holding fixture J 895 with cover end up.
2. Remove relief valve nut and relief valve.
3. Hold shock absorber arm firmly in vertical position to hold piston in cylinder and remove cover screws and cover.
4. Move arm toward piston side of housing so that the piston spring is compressed.
5. Install Delco hold down tool number 515 with leg down and loop out over edge of shock absorber on piston side.
6. Slide tool around edge of opening until the loop is locked under the shoulder at the corner of the shock absorber.
7. Remove shock absorber from holding fixture and place in an arbor press.
8. Move arm away from piston so that cam is turned up exposing the piston.
9. Place short length of cold rolled stock be-

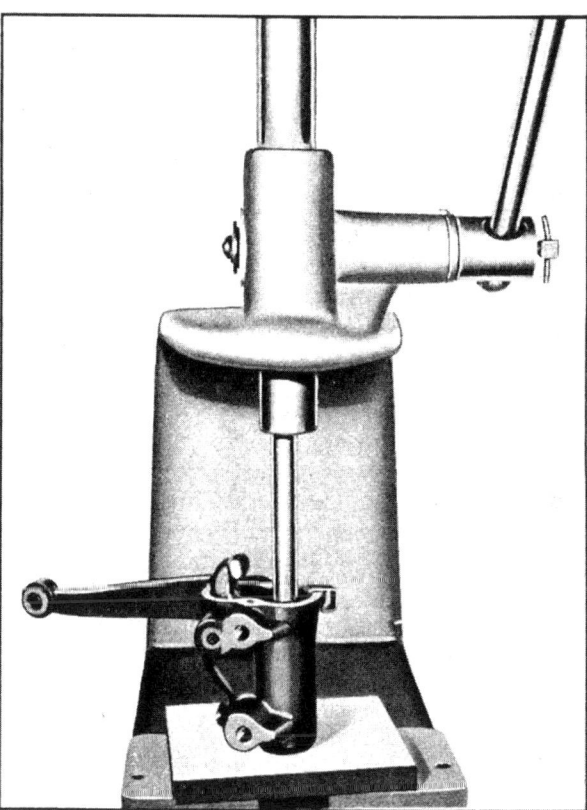

Fig. 7—Using Arbor Press to Compress Piston Spring

tween press and piston (fig. 7). Compress piston spring slightly and remove hold down tool number 515.
10. Raise press slowly until piston spring is fully extended and lift piston and spring out of shock absorber body.

Inspection

1. Wash all parts in cleaning solvent.
2. Blow out valve orifices with compressed air.
3. Check valves for dirt.
4. Inspect all parts for wear.
5. Check camshaft for wear in housing by mov-

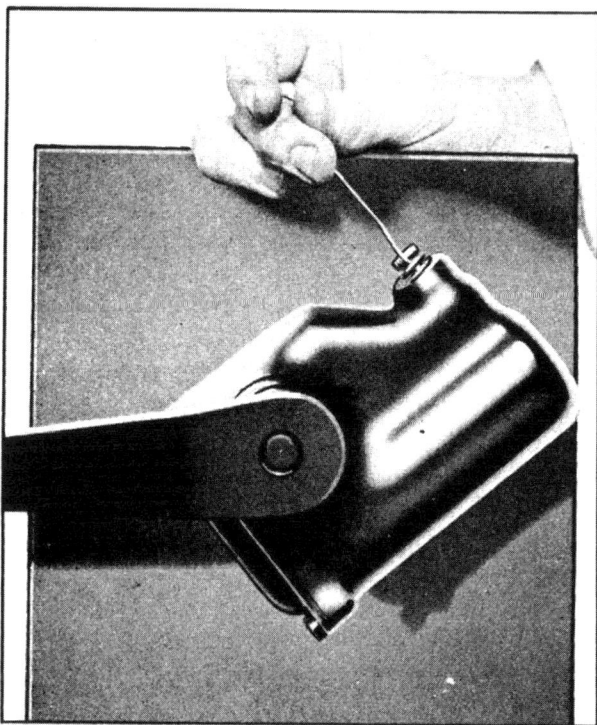

Fig. 6—Removing Shock Absorber Relief Valve

ing arm sideways. If shaft is galled or worn, replace complete shock absorber.

Assembly

1. Insert relief valve and relief valve nut, using a new gasket.
2. Insert intake valve and retainer in end of piston spring and install spring, valve and retainer into piston.
3. Install piston and spring into shock absorber body.
4. Compress piston and spring with arbor press as in disassembly, and insert hold down tool.
5. Remove shock absorber from arbor press; move arm so that cam is in operating position and mount shock with open side up on holding fixture J 895.

NOTE: If piston is loose in cylinder, an oversize piston may be installed. The oversize piston is distinguished from the standard piston by a blue paint mark on the top edge.

6. Hold down on shock absorber arm to compress piston spring and remove hold down tool.
7. Fill shock absorber to within one-half inch of top with fresh fluid.
8. Move arm through normal operating strokes to expel any trapped air and add fluid until level remains steady. Fill to within two tablespoons of capacity.
9. Replace cover, using a new gasket, and tighten securely with cover screws.
10. Remove shock absorber from holding fixture.

DIRECT DOUBLE-ACTING

General Description

Direct double-acting shock absorbers are used as regular equipment on the front of all ½, ¾ and 1 ton trucks and on the rear of the ½ and ¾ ton models. In addition, provision is made for the installation of a larger capacity unit of the same type as special equipment on the rear of the 1 ton series.

These shock absorbers are the non-adjustable direct acting bayonet type, consisting of three concentric tubes known as the piston tube, reservoir tube and dust shield tube. The shock absorbers are permanently sealed and require no maintenance other than replacement if necessary.

At the front, the shock absorbers are mounted outside the frame. The studs, which extend from each end of the shock absorber, are attached to an upper and lower bracket. The lower bracket is attached to the front "U" bolt of the spring and the upper bracket is bolted to the frame. The attachments are cushioned by rubber grommets.

Rear shock absorbers on ½ ton are mounted outside the frame and rear spring and are tilted forward at the upper end. Attachment at the upper end is to a bracket riveted to the frame. The attachment of the shock absorber to the bracket is cushioned with rubber grommets. The lower end of the shock absorber is fitted with an eye which slips over an anchor pin on the rear spring "U" bolt anchor plate. Natural rubber bushings fit in the shock absorber eye and over the anchor pin to cushion the attachment.

The rear shock absorbers on ¾ ton are mounted inside the frame and rear spring and the upper attachment is similar to that in the ½ ton. The lower end is fitted with a rubber bushed eye, which provides direct attachment to the rear axle housing. The eye of the shock absorber is attached, by means of a bolt, to a bracket welded to the rear axle.

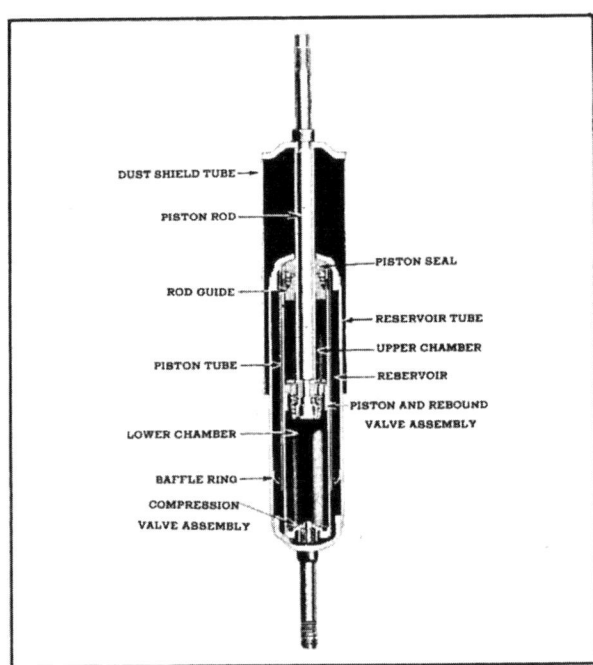

Fig. 8—Direct Acting Shock Absorber

The shock absorber (fig. 8) consists essentially of a cylinder and piston, the piston being attached to a steel rod which extends through a rubber seal in the top of the cylinder. The cylinder, or piston tube, is surrounded by a reservoir tube, the chamber between their walls serving as the fluid reservoir. A baffle ring in the reservoir prevents turbulence. Attached to the top of the piston rod is a third tube, called the dust shield, which is designed to protect the highly polished piston rod from dust and flying stones, *thus preserving its* smooth surface and insuring long life to the rubber seal.

The piston tube, or working cylinder, is divided into an upper and lower chamber by the combined piston and rebound valve assembly, which is attached to the lower end of the piston rod. The compression valve is fitted into the lower end of the piston tube, allowing the fluid to be forced back and forth between the reservoir and the piston tube.

Operation

When the spring is compressed, the shock absorber starts on its compression stroke, and the piston moves downward in its tube, displacing fluid in the lower chamber. Part of the fluid is forced upward through the outer holes in the piston, lifting the intake valve plate, and entering the upper chamber (fig. 9). Not all of the fluid that is displaced by the piston can pass into the upper chamber since the rod takes up part of the volume. Therefore, the remainder is forced out of the lower chamber through the compression valve orifice into the reservoir. As this opening is always below the reservoir fluid level, no emulsion of air and fluid can take place.

On the rebound stroke, the piston is pulled upward, and the fluid in the upper chamber is forced downward through the slot in the intake valve plate and the inner holes in the piston, exerting pressure against the rebound orifice disc. As the pressure builds up, fluid is forced through the rebound orifice, bending the orifice disc downward, and compressing the rebound relief valve spring, letting fluid pass into the lower chamber. Again, because of volume taken up by the rod, the displacement of fluid in the upper chamber is not as great as the displacement in the lower chamber. Therefore, as the piston moves upward, an additional amount of fluid is drawn into the lower chamber from the surrounding reservoir, through the compression valve assembly. The compression valve orifice plate is lifted from its seat, allowing the fluid to enter the chamber freely.

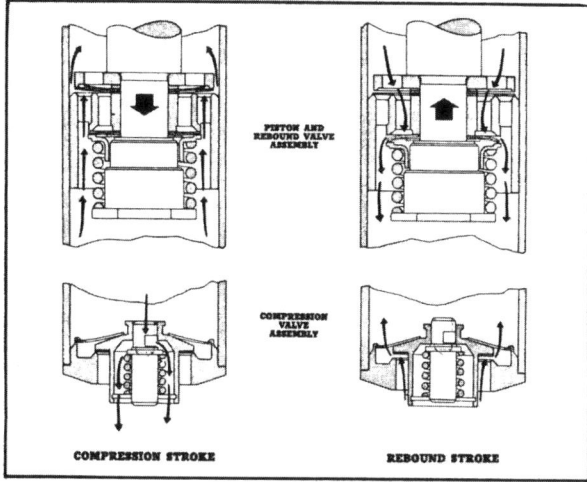

Fig. 9—Shock Absorber Valve Action

MINOR SERVICE OPERATIONS

Since the direct double-acting shock absorbers are permanently sealed, service operations are limited to replacement only. Shock absorbers may be replaced as follows:

FRONT SHOCK ABSORBER

Removal

1. Hold dust shield and upper stem from turning and remove upper stem retaining nut, grommet retainer and grommet.
2. Hold reservoir tube and lower stem from turning and remove lower stem retaining nut, grommet retainer and grommet.
3. Remove the shock absorber assembly from the vehicle and remove the grommets and retainers from shock absorber stems.
4. Inspect rubber grommets for condition and, if necessary, replace with new grommets.

Installation

1. Install grommet retainer and grommet on upper stem of shock absorber and insert upper stem through frame mounting bracket.
2. Install grommet and grommet retainer over upper stem and install retainer nut.
3. Install grommet retainer and grommet over lower stem of shock absorber and insert lower stem through lower mounting bracket.
4. Install grommet and grommet retainer on lower stem and install retainer nut to lower stem.
5. While holding each stem from turning, run upper and lower retainer nuts down until they bottom on the last thread. Apply 4-6 ft. lbs. torque to each nut to lock it on the last thread.

REAR SHOCK ABSORBERS

Removal—½ Ton

1. Hold dust shield and upper stem from turning and remove upper stem retaining nut, grommet retainer and grommet.
2. Remove nut, lockwasher and flat washer from shock absorber anchor bolt on rear spring "U" bolt anchor plate.
3. Pull shock absorber eye from anchor bolt and

lower assembly to disengage upper stem from frame mounting bracket.
4. Inspect rubber grommets for condition and, if necessary, replace with new grommets.

Installation—½ Ton

1. Install rubber bushings in shock absorber eye and install grommet retainer and grommet to shock absorber upper stem.
2. Install steel flat washer (21/32") on shock absorber anchor bolt and then install shock absorber, indexing upper stem through hole in frame mounting bracket and then install shock absorber eye to anchor bolt.
3. Install steel flat washer (½"), lockwasher and nut to anchor bolt and tighten securely.
4. Install grommet, grommet retainer and retainer nut to upper stem. Run retainer nut down until it bottoms on the last thread and then apply 4-6 ft. lbs. torque to the nut to lock it on the last thread.

Removal—¾ Ton

1. Hold dust shield and upper stem from turning and remove upper stem retaining nut, grommet retainer and grommet.
2. Remove lower shock absorber eye to axle bracket nut, lockwasher and bolt and lower assembly to disengage upper stem from frame mounting bracket.
3. Inspect rubber grommets for condition and, if necessary, replace with new grommets.

Installation—¾ Ton

1. Install grommet retainer and grommet to shock absorber upper stem and install rubber bushings and axle bracket spacer in shock absorber eye.
2. Install shock absorber, indexing upper stem through hole in frame mounting bracket and install axle bracket bolt through lower eye, bracket, bushings and spacer. Install lockwasher and nut and tighten securely.
3. Install grommet, grommet retainer and retainer nut on shock absorber upper stem. Run retainer nut down until it bottoms on the last thread and then apply 4-6 ft. lbs. torque to the nut to lock it on the last thread.

DOUBLE ACTING—CAM AND LEVER

General Description

Cam and lever double-acting shock absorbers, installed as special equipment are of two types, single external valve type and double external valve type.

Single External Valve Type

A cross section of the single external valve type double-acting shock absorber is shown in Figure 10.

This is an opposed cylinder design with an external rebound relief valve. The compression relief valve is carried in the compression piston.

Inside the body and pressed on the shaft is a cam which bears against one piston during compression and the other during rebound movement. The two pistons are held together by two screws, one in each piston, that pass through one piston and thread into the other.

The fluid reservoir is the space surrounding the shaft and cam inside the body, and an easily accessible filler plug is located in the upper part of this chamber. An end cap, plate and gasket is threaded over each end of the body and the caps must be removed for making valve changes.

The rebound valve is located in the end of a drilled passage cast on the outside of the body. This valve is held in place by a valve nut and gasket which are removed for changing this valve. Identification of valve assemblies is possible by the number stamped on the valve.

Double External Valve Type

The double external valve type double-acting shock absorber is shown in cross section in Figure 11 and is an opposed cylinder design with external relief valves.

The two pistons are held together by two screws, one in each piston, that pass through one piston and thread into the other.

End caps with gasket are threaded into the ends of the body and must be removed to make piston valve changes. However, on this type of opposed cylinder shock absorber, the rebound and com-

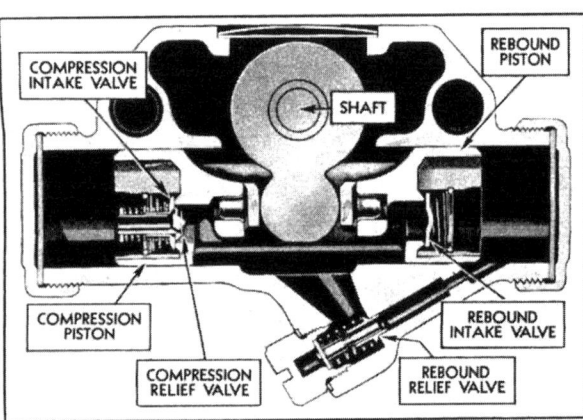

Fig. 10—Cross Section of Combination Internal-External Relief Valve Double-Acting Shock Absorber

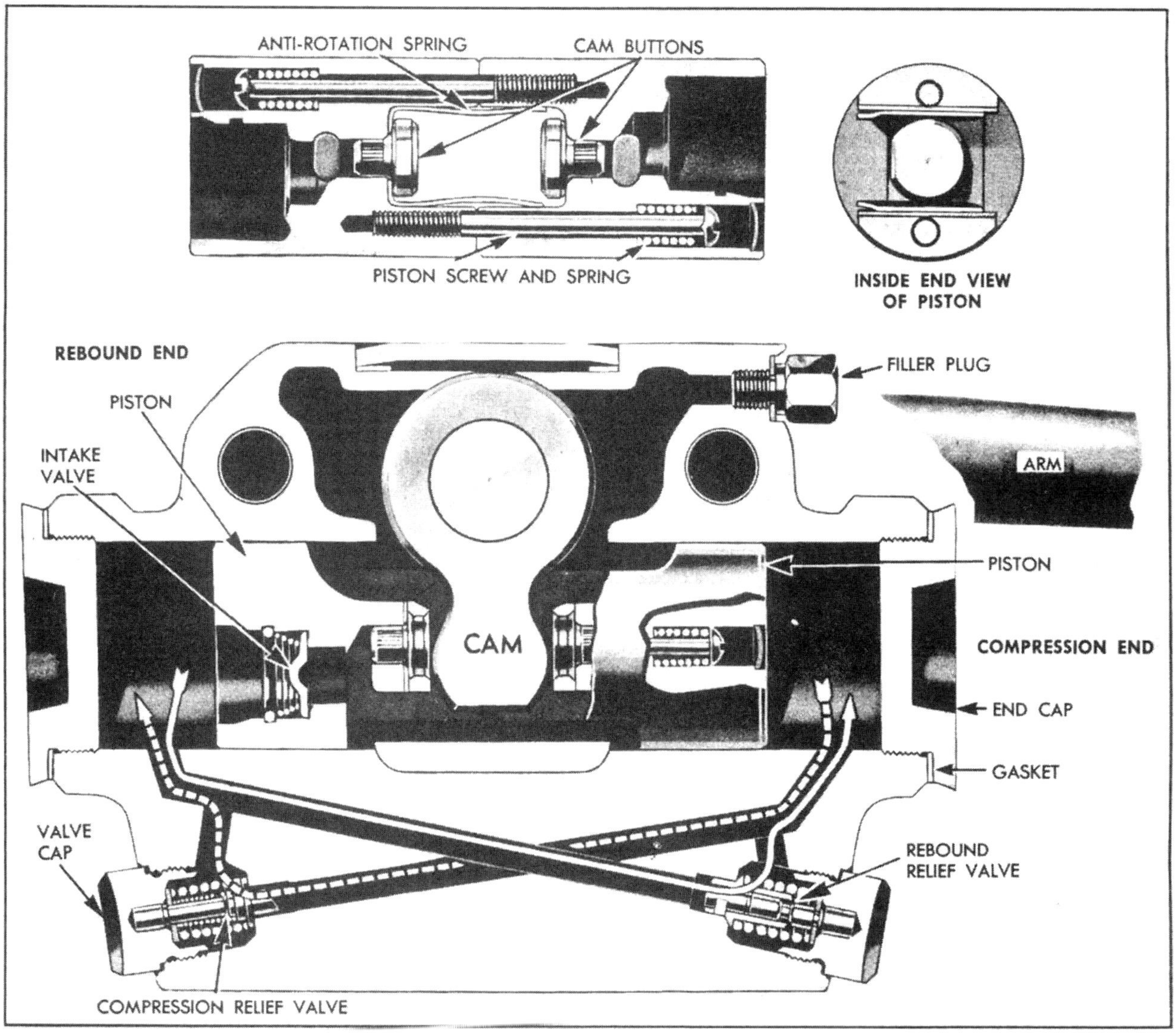

FRAME AND SHOCK ABSORBERS 2-9

Fig. 11—Action during Spring Compression

pression relief valves are located in the ends of drilled passages cast on the outside of the body. These valves are held in place by valve nuts and gaskets which are removable for changing valves. Valve identification is by the number stamped on valve nuts.

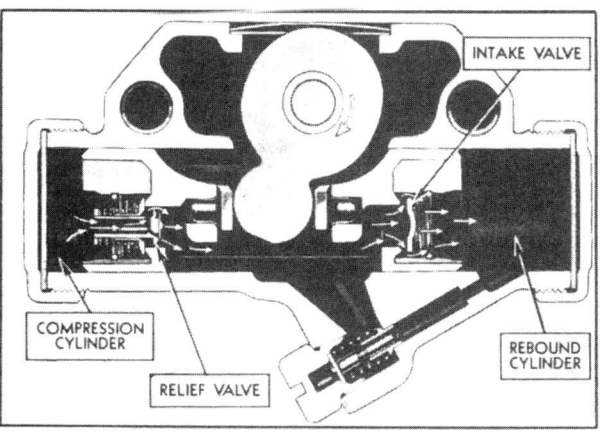

Fig. 12—Action during Compression Stroke

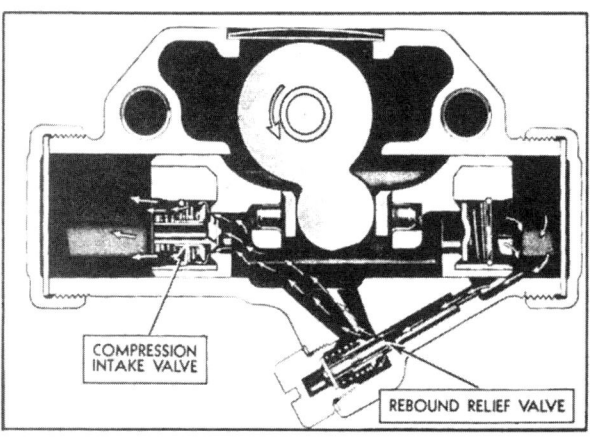

Fig. 13—Action During Rebound Stroke

Operation

Single External Valve Type

The compression piston is fitted with a spring-loaded compression relief valve which has a bleeder hole in the valve stem. Under normal compression, when the fluid pressure is applied by the piston, transfer of fluid takes place through the bleeder hole, but for violent road shocks the valve opens and allows a more rapid transfer of fluid past the valve seat, as well as through the bleeder hole. At the same time, fluid enters the rebound cylinder through the rebound piston intake valve (fig. 12).

During the rebound stroke, fluid is forced through the rebound relief valve at a pressure controlled by the relief valve spring tension. At the same time the intake valve in the compression piston opens allowing fluid to flow into the compression end of the cylinder (fig. 13).

Double External Valve Type

As the arm moves upward on the compression stroke, the compression piston moves toward the right (fig. 11), displacing the fluid in the compression end of the shock absorber. On very slight or slow axle movements, the fluid flows only through the bleeder hole of the compression valve, as indicated by the dotted arrow, and into the rebound end of the cylinder. Under the influence of rapid movement, the additional pressure lifts the valve from its seat against the tension of the valve spring and then flows into the rebound end of the cylinder. At the same time the rebound piston intake valve opens, allowing fluid to flow into the rebound end of the cylinder, as indicated by the white arrow (fig. 11).

During the rebound stroke, or as the arm moves downward, the direction of fluid flow is reversed. The piston moves away from the arm end of the shock absorber, forcing fluid from the rebound end of the cylinder. During slow action, fluid flows only through the bleeder hole of the rebound valve into the compression end of the cylinder. During rapid action, the rebound valve is lifted from its seat and the fluid passes at a pressure controlled by the relief valve spring into the compression end. At the same time, the intake valve of the compression piston opens, allowing fluid to pass into the compression end of the cylinder.

MINOR SERVICE OPERATIONS

Shock absorber service operations, because of the special equipment needed for complete disassembly, are limited to minor operations consisting of lubrication, correction of fluid leaks at end caps, valve plugs or filler caps, replacement of damaged or worn linkage and replacement of valves.

FLUID REQUIREMENT CHECKS

1. Disconnect shock absorber link from axle bracket.
2. Work shock absorber arm up and down. A resistance should be felt in both up and down movement of the shock absorber arm if shock absorber is functioning properly.

   NOTE: If arm travels easily part way in either direction and then comes to a stop and moves slowly for the rest of the arm travel, it indicates a need of fluid.

FILLING SHOCK ABSORBERS

1. Clean all dirt from around filler plug, using a suitable cleaning solvent. Remove plug and disconnect link at axle bracket.
2. Fill shock absorber to capacity, using fluid injector J-1026. Work shock absorber arm slowly up and down while filling.
3. Fill to level of filler plug hole. Air space above is sufficient to allow for expansion of fluid.
4. Replace filler plug, using a new gasket.
5. Attach shock absorber link to shock absorber axle bracket.

SHOCK ABSORBER LINKS

Shock absorber links are of two types, the link and clevis type or rod and taper stud type.

The rod and taper stud type is not serviced separately, but only as an assembly.

To check the link and clevis type for looseness, proceed as follows:

1. Move shock absorber arm up and down to determine tightness of bushings or wear in link pins or link pin holes.
2. Twist link with pliers or pry link connection with screwdriver to check for link or bushing wear.
3. Links which are bent or have elongated link pin holes should be replaced.

   NOTE: Link pins should fit tight in link pin holes to provide a tight link connection.

Link and Clevis Type—Replace

1. Disconnect link at lower end and remove mounting bolts and shock absorber from vehicle.
2. Remove nut and lockwasher and press out link pin attaching link to shock absorber arm.
3. Press worn bushing and grommet from shock

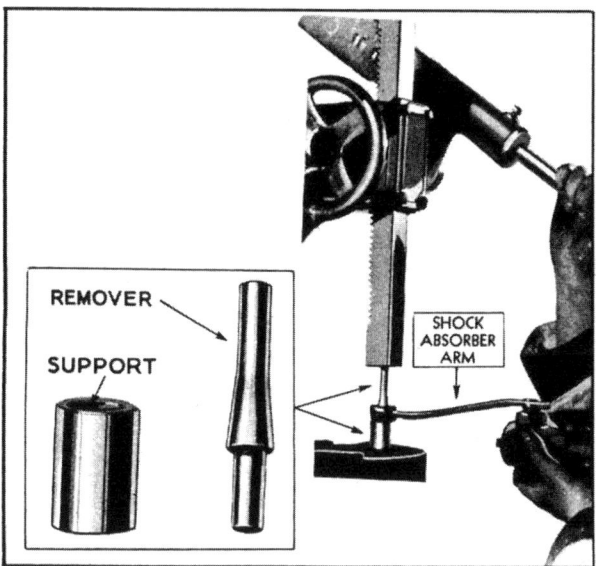

Fig 14—Removing Bushing and Grommet from Shock Absorber Arm

absorber arm using bushing remover and support J-903 in an arbor press (fig. 14).

4. Coat new rubber grommet with liquid soap for easy installation and press it into the shock absorber arm, using tool J-901 to insure proper seating of grommet.

5. Place a new bronze bushing on pilot of the bushing replacer J-899 and press bushing into grommet (fig. 15).

NOTE: This replacing tool expands the grommet and should be used for this operation to prevent damage to the grommet.

6. Reassemble link to shock absorber arm and install clevis pin using tool J-902.

NOTE: Pin should be started through link holes from side of link having punch mark.

7. After pin is installed, strike head of pin a sharp blow to properly seat clevis pin in link holes.

8. Install lockwasher and nut and replace shock absorber on vehicle.

9. Assemble lower end of link to axle fitting with retainer plates and new rubbers.

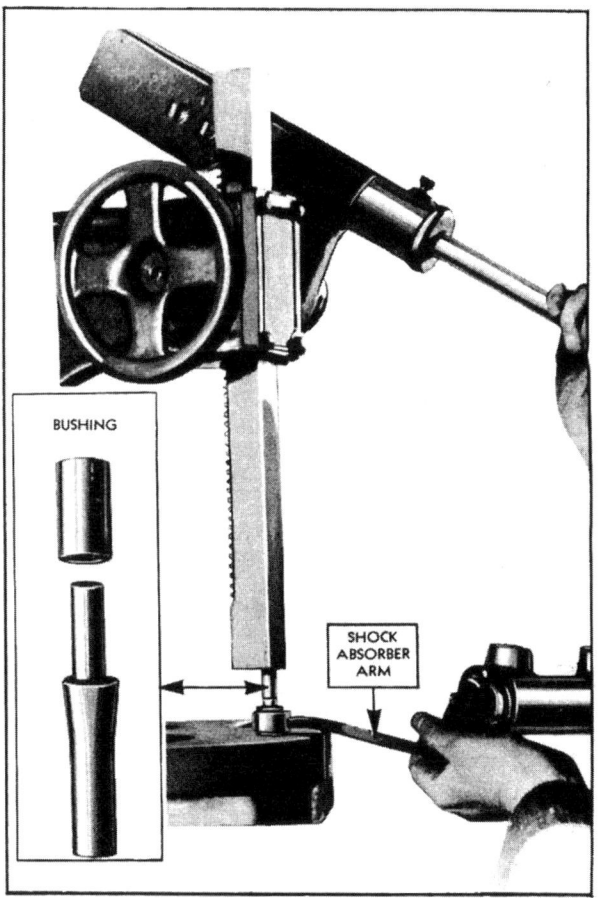

Fig. 15—Installing Bronze Bushing in the Grommet in Shock Absorber Arm

10. Tighten link nut until rubbers are compressed slightly.

Rod and Taper Stud Type—Replace

1. Complete link must be replaced. Upper and lower connections are integral parts of complete link.

2. Remove lockwashers and nuts retaining link end tapered studs to shock absorber arm and axle bracket.

3. Support link and tap end of tapered stud a sharp blow to remove from shock absorber arm and frame bracket.

4. Install new link assembly and draw tapered studs into place firmly with lockwasher and nut.

REPLACEMENT OF SHOCK ABSORBER PARTS

Because of special equipment needed for complete disassembly and assembly of shock absorbers, the body, arm, packing glands, camshaft and cam are not serviced separately. Other parts may be serviced as follows:

1. Disconnect shock absorber link from axle bracket.

2. Remove mounting bolts and shock absorber from vehicle.

3. Clean shock absorber thoroughly with cleaning solvent and drain fluid.

FRAME AND SHOCK ABSORBERS 2-12

4. Mount shock absorber on holding fixture J-895.

RELIEF VALVE REMOVAL

Single External Valve Type

Rebound Relief Valve (External)

1. Remove valve nut using offset screwdriver J-900.
2. Remove relief valve, using a small hooked tool or bent wire.
3. Insert new relief valve and replace valve nut, using a new gasket.

Compression Relief Valve (Internal)

1. Remove left end cap or cap that has valve identification marks stamped on it, using special end cap wrench J-766.

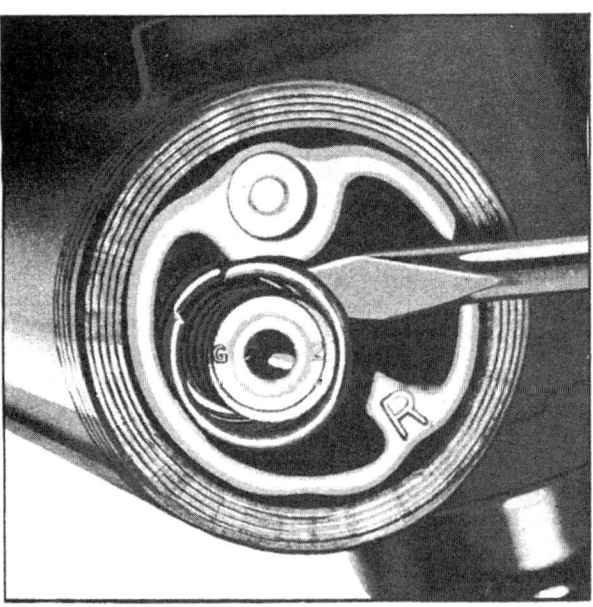

Fig. 16—Removing Valve Spring Retainer Clip

2. Remove valve spring retainer with a screwdriver (fig. 16) and lift out valve.
3. Install new valve and retainer, using valve installing tool J 896-A (fig. 17).

   NOTE: Be sure open side of retainer is installed (fig. 18) to assure easy removal.

4. Flip valve with screwdriver to make sure that the valve and spring are free.
5. Fill shock absorber to capacity with fresh fluid. While filling, move arm through complete strokes to expel air from unit.
6. Replace end cap, using a new gasket, and apply a small amount of grease between end cap and steel spacer.
7. Rotate fixture until arm is in same relation as when mounted in vehicle; remove filler

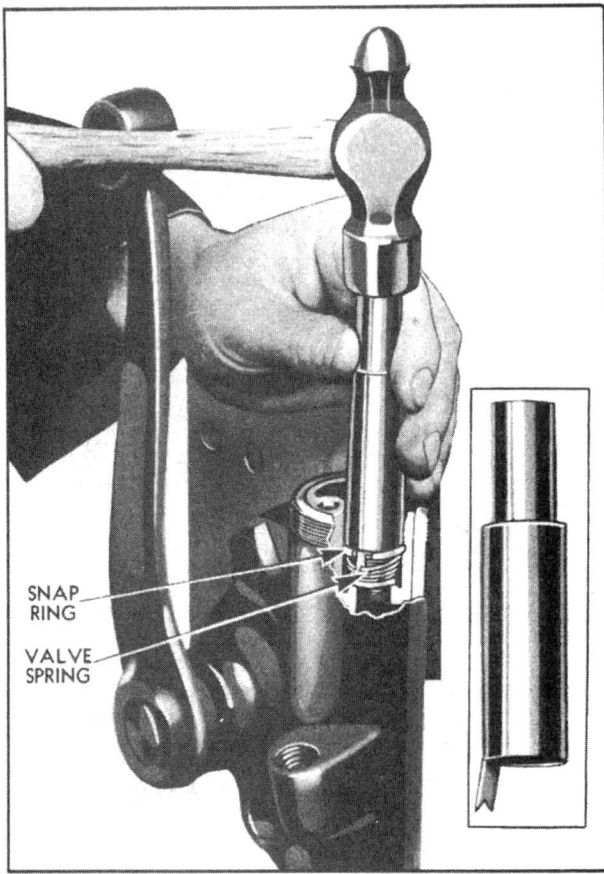

Fig. 17—Installing Valves and Snap Ring

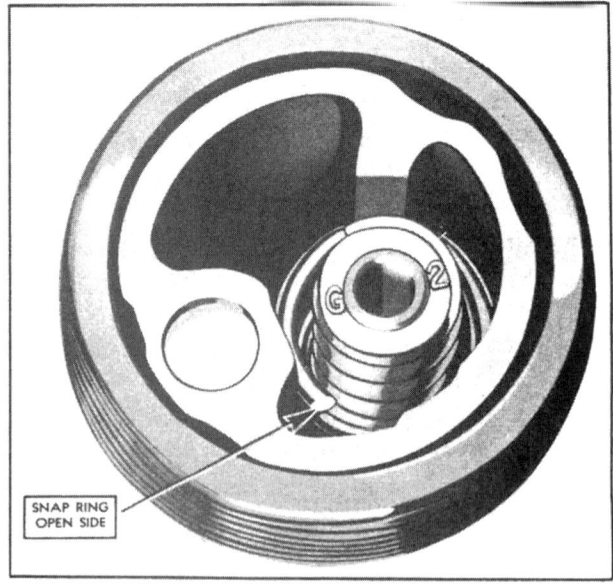

Fig. 18—Correct Position of Snap Ring

plug and allow fluid to drain down to level of reservoir to allow for normal expansion of fluid.

8. Replace filler plug, using a new gasket.

Double External Valve Type

1. Remove relief valve nuts.
2. Pick valves out, using a hooked tool or piece of wire.
3. Install new valves, making sure compression valve and rebound valves are located in proper passages.
4. Install relief valve nuts, using new gaskets.

Disassembly

1. Mount shock absorber on holding fixture J-895 and remove end caps.
2. Remove valve nuts and external valves.
3. Remove piston valve spring retainers with a screwdriver (fig. 16) and lift valves out.
4. Remove plugs over piston screws by piercing with a sharp tool and lifting out (fig. 19).
5. Disassemble pistons by removing piston screws.

Fig. 19—Piercing Piston Screw Plug

Inspection

1. Wash all parts in cleaning solvent.
2. Blow out valve orifices with compressed air.
3. Check valves for dirt.
4. Inspect all parts for wear.
5. Check camshaft for wear in housing by moving arm sideways. If shaft is galled or worn, replace complete shock absorber.

Assembly

1. Assemble external valves and nuts, using new gaskets.
2. File chamfer on rebound piston (the one without the anti-rotation spring) at point indicated in Figure 20.

   NOTE: This is necessary to allow the anti-rotation spring to enter the other piston during assembly.

3. Assemble piston with cam clearance up and also with high arch of anti-rotation spring up.
4. Install piston screws tightly, then back off from one to one-and-a-half turns to prevent a possible bind between cam and cam buttons.
5. Install new plugs over piston screws and expand in place.
6. Replace piston valves, using new valve retainers, installing retainers with installing tool J-896-A (fig. 17).

   NOTE: Be sure open side of retainer is installed (fig. 18) to assure easy removal.

7. Flip valves with screwdriver to make sure they are free.
8. Replace one end cap, using a new gasket. Turn shock so open end is up and fill to capacity.

   NOTE: Apply a small amount of grease between end cap and steel spacer.

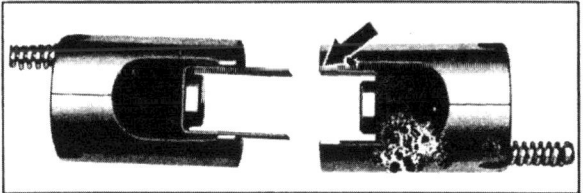

Fig. 20—Where to File Chamfer on Piston

9. Move shock absorber arm through its normal travel to expel any trapped air and refill to capacity.
10. Install remaining end cap, using a new gasket.
11. Rotate shock absorber to a position that is in same relation to mounted position and remove filler plug, allowing fluid to drain to level of reservoir.
12. Replace filler plug, using a new gasket.

TROUBLES AND REMEDIES
SHOCK ABSORBER

Symptom and Probable Cause

Hard Riding
    a. Shock absorber broken

    b. Vehicle springs and shackles improperly lubricated

Vehicle Too Flexible
    a. Lack of fluid in shock absorber

    b. Dirt in relief valve (Cam and lever type shock absorber)
    c. Shock absorber broken

Shock Absorber Noisy
    a. Insufficient fluid

    b. Shock absorber broken

    c. Grommets at upper or lower stems not compressed sufficiently or nut on rear shock absorber lever eye not tight (Direct-acting type shock absorbers)
    d. Shock absorber link bushings worn or mounting bolts loose. (Cam and lever type shock absorber)

Leaks Fluid
    a. Sealing welds broken loose (Direct-acting shock absorber)
    b. Packing gland worn (Direct-acting shock absorber)
    c. Cover screws loose (Cam and lever shock absorber)
    d. Cover on end gaskets damaged (Cam and lever shock absorber)
    e. Relief valve or filler plug leaks (Cam and lever shock absorber)
    f. Leaks at camshaft (Cam and lever shock absorber)

Probable Remedy

a. Disconnect shock absorber or shock absorber link and test action; replace inoperative Direct-acting shock absorbers, and replace or overhaul Cam and lever type shock absorber.
b. Lubricate springs and shackles

a. Replace Direct-acting shock absorber; fill Cam and lever type shock absorber.
b. Clean valves, flush shock absorber and refill with clean fluid
c. Replace Direct-acting shock absorber, replace or overhaul Cam and lever type shock absorber

a. Replace Direct-acting shock absorber; Fill Cam and lever type shock absorber
b. Replace Direct-acting shock absorber; Replace or overhaul Cam and lever type shock absorber
c. Tighten retainer nuts as specified or tighten rear shock eye retainer bolt nut

d. Rebush or replace links and tighten mounting bolts

a. Replace shock absorber
b. Replace shock absorber
c. Tighten screws
d. Replace gasket
e. Tighten plug
f. Replace shock absorber

FRAME AND SHOCK ABSORBERS 2-15

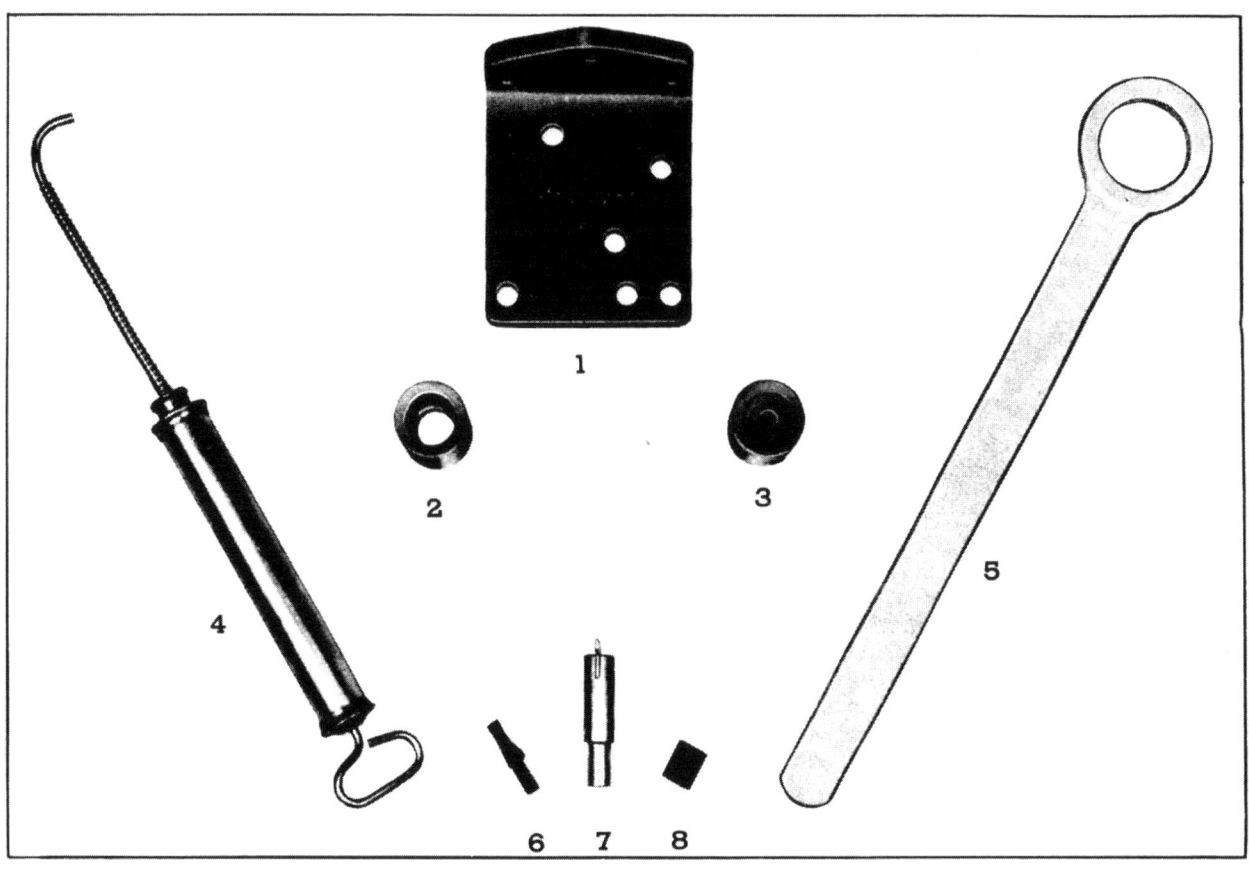

Fig. 21—Shock Absorber Special Tools

1. J895-1   Shock Absorber Holding Fixture
2. J903   Link Bushing Remover Support
3. J901   Shock Absorber Rubber Bushing Depth Spacer
4. KMO-1026   Oil Injector
5. J766   Knurled End Cap Wrench
6. J899   Link Bushing Remover and Replacer
7. J896A   Valve Installing Tool
8. J902   Link Removing Tool

SERVICE NEWS REFERENCE

Month	Page No.	Subject

SERVICE NEWS REFERENCE

Month	Page No.	Subject

SECTION 3

FRONT SUSPENSION

CONTENTS OF THIS SECTION

	Page
Front Axle Assembly	3-1
Front Springs	3-13
Troubles and Remedies	3-14
Special Tools	3-15
Front Axle Specifications	3-16
Front Spring Specifications	3-16
Torque Specifications	3-16
Service News Reference	3-16

FRONT AXLE ASSEMBLY

INDEX

	Page		Page
General Description	3-2	Front Wheel Bearings—Adjust	3-7
Minor Service Operations	3-3	Major Service Operations	3-8
Tie Rod	3-3	Front Axle Assembly	3-8
Removal and Installation	3-4	Removal	3-8
Steering Connecting Rod	3-4	Disassembly	3-8
Steering Knuckle Adjustment	3-5	Inspection	3-8
Stabilizer—½ Ton	3-5	Repairs	3-8
Stabilizer—Forward Control	3-6	Kingpin Bushings—Replace	3-8
Maintenance	3-6	Oversize Kingpins	3-9
Hubs and Drums	3-6	Straightening Front Axle "I" Beam	3-9
Removal	3-6	Assembly	3-9
Inspection	3-6	Installation	3-10
Repairs	3-6	Front End Alignment	3-10
Bearing Races—Replacement	3-6	Description	3-10
Brake Drum—Replacement	3-6	Service Operations	3-12
Installation	3-7	Correcting Front End Alignment	3-12

GENERAL DESCRIPTION

The front axle used on all truck models is the reverse Elliot type of construction (fig. 1). It is a steel drop-forging with the spring seats forged integral with the "I" beam. The "I" beam is heat treated to assure extreme toughness and is machined to very close limits.

Kingpin holes in each end of the "I" beam are bored at a slight angle to permit the kingpin to tilt inward at the top. This inward tilt of the kingpins is called Kingpin inclination.

Each steering knuckle is mounted to the front axle by means of the kingpin and rides against the kingpin thrust bearing. This bearing is a single row ball bearing, enclosed in a dust shield, on ½, ¾, 1 and 1½ ton trucks, except Forward Control models, the 1½ ton School Bus and 2 Ton. On Forward Control models, 1½ ton School Bus and on 2 ton models, this kingpin thrust bearing consists of two steel thrust washers separated by a leaded bronze washer and enclosed by two telescoping dust shields (fig. 2).

The brake flange is securely bolted to the steering knuckle and carries the brake shoes and wheel cylinders. The steering knuckle arm is also bolted

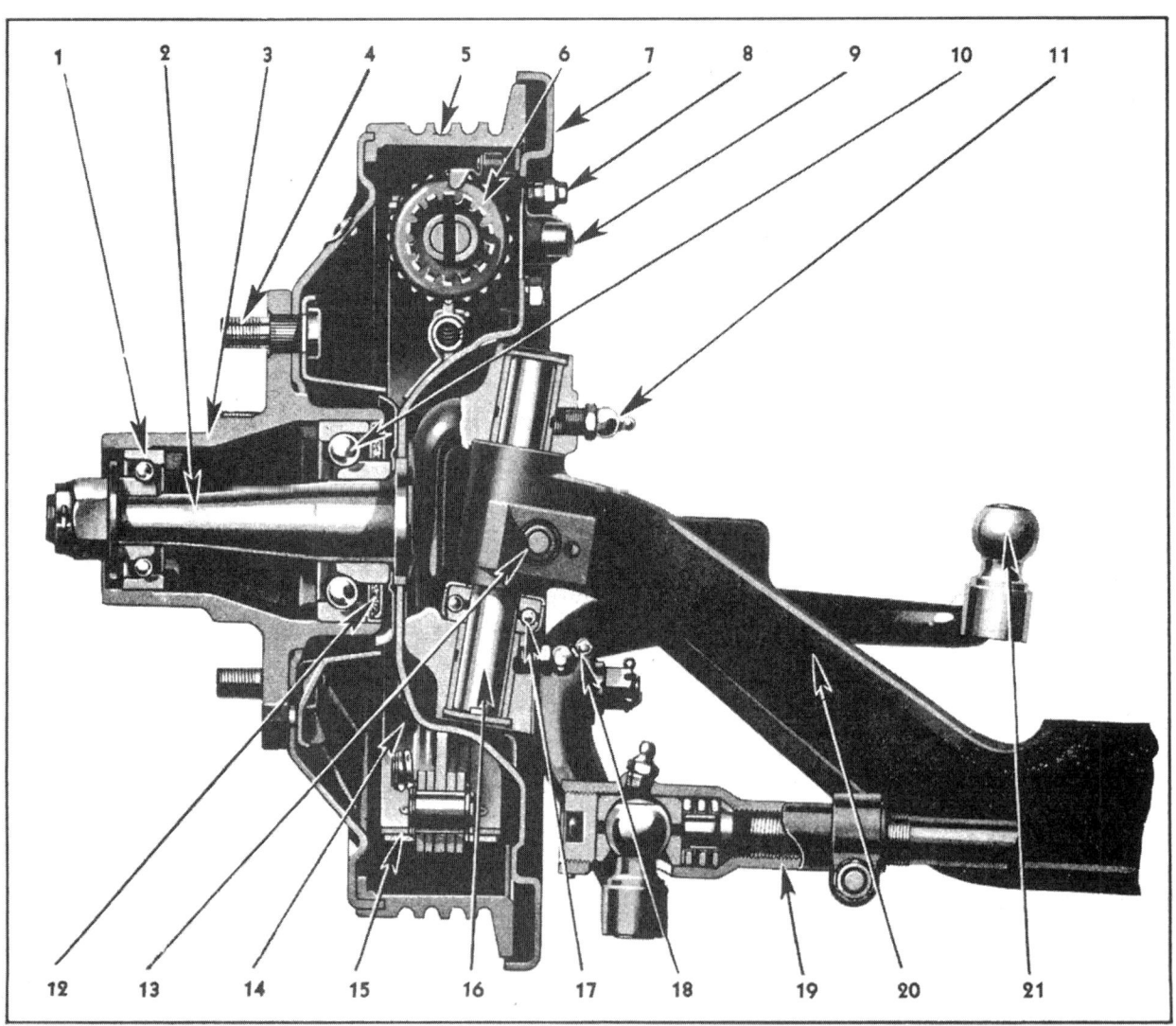

Fig. 1—Front Axle Assembly Cross Section

1. Outer Wheel Bearing
2. Wheel Spindle
3. Wheel Hub
4. Wheel Hub Bolt
5. Brake Drum
6. Brake Wheel Cylinder
7. Brake Flange Plate
8. Brake Bleeder Valve and Screw
9. Brake Wheel Cylinder Hose Connection
10. Inner Wheel Bearing
11. Lubrication Fitting
12. Inner Bearing Oil Seal
13. Kingpin Lock Pin
14. Brake Shoe
15. Brake Lining
16. Kingpin
17. Kingpin Thrust Bearing
18. Lubrication Fitting
19. Tie Rod End
20. Axle I-Beam
21. Steering and Third Arm

FRONT SUSPENSION 3-3

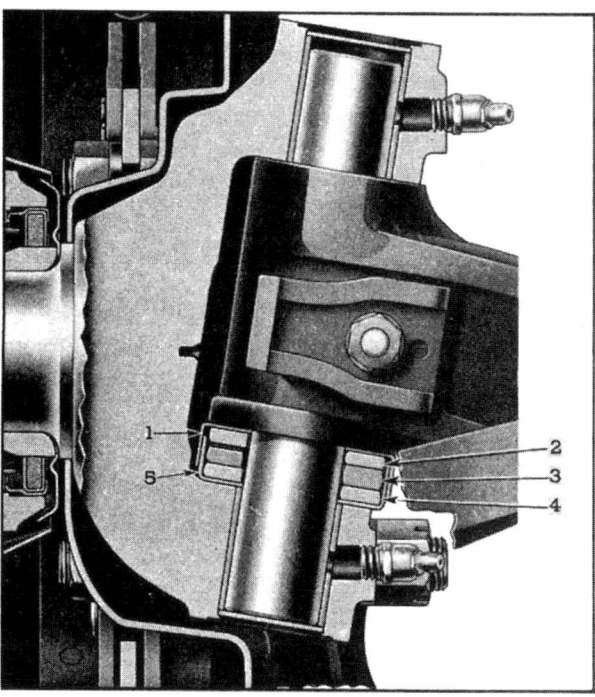

Fig. 2—Kingpin Thrust Bearing

1. Upper Dust Shield
2. Steel Thrust Washer
3. Leaded Bronze Washer
4. Steel Thrust Washer
5. Lower Dust Shield

to the steering knuckle and the steering knuckles are connected to each other by a tie rod. The tie rod is adjustable for length and being attached to the steering knuckle arms, controls the toe-in of the front wheels.

The steering third arm is forged integral with the left knuckle arm and is connected to the pitman arm by the steering connecting rod.

A caster shim or "I" beam spacer is inserted between the front springs and front axle. The installation of this shim controls the amount the top of the axle inclines or tilts backwards. This backward tilt of the axle is known as the caster angle.

The front wheel spindles, which are forged integrally with the steering knuckles, are tilted downward at their outer ends causing the front wheels to be farther apart at the top than they are at the bottom. This slight angular position of the front wheels is called camber.

The steering knuckle arms are installed on the knuckles at an angle, permitting the front wheels to toe-out when making turns. This is necessary so that when turning curves each wheel may travel in a different arc. This toe-out on curves is known as steering geometry.

Kingpin lock pins are tapered pins and are inserted from the front of the axle. Steering knuckle stops are installed over the rear end of the lock pin. Stop and lock pin are held in place with a nut and lockwasher. This nut should be inspected at regular intervals and tightened when necessary.

MINOR SERVICE OPERATIONS

TIE ROD

Tie rods used are three piece type consisting of a rod and two tie rod end assemblies. Right and left hand threads are provided to facilitate toe-in adjustment.

Two types of tie rod ends are used. Figure 3 illustrates the adjustable type used on all ½ and ¾ ton except the ¾ ton Forward Control. The

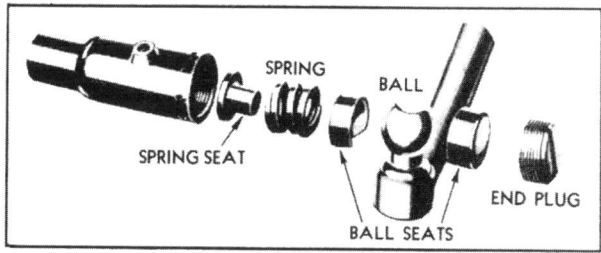

Fig. 3—Front Axle Tie Rod

other type (fig. 4) is used on the ¾ ton Forward Control and on all 1, 1½ and 2 ton.

The tie rod end used on the heavier models (fig. 4), is constructed with inner and outer seats tapered

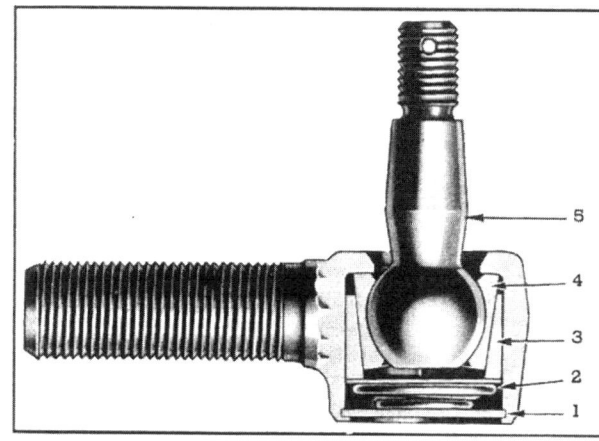

Fig. 4—Tie Rod End

1. Plug
2. Spring
3. Outer Ball Seat
4. Inner Ball Seat
5. Ball Stud

to fit together. These seats are split in half permitting spring pressure to force outer seat downward, thereby compressing inner seats in firm contact with ball at all times. This tie rod end is serviced as an assembly and should be replaced when excessive up and down motion is evident or if any lost motion or end play at ball end of stud exists. This type tie rod end is self-adjusting for wear and requires no attention in service other than periodic lubrication and occasional inspection to see that ball studs are tight.

(½ and ¾ Ton, except Forward Control)

Removal

1. Remove front wheels.
2. Remove cotter pin, end plug and ball seat.
3. Screw end plug back into end of tie rod until ball is in center of opening.
4. Pry tie rod from steering arm ball by placing a bar between tie rod end and steering arm.
5. Loosen tie rod end clamp bolt and unscrew end from tie rod.

Installation

1. If tie rod ends were removed, install ends on tie rod making sure both ends are threaded an equal distance on tie rod.
2. Install spring seat, spring and ball seat in both tie rod ends and install tie rod to steering arms.
3. Install outer ball seat and end plug into each tie rod end.
4. Screw plugs in tight until springs are compressed solid and back off to first cotter pin hole.
5. Insert and clinch cotter pins.
6. Lubricate both ends of tie rod.
7. Install front wheels.
8. Adjust toe-in as described under "Front Wheel Alignment."

(¾ Ton Forward Control and All 1, 1½ and 2 Ton)

Removal

1. Remove cotter pin from ball stud at each end of tie rod and remove ball stud nuts.
2. Screw J-1273 remover over threaded end of ball studs to protect the threads. Support steering arm and drive on remover with a hammer to loosen studs, then remove tie rod ends from steering arms.
3. To remove tie rod ends from tie rod, loosen clamp bolts, and unscrew end assembly from tie rod.

Installation

1. If tie rod ends were removed, install ends on tie rod making sure both ends are threaded an equal distance on tie rod and that both ends are in the same plane.
2. Make sure that threads on ball studs and in ball stud nuts are perfectly clean and smooth.

   NOTE: If threads are not clean and smooth, ball studs may turn in tie rod ends when attempting to tighten nuts.

3. Install ball studs in steering arms and install washers and nuts on studs.
4. Tighten nuts securely and install new cotter pins.
5. Adjust toe-in as described under "Front Wheel Alignment".

STEERING CONNECTING ROD

(½, ¾, 1 and (1948-50) 1½ and 2 Ton)

The steering connecting rod used on all ½, ¾, 1 and (1948-50) 1½ and 2 Ton trucks (fig. 5) is the

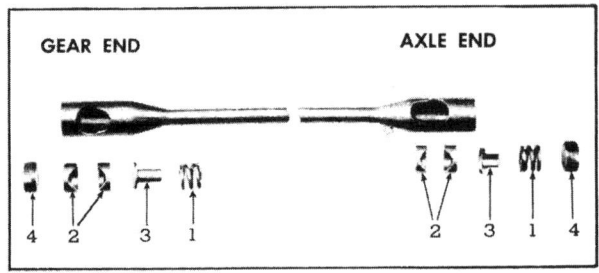

Fig. 5—Steering Connecting Rod

1. Spring
2. Ball Seats
3. Spring Seat
4. Screw Plug

adjustable ball and socket type. Adjustment is made manually by use of a screw plug (4) in each end of the rod assembly.

Adjustment of the steering connecting rod is required whenever the pitman arm ball or the steering arm ball is found to have end play in the connecting rod socket.

1. Remove cotter pin from end of socket; then, using a drag link bit in screw plug slot, tighten plug snugly to remove all end play of ball.
2. Back off screw plug one complete turn plus amount necessary to insert cotter pin and lock adjustment.

Ball joints must be tight enough to prevent end play and yet loose enough to allow free movement. Be sure sockets have ample lubrication.

(1951) 1½ and 2 Ton

The steering connecting rod used on all 1951 heavy duty trucks is designed with both studs permanently installed in the connecting rod and the assembly is furnished for service replacement as a unit. The ends of the studs are threaded and they are attached to the steering third arm and pitman arm with a nut and cotter pin.

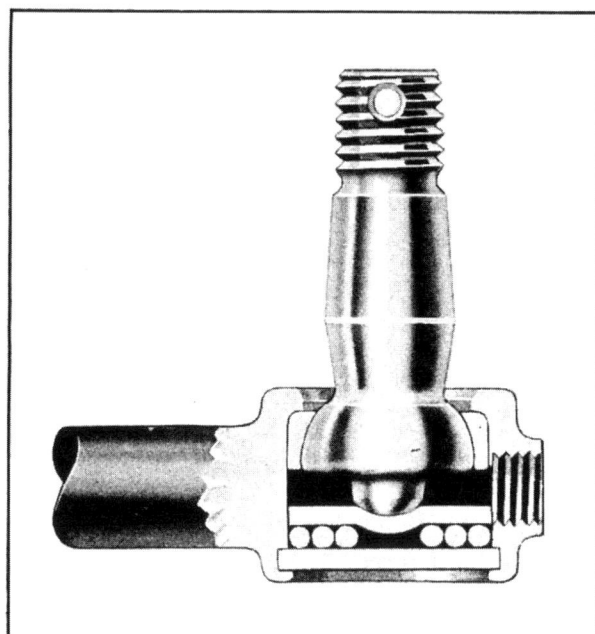

Fig. 6—Steering Connecting Rod

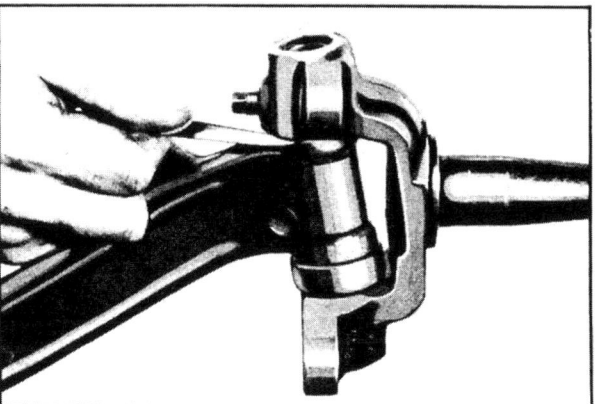

Fig. 7—Clearance between I-Beam and Steering Knuckle

In the assembly of the ball stud in each end of the connecting rod (fig. 6), the ball head fits on a spherical seat in the rod and is held tightly against the seat by a plate and spring, the spring itself being held in by a plug pressed and spun permanently in place.

STEERING KNUCKLE—ADJUSTMENT

As illustrated in Figures 1 and 2 steering knuckles are provided with thrust bearings or thrust washers mounted between the knuckle yoke and the lower face of the axle "I" beam. Up and down movement must be kept within proper limits to prevent pounding and consequent breakage. Shims placed between the upper face of the axle "I" beam and yoke are used to compensate for excessive movement.

This clearance should be checked as illustrated in Figure 7 and shims should be installed if this clearance exceeds .005". Shim installation is covered under "Major Service Operations."

STABILIZER

(1948-50) ½ Ton

The stabilizer bar used on the front of some (1948-50) ½ ton trucks is connected at the rear ends to the front spring bumper retainers by means of retainer caps. At the front it is attached to support brackets by means of a two-piece link at each side.

Removal or Replacement

1. Remove retaining caps at front spring bumper retainer and shock absorber link attaching plate.
2. Remove large bolts attaching upper end of the two-piece stabilizer shaft link to the support bracket.
3. Remove stabilizer assembly from vehicle.
4. Remove bolts holding two-piece bracket together to relieve pressure on rubber bushings and remove bracket and bushing from bar.
5. Replace bushing and bracket to stabilizer bar, but do not tighten bolts holding two-piece bracket together.
6. Replace stabilizer on vehicle and replace large bolt through stabilizer link and attach to support bracket.
7. Replace retaining caps securing shaft to front spring bumper retainer.
8. With weight of vehicle on wheels with no pay load, tighten bolts that hold two-piece bracket together.

NOTE: This must be done with no load in vehicle to allow rubber bushings to grip bar in proper relation to frame and axle.

(1951) ½ Ton

The transverse section of the stabilizer shaft is fitted in rubber bushings, retained in two U-shaped brackets and attached through a reinforcement plate to the underside of the front cross member. The two arms extend rearward and are fastened to the axle through rubber insulated links. These links are metal rods having a clevis at the bottom end which is attached through a rubber bushing and pin to an I-beam bracket which is fastened to the I-beam with a "U" bolt.

Removal

1. At the rear of each arm remove link nut, upper grommet retainer and grommet and disconnect arms from links.
2. Remove nuts and lockwashers retaining "U" shaped stabilizer shaft brackets to front cross member and remove stabilizer bar and

brackets. The split rubber bushings may now be removed from the stabilizer bar.

NOTE: Stabilizer shaft bracket reinforcements will drop off bracket bolts when bar is removed.

Installation

1. Place new rubber bushings on stabilizer bar and install support brackets over bushings.
2. Make sure bracket reinforcements are in place and then bolt brackets loosely to front cross member.
3. Place rear end of each arm over links. Install rubber grommet, upper grommet retainer and nut and tighten nut to limit of threads.
4. With wheels of truck on floor and supporting truck weight, bounce front end up and down several times to allow parts to seek proper relationship.
5. Tighten stabilizer shaft bracket mounting bolts securely.

Forward Control

Removal

1. Remove bolts attaching the stabilizer support brackets to mounting plates on the frame cross member. The brackets and the split rubber bushings on the stabilizer bar may now be removed.
2. Pull the stabilizer shaft toward the front of the vehicle, sliding the shaft ends out of the grommets in the spring bumper and stabilizer bar retainers.
3. Remove the rubber grommets in the spring bumper and stabilizer bar retainers by pushing them through the eye openings.

Installation

1. Replace the grommets in the spring bumper and stabilizer bar retainers. Lubricate the grommets with soap for ease in assembly.
2. Locate the ends of the stabilizer shaft in these grommets and move the shaft rearward until it is properly positioned under the mounting plates on the frame cross member.
3. Place the rubber bushings on the stabilizer shaft and the support brackets over the bushings. With the weight of vehicle on wheels and no payload, bolt the support brackets to the mounting plates and the cross member.

MAINTENANCE

At periodic intervals inspect front spring clips, "U" bolts, kingpin lock pins, turning stops and tie rod ends for looseness, excessive wear or damage. Tighten spring clips as required. Make certain that kingpin lock pins, turning stops and tie rod ends are secure and tightened properly. Also examine knuckle pin seals.

HUBS AND DRUMS

Removal

1. Loosen front wheel to hub bolts, raise vehicle from floor, place on stand jacks and remove front wheels.
2. Remove hub grease cap, cotter pin, spindle nut, spindle washer and remove hub and drum assembly.

   NOTE: In some cases it may be necessary to back off the brake adjustment because of scored drums or badly worn linings holding drum on.

3. Remove outer bearing from hub with fingers. The inner bearing will remain in the hub and may be removed by prying out the inner bearing felt retainer.
4. Wash all parts thoroughly in cleaning solvent.

Inspection

1. Check all bearings for cracked bearing cages, worn or pitted balls or rollers.
2. Check bearing races for cracks or evidence of scoring.
3. Check brake drums for out-of-round or scored condition.
4. Check bearing outer races for looseness in hubs.

REPAIRS

Bearing Races—Replacement

1. Insert front wheel bearing cup remover K-224 through hub, indexing end of tool with notches in hub shoulder behind bearing cup.
2. Tap lightly on cup through each notch to remove cup from hub.
3. Install new bearing cups in hub using K 463-A Bearing Cup Inserter Set (fig. 8).
4. Make sure that cups are not cocked and are fully seated against shoulder in the hub.

Brake Drum—Replacement

½ Ton Models

The brake drum is held to the hub by serrated hub bolts which in addition to the serrations are swedged into the countersink in the hub bolt hole.

1. Support hub and drum in an arbor press and press bolts from hub and drum.
2. Place new drum on hub, position new gasket and grease deflector on drum.

FRONT SUSPENSION 3-7

Fig. 8—Installing Bearing Cups

3. Use new hub bolts and press them into position making sure they bottom.
4. Using J-554 peening tool and anvil, swedge bolts into countersink in hub bolt holes.

¾ and 1 Ton Models

1. Remove two slotted head screws and remove brake drum.
2. Install new brake drum and retain in position with two slotted head screws.

1½, 2 Ton and C.O.E.

The brake drums are held to the hub by serrated bolts which are locked in position with lockwashers and nuts.

1. Remove brake drum to wheel hub bolt lockwashers and nuts.
2. Support drum in an arbor press with open side of drum up and press hub off of the serrated bolts. Tap studs out of drum with lead hammer.
3. Place new drum on hub, position new gasket and grease deflector on drum.
4. Replace hub bolts pressing them into position making sure they bottom.
5. Install retaining nuts and lockwashers and tighten securely.

Hub Assembly—Installation

1. Hand pack both inner and outer bearings. Front wheels equipped with ball bearings should be lubricated with a short fibre "High Melting Point Lubricant." Front wheels equipped with barrel type roller bearings should be lubricated with "Soft, Smooth Grease."
2. Place inner bearing in hub, then install a new felt retainer in hub.
3. Using a piece of fine sandpaper, lightly sand the inside braking surface of brake drum to insure a clean surface and proper brake operation.
4. Carefully position hub on spindle making sure the inner oil deflector is in proper position between inner bearing inner race and shoulder on the spindle.

NOTE: On vehicles equipped with a heavy duty front axle use a short length of 1¼" pipe to provide support for inner bearing and allow for easy installation of hub and drum assembly.

5. Install outer bearing pressing it firmly into the hub by hand.
6. Install adjusting nut washer, adjusting nut and adjust bearings.

Front Wheel Bearings—Adjust

The proper adjustment of front wheel bearings is one of the service operations that has a definite bearing on safety. Improperly adjusted front wheel bearings cause increased tire wear, lack of steering stability and a tendency of the truck to

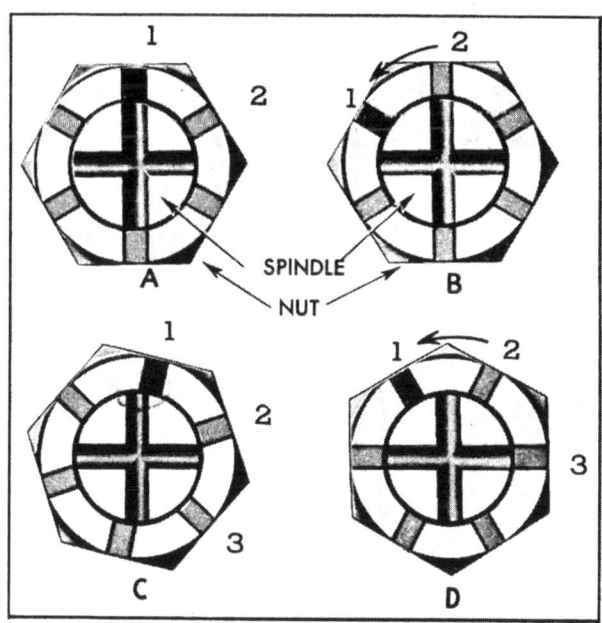

Fig. 9—Method of Adjusting Front Wheel Bearings

wander or shimmy. Therefore, it is important that the wheel and tire assembly be removed from the hub when making front wheel bearing adjustments. This eliminates the heavy drag of wheel

FRONT SUSPENSION 3-8

and tire and enables the workman to perform a much more accurate adjustment.

1. With front wheel and tires removed, tighten spindle nut to 33 ft. lbs. torque.
2. Check location of a slot in the nut with refence to a hole in the spindle. If a slot in the nut lines up with either the vertical or horizontal holes in the spindle (see "A," fig. 9), back off the nut (1/6 turn) until the next slot in the nut lines up with the same hole in the spindle and insert cotter pin (see "B," fig. 9).
3. If, when the spindle nut is tightened to 33 ft. lbs., the slot in the nut has passed beyond the vertical or horizontal holes in the spindle (see "C," fig. 9), back off nut a sufficient amount (between $\frac{1}{12}$ and $\frac{1}{6}$ turn) to line up the second next slot in nut and the other hole in the spindle.

NOTE: To illustrate this point the slots in the nut are indicated 1, 2, and 3 (see "D," fig. 9). If the slot marked 1 on the nut is slightly beyond the vertical hole in the spindle, the nut should be backed off until the slot marked 3 is in line with the horizontal hole in the spindle. It will be noted that the nut has been backed off slightly less than 1/6 turn.

4. Install wheels and tires and lower vehicle to the floor.

MAJOR SERVICE OPERATIONS

Steering knuckles, kingpins and bushings may be replaced as well as minor axle straightening without removing axle assembly from the vehicle. However, when the front axle assembly requires a complete overhaul the assembly can be removed, overhauled and installed as follows.

FRONT AXLE ASSEMBLY

Removal

1. Raise vehicle and support frame with blocks behind front spring rear brackets. Support axle on a suitable dolly.
2. Disconnect shock absorber lower stud or link from link attaching plate or lower attaching bracket and disconnect stabilizer bar if used.
3. Remove wheels, hubs, brake drums and bearings as outlined in this section.
4. Remove brake backing plates and wire up to frame to prevent damage to brake hose.
5. Disconnect steering connecting rod from steering arm.
6. Remove "U" bolts attaching axle to spring assembly.
7. Lower axle and remove from vehicle.

Disassembly

1. Remove tie rod as directed under "Tie Rod Removal" in this section.
2. Remove kingpin lock pin nut, washer and stop plate.
3. Replace nut on lock pin far enough to protect threads, then strike nut with a hammer to loosen lock pin.
4. Remove nut and drive lock pin out of axle using a hammer and small drift.
5. With a small chisel break kingpin plug stakes loose.
6. Remove either top or bottom plug by drilling through plug and then prying plug out with a drift.
7. Drive kingpin out of axle and knuckle using a brass drift. This will also remove other kingpin plug.
8. Remove steering knuckle and thrust bearing or thrust washers and dust shields from axle.

Inspection

1. Thoroughly clean all parts in cleaning solvent.
2. Examine thrust bearings or thrust washers for excessive wear, pitting or other damage.
3. Inspect steering knuckle bushings for excessive wear, scoring or other damage.

NOTE: If, when a new kingpin is tried in bushings, it is loose the bushings must be replaced.

4. Inspect kingpins for scoring or excessive wear.
5. Check kingpin holes in axle "I" beam using a new kingpin. If the kingpin is found to be loose in the "I" beam the axle end should be reamed for an oversize kingpin.

REPAIRS

Kingpin Floating Bushings—½ Ton Trucks

Bushings used on all ½ ton vehicles are the floating type and when replaced in service, either standard or .010" oversize, they need not be reamed to size as all service bushings are machined to finished dimensions. However, when replacing floating bushings care should be used to make sure that the oil groove in the bushing lines up with the lubrication fitting in the steering knuckle. These bushings should be free on the kingpin, but may be somewhat snug in the steering knuckle.

Kingpin Bushings—¾–1–1½–2 Ton Trucks

Removal

1. Support steering knuckle in bench vise.
2. Remove bushings from steering knuckle, by using driver K-318 on ¾, 1 and 1½ ton conventional models or J-2248 on ¾ and 1 ton Forward Control, 1½ ton school bus and all 2 ton models.

    NOTE: If tool is not available, thread a coarse tap into bushing and with a brass drift slightly smaller than knuckle pin diameter and long enough to extend 1" through opposite side of yoke, drive out tap and bushing.

Installation

1. Round off edges of new bushings slightly with a file.
2. Position bushings in knuckle pin hole so that oil hole in bushing will be aligned with lubrication fitting hole in steering knuckle.
3. Press bushing into place using an arbor press and bushing driver K-318 on ¾, 1 and 1½ ton Conventional models or J-2248 on Forward control, 1½ ton school bus and all 2 ton vehicles.

    NOTE: Do not attempt to drive bushings into place with a hammer.

4. Supporting steering knuckle in a bench vise, carefully ream bushings to size using J-3057 (.923") reamer on ¾, 1 and 1½ ton conventional models and KMO-654 (1.110") reamer on Forward Control, 1½ ton school bus and all 2 ton vehicles.

    NOTE: Bushing reamer must be long enough to ream both bushings at once in order to maintain alignment (fig. 10).

Oversize Kingpins

When installing oversize kingpins on ¾, 1 and 1½ ton models, except Forward Control, it is necessary to ream the steering knuckle bushings first with the reamer used for fitting a standard size kingpin and then with a special oversize reamer KMO-226-2 to fit the .010" oversize kingpin. A .020" oversize bushing must be used when installing .020" oversize kingpins and they must be reamed with KMO-312-2 reamer.

Reaming "I" Beam for Oversize Kingpins

When oversize kingpins are being installed on ¾, 1 and 1½ ton models, except Forward Control, it is necessary to ream the kingpin holes in the axle ends to accommodate the larger kingpins. The reamers are designed with long pilot diameters ahead and behind the cutting flutes to assure perfect alignment.

When installing .010" oversize kingpin use reamer KMO-226-1, and for .020" oversize kingpin use reamer KMO-312-1.

CAUTION: Use lard oil as a cutting fluid when reaming.

Straightening Front Axle "I" Beam

Front axle "I" beams which have been bent or twisted excessively from their original shape should be replaced with a new part. Experience has shown that parts excessively bent or twisted are generally distorted beyond their material elastic limit. As a general rule, when extreme bent conditions exist, minute fractures hardly visible, will occur. Failure under ordinary operating conditions usually results.

The straightening of any axle forging must be performed by mechanics who are thoroughly familiar with such operations and the use of special straightening tools.

Application of heat to assist straightening operations weakens the material strength of all axle forgings. ALWAYS STRAIGHTEN FORGINGS COLD—UNDER NO CIRCUMSTANCES SHOULD HEAT BE APPLIED.

Assembly

1. (a) On ½, ¾, 1 and 1½ ton (except Forward Control).

    Position steering knuckle on axle and then slide thrust bearing into place between lower face of axle end and steering knuckle lower yoke. Align holes in steering knuckle yoke, axle end and thrust bearing.

Fig. 10—Reaming Steering Knuckle Bushings

FRONT SUSPENSION 3-10

NOTE: Make sure closed side of the thrust bearing is at the top.

(b) On Forward Control, 1½ Ton School Bus and All 2 Ton:

Position steering knuckle on axle and then slide thrust washer assembly, consisting of a leaded bronze washer between two steel washers and enclosed by two telescoping dust shields, between the lower face of the axle end and the steering knuckle lower yoke. The chamfered edge of the upper steel washer should be up and that of the lower steel washer down. Align the holes in the steering knuckle yoke, axle end and the thrust washer assembly.

NOTE: Make sure the larger dust shield is at the top.

2. Hold axle rigid and place a jack under the steering knuckle and raise knuckle slightly to take up clearance between knuckle yoke, axle end and thrust bearing. Check clearance between upper face of axle end and knuckle upper yoke (fig. 7).

NOTE: This clearance should not exceed .005". If excessive clearance exists, a steel shim should be installed between upper face of the axle end and knuckle upper yoke.

3. Install kingpin making sure milled slot on side of pin will index with kingpin lock pin hole in axle "I" beam. Install kingpin from top, driving it down through the knuckle upper yoke, shim (if used), axle end, thrust bearing or thrust washer assembly and knuckle lower yoke, until milled slot in kingpins aligns with lock pin hole.

4. Install threaded end of kingpin lock pin through axle "I" beam from the front of axle. Install steering knuckle stop plate, lockwasher and nut on lock pin at rear of axle and tighten nut securely.

5. Install new bearing plugs in steering knuckle yokes. Make sure plugs are seated and stake in place at four points.

Installation

1. Place axle on dolly and roll it into position under vehicle.
2. Raise axle up against spring seats, making sure spring center bolts enter alignment holes in spring seats.

NOTE: On models using caster shims make sure shims are installed between spring and axle with thick end of shim toward rear of vehicle.

3. On 1948-50 models, place front spring bumper retainer on top of springs and install "U" bolts, shock absorber anchor plate spacer and anchor plate. On 1951 models, place shock absorber lower attaching bracket over the ends of the front "U" bolt. Then install lockwashers and nuts, and tighten securely.
4. On 1948-50 models equipped with shock absorbers attach links to shock absorber bracket or on 1951 models, lower stud to lower attaching bracket.
5. Install backing plate and brake assembly on steering knuckle with studs inserted through holes in knuckle. Install lockwashers and nuts on two upper studs and tighten securely.
6. Install steering arm on two lower studs and secure with lockwashers, nuts, and cotter pins.

NOTE: Steering arm with two ball studs goes on left hand knuckle and arm with single ball stud goes on right hand knuckle.

7. Install tie rod as outlined under "Tie Rod—Installation" in this section.
8. Install bearings, hubs and brake drums and adjust bearings as outlined in this section.
9. Connect and adjust steering drag link as outlined in Section 9.
10. Install wheels.
11. Remove blocks and dolly from under vehicle and re-tighten spring "U" bolt nuts.
12. On vehicles equipped with stabilizer, attach stabilizer bar as outlined under "Stabilizer, Removal and Replacement."
13. Adjust front wheel toe-in as outlined in "Front End Alignment—Toe-in Adjustment."

FRONT END ALIGNMENT

Correct alignment of front wheels must be maintained in order to insure ease of steering and satisfactory tire life. The most important factors of front wheel alignment are camber, caster and toe-in.

These factors should be checked at regular intervals, particularly when the axle has been subjected to heavy impacts. When checking wheel alignment it is important that wheel bearings and knuckle bearings be in proper adjustment. Loose bearings will affect instrument reading when checking camber, kingpin inclination and toe-in.

Toe-in—is the amount in fractions of an inch that the wheels are closer together in front "A" than at the rear "B" (fig. 11). The purpose of toe-in is to offset the effect of camber preventing side slippage and cross wear of tires. Camber and toe-in bear a definite relation to each other; therefore, both should be checked at the same time.

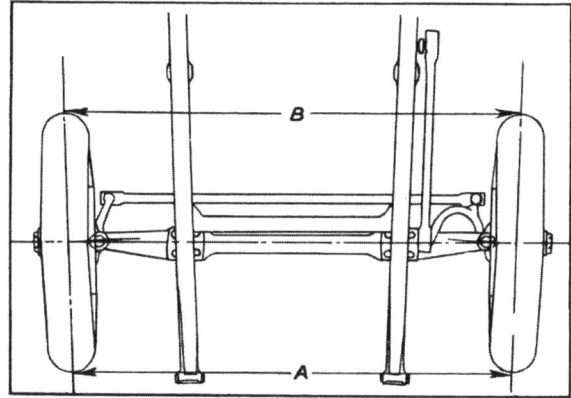

Fig. 11—Toe-In

Camber—is the amount in inches or degrees that the front wheels are tilted outward at the top from a vertical position (fig. 12). When a wheel is tilted too far out at the top, hard steering or wander will be experienced and tires will show excessive wear on outside shoulders.

Reverse camber or a wheel that is tilted too far in at the top will result in excessive tire wear on the inner shoulders.

Unequal camber may result in unstable steering, wandering, road shock, shimmy or unequal tire wear.

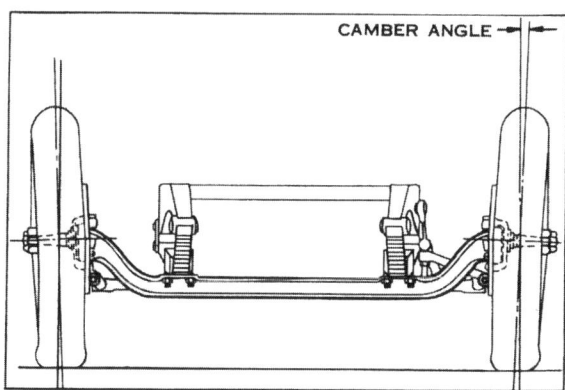

Fig. 12—Camber Angle

If wheels have a maximum or minimum of allowable camber they must have the maximum or minimum of allowable toe-in.

Caster—is the amount in degrees of the backward tilt of the axle and kingpin (fig. 13).

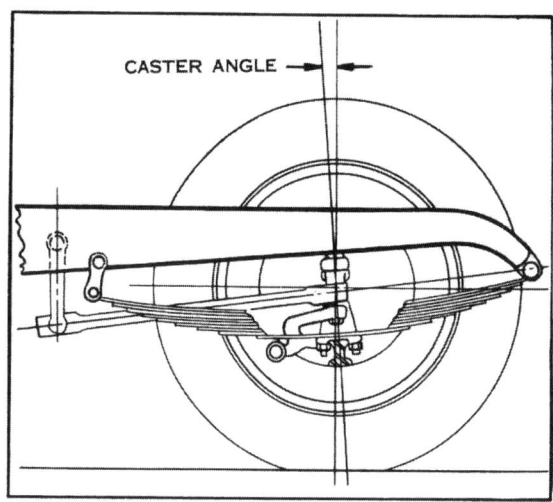

Fig. 13—Caster Angle

The purpose of caster is to provide steering stability which will keep the front wheels in a straight ahead position and to assist in bringing the wheels out of a turn on a curve.

A truck with no caster or negative caster would lack steering stability, would tend to wander and would be difficult to straighten out at the end of a curve or turn.

Unequal caster is apparent in causing the vehicle to pull to the right or left. The direction in which the vehicle tends to pull is toward the side with less caster.

Kingpin Inclination—is the amount in degrees that the tops of the kingpins are inclined toward the center of the vehcle (fig. 14).

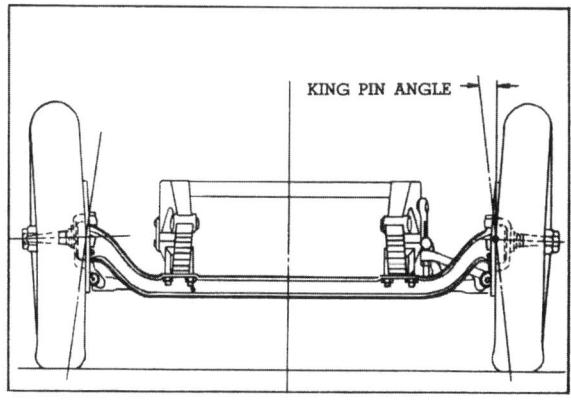

Fig. 14—Kingpin Inclination

The purpose of kingpin inclination is to keep the wheel spindles pointed outward in line with the axle to decrease frictional resistance of the tires against the road when turning right or left which results in easier steering.

Steering Geometry—is the mechanics of keeping the front wheels in proper relative alignment as the wheels are turned left or right (fig. 15). It is sometimes caller error or steering angularity. The governing factors in steering geometry are the length and angularity of the steering arms and linkage.

The front wheels when the vehicle is making a

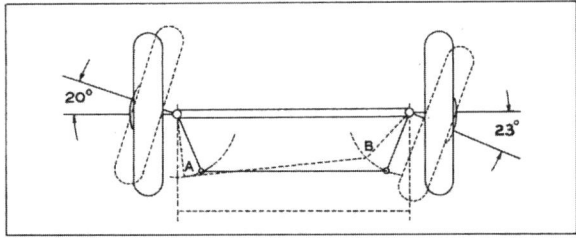

Fig. 15—Steering Geometry

turn are not on the same radius line drawn from the center around which the vehicle is turning. Because of this, it is necessary for the front wheels to assume a toed-out position when rounding curves. This position is governed by the angle of the steering arms.

The wheel of any vehicle, if properly set on the curves, will be at a right angle to the radius line from the center or point "D" around which the vehicle is turning (fig. 16).

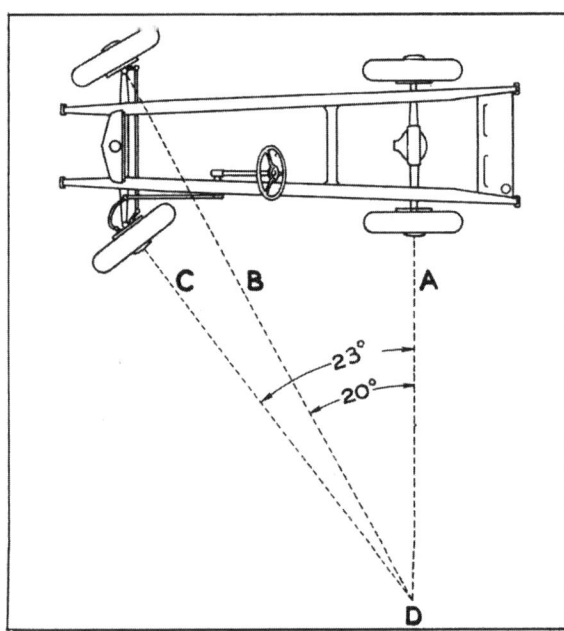

Fig. 16—Toe-Out on Curves

SERVICE OPERATIONS

There are several different types of front end alignment machines all of which outline proper procedure for checking factors of proper wheel alignment. The instructions furnished by each manufacturer for the operation of his particular machine should be followed. Regardless of type equipment used, all checks must be made with the vehicle level, with the weight of the vehicle on the wheels and with no pay load.

Bad steering complaints are not always the result of improper front wheel alignment, therefore it is recommended that the following factors be checked prior to placing vehicle on the front end machine.

1. Loose or improperly adjusted steering gear.
2. Steering housing loose at frame.
3. Play or excessive wear in kingpins or bushings.
4. Loose tie rod or steering connections.
5. Loose spring shackles.
6. Loose front spring "U" bolts.
7. Front spring slipped on spring seat due to sheared center bolt.
8. Over-lubricated front springs.
9. Sagging or broken front springs.
10. Underinflated tires.
11. Unbalanced or improperly mounted tires.
12. Motor mountings improperly adjusted.
13. Broken motor mountings.
14. Brakes dragging.
15. Hub bolt nuts loose.
16. Shock absorbers not operating properly.

CORRECTING FRONT END ALIGNMENT

Caster

Caster corrections in ordinary amounts may be made by the use of caster shims. To increase caster, place the thick side of the shim toward the back between the spring seat and the spring. To decrease caster, place the thick side of the shim toward the front. **The maximum amount of caster correction that should be made with the use of shims is 2° and anything over this amount should be corrected with the use of correcting tools.**

Changing the caster with the use of correcting tools is an operation of leveling the spring seats in those cases where the use of caster shims is not advisable.

Camber and Kingpin Inclination

From the definitions of "Kingpin Inclination" and "Camber"—one being the inward tilt of the kingpins and the other the outward tilt of the wheels—it is evident that one cannot be corrected without changing the other. For this reason these two factors of front end alignment must be considered together.

The ONLY instance in which a camber correction may be made at the "I" beam is where BOTH camber and kingpin inclination are off by the SAME amount. Then a correction of the "I" beam will take care of both conditions at the same time.

If a check shows that both camber and kingpin inclination are out, but NOT by the same amount, it means that not only the wheel spindle is bent and will have to be replaced, but also that a correction will have to be made at the "I" beam to correct the kingpin inclination. The same thing is true if the camber is all right but the kingpin inclination is out.

If a check shows that the camber is out but the kingpin inclination is all right, it indicates a bent wheel spindle which will have to be replaced.

Toe-in

Toe-in may be adjusted by loosening the clamp bolts at each end of the tie rod and turning the tie rod to increase or decease its length until proper toe-in is secured. Before locking the clamp bolts, make sure that the tie rod ends are in alignment with the studs. Misalignment of tie rod ends will result in binding.

Steering Geometry

If, when checking steering geometry (toe-out on turns), the reading does not fall within the limits given in the specifications it will be necessary to replace the steering arm that does not come within the limits.

FRONT SPRINGS

INDEX

	Page		Page
General Description	3-13	Repairs	3-14
Removal	3-13	Installation	3-14

GENERAL DESCRIPTION

Front springs on all truck models are of the single or two stage, semi-elliptic type.

Springs on all models, except Forward Control and C.O.E. are shackled at the front and pivoted at the rear. The Forward Control and C.O.E. front springs are shackled at the rear and pivoted at the front. Spring leaves are held in alignment with center bolts and spring clips.

All springs are constructed with a second leaf which partially wraps the main eye for additional safety. Shackles used are of the threaded bushing type (fig. 17), which favors a minimum of wear and long bushing life.

Removal

1. Raise vehicle with chain hoist enough to relieve spring tension.
2. On vehicles equipped with shock absorbers, disconnect stem or links from lower attaching bracket.
3. On vehicles equipped with stabilizer, disconnect stabilizer bar.
4. Remove "U" bolts, bumper retainer and shock absorber attaching plate, where used
5. Remove shackle draw bolt and shackle plates from shackle.
6. Remove shackle bolt at pivot end of spring by threading it out of hanger.
7. Remove front spring from vehicle.

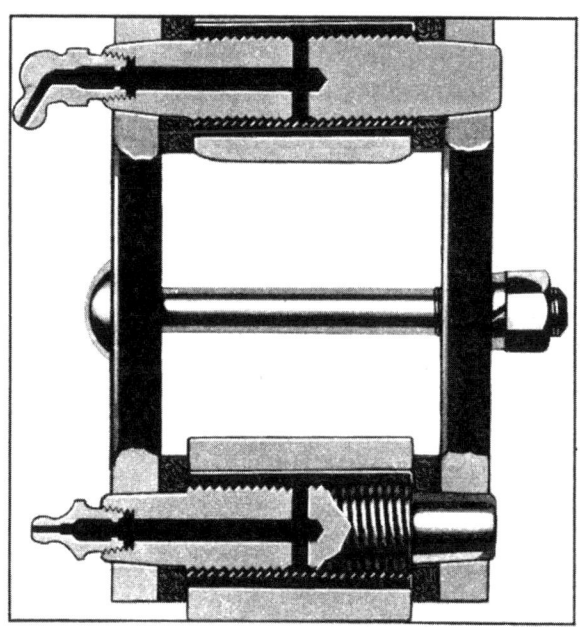

Fig. 17—Threaded Shackle

FRONT SUSPENSION 3-14

Repairs

All spring and shackle inspection and repairs are accomplished as outlined in Section 4.

Installation

1. Slide spring into position on front axle spring seat making sure spring center bolt positions in locating hole in axle spring seat.

   NOTE: On models using caster shims, make sure shims are installed between spring and axle with thick end of shim toward rear of vehicle.

2. Install bumper retainer, "U" bolts and shock absorber attaching plate or bracket if used.
3. Install "U" bolt lockwashers and nuts, and tighten securely.
4. On vehicles equipped with stabilizer, connect stabilizer bar.
5. On vehicles equipped with shock absorbers, attach shock absorber stem or links to attaching plate or bracket.
6. Attach pivot end of spring to spring hanger with shackle bolt and install lockwasher and nut; tighten securely.
7. Install shackle pins in spring support bushing and spring eye, and position pin so that each end projects 21/32" from the ends of the bushings.
8. Place new cork seals on the shackle pins, then install the shackle plates over tapered ends of shackle pins.
9. Install shackle draw bolt through shackle plates and install lockwasher and nut, and tighten securely.
10. Strike each end of shackle a sharp blow with a hammer to insure seating of the tapers and retighten draw bolt.
11. Install lubrication fittings and lubricate each shackle pin.
12. Lower vehicle to floor.

TROUBLES AND REMEDIES

FRONT AXLE AND WHEEL ALIGNMENT

Symptom and Probable Cause

Hard Steering
a. Lack of lubrication
b. Tight kingpin bushings

c. Underinflated tires
d. Improper toe-in
e. Improper steering adjustment
f. Tie rod ends out of alignment

Noisy Operation
a. Sharp squeak on rough roads
b. Rattles on rough roads

Front Wheel Shimmy
a. Underinflated tires
b. Broken or loose wheel bearings
c. Improper toe-in
d. Worn kingpin bushings
e. Improper caster
f. Unbalanced wheels
g. Steering gear loose
h. Tie rod ball studs loose

Road Wander
a. Underinflated tires
b. Lack of lubrication
c. Tight steering gear
d. Improper toe-in
e. Improper caster and camber
f. Worn tie rod ends

Probable Remedy

a. Lubricate chassis and steering gear
b. If not corrected by lubrication, replace bushings
c. Inflate tires to recommended pressure
d. Adjust toe-in
e. Adjust steering gear
f. Align tie rod ends with ball studs

a. Lubricate shackles
b. Tighten "U" bolts, tighten or replace tie rod ends, replace worn kingpin bushings, and replace worn shackle bolts or bushings

a. Inflate tires to recommended pressure
b. Replace or adjust wheel bearings
c. Adjust toe-in
d. Replace worn parts
e. Adjust caster
f. Balance wheel and tire assemblies
g. Adjust steering gear
h. Replace worn ball studs

a. Inflate tires to recommended pressure
b. Lubricate chassis and steering gear
c. Adjust steering gear
d. Adjust toe-in
e. Adjust caster and camber
f. Replace tie rod ends

FRONT SUSPENSION 3-15

Wheel Tramp
    a. Wheel assembly out of balance
    b. Blister or bump on tire

    a. Clean wheel and balance assembly
    b. Replace or repair tire

Excessive or Uneven Tire Wear
    a. Underinflated tires
    b. Improper camber
    c. Improper caster
    d. Improper toe-in
    e. Wheels out of balance

    a. Inflate tires to recommended pressure
    b. Adjust camber
    c. Adjust caster
    d. Adjust toe-in
    e. Balance wheels

Fig. 18—Front Suspension Special Tools

1. K-224   Front Wheel Bearing Cup and Pinion Bearing Remover
2. J-554   Hub Bolt Peening Tool and Anvil
3. J-1273   Steering Arm Ball Stud Remover
4. K-463-B   Front Wheel Bearing Cup Inserter Set
5. J-2248   Steering Knuckle Bushing Remover and Replacer
6. K-318   King Pin Bushing Driver
7. KMO-312-1   King Pin Bushing Reamer (.020" oversize)
8. KMO-226-1   King Pin Bushing Reamer (.010" oversize)
9. J-3057   King Pin Bushing Reamer (.923")
10. KMO-312-2   Steering Knuckle Bushing Reamer (.020" oversize)
11. KMO-226-2   Steering Knuckle Bushing Reamer (.010" oversize)
12. KMO-654   Steering Knuckle Bushing Reamer (1.110")

FRONT AXLE SPECIFICATIONS

	½ Ton	¾ Ton Conv.	¾ Ton Forward Control	1 Ton Forward Control	1 and 1½ Ton Conv.	2 Ton Conv.	2 Ton C.O.E.
Caster—Degrees	1¾ ± ½	2½ ± ½	3¼ ± ½	2¼ ± ½	2¾ ± ½	2¾ ± ½	3 ± ½
Camber—Degrees	1 ± ½	1 ± ½	1 ± ½	1 ± ½	1 ± ½	1 ± ½	1 ± ½
Kingpin Inclination—Degrees	7°10' ± 1°	7°10' ± 1°	7°10' ± 1°	7°10' ± 1°	7°10' ± 1°	7°10' ± 1°	7°10' ± 1°
Toe-In—Inches	1/16"–3/16"	1/16"–3/16"	1/16"–¼"	1/16"–¼"	1/16"–¼"	1/16"–¼"	1/16"–¼"
Steering Geometry (Toe-Out on Turns)							
Outside Wheel—Degrees	20	20	20	20	20	20	20
Inside Wheel—Degrees	23 ± 2	23 ± 2	23 ± 2	23 ± 2	23 ± 2	23 ± 2	23 ± 2
Knuckle Bushing Diameter—Inches	.868	.923*	1.111*	1.111*	.923*	1.111*	1.111*
Kingpin Diameter—Inches	.866	.921	1.109	1.109	.921	1.109	1.109

*Ream in place

FRONT SPRING SPECIFICATIONS

	½ and ¾ Ton	¾ and 1 Ton Forward Control	1 and 1½ Ton	1½ Ton Schoolbus Short Wheelbase C.O.E. and 2 Ton	Long Wheelbase C.O.E.
Length	38"	40"	40"	40"	40"
Leaf Width	1¾"	2"	2"	2"	2"
Type			Semi-Elliptic		
No. Leaves	8	8	7	9	11
No. Spring Clips	3	3	3	3	3
Spring Clip Type	Clinch	Bolt	Bolt	Bolt	Bolt
Shackle Type			Threaded		

TORQUE SPECIFICATIONS

Front Wheel Bearing Nut...33 ft. lbs.
  Tighten to 33 ft. lbs. then back off from 1/12 to 1/6 turn maximum to line up cotter pin hole

Spring "U" Bolt Nuts

½ Ton ....75-90 ft. lbs.

¾, 1, 1½ and 2 Ton ....125-150 ft. lbs.

SERVICE NEWS REFERENCE

Month	Page No.	Subject

SECTION 4

REAR AXLE AND SUSPENSION

CONTENTS OF THIS SECTION

	Page
½ Ton Rear Axle	4-1
¾ and 1 Ton Rear Axle	4-10
1½ and 2 Ton Rear Axle	4-20
Two-Speed Rear Axle	4-27
Rear Axle Troubles and Remedies	4-40
Rear Axle Special Tools	4-43
Rear Axle Specifications	4-47
Rear Axle Torque Specifications	4-48
Speedometer Gear	4-48
Propeller Shaft and Universal Joints	4-50
Propeller Shaft and Universal Joints Troubles and Remedies	4-58
Rear Springs and Shackles	4-59
Propeller Shaft and Spring Special Tools	4-63
Rear Spring Specifications	4-64
Service News Reference	4-64

½ TON REAR AXLE

INDEX

	Page		Page
General Description	4-2	Replacement	4-6
Minor Service Operations	4-3	1948-49 and Early 1950	4-6
Axle Shaft or Drum	4-3	1950-51	4-6
Axle Shaft—Bearing or Oil Seal	4-4	Propeller Shaft and Pinion	4-6
Major Service Operations	4-5	Differential Assembly	4-7
Rear Axle Assembly	4-5	Differential Carrier—Assembly	4-8
Removal	4-5	Ring Gear and Pinion Adjustment	4-9
Disassembly	4-5	Rear Axle	4-9
Inspection	4-5	Assembly	4-9
Propeller Shaft Bushings and Oil Seal	4-5	Installation	4-10

GENERAL DESCRIPTION

The rear axle on the ½-ton truck models is of the semi-floating type with Hypoid gears mounted in a pressed steel banjo type housing. The construction features are shown in Figure 1. Positive lubrication of the front pinion thrust bearing is accomplished by an oil passage drilled in the differential carrier. An oil retainer mounted in the carrier ahead of the pinion Hyatt roller bearing retards the return flow of lubricant to the carrier, thus assuring a continual bath of oil.

The drive pinion is overhung, the rear bearing is a Hyatt roller and the front bearing is a double row ball bearing. There are two differential pinion gears and two differential side gears. Barrel roller bearings are used in mounting the differential case. Both the pinion bearings and the differential bearings are preloaded in manufacture.

Wheel and axle shaft mountings are of the semi-floating design. Permanently lubricated and sealed Hyatt roller bearings are used at the rear wheels and the axle shaft oil seals are located at the outer ends of the axle tubes.

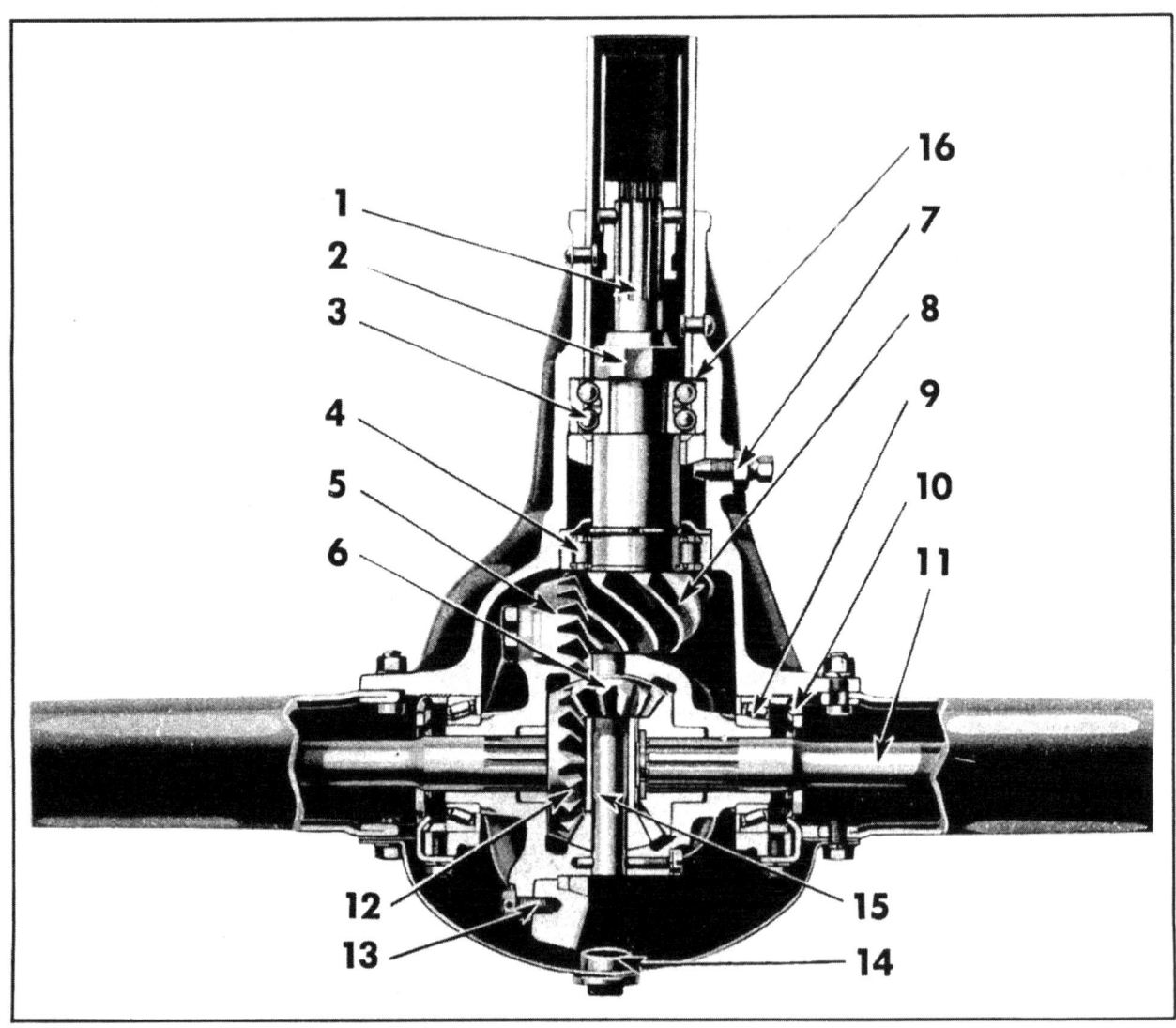

Fig. 1—½ Ton Rear Axle Assembly

1. Pinion Shaft
2. Pinion Bearing Retaining Nut
3. Front Pinion Bearing
4. Rear Pinion Bearing
5. Ring Gear
6. Differential Pinion Gear
7. Front Pinion Bearing Retaining Screw
8. Drive Pinion
9. Differential Side Bearing
10. Differential Side Bearing Adjusting Nut
11. Axle Shaft
12. Differential Side Gear
13. Ring Gear Cap Screw
14. Filler Plug
15. Differential Pinion Gear Shaft
16. Shims

MINOR SERVICE OPERATIONS

AXLE SHAFT OR DRUM

Removal

1. Remove wheel.
2. Remove two stamped brake drum retaining nuts (zipon type) from the two hub bolts (fig. 2).

Fig. 2—Rear Brake Drum Retaining Nuts

3. Remove brake drum from axle shaft.
4. On (1948-50) Models, install wheel cylinder clamp, KMO-145, on brake wheel cylinder.
5. Drain lubricant from differential and remove housing cover.
6. Remove the differential pinion shaft lock screw, the differential pinion shaft, axle shaft spacer and differential pinions (fig. 3).
7. Push axle shafts in toward the center of the axle and remove "C" washers from inner ends of the axle shafts.
8. Remove shafts from axle housing.

Replacement

1. Install gasket to hub aligning the center hole of the three holes closest together with the notch in the hub.

   NOTE: Apply heavy shellac or paint to both sides of gasket and oil deflector.

2. Install oil deflector over gasket aligning oil pocket with notch in the hub.
3. Insert six special bolts and force heads down to the deflector.
4. Peen end of shoulder on bolts into counter-

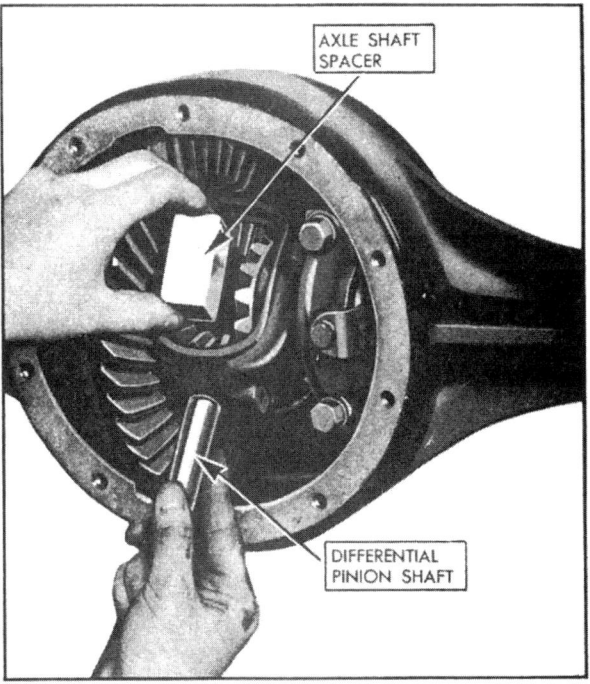

Fig. 3—Removing Axle Shaft Spacer

sink around bolt holes in the flange, using anvil and hub bolt peening tool J-554 (fig. 4).

   CAUTION: *This peening operation is very important from a safety standpoint.*

5. Inspect leather oil seal on inside of axle housing for excessive wear, damage or misplacement.
6. Slide axle shaft into place.

   CAUTION: *Exercise care that splines on end of shaft do not cut leather oil seal and that they engage with splines of differential side gears.*

7. Replace "C" washers on inner ends of shaft.
8. Pry shafts apart so that "C" washers are seated in counterbore in differential side gears and install differential pinions.

   CAUTION: *Exercise care to avoid scratching or damaging inner ends of shaft.*

9. Select axle shaft spacer to give free fit to .014" maximum clearance between ends of axle shaft and the spacer (fig. 5).

   NOTE: There are three sizes of axle shaft spacers available as follows:

Narrow . 1.147"-1.150" wide across ground surfaces
Medium 1.156"-1.159" wide across ground surfaces
Wide . . . 1.166"-1.169" wide across ground surfaces

10. Install spacer in place and assemble pinion shaft, locking in place with special screw, using lockwasher under head.

11. Replace axle housing cover using new gasket and refill differential.
12. On (1948-50) models, remove wheel cylinder clamps.
13. Replace brake drum and two brake drum retaining nuts.

CAUTION: *Make sure lug in web section of drum is aligned and extends into drain hole in axle shaft flange.*

14. Replace wheel.

AXLE SHAFT-BEARING OR OIL SEAL

Removal

1. Remove wheel and axle shafts (see Axle Shaft—Removal).
2. Insert special bearing puller J-1436 and remove bearing, bearing retainer and oil seal (fig. 6).

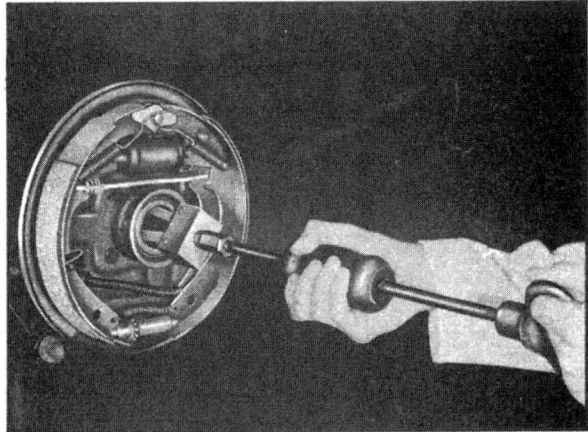

Fig. 6—Axle Shaft Bearing Puller

3. Inspect the bore and dress out the old stake points.

NOTE: *This is important as the old stake points can cut a definite groove in the new seal, thus making an ideal path for lubricant leakage.*

Replacement

1. Using bearing and retainer replacer J-270-7 (fig. 7) place oil seal, bearing and inside bearing retainer on tool in that order.

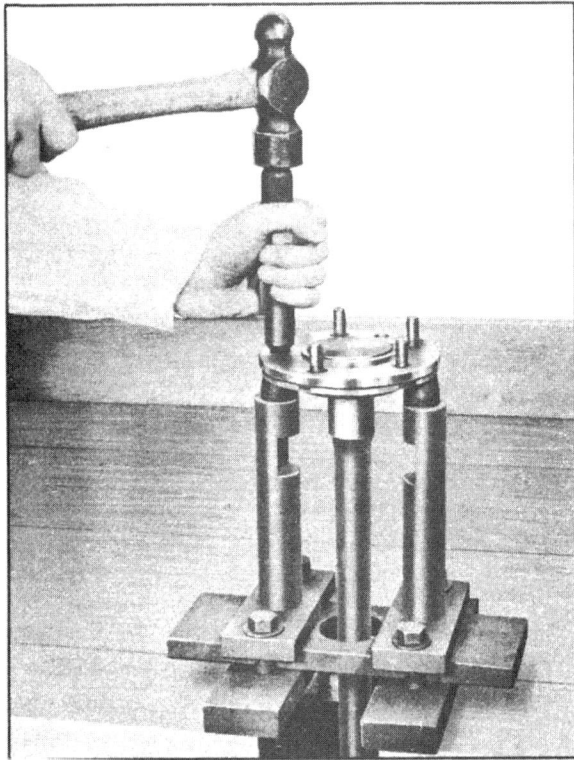

Fig. 4—Peening Flange Bolts

Fig. 5—Checking Clearance Between Axle Shaft and Spacer

Fig. 7—Axle Shaft Bearing and Oil Seal Replacer

NOTE: When installing a new seal, place a light coat of Permatex No. 2 on the oil seal O.D. to insure proper sealing of the seal in housing bore. However, be careful that no sealing material gets on leather lip of oil seal.

MAJOR SERVICE OPERATIONS

REAR AXLE ASSEMBLY

Removal

1. Raise vehicle from floor.
2. Remove rear wheels and brake drums.
3. On (1948-50) models, install wheel cylinder clamps KMO-145 on brake wheel cylinders.
4. Disconnect hand brake cables from cross-shaft lever.
5. Remove brake cables from cable clamp on frame side member.
6. Disconnect hydraulic brake line connection at rear axle housing.
7. Disconnect shock absorber link (1948-49 models) or shock absorber eye (1950-51 models) from anchor plate.
8. Remove spring "U" bolts and shock absorber attaching plate.
9. Disconnect spring shackles and drop springs.
10. Slide axle back to disconnect torque tube at front end, and remove from vehicle.
11. Place axle assembly in axle stand.

Disassembly

1. Drain lubricant and remove housing cover.
2. Remove axle shafts and differential gears (see Axle Shaft Removal).
3. Remove third member by removing nuts holding it to the front of the axle housing.
4. Remove the adjusting nut locks and four differential carrier cap screws.
5. Remove bearing caps and adjusting nuts and remove differential assembly.
6. Remove three tapered bearing retaining screws and tap splined end of propeller shaft allowing pinion shaft to slide out.
7. Remove shims from inside of propeller shaft housing making note of number and total thickness of shims removed.
8. Clean all parts in cleaning solvent.

Inspection

1. Check clearance between propeller shaft and its bushing.

NOTE: If this clearance exceeds .010" the bushings and oil seal should be replaced.

PROPELLER SHAFT BUSHINGS AND OIL SEAL—

Replacement (1948-49 and early 1950)

Propeller shaft bushings on (1948-49) and early (1950) models are doweled and dowels peened in place. New bushings must be drilled for redoweling, which operation must be done with care so as not to drill through the bushing wall.

1. Drill out dowel pins retaining bushings (fig. 8).
2. Drive out both bushings and oil seal from pinion end of housing.
3. Start a new oil seal into the housing with free side of the leather toward the front.
4. Install new rear bushing and drive both bushing and oil seal firmly against their seat, using bushing driver J-968.
5. Drill dowel hole in bushing being careful to control depth.

CAUTION: Do not drill completely through bushing.

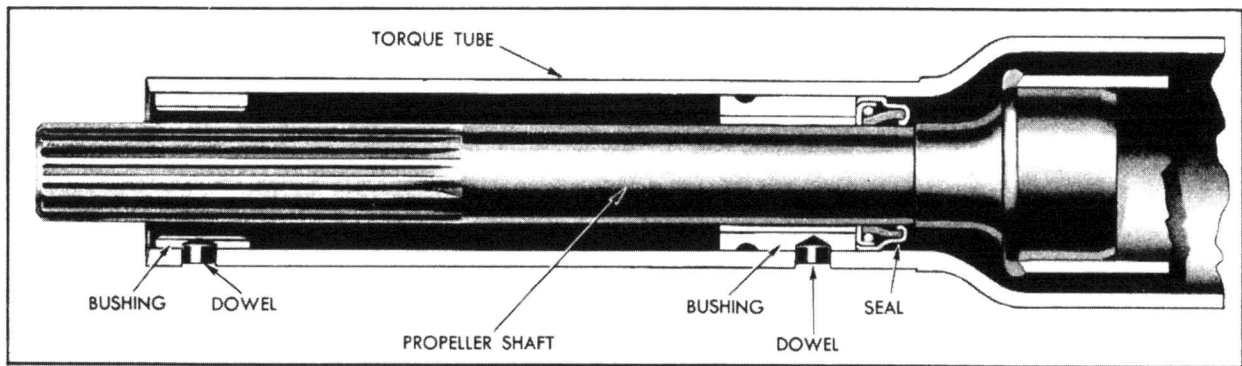

Fig. 8—Propeller Shaft Bushings and Oil Seal

6. Coat dowel with sealer to prevent leakage, install peen dowel in place.
7. Install front bushing using bushing driver J-968.
8. Drill dowel hole in bushing.

   CAUTION: *Extreme care must be used not to break through the wall of the bushing.*

9. Install and peen dowel in place.

   NOTE: *To prevent distortion of these bushings when peening the dowels an arbor or universal joint yoke should be inserted to support the bushing.*

10. Dress off with file any burrs set up during peening operation.

Replacement (1950-51)

Propeller shaft bushings are a press fit in the torque tube and require a special tool for removal and installation. To remove the propeller shaft bushings it is necessary to pull both bushings and the oil seal from the housing using special puller J-4258.

When installing new bushings, it is imperative that they be a tight fit. If there is any doubt, the bushings must be drilled and doweled in place as outlined under Bushing Replacement (1948-49).

1. Remove rear axle assembly from vehicle and remove differential assembly and propeller shaft and pinion from carrier.
2. Insert shaft with flanged end, which is part of J-4258, from pinion end of housing and position firmly against the oil seal.
3. Assemble puller flange on front of torque tube, then thread thrust bearing and nut on shaft. Turn nut to pull both bushings and oil seal from the torque tube (fig. 9).
4. Place a new oil seal on driver J-968 so that the free side of the leather is toward the head of the driver. Place the driver and seal into the housing and drive the seal against its seat.
5. Install new rear bushing using bushing driver J-4259 with spacer washer. Drive the bushing in until the stop on the driver is against end of torque tube (fig. 10).

Fig. 10—Installing Torque Tube Rear Bushing

NOTE: *It should be noted that rear bushing driver J-4259 includes a steel washer which must be used when installing the rear bushing to properly position it in the torque tube.*

6. Install new front bushing. Using bushing driver J-4290 drive the bushing in until the stop on the driver is against end of torque tube (fig. 11).

Fig. 11—Installing Torque Tube Front Bushing

PROPELLER SHAFT AND PINION

Disassembly

1. Drill end of rivet to clear countersink into which it is upset being careful to center the rivet with center punch.

Fig. 9—Removing Torque Tube Bushings

2. Drive out rivet.
3. Loosen pinion bearing lock nut and separate pinion from propeller shaft using tool J-4548 (fig. 12).

Fig. 12—Removing Pinion

4. Remove pinion bearing lock nut and press bearing from pinion shaft using pinion bearing remover, J-996.
5. Remove bearing lock sleeve and rear bearing lock ring.
6. Remove rear bearing oil retainer and bearing.

Inspection

1. Wash all parts in cleaning solvent.
2. Inspect splines for excessive wear or looseness.
3. Inspect shaft at propeller shaft bushing location for scoring or excessive wear.
4. After cleaning and oiling bearings, check for roughness, by slowly turning the outer race by hand.

   NOTE: Bearings should be cleaned in cleaning solvent and blown out with compressed air.

   CAUTION: Do not spin bearings with compressed air, as this will cause damage to races and balls.

5. Inspect double row front pinion bearing for end play.

   NOTE: Any end play in this bearing will allow the pinion to float in and out changing pinion depth in ring gear.

6. Inspect pinion for cracked, chipped or scored teeth.

Assembly

1. Install rear pinion bearing on pinion shaft and lock in place with lock ring.
2. Thread pinion bearing oil retainer over shaft with bevel of the large diameter of the retainer towards the pinion.
3. Coat beveled surface of pinion bearing lock sleeve with rear axle lubricant and install on shaft with beveled edge toward the pinion.
4. Press front (double ball) bearing on shaft and install bearing lock nut.
5. Install splined end of pinion shaft into coupling on end of propeller shaft and using tool J-4548 (fig. 13) press pinion into coupling until rivet hole is aligned.

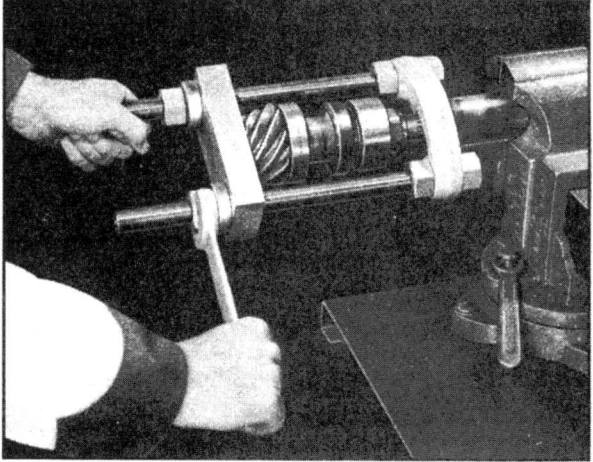

Fig. 13—Installing Pinion

6. Install new rivet and rivet both ends.
7. Tighten bearing lock nut to 200-240 ft. lbs. and lock in milled slot in pinion shaft.

DIFFERENTIAL ASSEMBLY

Inspection

1. Inspect differential side gears for scored hubs or thrust surfaces.
2. Inspect internal splines of side gears and check fit on axle shafts.
3. Inspect thrust surfaces on differential pinion gears and check their fit on pinion shaft.
4. Inspect differential side gear and pinion gear thrust faces in the differential case.
5. Using a torque wrench check each bolt for tightness (should be 85-95 ft. lbs.).
6. Clean differential side bearings, oil and check for roughness by rotating slowly by hand.

Differential Bearing Replacement

1. Install differential bearing puller TR-278-R making sure puller legs are fitted securely in notches in case and retaining yoke is tight.
2. Tighten puller screw and remove bearing. (fig. 14).
3. Replace bearing by placing on hub with the thick side of inner race toward case.
4. Drive bearing in place with differential side bearing replacer J-994. (fig. 15.)

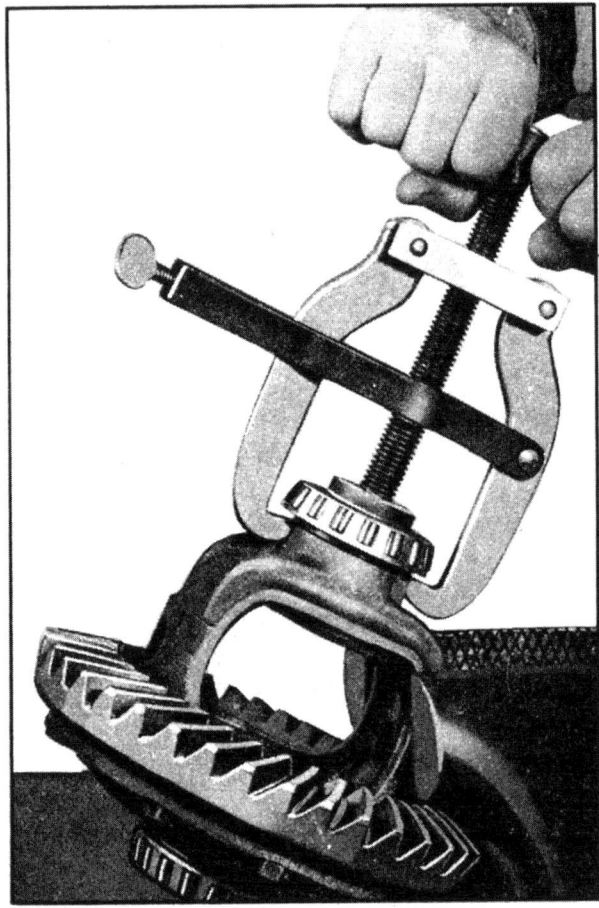

Fig. 14—Removing Differential Bearing

Fig. 15—Replacing Differential Bearings

Ring Gear Replacement

1. Remove ring gear bolts and lockwashers.
2. With soft hammer tap ring gear off the case.
3. Install guide pins made from 3/8"-24 x 1½" long capscrews with heads cut off and ends slotted to new ring gear.
4. Make sure back face of ring gear and face of case are free of dirt and burrs and slip gear over pilot diameter of the case.
5. Install every other ring gear bolt and lockwasher, then draw them up evenly and snugly so that ring gear face is flush with face of case.
6. Remove guide pins and install remaining bolts.

   NOTE: All bolts should be tightened to 85-95 ft. lbs.

DIFFERENTIAL CARRIER

Assembly

1. If original ring gear and pinion are to be used, replace same thickness of shims in propeller shaft housing counterbore that were removed.

   NOTE: As a means of adjusting pinion depth, shims are available in thicknesses of .012", .015", .018" and .021". By combining two shims a total shim thickness of .024" to .042" may be secured.

2. If new ring gear and pinion are used one .015" and one .018" shim should be used as a standard starting point.

   CAUTION: Make sure shims, when installed, are flat in the counterbore and not cocked.

3. Install propeller shaft and pinion assembly, driving it down until bearings are seated in the housing using spacer tool J-4050 to provide proper pinion to bearing clearance (fig. 16).
4. Check through the bearing lock screw holes to make sure lock sleeve is in position against back of front pinion bearing.
5. Install three tapered lock screws and draw them down evenly and tightly, then tighten lock screw nuts.
6. Install differential assembly in the carrier and install adjusting nuts.

CAUTION: *Carefully slide adjusting nuts alongside the bearing so that threads on nuts fit into threads in carrier.*

7. Install bearing caps aligning marks on cap with marks on carrier.
8. Install and tighten cap screws until lock washers just flatten out.

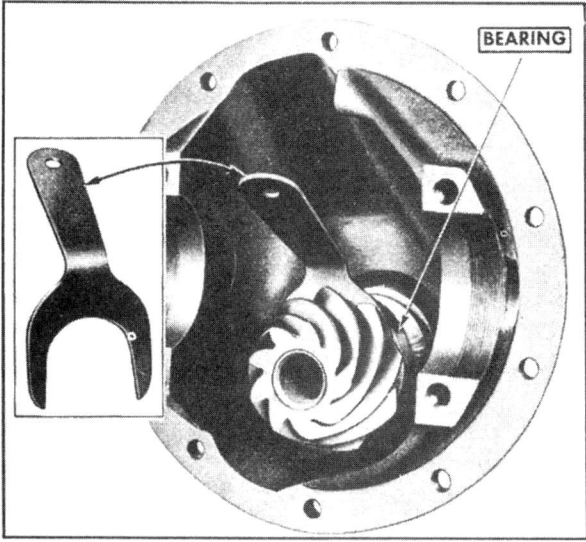

Fig. 16—Checking Pinion to Bearing Clearance

Ring Gear and Pinion Adjustment

1. Loosen right hand adjusting nut and tighten left hand adjusting nut using differential adjusting wrench J-972 while turning ring gear. Continue tightening left hand nut until all lash is removed, then back off the left hand nut one notch to a locking position.
2. Tighten right hand nut to force left bearing firmly into contact with left adjusting nut. Then loosen the right nut and again tighten snugly against the bearing.

   NOTE: This position may be easily determined as the nut comes to a definite stop.

3. Tighten right hand nut a minimum of one additional notch to maximum of two notches further to a locking position. (fig. 17). This operation preloads the differential bearings.
4. Mount a dial indicator on the carrier and check the back lash, (fig. 18) between the ring gear and pinion. The back lash should be from .005"-.008".

Fig. 18—Checking Ring Gear and Pinion Backlash

NOTE: If backlash is more than .008" loosen right hand adjusting nut one notch and tighten left hand adjusting nut one notch. If back lash is less than .005" loosen left hand adjusting nut one notch and tighten right hand adjusting nut one notch.

5. Tighten bearing cap bolts to 115-135 ft. lbs. Recheck back lash and install both adjusting nut locks.

REAR AXLE

Assembly

1. Clean out axle housing and cover and place new gasket over carrier mounting bolts.
2. Assemble differential carrier assembly to axle housing, install lock washers and nuts and tighten securely.

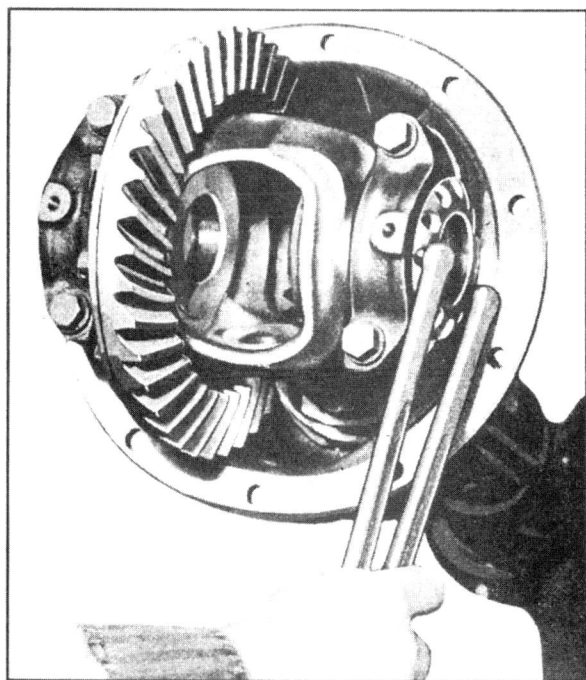

Fig. 17—Adjusting Ring Gear and Pinion

REAR AXLE 4-10

3. Lubricate hubs of differential side gears with hypoid lubricant and install them into differential case.
4. Install axle shafts, making sure the longer shaft is used on the right hand side and install "C" shaped axle shaft locks.
5. Spread shafts to make sure that the shafts, locks and differential side gears are in positive contact.
6. Roll the two differential pinions into position and install axle shaft spacer, pinion gear shaft and pinion gear shaft lock screw.

NOTE: Check clearance between end of axle shaft and spacer. This should be from free fit to .014" (fig. 5).

7. Install the axle housing cover using a new gasket and refill differential with 4½ pints of S.A.E. 90 "Multi-Purpose" gear lubricant.

Installation

1. Adjust universal ball joint as outlined in Transmission Section.
2. Slide axle assembly under vehicle and start propeller shaft into universal joint splines.
3. Raise axle assembly and replace rear spring shackles.
4. Remove square head pipe plug from rear of transmission case, lubricate the universal joint and propeller shaft bushings by inserting ½ pint of lubricant through the opening and replace the pipe plug.
5. Replace rear spring "U" bolts and place shock absorber attaching plate over front "U" bolt. Install nuts and tighten securely.
6. Attach shock absorber link (1948-49 models) or eye (1950-51 models) to anchor plate.
7. Connect hydraulic brake line to connector at rear axle housing.
8. Connect hand brake cables to cross-shaft lever, and adjust. See Brake Section.
9. Remove wheel cylinder clamps, if installed, and install brake drums and rear wheels.
10. Lower vehicle to floor.
11. Bleed brake lines at all four wheels. See Brake Section.

¾ AND 1 TON REAR AXLE

INDEX

	Page
General Description	4-10
Minor Service Operations	4-11
Axle Shaft Removal	4-11
Rear Wheel Bearings	4-11
Brake Drum	4-13
Major Service Operations	4-13
Rear Axle Assembly	4-14
Removal	4-14
Installation	4-14
Differential Carrier	4-14
Removal	4-14
Disassembly	4-15
Pinion	4-15
Pinion Bearing Retainer Oil Seal or Packing	4-15
Pinion Bearing Replacement	4-15
Differential	4-17
Ring Gear Replacement	4-17
Differential Bearing Replacement	4-17
Differential Carrier—Reassembly	4-17
Ring Gear and Pinion Adjustment	4-18
Ring Gear Thrust Pad	4-19
Installation	4-19

GENERAL DESCRIPTION

The rear axle used on all ¾ and 1 ton trucks is a full floating type with hypoid ring gear and pinion. The full floating construction enables easy removal of axle shafts without removing the truck load or jacking up the rear axle. The differential carrier is heavily ribbed to provide rigid support for the differential assembly and the differential bearing caps are dowled to the carrier to assure perfect alignment. With the exception of the ring gear and pinion gear ratios, the two carrier assemblies are identical.

The drive pinion is straddle mounted being supported at the rear end on a Hyatt roller bearing and at front on a Hyatt tapered roller bearing composed of two inner cone and roller assemblies with a one-piece outer race for both bearings. The outer race is drilled between the bearings to provide for efficient lubrication. The ring gear is bolted to the differential case and is provided with a ring gear thrust pad to prevent distortion when starting under heavy loads. This rear axle also has *four differential pinion gears* which are mounted on a differential pinion spider and two differential side gears. Barrel roller bearings are used in mounting the differential case in the carrier.

MINOR SERVICE OPERATIONS

AXLE SHAFT

Removal

1. Remove the eight-½" bolts and lockwashers which attach the axle shaft flange to wheel hub.
2. Install two ½"-13 bolts in the threaded holes provided in the axle shaft flange. By turning these bolts alternately the axle shaft may be easily started and then removed from the housing (fig. 19).

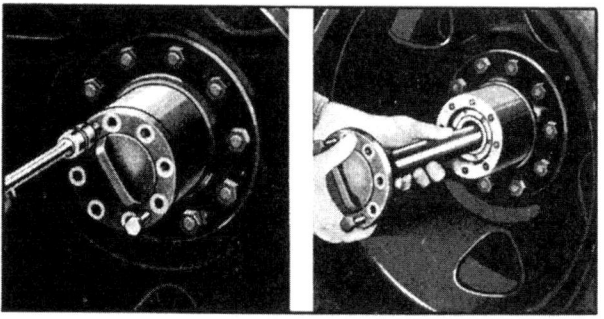

Fig. 15—Loosening and Removing Axle Shaft

Replacement

1. Thoroughly clean both the axle shaft flange and the end of the wheel hub.
   NOTE: Any lubricant on these surfaces tends to loosen axle shaft flange bolts.
2. Place a new gasket over the axle shaft and push the shaft into the housing until the splines enter the differential side gear. Insert two bolts with lockwashers through the flange and gasket and start the bolts into the hub. Install the remaining six bolts and lockwashers and tighten them alternately. The bolts should be finally tightened to a torque load of 85-95 ft. lbs. using a torque wrench.

   NOTE: To prevent lubricant leaking through the axle flange bolts, a small amount of Permatex should be applied to the bolt threads either with a small brush or with the finger. However, use care in the amount of sealer applied, as in too heavy an application, the sealer will be squeezed out as the bolt is installed and may get between the axle shaft flange and hub and thus destroy the sealing of the axle shaft flange to hub gasket.

REAR WHEEL BEARINGS

Removal

The exploded view of the wheel hub (fig. 20) shows the order in which the various parts are assembled.

1. Raise the truck with a floor jack and remove the wheel and axle shaft.

   NOTE: Removal of the wheel is important; it prevents damage to the oil seal and oil deflectors and also permits more accurate adjustment of the bearings.

2. Raise the lip of the special lock from the notch in the lock nut and remove the nut with special wrench J-2222 (fig. 21). Then remove the lock, inner adjusting nut and thrust washer.
3. Remove the hub and drum assembly.
4. Install brake wheel cylinder clamps to pre-

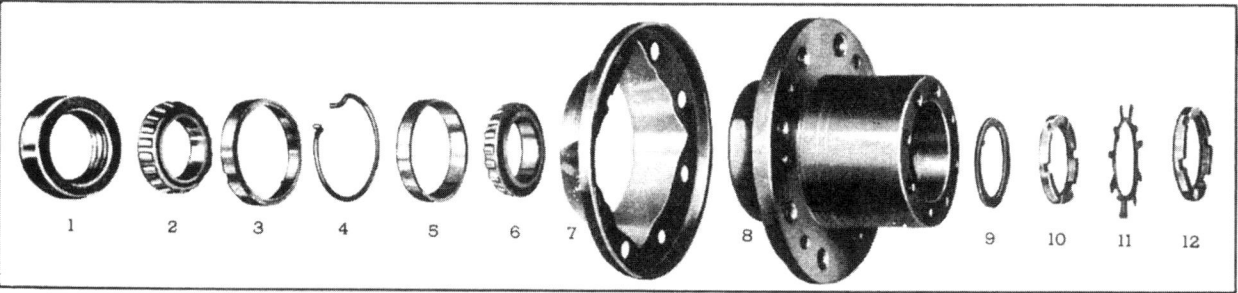

Fig. 20—Exploded View of Wheel Hub

1. Oil Seal
2. Cone and Roller, inner bearing
3. Outer Race, inner bearing
4. Snap Ring, outer bearing
5. Outer Race, outer bearing
6. Cone and Roller, outer bearing
7. Oil Slinger
8. Hub
9. Washer
10. Nut, bearing adjusting
11. Lock, bearing adjusting nut
12. Nut, adjusting nut lock

REAR AXLE 4-12

Fig. 21—Removing Bearing Adjusting Nut Lock

vent the brake fluid from leaking should the brake pedal be accidentally depressed.

5. To remove the inner bearing and oil seal, use driver J-2232 (fig. 22). The driver plate is installed by inserting it into the hub through the bearing and then pulling the plate into

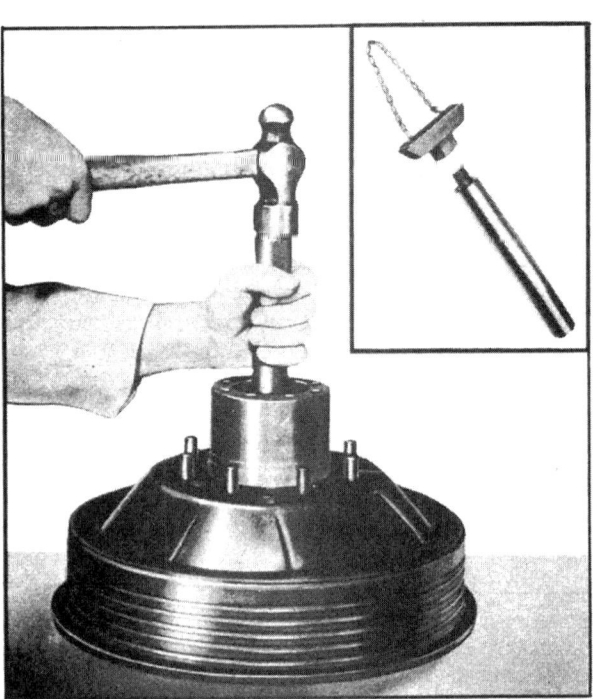

Fig. 22—Removing Inner Bearing Race and Oil Seal

contact with the outer race of the inner bearing using the chain attached. While holding the plate in contact with the bearing, thread the driver handle through the outer bearing and screw it into the plate. Drive the inner bearing and oil seal from the hub.

6. To remove the outer bearing proceed as follows; using a punch and hammer, tap the outer race away from the snap ring to relieve the tension; then remove the snap ring from the inside of the hub using a pair of pliers, (fig. 23). Using outer bearing remover J-2230 press the bearing from the hub.

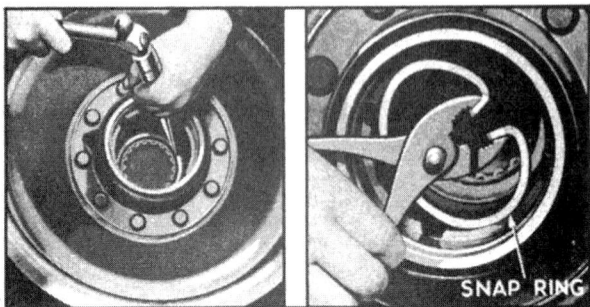

Fig. 23—Removing Outer Bearing Snap Ring

Cleaning and Inspection

Wash the bearings thoroughly in cleaning solvent. Inspect the races for cracks, chips and wear. Inspect the rollers and retainers for any damage. Lubricate the bearings with engine oil and check them for roughness. Any damaged parts should be replaced.

Replacement

1. Pack the roller assemblies with soft smooth cup grease.
2. To replace the outer bearing, first place the inner race and roller assembly in the wheel hub, then install the outer race of the bearing with the thin edge of the race toward outer end of hub. Press the race into the hub

Fig. 24—Replacing Outer Bearing Race

REAR AXLE 4-13

until it clears the snap ring groove using outer wheel bearing replacer J-2223 (fig. 24).

3. Install snap ring in groove on the inside of hub, then using outer bearing remover J-2230 through the bolt holes in end of hub, press the outer race into positive contact with the snap ring fig. 25).

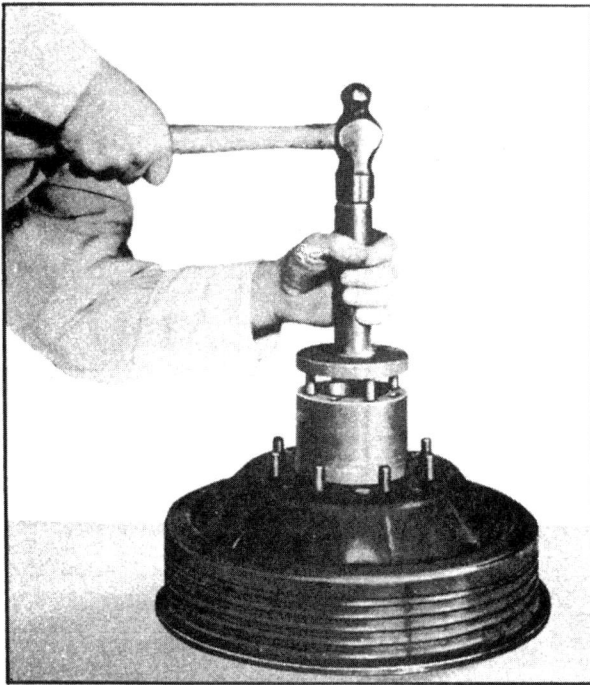

Fig. 25—Driving Outer Race into Contact With Snap Ring

NOTE: This operation must be performed to assure a wheel bearing adjustment that will not loosen up.

4. To replace the inner bearing, place the outer race in the wheel hub with wide side of the race down. Using inner bearing replacer J-872-1, press the outer race into the hub until it stops against its seat.

5. With a fine file, dress out old seal staking points and place the inner race and roller assembly in the hub. Place a light coating of Permatex around O. D. of seal and then install the oil seal using J-2221 Oil Seal Replacer (fig. 26). Lock the seal in place by prick punching edge of hub at three equally spaced places.

Fig. 26—Replacing Oil Seal

6. Install the wheel hub and drum on the end of axle housing; while installing turn the hub to aid in lining up the bearings.

7. Install the thrust washer and adjusting nut.

Adjustment

1. Using special wrench J-2222 (fig. 21) tighten the adjusting nut tight while turning the hub, then back off the adjusting nut a distance equal to that between two adjacent axle shaft flange bolt holes which is equal to 45 degrees. Turn the wheel hub by hand to make sure that it turns freely.

2. Install the adjusting nut lock, align nearest slot in nut with a tang on the lock, then bend tang into slot in nut.

3. Install the lock nut and tighten it securely. Lock it in position by bending a tang of the lock into a slot in lock nut.

4. Install the axle shaft and mount wheel on hub.

BRAKE DRUM

Replacement

The brake drum is held to the hub by two slotted screws which are easily removed with a screwdriver. It will be noticed on removing the brake drum that a soft paper gasket is used to insure a seal between the hub and drum. A new seal should be used in reassembly.

MAJOR SERVICE OPERATIONS

Major operations of this axle assembly may be performed without removing complete axle assembly from the vehicle. There may be occasions, however, when it will be necessary to remove the complete assembly as result of collision which may cause distortion of axle housing or axle shaft tubes. The following axle housing assembly removal, therefore, is to be used only when replacement of axle housing is necessary.

REAR AXLE ASSEMBLY

Removal

1. Raise vehicle from floor and support with stand jacks under frame siderails.
2. Remove rear wheels.
3. Remove two trunnion bearing "U" bolts from the rear yoke and split rear universal joint.

   NOTE: The bearings can be left on the trunnion and held in place with tape.

4. Disconnect hand brake cables from cross shaft levers and remove cables from cable clamps on frame.
5. Disconnect hydraulic brake line connection at rear axle housing.
6. Disconnect shock absorber links or eye from anchor plates or axle bracket.
7. While supporting axle assembly with hydraulic jack, remove spring "U" bolts, nuts and anchor plate, and lower axle assembly to the floor.

Installation

1. Slide axle assembly under vehicle, raise into position and install "U" bolts, anchor plates and nuts, and tighten securely.
2. Replace shock absorber links to anchor plates or connect shock absorber eye to axle bracket.
3. Connect hydraulic brake line to connector at rear axle housing.
4. Connect hand brake cables and adjust. See "Brake Section."
5. Reassemble the rear universal joint making sure "U" bolts are drawn up tight and locked properly.
6. Replace rear wheels and lower vehicle to floor.
7. Bleed brake lines at all four wheels. See "Brake Section."

The operations to follow are major service operations, but may be, as a result of axle construction, performed without raising vehicle from floor or removing axle assembly from the vehicle. An exploded view of the differential carrier assembly is shown in Figure 27.

DIFFERENTIAL CARRIER

Removal

1. Drain lubricant from differential, remove axle housing cover and axle shafts.
2. Remove two trunnion bearing "U" bolts from the rear yoke and split rear universal joint.

   NOTE: The bearings can be left on the trunnion and held in place with tape.

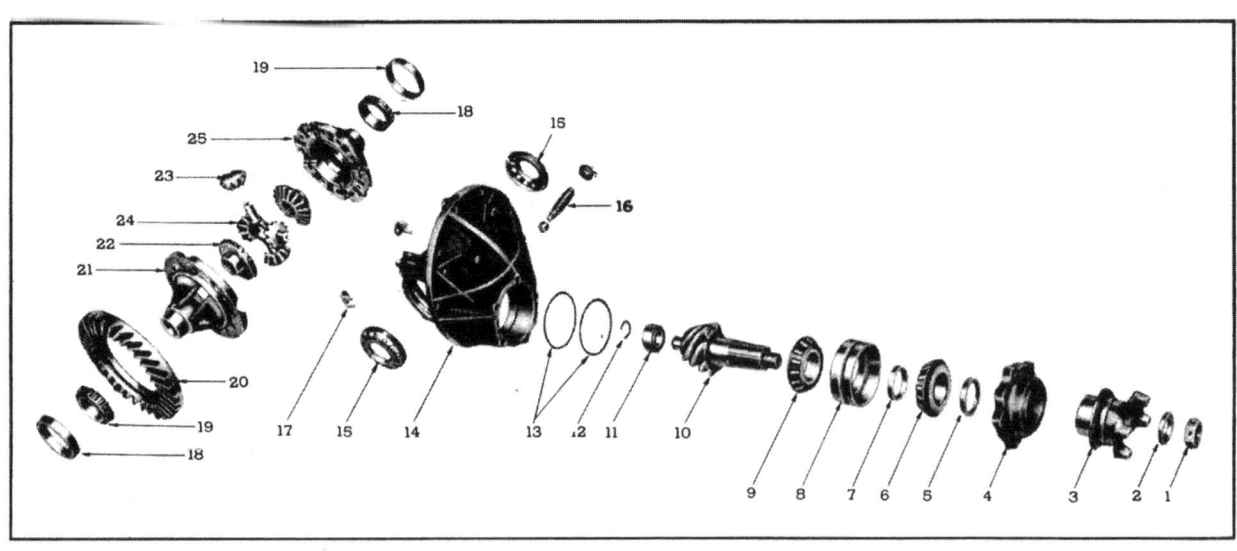

Fig. 27—Exploded View—¾ and 1 Ton Differential Carrier Assembly

1. Nut, pinion shaft
2. Washer, pinion shaft
3. Flange, pinion shaft
4. Retainer, pinion bearing and oil seal
5. Spacer
6. Inner Cone and Roller, pinion bearing
7. Spacer, bearing
8. Outer Race, pinion bearing
9. Inner Cone and Roller, pinion bearing
   Note: Items 6, 7, 8 and 9 are serviced as an assembly
10. Pinion
11. Bearing, pinion rear
12. Lock Ring, pinion bearing
13. Shims, pinion adjusting
14. Differential Carrier
15. Nut, differential bearing adjusting
16. Thrust Pad, ring gear
17. Lock, differential bearing adjusting nut
18. Outer Race, differential bearing
19. Inner Cone and Roller, differential bearing
20. Ring Gear
21. Differential Case Half, right
22. Side Gear, differential
23. Pinion, differential
24. Spider, differential pinion
25. Differential Case Half, left

3. Remove nuts and lockwashers which attach differential carrier to the axle housing and remove differential carrier assembly.

Disassembly

1. Mount carrier assembly in a bench vise or holding fixture.
2. Loosen ring gear thrust pad lock nut and remove thrust pad.
3. Remove differential adjusting nut locks and bearing cap bolts and lockwashers.
4. Remove bearing caps and adjusting nuts by tapping on bosses of caps until free from dowels.

   CAUTION: Do not use screwdriver to pry cap off as this may damage machined face of cap.

5. Remove differential and ring gear assembly from the carrier housing.

   CAUTION: Exercise care that differential side bearing outer races are not dropped in removing assembly from carrier housing.

6. Remove the bolts which attach the pinion bearing retainer to the carrier.
7. Remove the pinion and shaft assembly from the carrier.

   NOTE: It may be necessary to drive this unit from carrier. Use brass drift against pilot end of pinion shaft.

8. Remove shims from inside of carrier housing making note of number and total thickness of shims removed.
9. Wash all parts in cleaning solvent.

PINION

Disassembly

1. Clamp pinion shaft drive flange in bench vise.
2. Remove cotter pin, nut and washer from end of pinion shaft.
3. Remove drive flange and bearing retainer assembly from shaft.
4. Clean all parts thoroughly in cleaning solvent, blow out bearings with compressed air and oil lightly with engine oil.

   NOTE: Do not spin bearings when blowing out with air as this causes damage to races and balls.

Inspection

1. Inspect oil seal and packing in pinion bearing retainer.
2. Inspect splines on pinion shaft for excessive wear.
3. Inspect pinion teeth for scoring, cracked or chipped teeth.
4. Inspect rear pinion bearing for roughness by revolving by hand.

Pinion Bearing Retainer Oil Seal or Packing— Replacement

1. Drive oil seal and packing from retainer using chisel and hammer.
2. Soak new oil seal and packing in engine oil to provide initial lubrication.
3. Install packing and oil seal in retainer and press into position using Oil Seal Replacer J-2231 (fig. 28).

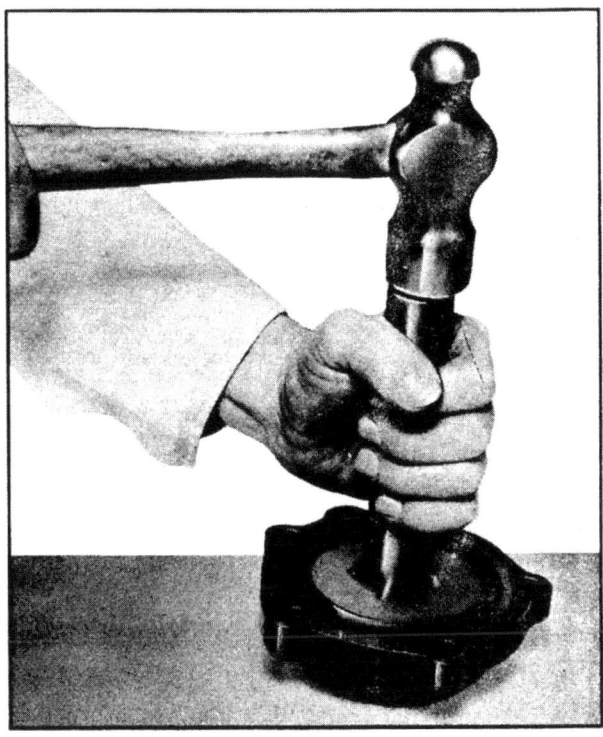

Fig. 28—Replacing Oil Seal

NOTE: Make sure free side of leather in oil seal is toward the pinion bearing.

Pinion Bearing Replacement

1. Remove rear pinion bearing snap ring and press rear pinion bearing from pinion shaft using press plate J-2229 (fig. 29).
2. Install pinion bearing remover J-2224 over pinion teeth of ¾ ton or J-2225 on 1 ton and press pinion bearing from shaft (fig. 30).

   NOTE: This bearing is serviced as a unit consisting of one double outer race, two inner race and roller assemblies and one spacer (fig. 31). These parts should always be installed as a group as the spacer is preselected to give proper pinion bearing adjustment.

REAR AXLE 4-16

3. Press one new inner race and roller assembly on pinion shaft using a piece of 2" pipe, applying pressure against inner race.

   NOTE: Large diameter of this race should be toward pinion.

4. Place bearing spacer and outer race on shaft and press other inner race and roller assembly on pinion shaft.

   NOTE: Small diameter of this race should be toward pinion.

5. Lubricate bearing with engine oil.
6. Lubricate rear pinion bearing and press on pinion shaft using driver to apply pressure to inner race.
7. Install lock ring using lock ring installer J-769 (fig. 32).

Fig. 29—Removing Rear Pinion Bearing

Fig. 31—Pinion Bearing Assembly

Fig. 30—Removing Pinion Bearing

Fig. 32—Rear Pinion Bearing Lock Ring Installer

Assembly

1. Place pinion bearing retainer with bolts and lockwashers installed over hub of pinion shaft drive flange.
2. Install spacer on pinion shaft and then install drive flange and pinion bearing retainer, washer and nut to pinion shaft.
3. Place pinion shaft drive flange in bench vise and tighten pinion shaft nut with torque wrench to 160-280 ft. lbs. Lock nut with cotter pin.

DIFFERENTIAL

Disassembly

1. Check differential case to make sure the two halves are marked so they may be reassembled in same relation (fig. 33).

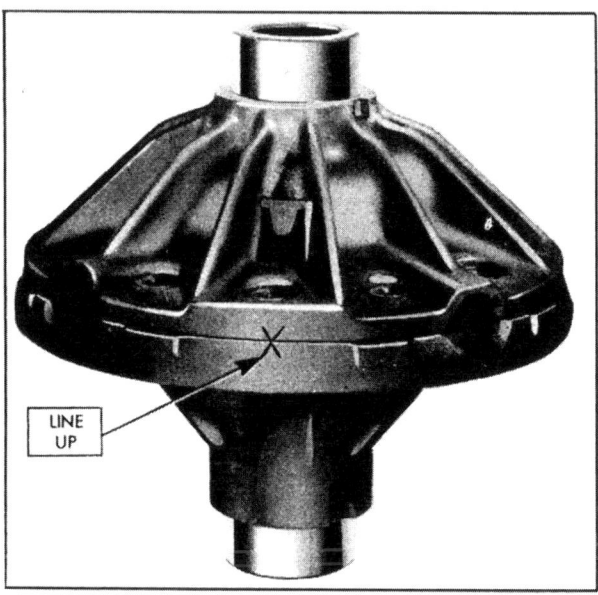

Fig. 33—Differential Case Line Up Marks

2. Remove twelve bolts holding case and cover together.

   NOTE: Ring gear is mounted on the case.

3. Separate cover from case and remove differential pinion gears, pinion gear spider and differential side gears.

Inspection

1. Wash all parts thoroughly in cleaning solvent.
2. Inspect ring gear for cracked, chipped or worn teeth.
3. Inspect differential case and cover for scored side gear and pinion thrust surfaces.
4. Check fit of differential side gear hubs in case and cover.
5. Inspect splines in differential side gears for excessive wear.
6. Inspect differential side gears and pinions for worn, cracked or chipped teeth.
7. Inspect hubs of differential pinion spider for scoring and check fit of pinions on these hubs.
8. Inspect differential case bearings for cracked or checked races and rollers for wear or damage.

Ring Gear Replacement

1. Remove ring gear from differential case by tapping the back of the gear with a soft faced hammer.
2. Inspect ring gear pilot, case flange and back of ring gear for dirt or burrs.
3. Install two guide pins made from ½"-20x2" long cap screws with heads cut off and ends slotted to new ring gear diametrically opposite each other.
4. Start guide pins through holes in case flange and tap ring gear on to case.

Reassembly

1. Lubricate differential side gears and pinions.
2. Place differential pinions on the spider.
3. Assemble side gears and pinions and spider to left half or cover of differential.
4. Assemble right half or case to left half or cover, being sure to line up marks on the two halves (fig. 33).
5. Install ten differential to ring gear bolts and lockwashers and tighten evenly until ring gear is flush with case flange.
6. Remove two guide pins and install remaining two bolts.

   NOTE: All bolts should be tightened with a torque wrench to 85-90 ft. lbs.

Differential Bearing Replacement

1. Install differential bearing puller TR-278-R making sure puller legs are fitted securely in notches in case and retaining yoke tight.
2. Tighten puller screw to remove bearing.
3. Place new bearing on hub with thick side of inner race toward case and drive in place with differential bearing driver J-2226 (fig. 34).

   NOTE: This tool is counterbored and has pilot to assure proper installation and seating of bearing.

DIFFERENTIAL CARRIER

Reassembly

To facilitate adjusting of pinion depth in the ring gear, there are four shims available for service use. They are .012", .015", .018" and .021".

If the original ring gear and pinion are to be used it is advisable to replace the same thickness

Fig. 34—Replacing Differential Bearing

of shims in the carrier housing counterbore that were removed.

If a new ring gear and pinion are used, one .015" and one .018" shim should be used as a standard starting setup.

1. Grease shims and place against bearing outer race.

    NOTE: It is important that shims be greased and stuck to bearing outer race to prevent damage to shims when pinion assembly is installed in carrier.

2. Place new pinion bearing retainer gasket on the retainer and install pinion assembly in carrier.

    NOTE: The pinion assembly should be pressed into the carrier to prevent the possibility of damaging the shims.

3. Install pinion bearing retainer bolts and lockwashers and tighten with a torque wrench to 85-95 ft. lbs.

4. Lubricate differential case bearing rollers with engine oil and place outer races over them.

5. Install differential assembly in carrier and install adjusting nuts.

    CAUTION: Carefully slide adjusting nuts alongside the bearings so that threads on nuts fit into threads in carrier.

6. Install differential bearing caps making sure the marks on the caps line up with the marks on the carrier.

7. Install bearing cap bolts and lockwashers and tighten until lockwashers just flatten out.

Ring Gear and Pinion Adjustment

1. Loosen right hand adjusting nut and tighten left hand adjusting nut using differential adjusting wrench J-972 while turning ring gear.

2. Continue tightening left hand nut until all backlash between ring gear and pinion is removed (fig. 35).

Fig. 35—Adjusting Ring Gear and Pinion

3. Back off left hand nut approximately two notches to point where notch in nut is aligned with lock.

4. Tighten right hand nut firmly to force the differential in solid contact with left hand adjusting nut. Loosen right hand adjusting nut until it is free of its bearing; then retighten snugly against bearing. Tighten right hand nut from one to two notches more to a position in which a notch in nut aligns with lock.

    NOTE: This method provides for the proper preload on the bearings.

5. Mount a dial indicator on the carrier and check the backlash between the ring gear and pinion (fig. 36) which should be from .005" to .008".

    NOTE: If backlash is more than .008" loosen the right hand adjusting nut one notch and tighten left hand adjusting nut one notch. If backlash is less than .005" loosen the left hand adjusting nut one

Fig. 36—Checking Ring Gear and Pinion Backlash

notch and tighten right hand adjusting nut one notch.

Checking Pinion Depth

1. Coat the ring gear teeth lightly with red lead or prussian blue. Then turn the pinion shaft several revolutions in both directions while applying considerable pressure to the ring gear to create a load.

2. Examine the pattern on the ring gear teeth. If the pinion depth is correct, the tooth pattern will be centered on the pitch line and toward the toe of the ring gear.

3. If the pattern is below the pitch line on the ring gear teeth, the pinion is too deep and it will be necessary to remove the pinion assembly and increase the shim thickness between the pinion bearing and the carrier.

4. If the pattern is above the pitch line on the ring gear teeth, the pinion is too shallow and it will be necessary to remove the pinion assembly and decrease the shim thickness between the pinion bearing and the carrier.

5. Changing the pinion depth will make some change in the backlash; therefore, it will be necessary to readjust the backlash.

6. Tighten bearing cap screws with a torque wrench to 95-105 ft. lbs. Again recheck the backlash and install the adjusting nut locks.

Ring Gear Thrust Pad

1. Inspect bronze tip on ring gear thrust pad and replace if worn.

Fig. 37—Ring Gear Thrust Pad Adjustment

2. Install thrust pad and tighten screw until bronze tip engages back of ring gear while rotating gear.

3. Back off screw one-twelfth (1/12) turn and tighten lock nut (fig. 37).

NOTE: Make sure screw does not turn during locking process. This adjustment provides .005" to .007" clearance between thrust pad and ring gear.

Installation

1. Clean out axle housing and cover and place new gasket over carrier mounting bolts.

2. Assemble differential carrier assembly to axle housing, install lockwashers and nuts, and tighten securely.

3. Replace axle housing inspection cover using new gasket.

4. Assemble trunnion bearings of the universal joint in the rear yoke. Install "U" bolts, lockwashers and nuts, and tighten nuts securely.

5. Clean axle shaft flange and end of wheel hub.

NOTE: These surfaces must be thoroughly cleaned of lubricant to prevent loosening of axle flange bolts.

6. Place new axle flange gaskets over axle shafts and push shafts into housing until splines enter differential side gears.

7. Install bolts and lockwashers and tighten them alternately.

NOTE: These bolts should be tightened with a torque wrench to 85-95 ft. lbs.

8. Fill rear axle with 6 pints of SAE 90 "Multi-Purpose" gear lubricant and lubricate the rear universal joint.

1½ AND 2 TON REAR AXLE

INDEX

	Page		Page
General Description	4-20	Disassembly	4-24
Minor Service Operations	4-21	Pinion	4-24
Axle Shaft	4-21	Pinion Bearing Retainer Oil Seal and Packing	4-25
Rear Wheel Bearings	4-22	Pinion Bearing Replacement	4-25
Adjustment	4-23	Differential	4-26
Brake Drum	4-23	Differential Bearing Replacement	4-26
Major Service Operations	4-23	Ring Gear Replacement	4-26
Axle Assembly	4-23	Differential Carrier	4-26
Removal	4-24	Assembly	4-26
Installation	4-24	Ring Gear and Pinion Adjustment	4-27
Differential Carrier	4-24	Installation	4-27
Removal	4-24		

GENERAL DESCRIPTION

The rear axle used on all 1½ and 2 ton trucks is full floating and incorporates the use of a hypoid ring gear and pinion. The construction features are shown in Figure 38. This axle is so constructed as to enable replacement of axle shafts without removal of truck load or jacking up the rear axle.

The axle incorporates involute splined axle shaft flanges and wheel hubs. The design provides for the driving torque to be transmitted from the axle shaft to the hub through the mating splines rather than through the attaching bolts. Inward thrust is controlled by a spacer that fits between the outer bearing outer race and the axle shaft flange. Outward thrust of the shaft is controlled by the hub cap which bolts to the hub (fig. 39).

Rigid support of the differential case is provided by heavy ribbing of the differential carrier and differential bearing caps are piloted to the carrier by sleeve dowels to prevent any possibility of bearing caps shifting. The differential case is a two-piece construction with the ring gear piloted or mounted to the right side. The case halves and the ring gear are bolted together permitting ring gear replacement without changing the differential case. A ring gear thrust pad is used to prevent ring gear distortion when starting under a heavy load.

The drive pinion is straddle mounted being supported at the rear by a roller bearing and at the front by a double row ball bearing. The differential case is mounted in the differential carrier on barrel roller bearings.

Four differential pinion gears are used which are mounted on a common differential pinion gear spider.

REAR AXLE 4-21

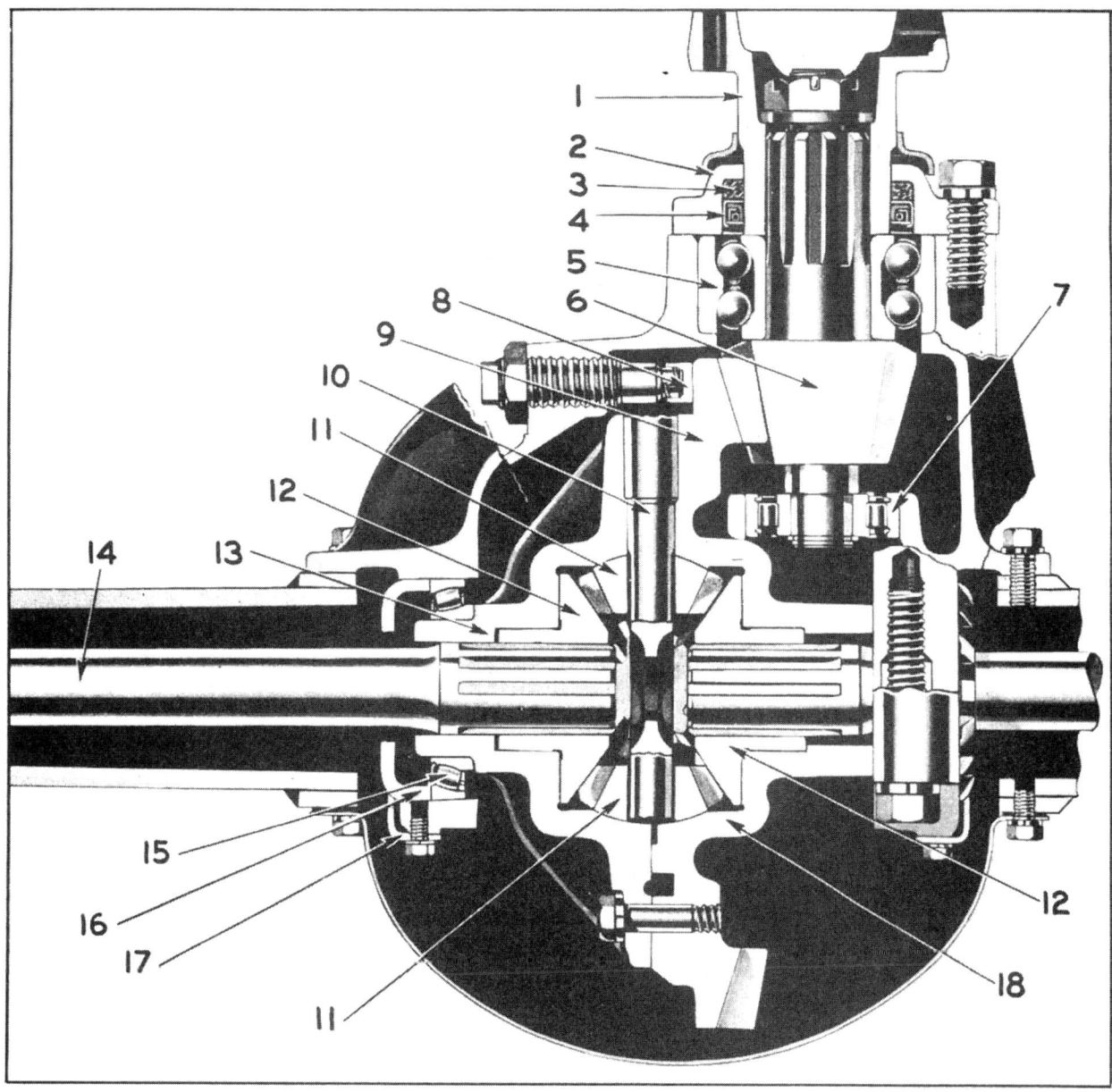

Fig. 38—1½ and 2 Ton Truck Hypoid Rear Axle

1. Universal Joint Yoke
2. Pinion Bearing Retainer and Oil Seal
3. Oil Seal Packing
4. Oil Seal
5. Front Pinion Bearing
6. Drive Pinion
7. Rear Pinion Bearing
8. Ring Gear Thrust Pad
9. Ring Gear
10. Differential Spider
11. Differential Pinion (Spider) Gear
12. Differential Side Gear
13. Differential Case—Left Half
14. Axle Shaft
15. Differential Bearing
16. Differential Bearing Adjusting Nut
17. Adjusting Nut Lock
18. Differential Case—Right Half

MINOR SERVICE OPERATIONS

AXLE SHAFT

Removal

1. Remove hub cap.
2. Remove jaws from J-1436, rear axle shaft bearing and oil seal remover, and install adapter J-1436-8 to puller handle.
3. Thread adapter into hole provided in end of axle shaft and remove shaft (fig. 40).

Replacement

1. Clean axle shaft flange and inside of wheel hub.
2. Install new shaft, indexing shaft flange splines with hub splines and tap into position.

NOTE: It may be necessary to move truck slightly in order to align splines on the axle shaft with those in the wheel hub and differential side gears.

REAR AXLE 4-22

Fig. 39—Splined Hub Parts

1. Hub
2. Spacer
3. Gasket
4. Axle Shaft
5. Hub Cap

3. Clean mating faces of hub cap and hub. Install new gasket and hub cap and tighten attaching bolts securely.

REAR WHEEL BEARINGS

Removal

1. Raise truck and place on stand jacks.
2. Remove wheel and axle shaft.

Fig. 40—Removing Splined Axle Shaft

3. Remove hub and drum assembly using special wrench J-870 to remove adjusting nut and lock nut.
4. To remove the inner bearing and oil seal, use puller J-918-A. The puller is installed by tilting the plate with the chain attached so that it may be slipped through the bearing and engage the outer race of the bearing. The plate is then held in this position by the chain while threading the puller shaft into the tapped hole. The puller body is then located against the hub and the bearing assembly and oil seal are removed by turning the puller handle (fig. 41).

Fig. 41—Removing Inner Bearing and Oil Seal

5. To remove the outer bearing, first tap the outer race to relieve the tension at the snap ring, then remove the snap ring on the inside of the hub (fig. 23). Remove the bearing by driving on the axle shaft spacer using a long 1/8" punch through splines in the hub. This will also bring out the inner race and roller assembly.

NOTE: Care must be taken to engage the edge of the spacer with the punch and not damage the bearing seat in the housing. The race must also be driven out evenly.

Cleaning and Inspection

Wash the bearings thoroughly in cleaning solvent. Inspect the races for cracks, chips and wear. Inspect the rollers and retainers for any damage. Lubricate the bearings with engine oil and check them for roughness. Any damaged parts should be replaced.

Replacement

1. Pack roller assemblies with soft smooth cup grease.

2. To replace the outer bearing, place the axle shaft spacer and the outer bearing with the thin edge of the outer race downward, into the wheel hub. Use outer wheel bearing replacer J-872-1 to press the bearing into the hub.

   CAUTION: Press the race only far enough to install the snap ring. This operation should be done in an arbor press.

3. Install the snap ring in the groove on inside of hub. Using a long 1/8" punch through the splines in the hub, drive on the axle shaft spacer to force the outer race into positive contact with the snap ring.

4. To replace the inner bearing, place the outer race of the bearing in the wheel hub with the wide side of the race down. Use special driver J-872-4 to press the race against its seat. Install the inner race and roller assembly.

5. Using a fine file, dress out old seal staking points. Then, coat the O.D. of the seal with a light coat of Permatex and install oil seal using oil seal replacer J-3067. Lock the seal in place by prick punching at three equally spaced places.

6. Install the wheel hub and drum assembly. Rotate assembly to properly line up the bearings.

7. Install thrust washer and adjusting nut (fig. 42).

Fig. 42—Installing Thrust Washer, Adjusting Nut, Lock Nut and Lock Nut Lock

Adjustment

1. Using special wrench J-870, tighten the adjusting nut tight, while turning drum by hand. Then back off the adjusting nut 45 degrees. Turn hub and drum by hand to make sure that it turns freely.

2. Install the adjusting nut lock and align nearest slot in nut with a tang on the lock and bend tang into slot in nut.

3. Install lock nut and tighten securely. Lock in position by bending a tang of the lock into a slot in the lock nut.

4. Install axle shaft, replace hub cap using a new gasket and mount wheel on hub.

BRAKE DRUM

Replacement—1948-50 Models

The brake drum is held to the hub by the hub bolts which must be pressed out of the hub or driven out with a hammer.

When replacing the drum or hub, the gasket between the inside of the brake drum and oil deflector should be coated with heavy shellac or paint on both sides to prevent oil leaking onto the braking surface of the drum. The small hole in the gasket and the channel in the oil deflector must be lined up with the oil relief hole in the drum. Insert eight new bolts through the oil deflector, brake drum and hub flange and press bolts in until they have bottomed and locked tight in the hub.

   NOTE: It is well to note, when studs have been removed, that the holes are not oversize. Bolts are no longer peened in place, but must fit tight to prevent their turning in the hub.

Replacement—1951 Models

The brake drum is held to the hub by three slotted screws which are easily removed with a screwdriver. It will be noticed on removing the brake drum that a soft paper gasket is used to insure a seal between the hub and drum. A new seal should be used in reassembly.

MAJOR SERVICE OPERATIONS

AXLE ASSEMBLY

Major operations of this axle assembly may be performed without removing the complete axle assembly from the vehicle. There may be occasions, however, when it will be necessary to remove the complete assembly as a result of a collision or other damage resulting in distortion of the axle housing or axle shaft tubes. The following axle housing assembly removal, therefore, is to be used only when replacement of axle housing is necessary.

Removal

1. Raise vehicle from floor and support with standjacks under frame side rails.
2. Remove rear wheels.
3. Remove two trunnion bearing "U" bolts from the rear yoke and split rear universal joint.

   NOTE: The bearings can be left on the trunnion and held in place with tape.

4. Swing the propeller shaft to one side and tie it to the frame side rail.
5. On 1948-50 models, disconnect parking brake cables at clevis and remove cable from cable clamp on frame.
6. Disconnect hydraulic brake line connection at rear axle housing.
7. Support rear axle assembly with hydraulic jack and remove spring "U" bolts, nuts and anchor plate and lower axle assembly to floor.

Installation

1. Slide axle assembly under vehicle, raise into position and install "U" bolt anchor plates and nuts and tighten securely.
2. Connect hydraulic brake line at rear axle housing.
3. On 1948-50 models, connect hand brake cables and adjust. See Brake Section.
4. Reassemble rear universal joint making sure "U" bolts are drawn up tight and locked properly.
5. Replace rear wheels and lower vehicle to floor.
6. Bleed brake lines at all four wheels. See Brake Section.

The following operations are MAJOR SERVICE OPERATIONS but may be, due to axle construction, performed without raising vehicle from the floor or removing axle assembly from the vehicle.

DIFFERENTIAL CARRIER

Removal

1. Drain lubricant from differential, remove axle housing cover and remove axle shafts. See Axle Shaft removal.
2. Remove two trunnion bearing "U" bolts from the rear yoke and split the rear universal joint (fig. 43).

   NOTE: The bearings can be left on the trunnion and held in place with tape.

3. Swing propeller shaft to one side and tie it to the frame side rail.
4. Remove bolts and lockwashers which retain carrier assembly to the axle housing. Support the differential carrier with a floor jack and roll it from under the truck.

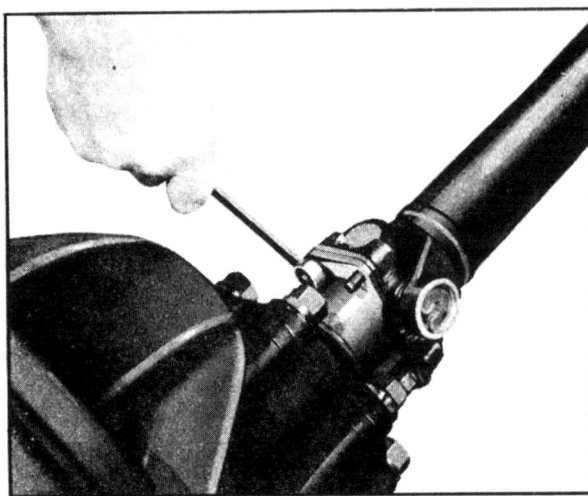

Fig. 43—Removing Rear Universal Joint "U" Bolts

Disassembly

1. Mount the assembly in a bench vise or holding fixture.
2. Loosen ring gear thrust pad lock nut and remove thrust pad.
3. Remove differential adjusting nut locks and bearing cap bolts and lockwashers.
4. Remove bearing caps and adjusting nuts by tapping on bosses of caps until free from dowels.

   CAUTION: Do not use screwdriver to pry cap off as this may damage machined face of cap.

5. Remove differential and ring gear assembly from carrier housing.

   CAUTION: Exercise care that differential side bearing outer races are not dropped in removing assembly from housing.

6. Remove bolts which attach the pinion bearing retainer to the carrier.
7. Remove the pinion and shaft assembly from carrier.

   NOTE: It may be necessary to drive this unit from the carrier. Use brass drift against pilot end of pinion shaft.

8. Wash all parts in cleaning solvent.

PINION

Disassembly

1. Clamp pinion shaft drive flange in bench vise.
2. Remove cotter pin, nut and washer from end of pinion shaft.
3. Remove drive flange and bearing retainer assembly from shaft.
4. Clean all parts *thoroughly in cleaning sol-*

REAR AXLE 4-25

vent. Blow out bearings with compressed air and oil lightly with engine oil.

NOTE: Do not spin bearings when blowing out with air as this causes damage to races and balls.

Inspection

1. Inspect oil seal and packing in pinion bearing retainer.
2. Inspect splines of pinion shaft for excessive wear.
3. Inspect pinion teeth for scoring, cracked or chipped teeth.
4. Inspect rear pinion bearing for roughness by revolving slowly by hand.
5. Inspect large front double row ball bearing for roughness by revolving slowly by hand.

Pinion Bearing Retainer Oil Seal and Packing—Replacement

1. Drive oil seal and packing from retainer.
2. Soak new oil seal and packing in engine oil to provide initial lubrication.
3. Install felt packing in bottom of bearing retainer recess and then the oil seal and press into position using oil seal replacer J-2231.

NOTE: Make sure open end of the leather in oil seal is toward pinion bearing.

Pinion Bearing Replacement

1. Remove rear pinion bearing snap ring and press rear pinion bearing from pinion shaft using press plate J-1453 (fig. 44).

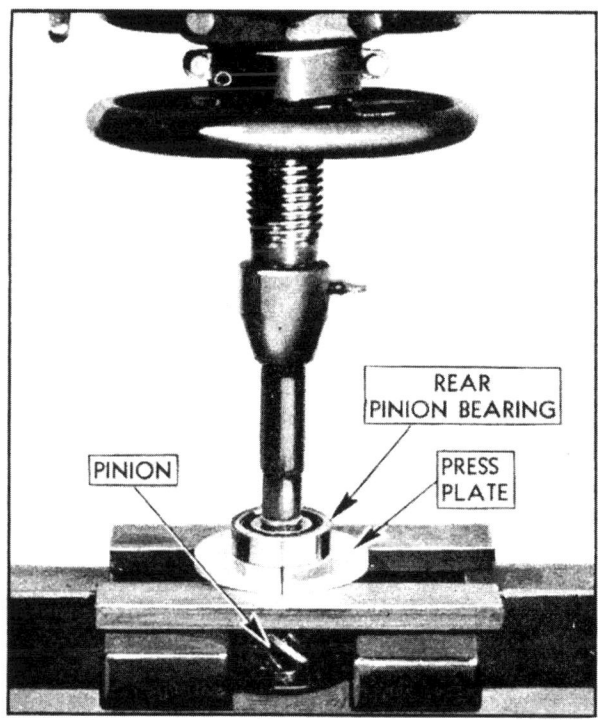

Fig. 44—Removing Rear Pinion Bearing

2. Install pinion bearing remover over pinion teeth and press front pinion bearing from shaft (fig. 45).

**NOTE: For 6-tooth pinion use tool J-1439
For 7-tooth pinion use tool J-1440**

3. Press a new double row pinion bearing on pinion shaft, using a piece of 2" pipe applying pressure against inner race.

NOTE: Bearing must be installed so that extended portion of inner race is toward the back of the pinion gear teeth.

4. Press rear pinion bearing on shaft using driver to apply pressure to inner race.

NOTE: Chamfered side of inner race should be toward pinion.

5. Install lock ring using lock ring installer J-1364 (fig. 46).
6. Lubricate both bearings with engine oil.

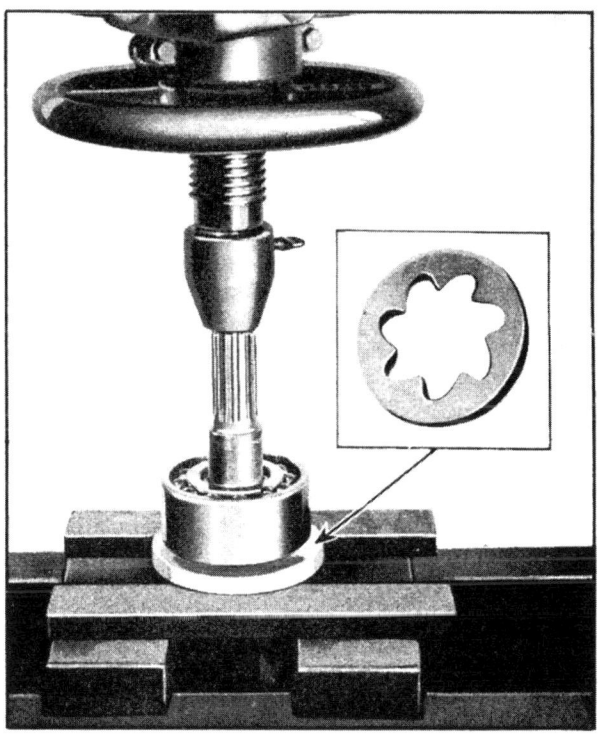

Fig. 45—Removing Pinion Bearing

Assembly

1. Place pinion bearing retainer over hub of pinion shaft drive flange.
2. Install drive flange and pinion bearing retainer, washer and nut to pinion shaft.
3. Place pinion shaft drive flange in bench vise and tighten pinion shaft nut with a torque wrench to 160-280 ft. lbs.
4. Lock nut in place with cotter key.

Fig. 46—Rear Pinion Bearing Lock Ring Installer

DIFFERENTIAL

Disassembly

1. Check differential case to make sure that the two halves are marked so they may be reassembled in same relation (fig. 33).
2. Remove twelve bolts holding case and cover together.

   NOTE: Ring gear is mounted on the case.

3. Separate cover from case and remove differential side gears, pinion gears and pinion gear spider.

Inspection

1. Wash all parts thoroughly in cleaning solvent.
2. Inspect ring gear for cracked, chipped or worn teeth.
3. Inspect case and cover for scored side gear or pinion gear thrust faces.
4. Check fit of side gear hubs in case and cover.
5. Inspect splines of side gears for excessive wear.
6. Inspect side gears and pinions for worn, cracked or chipped teeth.
7. Inspect hubs of spider for scoring and check fit of pinions on these hubs.
8. Inspect differential case bearings for cracked or checked, scored or broken races and rollers.
9. Check bearings for roughness by rotating by hand.

Differential Bearing Replacement

1. Install differential bearing puller TR-278-R making sure puller legs are fitted securely in case and retaining yoke is tight.
2. Tighten puller screw to remove bearing.
3. Place new bearing on hub with thick side of inner race toward case and drive in place with differential bearing driver J-1488 (fig. 34).

   NOTE: This tool is counterbored and has pilot to assure proper installation and seating of bearing.

Ring Gear Replacement

1. Remove ring gear from case by tapping the back of the gear with a soft faced hammer.
2. Inspect ring gear pilot case flange and back of ring gear for dirt or burrs.
3. Install two guide pins made from ½"-20x2" cap screws with heads cut off and ends slotted to new gear diametrically opposite each other.
4. Start guide pins through case flange and tap ring gear on to case.

Assembly

1. Lubricate differential side gears and pinions.
2. Place differential pinions on spider.
3. Assemble side gears and pinions to left half of differential case.
4. Assemble right half of case to left half being sure to line up marks on the two halves (fig. 33).
5. Install ten differential to ring gear bolts and lockwashers and tighten evenly until ring gear is flush with case flange.
6. Remove two guide pins and install remaining two bolts.

   NOTE: All bolts should be tightened with a torque wrench to 85-95 foot pounds.

DIFFERENTIAL CARRIER

Assembly

1. Mount carrier in bench vise or holding fixture.
2. Assemble pinion assembly to the carrier using a new gasket and tighten pinion bearing bolts securely.
3. Install differential assembly in carrier and install adjusting nuts.

   CAUTION: Carefully slide adjusting nuts alongside the bearings so that threads on nuts fit into threads in carrier.

4. Install differential bearing caps making sure the marks on the caps line up with marks on the carrier.
5. Install bearing cap bolts and lockwashers and tighten until lockwashers just flatten out.

Ring Gear and Pinion Adjustment

1. Loosen right hand adjusting nut and tighten left hand adjusting nut, using adjusting nut wrench J-972 until all lash between ring gear and pinion is removed (fig. 35).
2. Back off left hand adjusting nut two notches to a locking position.
3. Tighten right hand adjusting nut firmly to force differential in solid contact with left hand adjusting nut.
4. Back off right hand adjusting nut until free of bearing; then retighten snugly against bearing.
5. Tighten right hand nut from one to two additional notches to a locking position.

NOTE: This method of adjustment provides for proper preload of bearings.

6. Mount a dial indicator on the carrier and check the backlash between ring gear and pinion (fig. 36). Backlash should be from .005" to .008".

NOTE: If backlash is more than .008" loosen the right hand adjusting nut one notch and tighten left hand adjusting nut one notch. If backlash is less than .005" loosen the left hand adjusting nut one notch and tighten right hand nut one notch.

7. Tighten bearing cap bolts with a torque wrench to 130-160 foot pounds. Recheck backlash and install both adjusting nut locks.
8. Inspect bronze tip of thrust pad and if worn install a new one.
9. Install thrust pad and tighten screw until bronze tip engages back face of ring gear while rotating gear.
10. Back off screw one twelfth (1/12) turn and tighten lock nut (fig. 37).

NOTE: Make sure screw does not turn during locking process. This adjustment provides .005" to .007" clearance between thrust pad and ring gear face.

Installation

1. Clean out axle housing and cover and place new gasket over axle housing.
2. Assemble differential carrier to axle housing, install lockwashers and nuts and tighten securely.
3. Replace axle housing inspection cover using new gasket.
4. Assemble rear universal joint.
5. Clean axle flange and inside of wheel hub splines.
6. Install axle shaft, indexing shaft flange splines with hub splines and tap into position.

NOTE: It may be necessary to move truck slightly in order to align splines on the axle shaft with those in the wheel hub and differential side gears.

7. Clean mating faces of hub cap and hub. Install new gasket and hub cap. Tighten attaching bolts securely.
8. Fill axle assembly with 11 pints of SAE 90 "Multi-Purpose" gear lubricant on 1½ ton trucks and 12 pints on 2 ton and COE trucks.

TWO-SPEED REAR AXLE

INDEX

	Page		Page
General Description	4-27	Pinion Cage	4-32
Minor Service Operations	4-29	Repairs	4-32
Vacuum Cylinder Diaphragm	4-29	Double Reduction Shaft	4-34
Vacuum Cylinder Oil Seal	4-29	Differential	4-36
Shifter Spring	4-30	Repairs	4-37
Major Service Operations	4-30	Differential Carrier	4-37
Differential Carrier	4-30	Assembly	4-37
Removal	4-30	Ring Gear and Pinion Adjustment	4-38
Disassembly	4-30	Installation	4-39

GENERAL DESCRIPTION

The two-speed rear axle used as an option on all 2 ton conventional and Cab-Over-Engine trucks is a double reduction unit with variation of axle ratio of 6.13 to 1 in high gear to 8.10 to 1 in low gear. The construction features are shown in Figure 47. A hypoid ring gear and pinion are used, giving a reduction which operates in combination with either of two sets of helical gears to produce the selected low or high speed reduction. The drive pinion is mounted on two tapered roller bearings

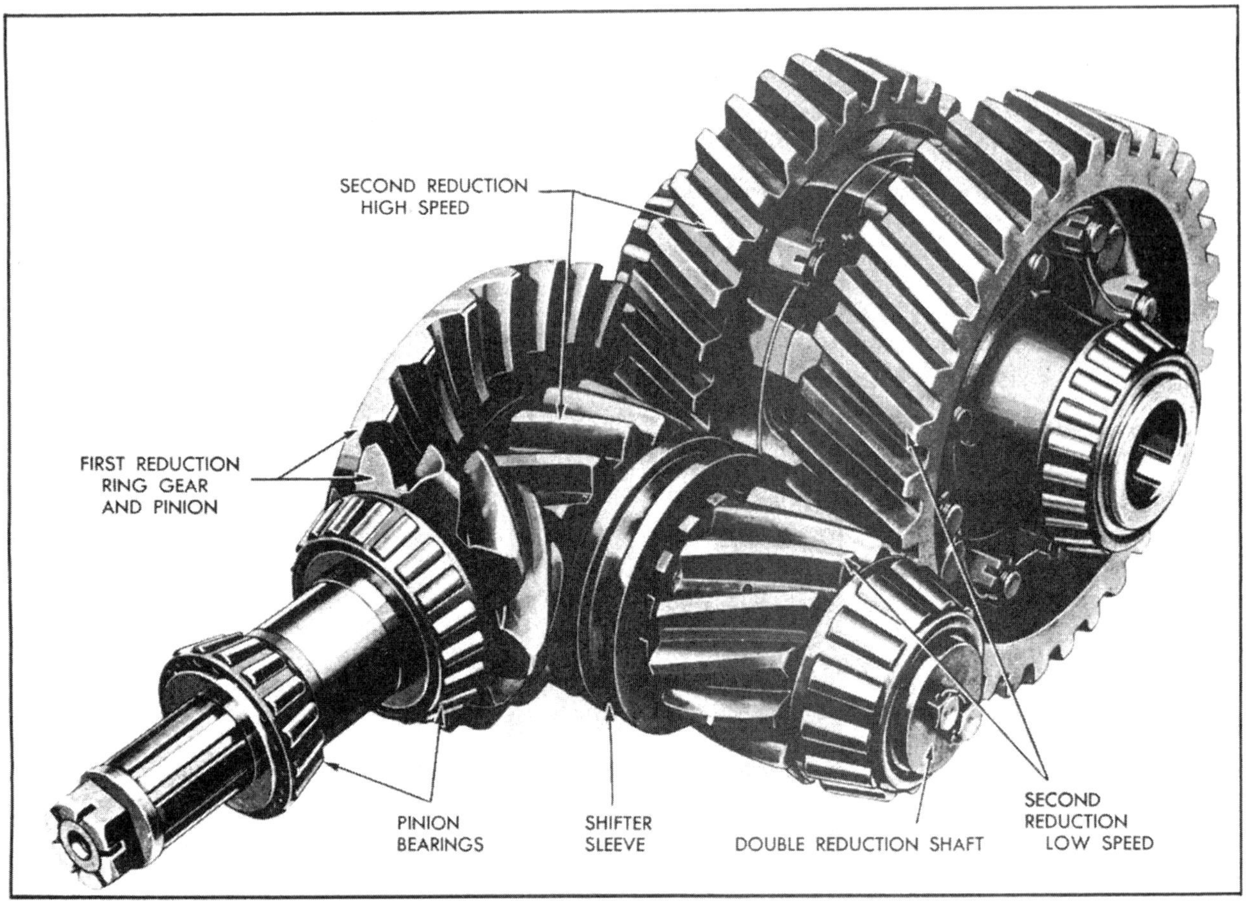

REAR AXLE 4-28

Fig. 47—Two-Speed Axle Drive Unit

and the ring gear is keyed and bolted to the double reduction shaft. The double reduction shaft, mounted on tapered roller bearings, has been designed for maximum strength and simplicity of servicing.

On the double reduction shaft are the two double reduction pinions, each of which has an integral spur pinion on one end. Between these two pinions are two sets of short splines integral with the reduction shaft. A shifter sleeve which is meshed with the splines on the reduction shaft is moved by a shifter mechanism to engage one or the other of the reduction pinions locking it to the shaft to give the gear ratio preselected by the driver.

Shifting from one axle ratio to the other is accomplished by a vacuum cylinder mounted on the differential carrier and connected directly to a shifter fork (fig. 48). A selector valve is mounted on the instrument panel and connected to the vacuum cylinder by two pipes and hose connections.

Through the use of this vacuum shift, the truck operator can quickly shift from low to high, or from high to low without declutching and without loss of headway, which results in a considerable savings in both time and operating costs.

With the selector valve in "Hi" range position, the shifter sleeve engages the high speed pinion which causes the pinion to be locked to the double reduction shaft through the medium of the splines on the shaft and internal teeth of the sleeve. The power from the engine is then transmitted through the propeller shaft to the pinion and ring gear to the double reduction shaft through the shifter sleeve to the high speed pin-

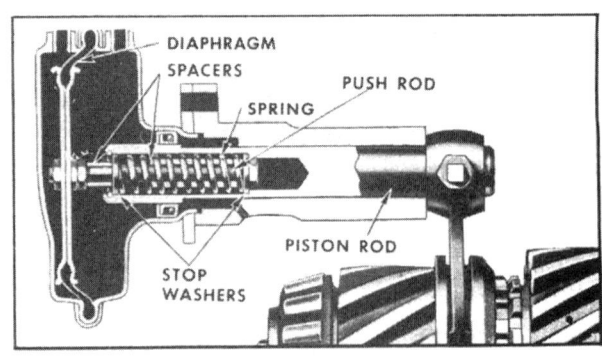

Fig. 48—Vacuum Shift Unit

ion to the high speed gear through the differential to the axle shafts and wheels.

With the selector valve in "Lo" range position, the shifter sleeve engages the low speed pinion which allows for flow of power through the low speed gear to the axle shafts and wheels.

Vacuum Control Operation

Operation and preselection of gear ratio is controlled by the driver through the use of a selector valve mounted on the dash of the vehicle. The center outlet of this valve is connected to the intake manifold through a vacuum check valve. With the selector lever set for low speed, vacuum is applied to the outer chamber of the vacuum cylinder and atmospheric pressure to the inner chamber. With the selector set for high speed, vacuum is applied to the inner chamber of the vacuum cylinder and atmospheric pressure to the outer chamber.

With the selector lever in the low-speed position, the spring-loaded poppets under the shifter sleeve hold it in position, centered under the shifter fork. This prevents wear of the fork by side contact with the sleeve.

When the operator desires to shift from low-speed to high-speed, he can preselect by moving the selector to the high-speed position. This applies vacuum to the inner chamber of the vacuum cylinder and atmospheric to the outer chamber and causes push rod to move inwards compressing the shifter spring. The low-speed pinion gear will continue to be locked in the low-speed position until driving torque is interrupted. When the operator desires to complete the shift to high gear, he merely lets up on the accelerator momentarily, thereby releasing the torque on the gears. This permits full force of the vacuum cylinder to move the shifter fork inward to disengage the shifter sleeve from the low-speed pinion gear into neutral.

When the speeds of the shifter sleeve and high-speed pinion are synchronized, the compressed shifter spring completes the shift by moving the shifter sleeve over the clutch teeth of the high-speed pinion. The poppets then move the shifter sleeve a little further, centering it under the shifter fork to prevent undue wear.

In shifting from high speed to low speed, the operator moves the selector lever to the low speed position. When he desires to complete the shift, he merely lets up on the accelerator momentarily to release the torque and disengage the shifter sleeve from the high speed pinion and steps down on the accelerator to speed up the engine which synchronizes the gears and allows for completion of the shift.

A speedometer adapter is used to secure proper speed and odometer readings with the rear axle in either high or low speeds. The shift rod which shifts the speedometer gear ratios in the adapter is connected to the selector valve so that whenever a change in ratio is made at the rear axle, a corresponding change is made at the speedometer adapter.

MINOR SERVICE OPERATIONS

VACUUM CYLINDER DIAPHRAGM

Replacement

1. Loosen clamps on hose connections at the vacuum cylinder and slip hoses off the connection fittings.
2. Remove the screws and nuts that attach the two halves of the vacuum cylinder and remove outer half.
3. Use two ½" end wrenches, one to hold the push rod inner nuts and the other to remove the outer nut from the push rod. Then remove diaphragm plates and diaphragm.
4. Install new diaphragm and plates to the push rod and tighten the retaining nut securely.

   NOTE: Apply Permatex around push rod hole between diaphragm plates.

5. Assemble outer half of vacuum cylinder to inner half, install retaining screws and nuts and tighten securely.

6. Replace hose connections and tighten clamp screws.

   CAUTION: Be careful not to transpose hose connections.

7. Test operation of shifting mechanism in high and low speeds.

VACUUM CYLINDER OIL SEAL

Replacement

1. Follow instructions given for the first three items under the heading Vacuum Cylinder Diaphragm Replacement.
2. Remove two nuts and washers that attach the vacuum cylinder to the differential carrier and remove inner half of vacuum cylinder.
3. Drive the damaged oil seal out of the inner half of the cylinder.
4. Soak new oil seal in engine oil to provide for initial lubrication. Coat outer diameter of

new seal with Permatex and place it in the inner half of the cylinder with the free side of the leather down and press into place with seal replacer J-968.
5. Assemble inner half of cylinder to the differential case, install lock washers and nuts and tighten securely.
6. Complete the assembly of the vacuum cylinder according to instructions given in items 4, 5, 6 and 7 under heading Vacuum Cylinder Diaphragm Replacement.

SHIFTER SPRING

Replacement

1. Follow instructions given in items 1, 2 and 3 under the heading Vacuum Cylinder Diaphragm Replacement.
2. Push in on end of push rod to relieve spring load and remove snap ring from inside of piston rod and pull push rod assembly out of piston rod.
3. Place head of push rod bolt in bench vise and remove two nuts, short spacer, stop washer, spring, long spacer and stop washer from push rod bolt.
4. Install stop washer, long spacer, new spring, stop washer and short spacer.
5. Install adjusting nut on push rod and tighten until distance between outer faces of stop washers is 3½" (fig. 49).

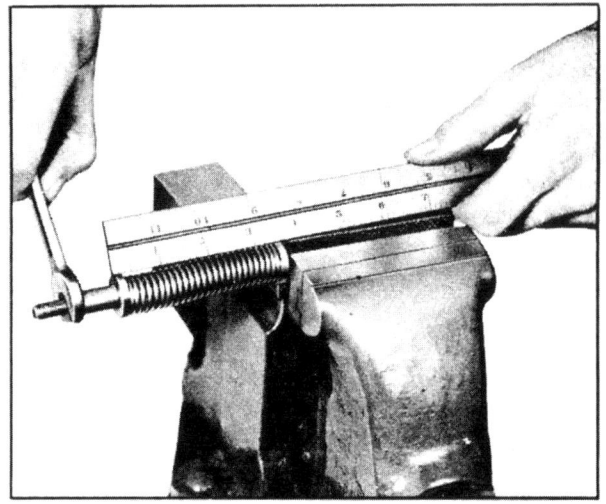

Fig. 49—Adjusting Push Rod

6. Install lock nut on push rod and tighten, being careful not to change 3½" adjustment.
7. Lubricate inside of piston rod with engine oil and install push rod assembly.
8. Push in on push rod to compress spring and install snap ring.
9. Complete the assembly of the vacuum cylinder according to instructions given in items 4, 5, 6 and 7 under the heading Vacuum Cylinder Diaphragm Replacement.

MAJOR SERVICE OPERATIONS

DIFFERENTIAL CARRIER

Removal

1. Drain the lubricant from the differential.
2. Remove hub caps. Remove jaws from J-1436, rear axle shaft bearing and oil seal remover, and install adapter J-1436-8 to puller handle. Install axle shaft puller adapter into hole provided in the end of the axle shaft and pull the shafts out about 8" to clear the differential.
3. Loosen the clamps on the hose connections at the vacuum cylinder and slip the hoses off the vacuum cylinder connection fittings.
4. Split the rear universal joint by removing the trunnion bearing "U" bolts from the rear flange. Slide the propeller shaft assembly forward and tape the universal joint bearings to trunnion to hold them in place and keep them clean. Swing the propeller shaft to one side and tie it to frame side rail.
5. Remove the capscrews attaching the differential carrier to axle housing.

   NOTE: Before removing the last capscrew, place a long drift punch through upper hole in differential carrier and housing to support carrier.

6. Place a roller jack under differential carrier and block between the jack and carrier to properly support it. Work the assembly forward until the differential clears the housing. Support the differential carrier on the jack and roll jack out from under truck.

The illustration (fig. 50) shows an exploded view of the differential carrier assembly.

Disassembly

1. Mark the differential bearing caps and carrier with a center punch or chisel for identification when reassembling.
2. Remove the adjusting nut locks and the differential bearing cap retaining nut tie wires. Then remove the nuts, bearing caps and differential assembly from the carrier.
3. Remove the pinion cage to carrier nuts and the lubrication plug. Install two ⅜" standard bolts in the tapped holes in cage flange and tighten the bolts to remove cage assembly. Remove the cage to carrier shims and note the number and thickness shims removed as this will aid in assembling and adjusting the unit.

REAR AXLE 4-31

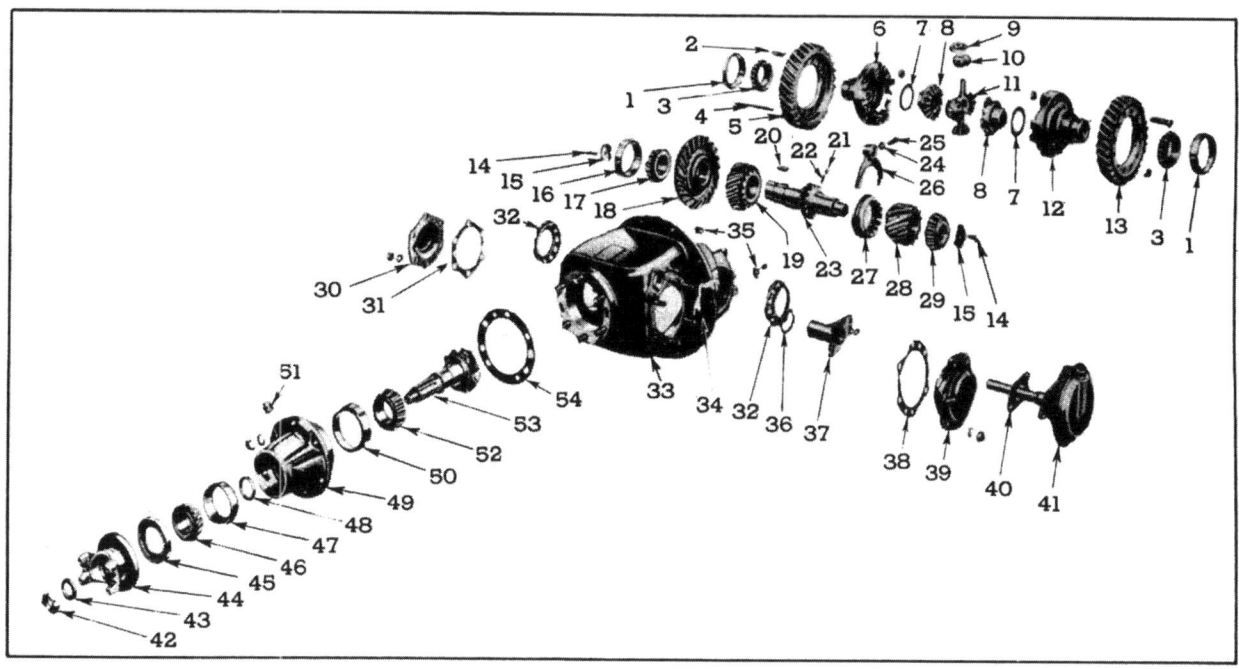

Fig. 50—Exploded View of Two-Speed Differential Carrier Assembly

1. Bearing Cup, differential side
2. Bolt, double reduction gear to case
3. Bearing, differential side
4. Bolt, reduction gear and differential case
5. Gear, high speed double reduction
6. Differential Case Half
7. Thrust Washer, differential side gear
8. Side Gear, differential
9. Thrust Washer, differential pinion
10. Pinion, differential
11. Spider, differential pinion
12. Differential Case Half
13. Gear, low speed double reduction
14. Cap Screw, reduction shaft bearing retainer
15. Washer, reduction shaft bearing retainer
16. Bearing Cup, reduction shaft right
17. Bearing, reduction shaft right
18. Ring Gear
19. Pinion, high speed double reduction
20. Key, ring gear to shaft
21. Poppet, shifter sleeve
22. Spring, shifter sleeve poppet
23. Shaft, double reduction
24. Nut, shifter fork bolt lock
25. Bolt, shifter fork lock
26. Shifter Fork
27. Shifter Sleeve
28. Pinion, low speed double reduction.
29. Bearing, reduction shaft left
30. Bearing Cap, double reduction shaft right
31. Shim, double reduction bearing cap right
32. Adjusting Nut, differential bearing
33. Carrier, differential
34. Shim, vacuum shift sleeve
35. Lock, differential bearing adjusting nut
36. Seal, vacuum shift sleeve
37. Sleeve, vacuum unit mounting
38. Shim, double reduction shaft cap left
39. Cap, double reduction shaft left
40. Gasket, vacuum shift flange
41. Vacuum Cylinder and Piston Rod
42. Nut, pinion shaft joint flange
43. Washer, pinion shaft joint flange
44. Flange, universal joint
45. Seal, pinion shaft oil
46. Bearing, pinion shaft front
47. Cup, pinion shaft front bearing
48. Spacer, pinion shaft bearing
49. Pinion Cage
50. Cup, pinion shaft rear bearing
51. Plug, pinion cage lubrication
52. Bearing, pinion shaft rear
53. Pinion and Shaft
54. Shim, pinion cage to carrier

4. Loosen the lock nut on the bolt that attaches the shifter fork to the vacuum shift piston rod and remove the bolt.
5. Remove the three nuts that attach the vacuum cylinder assembly to the differential carrier and remove cylinder, piston rod, mounting sleeve and shims. Remove shifter fork from inside of carrier.

    NOTE: It may be necessary to tap on end of piston rod to start it out of shifter fork.

6. Remove the nuts and lockwashers from the double reduction shaft bearing caps and remove caps and shims. Check the number and thickness shims removed at each cap for reference when reassembling.

    NOTE: Use two ⅜" standard cap screws in tapped holes in left bearing cap to remove it.

7. Slide the double reduction shaft assembly to the left in carrier and pull the ring gear end toward the rear to clear the differential bearing support and remove shaft assembly (fig. 51).

8. Drive the right bearing outer race out of carrier by driving it inside the carrier with J-872-1 driver (fig. 52). The left bearing race is pressed in the left bearing cap and cap and race are serviced as an assembly.

    NOTE: The above instructions cover the removal of the four assemblies from the differential carrier. Their disassembly, cleaning, inspection, reassembly and adjustment will be handled as individual units.

REAR AXLE 4-32

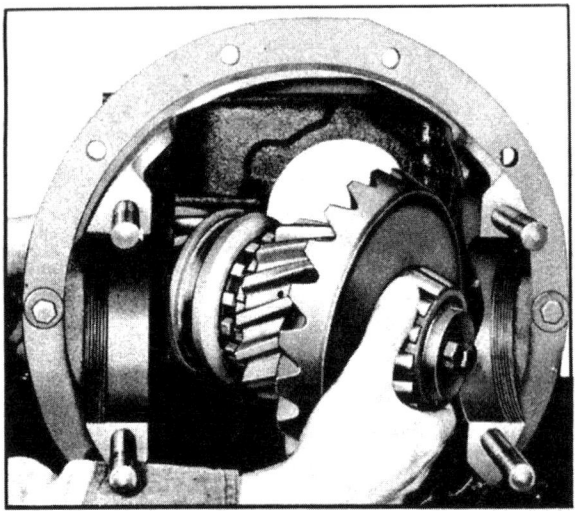

Fig. 51—Removing Double Reduction Shaft Assembly.

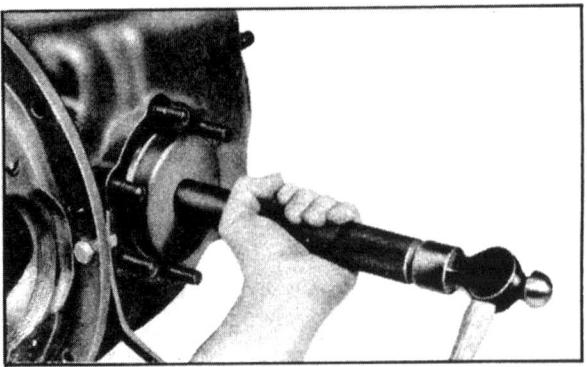

Fig. 52—Removing Right Bearing Race

PINION CAGE

Disassembly

1. Clamp the pinion shaft universal joint flange in a heavy vise and remove cotter pin, nut and washer. Remove joint flange.
2. Properly support the carrier end of pinion cage and press the pinion with rear bearing out of cage. Remove bearing spacer from pinion shaft.
3. Press the front bearing and oil seal out of the cage.

Inspection

1. Wash all parts thoroughly in cleaning solvent.
2. Inspect the drive pinion for chipped, cracked or worn teeth and inspect the splines for wear. Inspect both bearings for worn or pitted rollers or inner races. Inspect the cage for cracks, loose bearing races and for worn or pitted races. Inspect the universal joint rear flange for worn splines or damaged oil seal seat. Figure 53 shows layout of parts making up pinion cage assembly.
3. Replace all damaged parts including the oil seal or lay them aside for repairs.

Repairs

1. If the pinion or pinion rear bearing is found to be worn or damaged, the bearing can be pressed off the pinion shaft with J-2228 Pinion Bearing Remover in an arbor press. Replace damaged part and press bearing onto pinion shaft (fig. 54).

   NOTE: The pinion and ring gear are serviced in matched sets.

2. If the cage bearing outer races are found to be damaged they can be removed with a long drift and hammer.
3. Press the new bearing races squarely and firmly against their seats, using special driver J-1322 for the front race and J-2227 for the rear race (fig. 55).

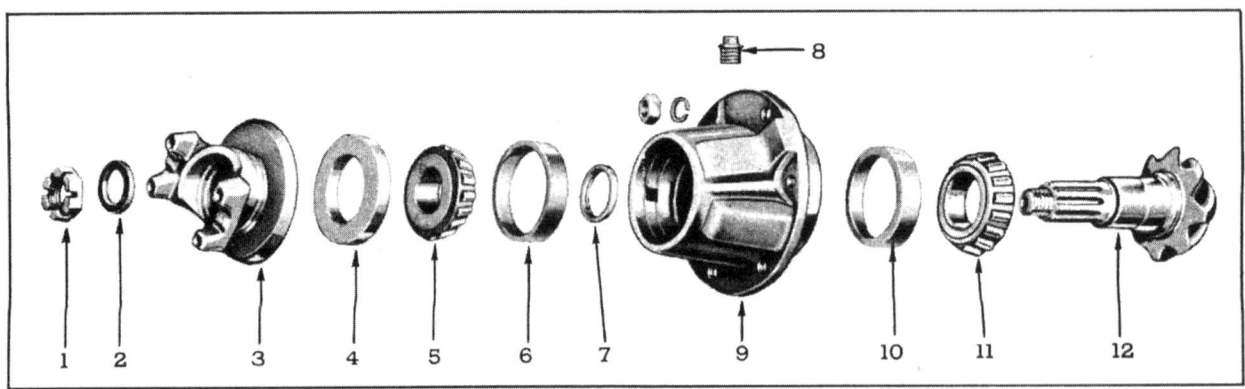

Fig. 53—Exploded View of Two-Speed Pinion Cage Assembly

1. Nut, pinion shaft joint flange
2. Washer, pinion shaft joint flange
3. Flange, universal joint
4. Seal, pinion shaft oil
5. Bearing, pinion shaft front
6. Cup, pinion shaft front bearing
7. Spacer, pinion shaft bearing
8. Plug, pinion cage lubrication
9. Pinion Cage
10. Cup, pinion shaft rear bearing
11. Bearing, pinion shaft rear
12. Pinion and Shaft

NOTE: Pinion cages are serviced through parts stock with bearing outer races pressed in place as part of the assembly.

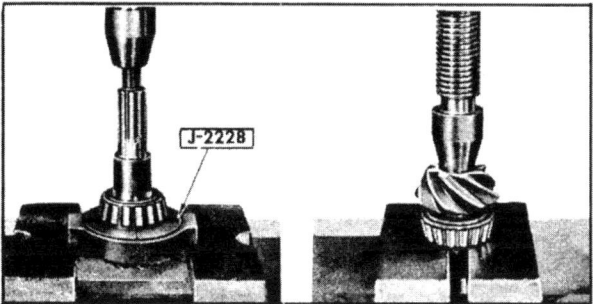

Fig. 54—Removing and Installing Pinion Rear Bearing

Assembly

1. Lubricate the pinion bearings. Place spacer on pinion shaft and install the shaft with spacer in pinion cage.
2. Place the front bearing on pinion shaft and drive it into position with a tubular driver. Install the universal joint flange. Install washer and nut, then tighten nut to 75 to 150 ft. lbs.
3. Clamp the cage web in a vise and check the load necessary to turn the pinion shaft which should be 12 to 18 inch pounds (fig. 56).

   NOTE: In production the pinion bearings are adjusted by the use of various thickness spacers which measure from .315" to .354". For convenience in making adjustments in service the following seven shims are available: 3847424—.157", 3847425—.159", 3847426—.163", 3847427—.167", 3847428—.171", 3847429—.175", and 3847430—.177".

4. If the load required to turn the pinion shaft is not within the limit of 12 to 18 inch pounds, it will be necessary to remove flange, press pinion out of cage and remove spacer. Check the thickness of the old spacer with a micrometer. By referring to the total thick-

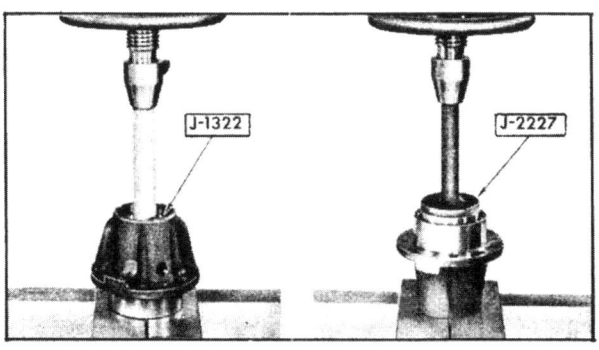

Fig. 55—Replacing Bearing Races

Fig. 56—Checking Pinion Shaft Bearing Load

ness column in the following table one can select the spacer and shim combination necessary to either tighten or loosen the bearing adjustment. It should be noted that seven shims will provide twenty different adjustments by .002" steps.

Total Thickness	Shims Used
.316"	1–3847424 and 1–3847425
.318"	2–3847425
.320"	1–3847424 and 1–3847426
.322"	1–3847425 and 1–3847426
.324"	1–3847424 and 1–3847427
.326"	2–3847426
.328"	1–3847424 and 1–3847428
.330"	1–3847426 and 1–3847427
.332"	1–3847424 and 1–3847429
.334"	2–3847427
.336"	1–3847425 and 1–3847430
.338"	1–3847427 and 1–3847428
.340"	1–3847426 and 1–3847430
.342"	2–3847428
.344"	1–3847427 and 1–3847430
.346"	1–3847428 and 1–3847429
.348"	1–3847428 and 1–3847430
.350"	2–3847429
.352"	1–3847429 and 1–3847430
.354"	2–3847430

5. Reassemble and check torque load as explained above. When correct adjustment is obtained remove universal joint flange and install a new oil seal, with the free edge of seal toward bearing, using driver J-971 (fig. 57) to prevent damaging the seal.

   NOTE: The seal should be presoaked in engine oil to provide initial lubrication.

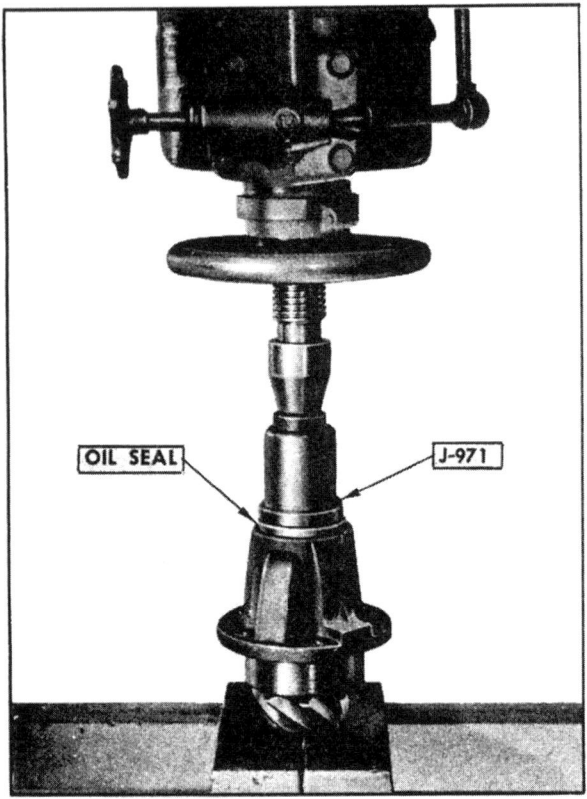

Fig. 57—Replacing Bearing Retainer Oil Seal

6. Install the joint flange, washer and nut. Tighten nut to between 75 and 150 ft. lbs. until a slot in nut lines up with cotter pin hole in shaft. Install cotter pin.

   NOTE: Do not back off nut to align cotter pin hole.

DOUBLE REDUCTION SHAFT

Disassembly

1. Remove the lock wires from the double reduction shaft bearing retainer washer cap screws, remove the screws and washers from both ends of shaft.

2. Support the tooth side of ring gear on hardwood blocks on an arbor press and press the reduction shaft out of ring gear and bearing (fig. 58). Remove the high speed pinion, shifter sleeve, shifter sleeve lock poppets and springs.

3. Place the shifter sleeve back on the shaft with tapered side against pinion, properly support it on an arbor press (fig. 59) and press the shaft out of bearing at low speed end of shaft. Remove low speed pinion and shifter sleeve.

Fig. 58—Removing Ring Gear and Bearing

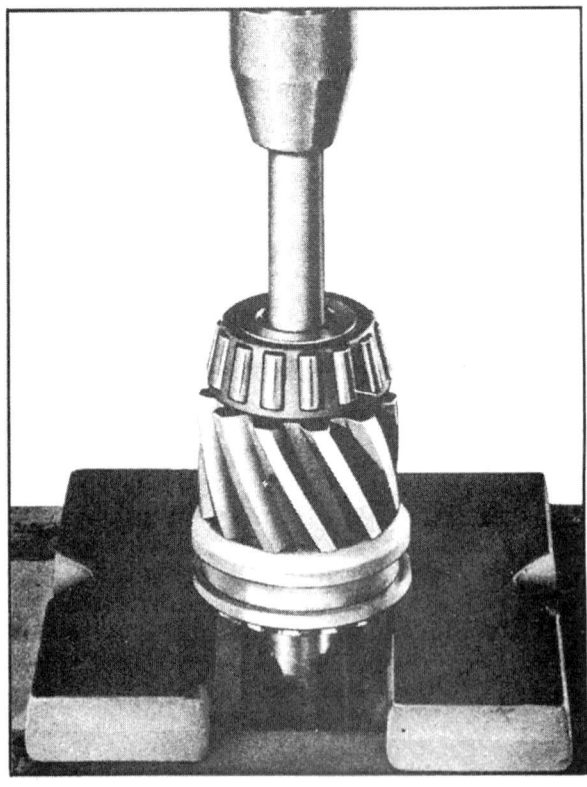

Fig. 59—Removing Bearing from Low Speed End of Shaft

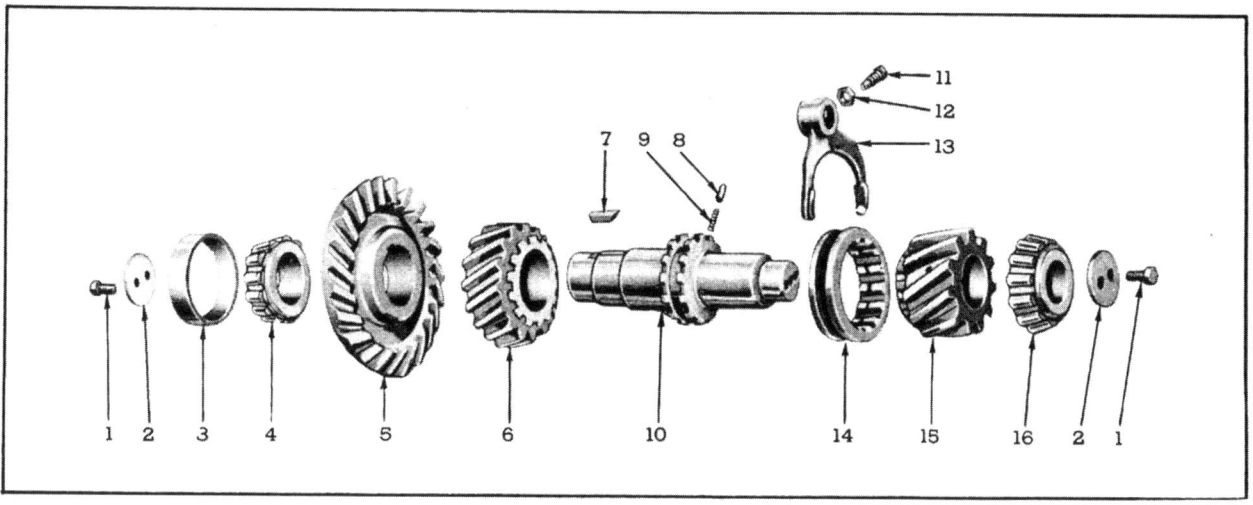

Fig. 60—Exploded View of Two-Speed Double Reduction Shaft Assembly

1. Cap Screw, reduction shaft bearing retainer
2. Washer, reduction shaft bearing retainer
3. Bearing Cup, reduction shaft right
4. Bearing, reduction shaft right
5. Ring Gear
6. Pinion, high speed double reduction
7. Key, ring gear to shaft
8. Poppet, shifter sleeve
9. Spring, shifter sleeve poppet
10. Shaft, double reduction
11. Bolt, shifter fork lock
12. Nut, shifter fork lock bolt
13. Shifter Fork
14. Shifter Sleeve
15. Pinion, low speed double reduction
16. Bearing, reduction shaft left

Inspection

1. Clean all parts thoroughly in cleaning solvent.
2. Inspect the ring gear and double reduction pinions for cracked, worn or chipped teeth, check the inner bearing surface of the pinions for being scored, check the pinion bearing surfaces on the shaft and check the pinion gear to shaft fit. Inspect the shaft for damage at the bearing seats and shifter sleeve splines.
3. Inspect the bearings for damaged rollers or cracked races. Any damaged parts should be replaced. Figure 60 shows parts making up double reduction shaft assembly. The double reduction shaft left bearing cap will be serviced only with the outer race in place.

Assembly

1. Lubricate the double reduction shaft pinion gear seats with hypoid lubricant for initial lubrication.
2. Place the high speed pinion on the long end of shaft with the end of pinion having the clutch teeth toward the splines on the shaft.
3. Place the ring gear key in shaft keyway and start the ring gear on the shaft. Press shaft into ring gear until shoulder contacts ring gear (fig. 61). Install the tapered roller bearing and press it down against gear. Install bearing retainer washer and cap screws.
4. Place the springs and poppets in their respective holes in the shaft. Locate the space on shaft between poppets having but four teeth and the space between the tapered teeth on shifter sleeve having but three splines (fig. 62).
5. Place the sleeve on shaft with the heavy tapered end of sleeve toward ring gear, mate the tapered teeth on the shifter sleeve with the poppets, then compress poppet springs and force sleeve into position.
6. Place the low speed pinion on the shaft and press the bearing down firmly against the

Fig. 61—Installing Ring Gear and Bearing

REAR AXLE 4-36

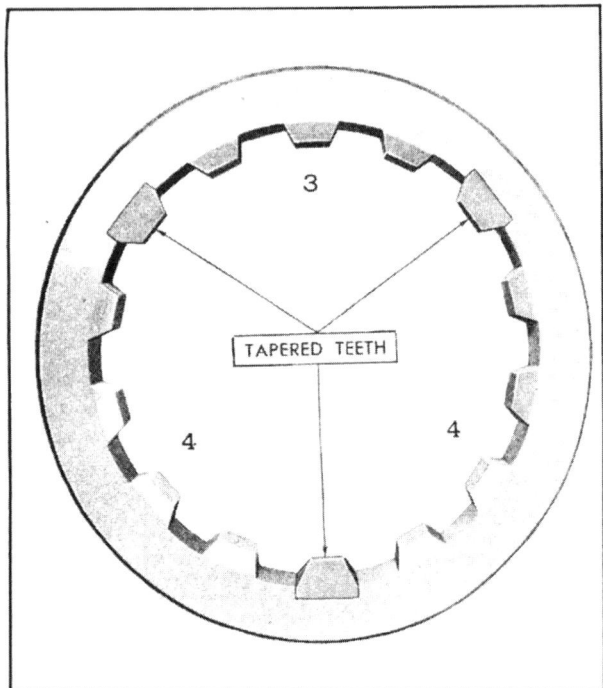

Fig. 62—Shifter Sleeve

shoulder (fig. 63) using bearing retainer washer as press plate.

7. Install the shaft bearing retainer washer and cap screws. Tighten screws on each end of shaft to 37-46 ft. lbs. torque and install lock wire.

DIFFERENTIAL

Disassembly

1. Make sure the two halves of case are properly marked for reassembly (fig. 67).
2. Remove the tie wires from all case bolts and

Fig. 63—Replacing Bearing on Low Speed End of Shaft

remove the 8 long through bolt nuts and bolts.
3. Separate the two halves of the case and remove the differential side gears, pinion gears, spider and all thrust washers.

Inspection

1. Thoroughly wash all parts with cleaning solvent. Inspect the reduction gears for chipped, worn or damaged teeth and for indication of

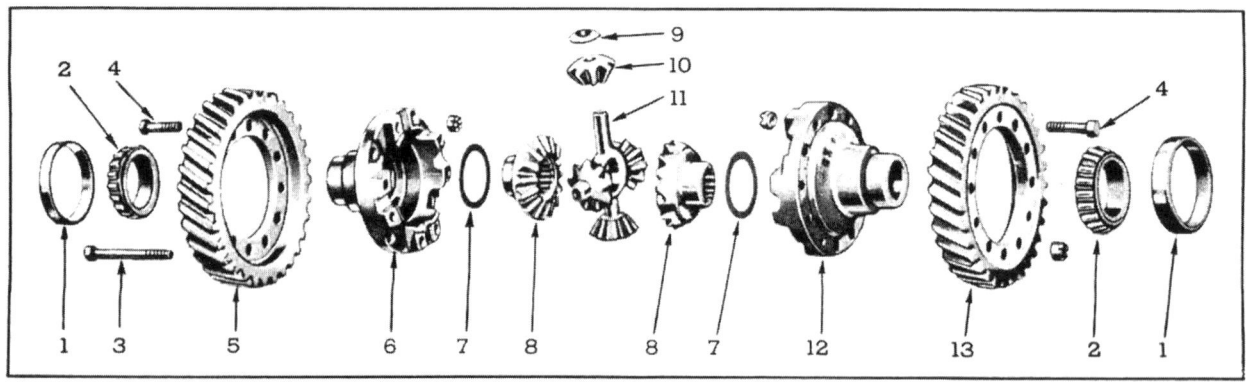

Fig. 64—Exploded View of Two-Speed Differential Assembly

1. Bearing Cup, differential side
2. Bearing, differential side
3. Bolt, reduction gear and differential case
4. Bolt, double reduction gear to case
5. Gear, high speed double reduction
6. Differential Case Half
7. Thrust Washer, differential side gear
8. Side Gear, differential
9. Thrust Washer, differential pinion
10. Pinion, differential
11. Spider, differential pinion
12. Differential Case Half
13. Gear, low speed double reduction

being loose on case. Inspect the case halves for damage or excessive wear at the thrust washer seats. Check the side bearings for damage or excessive wear.
2. Inspect the side and pinion gears for damaged teeth or excessive wear. Inspect the thrust washers for wear. Inspect the spider for wear or scored pinion bearing area. Figure 64 shows layout of parts which make up differential assembly.
3. Replace damaged parts or make repairs as follows:

Repairs

1. To replace a differential side bearing, clamp the two halves of J-1318 Differential Bearing Puller around the bearing (fig. 65) and support the case in an arbor press with the bearing puller down. Place a suitable drift through the case and press the bearing off.
2. Place new bearing on case and press it down against shoulder using J-1312 Replacer (fig. 66).
3. To replace a double reduction gear on either half of the case, remove the retaining bolt nuts and bolts and tap the gear off the case. Clean the mating flanges of case and new gear. Install the new gear on the case inserting as many of the four special hex head bolts as can be installed without forcing. Ream the remaining holes with a $9/16''$ reamer (.5625'') using the ring gear holes as a pilot.
4. To install a new case, remove the retaining bolt nuts and bolts. Tap the gear off the case. Clean the mating flanges of the new case and gear. Start the gear on the case using two or three of the long through bolts to line up the holes. Using a straight reamer $9/16''$ (.5625''),

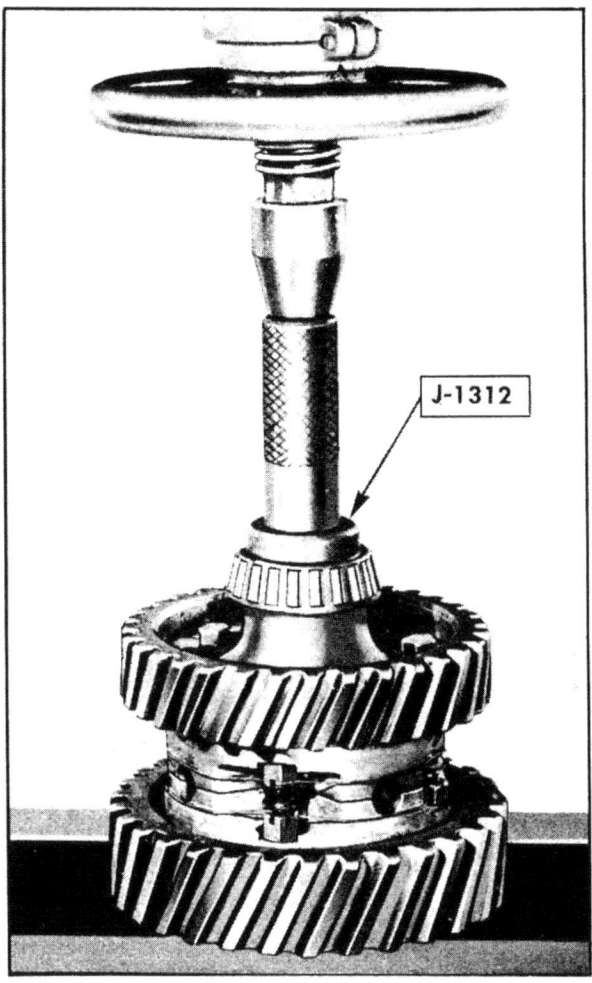

Fig. 66—Installing Differential Bearing

ream one of the four ring gear to case attaching bolt holes in the case (ring gear holes are already to size) using the ring gear as a pilot. Install a special hex head bolt and nut and tighten. Ream remaining three holes. Install special hex head bolts and tighten to 70 to 110 ft. lbs. Install the lock wires.

Assembly

1. Lubricate the thrust washers, side gear hubs, pinions and spider.
2. Assemble the above parts in one side of case. Place the other half of the case in position so that identification marks line up and install the eight case through bolts (fig. 67).
3. Tighten all nuts to a torque load of 70-110 ft. lbs. and install the lock wire.

DIFFERENTIAL CARRIER

Assembly

1. Install the double reduction shaft bearing outer race in the right side of carrier and tap it in flush with the carrier.

Fig. 65—Removing Differential Bearing

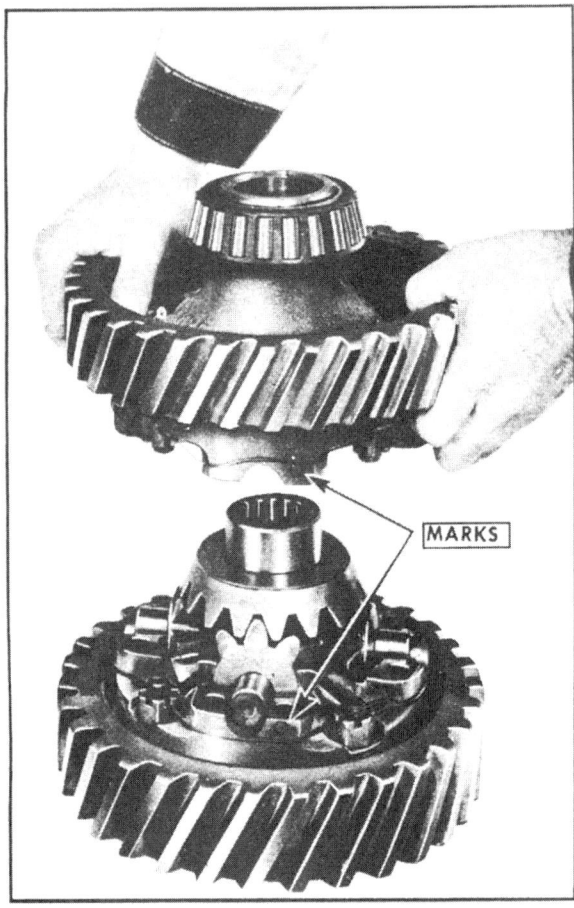

Fig. 67—Differential Case Line Up Marks

2. Start the left end of reduction shaft into carrier from differential end, and position right end of shaft in bearing race.
3. Install shims on each side, using the same number and thickness that were removed when disassembling.
4. Raise left end of shaft and install left bearing cap first, then install right bearing cap and install three lockwashers and nuts evenly spaced on each cap and tighten them securely.
5. Check the bearing adjustment. Correct adjustment of the double reduction shaft bearings will produce a slight drag when turning the shaft by hand. Correct adjustment can be secured by adding or removing .003" or .005" shims on either side.
6. Place the same number and thickness pinion cage shims that were removed when disassembling on the pilot of pinion cage. Assemble the cage to carrier. Install three lockwashers and nuts evenly spaced and tighten them securely.

Ring Gear and Pinion Adjustment

1. Paint the ring gear with red lead, or coat it lightly with Prussian blue. Turn the drive pinion first in one direction and then the other, at the same time applying pressure on the back of ring gear to bring a load on the gears.
2. Check the tooth bearing on the ring gear to determine adjustments required.
   a. If the tooth bearing is below the pitch line the pinion is too deep.
   b. If the tooth bearing is above the pitch line the pinion is too shallow.
   c. If the tooth bearing is on the pitch line, but toward the heel of the ring gear tooth, the pinion and ring gear backlash is too great.
   d. If the tooth bearing is on the pitch line, but toward the toe of the ring gear tooth, the pinion and ring gear backlash is insufficient.
3. To make pinion depth adjustment, remove the pinion cage and—
   a. Add shims between cage and carrier if the pinion is too deep.
   b. Remove shims if the pinion is too shallow.
4. Mount a dial indicator on the carrier and check the backlash between the ring gear and pinion. Correct backlash is from .008" to .013" (fig. 68).
   a. If backlash is insufficient, remove the double reduction shaft bearing caps and remove a shim from the left side and add a shim of the same thickness to the right side.
   b. If the backlash is excessive, remove a shim from the right side and add a shim of the same thickness to the left side. Continue these adjustments until the backlash is within limits.

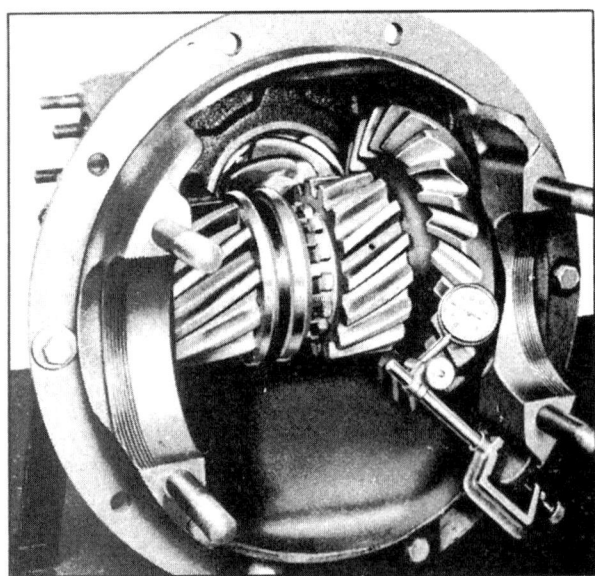

Fig. 68—Checking Backlash

NOTE: By following this method proper adjustment of the double reduction shaft bearings is maintained.

5. Install remaining washers and nuts at each reduction shaft cap and the pinion cage. Tighten reduction shaft cap nuts to a torque load of 75-95 ft. lbs. and the pinion cage nuts to a torque load of 115-130 ft. lbs.
6. Install pinion cage lubrication plug.
7. Shift the reduction shaft shifter sleeve into low speed position. Place the shifter fork in the shifter sleeve with the lock bolt hole toward the rear of carrier. Place the rubber oil seal over the vacuum unit mounting sleeve, install the same thickness shims that were removed when disassembling over the studs in carrier and install mounting sleeve.
8. Place new gasket over piston rod and start rod and cylinder assembly into mounting sleeve. Enter the end of piston rod into shifter fork, line up hole in rod with hole in fork and install the shifter fork to piston rod tapered bolt. Tighten lock nut securely.
9. Install the cylinder to carrier nuts and lockwashers and tighten them securely.
10. With the shifter sleeve in low speed position, check clearance on each side of shifter fork with a feeler gauge. There should be at least .010" clearance on each side of fork (fig. 69). If there is insufficient clearance on either side, loosen the cylinder and mounting sleeve attaching nuts and add or remove shims as necessary to provide a minimum of .010" clearance at each side of fork. Tighten cylinder and sleeve attaching nuts, then recheck clearance in both low and high speed positions.
11. Lubricate the differential bearings, assemble the outer races, and install the assembly in the carrier, then, assemble the adjusting nuts and caps. Make sure the cap and adjusting nuts are installed according to the marks made when disassembling and that the adjusting nuts are not cross-threaded. Tighten the bearing cap bolt nuts just "snug."
12. Check the position of the double reduction gears with the double reduction pinions. Move the differential by turning the adjusting nuts until the double reduction gears are centered with the double reduction pinions. Stop one adjusting nut in a locking position and tighten the other adjusting nut until all clearance is removed from the bearings; then, tighten each adjusting nut one notch to a locking position (fig. 70). This preloads the differential bearings.
13. Tighten the bearing cap bolts to a torque load of 150-170 ft. lbs. Install the adjusting nut locks and then lock cap bolt nuts with tie wire.

Installation

1. Place a new gasket on the flange of differential carrier. Place the differential carrier on a roller jack and roll it into position under the truck. Push the carrier back until the flange is against the axle housing, line up

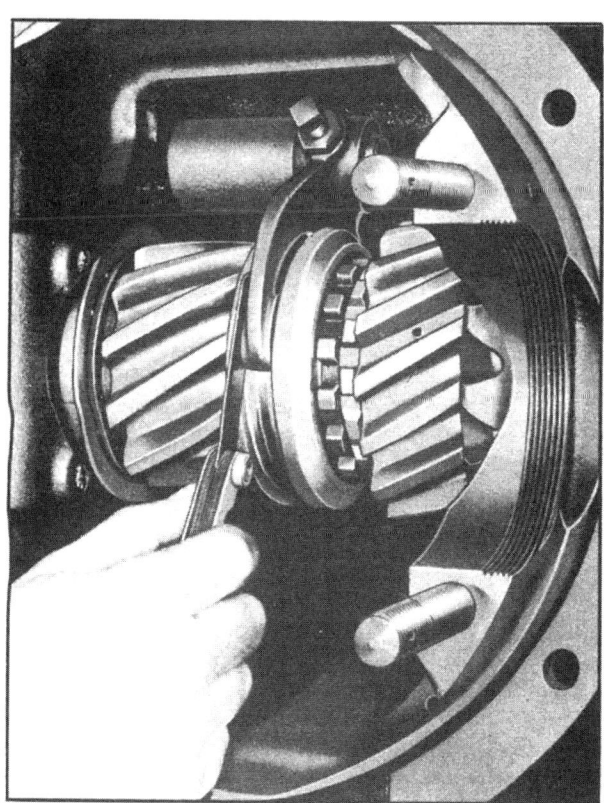

Fig. 69—Checking Shifter Fork Clearance

Fig. 70—Locking Adjusting Nut

the bolt holes with a taper punch and install cap screws near the top. Install and tighten all carrier to housing bolts.

2. Remove tape from universal joint trunnion bearings and seat them in the universal joint yoke on pinion shaft. Install "U" bolts, washers and nuts. Tighten securely.

3. Connect the vacuum hoses to fittings on the vacuum cylinder and tighten clamps securely.

NOTE: Be careful not to transpose hose connections.

4. Clean all lubricant from ends of hubs and axle shaft flanges, install shafts indexing shaft flange splines with hub splines and tap into position. Install new gaskets and hub caps and tighten attaching bolts securely.

5. Fill differential with 14½ pints of S.A.E. 90 "Multi-Purpose" gear lubricant.

6. Remove pipe plug in pinion cage, then using a lubricating gun fill the space between the pinion bearings with one pint of S.A.E. 90 "Multi-Purpose" gear lubricant.

7. Lubricate rear universal joint.

8. Drive the truck and check the operation of the axle in both low and high gear.

TROUBLES AND REMEDIES
REAR AXLE

Symptom and Probable Cause / **Probable Remedy**

Excessive Backlash

a. Loose Wheel bolts.
b. Loose axle flange to hub bolts.
c. Worn universal joint.
d. Loose propeller shaft to pinion splines.
e. Loose ring gear and pinion adjustment.
f. Worn differential gears or case.
g. Worn axle shaft or differential side gear splines.

a. Tighten nuts securely. Make sure the tapered end of nut is toward wheel.
b. Replace axle flange gasket and lock plate. Tighten bolts securely and lock.
c. Replace or overhaul joint.
d. Replace worn parts.
e. Adjust ring gear and pinion.
f. Replace worn parts.
g. Replace worn parts.

Klunking Noise in Axle or Vehicle Weight Shifts From Side to Side

a. Excessive end play in axle shafts.

a. Install thicker axle shaft spacer.

Axle Noisy on Drive

a. Ring gear and pinion adjustment too tight.
b. Pinion bearings rough.

a. Readjust ring gear and pinion.
b. Replace bearing and readjust ring gear and pinion.

Axle Noisy on Coast

a. Ring gear and pinion adjustment too loose.
b. Pinion bearings rough.
c. Excessive end play in pinion.
d. End play in double row bearing.

a. Readjust ring gear and pinion.
b. Replace bearing and readjust ring gear and pinion.
c. Tighten pinion bearing retaining screws or replace bearing.
d. Replace pinion bearing.

Axle Noisy on Both Drive and Coast

a. Pinion bearings rough.
b. Loose or damaged differential side bearings.
c. Damaged axle shaft bearing.
d. Worn universal joint or propeller shaft bushing.
e. Badly worn ring gear or pinion teeth.

a. Replace bearings and adjust ring gear and pinion.
b. Replace or adjust differential side bearings.
c. Replace bearing.
d. Replace worn parts.
e. Replace ring gear and pinion.

REAR AXLE 4-41

Symptom and Probable Cause	Probable Remedy
f. Pinion too deep in ring gear.	f. Double row ball bearing installed backwards—remove and install properly (see instructions).
g. Loose or worn wheel bearings.	g. Replace or adjust bearings.

TWO-SPEED REAR AXLE

Symptom and Probable Cause — **Probable Remedy**

Excessive Backlash

a. Loose wheel bolts.
b. Worn Universal joints.
c. Excessive ring gear and pinion backlash.
d. Worn differential gears or thrust washers.

a. Tighten bolts or, if necessary, replace worn parts.
b. Replace worn parts.
c. Adjust.
d. Replace worn parts.

Symptom and Probable Cause — **Probable Remedy**

Axle Noisy on Drive and Coast—High and Low Ratios

a. Pinion too deep in ring gear.
b. Ring gear and pinion adjusted too tight.
c. Pinion shaft; double reduction shaft, or differential bearings damaged or adjusted improperly.
d. Ring gear and pinion faulty.
e. Loose or damaged wheel bearings.

a. Shim between pinion cage and differential carrier and readjust backlash.
b. Adjust ring gear and pinion to correct lash.
c. Replace damaged bearings or adjust bearings correctly.
d. Replace ring gear and pinion.
e. Adjust or replace wheel bearings.

Axle Noisy on Drive—High or Low Ratio

a. Ring gear and pinion adjusted too tight.
b. Ring gear and pinion faulty.
c. Rear pinion bearing faulty.

a. Adjust gear and pinion to correct lash.
b. Replace ring gear and pinion.
c. Replace bearing.

Axle Noisy on Coast—High or Low Range

a. Excessive lash between ring gear and pinion.
b. End play in pinion bearings.

a. Adjust ring gear and pinion to correct lash.
b. Adjust or replace pinion bearings.

Axle Noisy in High Ratio Only

a. High speed reduction gear or pinion damaged.

a. Replace high speed reduction gears.

Axle Noisy in Low Ratio Only

a. Low speed reduction gear or pinion damaged.

a. Replace low speed reduction gears.

Axle Drives in One Gear but Locks When Shifted to the Other Gear

a. One reduction pinion frozen to double reduction shaft.

a. Replace pinion and shaft.

Won't Shift from Low Range to High Range

a. Diaphragm damaged.

a. Tighten retaining nuts.

Symptom and Probable Cause	Probable Remedy
b. Broken vacuum line.	b. Replace line.
c. Faulty dash control.	c. Tighten caps.
d. Shift rod in yoke loose or yoke broken.	d. Tighten shift rod to yoke set screw or replace shifter yoke.
e. Improperly adjusted push rod.	e. Readjust push rod.

Speedometer Does Not Register Correctly or At All in One Axle Ratio

a. Speedometer adapter or linkage faulty.

a. Replace damaged parts or adjust or replace linkage.

Lubrication Leaks

a. Pinion cage loose.
b. Carrier loose or gasket damaged.
c. Double reduction shaft bearing caps loose.
d. Pinion shaft oil seal damaged.

a. Tighten retaining nuts.
b. Replace gasket and tighten carrier nuts.
c. Tighten caps.
d. Replace oil seal.

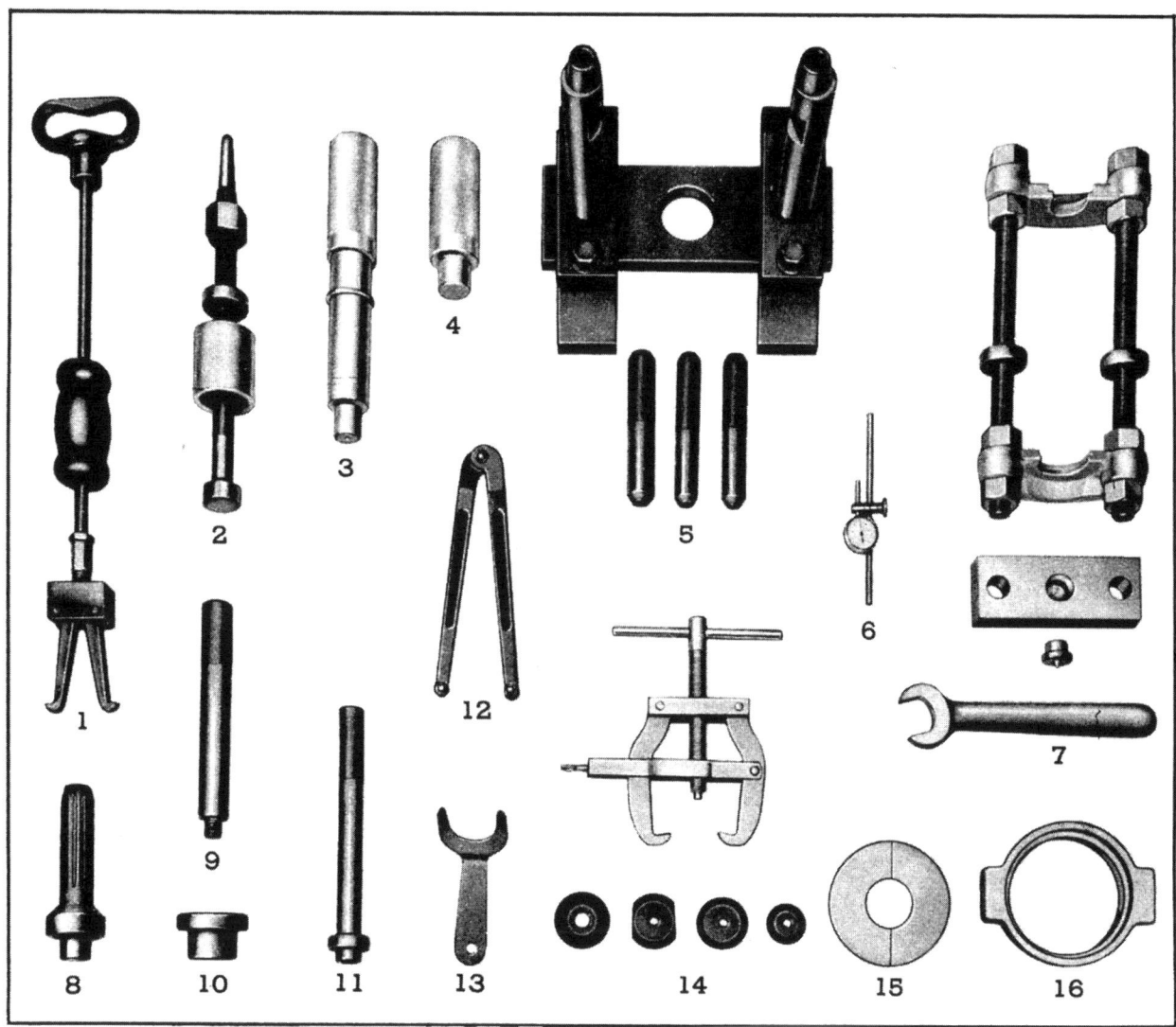

Fig. 71—Rear Axle Special Tools—½ Ton

1.	J-1436	Rear Axle Shaft Bearing and Oil Seal Remover		
2.	J-4258	Torque Tube Front and Rear Bushing Remover		
3.	J-4259	Torque Tube Rear Bushing Installer		
4.	J-4290	Torque Tube Front Bushing Installer		
5.	J-554	Hub Bolt Peening Tool and Anvil		
6.	KMO-30	Dial Indicator Set		
7.	J-4548	Pinion to Propeller Shaft Remover and Replacer		
8.	J-994	Differential Side Bearing Replacer		
9.	J-872-5	Driver Handle		
10.	J-270-7	Axle Bearing and Retainer Replacer		
11.	J-968	Propeller Shaft Bushing Replacer		
12.	J-972	Differential Adjusting Wrench		
13.	J-4050	Pinion Shaft Rear Bearing Spacer		
14.	TR-278-R	Differential Side Bearing Puller		
15.	J-996	Pinion Outer Bearing Remover Plate		
16.	J-358-1	Press Plate Holder		

REAR AXLE 4-44

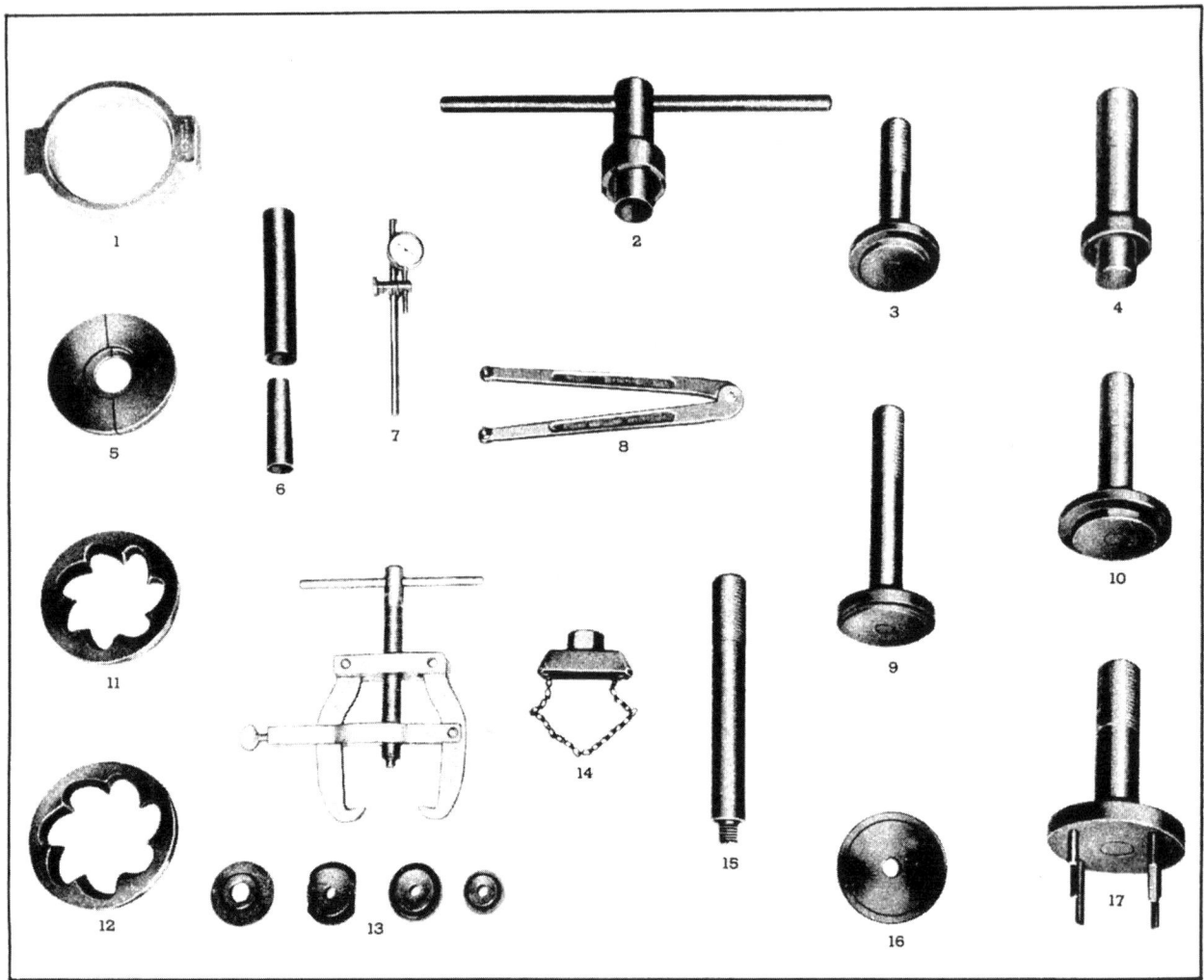

Fig. 72—¾ and 1 Ton Rear Axle Special Tools

1.	J-358-1	Press Plate Holder	10. J-2221	Wheel Hub Seal Replacer
2.	J-2222	Wheel Bearing Nut Wrench	11. J-2225	Pinion Front Bearing Remover Plate (1 ton)
3.	J-2231	Pinion Retainer Oil Seal Replacer	12. J-2224	Pinion Front Bearing Remover Plate (¾ ton)
4.	J-2226	Differential Side Bearing Replacer	13. TR-278-R	Differential Side Bearing Puller
5.	J-2229	Pinion Straddle Bearing Remover	14. J-2232	Wheel Bearing Inner Race Remover
6.	J-769	Bearing Lock Ring Installer	15. J-872-5	Driver Handle
7.	KMO-30	Dial Indicator Set	16. J-872-1	Outer Wheel Bearing Race Replacer
8.	J-972	Differential Adjusting Wrench	17. J-2230	Wheel Bearing Outer Race Remover
9.	J-2223	Wheel Hub Outer Bearing Race Replacer		

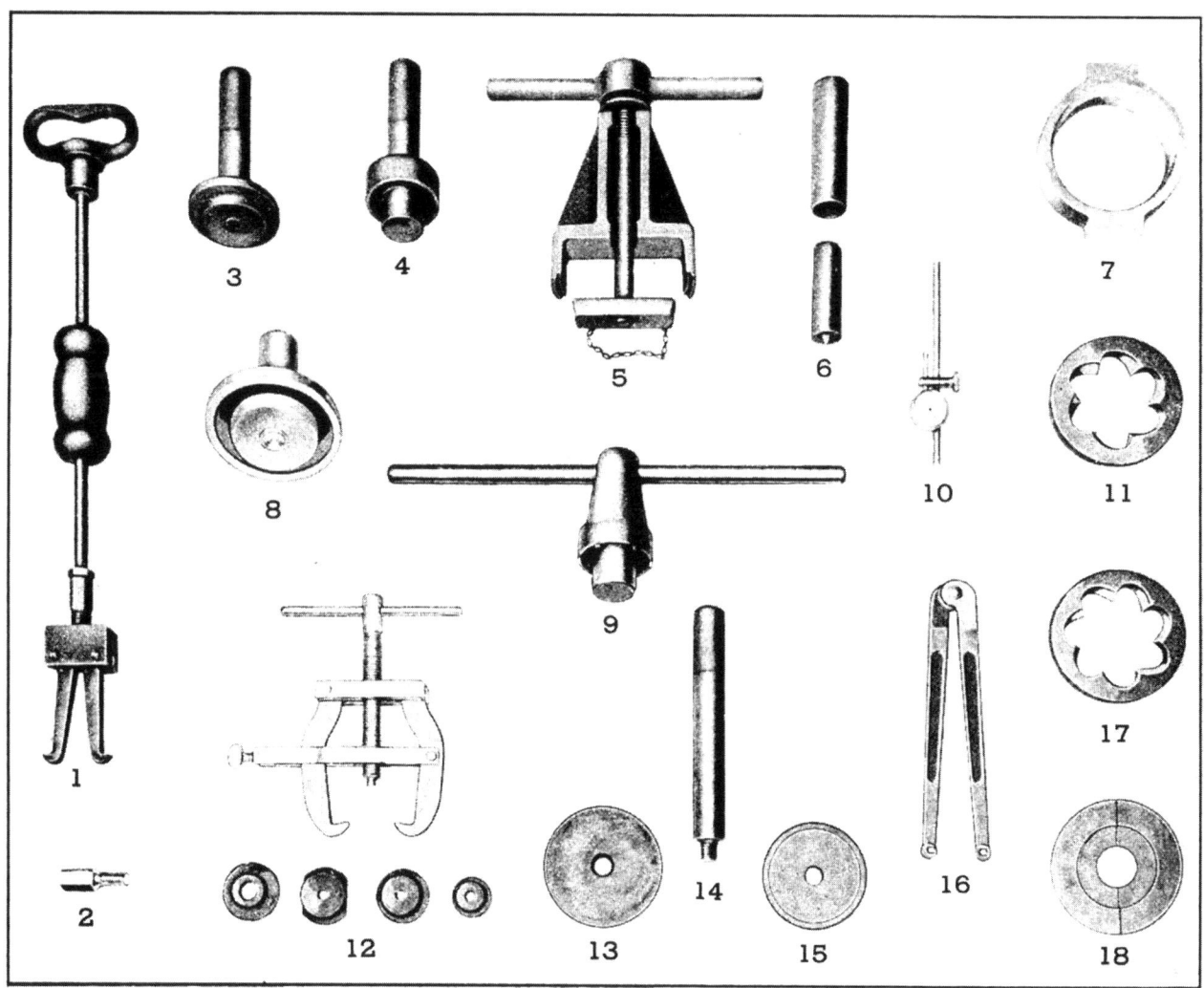

Fig. 73—Rear Axle Special Tools—1½ and 2 Ton

1. J-1436 — Rear Axle Shaft Bearing and Oil Seal Remover
2. J-1436-8 — Axle Shaft Remover Adapter
3. J-2231 — Pinion Retainer Oil Seal Replacer
4. J-1488 — Differential Side Bearing Replacer
5. J-918-A — Inner Wheel Bearing and Oil Seal Puller
6. J-1364 — Pinion Bearing Lock Ring Installer
7. J-358-1 — Press Plate Holder
8. J-3067 — Rear Hub Oil Seal Replacer
9. J-870 — Rear Axle Wheel Bearing Nut Wrench
10. KMO-30 — Dial Indicator Set
11. J-1439 — Pinion Bearing Remover Plate
12. TR-278-R — Differential Side Bearing Puller
13. J-872-4 — Inner Wheel Bearing Race Replacer
14. J-872-5 — Driver Handle
15. J872-1 — Outer Wheel Bearing Race Replacer
16. J-972 — Differential Adjusting Wrench
17. J-1440 — Pinion Bearing Remover Plate
18. J-1453 — Pinion Bearing Remover Plate

REAR AXLE 4-46

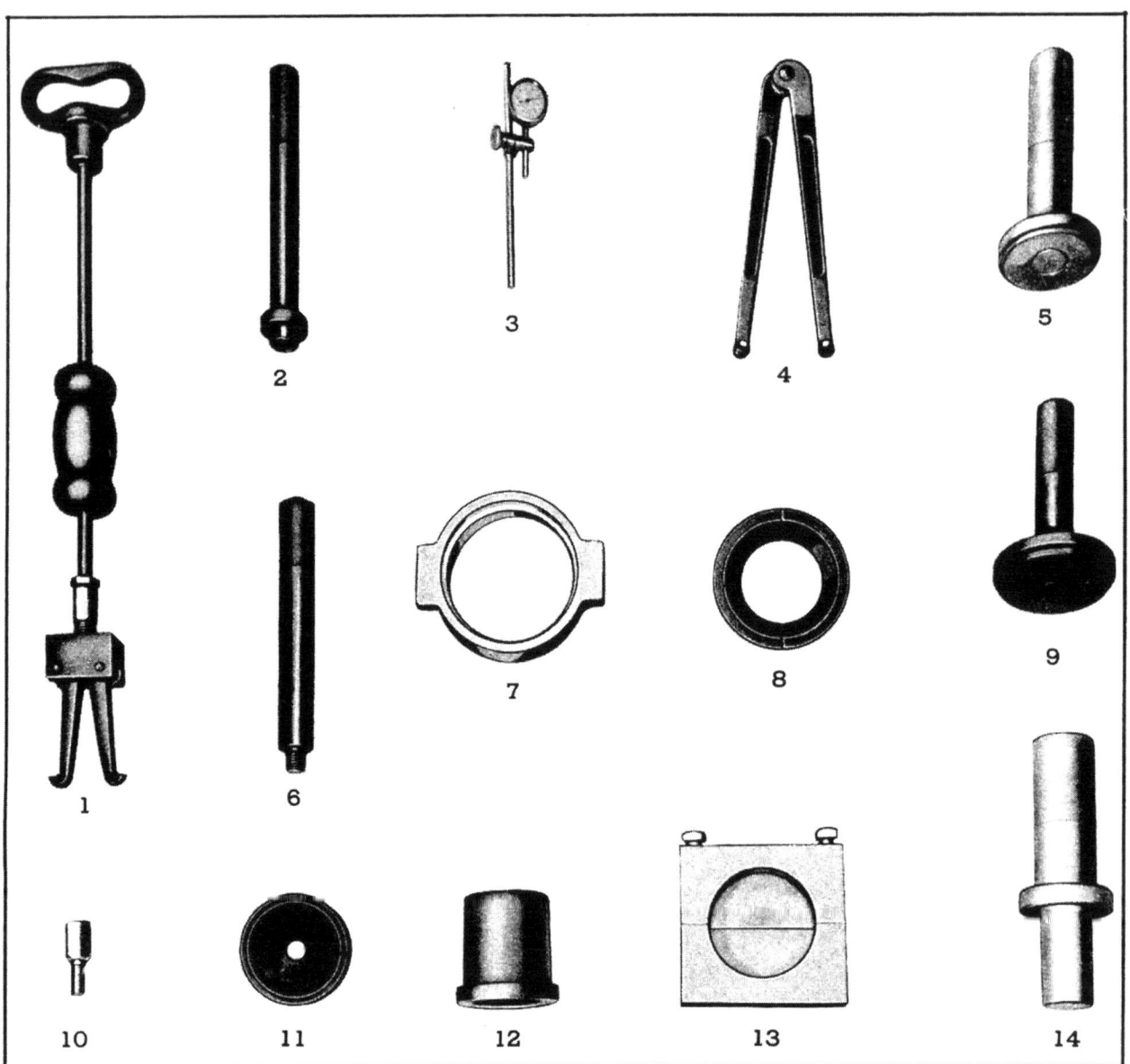

Fig. 74—Rear Axle Special Tools—2-Speed Axle

1. J-1436 — Rear Axle Shaft Bearing and Oil Seal Remover
2. J-968 — Propeller Shaft Bushing Replacer
3. KMO-30 — Dial Indicator Set
4. J-972 — Differential Adjusting Wrench
5. J-1322 — Pinion Front Bearing Race Replacer
6. J-872-5 — Driver Handle
7. J-358-1 — Press Plate Holder
8. J-2228 — Pinion Inner Bearing Remover
9. J-2227 — Pinion Cage Inner Bearing Race Replacer
10. J-1436-8 — Axle Shaft Remover Adapter
11. J-872-1 — Outer Wheel Bearing Race Replacer
12. J-971 — Camshaft Gear Remover and Replacer
13. J-1318 — Differential Case Bearing Remover
14. J-1312 — Differential Side Bearing Replacer

REAR AXLE SPECIFICATIONS

		½ Ton	¾ and 1 Ton	1½ and 2 Ton	Two Speed
Type		Semi-Floating	Full Floating		
Gears					
	Type		Spiral Hypoid		
	Ratio	4.11:1	4.57:1—3600 5.14:1—Others	6.17:1	6.13:1—High 8.10:1—Low
	Backlash		.005″-.008″		.008″-.013″
Pinion					
	Mounting	Overhung	Straddle		Overhung
	Adjustment	Shim and Tapered Collar	Shims	None	Shims
	Thrust		Against Pinion Front Bearing		
Differential Type		Two Pinion	Four Pinion		
Pinion Bearings					
Front	Part No.	N.D. 954394	HY 442093	N.D. 954237	
	Type	D. R. Ball	Taper R.	D. R. Ball	
Rear	Part No.	HY 125630	HY 189436	HY 144553	
	Type		ROLLER		
Differential Bearings					
	Part No.	HY 187434	HY 188930	HY 148399	
	Type		Barrel Roller		
2-Speed Axle	Drive Pinion Bearings	Front		Cup—Bearing Outer	128248
				Race—Assembly	147905
		Rear		Cup—Bearing Outer	189637
				Race—Assembly	189638
	Differential Bearings			Cup—Bearing Outer	135495
				Race—Assembly	435973
	Reduction Shaft Bearings	Right		Bearing Assembly	3651554
		Left		Race Assembly	436041
				Cover and Cup Assembly	3682496
Axle Shaft		Bolted to Hub	Splined to Hub		
	Type		Shaft and Drive Flange Integrally Forged		
	Diameter	1 5/32″	1 11/32″	1 7/16″—4000 1 9/16″—5-6000	1 9/16″
Bearings					
	Inner	—	HY 188930	HY 144527	
	Type	—		Barrel Roller	
	Outer	HY 111121	HY 188932	HY 144525	
	Type	Roller		Barrel Roller	
Drive Type		Torque Tube	Hotchkiss		
Lubricant Capacity		4½ pts.	6 pts.	11 pts.—4000 12 pts.—Others	14½ pts.

REAR AXLE 4-48

TORQUE SPECIFICATIONS
REAR AXLE

Ring Gear Bolts
   ½, ¾ and 1 Ton............. 40-60 ft. lbs.
   1½ and 2 Ton................ 85-95 ft. lbs.

Differential Side Bearing Cap Bolts
   ½ Ton .... 115-135 ft. lbs.
   ¾ and 1 Ton............... 95-105 ft. lbs.
   1½ and 2 Ton.............. 130-160 ft. lbs.

Pinion Bearing Retainer Bolts.... 85-95 ft. lbs.

Pinion Shaft Bearing Nut
   ½ Ton .... 200-240 ft. lbs.

Pinion Shaft Flange Nut
   ¾, 1, 1½ and 2 Ton........... 160-280 ft. lbs.

Spring "U" Bolts
   ½ Ton .... 75-90 ft. lbs.
   ¾, 1 and 1½ Ton............. 210-235 ft. lbs.
   2 Ton .... 375-400 ft. lbs.

Universal Joint Yoke Ball Retainer Bolts
   ½ and ¾ Ton.................. 8-12 ft. lbs.

Universal Joint Yoke Attaching Bolt
   ½ and ¾ Ton................. 15-20 ft. lbs.

(2-SPEED)

Universal Joint Flange Nut....... 75-150 ft. lbs.

Double Reduction Shaft Bearing
   Retainer Washer Cap Screw.... 37-46 ft. lbs.

Low or High Speed Gear to
   Differential Case Bolt Nut...... 70-110 ft. lbs.

Differential Case Bolt Nuts....... 70-110 ft. lbs.

Double Reduction Cap Nuts...... 75-95 ft. lbs.

Pinion Cage Nuts................. 115-130 ft. lbs.

Differential Side Bearing Cap
   Bolt Nuts .... 150-170 ft. lbs.

SPEEDOMETER GEARS—SPEED ADAPTERS

In some special types of operation, purchasers of Chevrolet trucks may desire to use tires of a different size or rear axles of different ratios than those furnished as standard equipment for the various units. Either one, or both, of these things will, of course, change tire revolutions per mile and result in speedometer inaccuracies.

When such change or changes are made, it is necessary to change the speedometer gears or to use a speedometer adapter with the present gears. In certain combination changes, of both rear axle and tires, it may be necessary to change the speedometer gears and use, in addition, an adapter to bring about proper speedometer readings.

Speedometer gears are serviced in sets to avoid inaccuracies that would naturally be caused by using just one new gear with a worn gear. The different service gear sets may be identified by the part number which is stamped on the face of the drive gear. If no number is found on the gear, the set may be identified by counting the number of teeth and referring to the following table:

Transmission	Gear Set Part No.	No. of Drive Gear Teeth	No. of Driven Gear Teeth	Gear Ratio
3-Speed	3695417	6	18	3.000
3-Speed	3692234	6	19	3.167
3-Speed	3692235	6	20	3.333
4-Speed	3689223	4	12	3.000
4-Speed	3689178	4	13	3.250
4-Speed	3689179	4	14	3.500
4-Speed	3689121	4	15	3.750

The following speedometer gear adapters are available, if needed, to be used separately or in conjunction with a change in speedometer gear sets.

Package Part Number:	1565812	1565814	1580273
Gear Ratio	17:16	16:17	15:17

The adapter is installed by removing the speedometer cable fitting from the transmission case and screwing the adapter into the case. The speedometer cable is then connected to the adapter.

When replacing speedometer gears it is very important that the drive gear be pressed onto the spacer or front yoke of the universal joint with the shoulder or chamfer on the gear away from the universal joint.

The following chart covers the various speedometer gear sets and adapters used on original production equipment according to rear axle ratio, transmission and regular production tires on the different models.

Rear Axle Ratio	Transmission	Tires	Speedometer Gear Set	Adapter Number
		½ TON		
4.11:1	3-Speed	All	3695417	None
	4-Speed	All	3689223	
		¾ TON		
4.57:1	3-Speed	15-6	3692234	None
		15-8		
		7.50 x 17-8		1565812
		7.00 x 17-6		
		7.00 x 17-8		
	4-Speed	15-6	3689178	None
		15-8		
		7.00 x 17-6	3689223	
		7.00 x 17-8		
		7.50 x 17-8		1565812
5.14:1	3-Speed	15-6	3692234	1580273
		15-8		
		7.50 x 17-8	3692235	None
		7.00 x 17-6		
		7.00 x 17-8		
	4-Speed	15-6	3689121	
		15-8		
		7.50 x 17-8	3689178	
		7.00 x 17-6		
		7.00 x 17-8		
		1 TON		
5.14:1	4-Speed	All	3689178	None
		1½ TON		
6.17:1	4-Speed	6.50 x 20-6	3689121	None
		7.00 x 20-8		
		7.00 x 20-10		
		7.50 x 20-8		1565812
		7.50 x 20-10		
5.43:1	4-Speed	6.50 x 20-6	3689178	None
		7.00 x 20-8		
		7.00 x 20-10		
		7.50 x 20-8		1565812
		7.50 x 20-10		

REAR AXLE 4-50

Rear Axle Ratio	Transmission	Tires	Speedometer Gear Set	Adapter Number
2 TON—C.O.E. AND CONVENTIONAL				
6.17:1	4-Speed	7.50 x 20-8	3689179	None
		7.50 x 20-10		
		8.25 x 20-10		
		8.25 x 20-12		
		9.00 x 20-10	3689178	
Two Speed* High 6.13 to 1 Low 8.10 to 1	4-Speed	7.50 x 20-8	3689179	
		7.50 x 20-10		
		8.25 x 20-10	3689178	1565814
		8.25 x 20-12		
		9.00 x 20-10		None

*Equipped with two-speed Axle Adapter, Part No. 3682957

PROPELLER SHAFTS AND UNIVERSAL JOINTS

INDEX

	Page
General Description	4-50
Service Operations	4-51
½ Ton Trucks	4-51
Propeller Shaft	4-51
Universal Joint	4-51
¾ Ton Trucks	4-52
Front Propeller Shaft	4-52
Oil Seal Replacement	4-53
Bushing Replacement	4-53
Rear Propeller Shaft	4-53
Trunnion Bearings	4-53
Front Universal Joint	4-54
Intermediate Universal Joint	4-54
1, 1½ and 2 Ton Conventional Trucks	4-55
Front Propeller Shaft	4-56
Trunnion Bearings	4-57
2 Ton C.O.E. Trucks	4-57
Propeller Shaft	4-57
Front Universal	4-58

GENERAL DESCRIPTION

Tubular type propeller shafts are used on all model trucks. All needle type universal joints are used with the exception of the bushing type used on the ½ and ¾ ton front joint.

The number of propeller shafts and universal joints used is dependent upon wheel base of the vehicle. The ½ ton vehicle which uses a torque tube drive is equipped with a universal ball and slip joint located at the transmission end of the shaft. All other model vehicles employ the Hotchkiss drive principle and they are equipped with universal joints at both ends of the propeller shaft. The ¾ ton models use an enclosed front propeller shaft which is mounted to the rear of the transmission through a universal ball similar to the ½ ton models.

Slip joints which compensate for variations in distance between rear axle and transmission and also facilitate transmission or power plant removal are located at forward ends of propeller shafts.

On vehicles which use two propeller shafts, an intermediate support bearing is used and is mounted in a support bracket. On vehicles that use three propeller shafts, such as the 2 ton 179" wheelbase models and the 2 ton School Bus, two intermediate support bearings are used. The ball bearings are a permanently sealed and lubricated type and each bearing is supported by a rubber cushion which fits inside a sleeve in the support bracket.

All needle bearing type universals have a trun-

REAR AXLE 4-51

nion which is drilled and fed by a central lubrication fitting (fig. 75) for lubricating the bearings.

A relief valve on the side opposite the lubrication fitting is also incorporated to prevent over-lubrication or damage to the trunion bearing oil seals. A lubrication fitting is also provided on the rear yoke of the intermediate universal to lubricate splines of slip joints. A plug is staked into the forward end of the splined opening to retain the lubricant. A small hole is drilled in the center of this plug to relieve trapped air. The rear end of the splined opening is sealed by means of a cork packing contained in a retainer cap which screws on the end of the yoke (fig. 76).

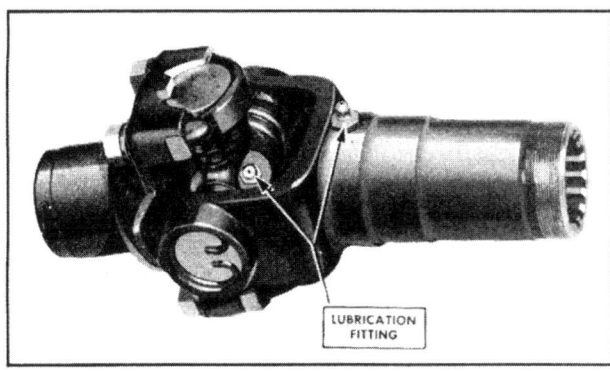

Fig. 75—Intermediate Universal Joint

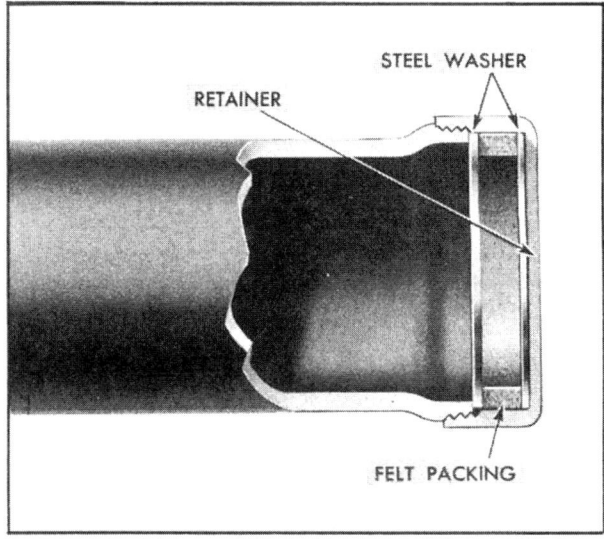

Fig. 76—Slip Joint Packing

SERVICE OPERATIONS

½ TON TRUCKS

PROPELLER SHAFT

Service operations on the ½ ton truck propeller shafts are covered in the Rear Axle Section.

UNIVERSAL JOINT

The universal joint on the ½ ton truck is a fully enclosed unit using bushings in place of needle bearings. Figure 77 shows construction details.

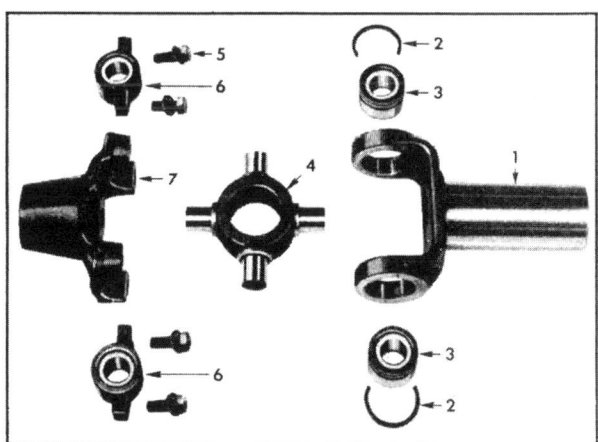

Fig. 77—Exploded View—½ Ton Universal Joint

1. Front Yoke
2. Trunnion Lock Ring
3. Trunnion Bearing and Bushing
4. Trunnion
5. Cap Screw
6. Rear Trunnion Bearing and Bushing
7. Rear Yoke

Disassembly

1. Remove floor mat and transmission hole cover.
2. Remove cap screws which retain ball collar to transmission and four bolts holding transmission support to frame cross member and slide collar and ball back on propeller shaft housing.
3. Remove cap screws which fasten front trunnion bearings to the front yoke.
4. Remove the two front yoke trunnion bearings and split the joint.
5. Raise propeller shaft and remove the rear yoke and trunnion from the propeller shaft splines.
6. Remove front yoke by removing bolt and lockwasher from ends of transmission main shaft.
7. Wash all parts in cleaning solvent.
8. Inspect yokes for excessive spline wear or damage.
9. Inspect trunnion yoke for scoring or excessive wear.
10. Inspect bushings for scoring or excessive wear.

Repairs

1. Remove lock rings from trunnion bearings.
2. With yoke supported in a bench vise, drive on

REAR AXLE 4-52

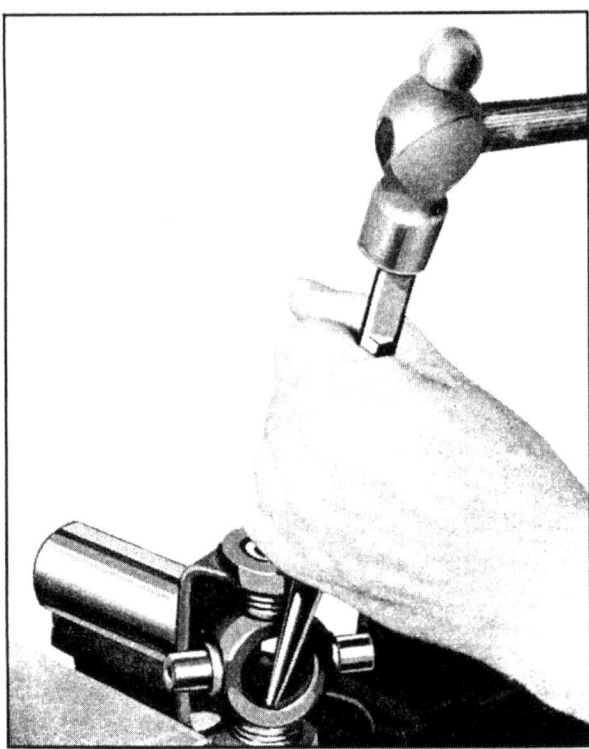

Fig. 78—Disassembly of Universal Joint

the center of the trunnion with a drift punch to remove rear trunnion bearings (fig. 78).
3. Press new rear trunnion bearings into yoke and over hubs of trunnion just far enough to install lock rings.
4. Install lock rings and while holding yoke in one hand, tap ends of trunnions with a hammer to firmly seat bushings against lock rings.

NOTE: Use new lock rings in reassembly.

5. Adjust Universal Ball joint as outlined in Transmission Section.

Assembly

1. Install front yoke on transmission main shaft and install universal joint yoke flat washer, lock washer and retainer bolt. Tighten bolt to 15-20 ft. lbs.
2. Raise front end of propeller shaft and slide rear yoke and trunnion on propeller shaft.
3. Install new front trunnion bearings to the trunnion, fasten front trunnion bearings to front yoke and tighten cap screws securely.

NOTE: Use new lock plates under cap screws and bend tangs up to lock cap screws after assembly.

4. Slide collar and ball forward on propeller shaft housing, assemble transmission support to frame cross member and install support to frame cross member bolts. Install collar cap screws and tighten to 8-12 ft. lbs.
5. Remove speedometer drive gear and fill housing with transmission lubricant.

¾ TON TRUCKS
PROPELLER SHAFTS

The front propeller shaft assembly on all ¾ ton trucks is of the enclosed type having a bushing type universal joint (fig. 79) with the housing incorporating a universal ball as part of the assembly. A thin wall bushing is pressed into the front end of the housing tube in which the hub of the rear yoke of the front universal joint takes its bearing. The rear end of the shaft is supported by a single roll bearing which is permanently lubricated and sealed.

FRONT PROPELLER SHAFT

Removal

1. Split intermediate universal joint by removing two trunnion bearing "U" clamps.
2. Tape bearings to keep them clean and from becoming damaged and drop front end of rear propeller shaft.
3. Remove bolts which attach universal ball collar to rear of transmission and slide collar back on tube.

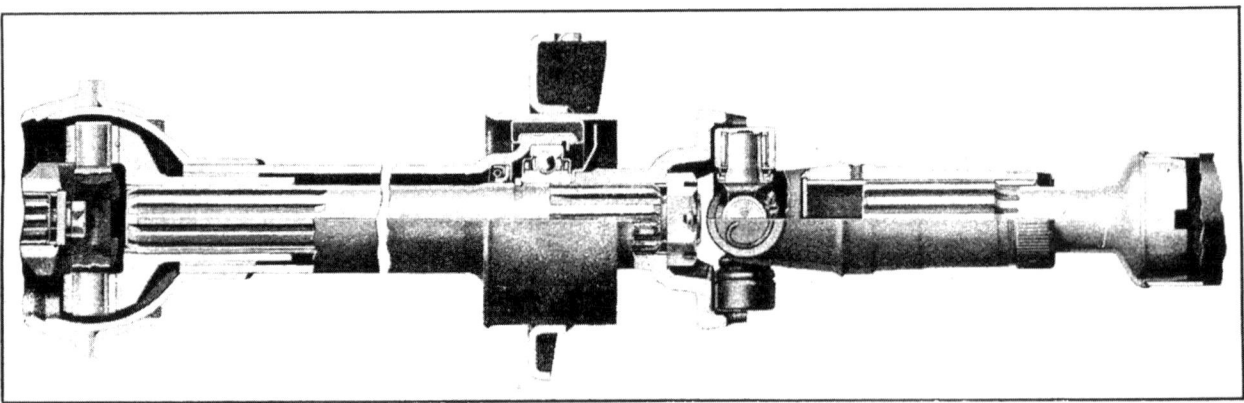

Fig. 79—Front Propeller Shaft Assembly—¾ Ton Trucks

REAR AXLE 4-53

4. Remove nuts attaching bearing support to frame cross member and pull entire assembly to the rear to clear splines of front universal joint.

Disassembly

1. Clamp one side of universal joint yoke in a bench vise and remove cotter pin and nut from shaft.
2. Tap yoke from shaft and remove dust shield.
3. Place bearing support bracket in vise and wet inside of sleeve and at the same time move propeller shaft housing from side to side to allow water to soften soap that was used at assembly.
4. Working the assembly in this manner will allow for removal of the propeller shaft housing from the support bracket.
5. Remove rubber cushion from the housing by slipping it off the machined section of the propeller shaft housing.
6. Remove universal ball collar and cork oil seal.
7. Compress tangs on end of bearing lock ring and remove.
8. Using a brass drift and hammer drive propeller shaft and bearing from housing.
9. Support bearing and press it off the shaft in an arbor press.
10. Wash all parts except bearing in cleaning solvent.
11. Inspect splines for excessive wear or damage.
12. Inspect bushing in front of housing for excessive wear.
13. Inspect oil seal in housing for damage.
14. Inspect bearing for roughness by turning it by hand.

REPAIRS

Oil Seal Replacement

1. Drive oil seal out from front of housing using a piece of shafting or a suitable driver.
2. Soak new oil seal in light engine oil thoroughly and install in housing with free end of leather toward the front end of housing. Use driver J-1362.

Bushing Replacement

1. Remove old bushing from housing using puller J-1436.
2. Install new bushing in housing using bushing replacer J-2243.

Assembly

1. Adjust the universal ball joint as outlined in Transmission Section, using the housing and ball collar without the cork seal.
2. Press bearing on shaft in an arbor press.
3. Assemble shaft and bearing into housing and seat bearing by tapping around its outer race using a drift punch and hammer.
4. Install bearing lock ring making sure ring is seated in ring groove.
5. Install new cork oil seal in universal ball collar.

   NOTE: It is recommended that the seal be shellaced to the retainer.

6. Install retainer over the housing.
7. Install rubber cushion over machined end at rear of housing.
8. Coat the outer diameter of the rubber cushion with soft soap and assemble the support bracket over the cushion.
9. Install bearing dust shield and universal joint front yoke.
10. Install nut and tighten securely and lock nut with cotter pin.

Installation

1. Place the proper number of ball collar gaskets, as determined at the time of adjustment, over the universal ball.
2. Place the transmission in gear and slide splines of front propeller shaft into rear yoke of front universal joint.
3. Bolt support bracket to frame cross member.
4. Lubricate the universal ball, position the gaskets, and bolt ball collar to rear face of transmission housing. Tighten the capscrews to 8-12 ft. lbs.
5. Raise rear propeller shaft, seat trunnion bearings in front yoke of universal, install "U" clamps and tighten securely.
6. Lubricate universal joint with S.A.E. 90 transmission lubricant and lubricate front universal by filling the housing with one pint of S.A.E. 90 transmission lubricant.

REAR PROPELLER SHAFT

Removal

1. Split the rear universal joint by removing trunnion bearing "U" clamps. Tape bearings to keep them clean and from becoming damaged and lower rear end of propeller shaft to floor.
2. Remove universal joint sleeve yoke dust cap and slide propeller shaft back disengaging splines from splines of yoke.
3. Wash splined end and trunnion end in cleaning solvent.
4. Check splines of shaft for excessive wear.
5. Check trunnion, trunnion bearings and yoke for damage or excessive wear.

REPAIRS

Trunnion Bearings

1. Remove lock rings from yoke and lubrication fitting from trunnion.
2. Support shaft yoke in a bench vise.
3. Using soft drift and hammer, drive on one end of trunnion bearing which will drive

opposite bearing from yoke.
4. Support the other side of yoke in bench vise and drive other bearing out using brass drift on end of trunnion hub.
5. Remove trunnion.
6. Replace trunnion and press new bearings into yoke and over trunnion hubs far enough to install lock rings.
7. Hold trunnion in one hand and tap yoke lightly to seat bearings against lock rings.
8. Replace lubrication fitting.

Installation

When installing splines of propeller shaft into splined end of universal joint, the rear yoke of the universal must be in line with the front yoke of the universal at rear of propeller shaft.
1. Slide splines of propeller shaft into splined end of intermediate universal joint and replace sleeve yoke dust cap.

   NOTE: Make sure seal in cap is in good condition before assembly (fig. 76).

2. Lift rear end of shaft and attach to rear axle flange with the "U" clamps and tighten securely.
3. Lubricate both points with transmission lubricant.

FRONT UNIVERSAL JOINT

The front universal joint on all ¾ ton vehicles is a fully enclosed unit of the trunnion bushing type and receives its lubrication from the transmission. Figure 80 shows construction details.

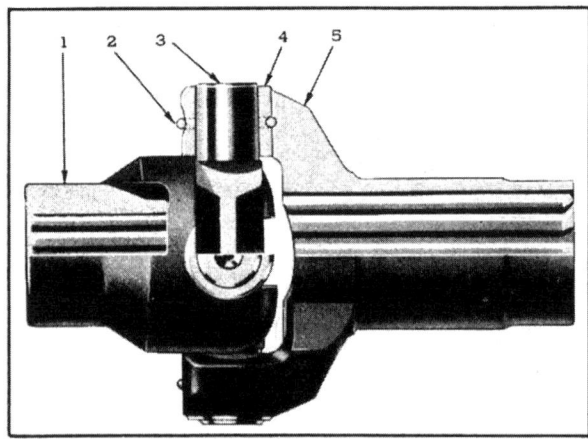

Fig. 80—Front Universal Joint—¾ Ton Trucks

1. Front Yoke
2. Trunnion Lock Ring
3. Trunnion
4. Trunnion Bushing
5. Rear Yoke

Removal

1. Remove front propeller shaft as outlined under "Front Propeller Shaft-Removal".
2. Remove bolt and lockwasher which attach joint assembly to transmission main shaft and slide universal joint from shaft.
3. Wash assembly in cleaning solvent.
4. Inspect yokes for excessive spline wear or damage.
5. Inspect assembly for excessive wear of bushings.

REPAIRS

1. Remove trunnion bushing lock rings.
2. Support front yoke in vise and drive bushings out using a drift punch (fig. 81).

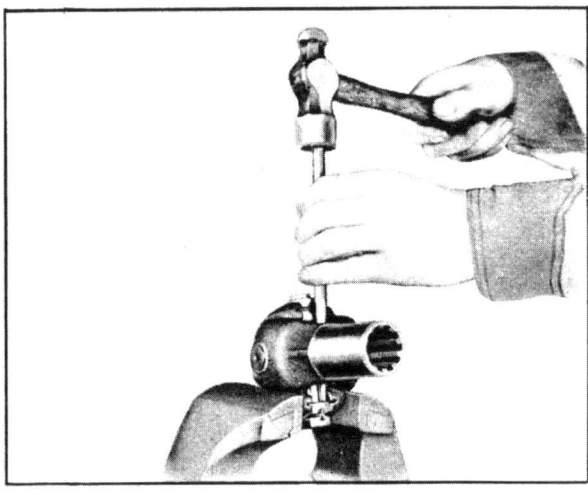

Fig. 81—Disassembly of Universal Joint

3. Support rear yoke in vise and drive bushings out using a drift punch and remove trunnion.
4. Press new trunnion bushings into yoke and over trunnion hubs (using an arbor press) just far enough to install new lock rings.

   NOTE: An old trunnion bearing may be used as a driver (fig. 82)

5. Install bushing retainer lock rings.

   NOTE: Use new lock rings in assembly.

Installation

1. Slide joint assembly over splines of main shaft and install retaining bolt, flat and lockwashers and tighten to 15-20 ft. lbs. torque.
2. Replace front propeller shaft as outlined under Front Propeller Shaft-Installation.

INTERMEDIATE UNIVERSAL JOINT (Fig. 83)

Removal

1. Split intermediate universal joint by removing two trunnion bearing "U" clamps.
2. Remove universal joint sleeve yoke dust cap and slide rear yoke assembly from splines of rear propeller shaft.
3. Wash parts in cleaning solvent.
4. Inspect splines for excessive wear or damage.
5. Inspect bearings and trunnion for excessive wear.

REAR AXLE 4-55

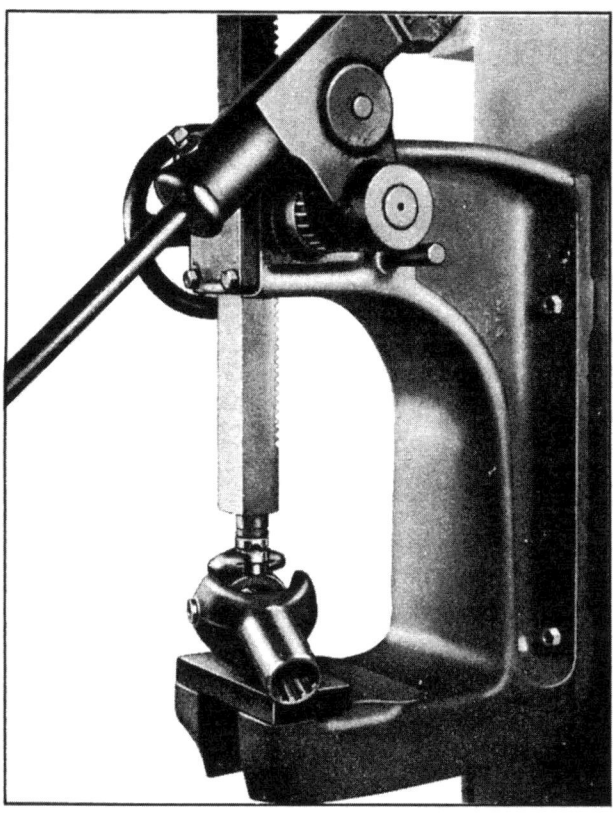

Fig. 82—Replacing Trunnion Bushings

Repairs

Overhaul of trunnion bearings is the same as covered under "Rear Propeller Shaft Repairs—Trunnion Bearings."

Installation

1. Slide yoke assembly onto splines of rear propeller shaft. The rear yoke of intermediate universal must be in line with the front yoke of the universal at the rear of the propeller shaft.
2. Replace universal joint sleeve yoke dust cap.

   NOTE: Make sure seal in cap is in good condition before assembling.

3. Attach rear yoke and trunnion to front yoke with two "U" clamps and tighten securely.
4. Lubricate joint with transmission lubricant.

1, 1½ and 2 TON CONVENTIONAL

All 1, 1½ and 2 ton conventional trucks use a similar type of propeller shaft and universal joint hook up. There are variations in length and the number of propeller shafts used, depending on the wheelbase of the vehicle, and the attachment of the front universal joint varies between the 1951, 1½ and 2 ton models and the 1948-50 models

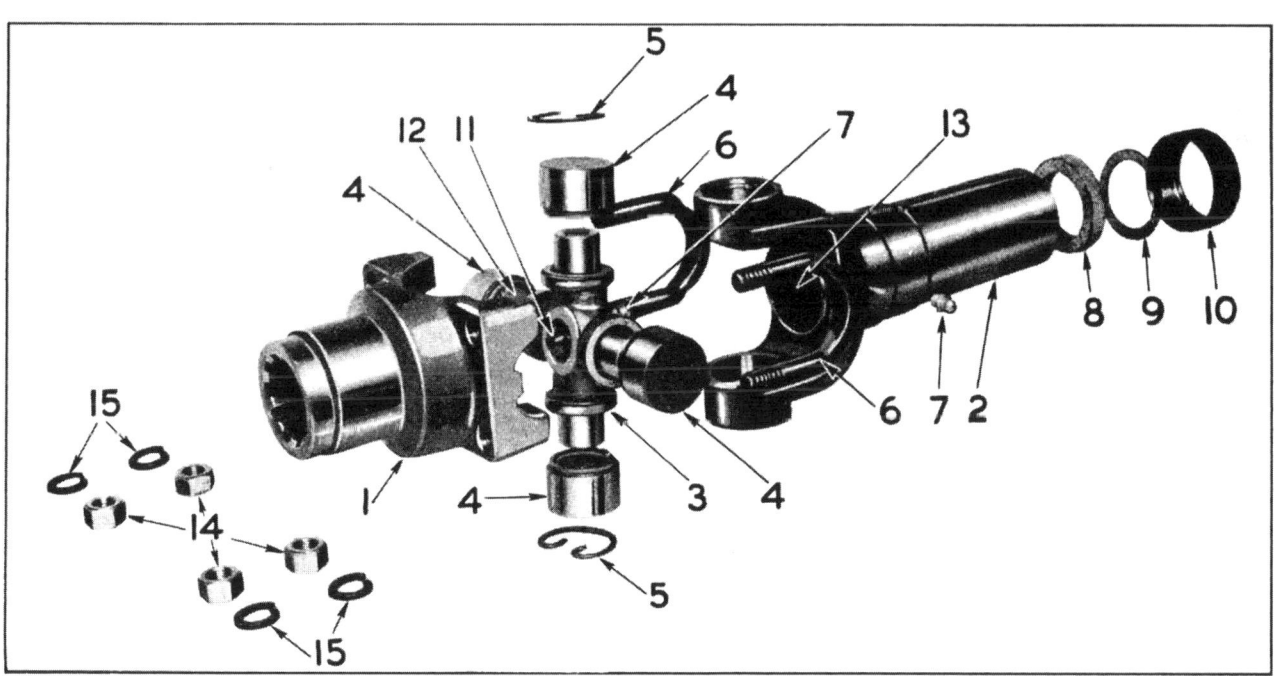

Fig. 83—Exploded View—Intermediate Universal Joint

1. Universal Joint Yoke	6. "U" Bolt	11. Relief Valve
2. Universal Joint Sleeve Yoke	7. Lubrication Fitting	12. Trunnion Bearing Rollers
3. Yoke Trunnion	8. Oil Seal	13. Air Vent
4. Trunnion Bearing	9. Washer	14. "U" Bolt Retaining Nut
5. Trunnion Bearing Lock Ring	10. Packing Retainer	15. Lockwasher

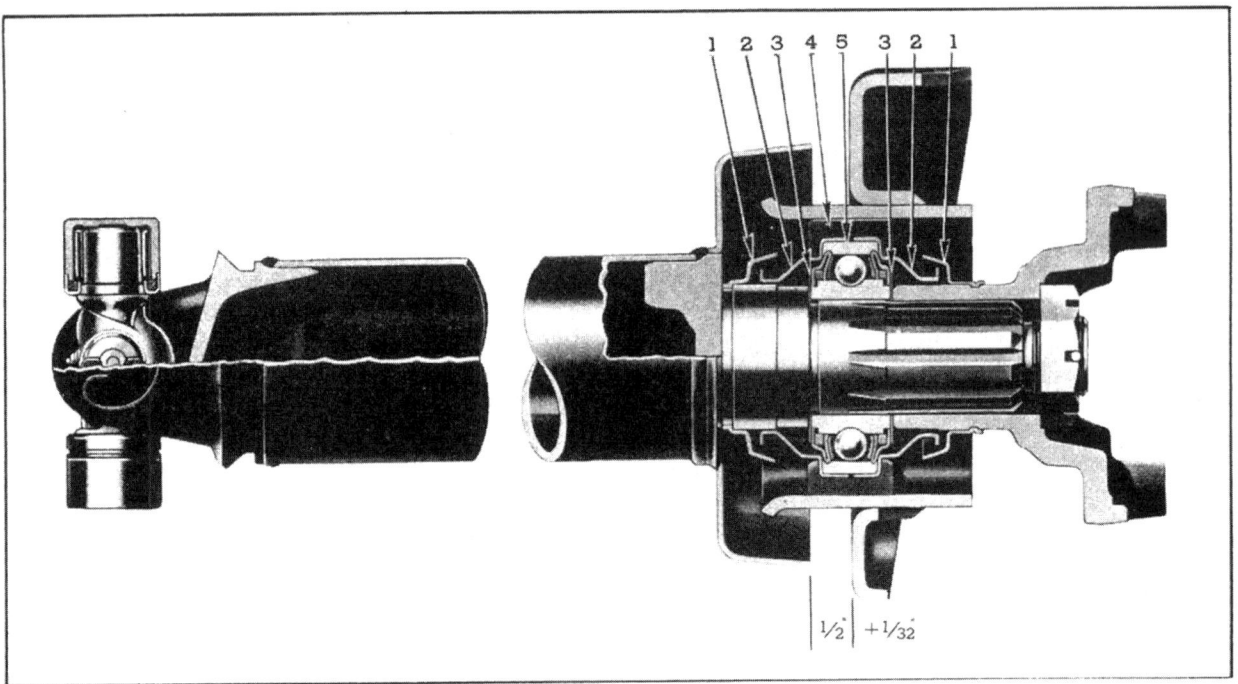

Fig. 84—Propeller Shaft Bearing Support Assembly

1. Grease Deflector
2. Grease Retainer
3. Grease Slinger
4. Bearing Cushion
5. Bearing

because of a propeller shaft brake that is used on the 1951, 1½ and 2 ton.

Service requirements for the rear propeller shaft are the same as those outlined for the ¾ ton rear propeller shaft removal, inspection, repairs and installation.

FRONT PROPELLER SHAFT

The front propeller shaft is supported at the rear in a bearing support consisting of a single row ball bearing which is permanently lubricated at the time of manufacture. This support also incorporates the use of grease traps which are packed with grease to eliminate entrance of water or dirt into the bearing (fig. 84).

Removal

1. Split intermediate joint by removing two trunnion bearing "U" clamps.
2. Tape bearings to keep them clean and from becoming damaged and drop front end of rear propeller shaft.
3. On all 1 ton and 1948-50, 1½ and 2 ton, split universal joint at transmission drive flange by removing two trunnion bearing "U" clamps and tape bearings.
4. On 1951, 1½ and 2 ton, remove the four front universal joint flange nuts.
5. Remove nuts attaching bearing support to frame cross member and remove shaft assembly from vehicle.

Disassembly

1. Place intermediate universal joint yoke in bench vise and remove cotter key and yoke retaining nut.
2. With brass drift drive front propeller shaft from universal joint yoke.
3. Pull support assembly off front propeller shaft.
4. Support assembly in an arbor press and with a piece of tubing, which will fit around slinger and inside the bracket, pressing on the rubber itself, remove bearing and rubber cushion assembly.
5. Remove flexible rubber cushion and grease retainers from ball bearing.
6. Clean rubber cushion in pure denatured alcohol only. Inspect cushion and replace if it shows any evidence of hardening or is cracked, torn or badly distorted.

NOTE: Any attempt to remove oil seal retainers from the ball bearing assembly will necessitate installation of a new bearing.

7. Check the bearing for broken balls and roughness by turning inner race slowly by hand.
8. Wash all other parts in cleaning solvent.
9. Inspect splines of shaft for excessive wear or damage.
10. Inspect propeller shaft front universal joint for excessive wear or damage.

REPAIRS
Trunnion Bearings
1. Remove trunnion bearing lock rings and remove lubrication fitting.
2. Support shaft yoke in a bench vise and using a soft drift and hammer, drive on one end of trunnion bearing to drive opposite bearing from yoke.
3. Support other side of shaft yoke in bench vise and drive opposite bearing out using brass drift on end of trunnion hub.
4. (a) On all 1 ton and 1948-50, 1½ and 2 ton, remove trunnion from shaft assembly.
   (b) On 1951, 1½ and 2 ton, remove trunnion and front yoke from shaft assembly.
5. On 1951, 1½ and 2 ton:
   (a) Support front yoke in a bench vise and using a brass drift and hammer and following the same procedure as outlined above, remove bearings and trunnion from front yoke.
   (b. Replace trunnion and press new bearings into front yoke and over trunnion hubs far enough to install lock rings.
   (c) Hold trunnion in one hand and tap yoke lightly to seat bearings against lock rings.
6. (a) On all 1 ton and 1948-50, 1½ and 2 ton, place new trunnion in rear yoke
   (b) On 1951, 1½ and 2 ton, place trunnion and front yoke into position in rear yoke.
7. Press new trunnion bearings into rear yoke and over trunnion hubs far enough to install lock rings.
8. Hold trunnion or front yoke in one hand and tap rear yoke lightly to seat bearings against the lock rings.

Assembly
1. Make sure grease deflectors are tight on propeller shaft end and universal joint yoke. These parts are secured by prick punching into propeller shaft end and yoke at two opposite points.
2. Place grease slingers, one on each side of bearing, and grease retainers over outside diameter of bearing. Force bearing and grease retainers into rubber bearing cushion and coat outside diameter of cushion with brake fluid.
3. Place bearing support bracket on bed of arbor press with flanged side up and place bearing with cushion squarely in flanged end of bore. Use piece of tubing which will contact rubber cushion only when pressing bearing into bracket.

NOTE: Flange of upper or front grease retainer must be flush with flanged end of bracket. If pressed in too far, invert bracket and press back again until these two surfaces are flush.

4. Pack grease retainers on both sides of bearing with a waterproof grease. This is not for lubrication purposes but only to exclude water and foreign matter from the bearing.
5. With grease slingers properly lined up with bearing hole, install support assembly over splined end of front propeller shaft; flanged end of support bracket is toward front of vehicle.
6. Install universal joint yoke so that yoke is at 90° to front propeller shaft front yoke.
7. Install yoke retaining nut, tighten to 160-280 ft. lbs. and install cotter pin lock.
8. Check clearance between propeller shaft bearing support and propeller shaft dust shield (fig. 84). This should be ½" ± 1/32".

Installation
1. On all 1 ton and 1948-50, 1½ and 2 ton:
   a. Position the propeller shaft and bearing support assembly under vehicle. Install bolts and nuts attaching bearing support to frame cross member.
   b. Connect universal joint to transmission drive flange. Install bearing "U" clamps, lockwashers and nuts.
2. On 1951 1½ and 2 ton:
   a. Install front propeller shaft and bearing support assembly, positioning the universal joint front yoke on the four flange bolts. Install bolts and tighten securely the nuts attaching propeller shaft support bracket to frame cross member.
   b. Install four universal joint flange lockwashers and nuts and tighten securely.
3. Raise front end of rear propeller shaft, install the trunnion bearing "U" clamps, lockwashers and nuts.

2 TON C.O.E. TRUCKS

Replacement of propeller shafts or repair of universal joints for the 134" wheelbase or 158" wheelbase C.O.E. trucks should be performed in the same manner as for conventional 1½ and 2 ton trucks.

The 110" wheelbase C.O.E. trucks have only one propeller shaft and the drive is of the Hotchkiss type. The front and rear universal joints are similar to those on conventional 1½ and 2 ton trucks.

PROPELLER SHAFT
Removal
1. Split the rear universal joint by removing trunnion bearing "U" clamps. Tape bearings to keep them clean and from becoming damaged and drop rear end of propeller shaft.
2. Remove front universal joint sleeve yoke dust cap and slide propeller shaft back disengaging splines from splines of yoke.

3. Wash splined end and trunnion end in cleaning solvent.
4. Check splines of shaft for excessive wear.
5. Check trunnion, trunnion bearings and yoke for damage or excessive wear.

NOTE: Trunnion bearings should be repaired as outlined in ¾ ton—"Rear Propeller Shaft—Repairs."

Installation

When installing the propeller shaft assembly, the front yoke of the rear universal must be in line with the rear yoke of the front universal.

1. Slide splines of propeller shaft into splined end of front universal joint and replace sleeve yoke dust cap.

   NOTE: Make sure seal in cap is in good condition before assembling (fig. 76).

2. Lift rear end of shaft and attach to rear axle flange with "U" clamps and tighten securely.
3. Lubricate both joints with transmission lubricant.

FRONT UNIVERSAL

Removal

1. Remove propeller shaft as outlined in this section.
2. On 1948-50 models, remove bolt, lockwasher and flatwasher which attach joint assembly to transmission mainshaft and slide universal joint from shaft.
3. On 1951 models remove the four front universal joint flange nuts and remove the universal.
4. Wash assembly in cleaning solvent.
5. Inspect yoke for excessive spline wear or damage.
6. Inspect bearings and trunnion for excessive wear.

NOTE: Trunnion bearings should be repaired as outlined under 1, 1½ and 2 ton Conventional Trucks — "Front Propeller Shaft — Repairs."

Installation

1. On 1948-50 models:
   a. Slide universal joint assembly over spline of transmission mainshaft and install retaining bolt, flat lockwashers and tighten to 15-20 ft. lbs.
   b. Replace the front propeller shaft as outlined under "Front Propeller Shaft—Installation."
2. On 1951 models:
   a. Slide yoke assembly onto propeller shaft splines so that the rear yoke of the front universal joint is in line with the front yoke of the universal at the rear of the propeller shaft.
   b. Replace universal joint sleeve dustcap.

   NOTE: Make sure seal in cap is in good condition before assembling (fig. 76).

   c. Install propeller shaft assembly, positioning the universal joint front yoke on the four flange bolts. Install lockwashers and nuts and tighten securely.
   d. Lift rear end of shaft and attach to rear axle shaft flange with "U" clamps and tighten securely.
   e. Lubricate both joints with transmission lubricant.

TROUBLES AND REMEDIES

PROPELLER SHAFT AND UNIVERSAL JOINTS

Symptom and Probable Cause

Excessive Vibration
- a. Worn universal joint.
- b. Bent propeller shaft.
- c. Propeller shaft bushings or universal joint yoke bushings worn.
- d. Universal joint yokes not installed on drive shaft in correct plane.
- e. Front propeller shaft intermediate bearing worn.

Excessive Backlash
- a. Worn universal joints.
- b. Worn drive shaft or joint splines.

Probable Remedy

- a. Replace worn parts.
- b. Replace bent shaft.
- c. Replace worn parts.
- d. Install yokes according to instructions in shop manual.
- e. Replace bearing.

- a. Replace worn parts.
- b. Replace worn parts.

REAR AXLE 4-59

REAR SPRINGS AND SHACKLES

INDEX

	Page		Page
General Description	4-59	Rear Spring Seat	4-61
Service Operations	4-60	¾, 1, 1½ and 2 Ton Rear Spring	4-62
½ Ton Rear Spring	4-60	Removal	4-62
Removal	4-60	Spring Eye Bushings—Replacement	4-62
Front Bushing Replacement	4-60	Spring Leaf Replacement	4-62
Rear Bushing Replacement	4-60	Rear Spring Shackle and Bushing	4-62
Spring Leaf Replacement	4-60	Installation	4-64
Installation	4-61		

GENERAL DESCRIPTION

The rear springs used on all truck models are of the semi-elliptic type and are designed for each individual unit to provide adequate load carrying capacity and a spring rate which is proportional to that of the front spring to give the smoothest ride possible.

Construction of rear spring assemblies is either single semi-elliptic, two stage semi-elliptic, or a combination semi-elliptic and auxiliary.

The single semi-elliptic spring may be of either light or heavy duty construction. Spring leaves are of variable lengths and assume entire deflection throughout varied load conditions.

The two stage spring construction allows for the reduction of the rebound or "throw" condition when the truck is not loaded and still allows for proper resistance to "bumping through" when the truck is loaded.

The combined auxiliary construction consists of variable length leaves that are assembled in such a manner as to assume a portion or all of the deflection depending upon road or load conditions. The auxiliary and main spring leaves are held together and in alignment by means of a center bolt passing through the center of leaves of both springs. Mounting "U" bolts hold spring and spacer plate firmly to the spring seat.

The spring leaves on all types are held in alignment with a center bolt and rebound clips.

Springs are designed to operate without lubrication between the leaves. Lubrication other than provided at the time of assembly will cause too lively spring action resulting in short spring life.

Shackles, bolts and pins are equipped with pressure gun lubrication fittings and should be lubricated at regular intervals.

Spring leaves, if broken, may be replaced with new parts; however, if spring assemblies have taken a set—that is—lost their resistance or elastic properties, they should be replaced with complete new assemblies.

There are two types of shackles used—the threaded bushing type, (fig. 85), and the clevis type (fig. 86).

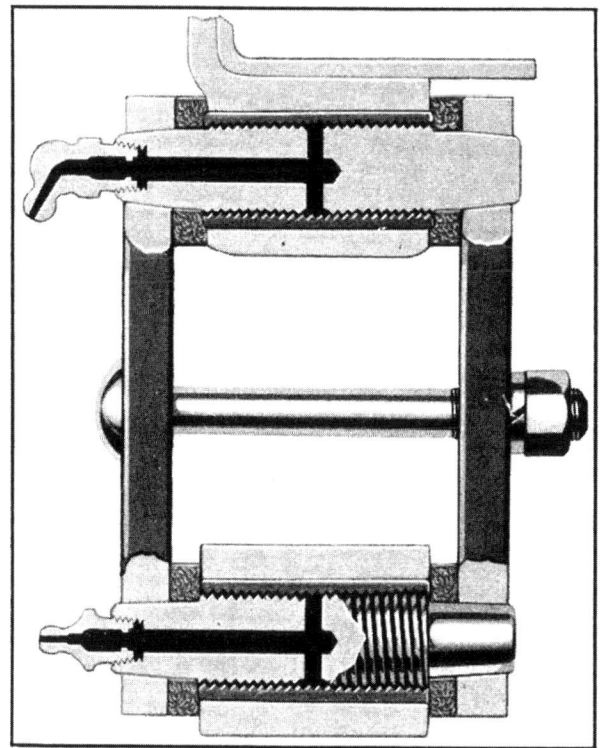

Fig. 85—Threaded Type Spring Shackle

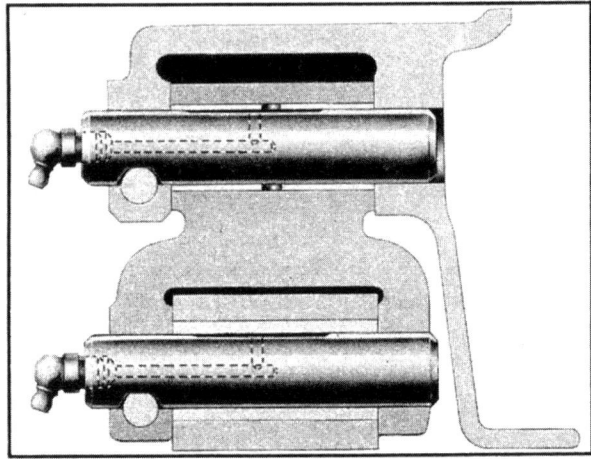

Fig. 86—Clevis Type Spring Shackle

The threaded type spring shackle has threaded bushings that are pressed into the spring hangers and into the spring eye. Threaded pins with tapered ends are screwed into the bushings with each end projecting the same distance. The shackles are plain heavy gauge steel stampings with tapered holes which fit tightly on the tapered ends of the shackle pins. A draw bolt is used to draw inner and outer shackles tightly on pins.

Shackle pins are drilled from their outer ends to the center where a cross hole connects it with the threaded portion. Lubrication fittings are assembled in the end of each central hole to provide lubrication of the threads. Cork washers are used at each end of shackle pin between the shackle and hanger or between shackle and spring to retain lubricant in the threaded portion.

In action, this shackle, being tight on the tapered pin end, oscillates the pin in the threaded portion. This design uses all the relatively large threaded surface of the shackle pin as a bearing reducing wear to a minimum and insures long bearing life of these bushings.

The clevis type shackle consists of a heavy malleable shackle bushed at the upper end to serve as a bearing for the upper shackle pin which passes through the shackle and the spring hanger, and a lower shackle pin which passes through the shackle and the spring eye bushing. A "pinch" bolt at the spring hanger keeps the upper shackle pin from turning, while the lower shackle pin is anchored in the same way by a "pinch" bolt at the shackle.

SERVICE OPERATIONS

½ TON REAR SPRING

Rear springs used on all ½ ton trucks are of the single stage type shackled at the rear by a threaded type shackle (fig. 85), and pivoted at the front on a shackle bolt anchored to a spring hanger.

Removal

1. Raise vehicle with chain hoist enough to relieve spring tension.
2. Disconnect shock absorber link or eye from rear shock absorber anchor plate.
3. Remove spring "U" bolts and shock absorber anchor plate.
4. Remove lubrication fittings, rear shackle draw bolt and shackle plates and lower rear end of spring to the floor.
5. Remove lubrication fitting from rear spring front shackle bolt and remove nut and lockwasher.
6. Thread shackle bolt out of front hanger and spring eye bushing.

NOTE: Bolt is threaded into spring hanger.

Inspection

1. Inspect bronze bushing in rear spring front eye for excessive wear or damage.
2. Remove spring shackle pin from rear spring eye and check for excessive looseness in threaded bushing.
3. Check spring leaves for breakage.
4. Check spring clips for tightness.

NOTE: Spring clips should be tightened sufficiently to maintain leaf alignment, but not tight enough to bind spring leaf action.

5. Check spring center bolt for tightness.

REPAIRS

Front Bushing (Plain)—Replacement

1. Install bushing remover J-1451 and remove bushing.
2. Install new bushing on bushing replacer J-1451 and install bushing in spring eye (fig. 87).

Rear Bushing (Threaded)—Replacement

1. Thread end of J-553 shackle bushing tool into bushing.
2. Turn pull nut on tool with wrench and remove bushing.
3. Insert end of J-553 shackle bushing tool through spring eye or spring hanger and screw new bushing on end of tool until it is centered with hole in spring or hanger.
4. Turn pull nut of tool to press bushing into place (fig. 88).

Spring Leaf—Replacement

1. Place spring in a bench vise and remove spring clips.

REAR AXLE 4-61

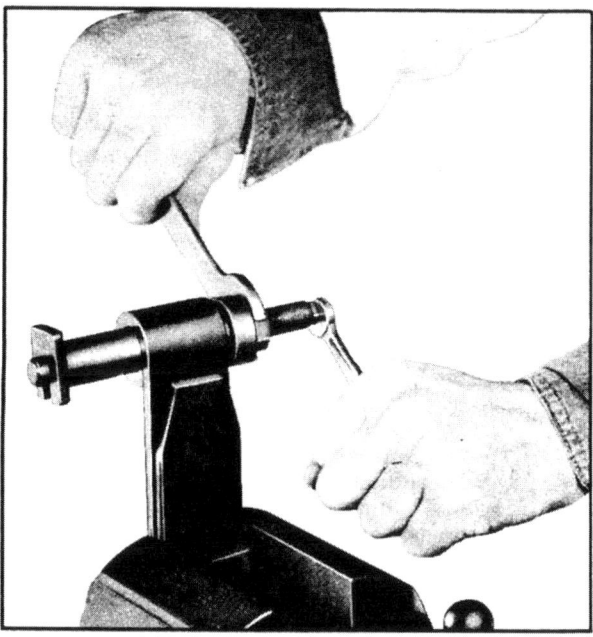

Fig. 87—Installing New Bushing (Plain)

NOTE: Spring clips will have to be bent open.

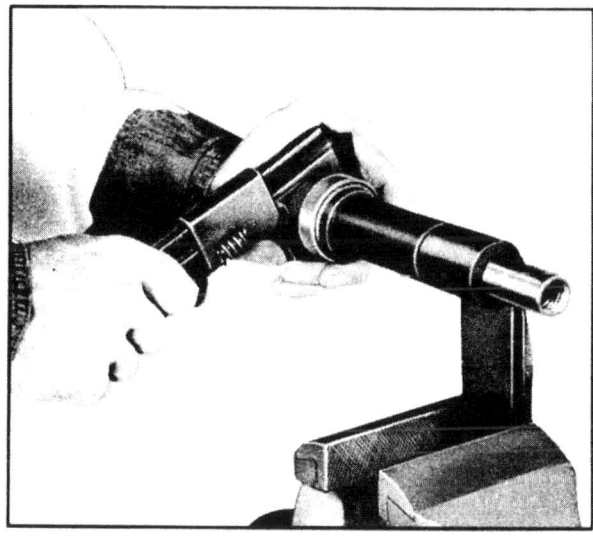

Fig. 88—Installing New Bushing (Threaded)

2. File peened end of center bolt and remove center bolt nut.
3. Open vise slowly and carefully to let spring assembly expand. Wire brush and clean spring leaves.
4. Replace broken spring leaf.
5. Align center holes in spring by means of a long drift and compress spring leaves in vise.
6. Remove drift from center hole and install new center bolt.
7. Install nut on center bolt and tighten se-

curely and peen end of bolt to keep nut from loosening.
8. Align springs by tapping with a hammer and bend spring clips back in position.

NOTE: Spring clips should be bent sufficiently to maintain alignment, but not tight enough to bind spring action.

Installation

1. Assemble front end of spring to spring hanger and install shackle bolt.
2. Install shackle bolt lockwasher and nut, and tighten securely. Replace grease fitting.
3. Raise spring assembly and locate center bolt in locator hole of spring seat.
4. Install shock absorber anchor plate and "U" bolts.
5. Install "U" bolt lockwashers and nuts, and tighten to 75-90 ft. lbs.
6. Connect shock absorber link or eye to shock absorber anchor plate.
7. Install new shackle pins in rear spring support bushing and in bushing in spring eye.
8. Locate shackle pins so that each end projects $21/32''$ from the ends of the bushings.
9. Place new cork seals and shackle plates over tapered ends of the shackle pins.
10. Install draw bolt through shackle plates, install lockwashers and nuts, and tighten securely.
11. Strike each end of shackle a sharp blow with a hammer to insure seating of the tapers and retighten draw bolt. Lower vehicle to the floor.
12. Install lubrication fittings in each shackle pin and lubricate shackles front and rear.

Rear Spring Seat

Rear springs on ½ ton trucks are completely insulated from the axle by means of a rubber core. At each side a bracket is welded on the front side of the axle housing (fig. 89). An eye bolt passes through this bracket and the spring seat in a manner similar to the way the front end of the

Fig. 89—Rear Spring Seat—½ Ton Trucks

rear spring is mounted. A steel spacer sleeve is used to prevent collapsing the walls of the axle bracket when the eye bolt and nut are pulled down tight. Between the spacer sleeve and the spring sleeve is a rubber bushing. Rubber washers at each end complete the installation.

The mounting effectively dampens out objectionable road noise at its source and in doing so prevents it from telegraphing through the frame and springs into the body.

Adjust this type seat as follows:
1. Weight of vehicle must be on the wheels.
2. Loosen hanger eye bolt nut and bounce vehicle up and down several times. This seats the rubber bushings in their normal position.
3. Tighten eye bolt nut securely and install cotter pin.

¾, 1, 1½, AND 2 TON

Service operations of rear springs and shackles are the same on all ¾, 1, 1½ and 2 ton vehicles. Although type and size of spring will be dependent upon the size of the vehicle the following procedures will cover removal and repairs of all types of rear springs. Shackles of these models are of the clevis type (fig. 86).

REAR SPRING

Removal

1. Raise vehicle with chain hoist enough to relieve spring tension.
2. Remove "U" bolts and anchor plate.
3. Remove pressure lubrication fittings from ends of rear spring pins at shackle and at rear spring front eye.
4. Remove lock bolt nut and lockwasher from rear spring pin lock bolt at front hanger. Drive lock bolt from hanger.

NOTE: The lock bolt body is tapered on one side to lock the rear spring pin more securely.

5. Remove the jaws from J-1436 bushing installer and install J-1436-9 adapter to installer handle.

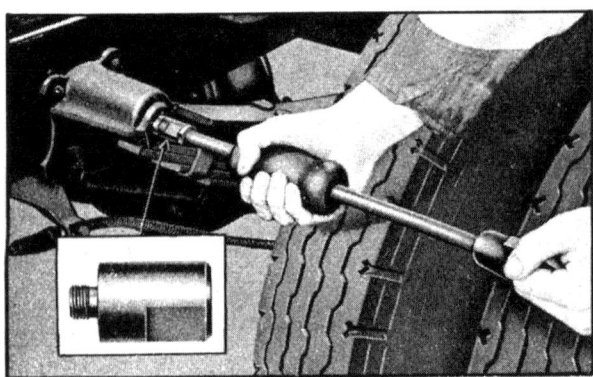

Fig. 90—Removing Rear Spring Pin

6. Thread adapter into rear spring pin lubrication threaded hole and remove pin (fig. 90).
7. Remove lock bolt nut and lockwasher from upper rear shackle pin lock bolt and drive bolt from shackle.
8. Thread adapter into upper shackle pin lubrication threaded hole and remove shackle pin.

NOTE: On ¾ and 1 ton, the spring leaf width is 2" as compared with 2½" on 1½ and 2 ton. A spacer is used therefore on the ¾ and 1 ton vehicles to permit the use of the same spring hangers on all vehicles. These spacers will be located on the inner side of the spring.

9. Lift rear spring assembly slightly to clear spring center bolt head from locating pocket in spring seat and remove spring assembly.

Inspection

1. Inspect bushings for excessive wear or damage.
2. Inspect shackle pins for scoring or damage.
3. Check spring leaves for breakage.
4. Check spring clips for tightness.
   NOTE: Spring clips should be tightened sufficiently to maintain leaf alignment, but not tight enough to bind spring leaf action.
5. Check spring center bolt for tightness.

REPAIRS

Spring Eye Bushings—Replacement

1. Support spring in arbor press and drive bushing out using suitable driver.
2. Place new bushing in spring eye and press into position using arbor press.

Spring Leaf—Replacement

Replacement of spring leaves may be accomplished in the same manner as spring leaf replacement on ½ ton vehicles. The only exception will be on vehicles equipped with the combined auxiliary type spring. This spring should be disassembled in an arbor press and care should be taken to install the spacer between the auxiliary spring and main spring at assembly.

Rear Spring Shackle and Bushing

1. Remove shackle and bushing assembly from rear spring by removing lock bolt nut and lockwasher and driving lock bolt from shackle. Then with a brass drift, drive shackle pin from shackle and spring eye.

NOTE: Bushings in shackle are line reamed after installation for perfect alignment and are therefore not replaceable in the field.

2. Assembly shackle and bushing assembly to rear spring and when spacer is used make sure spacer is located at inner side of spring.

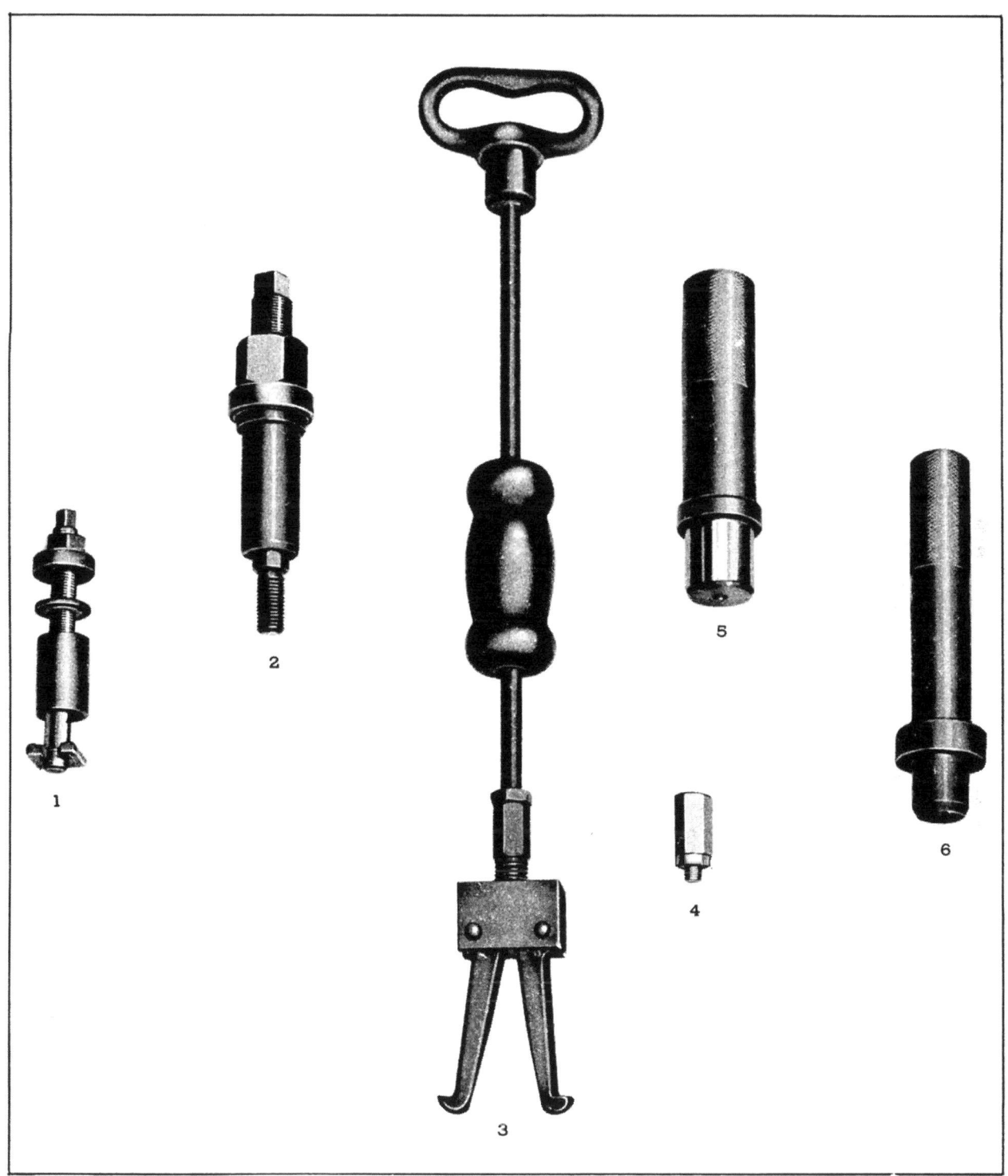

Fig. 91—Propeller Shaft and Rear Spring Special Tools

1. J-1451   Spring Hanger Bushing Remover and Replacer
2. J-553   Spring Shackle Bushing Remover and Replacer
3. J-1436   Axle Shaft Bearing and Oil Seal Remover
4. J-1436-9   Shackle Pin Remover Adapter
5. J-2243   Front Propeller Shaft Bushing Replacer
6. J-1362   Propeller Shaft Bushing and Oil Seal Replacer

Installation

1. Slide rear spring assembly over axle housing, locate center bolt in locating hole in spring seat.
2. Assemble front end of spring to spring hanger and install spring pin on adapter and drive into position.

   NOTE: Make sure taper on pin aligns with lock bolt hole in front spring hanger.

3. Install lock bolt, nut and lockwasher, and tighten securely.

   NOTE: Make sure taper on lock bolt aligns with taper on spring pin.

4. Replace "U" bolts and anchor plate, and tighten nuts securely.
5. Install rear spring rear shackle to spring hanger and install spring pin aligning taper on pin with shackle bolt hole in hanger.
6. Install shackle lock bolt so that taper aligns with taper on spring pin and install nut and lockwasher, and tighten securely.
7. Lower vehicle to floor.
8. Install lubrication fittings in each rear spring pin and lubricate shackles.

REAR SPRING SPECIFICATIONS*

	½ Ton	Forward Control	¾ Ton	1 Ton	1½ and 2 Ton School Bus	1½ Ton	2 Ton Main	2 Ton Auxiliary
Length	54	46	46	46	46	46	46	31
Leaf Width	1¾	2	2	2	2½	2½	2½	2½
Type	Semi-elliptic	Semi-elliptic	Semi-elliptic 2-stage	Semi-elliptic 2-stage	Semi-elliptic 2-stage	Semi-elliptic	Semi-elliptic	and Auxiliary
No. Leaves	8	8	7	8	11	11	11	6
No. Spring Clips	4	3	3	3	4	2	2	2
Spring Clip Type	Clinch	Bolt	Bolt	Bolt	Bolt	Bolt	Bolt	Clinch
Shackle Type	Threaded H	Clevis and Plain Bushings	Clevis and Plain Bushings	Clevis and Plain Bushings	Clevis and Plain Bushings	Clevis and Plain Bushings	Clevis and Plain Bushings	
Seat Type	Rubber Bushed	Fixed	Fixed	Fixed	Fixed	Fixed	Fixed	

*These specifications are for standard jobs. Different spring combinations are available as R. P. O.

SERVICE NEWS REFERENCE

Month	Page No.	Subject

SECTION 5

BRAKES

CONTENTS OF THIS SECTION

	Page
Hydraulic Brakes	5- 1
Troubles and Remedies	5-28
Hydrovac	5-29
Troubles and Remedies	5-36
Specifications	5-36
Special Tools	5-37

HYDRAULIC BRAKES

INDEX

	Page
General Description	5- 2
Front and Rear—(1951) ½ Ton	5- 2
Front and Rear—(1948-50) ½, 1½ and 2 Ton; (1948-51) ¾ and 1 Ton; Front—(1951) 1½ and 2 Ton	5- 3
Rear—(1951) 1½ and 2 Ton	5- 3
Main Cylinder	5- 4
Wheel Cylinders	5- 5
Hydraulic Operation	5- 5
Parking Brake	5- 6
Minor Service Operations	5- 7
Hydraulic Brake Fluid	5- 7
Bleeding Hydraulic System	5- 7
Toe Board Clearance Adjustment	5- 8
All except Forward Control	5- 8
Forward Control	5- 9
Hydraulic Brake Tubing	5- 9
Hydraulic Brake Adjustment	5-10
Front or Rear—(1951) ½ Ton	
Minor	5-10
Major	5-11
Front or Rear—(1948-50) ½ Ton (1948-51) ¾ Ton; Front—(1948-51) 1, 1½, 2 Ton	5-13
Rear—(1948-51) 1 Ton and (1948-50) 1½ and 2 Ton	5-13

	Page
Rear—(1951) 1½ and 2 Ton	5-13
Parking Brake Adjustment	5-14
All (1948-51) ¾ Ton and 1 Ton Forward Control; (1948-50) ½ Ton	5-14
All (1948-51) 1 Ton except Forward Control; (1948-50) 1½ and 2 Ton	5-14
All (1951) 1½ and 2 Ton	5-14
Major Service Operations	5-15
Brake Shoe Replacement	5-15
Front or Rear—(1951) ½ Ton	5-15
Front—(1948-50) ½ Ton; (1948-51) ¾, 1, 1½ and 2 Ton	5-17
Rear—(1948-50) ½ Ton; (1948-51) ¾ and 1 Ton; (1948-50) 1½ and 2 Ton	5-19
Rear—(1951) 1½ and 2 Ton	5-20
Brake Shoe Relining	5-21
Bonded Linings	5-21
Riveted Linings	5-21
Parking Brake—(1951) 1½ and 2 Ton	5-21
Brake Cable—Lubrication	5-22
Parking Brake Toggle Lever Adjustment	5-22
Main Cylinder	5-23
Wheel Cylinder	5-25
Brake Drums	5-27
Removal	5-27
Inspection and Reconditioning	5-27
Installation	5-28

GENERAL DESCRIPTION

½ TON—FRONT AND REAR (1951)

The brakes used on both front and rear of all ½ ton trucks are the Duo-Servo single anchor type which utilize the momentum of the vehicle to assist in the brake application. This self-energizing or self actuating force is applied to both brake shoes at each wheel in both forward or reverse motion.

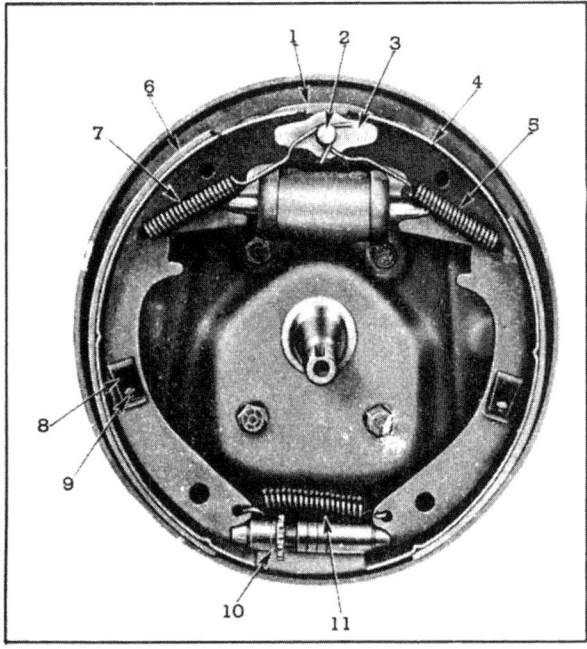

Fig. 1—Brake Mechanism (1951) ½ ton

1. Wheel Cylinder Stop
2. Anchor Pin
3. Guide Plate
4. Primary Shoe
5. Primary Shoe Pull Back Spring
6. Secondary Shoe
7. Secondary Shoe Pull Back Spring
8. Shoe Hold Down Spring
9. Shoe Hold Down Pin
10. Adjusting Link
11. Adjusting Link Pin

Each brake (fig. 1) has one wheel cylinder located near the top of the brake flange plate just below the anchor pin. Each wheel has two shoes with a pull back spring installed between each shoe and the anchor pin to hold the upper ends of the shoes against the anchor pin when the brakes are released. The lower ends of the shoes are connected by a link and a helical spring. The link is made up of an adjusting screw, riding in a socket at one end, and threaded into a pivot nut at the other. The outer ends of the socket and pivot nut are notched to fit the webs of the brake shoes, providing freedom of motion between the link and the shoes. The spring is stretched from one shoe web to the other, crossing over the notched head of the adjusting screw. It bears against one of the notches in the head, and thus acts as a lock for the adjusting screw.

Bonded brake linings are used and brake drums are 11" in diameter. The front brakes are 2" wide while the rear are 1¾".

In each brake assembly the linings for the front and rear shoes differ in length with the secondary facing being longer than the primary, because in operation, a greater force is applied to the secondary facing than to the primary.

The brake flange plate has six bearing surfaces, three for each shoe, against which the inner surfaces of the shoes bear to maintain alignment. Slightly below the center of each shoe web is a hole through which a hold down pin is inserted. A spring fitted over the outer end of the pin, holds the shoe against the bearing surfaces. At the top of the brake where the shoes butt against the anchor pin, a guide plate separates the pull back springs from the shoe webs, and assists in keeping the shoes properly aligned.

The brake mechanism is effectively sealed against the entrance of dirt or mud by the joint between the brake flange plate and the drum. The outside edge of the flange plate fits over the edge of the drum which has an annular groove located between two flanges. The outer flange is of a larger diameter than the inner one, so that dirt and moisture which collect in the groove are thrown off the larger flange by the centrifugal force of the rotating drum, thus keeping foreign matter away from the drum-to-flange plate joint.

To keep out dust and moisture, and to prevent gumming of the brake fluid, both ends of each wheel cylinder are sealed with a rubber boot.

When the brakes are applied, the pistons in the wheel cylinder, acting on the brake shoes through the connecting links, force the shoes against the drum. Since the shoes float free in the brake, the force of friction between the shoes and the rotating drum turns the entire assembly in the direction of the wheel rotation. The front or primary shoe moves downward, and the back or secondary shoe is carried upward until its upper end butts against the anchor pin. The friction between the moving drum and the stationary shoes now tends to roll both shoes toward the drum with increased pressure. The secondary shoe pivots on the anchor pin at the top, and the primary shoe tends to turn about the adjusting link at the bottom which is held stationary by the secondary shoe. This self-energizing effect, greatly increases the pressure of the shoes against the drum and reduces the physical force required on the brake pedal.

Inasmuch as the brake shoes are freely connected at the bottom by the adjusting link, the self-energizing or friction force, which is applied to the primary shoe by the brake drum, is transmitted to the secondary shoe through the link.

The effectiveness of the secondary shoe is nearly doubled, because the total force applying this shoe becomes the sum of the force which is received from the primary shoe and the self energizing effect that is derived from the rotating drum.

When backing the car, the brake action is reversed. The rear shoe becomes the primary shoe and the front shoe becomes the secondary, butting up against the anchor pin during braking and being forced against the drum with great pressure.

FRONT AND REAR—(1948-50) ½, 1½ and 2 Ton; (1948-51) ¾ and 1 Ton; FRONT—(1951) 1½ and 2 Ton

The brakes used on the front and rear of all (1948-51), ¾ and 1 ton vehicles; (1948-50), ½ Ton, 1½ and 2 Ton vehicles and front only on (1951), 1½ and 2 Ton are of the double articulating Huck type (fig. 2). Bonded linings are used on the ¾ and 1 ton and riveted linings on the 1½ and 2 ton.

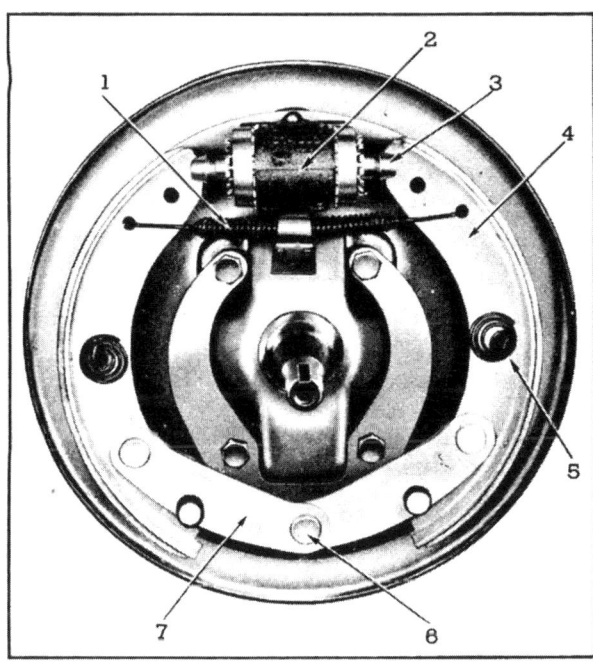

Fig. 2—Front Brake Mechanism

1. Retracting Spring
2. Wheel Cylinder
3. Adjusting Screw
4. Brake Shoe
5. Conical Spring
6. Anchor Pin
7. Articulating Link

REAR ONLY—(1951) 1½ and 2 Ton

The brakes used on the rear only of all (1951), 1½ and 2 ton trucks are the Twinplex four anchor type and are radial self-centering in operation utilizing the momentum of the vehicle to assist in the brake application. This self-energizing or self-actuating force is applied to both brake shoes at each wheel in both forward or reverse motion.

Fig. 3—Brake Mechanism Rear (1951) 1½ and 2 ton

1. Shield
2. Wheel Cylinder (Rear)
3. Dust Shield
4. Adjusting Screw Head
5. Brake Shoe
6. Shoe Pull Back Spring
7. Shoe Hold Down Bolt
8. Shoe Pull Back Spring
9. Fluid Line
10. Wheel Cylinder (Front)

Each brake (fig. 3), has two wheel cylinders which are mounted vertically, one at the front and one at the rear of the brake assembly. The two brake shoes are mounted between the wheel cylinders, one being located at the top and the other at the bottom. There are two primary or sliding pivot anchors, one at the front of the upper shoe and one at the rear end of the lower shoe; and two secondary or adjustable anchors, one at the front end of the lower shoe and one at the rear end of the upper shoe. There are four hold-back springs which normally hold each end of each shoe against its respective anchor.

Anchor brackets are steel forgings, bolted directly to the flange plate and are very rigid. The pivot of each forward motion anchor is a circle segment inserted in a slot in one end of the anchor bracket. Its flat edge bears against the anchor bracket and is free to move in an approximately radial direction. Its round edge bears against the web of the brake shoe, which is shaped to fit. Each reverse motion anchor is an adjusting screw threaded into the anchor bracket. The shoe web bears against the flat head of the screw and is rounded so that it can rock on the screw head anchor. With one end of the shoe web free to seek its own position on the adjustable anchor head and the sliding pivot anchor free to move in and out, the shoes are radially self centering and tend to assume the most favorable position for best contact with the drum. This provides uniform contact throughout the length of the facing, which results in even wear and long life. Since the anchors are located close to the axle, there is effective wrap-in which helps provide full contact and even wear of the facings.

The adjusting screw head of the front and rear secondary anchors have twelve notches and are rotated for shoe adjustment through access holes in the flange plate.

The brake flange plate has six bearing surfaces, three for each shoe, against which the inner edge of each shoe bears to maintain alignment. Two hold down bolts project from the flange plate, one passing through a hole in the middle of each shoe web. The hole in the shoe web is large and oblong, and there is approximately .010" clearance between the washer and shoe web, thus eliminating any interference with braking action.

Both ends of the wheel cylinders are sealed with a rubber boot to keep out dust and moisture and prevent gumming of the brake fluid. A flat shield fits over the upper end of each cylinder to protect the boot from brake facing dust and from foreign matter that might enter the brake.

The inlet for the hydraulic fluid is through the flange plate into the rear cylinder and a steel tube connects the two cylinders. Steel stampings shield each cylinder from heat radiating from the drum, thus assuring that the brake fluid will not become excessively hot and possibly boil away.

The outside edge of the brake flange plate is formed to fit into a groove in the edge of the drum rim so that, while maintaining clearance, it provides an effective seal against the entrance of dirt or mud into the brake mechanism. (Fig. 4).

Fig. 4—Sealing of Brake Mechanism

Wheel cylinders are 1½" in diameter, brake drum diameter is 15" with a 4⅜" rim width and brake facings are moulded, 4" wide, ⅜" thick, fastened to the shoe with 14 rivets.

The brake drum is of one-piece cast iron construction which provides much more metal for absorbing and conducting heat. Handholes in the wheel provide a certain amount of air flow which carries away heat that has been conducted from the rim into the web of the drum.

Adjustment of the brakes is accomplished by inserting an adjusting tool through the brake flange plate into one of the notches on the adjusting screw and rotating the screw. A click spring provides equal increments of movement and an audible measurement of the number of notches that the screw is rotated, and locks the adjusting screw in position.

MAIN CYLINDER

Operation of the hydraulic system is dependent upon the proper functioning of main and wheel cylinders. The main cylinder (fig. 5) contains a

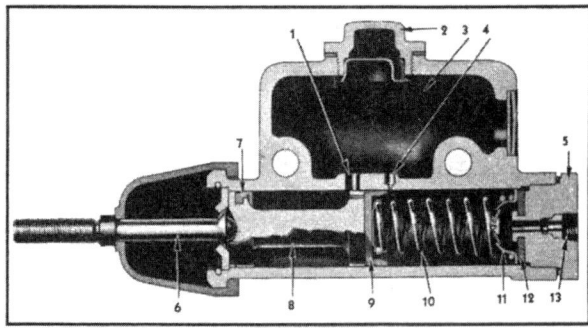

Fig. 5—Main Cylinder Cross Section

1. Inlet
2. Filler Plug
3. Reservoir
4. Compensating Port
5. End Plug
6. Push Rod
7. Piston Cup—Secondary
8. Piston
9. Piston Cup—Primary
10. Spring
11. Valve
12. Valve Seat
13. Outlet

piston which receives mechanical pressure from the push rod and exerts pressure on the fluid in the lines, building up the hydraulic pressure, which moves the wheel cylinder pistons. The primary cup is held against the piston by the piston return spring which also retains the return valve against its seat. The spring maintains a slight pressure in the lines and in the wheel cylinders to prevent the possible entrance of air into the system. The secondary cup, which is secured to the opposite end of the piston, prevents the leakage of fluid into the rubber boot. The holes in the piston head are for the purpose of allowing the fluid to flow from the annular space around the piston into the space between the primary cup and the check valve, keeping sufficient fluid in the lines at all times. The holes in the valve cage allow the fluid to flow through the cage and around the lip or the rubber valve cup and out into the lines during the brake application. When the brake is released, the lip of the rubber valve cup seals the holes in the valve cage and the valve is forced off its seat, permitting the fluid to return to the main cylinder.

The push rod assembly is held in the opposite end of the housing by means of a snap ring. A rubber boot that fits around the push rod and over the end of the housing prevents dirt or any other foreign matter from entering the main cylinder.

WHEEL CYLINDERS

Wheel cylinders are the double piston type permitting even distribution of pressure to each brake shoe. Rubber piston cups maintain pressure on the pistons and prevents leakage of fluid past the pistons. Design of the wheel cylinders

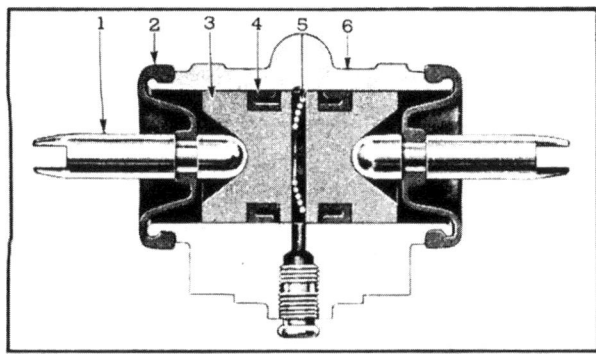

Fig. 6—Wheel Cylinder Rear (1951) 1½ and 2 ton

1. Connecting Link
2. Rubber Boot
3. Piston
4. Piston Seal
5. Spring
6. Cylinder

used on the (1951) 1½ and 2 ton rear brakes (fig. 6) differ somewhat from the design used on the (1951) ½ ton (fig. 7) and the (1948-51) ¾ and 1

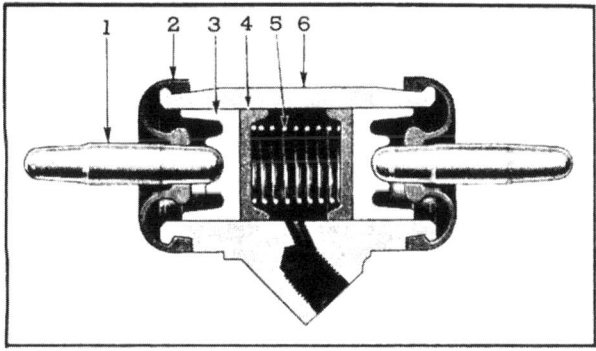

Fig. 7—Wheel Cylinder—Front and Rear (1951) ½ ton

1. Connecting Link
2. Rubber Boot
3. Piston
4. Piston Cup
5. Spring
6. Cylinder

ton and (1948-50) ½, 1½ and 2 ton (fig. 8) insofar as the placement and design of the rubber piston cups. In addition, both ends of the wheel cylinders used on (1951), ½ ton front and rear and 1½ and 2 ton rear brakes are sealed with a rubber

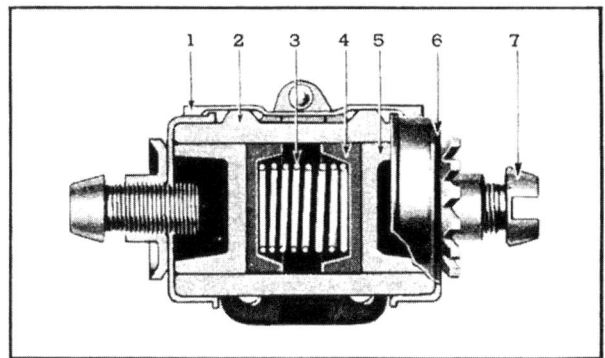

Fig. 8—Wheel Cylinder (1948-51) ¾ and 1 ton; (1948-50) ½, 1½ and 2 ton

1. Lock Spring
2. Cylinder
3. Spring
4. Piston Cup
5. Piston
6. Cover
7. Adjusting Screw

boot and have no external adjustments. The wheel cylinders used on (1948-51) ¾ and 1 ton, (1948-50) ½, 1½ and 2 ton models (fig. 8), however, have metal adjusting covers at each end which prevent the entrance of dirt and foreign material and at the same time allow a means of adjusting the brake shoes. These covers are threaded to receive the slotted adjustment screws which fit the webs of the brake shoes.

HYDRAULIC OPERATION

In operation, pressure is applied to the brake pedal and transmitted to the push rod and the piston in the main cylinder. This pressure on the piston causes the primary cup to close the compensating port and fluid is forced through the holes in the valve cage, around the lip of the rubber valve cup, into the pipe lines and into the wheel cylinders. This fluid pressure forces the pistons in the wheel cylinders outward, expanding the brake shoes against the drums. As the pedal is depressed further, higher pressure is built up within the hydraulic system, causing the brake shoes to exert greater pressure against the brake drums.

As the pedal is released, the hydraulic pressure is relieved and the brake shoe retracting springs draw the shoes together, pressing the wheel cylinder pistons inward and forcing the fluid out of the wheel cylinder back into the lines toward the main cylinder. The piston return spring in the main cylinder returns the piston to the pedal stop faster than the brake fluid is forced back into the lines, creating a partial vacuum in that part of the cylinder ahead of the piston. This vacuum causes a small amount of fluid to flow through the holes in the piston head past the lip of the primary cup and into the forward part of the cylinder. This action keeps the cylinder full of fluid at all times, ready for the next brake application. As fluid is drawn from the space behind the piston head, it is replenished from the reservoir through the inlet or breather port. When the piston is in a fully released position, the primary cup clears the compensator port, allowing excess fluid to flow from the cylinder into the reservoir as the brake shoe retracting springs force the fluid out of the wheel cylinders.

PARKING BRAKE

A pedal operated parking brake is used on all (1948-51) ½ and ¾ ton trucks and on 1 ton Forward Control models (fig. 9). The other 1 ton

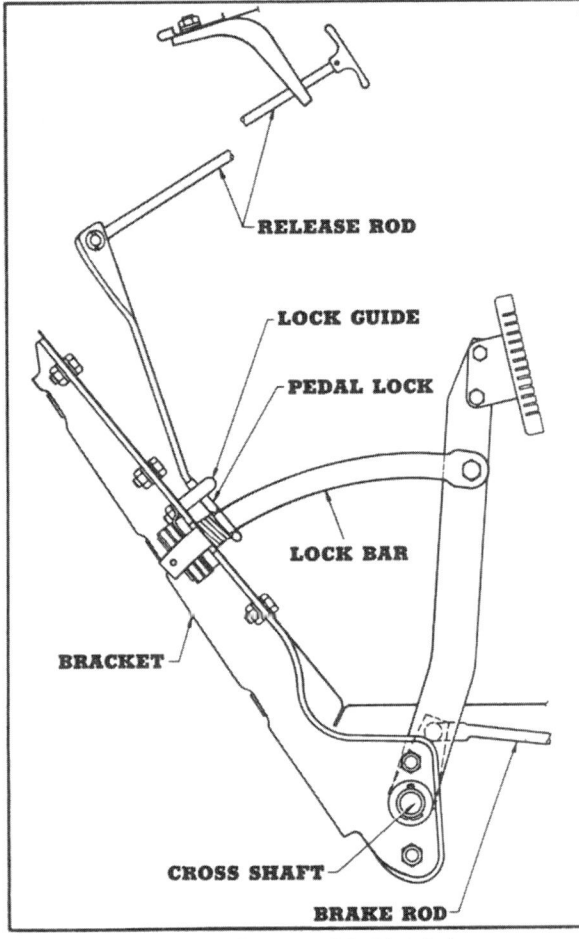

Fig. 9—Pedal Operated Parking Brake

Fig. 10—Propeller Shaft Parking Brake

truck models and the (1948-50) 1½ and 2 ton use the hand brake lever. Both are connected to the rear brake shoes by means of interconnecting rods and cables. Application of the parking brakes is independent of the hydraulic brake system.

The parking brake on all (1951) 1½ and 2 ton vehicles (fig. 10) is applied to the propeller shaft. The brake consists of a brake drum which is attached to the output shaft of the transmission ahead of the universal joint and an internal and external shoe which grip the drum between them, contacting about ¼ of the drum circumference.

The outside shoe is fulcrumed at the left of the drum a little above the centerline of the propeller shaft. It curves down, covering about 115° of the drum circumference. The brake shoe lever is a forged steel bell crank fulcrumed on the outer shoe below the drum and a little to the left of the centerline. The horizontal arm of the lever extends out to the right of the brake and the vertical arm, much shorter, extends up so that its end is fulcrumed on the inner shoe. Thus, when the horizontal arm of the brake shoe lever is raised, the vertical arm is rotated, shortening the vertical distance between its points of attachment to the shoes and squeezing the drum rim between the shoes.

The horizontal arm of the brake shoe lever is connected by a vertical link to the horizontal arm of a bell crank mounted on the transmission. On conventional models, the vertical arm of this bell crank is connected by a link directly to the hand brake lever, also mounted on the transmission. On C.O.E. models, the bell crank is linked to a cross shaft which is connected to linkage from the hand brake lever on the left side of the truck.

Both the inner and outer brake facings are ¼" thick by 2¼" wide. The inner facing is 7" long and the outer facing is about 1" longer with each facing being riveted to its shoe with six rivets.

The brake drum has an inside diameter of 9½" with a brake surface 2½" wide and is bolted to the transmission output flange with four bolts which also hold the universal joint. A cylindrical cup is bolted inside the drum and covers the universal joint to protect the drum and shoes from splashing lubricant.

For shoe adjustment, an adjusting screw, which is threaded through a bracket bolted to the rear of the transmission housing, bears against the underside of the outer shoe. A return spring connects the outer shoe to the bracket.

MINOR SERVICE OPERATIONS

In any service operation it is extremely important that absolute cleanliness be observed. Any foreign matter in the system will tend to clog the lines, ruin the rubber cups of the wheel and main cylinders and cause inefficient operation or even failure of the braking system. Dirt or grease on a brake lining will cause that brake to grab first on brake application and fade out on heavy brake application.

HYDRAULIC BRAKE FLUID

Only G.M. Hydraulic Brake Fluid Super No. 11 should be used when bleeding brakes. This brake fluid is satisfactory for any atmospheric temperature, hot or cold, and has all the qualities necessary for satisfactory operation, such as a high boiling point to prevent evaporation and tendency to vapor lock and still remain fluid at low temperatures.

In the event that improper fluid has entered the system, it will be necessary to—
1. Drain the entire system.
2. Thoroughly and vigorously flush the system with clean alcohol, 188 proof, or a hydraulic brake system cleaning fluid such as "Declene."
3. Replace all rubber parts of the system, including brake hoses.
4. Refill the system with G.M. Hydraulic Brake Fluid Super No. 11.

BLEEDING HYDRAULIC SYSTEM

The hydraulic brake system must be bled whenever a pipe line has been disconnected, when a leak has allowed air to enter the system or at any time the system has been opened. For satisfactory brake operation, the system must be completely free of all air.

Bleeding which may be accomplished by one of two methods; Pressure or Manual, should be done on the longest line first, the proper sequence being left rear, left front, right rear and right front.

Pressure Bleeding (except 1951, 1½ and 2 ton)

1. Clean all dirt from top of main cylinder and remove filler plug.
2. Connect hose from bleeder tank to main cylinder filler plug opening and open valves at both ends of hose.

    NOTE: Make sure fluid in tank is up to petcock above outlet and that tank is charged with 20 pounds air pressure.

3. Remove bleeder valve screw and screw bleeder hose into bleeder valve, placing other end of hose in a container having sufficient fluid to cover end of hose (fig. 11).
4. Open bleeder valve by turning ¾ turn in a

Fig. 11—Bleeding Brake System at Wheel Cylinder

counterclockwise direction and watch flow of fluid at end of bleeder hose.

5. Close bleeder valve tightly as soon as bubbles stop and fluid flows in a solid stream.
6. Remove bleeder hose and install bleeder valve screw in bleeder valve.
7. Repeat above operations at each wheel.

Manual Bleeding (except 1951, 1½ and 2 ton)

1. Clean all dirt from top of main cylinder and remove filler plug.

Fig. 12—Filling Main Cylinder Reservoir

2. Install adapter and automatic filler J-713 (fig. 12).
3. Follow bleeding operations as outlined in Steps 3 through 7 under "Pressure Bleeding."

Pressure Bleeding (1951, 1½ and 2 ton)

To bleed the hydraulic system on 1951 1½ and 2 ton trucks, a pressure bleeder tank should be used and in accordance with the following procedure:

1. Back off adjustment all the way on the upper shoe on both rear wheels.
2. Remove filler cap from main cylinder and fill the reservoir to the top of filler plug opening.
3. Connect pressure bleeder to main cylinder and open valve in the bleeder tank line.

   NOTE: The bleeder tank should be charged with 20 pounds air pressure and kept at approximately this pressure during bleeding operation. The end of the bleeder tube must be in a bleeder jar or bottle and covered with fluid while performing all bleeding operations.

4. Connect bleeder tube to hydrovac slave cylinder, open bleeder valve and bleed until all air bubbles disappear. Close bleeder valve.
5. Connect bleeder tube to hydrovac valve bleeder valve, open bleeder valve and bleed until all air bubbles disappear. Close bleeder valve.
6. Connect bleeder tube to the rear, rear wheel cylinder on left side, open bleeder valve and bleed until all air bubbles disappear. Close bleeder valve.
7. Connect bleeder tube to the front, rear wheel cylinder on left side, open bleeder valve and bleed until all air bubbles disappear. Close bleeder valve.
8. Connect bleeder tube to left front wheel cylinder, open bleeder valve and bleed until all air bubbles disappear. Close bleeder valve.
9. Connect bleeder tube to the rear, rear wheel cylinder on the right side, open bleeder valve and bleed until all air bubbles disappear. Close bleeder valve.
10. Connect bleeder tube to the front, rear wheel cylinder on the right side, open bleeder valve and bleed until all air bubbles disappear. Close bleeder valve.
11. Connect bleeder tube to the right front wheel cylinder, open bleeder valve and bleed until all air bubbles disappear. Close bleeder valve.
12. Connect bleeder tube to hydrovac slave cylinder, open bleeder valve and bleed until all air bubbles disappear. Close bleeder valve.
13. Connect bleeder tube to hydrovac bleeder valve, open bleeder valve and bleed until all air bubbles disappear. Close bleeder valve.

    NOTE: It is important to bleed the hydrovac both before and after bleeding the wheel cylinders.

14. Adjust upper shoe on each rear wheel.
15. Push down hard on the brake pedal several times to centralize the shoes, then readjust all brake shoes.
16. Apply approximately 75 pounds pressure on the brake pedal and check the pedal clearance from the toe board to the forward edge of the pedal pad. This clearance should be a maximum of 3½ inches with the floor mat in place.

If the pedal clearance is less than 3½ inches the hydraulic system should be rebled in accordance with the foregoing procedure.

TOE BOARD CLEARANCE ADJUSTMENT

Toe board clearance very seldom needs adjustment. The main cylinder push rod has a definite stop which is permanent and not adjustable. This stop is used in conjunction with a clevis attachment from the brake pedal to the push rod and toe board clearance is made at this clevis (fig. 13).

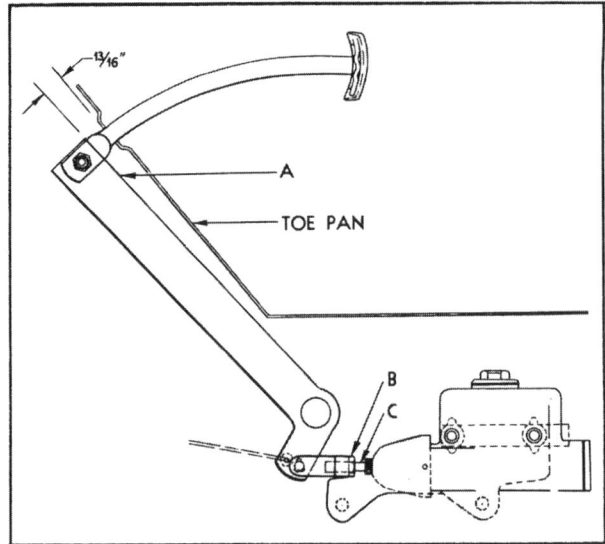

Fig. 13—Toe Board Clearance Adjustment

Before adjusting toe board clearance, make sure brake pedal returns to the fully released position freely, with no binding, and that the pedal retracting spring has not lost its tension.

All Models except Forward Control

1. Brake pedal "A" should be adjusted to give 1 13/16" clearance between top of the pedal arm and toe pan (fig. 13).
2. Loosen check nut "B" at rear of clevis on main cylinder push rod "C".

3. Turn main cylinder push rod "C" by knurled portion ahead of boot, in the proper direction to secure desired clearance.
4. Tighten check nut "B" against the clevis.

NOTE: Hold main cylinder push rod while tightening check nut.

Forward Control Models

1. Remove front floor pan.
2. Remove cotter pin and clevis pin from upper end of brake pedal lever rod.
3. Adjust brake rod clevis to give 1" pedal to floor board clearance and install upper end to brake pedal, inserting clevis pin and cotter pin.
4. Replace front floor pan.

HYDRAULIC BRAKE TUBING

Hydraulic brake tubing used on all trucks is a double layer flexible steel, copper coated and tin plated tubing which resists corrosion and also stands up under the high pressures which are developed when applying the brakes. Brake tubing 3/16" in diameter is used on all lines of (1951), 1/2 ton and on rear wheel cylinder connecting pipe on (1951), 1 1/2 and 2 ton trucks. Tubing 1/4" in diameter is used on all other models (1948-51). In making up hydraulic brake pipes, it is important that the ends of the tubing be flared properly for the compression couplings. Unless the tubing is properly flared, the couplings will leak and the brakes will become ineffective.

This safety steel tubing must be double-lap flared at the ends in order to produce a strong leak-proof joint.

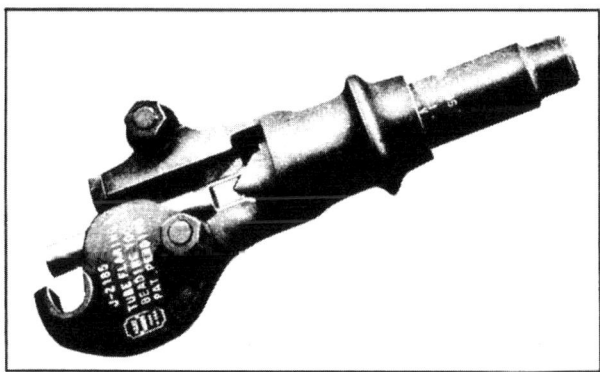

Fig. 14—Hydraulic Brake Tube Flaring Tool

The brake tube flaring tool J-2185-C (fig. 14) is a basic unit and must be equipped with the proper size die block and upset flare punch for each size tubing to form the double-lap flare.

The proper size die blocks and upset flare punches are as follows:

Tubing Size	Die Block	Upset Flare Punch	Finish Flare Punch
3/16"	J-2185-27	J-2185-3	J-2185-26
1/4"	J-2185-28	J-2185-37	J-2185-26

Figure 15 shows two pieces of tubing—one with a single-lap flare "A" and the other with a double-lap flare "B". It will be noted that the single-lap flare split the tubing while the one shown in "B" was a heavy, well-formed joint.

The following procedure should be followed in making up hydraulic brake pipes:

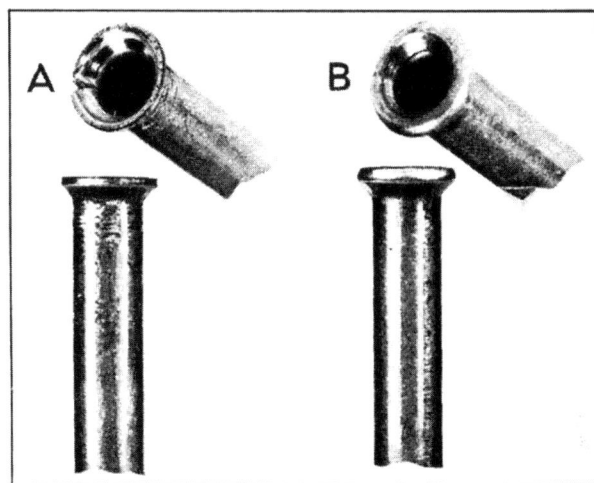

Fig. 15—Single and Double Lap Flare on Tubing End

1. Cut the tubing to the desired length, using tube cutter KMO-3-A. Square off ends of tube and ream sharp edges with reamer tool provided on the tube cutter.
2. Install compression couplings on tubing and dip end of tubing to be flared in hydraulic brake fluid. This lubrication results in better formation of the flare.
3. Select the correct size upset flare punch. One end of this punch is hollowed out to gauge the amount of tubing necessary to form a double-lap flare.
4. Slip the punch into the tool body with the gauge end toward the die blocks, install the ram and tap lightly until the punch meets the die blocks and they are forced securely against the stop plate (fig. 16).

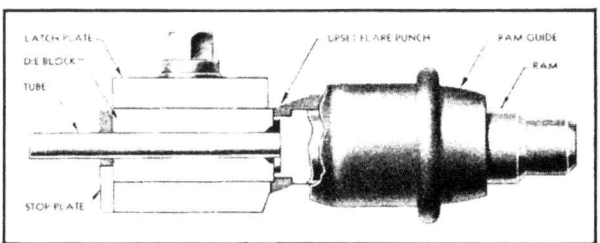

Fig. 16—Flaring Operation—Positioning Tubing

5. Draw latch plate nuts down tight to prevent tube from slipping. Draw nuts down alternately beginning with nut on closed side to prevent distortion of plate.
6. Remove punch and ram. Reverse punch and

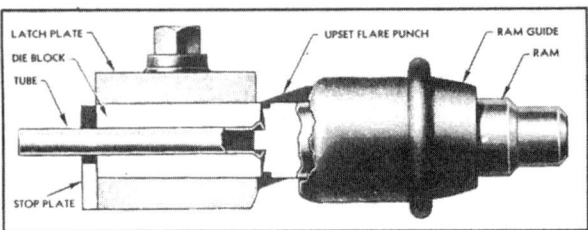

Fig. 17—Flaring Operation—First Flare

place back in tool body. Install ram and tap lightly until face of punch contacts face of die blocks to complete first flare operation (fig. 17).

7. Remove ram and punch.
8. Insert finish flare and ram in tool body and tap ram until a good seat is formed (fig. 18).
9. Blow tubing out with compressed air.

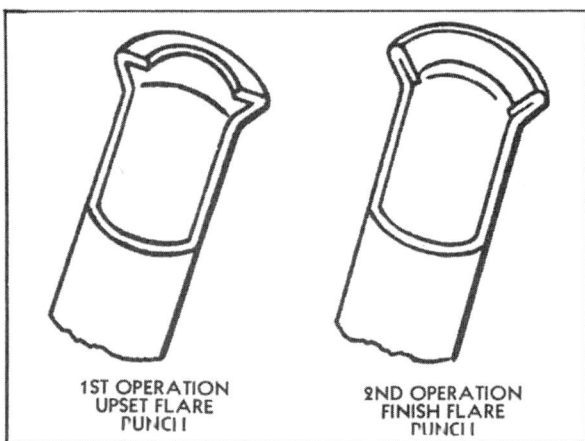

Fig. 18—Flaring Operation—First and Second Flare

HYDRAULIC BRAKE ADJUSTMENT

All truck hydraulic brakes can be adjusted without removal of the wheels as all brake flange plates have either openings with spring snap covers or are equipped with an exterior adjusting pinion.

Adjustment of front and rear brakes on all (1951) ½ ton truck models is accomplished by adjustment of a single adjusting screw at the bottom of the assembly.

Adjustment of front brakes on (1948-51) 1, 1½ and 2 ton and front and rear of all (1948-51) ¾ ton and (1948-50) ½ ton truck models is accomplished by direct adjustment of adjusting wheels at either end of each wheel cylinder.

Adjustment of rear brakes on the (1948-51) 1 ton truck models and (1948-50) 1½ and 2 ton is accomplished by external adjusting pinion studs at either end of each wheel cylinder.

Rear brakes on all (1951) 1½ and 2 ton vehicles are actuated by two wheel cylinders and each shoe is adjusted by means of an individual adjusting screw.

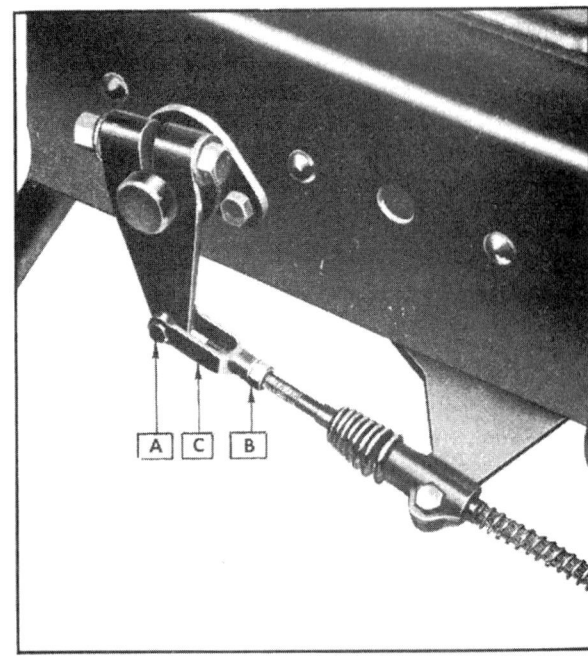

Fig. 19—Emergency Brake Adjustment

Adjustment—Front or Rear—(1951) ½ Ton Minor

1. Jack all wheels clear of floor.
2. Loosen brake cable clevis lock nuts "B" (fig.

Fig. 20—Adjusting ½ Ton Brakes

19) and then remove cotter pin and clevis pin "A" disengaging clevis "C" from cross shaft outer levers.

NOTE: If cables have been adjusted too short, the rear brake shoes will be forced away from the anchor pins in brake release position, making correct shoe adjustment impossible.

3. Remove adjusting hole covers from flange plate on all four wheels. Expand brake shoes by turning adjusting screw with tool J-4707 until a light drag is felt on the brake drum (fig. 20).

NOTE: Moving the outer end of tool toward center of wheel, expands shoes.

4. Turn the adjusting screw in opposite direction on all four wheels 14 notches. Brake drum must be free of drag.
5. Replace adjusting hole covers.
6. After brakes are adjusted, set parking brake foot pedal in the fully released position.
7. With foot pedal in fully released position, adjust brake pedal pull rod clevis to give 1/8" clearance between cross shaft and frame cross member at center.
8. Depress foot pedal 1½" (fig. 21) and then pull cables from conduit as far as possible

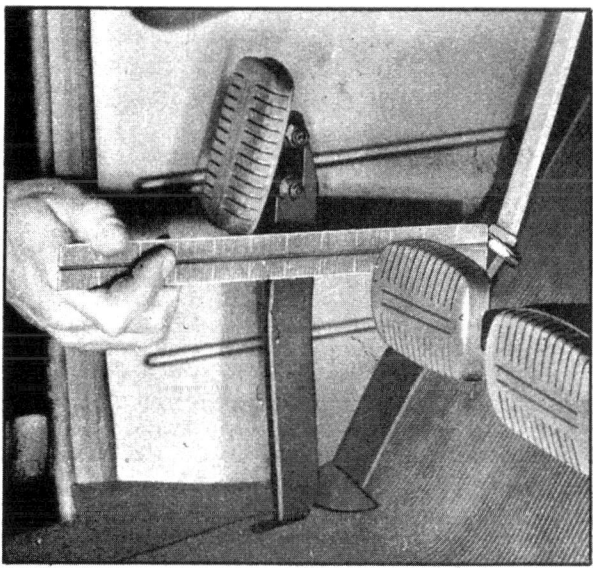

Fig. 21—Positioning Foot Pedal for Parking Brake Adjustment

and adjust cable clevis until hole in clevis registers with hole in cross shaft outer levers and install clevis pins.

9. Depress foot pedal until heavy drag is felt at one wheel. Check opposite wheel for equal drag and readjust clevis if necessary.
10. Install cotter pin in clevis pin and tighten clevis lock nut.

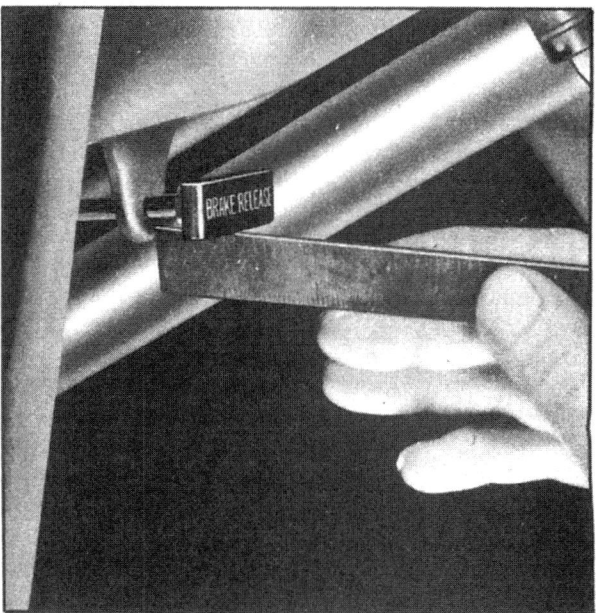

Fig. 22—Checking Release Rod Handle Clearance

11. Check clearance between parking brake release rod handle and rod support bracket. This clearance should be minimum of ½" (fig. 22). If necessary, correct by adjusting release rod handle.
12. Lower truck to floor and test brakes.

Adjustment—Front or Rear—(1951) ½ Ton Major

The major brake adjustment is intended for use when braking action is unequal, severe or otherwise unsatisfactory. This major adjustment must also be performed after new brake shoes have been installed or when the car has been driven sufficient mileage to warrant thorough inspection and cleaning of the brake assemblies and drums.

1. Raise vehicle place on stand jacks and remove all wheels.
2. Check fluid in main cylinder reservoir and add fluid if necessary.
3. Check brake pedal for free action, proper return to stop and proper clearance at toe-board.
4. Check for proper release of main cylinder or leakage within cylinder by action of brake pedal. If improper release or leakage is found, overhaul main cylinder.
5. Inspect all brake hoses, pipes and connections for evidence of fluid leakage. Tighten any leaking connections, apply heavy pressure to brake pedal to build up pressure in system and recheck connections.
6. Remove rear brake drums and front hub and drum assemblies.

NOTE: Since stops are located on brake backing plates to prevent pistons from leaving wheel cylinders, it is not necessary to install wheel cylinder clamps

when drums are removed; however, brake pedal must not be depressed while drums are removed.

7. Clean all dirt out of brake drums being careful not to get dirt in front wheel bearings. Inspect drums and replace or recondition if required.
8. Inspect front wheel bearings and oil seal and if damaged replace.
9. Blow all dirt from brake assemblies. Inspect brake linings for excessive wear, oil soaking and embedded foreign particles. If linings are worn excessively or are oil soaked, replace shoes.
10. Carefully pull lower edges of wheel cylinder boots away from cylinders and note whether interior is wet excessively with brake fluid. Excessive fluid at this point indicates leakage past the piston cup, requiring overhaul of wheel cylinder.

   NOTE: A slight amount of fluid is nearly always present and acts as lubricant for the piston.

11. Inspect rear brake flange plates for oil leaks past axle shaft oil seal. If leakage is evident, replace seal.
12. Tighten brake flange plate attaching bolts.
13. Loosen brake cable clevis lock nuts and then remove cotter pin and clevis pin, disengaging clevis from cross shaft outer levers.
14. If shoes are not removed for additional work, pry shoes away from brake flange plates and clean all rust and dirt from contact surfaces on shoes and flange plates, using fine emery cloth. Lubricate contact surfaces sparingly with Bendix or Delco brake lubricant or Lubriplate. On rear brakes, sparingly apply the same lubricant to parking brake strut and flange plate boss under the brake cable.
15. Lubricate front wheel bearings, install hub and drum assemblies and adjust wheel bearings.
16. Install rear brake drums using three wheel nuts to hold drum in position and remove adjusting hole covers from all brake flange plates.

    NOTE: Stamped nuts will not hold drum securely enough during adjustment.

17. Loosen anchor pin nut just enough so that pin can shift in slotted hole in backing plate.

    NOTE: If nut is loosened too much, the anchor pin will tilt due to pull of brake pull back springs.

18. Using tool J-4707, turn brake adjusting screw to expand brake shoes until a heavy drag is felt on drum.

19. Tap anchor pin and backing plate lightly to allow shoes to center in drum. If drag on drum changes, tighten adjusting screw a few more notches and again tap anchor pin and backing plate. Repeat this operation until drag remains constant. Then tighten anchor nut snugly.
20. Back off adjusting screw 10 notches and check clearance at toe and heel of secondary shoe with a .010" feeler (fig. 23). If clear-

Fig. 23—Checking Secondary Shoe Clearance

ance at each end of shoe is not equal, tap anchor pin up or down to equalize clearance

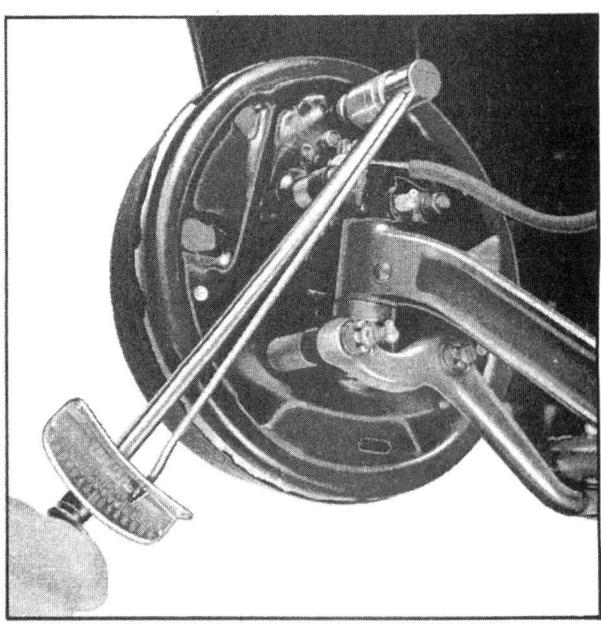

Fig. 24—Tightening Anchor Nut

and then tighten anchor nut to 60-80 ft. lbs. torque (fig. 24).
21. Install wheels and tighten adjusting screw until a light drag is felt. Then back off 14 notches and replace hole covers.
22. After service brakes are adjusted, set parking brake foot pedal in fully released position.
23. With foot pedal in fully released position, adjust brake pedal pull rod clevis to give ⅛" clearance between cross shaft and frame cross member at center.
24. Depress foot pedal 1½" (fig. 21) and then pull cables from conduit as far as possible and adjust cable clevis until hole in clevis registers with hole in cross shaft outer levers and install clevis pin.
25. Depress foot pedal until a heavy drag is felt at one wheel. Check opposite wheel for equal drag and readjust clevis if necessary.
26. Install cotter pin in clevis pin and tighten clevis lock nut.
27. Check clearance between parking brake release rod handle and rod support bracket. This clearance should be ½" (fig. 22). If necessary, correct by adjusting the release rod handle.
28. Lower truck to floor and test brakes.

Front and Rear—(1948-50) ½ ton, (1948-51) ¾ ton; Front—(1948-51) 1, 1½ and 2 ton.

1. Jack all wheels clear of floor and remove adjusting hole covers from flange plate.

Fig. 25—Adjusting Brakes

2. Through hole in flange plate, insert tool J-4707 and engage teeth of adjusting wheel on wheel cylinder (fig. 25).
3. Turn adjusting wheel until shoe drags slightly and then turn adjusting wheel back five notches to insure running clearance.

NOTE: Turn adjusting wheel in a clockwise direction looking toward center of brake from end of cylinder being adjusted to expand shoe.

4. Repeat this operation on each shoe in each brake and replace hole covers in flange plate.
5. Lower truck to floor.

Rear—(1948-51) 1 ton and (1948-50) 1½ and 2 ton.

1. Jack rear wheels clear of floor.
2. With an open end wrench, engage adjusting pinion stud (fig. 26).

Fig. 26—Adjusting Heavy Duty Truck Rear Brakes

3. Turn this stud in a clockwise direction, looking directly at flange plate, from center of truck, until shoe drags slightly.
4. Back off stud ⅔ of a turn or four sides of the hex stud to insure proper running clearance.
5. Repeat this operation on each shoe in each brake.
6. Lower rear of truck to floor.

Rear—(1951) 1½, 2 ton.

1. Jack rear wheels clear of floor and remove adjusting hole covers from flange plates.
2. Using tool J-4707 (fig. 27), turn rear adjusting screw until a light dragging contact is felt on the brake drum and then back off 3 notches. Turn front adjusting screw until a light dragging contact is felt on the brake drum and back off 3 notches. Install adjusting hole covers.
3. Repeat above operation on the other rear wheel.

NOTE: Moving the outer end of the adjusting tool toward the center of the wheel expands the shoes.

4. Lower rear of truck to floor.

BRAKES 5-14

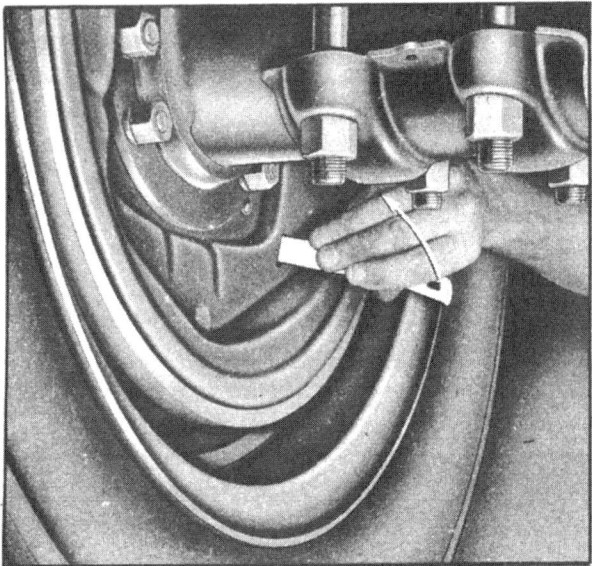

Fig. 27—Adjusting (1951) 1½ and 2 Ton Rear Brakes

PARKING BRAKE ADJUSTMENT

The parking brake on all (1951) ½ ton trucks must be adjusted **each time** the service brakes are adjusted as outlined under "Adjustment—Front and Rear (1951) ½ Ton". The parking brake used on all (1951) 1½ and 2 ton trucks, being a propeller shaft brake, entirely independent of the service brakes, must be adjusted as required. On all other truck models the parking brake adjustment should be checked and readjusted, if necessary, each time the hydraulic service brakes are adjusted.

All (1948-51) ¾ and 1 Ton Forward Control; (1948-50) ½ Ton.

1. With the hydraulic brakes adjusted, set parking brake foot pedal in the fully released position.
2. Loosen check nut "B" and remove cotter pin and clevis pin at "A" (fig. 19).
3. Turn clevis "C" to adjust cable length so that hole in clevis registers with hole in cross shaft lever when cable is pulled out of conduit by hand until a positive stop is felt.
4. Replace clevis pin "A" and cotter pin and tighten check nut "B".
5. If further adjustment is necessary, proceed as in step No. 3.

   NOTE: Never attempt to eliminate either shoe drag or unequal braking by using wheel cylinder adjustment. Hand brake adjustments must be made at points "A", "B", and "C".

6. On (1948-50) models, check the parking brake release rod handle for a minimum clearance of ½" with the rod support bracket (fig. 22).

Adjust at the release rod lower end. The (1951) models have no adjustment of this rod, but handle may be adjusted.

All (1948-51) 1 Ton except Forward Control; (1948-50) 1½ and 2 Ton

The parking brake cables on the 1 ton are located outside the frame while the cables on the 1½ and 2 ton models are located inside the frame.

1. With hydraulic brakes adjusted, set hand brake lever in the fully released notch of the ratchet sector.
2. Loosen the check nuts at the cable ends and remove cotter pin and clevis pin.
3. Pull the cables out of the conduit by hand until a positive stop is felt. While holding the cable in this position, adjust the clevis until hole in clevis registers with hole in cross shaft lever. Then tighten the check nuts securely.

All (1951) 1½ and 2 Ton

1. Set hand brake lever in the fully release notch of the ratchet sector.
2. Loosen lock nut "D" and draw up adjusting bolt "A" (fig. 28) to secure clearance between outer shoe facing and brake drum of .010"-.015" measured at a point directly above bolt "A". Then hold bolt and tighten lock nut securely.

Fig. 28—Propellor Shaft Brake

3. Loosen lock nut "C" and draw up nut "B" to secure .010"-.015" clearance between inner shoe facing and brake drum. Then hold nut "B" and tighten lock nut "C" securely.
4. Recheck both facing to drum clearances.

MAJOR SERVICE OPERATIONS

In all cases of brake complaints denoting actual brake lining or shoe failure, the brake drums should be removed and before disassembly of the shoes from the flange plate, all linings should be inspected for wear, improper alignment causing uneven wear and oil and grease on the linings. If any of these conditions exist, it will be necessary to replace or reline the shoes. If, in checking the linings, it is noticed that they have the appearance of being glazed, this is a normal condition with the type lining used. Do not use a wire brush or an abrasive on the lining to destroy this glazed surface as it is essential for proper operation.

On the front and rear of all (1948-51) ¾ and 1 ton trucks, (1948-50) ½, 1½ and 2 ton, and the front only of all (1951) 1½ and 2 ton, satisfactory performance can be obtained by replacing only the forward shoes when the reverse shoe linings do not show excessive wear. Tests have shown that in most cases, on these models, the reverse shoe lining will outlast two sets of forward shoe linings. This is true of both front and rear wheel brakes.

Shoes should be replaced in sets—that is, both forward shoes on the front wheels or both forward and reverse shoes on the front wheels. The same is true on the rear wheels.

The brakes as used on the front and rear of all (1951) ½ ton trucks and the brakes used on the rear of all (1951) 1½ and 2 ton trucks differ in construction and wear characteristics from all other truck models and when brake lining replacement is necessary, all shoes and linings should be replaced. In no case should a single lining and shoe be replaced. In exceptional cases, on ½ ton models, it may be satisfactory to replace the shoes and linings on both front wheels or both rear wheels.

BRAKE SHOE REPLACEMENT

(1951) ½ TON—FRONT OR REAR

Removal

1. Raise vehicle and place on stand jacks.
2. Disconnect parking brake cables from parking brake cross shaft outer levers.
3. Remove wheels, back off brake adjustment and remove rear brake drums and front wheel hub and drum assemblies.

   NOTE: Since stops are located on brake backing plates to prevent pistons from leaving wheel cylinders, it is not necessary to install wheel cylinder clamps when drums are removed; however, brake pedal must not be depressed while drums are removed.

4. Unhook brake shoe pull back springs from anchor pin using Brake Spring Remover and Replacer KMO-526 (fig. 29).

Fig. 29—Removing Shoe Pull Back Spring

5. Remove brake shoe hold down pins and springs using Hold Down Spring Assembly Tool J-4712 (fig. 30).

Fig. 30—Removing Brake Shoe Hold Down Spring

6. Spread shoes to clear wheel cylinder connecting links and remove shoes from backing plate (fig. 31).
7. Separate the brake shoes by removing adjusting screw and spring.
8. Remove parking brake lever from secondary brake shoe (rear only).
9. Clean all dirt out of brake drum using care to avoid getting dirt into front wheel bearings. Inspect drums for roughness, scoring or

BRAKES 5-16

Fig. 31—Removing Shoe Assemblies

out-of-round. Replace or recondition drums as necessary.

10. Inspect wheel bearings and oil seal and replace any necessary parts.
11. Carefully pull lower edges of wheel cylinder boots away from cylinders and note whether interior is wet excessively with brake fluid. Excessive fluid at this point indicates leakage past piston cups, requiring overhaul of wheel cylinder.

NOTE: A slight amount of fluid is nearly always present and acts as lubricant for the piston.

12. If working at rear wheels, inspect backing plate for oil leakage past axle shaft oil seals. Install new seals if necessary.
13. Check all brake flange plate attaching bolts to make sure they are tight. Clean all rust and dirt from shoe contact faces (fig. 32) on flange plate, using fine emery cloth.

Installation

1. Inspect new linings and make sure there are no nicks or burrs or bonding material on shoe edge where contact is made with brake flange plate or on any of the contact surfaces.

NOTE: Keep hands clean while handling brake shoes. Do not permit oil or grease to come in contact with linings.

2. If working on rear brakes, lubricate parking brake cables.
3. On rear brakes only, lubricate fulcrum end of parking brake lever and the bolt with Bendix or Delco brake lube or Lubriplate, then, attach lever to secondary shoe with bolt, spring washer, lockwasher, and nut. Make sure that lever moves freely.
4. Lubricate threads and socket end of adjusting screw with Bendix or Delco brake lube or Lubriplate.
5. Connect brake shoes together with adjusting screw spring, then place adjusting screw, socket and nut in position (fig. 33).

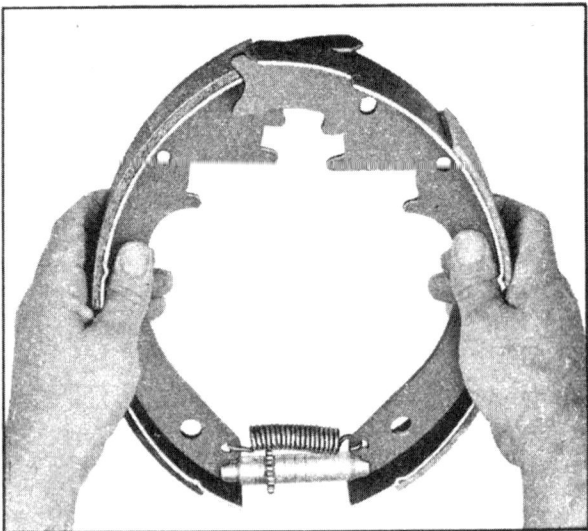

Fig. 33—Brake Shoe Assembly

CAUTION: The socket and star wheel must be adjacent to the primary (front) shoe on the brakes on the left side and adjacent to the secondary (rear) shoe on the brakes on the right side.

6. Attach brake shoes to brake flange plates with the hold down pins and springs using tool J-4712, at the same time engaging shoes with wheel cylinder connecting links. The primary shoe (short lining) goes forward.

Fig. 32—Brake Shoe Contact Faces

7. On rear brakes, connect cable to parking brake lever and install strut between lever and primary shoe as installation is made.
8. If old brake pull back springs are nicked, distorted, or if strength is doubtful, install new springs. Hook springs in shoes and using Brake Spring Remover and Replace KMO 526, install spring connected to primary shoe over anchor (fig. 34) and then spring connected to secondary shoe over anchor.

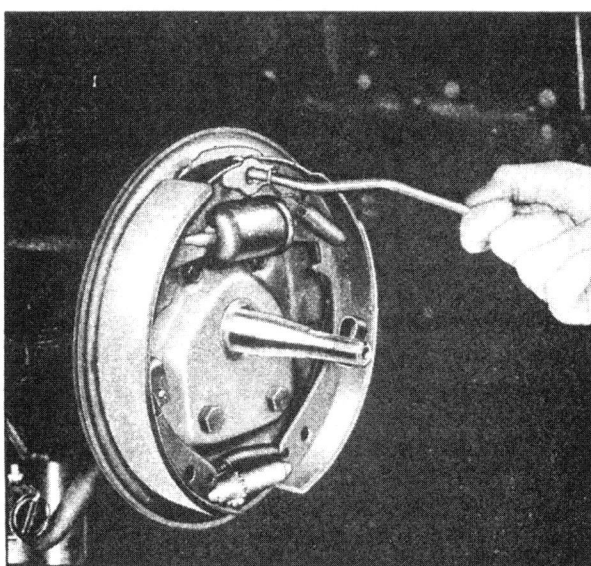

Fig. 34—Installing Shoe Pull Back Spring

9. Pry shoes away from backing plate and lubricate shoe contact surfaces with a thin coating of Bendix or Delco brake lube or Lubriplate. On rear wheels, sparingly apply this same lubricant where brake cable contacts brake flange plate.

CAUTION: Be careful to keep lubricant off facing.

10. Install brake drums. If working on front brakes, lubricate and adjust wheel bearings. Remove adjusting hole covers from backing plates.

NOTE: Use three wheel nuts to hold rear drums in position.

11. Centralize brake shoes and set anchor pin, then adjust all brakes and brake cables as outlined under "Minor Service Operations, Adjustment—Front or Rear—(1951) ½ Ton—Major" steps 17 through 28.

FRONT (1948-50) ½ TON; (1948-51) ¾, 1, 1½ AND 2 TON

Removal

1. Raise vehicle and place on stand jacks.
2. Remove wheels, back off brake adjustment and remove drums.

NOTE: Front brake drums are non-demountable on all models except ¾ and 1 ton and are removed with front wheel hubs and bearings.

3. Install wheel cylinder clamps KMO-145 (fig. 35), to keep wheel cylinder pistons in place

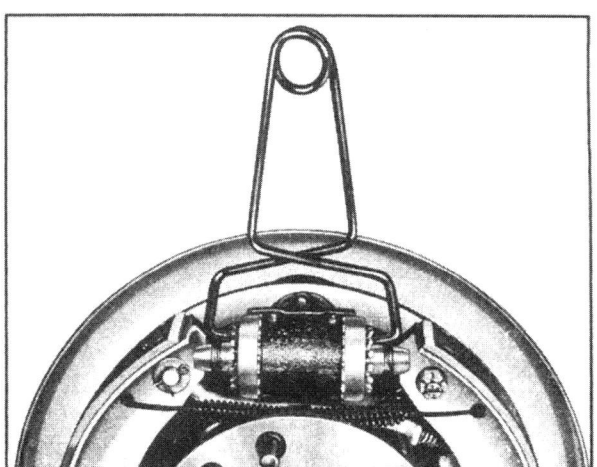

Fig. 35—Brake Wheel Cylinder Clamp

and to prevent leakage of fluid while replacing shoes.

4. Remove brake shoe retracting spring with Brake Spring Pliers KMO-142 (fig. 36).

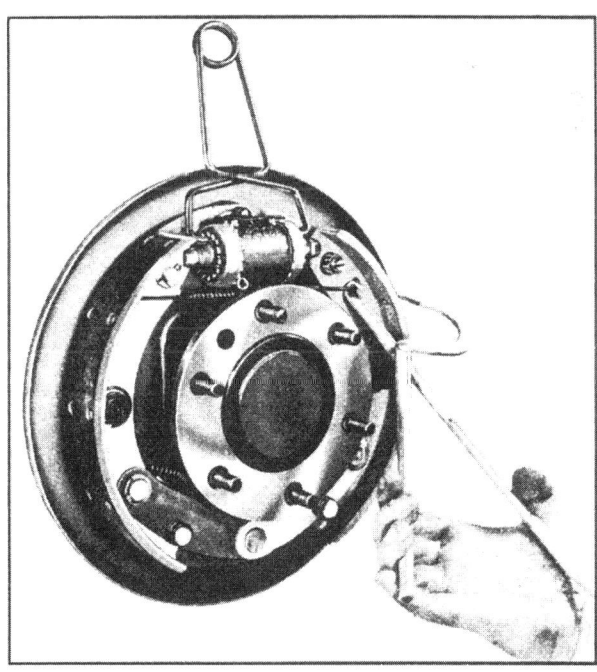

Fig. 36—Removing Brake Shoe Retracting Spring

5. On (1948) ½ and ¾ ton vehicles, remove brake shoe conical springs and pins.
6. Remove brake shoe anchor pin lock and pin and remove shoes.

7. Disassemble articulating links from shoes by removing friction spring locks, pins and springs.

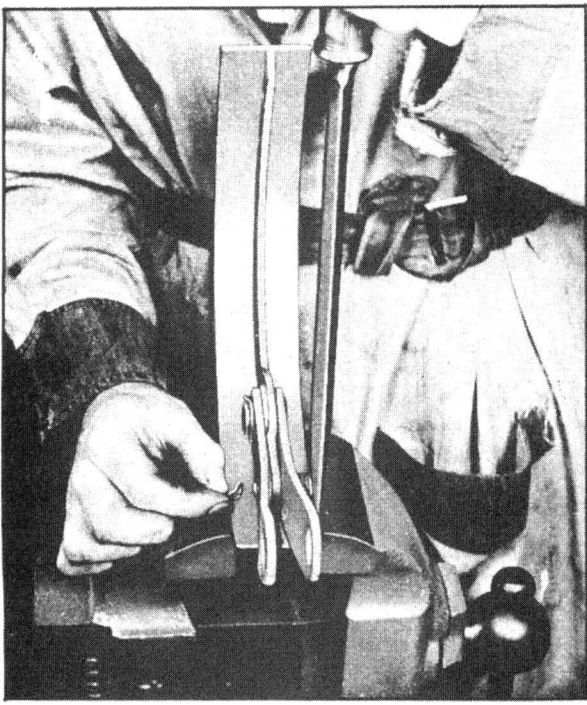

Fig. 37—Installing Articulating Link Pin Retainer

Installation

1. Assemble articulating links, pins, friction springs and locks to new brake shoes.

   NOTE: To facilitate installation of link pin lock, install shoe in vise and compress spring with screwdriver (fig. 37).

2. Attach new brake shoe assemblies to the anchor plate with anchor pin and anchor pin lock.

3. Engage ends of shoes in the slots in ends of wheel cylinder adjusting screws.

   NOTE: On 1, 1½ and 2 ton vehicles, shoes must also enter the shoe guides on anchor plate.

4. Install brake shoe retracting spring, using Brake Spring Pliers, KMO-142.

   NOTE: Use metal strip between point of pliers and lining.

5. On (1948) ½ and ¾ ton vehicles, install brake shoe guide pins and conical springs.
6. Remove Wheel Cylinder Clamp KMO-145.
7. On (1948) ½ and ¾ ton vehicles, check with a .002″ feeler to make certain shoes are against the pads on the brake flange plate (fig. 38). If the shoes do not touch all the pads, use a screwdriver to raise pad that is low.

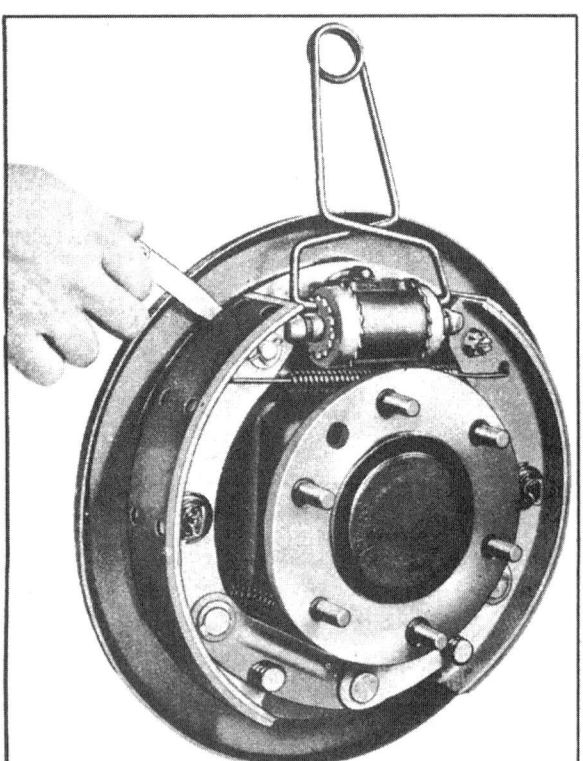 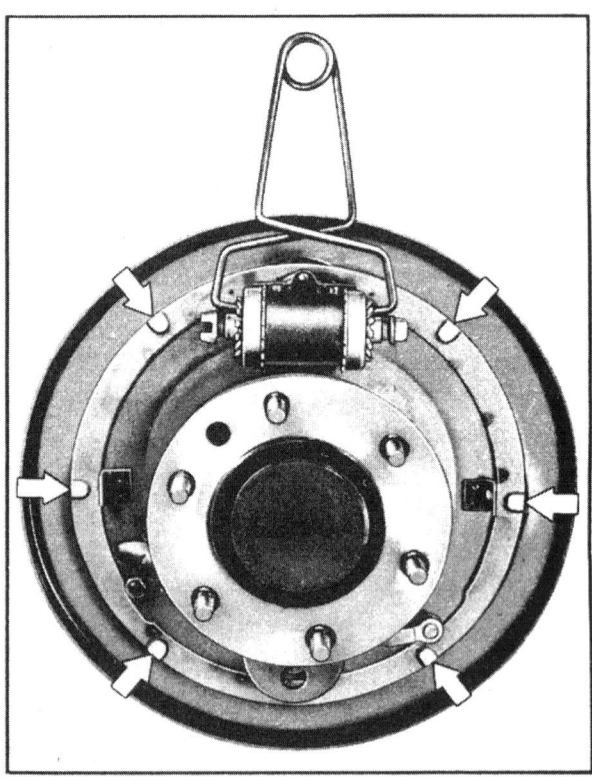

Fig. 38—Checking Alignment of Brake Shoes with Flange Plate

BRAKES 5-19

8. On 1, 1½ and 2 ton vehicles, shoes should move freely without bind in shoe guides.
9. Install drums on ¾ and 1 ton and hub and drum assembly on ½, 1½, and 2 ton and adjust wheel bearings as outlined in section 3.
10. Install wheels.
11. Depress foot pedal several times to align the brake shoe articulating links. Adjust brakes and bleed lines as outlined in this section.
12. Lower vehicle to floor.

REAR (1948-50) ½ TON; (1948-51) ¾ and 1 TON; (1948-50) 1½ AND 2 TON

Removal

1. Raise vehicle and place on stand jacks.
2. Remove wheels, back off brake adjustment and remove drums.

   NOTE: Rear brake drums on ½, ¾ and 1 ton vehicles may be removed without pulling rear hubs by removing retaining screws. On 1½ and 2 ton vehicles, hub and drum assembly must be removed.

3. Install Wheel Cylinder Clamps, KMO-145, to keep wheel cylinder pistons in place and to prevent leakage of fluid while replacing shoes.
4. Remove brake shoe retracting spring with Brake Spring Pliers, KMO-142.
5. On (1948) ½ ton, remove brake shoe conical spring and pins.
6. Remove brake shoe anchor pin lock and pin, one on ½, ¾, and 1 ton, and two on all other models.
7. Unhook toggle lever from parking brake cable on ½, ¾, and 1 ton. Disengage shoes from parking brake links on 1½ and 2 ton and remove brake shoes.
8. Remove toggle lever eccentric bolt and nut from brake shoe on ½, ¾, and 1 ton vehicles, and remove toggle lever from shoe; also, remove parking brake extension link.
9. Disassemble articulating links from shoes by removing friction spring locks, pins and springs.

REAR—(1948-50) ½ TON; (1948-51) ¾ AND 1 TON

Installation

1. Assemble articulating links, pins, friction springs, locks and parking brake extension link to new shoes.
2. Assemble toggle lever to new shoe, making sure that the high side of the eccentric attaching bolt is toward the brake shoe facing.

   NOTE: A flat has been ground on the bolt head to indicate the high side of the eccentric.

3. Assemble shoes to anchor plate with anchor pin and anchor pin lock.
4. Hook toggle lever to parking brake cable.
5. Place spring on parking brake extension link and line up slot of the link so it will straddle the toggle lever.
6. Engage ends of shoes in the slots in ends of wheel cylinder adjusting screws and using a metal strip between point of pliers, KMO-142, and lining, install brake shoe retracting spring.

   NOTE: On ¾ and 1 ton vehicles, shoes must also enter the shoe guides on anchor plate.

7. On (1948) ½ ton, install brake shoe guide pins and conical springs.
8. Remove wheel cylinder clamp.
9. On (1948) ½ ton, check with a .002" feeler to make certain that shoes are against the pads on the brake flange plate (fig. 38). If the shoes do not touch all pads, use a screwdriver to raise pad that is low.
10. On ¾ and 1 ton vehicles, the shoes should move freely without bind in the shoe guides.
11. Replace brake drum, making sure tang in drum is aligned with drain hole in axle flange on ½ ton.
12. Depress foot pedal firmly several times to align brake shoe articulating links; adjust brakes and bleed lines.
13. Adjust parking brake toggle lever and parking brakes. See instructions in this section.

REAR—(1948-50) 1½ and 2 TON

Installation

1. Assemble articulating links, pins, friction springs and locks to new shoes.
2. Assemble shoes to anchor plate with anchor pins and anchor pin locks.
3. Inspect emergency brake lines and link assembly and make sure these parts operate freely without binding.
4. Engage ends of shoes in the slots in ends of wheel cylinder adjusting screws.

   NOTE: Shoes must also be aligned in shoe guides and must move freely in guides without binding.

5. Install brake shoe retracting spring and remove wheel cylinder clamps.
6. Replace brake drums and hub assembly. See Section 4 for adjustment.
7. Depress foot pedal firmly several times to align brake shoe articulating links; adjust brakes and bleed lines.
8. Adjust parking brake; install wheel assembly and lower vehicle to the floor.

REAR—(1951) 1½ AND 2 TON

Removal

1. Raise rear of vehicle and place on stand jacks.
2. Remove wheels, back off brake adjustment, remove three drum retaining screws and remove brake drums.
3. Remove brake shoe pull back springs using Brake Spring Remover and Replacer KMO-526 (fig. 39).

Fig. 39—Removing Brake Shoe Pull Back Springs

4. Remove brake shoe hold down bolt nut and washer and remove brake shoes.

   NOTE: Since stops are located on brake backing plates to prevent pistons from leaving wheel cylinders, it is not necessary to install wheel cylinder clamps when drums are removed; however, brake pedal must not be depressed while drums are removed.

5. Clean all dirt out of brake drums. Inspect drums for roughness, scoring or out-of-round. Replace or recondition drums as necessary.
6. Inspect brake flange plate for oil leakage past axle shaft oil seal. Install new seals if necessary.
7. Check brake flange plate attaching bolts to make sure they are tight. Clean all dirt and rust from shoe contact faces on flange plate, (fig. 40), using fine emery cloth.
8. Carefully pull lower edge of wheel cylinder boots away from cylinders and note whether interior is wet excessively with brake fluid. Excessive fluid at this point indicates leakage past piston cups requiring overhaul of wheel cylinders.

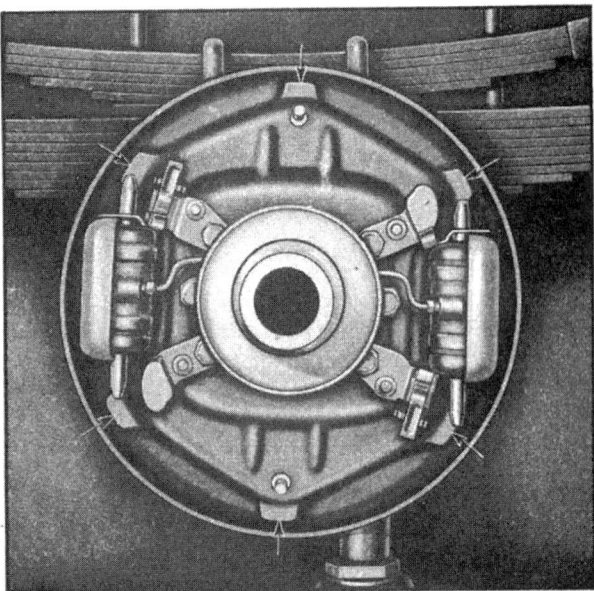

Fig. 40—Flange Plate Shoe Contact Faces

NOTE: A slight amount of fluid is nearly always present and acts as lubricant for the piston.

9. Inspect wheel cylinder pipe connections for brake fluid leak. If leaking, tighten connections or replace fluid line.

Installation

1. Inspect new linings and make sure there are no nicks or burrs on shoe edge where contact is made with the brake flange plate or on any other contact surfaces.

   NOTE: Keep hands clean while handling brake shoes. Do not permit oil or grease to come in contact with linings.

Fig. 41—Installing Brake Shoe Pull Back Springs

2. Place light film of Bendix or Delco brake lube or Lubriplate on primary (sliding pivot) anchors and on shoe bearing surfaces on brake flange plate. Then install shoes, indexing shoe ends with anchors and slotted ends of wheel cylinders and indexing hole in shoe web over hold down bolt.
3. Place light film of Bendix or Delco brake lube or Lubriplate on hold down bolts and washers. Place washer over bolt and install bolt nut loosely.
4. Using Brake Spring Remover and Replacer, KMO-526, install brake shoe pull back springs (fig. 41).
5. Tighten shoe hold down bolt nuts to give .010" clearance between shoe edge and flange contact faces (fig. 42).

Fig. 42—Checking Shoe to Flange Plate Clearance

6. Carefully install drum assemblies and adjust brakes as outlined under, Minor Service Operations, "Adjustment—Rear—(1951) 1½ and 2 Ton."

BRAKE SHOE—Relining

Bonded Linings

Brake linings on the front and rear brake shoe assemblies of all ½, ¾ and 1 ton trucks are bonded to the shoe which greatly increases the useful lining life. When the brake shoe lining becomes worn to a point where replacement is necessary, it is recommended that factory bonded shoes be used for replacement.

Riveted Linings

Brake linings on the front and rear brake shoe assemblies of all 1½ and 2 ton trucks are riveted to the shoe and replacement of these linings may be accomplished in the field. Care should be exercised that shoes are clean and that linings are installed in a manner that will prevent air pockets between the lining and shoe.

1. Remove the rivets using the deliner punches in a brake shoe relining machine.
2. Wash shoes in cleaning compound and buff them on a wire buffer.
3. Install new lining in place on shoe and rivet two holes at center.
4. In order to eliminate air pockets between lining and shoe which might cause uneven contact or squeaky brake, a brake shoe lining clamp should be used to force the lining against the shoe (fig. 43).

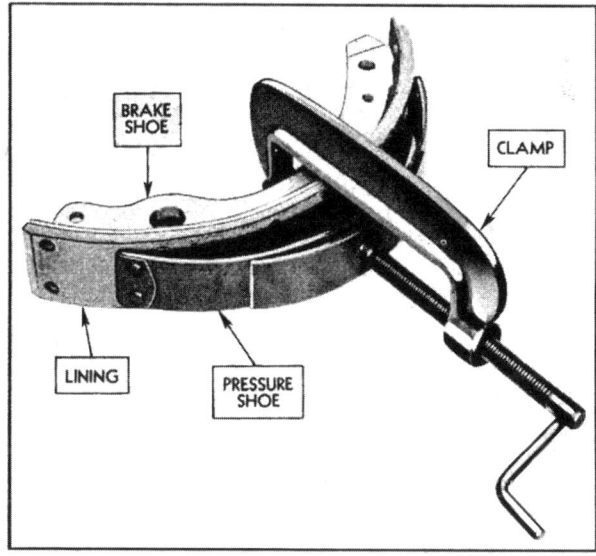

Fig. 43—Installing Brake Lining Clamp

5. After the end holes in the lining and shoe are in alignment, the rivets may be installed in both ends (fig. 44).
6. Remove the clamp and install the remaining rivets.

PARKING BRAKE—(1951) 1½ and 2 Ton

Linings on the propeller shaft parking brake are riveted to the shoes. Removal and replacement of the linings may be accomplished as follows.

1. Remove lever adjusting nut and disengage link from shoe lever.
2. Loosen outer shoe adjusting bolt lock nut and back off adjusting bolt until it clears the shoe web.
3. Remove pin lock from outer shoe upper pivot and slide shoe assemblies from brake drum.
4. Place assembly on bench and remove parking

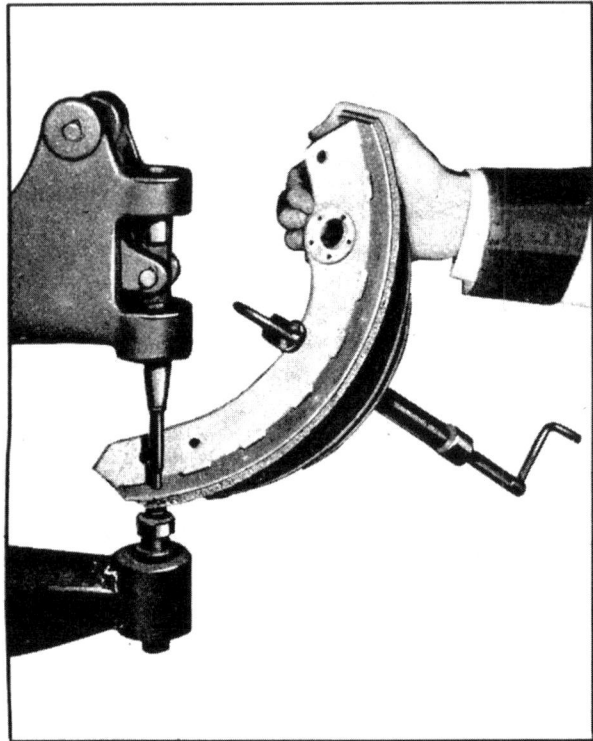

Fig. 44—Riveting Brake Lining to Shoe

brake shoe lever lock rings from shoe lever pins and separate inner and outer shoes from the shoe lever.

5. Remove the rivets, using the deliner punches in a brake shoe relining machine.
6. Wash shoes in cleaning compound and buff them on a wire buffer.
7. Install new linings in place and starting at center rivet holes, rivet linings to shoe securely.
8. Check lining to shoe for air gap, a .010" feeler must not enter at any point.
9. Connect shoes together with shoe lever pins and install lock rings.
10. Slide shoe assemblies on brake drum and index outer shoe upper pivot with pivot pin.
11. Install outer shoe upper pivot pin lock.
12. Engage outer lever with operating link, install adjusting nut and adjust parking brake as outlined under Minor Service Operations, "Parking Brake Adjustment, (1951) 1½ and 2 Ton."

BRAKE CABLE—LUBRICATION

Hand brake cables should be lubricated during a brake reline job or when adjusting brakes if cables feel sticky. Cable lubricators are available from jobbers and should be used to secure a satisfactory job of lubrication.

When lubricating the brake cables, the rear brake drums must be removed on ½, ¾ and 1 ton vehicles in order to make sure that lubricant is not forced into the brake assembly during lubrication.

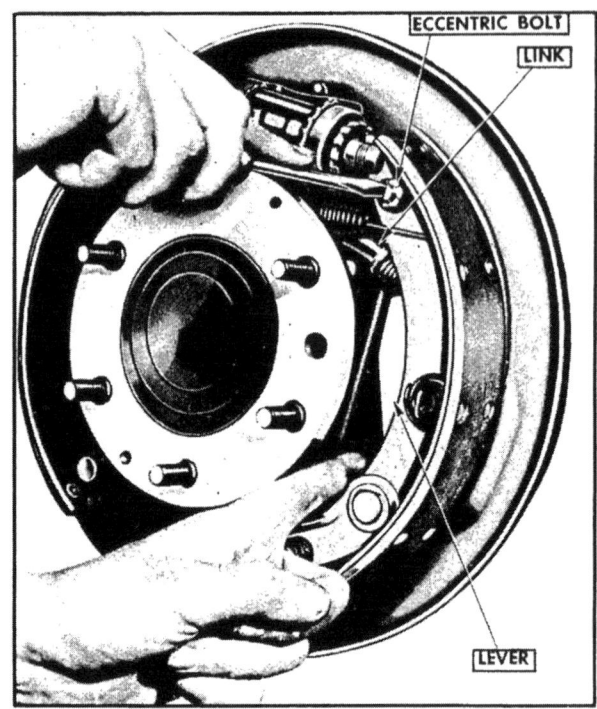

Fig. 45—Adjusting Rear Brake Toggle

CAUTION: A hand gun should be used when lubricating cables as power guns build up high pressures which are liable to damage the brake cable conduit or the lubricator.

PARKING BRAKE TOGGLE LEVER ADJUSTMENT

(1948-50) ½ TON; (1948-51) ¾ AND 1 TON

Whenever new rear brake shoes are installed, it is necessary to adjust the toggle lever with the parking brake extension link, by means of the eccentric bolt. This can only be done correctly AFTER the hydraulic service brake adjustment has been made and the brake shoes are in a fully released position.

1. Remove brake drum and loosen eccentric bolt lock nut.
2. Hold the toggle lever against the shoe and turn the eccentric bolt until there is only a slight clearance between the lever and the bottom of the slot in the parking brake extension link (fig. 45).
3. Tighten the eccentric bolt lock nut and again check for clearance.
4. Replace brake drum and adjust parking brake.
5. Install wheel assembly and lower vehicle to the floor

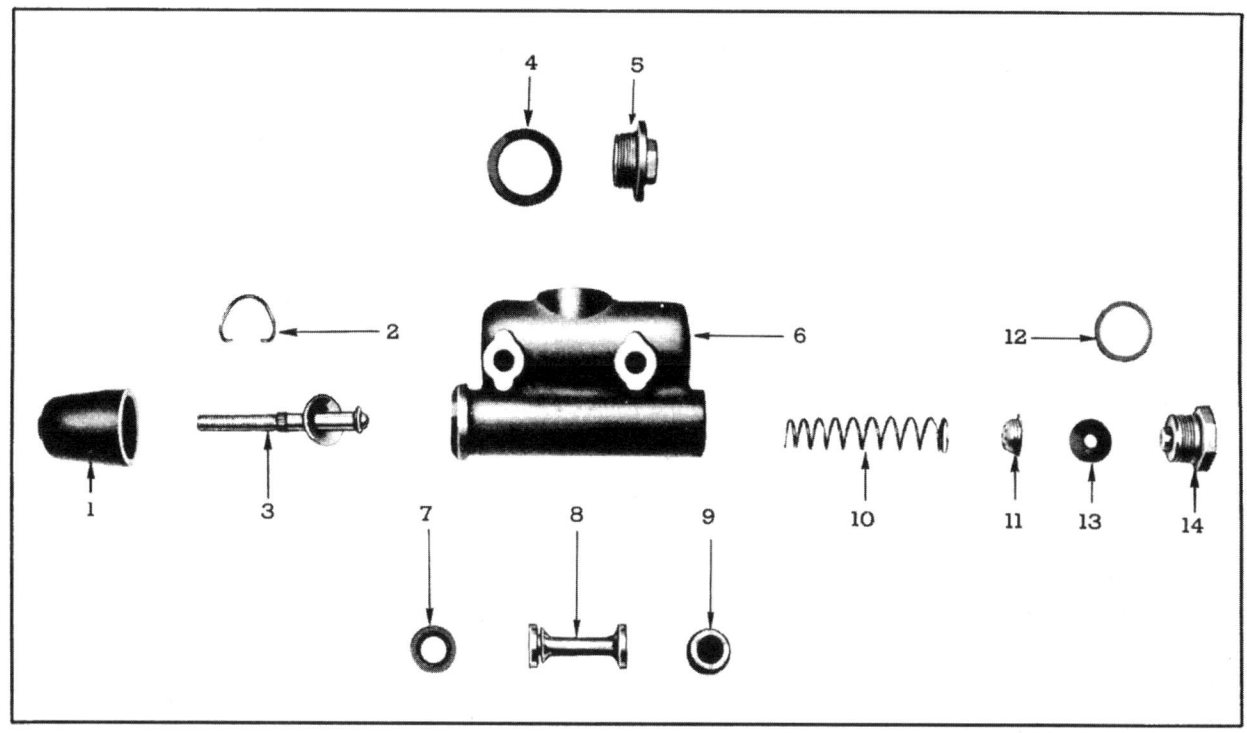

Fig. 46—Main Cylinder Parts Layout

1. Rubber Boot
2. Lock Ring
3. Push Rod Assembly
4. Filler Plug Gasket
5. Filler Plug
6. Body
7. Secondary Cup
8. Piston
9. Primary Cup
10. Spring
11. Valve Assembly
12. End Plug Gasket
13. Valve Seat

MAIN CYLINDER

Removal

1. Disconnect hydraulic line from end of cylinder.
2. Disconnect piston push rod yoke from brake pedal extension.
3. Remove mounting bolts and remove unit from vehicle.
4. Remove push rod yoke and lock nut from push rod.

Disassembly—

Figure 46 shows construction details

1. Remove the end plug and valve seat washer.
2. Remove the valve seat washer from the button on the end plug (fig. 47).

Fig. 47—Valve Seat and End Plug Relation

3. Remove the valve assembly and spring.
4. Remove the main cylinder boot.
5. Remove the pedal stop snap ring with a screwdriver and remove the pedal stop and push rod assembly.
6. Remove the piston with the secondary cup.
7. Remove the primary cup.
8. Remove filler plug.

Inspection

1. Wash all parts in clean alcohol. Make sure that compensating port in main cylinder housing and bleeder holes in piston are clean and open.

   NOTE: Before washing parts, hands must be clean. Do not wash hands in gasoline or oil before cleaning parts. Use soap and water to clean hands.

2. Inspect cylinder bore to make sure it is smooth.
3. Inspect primary and secondary cups, valve and valve seat for damage or swelling. Swelling of rubber parts is due to the use of improper brake fluid or washing parts in gasoline or kerosene.

   NOTE: The primary cup has a brass support ring vulcanized in its base to prevent it from imbedding in the bleeder holes during braking action.

4. Check piston fit in cylinder bore (fig. 48). The clearance between piston and wall of the cylinder should be from .001" to .005".

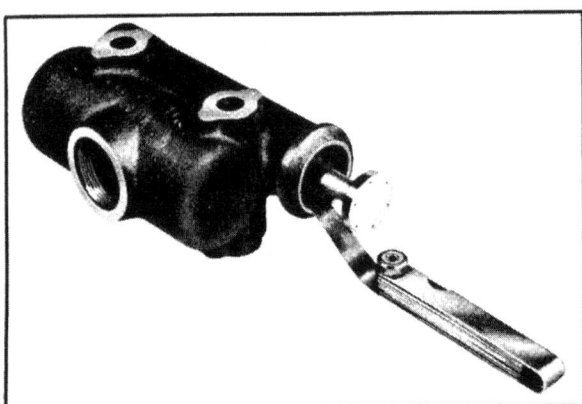

Fig. 48—Checking Main Cylinder Piston Fit

5. Check clearance between the edge of the primary cup and the center of the compensating port. To check this clearance, proceed as follows:
   a. Install pedal stop and push rod assembly and lock in place with snap ring.
   b. Assemble secondary cup on piston and install assembly in housing. Place primary cup in the housing with the flat side of the cup against the piston.
   c. Push the piston cup against the pedal stop and check clearance between edge of primary cup and center of the compensating port. This clearance should be a minimum of .035". If clearance is less than .035", the primary cup must be replaced.

   NOTE: This check can be made by using a small mirror.

6. After clearance is checked, again completely disassemble main cylinder.

Assembly

Whenever a hydraulic brake main cylinder is overhauled, care must be taken to reassemble the valves and seats correctly. Improper assembly of the check valve seat rubber washer will result in its distortion. When the check valve seat is distorted, there will be no check valve seal and there will be a loss of brake pedal travel, and the pedal will have to be depressed or pumped one or more times before actual car braking occurs.

1. Dip a new check valve seat washer in genuine hydraulic brake fluid and assemble over the button on the end of the end plug.
2. Assemble a new gasket over the end plug and screw the plug, valve seat washer and gasket into the main cylinder housing and tighten securely.
3. Inspect valve seat washer through push rod end of the housing to make sure the washer is properly seated.
4. Dip the rubber cups and valves in hydraulic brake fluid.
5. Install valve assembly from push rod end of main cylinder.
6. Install piston spring.
7. Place the primary cup in the housing with the cupped side against the spring.

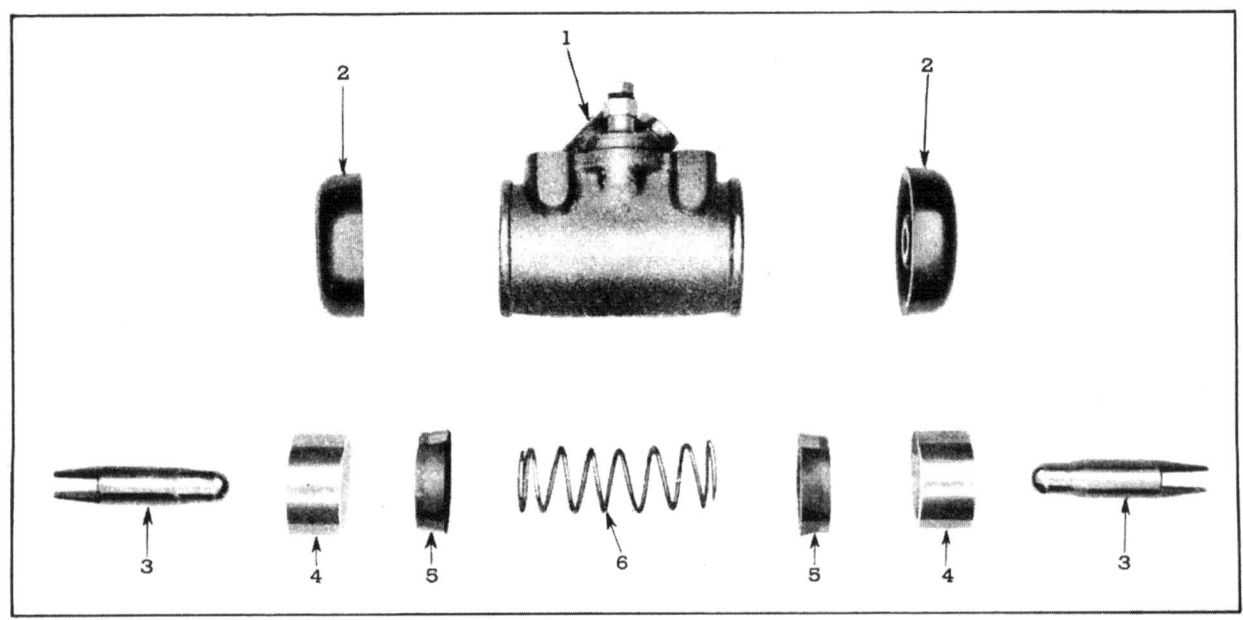

Fig. 49—Wheel Cylinder (1951) ½ ton

1. Cylinder
2. Rubber Boot
3. Connecting Link
4. Piston
5. Piston Cup
6. Spring

BRAKES 5-25

Fig. 50—Wheel Cylinder Parts Layout

8. Assemble secondary cup to the piston and install assembly in the housing so that the bleeder hole end of the piston will be against the flat side of the primary cup.
9. Install the pedal stop and push rod assembly and lock in place with a snap ring.
10. Install the rubber boot over pedal stop and push rod, making sure this seal is tight on the housing. This seal must be tight to keep water and other foreign matter from entering the main cylinder through the pedal stop.

Installation

1. Replace yoke and lock nut on push rod.
2. Replace unit in vehicle and tighten attaching bolts securely.
3. Connect piston push rod yoke to pedal extension and adjust to give proper toe board clearance, as outlined under "Minor Service Operations."
4. Connect hydraulic brake line to cylinder.

5. Refill main cylinder and bleed all brake lines, as outlined in this section.

WHEEL CYLINDER

There are four design types of wheel cylinders used on the various truck models. Cylinders used on the front and rear of all (1951) ½ ton trucks (fig. 49) are sealed at each end by a rubber boot and have no adjustment. Those used on the front and rear of the (1948-50) ½ ton and (1948-51) ¾ ton and on the front only of (1948-51) 1, 1½ and 2 ton trucks (fig. 50) have metal end covers and are adjustable at each end internally. Cylinders used on the rear of all (1948-51) 1 ton and (1948-50) 1½ and 2 ton, also have metal end covers which, however, are adjustable at each end externally by means of an adjusting pinion stud. The wheel cylinders (fig. 51) used on the rear of all (1951) 1½ and 2 ton trucks (two to each wheel) are, like those used on the (1951) ½ ton, sealed at each end by a rubber boot and have no adjustment.

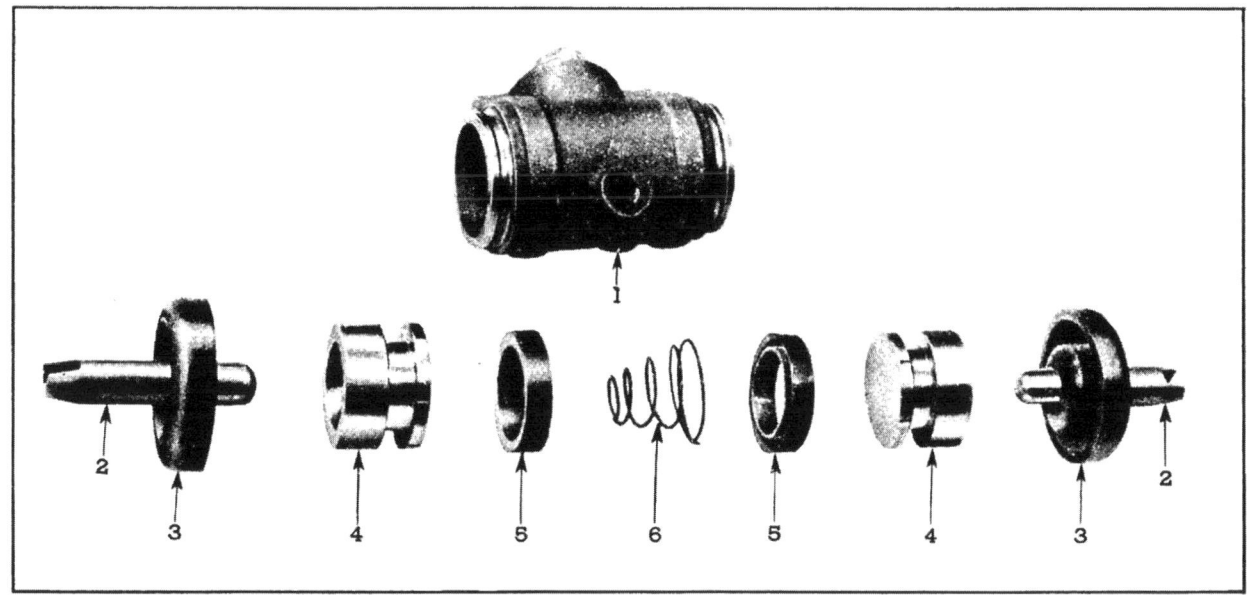

Fig. 51—Wheel Cylinder (1951) 1½ and 2 ton Rear

1. Cylinder
2. Connecting Link
3. Rubber Boot
4. Piston
5. Piston Seal
6. Spring

Removal

1. Raise vehicle and place on stand jacks.
2. Remove wheels, back off brake adjustment and remove drums.

   NOTE: Front drums are non-demountable on all models except ¾ and 1 ton and are removed with wheel hubs. Front drums on ¾ and 1 ton and rear drums on ½, ¾, 1 and (1951) 1½ and 2 ton may be removed by removing retaining screws. On (1948-50) 1½ and 2 ton, hub and drum assemblies are removed.

3. Disconnect brake system wheel cylinder hose from fitting at frame bracket on front brakes and then remove hose from wheel cylinder. On rear brakes, disconnect brake line from wheel cylinder.

4. On (1951) ½ ton trucks, disconnect pull back springs from anchor using tool KMO-526, remove hold down pins and springs using tool J-4712 and remove shoes. On (1948-50) ½ ton, (1948-51) ¾ and 1 ton front and rear and 1½ and 2 ton front, disconnect brake shoe retracting spring from brake shoes using tool KMO-142 and spread shoes. On (1951) 1½ and 2 ton rear, remove pull back springs from both shoes using tool KMO-526, remove shoe hold down bolt nuts and washers and remove shoes.

5. Remove capscrews which hold wheel cylinder to brake flange plate and remove wheel cylinder.

   NOTE: On (1951) 1½ and 2 ton rear brakes, which have two wheel cylinders connected by a fluid line, remove both cylinders and line together.

Disassembly

1. On (1951) 1½ and 2 ton remove fluid line that connects the rear wheel cylinders.
2. Remove the cylinder adjusting covers and adjusting screws or the rubber boots and connecting links.
3. Remove the pistons, rubber cups and spring.

   NOTE: The rubber cups in the (1951) 1½ and 2 ton rear wheel cylinders fit into a ring groove in the piston and should not be removed except for replacement.

4. Wash all parts in clean alcohol.

   NOTE: Do not use gasoline, kerosene, or any other cleaning fluid that might contain even a trace of mineral oil.

Inspection

1. Inspect pistons and cylinder bore for scores, deep scratches, or corrosion. Light scratches and slightly corroded spots in the cylinder bore may be polished with crocus cloth (never use emery cloth or sandpaper). If scratches or corroded spots are too deep to be polished satisfactorily with crocus cloth, the cylinder should be replaced since honing is not recommended.
2. Check rubber cups and cylinder boots for damage or swelling due to improper brake fluid. Replace when necessary.
3. Check fit of piston in cylinder bore using a feeler gauge (fig. 52). This clearance should be .002" to .004".

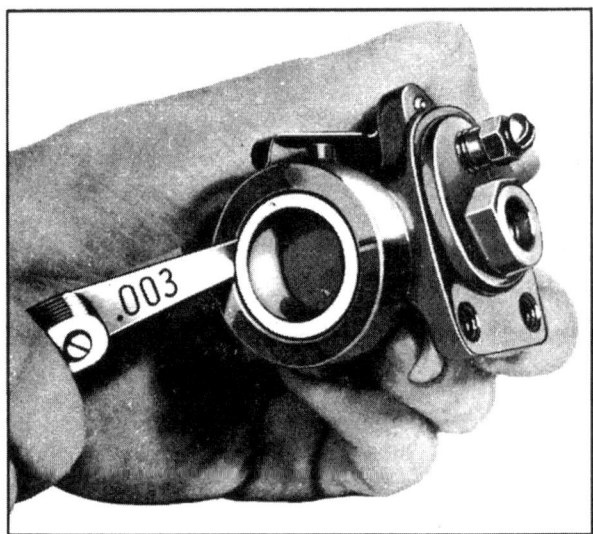

Fig. 52—Checking Wheel Cylinder Piston Fit

Assembly

1. Dip internal parts in brake fluid.
2. Place spring in center of housing.
3. Install rubber cups into cylinder at each end of spring with cupped side toward spring being careful not to damage edges of cups.

   NOTE: On (1951) 1½ and 2 ton rear, where cups required replacement, install new cup on piston so open end of cup will be toward flat end of piston using tool J-4705 (fig. 53).

4. Install pistons with flat side against the flat side of the rubber cups.

   NOTE: On (1951) 1½ and 2 ton rear install pistons with cups in grooves into cylinder with flat end of pistons toward spring.

5. Replace adjusting covers with adjusting screws in place or on (1951) ½ ton and

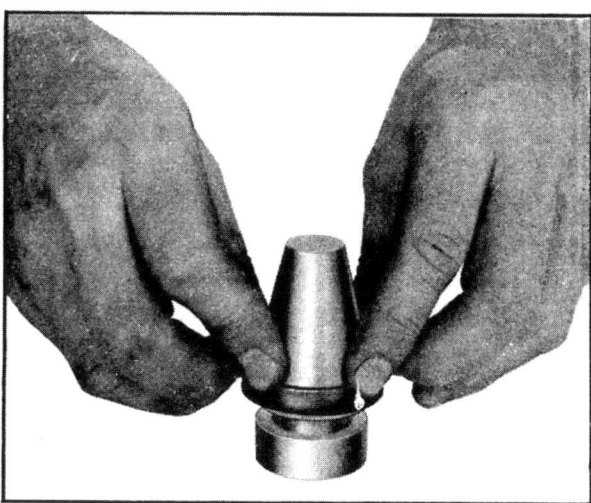

Fig. 53—Installing Piston Cup (1951) 1½ and 2 ton Rear

(1951) 1½ and 2 ton rear, install rubber boots with connecting links in place.

Installation

1. Mount wheel cylinders to brake flange plate, install capscrews and tighten securely.
2. On (1951) 1½ and 2 ton rear, install fluid line connecting rear cylinder to front cylinder.
3. On (1951) ½ ton, replace shoes, connect pull back springs to anchor and install hold down pins. On (1948-50) ½ ton and (1948-51) ¾ and 1 ton front and rear and 1½ and 2 ton front, rotate shoes together indexing webs with guides and shoe ends with slots in adjusting screws and install brake shoe retracting spring. On (1951) 1½ and 2 ton rear, install brake shoes indexing shoe ends with slots in cylinder connecting links, install shoe hold down bolt washers and nuts and pull back springs.
4. Connect wheel cylinder hose to front brake wheel cylinder and to frame bracket. Connect brake tube to rear wheel cylinder.
5. Check and adjust parking brake toggle lever on (1948-51) ¾ and 1 ton and (1948-50) ½ ton.
6. Install brake drums on ½ ton rear, ¾ and 1 ton front and rear and (1951) 1½ and 2 ton rear and install retaining nuts or screws.
7. Install hub and drums on ½, 1½ and 2 ton front and on rear of (1948-50) 1½ and 2 ton and adjust bearings.
8. Bleed all brake lines and adjust brakes as outlined under Minor Service Operations.

BRAKE DRUMS

All front brake drums except those used on ¾ and 1 ton trucks are the non-demountable type, that is, they cannot be removed without removing the hub. Whenever this type drum is removed, wheel bearings must be adjusted as outlined in Section 3. Rear brake drums on ½, ¾, 1, and (1951) 1½ and 2 ton are demountable, that is, they may be removed without removing the wheel hub. On (1948-50) 1½ and 2 ton, the drum and hub must be removed. See Section 4 for procedure.

REMOVAL

Front

1. Jack up front end of vehicle and remove wheel.
2. Remove hub and brake drum asssembly.

   NOTE: ¾ and 1 ton drums may be removed by removing 2 slotted head screws which retain drums to hub. On ½, 1½ and 2 ton, hub and drum are removed as an assembly.

3. Remove brake drum from hub as outlined in Section 3.

Rear

1. Jack up rear end of vehicle and remove wheel.
2. On ½ ton vehicles, remove two stamped brake drum retaining nuts, two countersunk screws on ¾ and 1 ton models, three countersunk screws on (1951) 1½ and 2 ton, and remove brake drum from outer flange of hub. On (1948-50) 1½ and 2 ton, remove drum and hub assembly and remove drum from hub as outlined in Section 4.

Inspection and Reconditioning

Whenever brake drums are removed they should be thoroughly cleaned and inspected for cracks, scores, deep grooves, and out-of-round. Any of these conditions must be corrected since they can impair the efficiency of brake operation and also can cause premature failure of other parts.

Smooth up any slight scores by polishing with fine emery cloth. Heavy or extensive scoring will cause excessive brake lining wear and it will probably be necessary to rebore in order to true up the braking surface.

An out-of-round drum makes accurate brake shoe adjustment impossible and is likely to cause excessive wear of other parts of brake mechanism due to its eccentric action.

A drum that is more than .010" out-of-round on the diameter is unfit for service and should be rebored. Out-of-round, as well as taper and wear can be accurately measured with an inside micrometer fitted with proper extension rods.

If drum is to be rebored for use with standard size brake facings which are worn very little, only enough metal should be removed to obtain a true smooth braking surface. If drum has to be rebored more than .010" over the standard diameter, however, it should be rebored to .060" oversize on the diameter and the brake facing should be replaced with .030" oversize facings.

A brake drum must not be rebored more than .060" over the maximum standard diameter, since removal of more metal will affect dissipation of heat and may cause distortion of drum. Chevrolet brake facing is not furnished larger than .030" oversize and this will not work efficiently in drums bored more than .060" oversize.

Brake drums may be refinished either by turning or grinding. Best brake performance is obtained by turning drums with a very fine feed. To insure maximum lining life, the refinished braking surface must be smooth and free from chatter or tool marks, and run-out must not exceed .005" total indicator reading.

INSTALLATION

1. Make sure mating surfaces of hub, drum and oil deflector are clean and smooth and assemble as outlined in Section 3 or 4.
2. On front, install drum and hub assembly to wheel spindle and adjust bearings on ½, 1½ and 2 ton as outlined in Section 3. On ¾ and 1 ton install drum and retain in place with retaining screws.
3. On rear, assemble drum assembly over hub studs on ½, ¾, 1 ton and (1951) 1½ and 2 ton models and install retaining nuts or screws. On (1948-50) 1½ and 2 ton, install hub and drum assembly, and adjust bearings as outlined in Section 4.
4. Replace wheel assembly and lower vehicle to floor.

TROUBLES AND REMEDIES

BRAKE SYSTEM

Symptom and Probable Cause	Probable Remedy
Pedal Spongy	
a. Air in brake lines	a. Bleed brakes
All Brakes Drag	
a. Mineral oil in system	a. Flush entire brake system and replace all rubber parts
b. Improper pedal toe-board clearance	b. Adjust pedal toe-board clearance
c. Compensating port in main cylinder restricted	c. Overhaul main cylinder
d. Anchor pin improperly adjusted—½ ton	d. Readjust anchor
One Brake Drags	
a. Loose or damaged wheel bearings	a. Adjust or replace wheel bearings
b. Weak, broken or unhooked brake retractor spring	b. Replace retractor spring
c. Brake shoes adjusted too close to brake drum	c. Correctly adjust brakes
d. Anchor pin improperly adjusted—½ ton	d. Readjust anchor
Excessive Pedal Travel	
a. Normal lining wear or improper shoe adjustment	a. Adjust brakes
b. Fluid low in main cylinder	b. Fill main cylinder and bleed brakes
Brake Pedal Applies Brakes But Pedal Gradually Goes to Floor Board	
a. External leaks	a. Check main cylinder, lines and wheel cylinder for leaks and make necessary repairs
b. Main cylinder leaks past primary cup	b. Overhaul main cylinder
Brakes Uneven	
a. Grease on linings	a. Clean brake mechanism; replace lining or shoe assembly and correct cause of grease getting on lining.
b. Tires improperly inflated	b. Inflate tires to correct pressure
c. Spring center bolt sheared and spring shifted on axle	c. Replace center bolt and tighten "U" bolts securely
d. Anchor pin improperly adjusted—½ ton	d. Readjust anchor

Excessive Pedal Pressure Required, Poor Brakes

a. Grease, mud or water on linings

b. Full area of linings not contacting drums

c. Scored brake drums
d. Vacuum brakes not functioning
e. Leak in vacuum lines
f. Vacuum valve sticking

a. Remove drums—Clean and dry linings or replace

b. Free up shoe linkage, sand linings or replace shoes

c. Turn drums and install new linings
d. Lubricate, adjust and test vacuum brakes
e. Test and correct leaks
f. Remove valve, clean, reassemble and test

HYDROVAC

INDEX

General Description	5-29
Construction	5-29
Operation	5-29
Bleeding Hydraulic System	5-31
Maintenance	5-32
Removal	5-32
Disassembly	5-32
Cleaning	5-33
Inspection and Repair	5-33
Power Cylinder Parts	5-33
Control Valve Parts	5-33
Power Brake Hydraulic Cylinder Parts	5-33
Assembly	5-34
Control Valve	5-34
Power Cylinder End Plate	5-35
Hydraulic Cylinder	5-35
Power Cylinder	5-35
Replacement	5-35

GENERAL DESCRIPTION

A hydrovac braking system is used as standard equipment on the 2 ton and 1½ ton special models; it is also available as optional equipment on 1 ton and 1½ ton regular models.

This system makes available to the driver a greater pressure on the hydraulic brake system than he could possibly exert by foot pressure on the brake pedal, thereby greatly increasing the driver's ability to stop the truck quickly when driving at high speeds or when heavily loaded on steep grades.

The hydrovac is a combined hydraulic and vacuum power braking system which uses the vacuum created in the engine intake manifold as an operating force. It is a self-contained unit placed between the regular main cylinder and the main line leading to the wheel cylinders.

The hydrovac is so constructed that in case of engine failure and consequent loss of vacuum, the hydraulic fluid from the main cylinder bypasses the hydrovac unit and the brakes will function with the regular hydraulic system.

CONSTRUCTION

The hydrovac unit consists of three operating units built into one assembly, namely — the vacuum power cylinder, control valve assembly and power brake hydraulic cylinder.

1. The vacuum power cylinder contains a piston and push rod assembly and a piston return spring. When the brakes are in the released position, vacuum is impressed on both sides of the piston in the cylinder and the return spring holds the piston in the off position.

2. The control valve assembly contains a hydraulic cylinder and piston which is connected with a diaphragm, a coil spring which holds the diaphragm and hydraulic piston in the off position except when brakes are applied, vacuum and atmospheric valves attached to a common stem and a valve return spring.

3. The power brake hydraulic cylinder contains a piston and valve assembly and a synthetic rubber seal which prevents the brake fluid from leaking into the power cylinder. A spring loaded rawhide seal mounted in the power cylinder cover prevents the cylinder lubricant from entering the hydraulic cylinder.

OPERATION

In order to simplify the explanation of the operation of the hydrovac, reference will be made

BRAKES 5-30

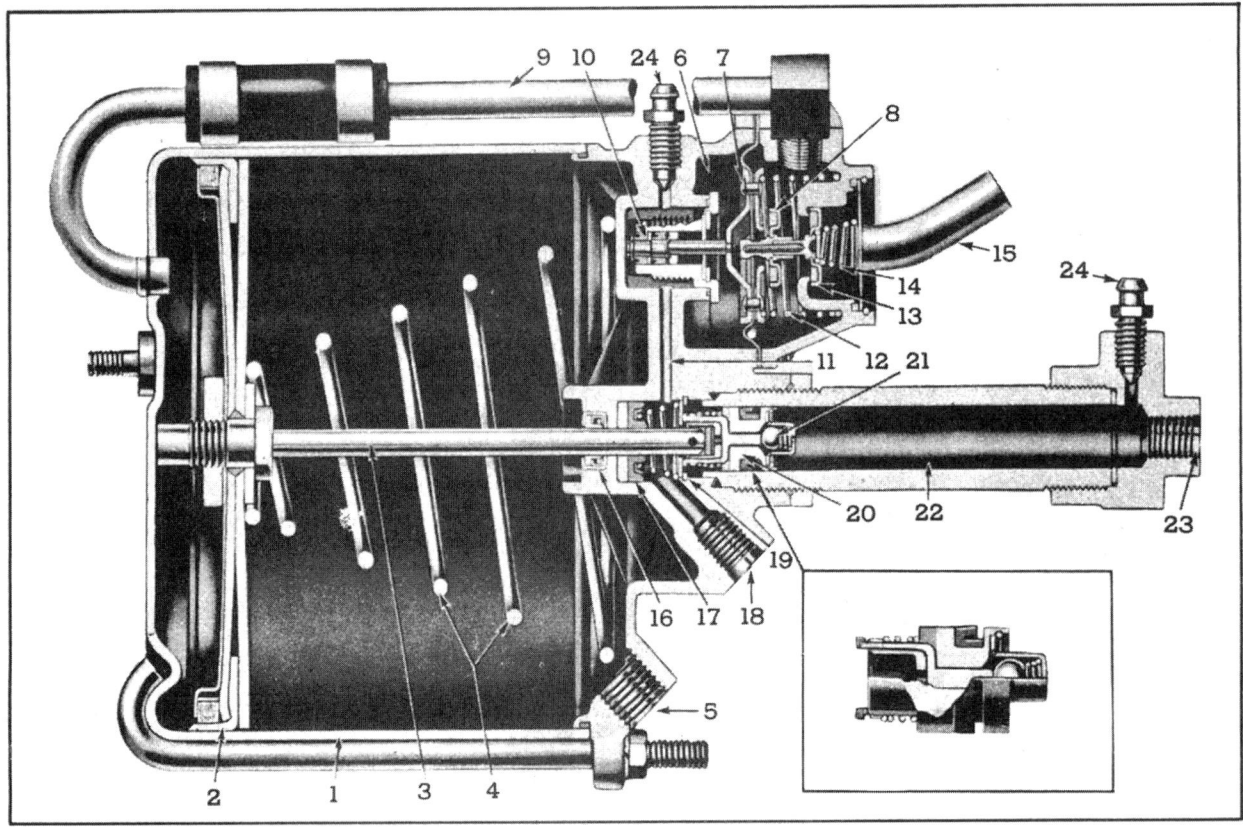

Fig. 54—Hydrovac Unit Cross Section

1. Power Cylinder
2. Power Cylinder Piston
3. Piston Push Rod
4. Piston Return Spring
5. Connection (Vacuum)
6. Cast Opening in End Plate
7. Diaphragm
8. Valve (Vacuum)
9. Pipe Connection
10. Piston (Control Valve Hydraulic Cylinder)
11. Passage
12. Spring (Diaphragm)
13. Valve (Atmospheric)
14. Spring
15. Air Intake
16. Seal (Push Rod, leather)
17. Seal (Push Rod, rubber Hydraulic Cylinder Piston)
18. Connection (Hydraulic, from main cylinder)
19. Stop Washer (Brake)
20. Piston, Brake Hydraulic Cylinder
21. Check Valve
22. Brake Hydraulic Cylinder
23. Connection (Hydraulic to Wheel Cylinders)
24. Bleeder Valves

to the numbers shown on the cross section illustration (fig. 54).

When engine is running, vacuum from the intake manifold is transmitted through the vacuum line to the vacuum connection No. 5 on the power cylinder; thence to the forward end of the cylinder and through the cast opening in the cylinder end plate to the vacuum chamber No. 6 in the control valve body. At this time, the control valve diaphragm and hydraulic piston are being held in the off position by the diaphragm spring No. 12 and the vacuum valve No. 8 is in its open position. This allows vacuum to be impressed on the rear end of the power cylinder through the connecting pipe No. 9. With vacuum impressed on each side of the power cylinder piston the pressure on each side is equal. In other words, the piston is suspended in vacuum. The piston return spring No. 4 holds the piston in the brake released position.

Brake Application

As the brake pedal is depressed by the driver, hydraulic pressure is built up in the brake main cylinder and is transmitted through the hydraulic line to the connection No. 18 on the end plate; thence through the by-pass passages and the open valve in the brake hydraulic cylinder piston assembly No. 20; thence through the cylinder and into the hydraulic line No. 23 leading to the wheel cylinders, thus starting the brake application in the same manner as in the regular hydraulic brake system.

At the same time, the hydraulic pressure from the brake main cylinder is also conducted through the drilled passage No. 11 to the hydraulic cylinder in the control valve body and is impressed on the hydraulic piston No. 10. When the pressure from the brake main cylinder reaches approximately 40 pounds per square inch, it starts to overcome the pressure of the diaphragm spring No. 12 and the hydraulic piston No. 10 starts to move down in its cylinder. This results in moving the diaphragm with vacuum valve seat into contact with the vacuum valve No. 8, thus shutting off the vacuum to the rear end of the power cylinder through pipe No. 9.

Additional pressure applied to the brake pedal causes further movement of the piston No. 10 in the control valve hydraulic cylinder. This in turn moves the atmospheric valve No. 13 off its seat and allows air to pass through the valve and pipe No. 9 to the rear end of the power cylinder.

Atmospheric pressure applied to the rear of the power cylinder piston No. 2 starts to move it toward the front of the cylinder. As the piston moves forward, the push rod No. 3 starts to move the piston No. 20 in the brake hydraulic cylinder No. 22. When the piston No. 20 is moved away from its stop, the hydraulic piston check valve No. 21 is closed by the pressure of its spring. Continued movement of the push rod No. 3 moves the hydraulic piston No. 20 toward the end of the brake hydraulic cylinder No. 22, forcing the brake fluid through the lines to the wheel cylinders for additional braking pressure. The pressure applied to the wheel cylinders is the sum of the pressure exerted by the power cylinder and the fluid pressure from the main cylinder acting on the back of the brake hydraulic cylinder piston No. 20.

To secure partial brake application, it is only necessary for the driver to stop pushing on the brake pedal when the desired rate of deceleration is obtained. Whenever the line pressure from the brake main cylinder stops increasing, the air pressure entering the control valve assembly through the atmospheric valve No. 13 and applied to the diaphragm No. 7, reacts against the pressure delivered by the control valve hydraulic piston No. 10; this tends to close the atmospheric valve No. 13, thus bringing the control valve assembly to its holding position with both vacuum and atmospheric valves closed.

When greater braking effort is desired, pushing farther down on the brake pedal increases the fluid pressure in the brake main cylinder which will again cause the atmospheric valve in the control valve assembly to open and admit additional air to the power cylinder which causes an additional movement of the power cylinder piston. This in turn forces the piston No. 20 farther down the brake hydraulic cylinder, thereby increasing the fluid pressure applied to the wheel cylinders for brake application.

Brake Release

When foot pressure is released from the brake pedal, the pressure in the main cylinder line is released; this in turn removes the hydraulic pressure from the back of the brake hydraulic cylinder piston No. 20, and also from the hydraulic piston No. 10 in the control valve assembly. This allows the diaphragm spring No. 12 to return the diaphragm No. 7 and the hydraulic piston No. 10 to their normal position and in so doing, allows the atmospheric valve No. 13 to close and the diaphragm with vacuum valve seat to move away from the vacuum valve No. 8 opening the vacuum valve, thereby allowing vacuum to be impressed on the rear end of the power cylinder. The vacuum from the engine intake manifold withdraws the air from the rear of the power cylinder, thus balancing the pressure on each side of the power cylinder piston No. 2, allowing the piston spring No. 4 to return the piston No. 2 to its normal position at the rear end of the power cylinder. During this operation the piston push rod No. 3 pulls the brake hydraulic cylinder piston No. 20 with it, thereby returning the piston to its normal position at the inner end of the cylinder. As soon as the brake hydraulic cylinder piston reaches its stop, the yoke in the piston pushes the check valve No. 21 off its seat, allowing the entire hydraulic system to return to its original line pressure and ready for the next brake application.

BLEEDING HYDRAULIC SYSTEM

To bleed the entire hydraulic system, the hydrovac unit must be bled at both bleeder valves before attempting to bleed at the wheel cylinders.

CAUTION: The entire bleeding operation must be performed with the engine shut off and no vacuum in the power system.

1. Remove the filler plug from the brake main cylinder and fill it with hydraulic brake fluid.
2. Attach bleeder drain hose to No. 1 bleeder valve (fig. 55); keep end of the drain hose below the surface of fluid in the drain jar.
3. Loosen No. 1 bleeder valve ½ to ¾ turn.
4. Depress the brake pedal slowly by hand to expel air. When the pedal has reached the toe board, close bleeder valve before returning pedal to release position. Repeat this procedure until air bubbles cease to appear at the end of the bleeder drain hose in the jar and the stream is a solid fluid mass; then tighten bleeder valve and remove drain hose.

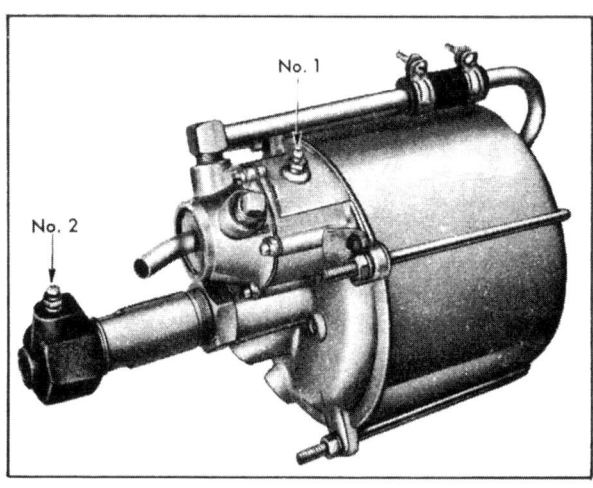

Fig. 55—Hydrovac Unit Bleeder Valves

BRAKES 5-32

NOTE: During the operation the brake main cylinder must be filled with fluid.

5. Following the procedure given above, bleed at the No. 2 bleeder valve (fig. 55), then proceed to bleed at the wheel cylinders according to instructions as outlined under "Bleed Brakes" in this section.

MAINTENANCE

The outside of the hydrovac unit should be cleaned thoroughly at least every six months. All hose connection clamps should be tightened and all pipe fittings and hydraulic connections checked for looseness. One ounce of Bendix Vacuum Cylinder Oil should be added to the power cylinder at the lubrication plug at 10,000 mile intervals or each six month period especially prior to the start of cold weather. The air cleaner should be removed, disassembled and cleaned at least twice a year. If the truck is operating under dusty conditions, the air cleaner should be cleaned more frequently.

To keep this unit in proper operating condition so that it may continue to provide trouble free service, regular maintenance should be performed. If, however, trouble should develop in the system reducing its efficiency, it is recommended that before actually checking for trouble within the hydrovac unit itself, the following points be checked which contribute to improper operation.

1. *Main Cylinder Primary Cup to Compensating Port Clearance*—Make certain linkage is properly adjusted to permit opening of compensating port with brake pedal in normal full released position. Failure to properly uncover the compensating port may cause sufficient pressure to be maintained in the brake system to hold the hydrovac valve in a partially applied position and thus cause dragging brakes.
2. *Restricted Vacuum Lines*—Check for vacuum at the hydrovac by disconnecting the vacuum line at the hydrovac vacuum connection fitting and holding a thumb over the line with the engine running. If no vacuum exists, or if air flow is slow, check vacuum line to manifold for kinks in tubing and collapsed liners in hoses. Also test the check valve to be sure it opens.
3. *Restricted Air Line and Air Cleaner*—Disconnect the air cleaner line at the hydrovac and blow into the line. If the line is restricted check for collapsed hose or tubing. Clean or replace air cleaner.
4. *Brakes*—Check brake shoe adjustment for proper clearances. These clearances should be in accordance with the recommendations given in Hydraulic Brake Adjustment. Excessive shoe clearance will cause loss of pedal, reserve travel. Insufficient shoe clearance may cause dragging brakes.

Removal

1. Remove vacuum line, brake fluid line to wheel cylinders and main cylinder and air cleaner hose from the hydrovac unit.
2. Remove the two nuts and one bolt which attach the hydrovac unit to its mounting bracket on the right side rail of the frame.

Disassembly

1. Remove the bleeder valves from the power brake hydraulic cylinder and the control valve assembly.
2. Place the hexagon end of the brake hydraulic cylinder in a bench vise; then using a 1⅝" wrench, loosen the lock nut on the cylinder tube. Then unscrew the cylinder tube from the power cylinder end plate.
3. Loosen the two clamps on the hose that connect the pipes from the control valve and power cylinder; then slide the hose connection along the pipe connected to the control valve.
4. Loosen the nuts on the power cylinder to end plate hook bolts and remove them by threading through holes in end plate. Remove end plate from power cylinder with piston assembly attached.
5. With the assembly resting on end of piston rod, push down on cylinder end plate until brake hydraulic cylinder piston rod protrudes

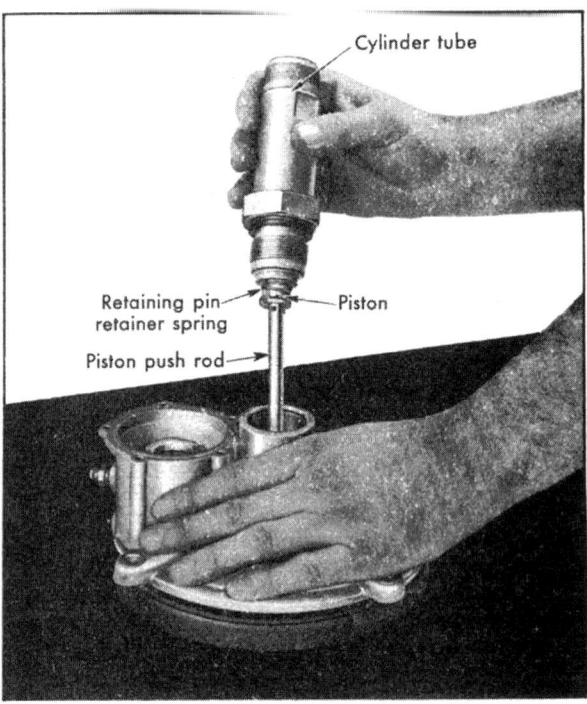

Fig. 56—Method of Removing or Installing Hydraulic Piston on Push Rod

out of end plate (fig. 56). Then compress spring which retains the push rod to piston connecting pin. Remove pin and release pressure on end plate. The brake hydraulic cylinder piston, power cylinder piston and return spring may now be removed from the end plate. Remove brake hydraulic cylinder rubber gasket from end plate.
6. Place brake hydraulic cylinder end plug in a bench vise and unscrew the cylinder tube using a 1⅛" end wrench.
7. Using a pair of long nose pliers, remove the snap ring that retains the brake hydraulic cylinder piston stop washer; then remove the washer, coil spring, spring retainer, push rod hydraulic seal and seat washer from the end plate.
8. Remove the five screws that attach the control valve and poppet assembly to the power cylinder end plate and remove the diaphragm spring, diaphragm and gasket.
9. Remove the snap ring which retains the cover on the control valve and poppet assembly and remove the cover, valve spring and gasket.
10. Using a 1⅛" socket wrench remove the control valve hydraulic cylinder and piston from the power cylinder cover. Remove the piston by pushing it out of the cylinder.
11. Remove C-washer, rubber cup, spacer washer and second rubber cup from hydraulic piston.

Cleaning

Clean all parts by washing the power cylinder, piston and spring in cleaning solvent and the hydraulic parts in alcohol; then dry all parts thoroughly.

CAUTION: It is important that the cleaned parts be placed on clean paper or cloth prior to assembly, to prevent the possibility of dirt being assembled into the hydrovac.

INSPECTION AND REPAIR

Power Cylinder Parts

1. Inspect cylinder for dents and scored surfaces.
2. Inspect piston packing for wear or damage and the piston push rod for wear and scores. If the piston packing is worn it may be replaced as follows:
   a. Place the hexagon nut on the piston rod in a bench vise and remove the nut that retains the piston plates to the piston rod and remove wicking retainer plate, expander ring, cotton wicking, outer plate, piston packing seal and inner plate.
   b. Place the large diameter piston plate in an assembly ring with the chamfered inside diameter up. Place the 3-cornered seal on this chamfered section.

   NOTE: An assembly ring may be made by cutting a 1" section from the end of a power cylinder.

   c. Place the leather packing on top of piston plate with the lip upward.
   d. Place small diameter piston plate on the leather packing with its lip toward the packing.
   e. Install the cotton wicking.
   f. Install wicking expander ring with the grippers pointing upward. Hook the expander ring securely in notch provided near the loop.
   g. Place wicking retainer plate over wicking and expander ring. Register opening squarely over loop in the expander ring.
   h. With the piston assembly still in the assembly ring, place the flat washer and piston on the piston rod. The lip of the leather must extend away from the length of piston rod.
   i. Install the end nut and tighten it securely. Remove assembly ring. Stake nut using a center punch.
3. Inspect cylinder end plate for cracks and the push rod seal for wear or damage. If it is necessary to replace the push rod rawhide seal, it may be driven out with a punch.

NOTE: The seal cannot be removed without damaging it. When installing a new seal, start the end in which the rawhide is free into the end plate, then using a punch whose diameter is equal to that of the seal, press into the end plate until it is seated.

Control Valve Parts

1. Inspect control valve hydraulic cylinder and piston for scored surfaces and the piston rubber cups for wear or damage.
2. Inspect the diaphragm for pin holes or abrasions. Check the vacuum valve seat for corrosion. If the diaphragm is damaged in any way it should be replaced. If the vacuum valve seat is slightly corroded, it may be cleaned with fine steel wool.
3. Inspect the vacuum and atmospheric poppet valves for damage. If the valves are damaged it will be necessary to replace the control valve cover and poppet assembly.

Power Brake Hydraulic Cylinder Parts

1. Inspect the cylinder for scores or corrosion. A badly pitted cylinder should be replaced.
2. Inspect hydraulic cylinder piston for scored surface. Check operation of check valve. If it

BRAKES 5-34

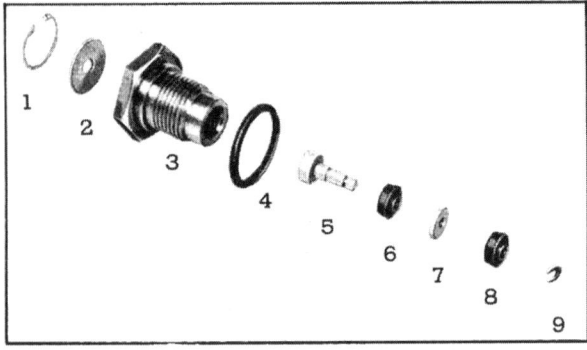

Fig. 57—Hydraulic Cylinder Parts

1. Snap Ring
2. Washer (Piston Stop)
3. Hydraulic Cylinder
4. Rubber Gasket
5. Hydraulic Piston
6. Rubber Piston Seal
7. Spacer Washer
8. Rubber Piston Seal
9. "C" Washer

is not functioning properly, remove snap ring, retainer, spring and ball from piston.

NOTE: Piston rubber cups should be replaced when overhauling hydrovac unit.

3. Inspect push rod synthetic rubber seal and spring for damage.

ASSEMBLY

It is good practice when overhauling a hydrovac unit to replace all rubber parts and make sure all parts are kept clean.

All rubber parts should be dipped in hydraulic brake fluid before assembly.

Control Valve

1. Assemble rubber cup, spacer washer, second rubber cup and C-washer on hydraulic piston. Coat cups with hydraulic brake fluid and install piston in cylinder. Figure 57 shows hydraulic cylinder parts.

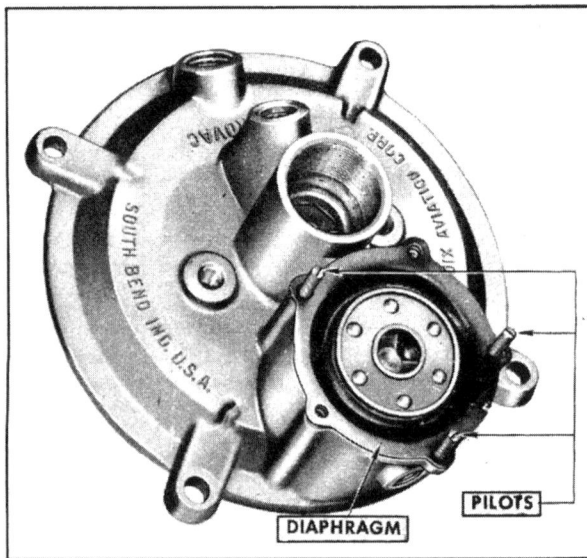

Fig. 58—Diaphragm Assembly Pilots

2. Assemble rubber gasket on hydraulic cylinder and screw it into power cylinder end plate using a 1⅛" socket wrench.
3. Install diaphragm gasket and diaphragm. To prevent damage to the diaphragm when installing the control valve and poppet assembly, install three pilot screws (fig. 58). These pilots may be made by cutting the heads off three 8-32x1" machine screws.

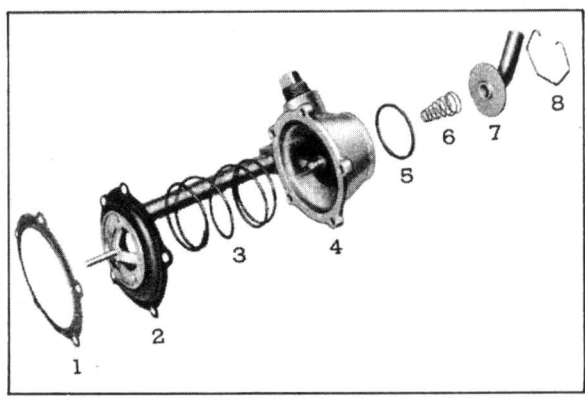

Fig. 59—Control Valve and Poppet Assembly

1. Diaphragm Gasket
2. Diaphragm
3. Spring (Diaphragm)
4. Control Valve Cover and Poppet Assembly
5. Gasket
6. Spring (Atmospheric Valve)
7. Cover with Air Intake
8. Snap Ring

4. Assemble diaphragm spring and control valve and poppet assembly to power cylinder end plate. Install screws and tighten them securely. Figure 59 illustrates the control valve and poppet assembly parts.
5. Install gasket, spring and end cover with air intake tube to the control valve and poppet assembly and lock in place with snap ring.
6. Install bleeder valve.

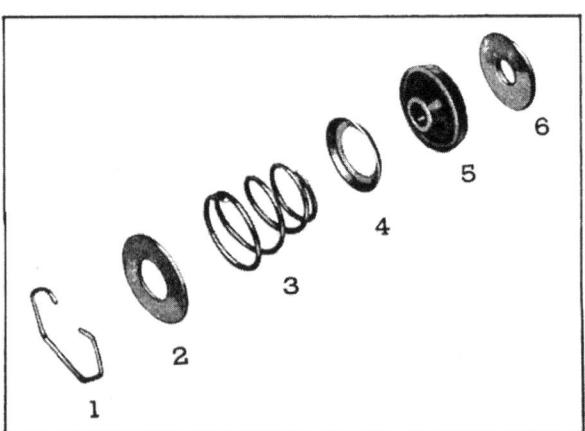

Fig. 60—Power Cylinder End Plate Parts

1. Snap Ring
2. Washer (Piston Stop)
3. Spring
4. Spring Retainer
5. Seal
6. Seat Washer

Power Cylinder End Plate

1. Assemble seat washer, rubber cup, retainer, spring and piston stop washer in power cylinder end plate (fig. 60). Push down on washer to compress the spring and install the snap ring which retains the assembly.
2. Place hydraulic cylinder seal in power cylinder end plate.

Brake Hydraulic Cylinder

1. Install the rubber cup on brake hydraulic cylinder piston. The illustration (fig. 61) shows the piston assembly parts.

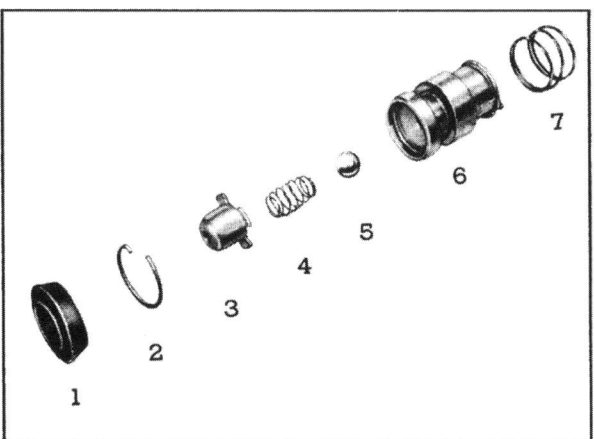

Fig. 61—Hydraulic Cylinder Piston Parts

1. Rubber Cup Seal
2. Snap Ring (Check Ball Retainer)
3. Retainer (Check Ball)
4. Spring
5. Ball Check
6. Piston
7. Spring (Piston to Push Rod Pin Retainer)

2. Thread lock nut on inner end of brake hydraulic cylinder tube and assemble seal ring.
3. Push the piston into the outer end of the brake hydraulic cylinder, then continue to push it through the cylinder until the end of piston protrudes from its inner end.

   NOTE: If assembly of the piston to the inner end of the cylinder is attempted, the rubber cup will be damaged.

4. Place piston return spring over power cylinder piston push rod, then place end of piston rod on a bench and thread the power cylinder end plate over the piston push rod.
5. Push down on end plate until piston push rod extends out of opening in end plate, then assemble hydraulic cylinder piston on end of push rod (fig. 56). Compress spring, install piston to push rod retaining pin, and release spring.
6. While still maintaining pressure on the end plate, screw hydraulic cylinder tube into end plate until it bottoms on seal, then release pressure on end plate.
7. Place copper gasket in cylinder end plug and screw it on to the cylinder tube.
8. Place the end plug in a bench vise, then tighten the brake hydraulic cylinder tube into the end plug using a 1⅛" end wrench.
9. Tighten the hydraulic cylinder tube in the end plate using a 1⅛" end wrench. Then tighten the cylinder lock nut using a 1⅝" end wrench.
10. Install bleeder valve in brake hydraulic cylinder end plug.

Power Cylinder

1. Slide hose connection over pipe extending from control valve assembly.
2. Place cylinder gasket over shoulder on end plate, then dip piston in Bendix Vacuum Cylinder Oil to saturate the piston leather and cotton wicking. Allow excess to drain off.
3. Assemble cylinder over piston assembly. Line up pipe in cylinder with pipe from control valve and slide hose connection into position. Install the hook bolts and tighten nuts securely.
4. Tighten clamp screws on hose connection.

REPLACEMENT

1. Assemble hydrovac unit to its mounting bracket on the frame side rail, then install and tighten the attaching nuts and bolts.
2. Connect air cleaner hose, brake fluid line to wheel cylinders, brake fluid line from brake main cylinder and vacuum line to their connections on the hydrovac unit.
3. Fill vacuum power cylinder with Bendix Vacuum Cylinder Oil to the level of the lubrication plug.
4. Fill the brake main cylinder with hydraulic brake fluid and bleed the entire braking system according to instructions given under the heading "Bleeding Hydraulic System."

TROUBLES AND REMEDIES

HYDROVAC

Symptom and Probable Cause | **Probable Remedy**

Brakes Won't Release or Dragging Brakes

a. Insufficient vacuum cylinder shell length

b. Sticking control valve piston

c. Bent or broken vacuum cylinder push rod

a. Check by measuring the distance from the center of the closed portion of the shell to the open end. Minimum of 5 29/64". Replace shell if less

b. Clean piston and bore. Replace swollen cup and determine cause of swelling. Flush complete brake system with clean brake fluid

c. Replace all damaged parts

Brakes Apply When Engine Is Started

a. Broken or improperly assembled atmospheric valve return spring

a. Replace spring or reassemble correctly

Brake Pedal Kickback

a. Defective or damaged brake hydraulic cylinder piston cup

b. Improperly seated brake hydraulic cylinder ball check valve

a. Clean all parts and replace cup

b. Clean ball and seat. Replace piston assembly

Loss of Fluid from Brake System

a. Defective or damaged brake hydraulic cylinder push rod rubber seal

b. Defective or damaged control valve piston cups

c. Foreign matter under lip of brake hydraulic cylinder push rod seal or valve piston cups

a. Clean all parts and replace seal

b. Clean all parts. Replace all damaged parts

c. Clean all parts. Replace both brake hydraulic cylinder valve piston cups and push rod rubber seal

Air in Hydraulic System

a. Improperly assembled, defective or missing control valve piston secondary cup

a. Provide good cup properly assembled

BRAKE SPECIFICATIONS

Model	Brake Drum Diameter	Facing		Clearance		Wheel Cyl.	Main Cyl.
		Thickness	Width	Main Cyl. Piston	Wheel Cyl. Piston	Size	Size
½ Ton Front Rear	11 11			.001" to .005"	.002" to .004"	1⅛" 1"	1"
¾ Ton Front Rear	11 12			.001" to .005"	.002" to .004"	1¼" 1⅜"	1¼"
1 Ton Front Rear	12 14			.001" to .005"	.002" to .004"	1⅜" 1⅜"	1¼"
1½-2 Ton Front Rear	14 15	.265"-.272" .392"-.412"	2" 4"	.001" to .005"	.002" to .004"	1⅜" 1½"	1¼"

BRAKES 5-37

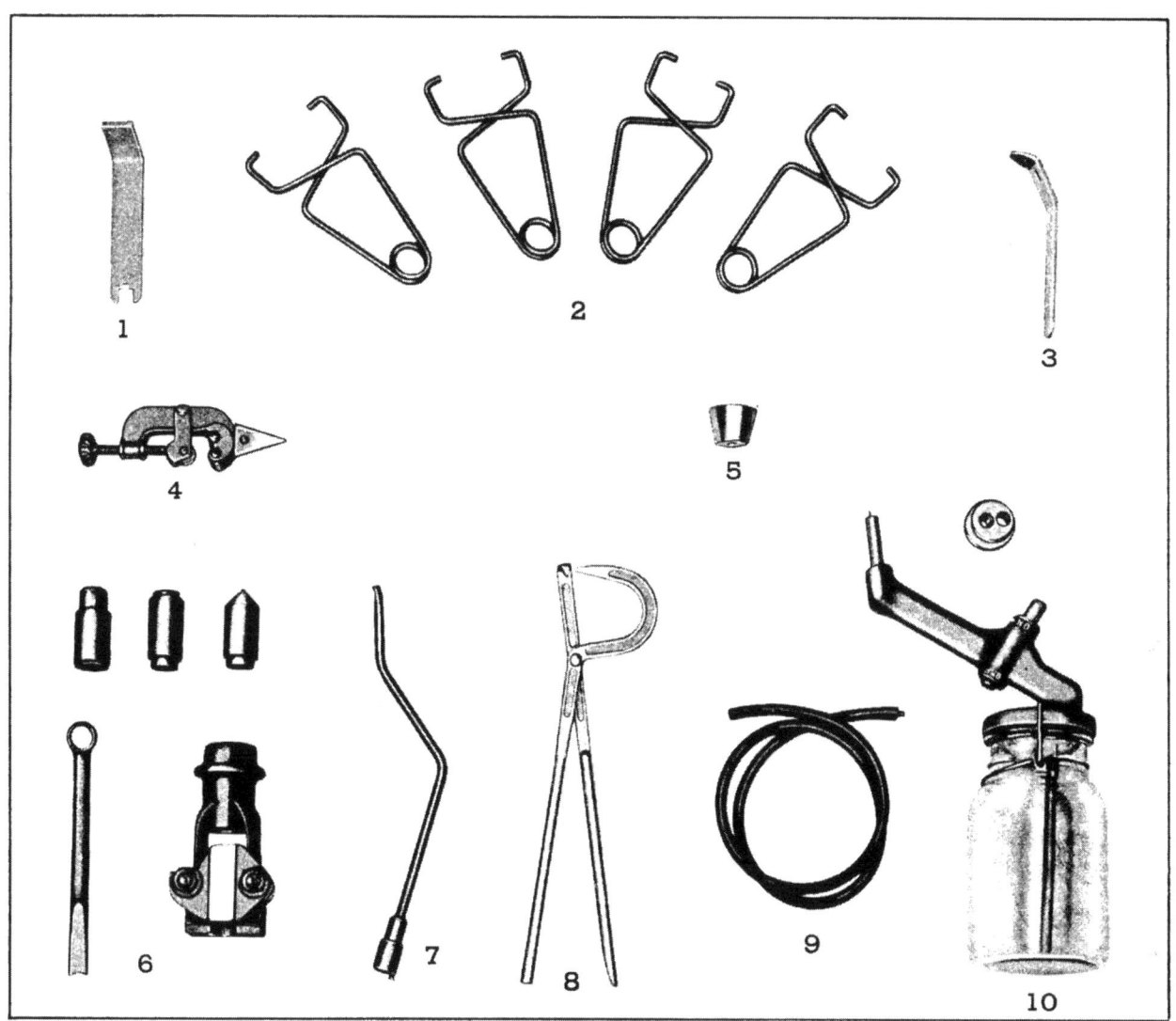

Fig. 62—Brake Special Tools

1. J-4712	Brake Shoe Hold Down Spring Remover and Replacer		6. J-2185-C	Brake Tube Flaring Tool
2. KMO-145	Wheel Cylinder Clamps		7. KMO-526	Brake Spring Remover and Replacer
3. J-4707	Brake Adjusting Tool		8. KMO-142	Brake Spring Pliers
4. KMO-3A	Brake Tube Cutter		9. J-747	Brake Bleeder Tube
5. J-4705	Wheel Cylinder Piston Cup Installer		10. J-713	Brake Main Cylinder Filler

SERVICE NEWS REFERENCE

Month	Page No.	Subject

SECTION 6
ENGINE ASSEMBLY

CONTENTS OF THIS SECTION

	Page
Engine	6- 1
Tune-Up	6-18
Troubles and Remedies	6-41
Engine Special Tools	6-46
Specifications	6-47
Fuel System	6-49
Carter Downdraft Carburetor	6-49
GM Model "B" Downdraft Carburetor	6-58
Updraft Carburetor	6-65
Fuel Pump	6-70
Air Cleaner	6-76
Governor	6-78
Troubles and Remedies	6-79
Carburetor Special Tools	6-80
Specifications	6-80
Cooling System	6-81
Troubles and Remedies	6-87
Specifications	6-88
Clutch	6-88
Troubles and Remedies	6-93
Clutch Special Tools	6-94
Specifications	6-95
Service News Reference	6-95

ENGINE

INDEX

	Page		Page
General Description	6- 2	Rear Mounts—Insulation	6-14
Minor Service Operations	6- 6	Oil Pump	6-14
Valve Timing	6- 6	Removal and Disassembly	6-14
Valve Adjustment	6- 7	Inspection	6-14
Cylinder Head and Valve Conditioning	6- 7	Assembly	6-15
Removal and Disassembly	6- 7	Connecting Rod Bearing Lubrication	6-15
Cleaning	6- 8	Checking Dipper Height	6-15
Inspection	6- 8	Checking Oil Pan Troughs	6-15
Repairs	6- 8	Checking Oil Pan Nozzles	6-16
Replace Valve Guides	6- 8	Connecting Rod Bearings—Adjust	6-16
Reseating Valve Seats	6- 9	Main Bearings—Adjust	6-17
Refacing Valves	6-10	Oil Seal—Rear Bearing Cap—Replace	6-17
Rocker Arms and Shafts	6-10	Engine Tune-Up	6-18
Cylinder Head	6-11	Compression	6-18
Assembly	6-11	Spark Plugs	6-18
Installation	6-11	Battery Test	6-18
Engine Mountings	6-13	Ignition Distributor	6-18
Checking Clearance of New Front Mount	6-13	Coil and Condenser	6-19
Checking Clearance of Used Front Mount	6-13	Ignition Timing	6-19
Rear Mounts—Removal	6-14		

ENGINE ASSEMBLY 6-2

	Page		Page
Fuel Pump	6-19	Oil Seal—Rear Bearing Upper—Replace	6-27
Air Cleaner	6-20	Crankshaft	6-27
Carburetor	6-20	Main Bearings—Install and/or Adjust	6-28
Manifold Heat Valve	6-20	Timing Gear Oil Nozzle	6-30
Valve Adjustment	6-20	Cylinder Block Front End Plate	6-30
Idling Adjustment	6-20	Crankshaft Gear—Install	6-31
Cooling System	6-20	Camshaft, Camshaft Gear and/or Thrust Plate—Install	6-31
Current and Voltage Regulator	6-20	Timing Gear Cover	6-32
Road Test	6-20	Harmonic Balancer—Install	6-33
Major Service Operations	6-20	Clutch Housing—Install	6-33
Engine	6-20	Alignment Correction	6-33
Removal	6-20	Flywheel—Install	6-33
Disassembly	6-21	Connecting Rod Alignment	6-34
Cleaning and Inspection	6-23	Assembly—Connecting Rod to Piston	6-35
Repairs	6-24	Connecting Rod and Piston Alignment	6-35
Cylinder Conditioning	6-24	Piston Ring Fitting	6-36
Cylinder Boring	6-24	Connecting Rod and Piston—Assembly to Engine	6-37
Cylinder Honing and Piston Fitting	6-25		
Piston Pin Fitting	6-25	Oil Pump Assembly	6-37
Camshaft	6-26	Cylinder Head	6-38
Camshaft Bearings	6-26	Rocker Shaft Oil Line Pipe	6-38
Removal	6-26	Engine Assembly	6-38
Replacement	6-27	Engine Installation	6-40
Reaming	6-27		

ENGINE

GENERAL DESCRIPTION

Chevrolet truck engines (fig. 1) are available in two types, both being of six cylinder valve-in-head construction. Engines used on all trucks except the 2 ton models have a displacement of 216.5 cubic inches using a 3½" bore and a 3¾" stroke. The engine used on all 2 ton trucks, which is optional on all 1½ ton models, has a displacement of 235.5 cubic inches using a 3 9/16" bore and a 3 15/16" stroke.

Service operations on the two engines are performed in the same manner and all checks and clearances, except positioning dimensions for the valve guides and adjustments for the connecting rod oiling system, are the same.

The cylinder head assembly as installed on the engine, includes the valve guides, valves, valve springs, rocker arm and shaft assemblies, spark plugs, temperature indicator fitting, water outlet, exhaust and intake manifolds and other assembling parts. The carburetor and air cleaner assembly bolt to the top of the manifold and the rocker arm cover attaches to the top of the head to enclose the valve mechanism.

The cylinder block and crankcase assembly is the major section of the engine as it is fitted with the camshaft, crankshaft, timing gear plate, timing gears, pistons, piston rings, piston pins, connecting rods and miscellaneous parts.

In addition to the above parts, which are part of a cylinder block assembly, the following units are attached to this assembly when in the vehicle; water pump, oil pump, distributor, starter, generator, flywheel, clutch, clutch housing, harmonic balancer, fuel pump and other miscellaneous parts.

The oil pan is fitted with oil troughs and oil pipes for connecting rod bearing lubrication.

A "V" type fan belt operating from a combined harmonic balancer and pulley on the front of the crankshaft, drives the generator, water pump and fan.

The distributor, mounted on the right side of the engine, is gear driven from the camshaft. The oil pump connects to the lower end of the distributor shaft and is driven at distributor speed. The fuel pump mounts on the right side of the engine and is operated by a special cam on the camshaft.

Pistons are cast alloy iron, cam ground to provide slightly greater diameter at right angles to the piston pin. Pistons have three piston ring

ENGINE ASSEMBLY 6-3

Fig. 1—Engine Cross Section

grooves above the piston pin bosses and the bosses have cast bronze bushings installed.

One oil control ring and two compression rings are used on each piston. The oil control ring is used in the bottom groove where the piston is drilled to permit the oil wiped by the ring to return to the oil pan. Both compression rings of the 216 engine are the taper-face type. For (1948-49) models, both compression rings of the 235 engine are the taper-face type, and for the (1950-51) models, the top ring of the 235 engine is a twist-type and the second compression ring is a taper-face type.

Camshaft bearings are steel backed and babbitt lined, providing uniform expansion and long life. The bearings are installed in the cylinder block and finish bored for perfect alignment.

Main bearings are precision interchangeable, thin walled babbitt type with dual advantages of longer life and simplified installation. Babbitt thickness is .003" to .007". This thickness has been determined by test to give increased bearing life and at the same time sufficient metal has been retained to provide for embedability or the ability of the babbitt to absorb foreign particles and so prevent scoring.

The precision interchangeability features of the bearings facilitate engine repair as well as engine assembly because the bearings are accurately machined to tolerances of .0003" and are ready for installation as received.

The crankshaft has four unusually large bearing journals, it is heavily counterbalanced and weighs approximately 70 pounds, all of which contributes to Chevrolet's smooth engine performance.

The four bearing camshaft is designed to provide accurate, quiet valve action and hold the valves open long enough to provide complete discharge of the exhaust gases and allow a full charge of fuel mixture. The cams have a wear resisting treatment, which combined with off-center lifters, provide unusually long life and quiet operation.

Connecting rods are of drop forged steel "I" beam construction for rigidity. The upper end is fitted with a clamp bolt for securely attaching the rod to the piston pin. The connecting rod bearing is of thin wall babbitt with the bearing being centrifugally cast in the rod and an integral part of the rod assembly. This "spun-in" type rod bearing is accurately diamond bored for journal fit and alignment.

A heavy cast iron flywheel bolts to the flange at the rear end of the crankshaft and a steel ring gear is shrunk on the outer diameter of the flywheel; the starting motor drive pinion engages this ring gear when cranking the engine. Flywheel and crankshaft are accurately balanced to prevent engine vibration and the rear flywheel face is accurately machined for clutch mounting.

The front end of the crankshaft is fitted with a harmonic balancer. This balancer consists of a hub attached to the crankshaft and a small flywheel connected to the hub by two rubber annular rings. This rubber mounted flywheel tends to resist quick changes in crankshaft speed caused by the power impulses, and thereby dampens out or absorbs crankshaft vibration.

In the cylinder head for the 216 engine and (1948-49) 235 engine, "nozzle jets" direct water under pressure against the valve seats (fig. 2). These nozzles are not in the (1950-51) 235 engine,

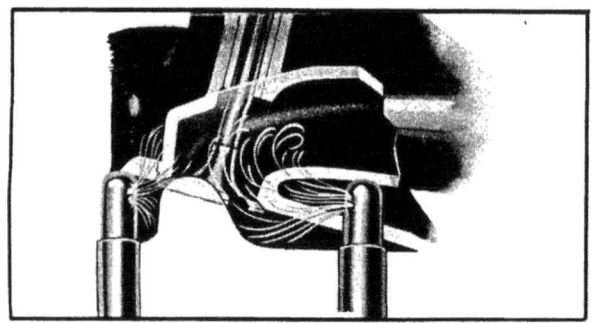

Fig. 2—Cylinder Head Water Nozzles

for larger water passages in the cylinder head provide adequate cooling of the valve seats.

For the 216 engine and (1948-49) 235 engine, the intake manifold passages have a "D" shape cross-section, whereas for the (1950-51) 235 engine, the manifold passages are circular in cross-section. Also, on the (1950-51) 235 engine, the manifold is mounted so that its main passage is parallel to the ground.

The exhaust manifolds are interchangeable between the 216 and 235 engines for (1948-49) models. However, for (1950-51) engines although similar, the exhaust manifold on the 235 engine is proportionately larger.

Located on the inside of the exhaust manifold is the thermostatically operated heat control valve. This valve in the exhaust manifold, directs the hot exhaust gases against the center of the intake manifold when the engine is cold as shown at the left of Figure 3. As the engine warms up, the thermostatic spring closes the valve and directs the exhaust gases away from the intake manifold as shown at the right of Figure 3. This thermostatic control results in the proper temperature of the incoming gases under all operating conditions.

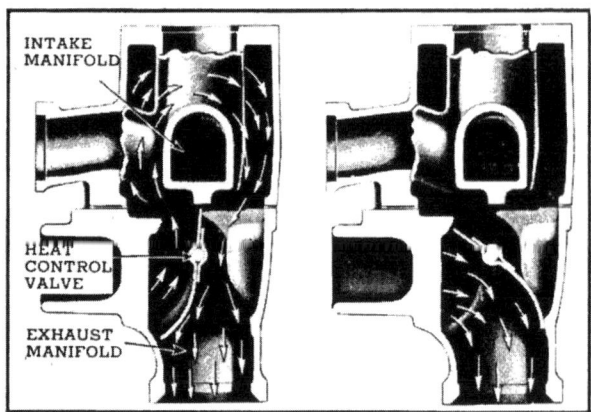

Fig. 3—Manifold Heat Riser and Heat Control Valve

The tension of the thermostatic spring is very important. When too tight, the heat will not be turned off the intake heat riser as the engine warms up, with the result that the incoming gases will be expanded several times greater than normal and it will be impossible to get a normal fuel charge into the cylinders. This condition will reduce power and maximum speed and cause detonation as well as sticking valves. Therefore, it is important that the thermostatic spring be wound up just enough to slip its outer end over the anchor pin (fig. 4) and no more. This is approximately ½ turn of the spring from its position when unhooked.

Sometimes the heat control valve shaft becomes frozen in the manifold; when this condition occurs the valve may stick in either the "heat on" or "heat off" position.

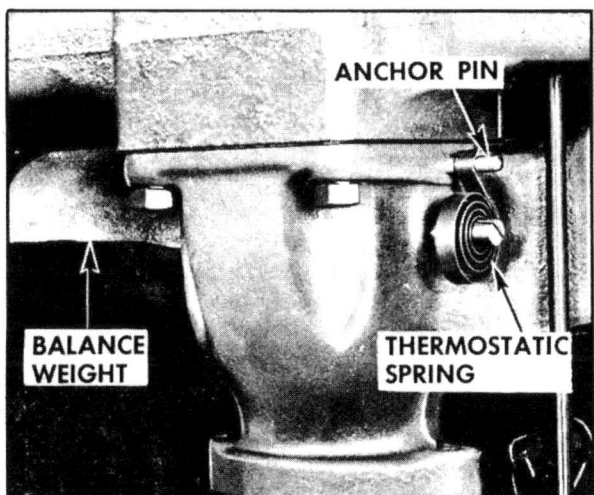

Fig. 4—Manifold Heat Valve Anti-Rattle Spring

If it sticks in the "heat on" position, it will result in poor engine performance, overheating and detonation. On the other hand, if it should stick in the "heat off" position, the heat will be turned off the intake heat riser at all times and result in poor performance, particularly while the engine is warming up and driving at lower speeds.

On all engine tune-up jobs and also on complaints of poor performance, overheating and detonation, the operation and adjustment of the manifold heat control valve should be closely checked and any necessary corrections made.

Engine lubrication is supplied by a positive driven gear pump equipped with a spring loaded by-pass valve to control the maximum pressure at high speeds and when the engine oil is cold and sluggish during cold weather starting.

The engine oiling system provides positive pressure lubrication to the main bearings and camshaft bearings. The connecting rod bearings are lubricated at low speeds by means of dippers on the rod bearing caps which dip into oil filled troughs in the oil pan. At high speeds, lubrication is amply maintained by oil nozzles, which direct a stream of oil that is intercepted by the dippers, thereby, forcing oil into the bearings under high pressure. Cylinder walls, pistons and piston pins are lubricated by the oil spray thrown off by the connecting rods. Lubrication of the valve mechanism is accomplished by metered oil pressure pumped to the hollow rocker arm shafts.

Improved lubrication control of the inlet and exhaust valve stems is provided by a synthetic rubber oil seal which is assembled between the valve stem and the valve spring cap. An extra groove is provided on the valve stem to accommodate the rubber seal. Both seal and cap are interchangeable between intake and exhaust valves. The valve spring cap is identified by an annular groove $\frac{1}{16}''$ deep in the top of the cap.

Valve stem tips are hardened to prevent wear from contact with the rocker arms.

Full pressure lubrication to the main and camshaft bearings is provided by oil flowing from the oil pan through the pump screen, oil pump and passage in cylinder block to the main oil supply gallery on the left side of the engine. From the oil gallery, the oil goes through drilled passages that extend to the groove in each of the four main bearings and from these to the groove in each of the adjacent camshaft bearings (fig. 5). In this manner, full pressure feed lubrication is supplied to all main and camshaft bearings.

Pressure lubrication of the timing gears is provided for on (1949-51) engines, by an oil passage from the front camshaft bearing, through a milled slot in the rear surface of the engine front plate, to a nozzle extending out from the front plate and so aimed that the oil stream effectively lubricates the timing gears. All the oil entering the passage is delivered to the timing gears.

Oil for lubrication of the valve mechanism of the (1950-51) 235 engine, is tapped from the rear camshaft bearing (fig. 5). An oil passage drilled through the tappet ledge intersects the oil groove

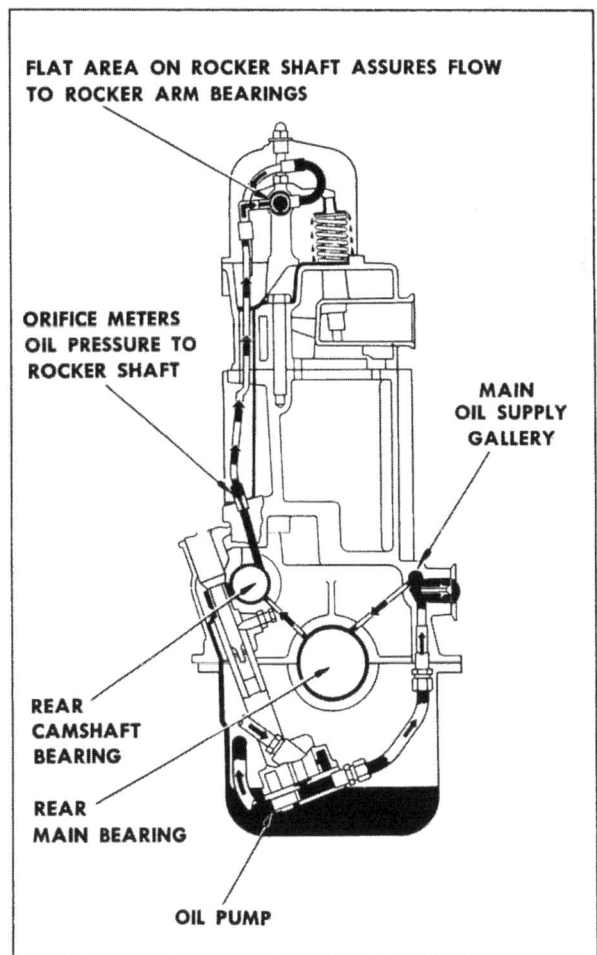

Fig. 5—Lubrication System

of the rear camshaft bearing. An oil tube connected to this drilled passage extends forward in the push rod compartment to the center and then upward to a fitting between the two hollow rocker arm shafts, through which oil is directed to the rocker arm bearings. A bleeder hole in each rocker arm supplies oil for lubrication of valve stems and push rod sockets. To prevent excess oil at the rocker arms, this supply of oil is metered by a restricted fitting at the connection directly above the rear camshaft bearing.

Oil for lubrication of the valve mechanism of the 216 engine and (1948-49) 235 engine, is tapped from a small diameter by-pass at the oil distributor valve and carried by a pipe, passing through the water jacket, to a fitting between the two hollow rocker arm shafts, from which it is distributed to all rocker arm bearings. A bleeder hole in each rocker arm supplies oil for lubrication of the valve stems and push rod sockets.

Oil for the connecting rod bearings passes from the oil pump through a passage in the block to the oil distributor. As the oil pressure builds up, the oil distributor valve opens and releases the oil into another drilled passage in the block; this passage connects by short pipe fitting into the main supply pipe in the oil pan. From the main supply pipe, the oil passes to the oil distributor pipe in the oil pan where it is distributed to the six oil nozzles.

As the engine speed is increased and the oil volume is built up, the nozzle oil streams rise and are caught by the dippers, forcing oil into the connecting rod bearings under high pressure (fig. 6).

Fig. 6—Connecting Rod Bearing Lubrication

MINOR SERVICE OPERATIONS

VALVE TIMING

Valve timing diagram (fig. 7) is applicable to all truck models. Note that the intake valve starts to open 1° after upper dead center and remains open for 218°, closing 39° past lower dead center.

The exhaust valve starts to open 42° before lower dead center and remains open for 231°, closing 9° past upper dead center.

Both the exhaust and intake valves must open and close at the correct time in relation to piston position or lack of power and overheating will result. To check the valve timing, use the number one cylinder exhaust valve.

1. Remove rocker arm cover, crank engine until number one exhaust valve is closed and tighten adjusting screw to just remove all tappet clearance.

2. Crank the engine until the number one cylinder exhaust valve opens and just starts to close.

3. Continue to crank the engine until the triangular mark on the flywheel lines up with the pointer on the flywheel housing.

4. Mount a dial gauge on the rocker shaft support with the spindle of the indicator on top of the number one cylinder exhaust valve adjusting screw.

5. Set the indicator at .044" (fig. 8).

6. Continue to crank the engine until the indicator hand just stops moving. At this point the indicator should read zero plus or minus .004".

7. If indicator reading is greater or less than .004", it indicates excessive timing gear wear or improperly installed timing gears. Refer to timing gear installation under "Major Service Operation."

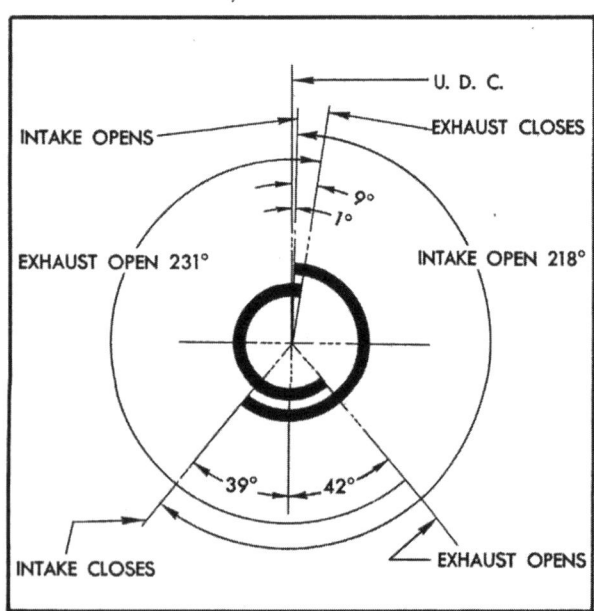

Fig. 7—Valve Timing Diagram

ENGINE ASSEMBLY 6-7

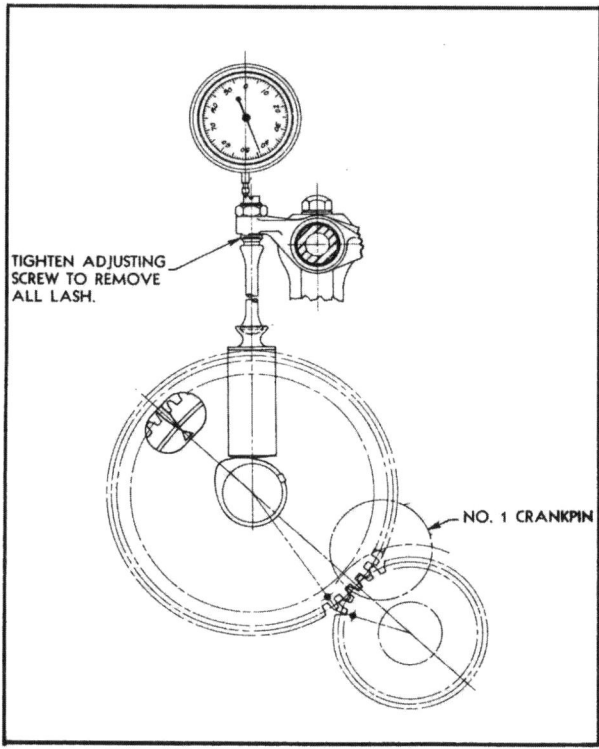

Fig. 8—Checking Valve Timing

VALVE ADJUSTMENT

Before adjusting the valve stem to rocker arm clearance, it is extremely important that the engine be thoroughly warmed up to normalize the expansion of all parts. This is very important because during the warm-up period, the valve clearances will change considerably. To adjust the valves during or before this warm-up period, will produce clearances which will be far from correct after the engine reaches normal operating temperature.

Tests have shown that valve clearances will vary as much as .005" from a cold check through the normalizing range; consequently the engine should be run approximately 30 minutes to properly normalize all parts.

Covering the radiator will not materially hasten this normalizing process because even with the water temperature quickly raised to 185° it does not change the rate at which the oil temperature increases or the engine parts become normalized.

The actual temperature of the oil is not as important as stabilizing the oil temperature. The expansion or contraction of the valves, rocker arm supports, push rods, cylinder head and cylinder block are relative to this oil temperature. Therefore, only after the oil temperature is stabilized, do these parts stop expanding and valve clearance changes cease to take place.

1. Remove rocker arm cover attaching nuts and cover.

2. Run engine at fast idle (approximately 600 RPM) and check oil temperature with a thermometer at the overflow pipe on the valve rocker shaft connector.

   NOTE: When oil temperature remains constant for five minutes, engine is normalized and ready for valve adjustment.

3. Tighten all manifold bolts, valve rocker arm stud nuts and cylinder head bolts.

   NOTE: Cylinder head bolts should be tightened to 70-80 ft. lbs. tension, rocker shaft support bolts and stud nuts to 25-30 ft. lbs. and manifold clamp bolts to 15-20 ft. lbs.

4. Lubricate valve stems with engine oil to insure free movement of valves in their guides.

5. Adjust valve clearances as follows:

	Normal Operation	Heavy Duty Operation
Intake	.006" to .008" Hot	.010" Hot
Exhaust	.013" to .015" Hot	.020" Hot

6 Install rocker arm cover using a new gasket and check for oil leaks.

CYLINDER HEAD AND VALVE CONDITIONING

The condition of the cylinder head and valve mechanism, more than anything else, determines the power, performance and economy of a valve-in-head engine. Extreme care should be exercised when conditioning the cylinder head and valves to maintain correct valve stem to guide clearance, correctly ground valves, valve seats of correct width and correct valve adjustment.

Removal and Disassembly

1. Drain radiator, raise hood, loosen air cleaner clamp and remove air cleaner. Disconnect choke and throttle wires from carburetor.

2. Remove cotter pin at lower end of throttle rod and disconnect rod from bell crank and disconnect throttle return spring.

3. Disconnect gas and vacuum lines from carburetor, 2-speed and hydrovac vacuum line from manifold fitting.

4. Remove gas and vacuum line retaining clip from water outlet.

5. Remove nuts, cap screws, washers and clamps that attach manifold assembly to cylinder head and pull manifold assembly off the manifold studs. Let curve of exhaust pipe rest on steering gear housing to support it.

6 Disconnect radiator hose from water outlet, remove outlet to cylinder head bolts and remove outlet and thermostat.

7. Remove rocker arm cover attaching nuts and remove cover and gasket.
8. Disconnect wires and remove all spark plugs.
9. Remove high tension wire from coil, remove coil attaching screws and lay coil down out of the way.
10. Remove push rod cover attaching screws and remove cover and gasket.
11. Disconnect rocker arm oil line from rocker arm connector.
12. Remove temperature indicator element from cylinder head.
13. Remove bolts and nuts which retain rocker arm assembly to cylinder head and remove rocker arm assembly.
14. Remove twelve push rods and twelve valve lifters.
15. Remove the cylinder head bolts, cylinder head and gasket.
16. Using valve lifter, KMO-642, compress the valve springs and remove valve keys, spring caps, oil seals, springs, and valves (fig. 9).

Fig. 9—Use of Valve Lifter Tool

Cleaning
1. Clean all carbon from combustion chambers and valve ports using carbon removing brush KMO-7004.
2. Thoroughly clean the valve guides using valve guide cleaner KMO-122.
3. Clean all carbon from push rods and valve lifters.
4. Clean valve stems and heads on a buffing wheel.
5. Clean carbon deposits from pistons and cylinders.
6. Wash all parts in cleaning solvent and dry them thoroughly.

Inspection
1. Inspect the cylinder head for cracks in the exhaust ports, combustion chambers, or external cracks to the water chamber.
2. Inspect the valves for burned heads, cracked faces or damaged stems.
3. Check fit of valve stems in their respective guides.

    NOTE: Excessive valve to guide clearance will cause lack of power, rough idling and noisy valves. Insufficient clearance will result in noisy and sticky functioning of the valve and disturb engine smoothness of operation. Intake valve stem to guide clearance should be .001" to .003" while exhaust stem clearance should be .002" to .004". By trying new valves in the old guides it can be determined whether the valves or guides or both should be replaced.

4. Check valve spring tension with KMO-607 spring tester (fig. 10).

    NOTE: Spring should be compressed to 1½" at which height it should check from 124 to 140 pounds. Weak springs affect power and economy and should be replaced if not within the above limits.

5. Check valve lifters for free fit in block. The end that contacts the camshaft should be smooth. If this surface is worn or rough the lifter should be replaced.
6. Check push rods for bent condition.

REPAIRS

Replace Valve Guides
1. Place the cylinder head on the table of an arbor press and press the old valve guides out using remover J-267 (fig. 11).
2. Press new precision exhaust (short) guides and new precision intake (long) guides into the cylinder head.

ENGINE ASSEMBLY 6-9

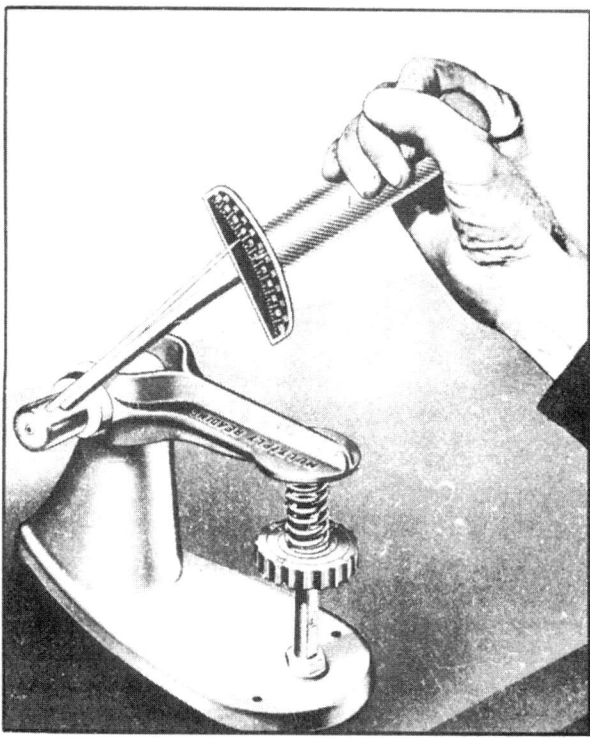

Fig. 10—Valve Spring Tension Gauge

Fig. 11—Removing Valve Guide

NOTE: The guides should be pressed into the cylinder head until the tops of the guides extend above the head as follows (fig. 12):

	Intake	Exhaust
216 engine	1 1/16"	61/64"
1948-49, 235 engine	1 1/16"	61/64"
1950-51, 235 engine	1"	55/64"

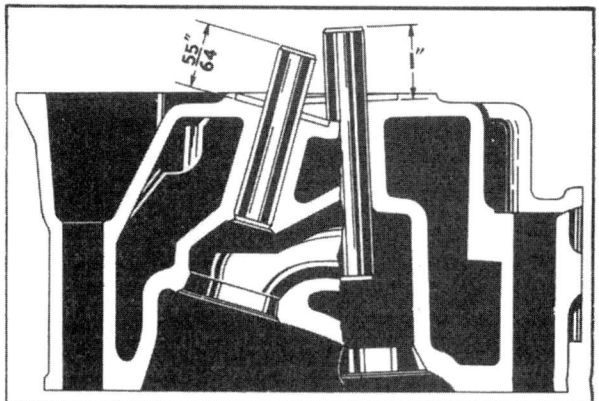

Fig. 12—Valve Guides—1950-51, 235 Engine

For the 216 engine and (1948-49) 235 engine, replacer tools J-1089 (for exhaust guides) and J-1090 (for intake guides) may be used. These tools have stop collars for proper positioning of the guides.

3. Finish ream all guides with a .343" hand reamer.

Reseating Valve Seats

Reconditioning the valve seats is very important, because the seating of the valves must be perfect for the engine to deliver the power and performance built into it.

Another important factor is the cooling of the valve heads. Good contact between each valve and its seat in the head is imperative to insure that the heat in the valve head will be properly carried away.

Several different types of equipment are available for reseating valve seats; the recommendations of the manufacturer of the equipment being used should be carefully followed to attain proper results.

Valve reseater set, KMO-150-B, contains all necessary valve seat reconditioning equipment necessary for proper renewing of valve seats. Regardless of what type of equipment is used, however, it is essential that valve guides are free from carbon or dirt to insure proper centering of pilot in the guide.

1. Install expanding pilot in the valve guide and expand pilot by tightening nut.
2. Place roughing or forming cutter over pilot and just clean up the valve seat.
3. Remove roughing or forming cutter from pilot, install finishing cutter on pilot and cut just enough metal from the seat to provide a smooth finish.
4. Narrow down the valve seats to the proper width of 3/64" to 1/16" for the intake and 1/16" to 3/32" for the exhaust.

NOTE: This operation is done by machining both port and top of valve seat.

5. A form cutter must be used to thin down the intake seats from the top. This cutter also machines the edge of the valve recess in the head smoothing this passage for the free flow of incoming gases.
6. Remove expanding pilot and clean head carefully, to remove all chips from above operations.

NOTE: Valve seats should be concentric to within .002" total indicator reading (fig. 13).

Fig. 14—Valve Refacing Machine

Fig. 13—Checking Valve Seat with Indicator

Refacing Valves

Valves that are pitted can be refaced to the proper angle, insuring correct relation between the head and stem, on a valve refacing machine (fig. 14).

1. If necessary, dress the valve refacing machine grinding wheel to make sure it is smooth and true. Set the chuck at the 30° mark for grinding 30° valve seats and at the 45° mark for grinding 45° valve seats.
2. Clamp the valve stem in the chuck of the machine.
3. Start the grinder and move the valve head out in line with the grinder wheel by moving the lever to the left.
4. Turn the feed screw until the valve head just contacts wheel. Move valve back and forth across the wheel and regulate the feed screw to provide light valve contact.
5. Continue grinding until the valve face is true and smooth all around valve. If this makes the valve head thin the valve must be replaced as the valve will overheat and burn.
6. Remove valve from chuck and place stem in "V" block. Feed valve squarely against grinding wheel to grind any pit from rocker arm end of stem.

NOTE: Only the extreme end of the valve stem is hardened to resist wear. Do not grind end of stem excessively.

7. Make pencil marks about ¼" apart across the valve face, place the valve in cylinder head and give the valve ½ turn in each direction while exerting firm pressure on face of valve.
8. Remove valve and check face carefully. If all pencil marks have not been removed at the point of contact with the valve seat, it will be necessary to repeat the refacing operation and again recheck for proper seating.
9. Grind and check the remaining valves in the same manner.

Rocker Arms and Shafts

Sludge and gum formation in the rocker arm shafts and rocker arms will restrict the normal flow of oil to the rocker arms and valves. Each time the rocker arm and shaft assemblies are removed they should be disassembled and thoroughly cleaned.

1. Remove the support bolts, hairpin locks, springs, rocker arms and supports.
2. Clean all sludge or gum formation from the inside and outside of the shafts.
3. Clean oil holes and passages in the shafts and rocker arms.
4. Clean the rocker arm shaft oil connector assembly.
5. Inspect the shafts for wear. Check the fit of rocker arms on the shafts and check the

valve end of rocker arms for excessive wear. Replace all worn parts.

6. There are three each of eight different type rocker arms used—right and left hand exhaust and right and left hand intake for both 216 and 235 engines. They must be installed on the shafts in correct position. For identification, each type rocker arm carries a different number stamped on the side (fig. 15).

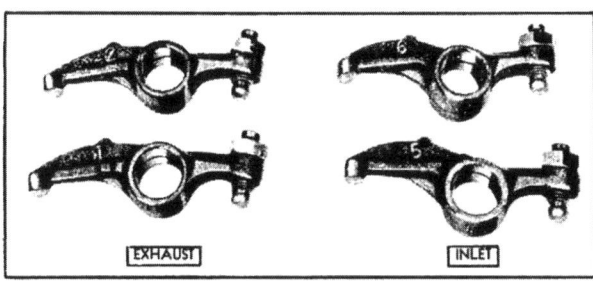

Fig. 15—Valve Rocker Arm Identification

7. The proper locations of the rocker arms according to number are as follows:

216 Engine and (1948-49) 235 Engine

No. on Rocker Arm	Type Rocker Arm	For Cylinder No.	Part Number
1	L.H. Exhaust	1-3-5 Exhaust	839459
2	R.H. Exhaust	2-4-6 Exhaust	839460
5	L.H. Intake	2-4-6 Intake	839463
6	R.H. Intake	1-3-5 Intake	839464

(1950-51) 235 Engine

No. on Rocker Arm	Type Rocker Arm	For Cylinder No.	Part Number
9	L.H. Exhaust	1-3-5 Exhaust	3835547
0	R.H. Exhaust	2-4-6 Exhaust	3835548
3	L.H. Intake	2-4-6 Intake	3835551
4	R.H. Intake	1-3-5 Intake	3835552

8. One end of each rocker arm shaft is plugged; the open end of each shaft must be toward the center.

9. Install the rocker arms, springs, supports, support bolts and locks in their correct position by referring to the above chart and Figure 16. Figure 19 shows the rocker arm and shaft assemblies correctly installed on the cylinder head.

CYLINDER HEAD

Assembly

1. Clean valves, valve seats, valve guides and cylinder head thoroughly.
2. Starting with No. 1 cylinder, place the exhaust valve in the port and place the valve spring and cap in position. Then using valve lifter, KMO-642, compress the spring and install the oil seal and valve keys (fig. 17). See that the seal is flat and not twisted in the valve stem groove and that the keys seat properly in the valve stem groove.

NOTE: Place valve springs in position with the closed coil end toward the cylinder head.

3. Assemble the remaining valves, valve springs, spring caps, oil seals and valve keys in the cylinder head using tool, KMO-642.

Installation

1. Place a new cylinder head gasket in position on the cylinder block following the instructions stamped on the gasket. This assures alignment of water passages and bolt holes in the block and head with openings in the gasket.
2. Place two cylinder head guide pins through the gasket and screw them into the cylinder block front and rear holes on the manifold side to hold the gasket in position and guide the cylinder head into place.

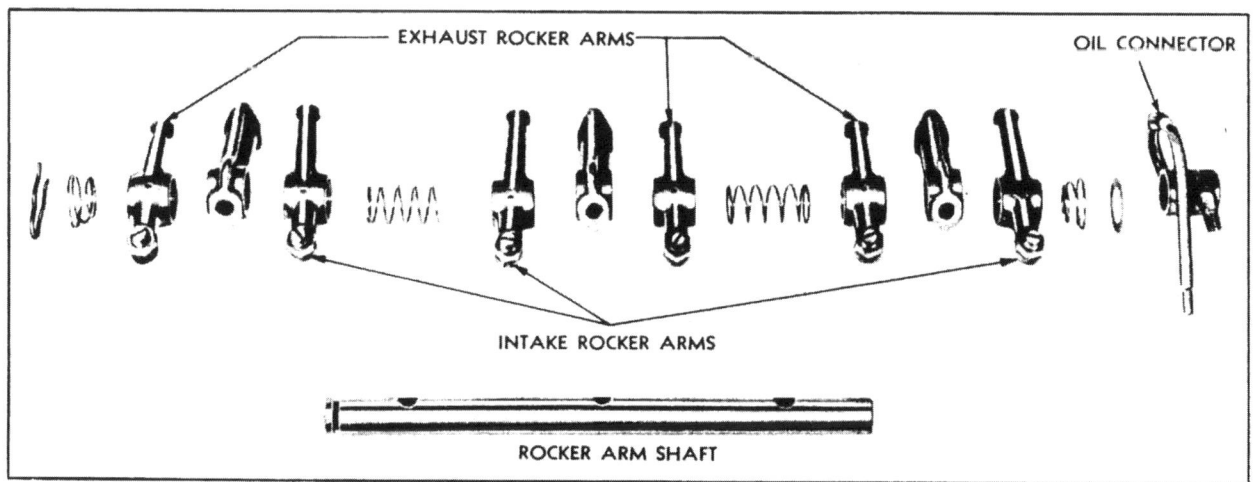

Fig. 16—Layout of Rocker Arm and Shaft Parts

ENGINE ASSEMBLY 6-12

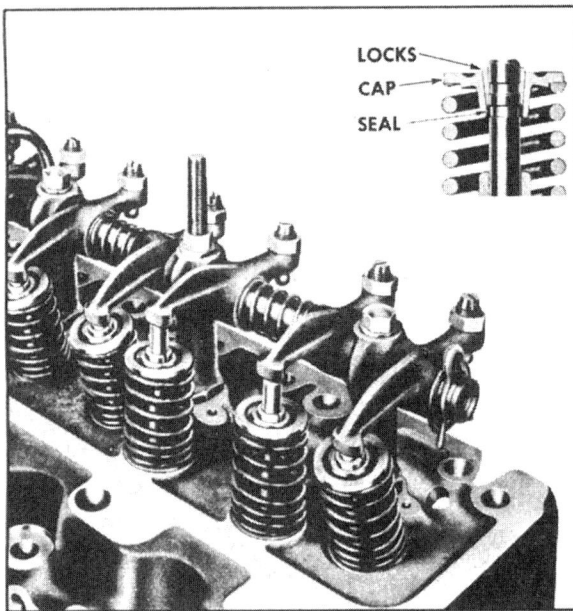

Fig. 17—Correct Installation of Seal, Cap and Lock

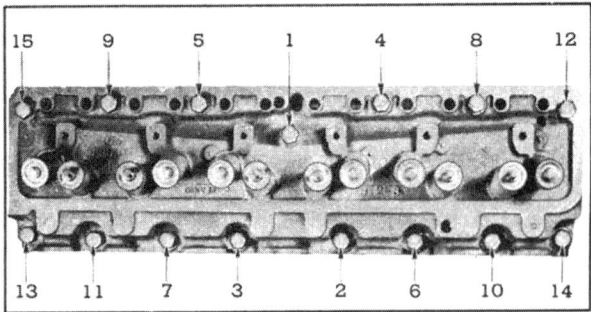

Fig. 18—Cylinder Head Bolt Tightening Diagram

3. Place the cylinder head in position over the guide pins, pilot the rocker arm feed pipe up through hole in head and lower the head into position.
4. Install cylinder head bolts finger tight. Remove guide pins and install two remaining bolts.
5. Tighten the cylinder head bolts a little at a time in the order shown in Figure 18. The final tightening should be to 70-80 ft. lbs.
6. Install 12 valve lifters in right side of block and drop the 12 valve push rods down through the openings in the cylinder head and seat them in the lifters.
7. Install and tighten two rocker arm shaft studs in cylinder head.
8. Place the oil connector over open ends of the two rocker shaft assemblies and place this assembly on the cylinder head so that the studs will enter the center support on each shaft.
9. Install four bolts and two stud nuts which retain rocker arm assembly to cylinder head and tighten evenly to 25-30 ft. lbs. torque.
10. Connect rocker arm oil line to oil connector and tighten securely. Figure 19 shows rocker arm and shaft assemblies correctly installed on head.
11. Install temperature indicator fitting and tighten securely.
12. Install thermostat and thermostat housing using a new gasket and connect radiator hose.
13. Install push rod cover using a new gasket. On the 216 engine and (1948-49) 235 engine, make sure the cork seals are properly positioned around the spark plug openings. Place coil in position and install attaching screws. Tighten push rod cover screws to 6-7½ ft. lbs. and coil mounting bolts to 5-8 ft. lbs. torque.

Fig. 19—Valve Rocker Arms Correctly Assembled

ENGINE ASSEMBLY 6-13

14. Clean all spark plugs with abrasive type cleaner, inspect for damage and using a round feeler gauge, set the spark gap as follows: on (1948) models, .040"; on (1949-51) models, .035".
15. Place new gaskets on plugs and install. Tighten to 12-15 ft. lbs. torque on (1948) models, and 20-25 ft. lbs. on (1949-51) models. If torque wrench is not available, tighten finger tight and ½ turn more.
16. Connect spark plug wires to their respective terminals and the high tension wire to the coil.
17. Clean gasket flanges on cylinder head and manifold, and install new gaskets, intake manifold pilot sleeves, and the center cap screws with clamps loosely. Position the manifold and slide it into place over the end studs and pilot sleeves, making sure it seats against the gaskets.
18. Install the two end cap screws with clamps and turn the center clamps into position against manifold. Tighten the center clamp bolts to 15-20 ft. lbs. torque and the two end clamp bolts to 25-30 ft. lbs. torque.
19. Connect choke and throttle wires to the carburetor. Connect lower end of throttle rod and install a new cotter pin.
20. Connect gas and vacuum lines to carburetor, 2-speed and hydrovac vacuum line to manifold fitting.
21. Attach gas and vacuum line retaining clip to water outlet.
22. Fill cooling system and check for water leaks.
23. Clean air cleaner and install.
24. Roughly set all valve clearances to make sure that all valves have clearance.
25. Normalize engine and adjust valves as instructed under "Minor Service Operations, Valve Adjustment."

ENGINE MOUNTINGS

The engine is rubber mounted in three places. The front engine mount is through the engine front plate, oil shield and rubber insulator to the frame cross member (fig. 20). Two mounting insulators are used at the rear and are either bolted to the clutch housing and to the frame cross member or are mounted to brackets bolted to the clutch housing and to brackets riveted to the frame side member (fig. 21).

Fig. 21—Engine Rear Mount

Mounting brackets should be inspected at regular intervals to be sure that they are tight. Insulator bolts should also be inspected for evidence of looseness.

All bolts should be kept tight except the two self-locking end nuts on front motor support. Self-locking nuts should be tightened securely but not too tight to cause damage to the front support assembly.

All parts of the front support should be kept clean and free of oil to prevent deterioration of rubber portion of support.

Engine oil leaks, if any, should be eliminated prior to installation of a new support.

Checking Clearance of New Front Support

1. Check clearance between upper plate and lower retainer before tightening bolts or applying engine weight on support.
2. Clearance at this point should be between ³⁄₆₄" and ⁵⁄₆₄" as indicated in Figure 20.
3. If clearance is less than ³⁄₆₄" file or grind top of lower retainer until proper clearance is obtained.
   NOTE: Do not shim.
4. If clearance is more than ⁵⁄₆₄" a new lower retainer must be installed.

Checking Clearance of Used Front Support

1. Drain radiator and remove radiator inlet and outlet hoses.
2. Loosen rear engine mountings and remove

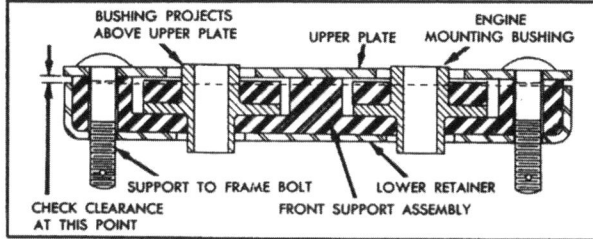

Fig. 20—Engine Front Mounting

engine front support from engine and frame cross member.
3. Fit front support assembly into lower retainer and position upper plate on top.
4. With parts held together firmly, determine if rubber support assembly fits tight between upper plate and lower retainer.
5. Check engine mounting bushings to be sure they project above upper plate.

   NOTE: This will prevent oil shield contacting upper plate and resultant improper cushioning effect of support.

6. If rubber support is loose between upper plate and lower retainer or if bushings do not project above upper plate, install new front support assembly.
7. Check clearance between upper plate and lower retainer (fig. 20). If clearance is more than $5/64''$ new lower retainer must be installed.
8. Install front support, tighten rear engine mountings, replace radiator inlet and outlet hoses and refill radiator.

Rear Mounts—Removal

1. Disconnect clutch pedal pull back spring and remove clutch link.
2. Remove motor mount to cross member nut, lockwasher and bolt for each mount.
3. Raise engine slightly (approximately $3/4''$) to obtain wrench clearance for removal of side mount to clutch housing bolts.

   NOTE: On (1951) 1½ or 2 ton models, or any model using a propeller shaft brake of any type, it will be necessary to remove screws from transmission hole cover to allow raising of engine due to limited clearance between brake and hole cover.

Rear Mounts—Installation

1. Install top mount to clutch housing bolt to secure alignment of mount.
2. Install lower mount to clutch housing bolt and then tighten both bolts securely.
3. Lower engine and install mount to cross member bolt, lockwasher and nut for each mount and tighten securely.

   NOTE: It is imperative that bolts be securely tightened or early mount failure will result.

OIL PUMP

Oil pump (fig. 22) consists of two gears and a pressure relief valve enclosed in a one-piece housing and driven from the distributor drive shaft which in turn is driven by a helix gear on the camshaft. Pump inlet is fitted with a fine mesh

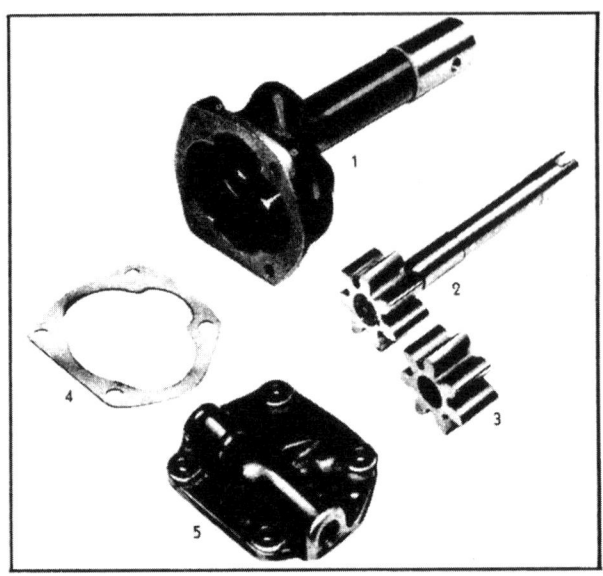

Fig. 22—Layout of Oil Pump Parts
1. Oil Pump Body
2. Drive Gear and Shaft
3. Idler Gear
4. Cover Gasket
5. Cover

screen to prevent entry of small particles of sludge, etc., into the oil lines.

Inasmuch as the oil pump is serviced on an exchange basis no repair operations other than disassembly and inspection operations are covered in this manual.

Removal and Disassembly

1. Drain oil and remove flywheel housing underpan, flywheel underpan extension and oil pan.
2. Disconnect oil pump to block oil line at the block and disconnect oil line from pump to screen at pump.
3. Remove oil pump retaining sleeve lock screw and remove oil pump and pump to block oil line.
4. Remove oil line from pump and remove pump cover attaching screws, cover, gasket, idler gear and drive gear and shaft.
5. Remove oil pump inlet screen.
6. Wash all parts in cleaning solvent and dry by using compressed air, if available.

Inspection

Should any of the following conditions be found during inspection operations, the pump assembly should be replaced.

1. Inspect pump body for cracks or excessive wear.
2. Inspect oil pump gears for excessive wear or damage.
3. Check shaft for looseness in the housing.
4. Check inside of cover for wear that would permit oil to leak past the ends of gears.

Assembly

1. Place drive gear and shaft in pump body.
2. Install idler gear so that smooth side of gear will be toward the cover.
3. Install a new GENUINE Chevrolet gasket to assure correct end clearance of the gears.
4. Install cover and attaching screws. Tighten screws securely and check to see that shaft turns freely.
5. Install oil line to pump body loosely.
6. Place oil pump in block fitting, aligning oil lines and install oil pump retaining sleeve lock screw and tighten it securely.

   NOTE: Make sure that tapered end of lock screw draws down into hole in oil pump body. Tighten lock nut securely.

7. Tighten oil pump to block oil line and pump to screen oil line connector nuts securely and replace oil pump screen.
8. Install oil pan using a new oil pan gasket. Tighten oil pan flange bolts to 6-7½ ft. lbs. and oil pan corner bolts to 12½-15 ft. lbs. torque. Install flywheel underpan extension and flywheel housing underpan. Refill with oil.

CONNECTING ROD BEARING LUBRICATION

Proper lubrication of the connecting rod bearings depends upon accurate adjustment of connecting rod dippers, depth of oil pan troughs and aiming nozzles in the oil pan.

The oil pans on both engines are the same; however, there are differences in the dipper height due to the difference in the length of the engine stroke. When checking oil pan troughs and dipper height, use the gauges as listed below:

Tool No.	Engine
J-969-2A	216
J-1541	235

These gauges have "Go" and "No Go" limits for the dipper height incorporated in them.

Checking Dipper Height

1. With oil pan removed, turn crankshaft until connecting rod is at bottom dead center.
2. With the oil pan gasket removed, place the two side pins of the gauge on the pan rail adjacent to the connecting rod dipper being checked.
3. Slide the gauge over the dipper being checked (fig. 23). If the dipper is properly adjusted, the low (or "Go") step of the gauge will pass over the dipper, but the high (or "No Go") step will not pass over it.
4. If the low (or "Go") step of the gauge will not pass over the dipper it may be lowered by a light tap with a hammer.

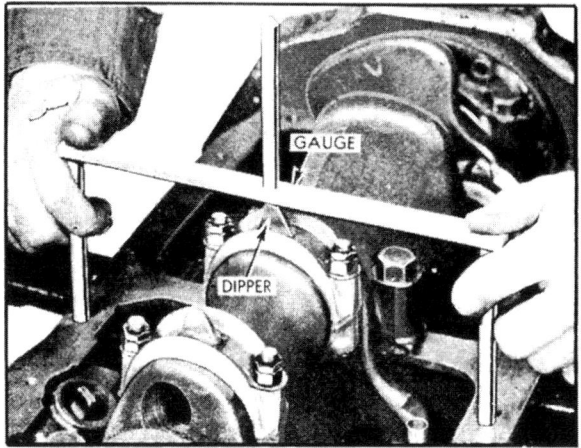

Fig. 23—Checking Connecting Rod Dipper Height

5. If the high (or "No Go") step passes over the dipper, a new dipper should be installed.

Each connecting rod dipper should be checked in this manner.

Checking Oil Pan Troughs

1. With the oil pan gasket removed, place the gauge on the side rails with the center pin extending into the oil pan.
2. Slide the gauge so that the pin passes over the edge of the trough at its center (fig. 24).
3. Check clearance between end of pin on gauge and edge of oil trough. This should not exceed .015" if the trough is in proper adjustment.

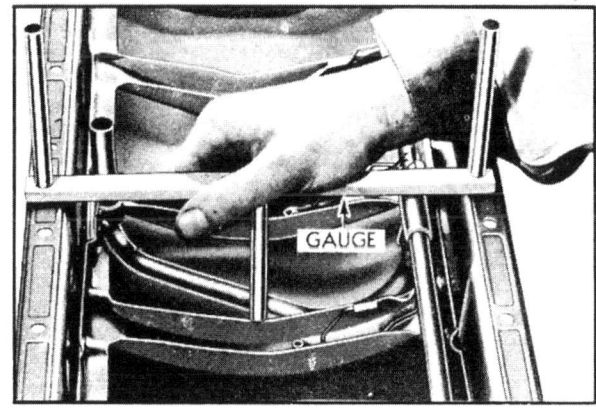

Fig. 24—Checking Oil Trough Depth

4. If the gauge does not pass over the trough, it may be corrected by carefully grinding the edge of the trough.
5. If there is more than .015" clearance between end of gauge and edge of oil trough, check for loose spot welds where trough is welded to the oil pan. A loose trough should either be rewelded or the oil pan replaced.

ENGINE ASSEMBLY 6-16

Checking Oil Pan Nozzles

1. Install oil pan target gauge J-969-1 on the oil pan with the target plate on the side of the pan opposite the oil nozzles; locate the dowels of the gauge in the screw holes in the oil pan rail.
2. Insert water nozzle J-793-3 in the main oil pipe.
3. Tip the oil pan about 45 degrees to prevent the water from covering the ends of the nozzles.
4. Open the water nozzle just enough to straighten the water streams at the ends of the nozzles. If the oil nozzles are properly adjusted, the water stream will pass through the centers of the target holes. Correct and incorrect aiming of the nozzles is shown in Figure 25.

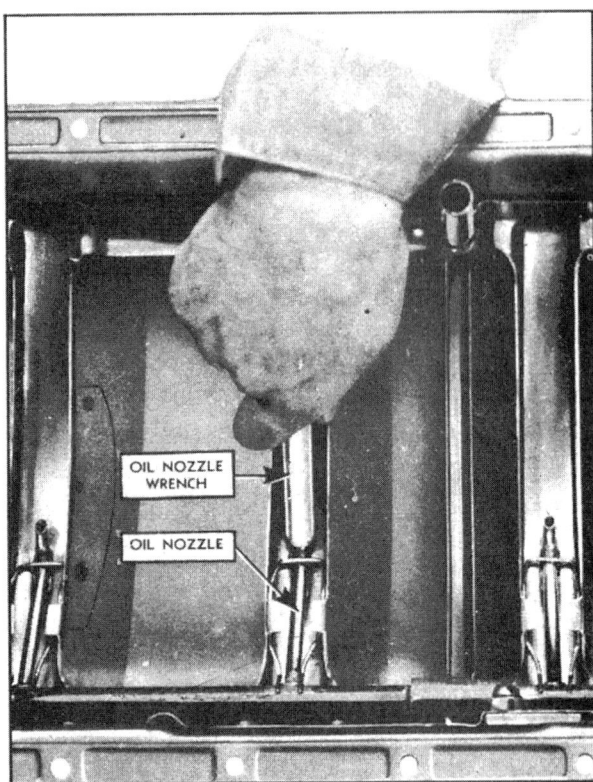

Fig. 26—Adjusting Aim of Oil Nozzles

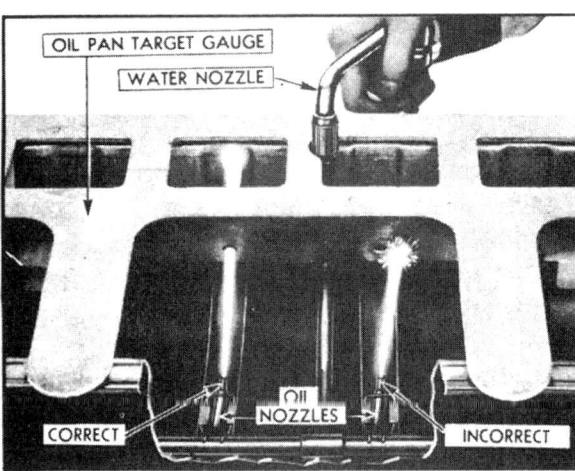

Fig. 25—Checking Aim of Oil Nozzles

5. The aiming of the oil nozzles may be adjusted by using the oil nozzle wrench J-793-5 as shown in Figure 26. Continue adjusting and checking the oil nozzles until each water stream passes through the center of its target hole.

CONNECTING ROD BEARINGS—ADJUST

1. Drain oil and remove oil pan.
2. Remove bearing cap and remove an equal number of shims from each side of bearing until the rod cannot be moved by hand but can be tapped back and forth with a light blow with an 8-ounce hammer.
3. Replace one .002" shim on one side, being careful to keep the number of shims equal on each side if possible.
4. When the bearing is properly fitted, it should be possible to snap the rod back and forth on the crankpin with one hand (fig. 27).

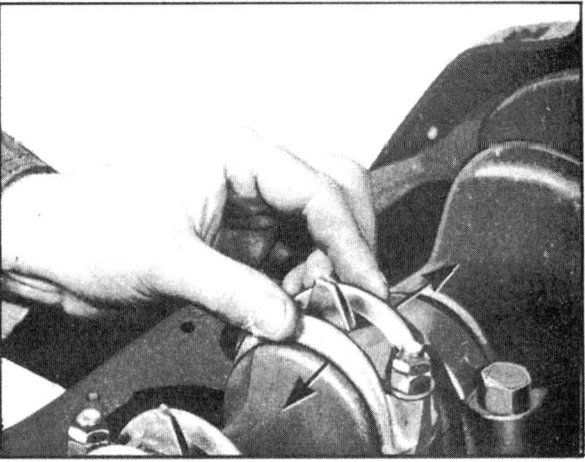

Fig. 27—Checking Connecting Rod Bearing Fit

5. If it is not possible to keep the number of shims equal on each side of all bearings, it is preferable to have the greater number of shims on the camshaft side.
6. Check the connecting rod clearance between the upper half of the connecting rod and the side of the crankpin with a feeler gauge. This clearance should not be less than .004" nor more than .012" (fig. 28).
7. Tighten connecting rod bolt nuts to 40-50 ft. lbs. torque with oiled threads and lock the nuts by installing new "pal" locking nuts.

ENGINE ASSEMBLY 6-17

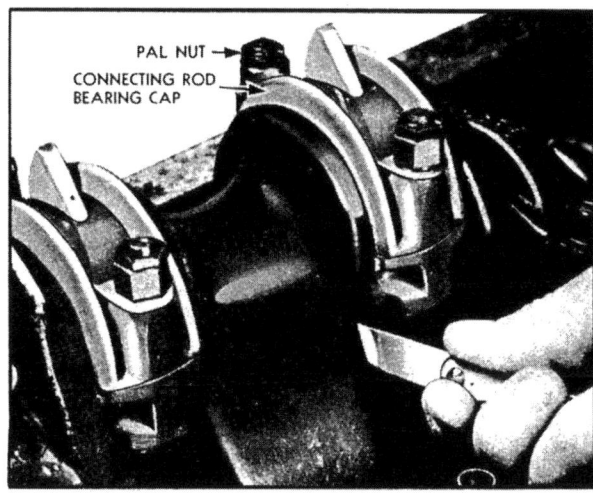

Fig. 28—Checking Connecting Rod End Clearance

The "pal" nuts must be installed with the open side of the nut toward the end of the bolt. Turn the pal nut up finger tight and then ½ turn more.

8. As a final check to be sure that the piston and rod assembly will travel true with the bore, check the clearance between the piston pin end of the connecting rod and the piston pin bosses of the piston with a feeler gauge. This clearance should not be less than .025".
9. Install oil pan using a new oil pan gasket and refill with oil.

MAIN BEARINGS—ADJUST

1. Drain oil and remove oil pan.
2. Disconnect spark plug wires and remove spark plugs.
3. Loosen oil screen to pump oil line and remove oil screen and oil screen cover from cover support.
4. Remove cover support from bearing cap and rotate out of way.
5. Remove two bolts and lock plate that hold timing gear cover to front main bearing.
6. Loosen all bearing cap bolts and then draw them up snugly. Check to see that crankshaft rolls freely.
7. Starting with the rear bearing, remove cap and remove one shim at a time from each side until there is a slight drag on the crankshaft (when hand cranking engine) with the cap bolts pulled down tight, 100-110 ft. lbs. torque.
8. Replace one .002" shim on one side for clearance, retighten the bolts and check for drag. The crankshaft should now roll freely without excessive drag when rotated by hand.
9. Loosen bolts on bearing that has just been adjusted and proceed to adjust remaining bearings in the same manner.
10. When adjusting the bearings, the shims should be removed evenly. If an uneven number of shims have to be used, it is good practice to have the greater number of shims on the same side of all bearings.
11. If the shaft turns without excessive drag when turned by hand after all bolts have been tightened to 100-110 ft. lbs. torque with a torque wrench, the bearings are properly adjusted.
12. Replace oil screen cover support to bearing cap, attach cover support, install oil screen and tighten oil screen to pump oil line.
13. Replace two bolts and lock plate that hold timing gear cover to front main bearing cap.
14. Install oil pan using a new oil pan gasket and refill crankcase.
15. Replace spark plugs and attach spark plug wires.

OIL SEAL—REAR BEARING CAP—REPLACE

Sealing at the crankshaft rear bearing is made very effective due to machining the rear bearing cap and cylinder block to receive a wick type seal (fig. 29).

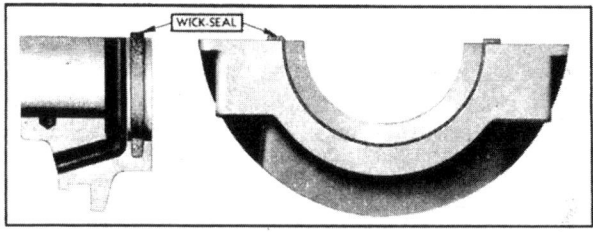

Fig. 29—Rear Main Bearing Oil Seal

To install a new wick seal in the rear main bearing cap proceed as outlined below.

1. Remove rear bearing cap.
2. Remove old seal from groove and make sure groove is clean.
3. Insert new seal in groove with the fingers.
4. Using a rounded tool, roll the seal into the groove.

NOTE: When rolling the seal start at one end and roll it to the center of the groove. Then starting from the other end, again roll toward the center (fig. 30).

5. Cut the small portion of the seal that protrudes from the groove flush with the surface of the bearing cap.

NOTE: To prevent possibility of pulling seal out of groove a round block of wood the same diameter as the crankshaft flange may be used to hold packing firmly in place while the ends are being cut off.

ENGINE ASSEMBLY 6-18

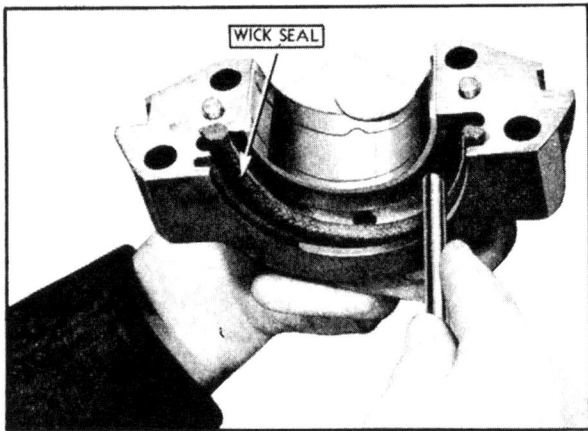

Fig. 30—Rolling Rear Bearing Cap Oil Seal into Groove

6. If it should be necessary to replace the upper half of the seal, it will be necessary to remove the engine from the chassis and remove the crankshaft as outlined under "Major Service Operations" in this section.
7. Replace cap and adjust bearing.

ENGINE TUNE-UP

One of the most important duties to perform on modern high compression engines is proper engine tune-up. This operation more than any other determines whether or not the truck will produce the maximum amount of performance with the greatest amount of economy. Only by performing these operations and staying within limits, clearances and specifications, is it possible to obtain the performance and economy built into the Chevrolet engine.

Compression

Before making any checks on an engine it should be run for several minutes and allowed to warm up and lubricate the valve mechanism. The compression of each cylinder should be checked first because AN ENGINE WITH UNEVEN COMPRESSION CANNOT BE TUNED SUCCESSFULLY.

1. Turn the ignition off and pull the hand throttle control out to open position.
2. Remove all spark plugs from engine.
3. Insert compression gauge in a spark plug hole and hold it tightly in position. Crank the engine with the starting motor until gauge reaches its highest reading, which requires only a few turns of the engine.
4. Repeat this test on all cylinders and make a note of the compression reading on each cylinder.
5. Compression on all cylinders should be 110 pounds or better and all cylinders should read alike within 5 to 10 pounds for satisfactory engine performance.

Should a low compression reading be obtained on two adjacent cylinders, it indicates the possibility of a leak from one cylinder to the other, usually caused by a leak at the cylinder head gasket. If the compression readings are low, or vary widely, the cause of the trouble may be determined by injecting a liberal supply of engine oil on top of the pistons of the low reading cylinders. Crank the engine over several times, and then take a second compression test. If there is practically no difference in the readings when compared with the first test, it indicates sticky or poorly seating valves. However, if the compression on the low reading cylinders is higher and about uniform with the other cylinders it indicates compression loss past the pistons and rings.

The cause of low or uneven compression must be corrected before proceeding with an engine tune-up.

Spark Plugs

Clean the spark plugs thoroughly, using an abrasive type cleaner. If the porcelains are badly glazed or blistered, the spark plugs should be replaced. All spark plugs must be of the same make and number or heat range. Using a round feeler gauge adjust the spark plug gaps as follows: on (1948) models, .040"; on (1949-51) models, .035".

CAUTION: In adjusting the spark plug gap never bend the center electrode which extends through the porcelain center. Always make adjustment by bending the side electrode.

Install the spark plugs in the engine using new gaskets and tighten to 12-15 ft. lbs. torque on (1948) models, and 20-25 ft. lbs. torque on (1949-51) models. If torque wrench is not available, tighten finger tight and ½ turn more.

Battery Test

Connect the positive terminal of a voltmeter to the starting switch terminal and the negative terminal of the voltmeter to a good ground.

Close the starting motor switch and crank the engine for 15 seconds. If the starting motor cranks the engine at a good rate of speed during this period with the voltmeter reading 5 volts or better, it indicates a satisfactory starting circuit, which includes the condition of the battery terminals and cables. However, if the cranking speed is slow, or the voltmeter reading is under 5 volts, the starting motor, battery and battery terminals should be checked individually to locate the source of the trouble.

Ignition Distributor

1. Remove the spark plug wires from the distributor cap and examine the terminals for

corrosion. The wires should be checked for damaged insulation and oil soaked condition.
2. Remove the distributor cap. Check the cap and distributor rotor for cracks or burned or pitted contacts.
3. Check the distributor automatic advance mechanism by turning the distributor cam in a clockwise direction as far as possible, then release the cam and see if the springs return it to its retarded position. If the cam does not return readily, the distributor must be disassembled and the cause of the trouble corrected. See Section 12 for "Distributor Repair."
4. Examine the distributor points. Dirty points should be cleaned, and pitted or worn points should be replaced. Check the points for alignment and align them if necessary.
5. Crank the engine until the distributor point cam follower rests on the peak of the cam. Adjust the point gap to .018" (fig. 31) using a

Fig. 31—Adjusting Distributor Points

feeler gauge. This operation must be performed very accurately because it affects the point dwell or length of time the points remain closed in operation and, in turn, ignition coil performance.

NOTE: The standard point setting is .018". Whe new points are installed, adjust points to .022" as the cam follower will wear down slightly while seating to the cam.

6. Crank the engine until the cam follower is located between the cams. Hook the end of a distributor point scale over the movable point and pull steadily on the spring scale until the points just start to open. At this point the reading on the scale should be between 17-21 ounces.
7. Check to see that the vacuum spark control operates freely by turning the distributor body counterclockwise and see that the spring returns it to the retarded position. Any stiffness in the operation of the vacuum spark control will affect the ignition timing.
8. Install the rotor and distributor cap to the distributor body and spark plug wires to cap. Make sure that all terminals of the primary wire at the ignition coil and distributor are clean and tight.

Coil and Condenser

The ignition coil and condenser should be checked following the instructions given by the manufacturer of the test equipment being used.

Ignition Timing

1. Set the octane selector at "O" on the scale (fig. 32) and attach a timing light to the No. 1 spark plug and a good ground. Start the engine and run it at idling speed with light aimed at flywheel housing opening.

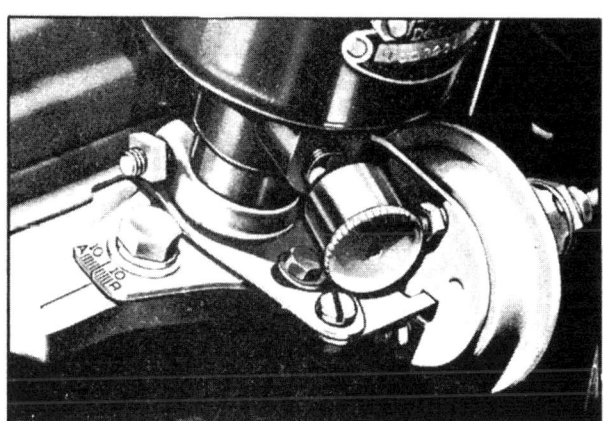

Fig. 32—Octane Selector

2. Loosen distributor clamp and rotate distributor body clockwise or counterclockwise until the steel ball in the flywheel lines up with the pointer on the flywheel housing.
3. Tighten distributor clamp screw and remove timing light.

Fuel Pump

1. Remove pump filter bowl and screen and wash them thoroughly in cleaning solvent.
2. Reassemble bowl and screen making sure that the cork gasket is in good condition and properly seated.

ENGINE ASSEMBLY 6-20

3. Tighten all fuel pump connections.

Air Cleaner

1. Remove cover wing nut, cover and filter element.
2. Wash filter element thoroughly in cleaning solvent.
3. Let element dry and dip in engine oil and allow excess oil to drain.
4. Install element and cover and secure with wing nut.

    NOTE: If oil bath air cleaner is used, see instructions under "Fuel Section."

Carburetor

1. Remove carburetor from engine, disassemble, inspect and reassemble as outlined in "Fuel Section."
2. Reassemble carburetor and air cleaner to the engine.

Manifold Heat Valve

1. Unhook the thermostat spring from its anchor pin and check the adjustment.
2. Proper adjustment requires only ½ turn of the spring from its unhooked position to slip it over the anchor pin.

    NOTE: Should this spring be distorted in any way it should be replaced.

3. Check valve shaft to make sure it is free in the manifold. If shaft is sticking, free it up with kerosene containing a small amount of baking soda.

Valve Adjustment

Normalize the engine and adjust the valves according to procedure under "Minor Service Operations, Valve Adjustment."

Idling Adjustment

1. Warm up engine to normal operating temperature.
2. Attach vacuum gauge to intake manifold fitting.
3. Set idling speed to approximately 450-500 R.P.M. by adjusting stop screw on carburetor throttle lever.
4. Turn idling screw gradually to right or left to give highest reading on vacuum gauge. This reading should range between 17-21 inches.
5. If engine idles too fast after this adjustment, readjust throttle stop screw until correct idling speed is obtained.

Cooling System

1. Tighten all cooling system hose connections and check for indications of leakage.
2. Check fan belt for proper tension and adjust if necessary. See "Cooling System, Fan Belt Adjustment."

    NOTE: With correct adjustment, a light pressure on the belt at a point midway between the pulleys should cause ¾" deflection.

Current And Voltage Regulator

Check the adjustment of the current and voltage regulator as outlined in Section 12 of this manual.

Road Test

After completion of the above operations, the truck should be road-tested for performance.

MAJOR SERVICE OPERATIONS

ENGINE

Removal

1. Drain radiator, cylinder block, oil pan and transmission.
2. Disconnect hood springs and hinges and remove hood.
3. Remove radiator support bracket to fender bolts, radiator support to frame cross member bolts and remove radiator and radiator support.
4. Remove the battery cable and ammeter wire from the starter switch terminal. On vehicles equipped with push button starter, remove battery cable and ammeter wire from large terminal on solenoid and starter switch wire from small terminal. Tape end of battery cable to prevent possibility of shorting.
5. Disconnect the coil lead from distributor terminal and pull the coil high tension wire from the center of the distributor cap.
6. Remove two coil mounting screws and lay coil with wires attached on top of dash.
7. Disconnect engine ground strap from frame.
8. Disconnect gasoline line from fuel pump.
9. Disconnect the generator and field wires from the generator.
10. Disconnect wires from horn.
11. Remove air cleaner and disconnect choke and throttle control cables from carburetor.
12. Remove temperature indicator element from cylinder head and disconnect oil pressure line at cylinder block.
13. Disconnect windshield wiper vacuum line and vacuum line to hydrovac on vehicles so equipped.

14. Remove exhaust pipe flange to manifold bolts.
15. Remove starter pedal and remove accelerator pedal from accelerator rod.
16. (a) On ½ and ¾ ton, remove 1st and reverse control rod from shifter lever on left side of the transmission and remove 2nd and 3rd control rod from bell crank on left side of clutch housing.
    (b) On other models, remove floor mat and transmission floor pan cover.
17. (a) On all 1 ton, and (1948-50) 1½ and 2 ton, remove cotter key and pin attaching parking brake pull rod assembly to parking lever.
    (b) On (1951) 1½ and 2 ton, disconnect parking brake lever return spring from brake operating lever and remove cotter key and pin attaching inner and outer levers to parking brake operating lever.
18. On 1, 1½ and 2 ton, remove transmission cover with parking lever and gearshift lever. Place piece of cardboard on top of transmission to prevent possibility of dirt falling in during removal.
19. Disconnect speedometer cable from transmission and disconnect clutch link to clutch pedal arm.
20. On ½ ton:
    (a) Remove bolts from universal ball collar and bolts holding transmission support to frame cross member. Slide collar and ball back on propeller shaft housing.
    (b) Remove capscrews which fasten front trunnion bearings to the front yoke, remove bearings and split the joint.
21. On ¾ ton:
    (a) Split intermediate universal joint, tape bearings to keep clean and drop front end of rear propeller shaft.
    (b) Remove bolts which attach universal ball collar to rear of transmission and slide collar back on tube.
    (c) Remove nuts attaching propeller shaft bearing support to frame cross member and pull front propeller shaft assembly to the rear to clear splines of front universal joint.
22. On all 1 ton and (1948-50) 1½ and 2 ton, split the universal joint back of the transmission and tape the bearings to keep clean.
23. On (1951) 1½ and 2 ton:
    (a) Split intermediate universal joint by removing two trunnion bearing "U" clamps, tape bearings to keep clean and lower front end of rear propeller shaft to floor.
    (b) Remove the four front universal joint flange nuts.
    (c) Remove nuts attaching propeller shaft bearing support bracket to frame cross member and remove front propeller shaft and bearing assembly.

24. Remove rocker arm cover, disconnect oil line from rocker arm connector, remove rocker arm attaching bolts and stud nuts, rocker arm and shaft assembly and push rods.
25. Remove the third cylinder head bolt from the rear on the left and the fourth from the rear on the right. Then using lift kit J-4536, install the proper lifting tool (fig. 33) and raise engine slightly.

Fig. 33—Lifting Attachment

26. Remove bolts from rear engine mountings, remove front engine mounting and raise the engine, clutch and transmission from the chassis as a unit.
27. Remove crankcase ventilator pipe.
28. Remove starting motor, generator and fan belt.

Disassembly

1. Mount engine in stand and clamp it securely so that the engine can be turned over when necessary. Remove the lifting attachment.
2. Remove flywheel underpan extension and bolts attaching transmission to clutch housing. Remove transmission.

    NOTE: Support the transmission as the last mounting bolt is removed and as it is being pulled away from the engine to prevent damage to clutch disc.

3. Remove clutch release link from clutch fork.
4. Remove throwout bearing from clutch fork and remove fork by forcing it away from ball mounting with a large screwdriver.
5. Install clutch pilot K-411 to support clutch during disassembly. Loosen clutch to flywheel bolts a turn at a time (to prevent distortion of clutch cover) until the diaphragm spring pressure is released. Remove all bolts, pilot tool, cover assembly and disc.

6. Remove starter shaft and bracket assembly and engine ground strap.
7. Remove the flywheel and clutch housing.
8. Remove octane selector retaining screw and disconnect vacuum line from vacuum spark control. Disconnect spark plug wires from spark plugs and lift the distributor up out of engine.
9. Disconnect gas line from fuel pump, remove fuel pump mounting bolts and fuel pump.
10. Disconnect fuel and vacuum lines from clip at water outlet and from carburetor and remove lines.
11. Remove spark plugs, push rod cover, and oil gauge rod.
12. Remove two bolts attaching water outlet to thermostat housing and remove water outlet and thermostat.
13. Remove two bolts attaching thermostat housing to cylinder head and remove housing.
14. Remove water pump retaining bolts and remove generator brace and pump.
15. Attach harmonic balancer puller J-1287 to balancer and turn puller screw to remove balancer and pulley assembly (fig. 34).

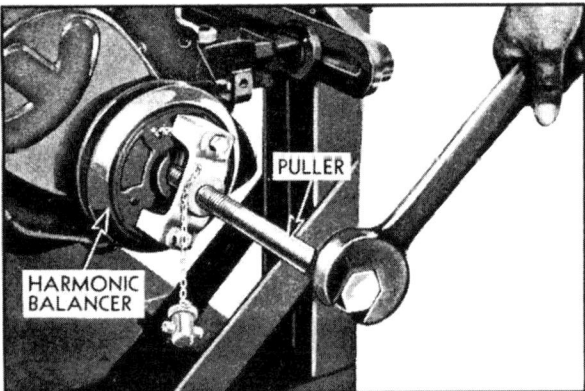

Fig. 34—Harmonic Balancer Puller and Driver

16. Disconnect throttle rod from throttle and accelerator lever and remove throttle rod.
17. Remove throttle and accelerator lever, stud, and accelerator rod from cylinder block.
18. Remove carburetor attaching nuts and carburetor.
19. Remove nuts and cap screws attaching manifold to cylinder head and remove manifold assembly and gaskets.
20. Remove screws attaching oil distributor to block and remove cover, gasket, plate with valve and gasket.
21. On the (1950-51) 235 engine only, disconnect rocker arm shaft oil line at cylinder block and remove oil line.
22. Remove valve lifters.
23. Remove the cylinder head attaching bolts, cylinder head and gasket.
24. Using valve lifter KMO-642, compress the valve springs and remove valve keys, spring caps, oil seals, springs and valves (fig. 9).
25. Turn the block assembly over in the engine stand and remove oil pan attaching screws, oil pan and gasket.
26. Remove the timing gear cover attaching screws and the two bolts that are installed from the back through the front main bearing cap and remove cover and gasket.
27. Pull the crankshaft gear with gear puller T-126-R by attaching it to the gear and turning the puller handle (fig. 35).

Fig. 35—Using Puller to Remove Crankshaft Gear

28. Remove the two crankshaft thrust plate screws by working through holes in the camshaft gear.
29. Remove the camshaft and gear assembly by pulling it out through the front of the block.

NOTE: Support shaft carefully when removing so as not to damage camshaft bearings.

30. Remove the engine front mounting plate attaching screws and remove plate and gasket.

31. Disconnect oil pump to block and oil pump to screen oil lines from pump and block fitting and remove oil line.
32. Remove oil pump retaining screw and remove oil pump.
33. Remove oil screen and body assembly.
34. Remove oil pump cover attaching screws, cover, gasket, idler gear and drive gear and shaft.
35. Check the connecting rods and pistons for cylinder number identification and, if necessary, mark them.
36. Remove connecting rod pal nuts, nuts, oil dippers and rod caps. Push the rods away from the crankshaft and install caps and nuts loosely to their respective rods.
37. Push piston and rod assemblies away from crankshaft and out of the cylinders.

    NOTE: It will be necessary to turn the crankshaft slightly to disconnect some of the rods and to push them out of the cylinder.

38. Remove piston rings by expanding them and sliding them off the ends of the pistons.
39. Clamp the piston in piston vise J-1218 (fig. 36), remove the connecting rod to piston pin clamp bolt and push the piston pin out (all pistons).
40. Remove main bearing cap bolts and remove the bearing caps and shims.
41. Lift the crankshaft out of the block and place it where it will not get damaged.
42. Lift bearing shells from the block.

Cleaning and Inspection

1. Wash all parts thoroughly in cleaning solvent.
2. Remove oil gallery plugs located one at front and one at rear face of cylinder block. These plugs may be removed with a sharp punch or they may be drilled and pried out. This oil passage should be thoroughly cleaned either by using compressed air or wire brush.
3. Clean all oil passages in the cylinder block by blowing them out with compressed air. It is good practice to blow them out separately. This can be done by plugging the holes in three of the bearings and placing the nozzle of the air gun in the oil inlet of the cylinder block and blowing through the remaining bearing oil passages. Continue this until all passages are clean. Blow through the passages to the camshaft bearings.
4. Blow out the rocker arm shaft oil line, and for the (1950-51) 235 engine, also the passage up from the rear camshaft bearing. Blow out the pipes in the oil pan.

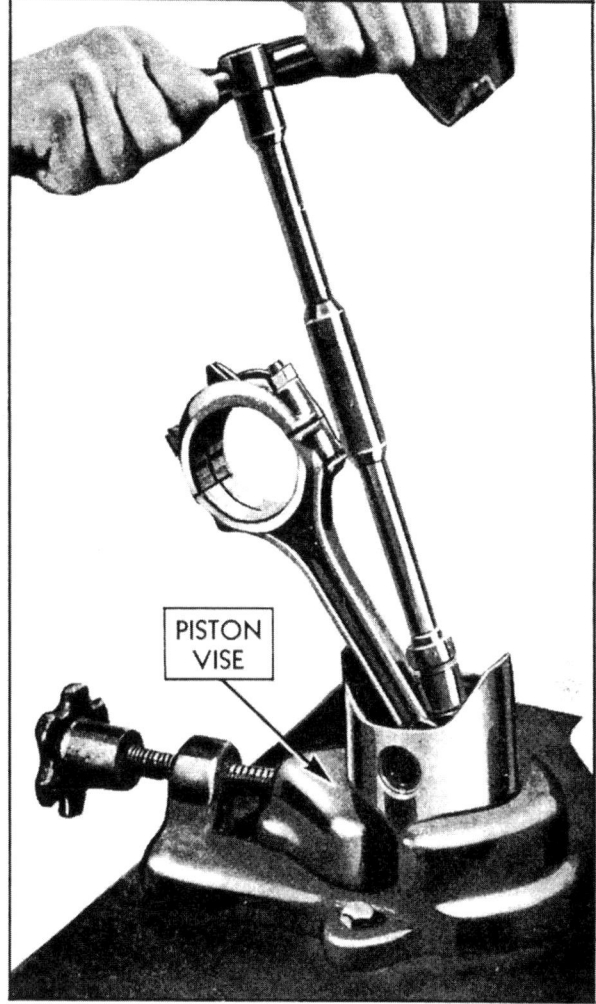

Fig. 36—Piston in Piston Vise

5. Clean carbon from piston heads, ring grooves and inside of piston head. Clean carbon from cylinder head combustion chambers and valve ports with carbon removing brush KMO-7004. Clean valve guides with valve guide cleaner KMO-122. Clean valve stems and heads on a buffing wheel.
6. Check the cylinder block for cracks in the cylinder walls, water jacket and main bearing webs.
7. Check the cylinder walls for taper, out-of-round or excessive ridge at top of ring travel. This should be done with a dial indicator (fig. 37). Set the gauge so that the thrust pin must be forced in about ¼" to enter gauge in cylinder bore. Center gauge in cylinder and turn dial to "0." Carefully work gauge up and down cylinder to determine taper and turn it to different points around cylinder wall to determine the out-of-round condition.
8. Set the indicator to the standard cylinder size using a pair of micrometers. Then, by

Fig. 37—Checking Cylinder Bore with Dial Gauge

checking the cylinders, the oversize pistons required and the amount necessary to be removed from the cylinders can be determined.

9. Inspect the main bearing shells for wear or damage that would make replacement necessary.
10. Inspect camshaft bearings for wear or damage that would make replacement necessary.

NOTE: Camshaft bearings should not be removed from the case unless new bearings are to be installed.

11. Inspect the camshaft for damaged cams or bearing journals. If the journals are out-of-round more than .001" the shaft should be replaced. Check the fit of the camshaft in the bearings.
12. Inspect the crankshaft journals and crank pins for roughness and scores. Check them with a micrometer for out-of-round or taper. If out-of-round more than .001" or tapered, the shaft should be replaced or reconditioned.
13. Inspect the connecting rod bearings for damage that would make replacement necessary.
14. Determine whether or not pistons are to be replaced. New piston assemblies and rings are required when the cylinders are to be honed or rebored. If the pistons are to be used again, check the piston pin fit in the bushings.
15. Inspect the timing gears for excessive tooth wear and for loose hub in camshaft gear. Inspect the camshaft thrust plate for excessive wear.
16. Check the cylinder head for being warped, for having clogged water passages, cracked valve seats or worn valve guides.
17. Inspect the manifolds for excessive carbon in the ports. Check the operation of the heat control valve and make sure that the gasket between the manifolds is in good condition.
18. Inspect the oil pump gears for wear, check the shaft for looseness in the housing and the inside of cover for wear that would permit oil to leak past end of gears.
19. Instructions for inspection and repair of the fuel pump, carburetor, air cleaner, generator, starting motor, distributor, clutch and water pump will be found in their respective sections of this manual.

REPAIRS

Some of the following repair operations may not be required on all engine overhauls, depending upon the result of the inspections made. In making some of the repairs, certain engine assembling operations must be performed; therefore, the assembling operations will start with the engine partly assembled as covered under repair operations.

Cylinder Conditioning

If the cylinder block inspection indicated that the block was suitable for continued use, except for out-of-round or tapered cylinders, they can be conditioned by honing or boring and honing. Pistons are serviced in .005", .010", .020", .030", and .040" oversize. If the cylinders were found to have less than .005" taper or wear they can be conditioned with a hone and .005" oversize pistons would be used. If more than .005" taper or wear they should be bored and honed to the smallest oversize that will permit complete resurfacing of all cylinders. The use of a dial gauge set up with a pair of micrometers to the standard cylinder bore size as outlined under "Cleaning and Inspection," will aid in determining the size pistons for which the cylinders must be bored.

Cylinder Boring

1. Before using any type boring bar, the top of the cylinder block should be filed off to remove any dirt or burrs. This is very important, otherwise the boring bar may be tilted which would result in the rebored cylinder wall not being at right angles to the crankshaft.
2. In Chevrolet engines, the piston clearance is provided for on the piston and this must be taken into consideration when setting the cutter in the boring bar. The piston to be fitted should be checked with a micrometer, measuring just below the lower ring groove and at right angles to the piston pin. The cylinder should be bored to the same diameter as the piston.

3. If a micrometer is not available to measure the piston, the cylinder should be bored .002" less than the oversize piston to be fitted. For example, when fitting a .020" oversize piston, the cylinder should be bored .018" oversize.
4. The instructions furnished by the manufacturer of the equipment being used should be carefully followed.

Cylinder Honing and Piston Fitting

1. When the cylinders are to be honed only for .005" oversize pistons or for final finishing after they have been rebored to within .002" of the desired size, they should be finish honed and polished with a hone. Rough stones may be used at first and fine stones for the polishing operation.
2. Place the hone into a cylinder bore and expand the stones until the hone can just be turned by hand. Connect a ¾" electric drill to the hone and drive hone at drill speed while slowly moving hone up and down entire length of cylinder until hone begins to run free. During this operation a liberal amount of kerosene should be used as a cutting fluid to keep the stones of the hone clean.
3. Expand the stones against the cylinder bore and repeat the honing operation until the desired bore diameter is obtained.
4. Occasionally during the honing operation the cylinder bore should be thoroughly cleaned and the piston selected for the individual cylinder checked for correct fit.
5. Correct piston fit is determined by placing a long, ½" wide feeler along the side of the piston 90° around the piston from the piston pin (fig. 38) and inserting the piston and feeler into the cylinder bore. The piston should push through the cylinder with light pressure when a .002" feeler is used and should lock with a .003" feeler.
6. Permanently mark the piston for the cylinder to which it has been fitted and proceed to hone cylinders and fit the remaining pistons.

    CAUTION: *Handle the pistons with care and do not attempt to force them through the cylinder until the cylinder has been bored to correct size as this type piston can be distorted through careless handling.*

7. Clean the cylinder bores and block to remove all cuttings.

Piston Pin Fitting

All new Chevrolet pistons are serviced with properly fitted piston pins and bushings; therefore, pin fitting is unnecessary when new pistons are installed. Where cylinder condition and piston fit justify the use of old pistons, it may be desirable to install new piston pins which are available

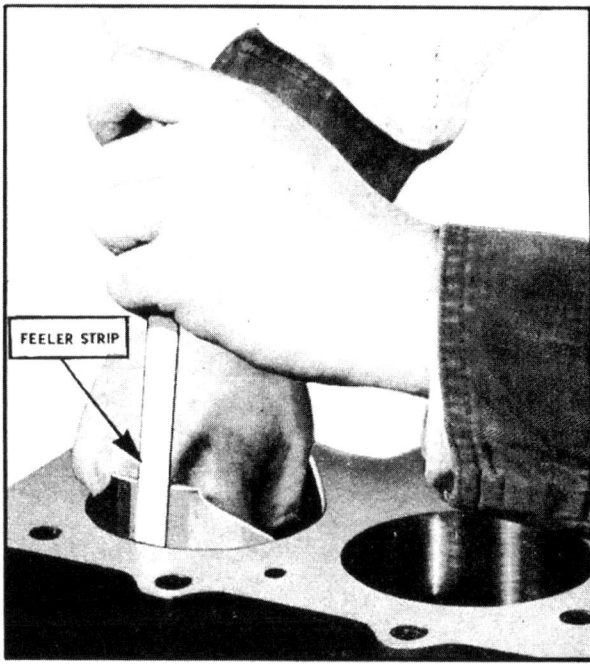

Fig. 38—Fitting Pistons

in .003", .005" and .010" oversize. Correct alignment of the bushing bores is essential; therefore, the following procedure should be carefully followed.

1. Place the piston pin bushing reaming fixture J-965 in a bench vise.
2. Adjust the expansion reamer for a light cut.
3. Insert the reamer in the piston bushings and start the reamer pilot into the guide in the fixture.
4. Hold the piston in the V-block of the fixture with one hand and turn the reamer handle with the other hand until the reamer has passed through both bushings (fig. 39).

Fig. 39—Reaming Piston Pin Bushings

5. Expand the reamer by easy stages and repeat the reaming operation until the piston pin is fitted. The proper fit of the piston pin is a "thumb push" fit as shown in Figure 40.

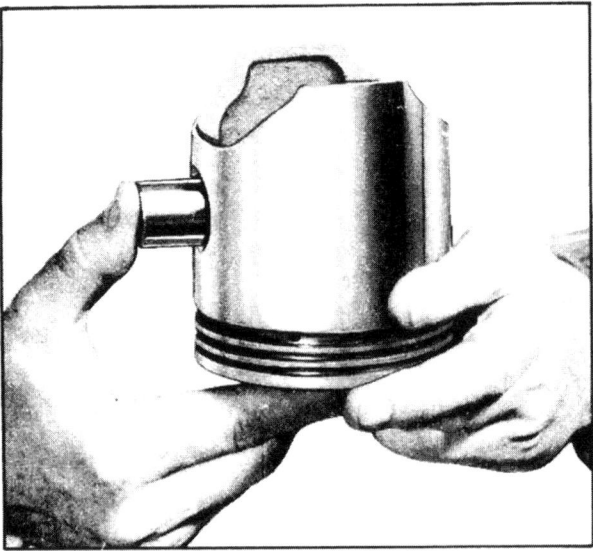

Fig. 40—Fitting Piston Pin

6. After fitting the first piston pin, the other bushings may be reamed quickly by reducing the diameter of the reamer approximately .0005" (half a thousandth) by backing off the expansion screw. This permits quick roughing out of all bushings leaving about half a thousandth for the finish cut.
7. It is good practice to check the diameter of all piston pins with a micrometer. In case there should be a slight variation in diameter, consideration must be taken when adjusting the reamer for the finish cut.
8. The purpose of the piston pin reaming fixture is to make sure that the piston pin bushings will be reamed at right angles to the skirt of the piston, assuring proper alignment of the piston in the cylinder.

CAMSHAFT

The camshaft bearing journal sizes are as follows: front, 2.0282"-2.0292"; front intermediate, 1.9657"-1.9667"; rear intermediate, 1.9032"-1.9042"; rear, 1.8407"-1.8417".

These dimensions should be checked with a micrometer for an *out-of-round* condition. If the journals exceed .001" out-of-round, the camshaft should be replaced.

The camshaft should also be checked for alignment. The best method is by use of "V" blocks and a dial indicator (fig. 41). The dial indicator will indicate the exact amount the camshaft is out of true. If it is out more than .002" dial indicator reading, the camshaft should be straightened. When checking, the high reading of the dial indicator indicates the high point of the shaft. This point should be chalk marked to tell exactly where to apply pressure when straightening.

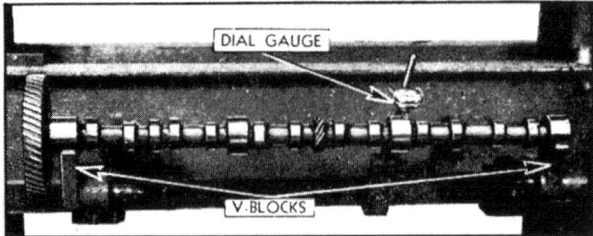

Fig. 41—Checking Camshaft Alignment

NOTE: During the straightening operation, care should be taken to protect the bearing journals and prevent damage of their surfaces.

After the camshaft has been straightened, it should be rechecked to be sure it is within .002" dial indicator reading for alignment.

CAMSHAFT BEARINGS

All four of the steel backed, babbitt lined camshaft bearings are pressed into the crankcase and staked in place to prevent rotation or endwise movement in the bores. The camshaft bearings are lubricated through holes that line up with oil passages leading from the main bearings.

Replacement of these bearings is seldom necessary; however, if the inspections previously made indicate that replacement is necessary, the camshaft bearing removing and replacing tools shown in Figure 42 must be used. These tools are not considered essential as far as dealers are concerned and when this job is necessary they may be obtained from the Chevrolet Zone Offices.

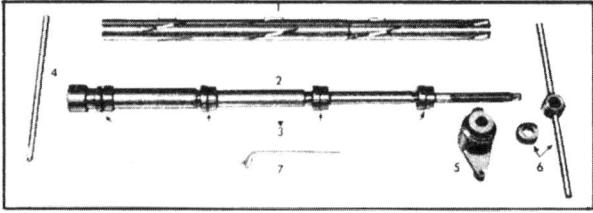

Fig. 42—Camshaft Bearing Removing and Replacing Tools

1. Reamer
2. Removing and Replacing Bar
3. Removing and Replacing Sleeves
4. Extension Handle
5. Bracket
6. Handle and Thrust Bearing
7. Staking Tool

Removal

1. With camshaft removed, drive out expansion plug from cylinder block at the rear of the rear camshaft bearing, by driving it out from the inside.

2. Assemble the camshaft bearing remover bracket loosely to the rear of the cylinder block.
3. Start the bearing puller bar through the front bearing and install the puller sleeve for each bearing over the bar before it passes through that particular bearing. Then pass the bar through the hole in the bracket. Tighten the bolts that hold the bracket to the cylinder block. Then install the thrust bearing and puller handle on the end of the bar.
4. Turning the puller handle clockwise will now remove all four bearings at one time. An extension handle is provided to aid in starting bearings that may have corroded in the block.

Replacement
1. To make sure that the oil holes in the camshaft bearing bores will line up with the oil holes in the camshaft bearings after the bearings have been installed, mark the position of the oil hole in the bore on the front face of each bearing bore.
2. Place puller sleeve and new front camshaft bearing over the puller bar and start the bar through the front bearing bore. Place the puller sleeve with a new bearing over the bar before passing the bar through the other bearing bores in the cylinder block. Pass the end of the bar through the puller bracket, install the thrust bearing and turning handle.
3. Line up the oil holes in each bearing with the oil hole location marks previously made. All four bearings can now be pulled into place at the same time.
4. Remove the puller bar and bracket and stake each bearing into the hole provided in the bore for that purpose.

Reaming
The special camshaft bearing line reamer has all four cutters mounted on one bar so that all bearings will be in perfect alignment after the reaming operation.
1. Pass the reamer through the first, second and third bearings. Turn the cylinder block to a vertical position so the reamer will feed through the bearings by its own weight. Then start the reamer cutter into all four bearings and turn the reamer slowly until the cutters have passed through the bearings. While the bearings are being reamed, a liberal amount of kerosene should be used to wash out all metal cuttings.
2. Remove the reamer by pulling it back through the bearings, at the same time turning the reamer slowly in the same direction as when reaming the bearings.

3. Blow all cuttings from the bearings with compressed air and wash cylinder block out thoroughly with cleaning solvent. Blow out all oil passages. Install the camshaft and check all bearing clearances with a narrow feeler gauge. The proper clearance is from .002" to .004". Install a new camshaft end plug in the back end of the cylinder block at the rear camshaft bearing.

NOTE: Camshaft end plug must be assembled flush to $1/32$" deep from clutch housing face of case.

OIL SEAL—REAR BEARING—UPPER

The upper half of the rear bearing cap oil seal, located in the cylinder block, can only be replaced with the crankshaft removed from the block.

See "Minor Service Operations, Oil Seal—Rear Bearing Cap" for replacing oil seal in bearing cap.
1. Remove old wick seal from groove in block and make sure groove is thoroughly cleaned.
2. Install new wick seal in groove with the fingers.
3. Use a rounded tool and roll the seal into the groove starting at one end and roll it to the center. Then starting from the other end again roll to the center.
4. Cut the small portion of the seal that protrudes from the groove off flush with surface of the bearing.

NOTE: A round block of wood the same diameter as the crankshaft flange should be used to hold the packing firmly in position in the groove while the ends are being cut off.

CRANKSHAFT

The crankshaft main bearing journal and connecting rod journal sizes are as follows: front, 2.6835"-2.6845"; front intermediate, 2.7145"-2.7155"; rear intermediate, 2.7455"-2.7465"; rear, 2.7765"-2.7775" connecting rod journal, 2.311"-2.312".

These dimensions should be checked with a micrometer for out-of-round, taper or undersize. If the journals exceed .001" out-of-round or taper the crankshaft should be replaced or reconditioned to an undersize figure that will enable the installation of undersize precision type bearings.

The crankshaft should also be checked for runout. To perform this operation, support the crankshaft at the front and rear main bearing journals in "V" blocks and indicate the runout of both the rear intermediate and front intermediate journals, using a dial indicator. The runout limit of each of these journals is .002". If the runout exceeds .002", the crankshaft must be straightened.

ENGINE ASSEMBLY 6-28

MAIN BEARINGS

Precision type main bearings used as service replacement are of high quality with close tolerances of fit and will not require line reaming on installation. The close dimensional tolerances assure an equalized bearing surface at all points on the crankshaft when replaced in sets.

Bearings are available in standard sizes and undersizes of .002", .010", .020" and .030".

Precision type main bearings may be replaced either with the engine in the vehicle or with the engine removed. With the engine in the vehicle, proceed as outlined below.

1. Drain radiator and remove drain cock and upper and lower radiator hoses.
2. On vehicles equipped with a fan shroud, remove fan blades and then remove radiator body assembly and shroud.
3. Remove fan belt and harmonic balancer.
4. Remove rocker arm cover and loosen all rocker arm screws to relieve tension on camshaft.
5. Remove spark plugs.
6. Remove transmission floor pan hole cover.
7. Remove flywheel underpan and extension.
8. On ½ and ¾ ton, disconnect control rods from shifter levers on transmission.
9. (a) On all 1 ton and (1948-50) 1½ and 2 ton, remove cotter key and pin attaching parking brake pull rod assembly to parking lever.
    (b) On (1951) 1½ and 2 ton, disconnect parking brake lever return spring from parking brake operating lever and remove cotter key and pin attaching inner and outer levers to parking brake operating lever.
10. On 1, 1½ and 2 ton, remove parking brake lever lock, flat washer and spring and remove parking brake lever.
11. (a) On ½ ton, disconnect ball collar, remove bolts retaining transmission support to cross member, split the joint and raise front end of propeller shaft to gain clearance for transmission removal.
    (b) On ¾ ton, disconnect ball collar, disconnect intermediate universal joint, remove bolts retaining intermediate support to cross member and remove front propeller shaft.
    (c) On all 1 ton and (1948-50) 1½ and 2 ton, split universal joint at transmission, remove nuts retaining intermediate bearing support to cross member and drop front propeller shaft.
    (d) On (1951) 1½ and 2 ton, split the intermediate universal joint by removing the trunnion bearing "U" clamps, tape the bearings and lower front end of rear propeller shaft to floor. Remove the four front universal joint flange nuts. Remove nuts attaching propeller shaft bearing support bracket to frame cross member and remove front propeller shaft assembly.
12. Disconnect speedometer cable at transmission.
13. Remove two top transmission to clutch housing bolts and install guide pins J-1116.
14. (a) On ½ and ¾ ton, remove two lower transmission to clutch housing bolts, slide transmission straight back on guide pins until clutch gear shaft is free of splines in the clutch disc and remove transmission through opening in body floor.
    (b) On all other models, place jack under transmission, remove two lower transmission to clutch housing bolts, slide transmission straight back on guide pins until clutch gear shaft is free of splines in the clutch disc and lower transmission to the floor.
15. Drain the oil, remove the oil pan, oil pump, screen and lines.
16. Remove the timing gear cover.
17. Rotate crankshaft to best possible position for removal of all bearing caps and mark the meshing teeth of the timing gears so that they can be remeshed in the same position.
18. Loosen all four main bearing cap bolts evenly until the crankshaft is lowered approximately ⅜".
19. Remove front intermediate and rear bearing caps and remove upper and lower bearing shells. If upper bearing shells do not come away with the crankshaft, tap lightly to loosen.

NOTE: Always replace bearings in pairs. In this way two bearings are supporting the crankshaft while you are working on the other two.

20. Install new upper half bearing shells in rear and front intermediate bearing bores by rolling into position, centering, and pressing up into place. If the bearings have the correct spread, they will snap into place and stay there.

NOTE: Be sure to install all upper bearing halves so the smaller of the two oil holes will be toward the camshaft when the bearing halves are rolled into place.

21. Install new lower half bearing shells in rear and front intermediate bearing caps and replace caps, using three .002" shims on each side of bearing as a starting point for adjust-

ment. Lubricate bearings with light engine oil. Draw bolts up until caps are snug to crankshaft bearing journals.

22. Remove front and rear intermediate bearing caps and remove upper and lower bearing shells. If upper bearing shells do not come away with the crankshaft, tap lightly to loosen.

23. Install new upper half bearing shells in front and rear intermediate bearing bores by rolling into position, centering, and pressing up into place.

   NOTE: Due to close side fit, the upper half of the rear intermediate bearing may not go all the way into place. Start it evenly and it will go all the way into place when the crankshaft is raised.

24. Install new lower half bearing shells in front and rear intermediate bearing caps and replace caps using three .002" shims on each side of bearing. Draw bolts up until caps are snug to crankshaft bearing journals.

25. After all main bearings have been replaced, raise the crankshaft by tightening the bearing cap bolts alternately and evenly.

   NOTE: At the same time, check the meshing of the timing gears, turning the camshaft gear as necessary so that the gears engage with the previously installed marks (step 17) aligned.

26. With the crankshaft up in place, force it all the way fore or aft and check the end clearance at the rear intermediate bearing. This should be .003" to .009".

27. Adjust main bearings as outlined under "Minor Service Operations, Main Bearings—Adjust."

28. Replace oil pump, screen and lines.

29. Replace timing gear cover and oil pan.

30. On ½ and ¾ ton:
    (a) Install transmission through opening in floor.
    (b) Place the transmission on the guide pins and start clutch gear shaft in clutch disc and slide forward making sure the step at the end of the countershaft is flush with the face of the transmission and engages properly with the clutch housing. This keeps the shaft from turning as well as helps align transmission properly.
    (c) Install two lower transmission mounting bolts and tighten securely. Remove two guide pins and install two upper transmission mounting bolts and tighten securely.

31. On all other models:
    (a) Raise transmission with jack, place on guide pins, start clutch gear shaft in clutch disc and slide transmission forward till it engages clutch housing.
    (b) Install two lower transmission mounting bolts and tighten securely. Remove two guide pins and install two upper transmission mounting bolts and tighten securely.

32. On ½ ton, lower propeller shaft, connect front universal, connect ball collar and replace transmission support to cross member bolts.

33. On ¾ ton:
    (a) Install front propeller shaft engaging splines to transmission yoke, lift rear of shaft and replace intermediate bearing support to cross member bolts and connect ball collar.
    (b) Raise front of rear propeller shaft, align rear joint and intermediate joint for balance and install trunnion bearing "U" clamps.

34. On all 1 ton and (1948-50) 1½ and 2 ton, raise and connect front of propeller shaft to transmission universal joint flange, replace intermediate support bracket to cross member bolts and nuts and tighten securely.

35. On (1951) 1½ and 2 ton, install front propeller shaft and bearing support assembly positioning the universal joint front yoke on the four flange bolts. Install and tighten securely the nuts attaching propeller shaft support bracket to frame cross member. Install four universal joint flange lockwashers and nuts and tighten securely. Raise front end of rear propeller shaft, align trunnion bearings with front yoke and install trunnion bearing "U" clamps and tighten securely.

36. On ½ and ¾ ton, connect control rods to shifter levers on transmission.

37. On 1, 1½ and 2 ton, install parking brake lever and install spring, flat washer and parking brake lever lock.

38. (a) On all 1 ton and (1948-50) 1½ and 2 ton, connect parking brake pull rod assembly to parking lever.
    (b) On (1951) 1½ and 2 ton, connect inner and outer levers to parking brake operating lever and connect brake lever return spring to brake operating lever.

39. Replace flywheel underpan and extension.

40. Replace transmission floor pan hole cover.

41. Adjust and replace spark plugs.

42. Replace harmonic balancer and fan belt.

43. On vehicles with shroud, place shroud and radiator core in position and install fan blades, then install radiator core attaching bolts.
44. Replace upper and lower radiator hoses and replace drain cock.
45. Refill the crankcase and cooling system.
46. Tighten rocker arm screws, start the engine and after it has normalized, adjust the valve clearances. Install the valve cover.

With the engine removed from the vehicle—The procedure for replacing main bearing is as follows:

1. Remove old bearing shells from cylinder block and caps. Make sure that cylinder block and caps are well cleaned.
2. Install the new bearing shells in cylinder block and caps.

   NOTE: The front and front intermediate bearing shells are very similar in appearance and it is possible to get them mixed. The front intermediate shells are identified by the letter "I" in the bottom of the oil groove.

3. Lubricate all four bearings with light engine oil and place the crankshaft in the bearings.
4. Place three .002" shims on each side of each bearing and install bearing caps.

   NOTE: The intermediate bearing caps are marked "front" and "rear" for identification purposes. The front intermediate bearing cap is installed with the "Front" mark to the front of the engine and the rear intermediate bearing cap is installed with the "Rear" mark to the rear of the engine.

5. Force the crankshaft to its extreme rear position and check the end clearance at the rear intermediate bearing (fig. 43). This end clearance should be .003" to .009".
6. Adjust bearings as outlined under "Minor Service Operations, Main Bearings—Adjust."

TIMING GEAR OIL NOZZLE

Examine the timing gear oil nozzle which is of tubular construction and pressed and flared in place in the cylinder block front end plate.

In the event the oil nozzle is damaged it will be necessary to replace the front end plate assembly as it is not practical to replace the nozzle only without the use of special equipment.

CYLINDER BLOCK FRONT END PLATE

1. Install new oil gallery plugs at front and rear face of block making sure they seat properly.
2. Install new front end plate gasket and end plate, and hold in position with three screws and two hex head bolts. Tighten screws to 15-20 ft. lbs. and stake securely at bottom of slot.

   NOTE: Make sure gasket surfaces on block and on end plate are thoroughly cleaned.

3. Place two camshaft thrust plate gaskets and a new thrust plate over camshaft hole in end plate.

Fig. 43—Checking Crankshaft End Play

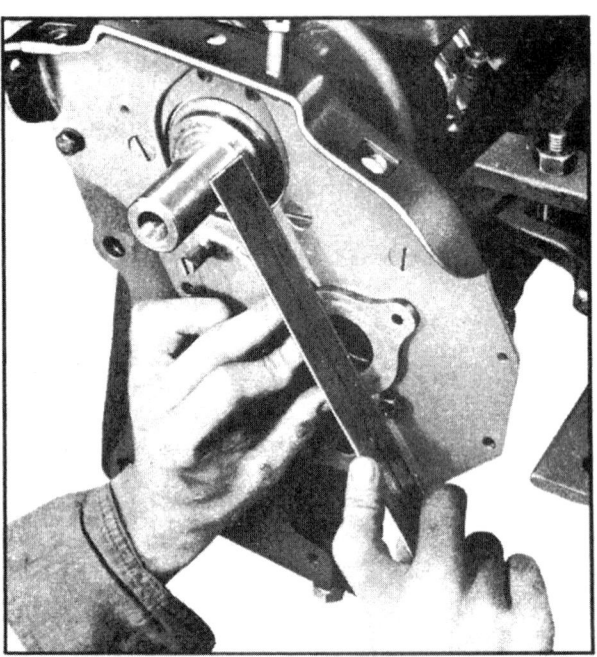

Fig. 44—Checking Timing Gear Alignment

4. Lay a straight edge against the thrust plate and over to the gear shoulder on the crankshaft. Check to see whether their two surfaces are flush (fig. 44).
5. If scale strikes the shoulder on the crankshaft, add another gasket beneath the thrust plate.
6. When number of thrust plate gaskets necessary to obtain this proper alignment is determined, note the number so that when camshaft is installed the proper number of gaskets will be used between the thrust plate and the front end plate.

CRANKSHAFT GEAR—INSTALL

1. Place the two woodruff keys in their respective keyways in the crankshaft.
2. Place the crankshaft gear on the end of crankshaft with keyway in line with key.
3. Drive the gear onto the shaft, using a suitable driver until gear bottoms against shoulder on shaft.

Camshaft, Camshaft Gear and Thrust Plate

1. If the inspection indicated that the camshaft, gear and thrust plate were in good condition, the camshaft end play should be checked (fig. 45). This clearance should be .001" to .005".

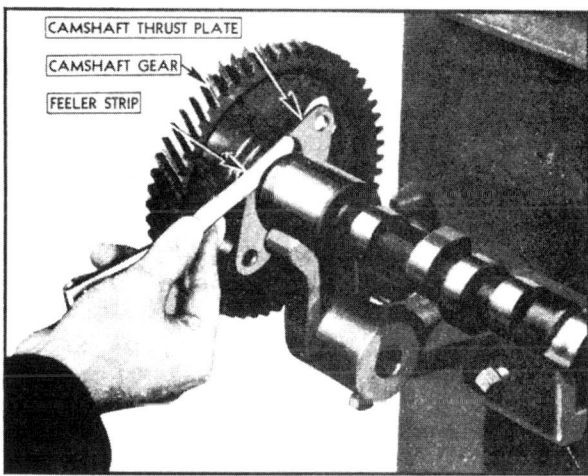

Fig. 45—Checking Camshaft End Play

2. If the inspection indicated that the shaft, gear or plate should be replaced, the gear must be removed from the shaft. This operation requires the use of camshaft gear remover J-971.
3. Place the camshaft through the gear remover, place end of remover on table of a press and press shaft out of gear (fig. 46).

CAUTION: Thrust plate must be so positioned that woodruff key in shaft does not damage it when the shaft is pressed out of gear.

4. To assemble camshaft gear and thrust plate to camshaft of 216 engine or 235 engines which are equipped with aluminum alloy gear with steel hub, proceed as follows:
   (a) Firmly support shaft at back of the front journal in an arbor press.
   (b) Place thrust plate over end of shaft and install woodruff key in shaft keyway.
   (c) Install camshaft gear and press into position. As the gear is being pressed onto the shaft, check space between thrust plate and shoulder of shaft. The plate must turn freely, but must not have more than .001" to .005" clearance.

NOTE: Press on the hub of the gear or the gear will be seriously damaged.

5. To assemble camshaft gear, thrust plate and gear spacer ring to camshaft of 235 engines which are equipped with all aluminum alloy gear, proceed as follows:
   (a) Firmly support shaft at back of the front journal in an arbor press.

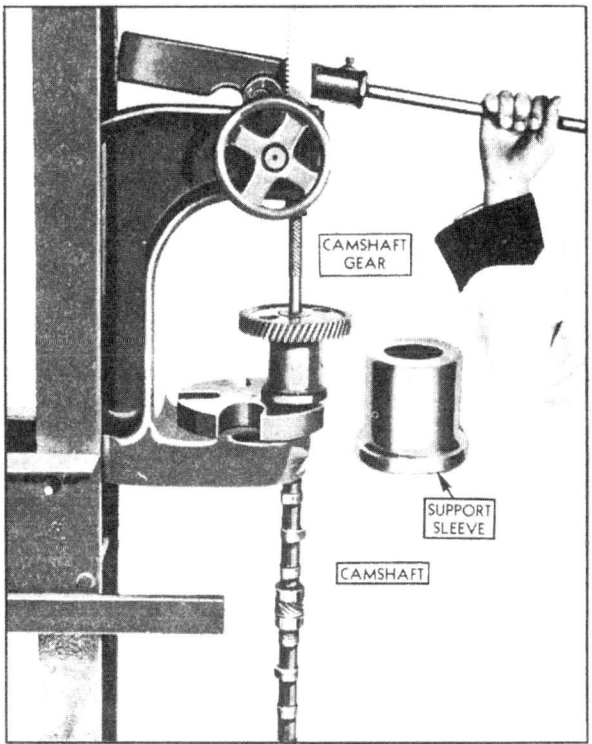

Fig. 46—Removing Camshaft Gear

   (b) Place gear spacer ring and thrust plate over end of shaft, and install woodruff key in shaft keyway.
   (c) Install camshaft gear and press it onto the shaft until it bottoms against the gear spacer ring. The end clearance of the thrust plate should be .001" to .005".

6. Place the thrust plate gaskets, proper quantity previously determined, over camshaft and install camshaft assembly being careful not to damage bearings or cams.

7. Turn crankshaft and camshaft so that the valve timing marks on the gear teeth will line up and push camshaft into position. Install camshaft thrust plate to block screws and tighten them securely.

8. Check camshaft and crankshaft gear runout with a dial indicator (fig. 47). The camshaft

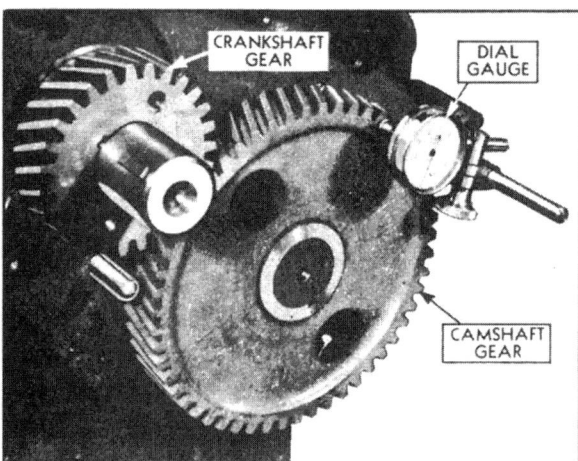

Fig. 47—Checking Runout of Timing Gears

gear runout should not exceed .004" and the crankshaft gear runout should not exceed .003".

9. If gear runout is excessive, the gear will have to be removed and any burrs cleaned from the shaft or the gear replaced.

Fig. 48—Checking Timing Gear Backlash

10. Check the backlash between the timing gear teeth with a narrow feeler gauge (fig. 48). The backlash should not be less than .003" nor more than .005" with a Bakelite timing gear (216 engine). With an aluminum timing gear (235 engine) the backlash should not be less than .004" and not more than .006".

TIMING GEAR COVER

1. A spring loaded leather oil seal is pressed into the crankshaft opening of the timing gear cover to prevent oil leakage around the hub of the harmonic balancer.

2. If this seal shows signs of wear or damage, it should be replaced by prying it out of the cover from the front with a large screwdriver.

3. Install new seal so that open end of the leather is toward the inside of the cover and drive in place with oil seal driver J-995 (fig. 49).

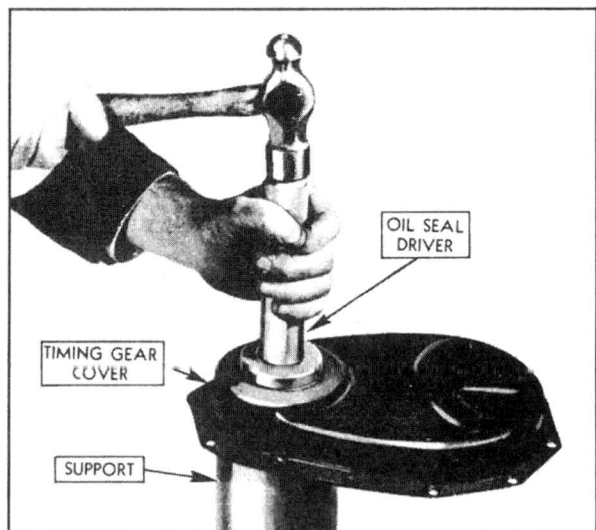

Fig. 49—Installing Timing Gear Cover Oil Seal

4. Make certain that cover mounting face and cylinder block front end plate face are clean.

5. Install timing gear cover centering gauge J-966 over end of crankshaft.

6. Coat the leather oil seal with light grease and using a new cover gasket, install cover and gasket over centering gauge.

7. Install cover screws and two bolts through bearing cap and tighten to 6-7½ ft. lbs. torque, using a torque wrench. Remove centering gauge.

NOTE: It is important that the centering gauge be used to align the timing gear cover so that the harmonic balancer installation will not damage the seal and to provide uniform seal tension on the hub of the balancer.

HARMONIC BALANCER INSTALLATION

1. Remove puller screw from harmonic balancer.
2. Place driver adapter of puller J-1287 in starting crank jaws of balancer. Install puller body to balancer and tighten attaching screws securely.
3. Line up keyway in balancer with key on crankshaft and drive balancer onto shaft until it bottoms against crankshaft gear using puller screw as a driver.

CLUTCH HOUSING—INSTALL

1. Install clutch housing and attaching bolts and tighten to 45-55 ft. lbs. with a torque wrench.
2. Install indicator extension in a crankshaft stud hole, attach indicator to extension and check pilot hole runout (fig. 50). This runout

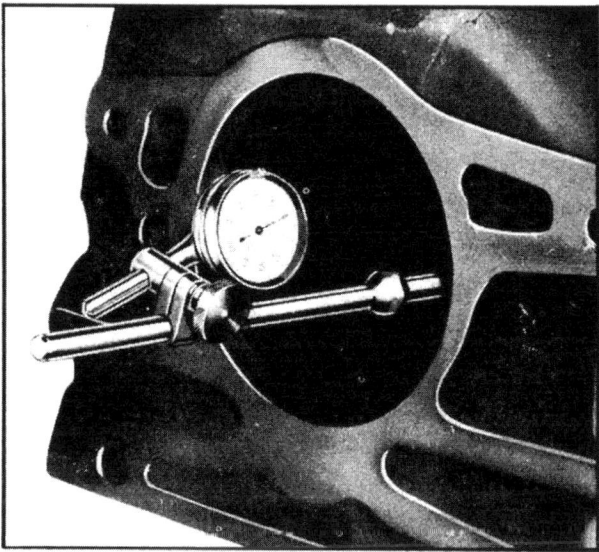

Fig. 50—Checking Runout of Transmission Pilot Hole

should not exceed .008". Also check face runout which should not exceed .010".

3. Should pilot hole runout exceed .008" or face runout exceed .010" the clutch housing should be realigned as outlined under "Alignment Correction."

Alignment Correction

1. If bore runout is in excess of .008" or if housing face parallelism exceeds .010", remove indicator and the flywheel housing from the engine block.
2. Remove the lower left hand dowel by driving it out, using a drift punch through hole in cylinder block flange.
3. Center punch the other two dowels and then drill through the dowels using a 7/32" drill.
4. Run a 1/4"-28 tap through drilled holes in dowels.
5. Install a 1/4"-28 x 2" capscrew into each dowel. Tightening capscrew will push dowels out of block.
6. Clean mating faces of flywheel housing and engine block and make certain there are no burrs or metal extrusion around dowel or bolt holes.
7. Install flywheel housing and tighten attaching bolts evenly to 45-55 ft. lbs. torque.
8. Mount indicator on indicator post and indicate flywheel housing face. Set indicator at zero at the six o'clock position and carefully check indicator readings at the 9, 12, and 3 o'clock positions. The runout limit is .010".

NOTE: Care should be exercised so that the indicator button is not on the edge of a bolt hole when the readings are taken.

9. If the face runout exceeds .010", shim as necessary, using main bearing shim No. 3847687 between the housing and block at the attaching bolt locations.
10. After the housing face has been brought within the .010" limit, with bolts tightened to required torque, reset indicator to read zero at the six o'clock position on the machined inside diameter of the flywheel housing bore.

NOTE: Be careful that the indicator button is centered on the narrow machined flange and does not touch flange step.

11. Check indicator readings at the 9, 12, and 3 o'clock positions, carefully lifting indicator button over each cutaway section of flange. The runout should not exceed .008".
12. If the readings exceed the .008" runout limits, loosen bolts slightly and tap housing with a soft hammer in required direction until runout is within limits. Tighten attaching bolts evenly to 45-55 ft. lbs. torque and recheck.
13. With flywheel housing in proper alignment, carefully drill through dowel holes in housing and into block using a 13/32" drill.

CAUTION: When drilling into lower right blind hole in block, be careful not to drill through.

14. Carefully ream holes using J-4628 reamer (27/64").
15. Blow out holes and then install 27/64" oversize dowels.
16. Recheck flywheel housing bore and the face to make sure they are still within proper limits.

FLYWHEEL INSTALLATION

1. Clean the mating flanges of flywheel and crankshaft carefully and make sure there are no burrs on either mounting face.

2. Place the flywheel in the clutch housing and position it so that the three unevenly spaced dowels in crankshaft flange will enter the dowel holes in the flywheel.
3. Install the six bolts using new lock plates under each pair of bolts.
4. Tighten bolts to 50-65 ft. lbs. with a torque wrench.
5. Mount a dial indicator on the clutch housing so that the button of the indicator will contact the machined surface of flywheel (fig. 51), and check the flywheel runout.

Fig. 51—Checking Flywheel Runout

6. Runout should not exceed .008". If excessive, remove flywheel and recheck for burrs or replace flywheel.
7. Securely lock the mounting bolts by bending the locks up against the bolt heads.

CONNECTING ROD ALIGNMENT

Correct alignment of the connecting rods is important. Whether new rods are being used or the old ones reinstalled, they must be checked for alignment.

1. Place the piston pin in the eye of the connecting rod and tighten the clamp bolt.
2. Place the connecting rod on the arbor of the aligning fixture J-874-C, and tighten the connecting rod bolts.
3. Place the "V" block on the piston pin and move the rod and arbor toward the face plate until the pins on the "V" block just engage the face plate (fig. 52). If all pins touch the face plate the rod is in alignment.
4. If either the top or the bottom two pins touch the face plate, but the other two do not, the rod is bent.
5. If only the two pins on the front or the two on the back side of the "V" block touch the face plate, the rod is twisted.
6. The fixture is sufficiently strong to hold the connecting rod for straightening. Place a bending bar on the rod and twist or bend the

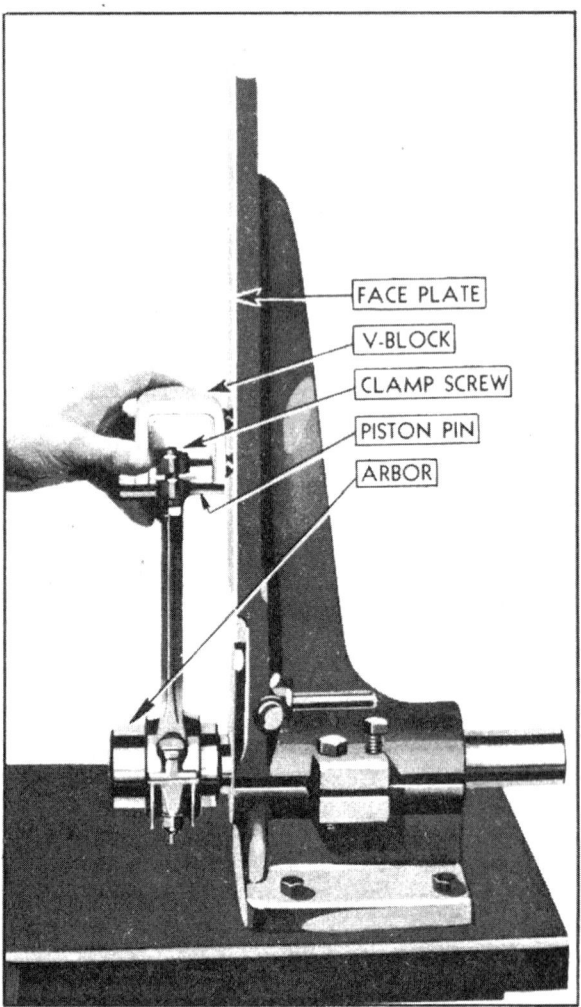

Fig. 52—Connecting Rod Alignment Fixture

rod as required and recheck. Continue this operation until all pins just touch the face plate.

7. Place the "V" block on the piston pin so that the "V" block rests against the outside edge of the connecting rod and move the rod and "V" block toward the face plate until all four pins touch.
8. Place the index on the bottom of the fixture so that it touches the large end of the connecting rod bearing. Remove the rod from the arbor and turn it around.
9. Assemble it again to the arbor and place the "V" block on the piston pin in the same place as when checking the other side. Move rod and "V" block toward the face plate until either the index touches the bearing or the pins touch the face plate.
10. If the index does not touch the rod bearing with the four pins touching the face plate, check the distance between the rod bearing and the index with a feeler gauge. If this distance is greater than .025" the rod should be

straightened until pins touch the face plate and the index touches the rod bearing within .025".

11. If the index touches the rod bearing and the four pins do not touch the face plate, the distance between the pins and the face plate should also be checked with a feeler gauge. If this distance is more than .025" the rod should be straightened until the pins on the "V" block touch the plate and the index touches the rod bearing within .025".

Assemble Connecting Rod to Piston

1. Place the piston in piston vise J-1218. Assemble the rod to the piston and install the piston pin. Before tightening the clamp screw, center the piston pin in the piston and the connecting rod in the center of the two piston pin bosses.

2. Tighten the clamp screw and move piston on pin from side to side, checking to see that the piston pin does not extend beyond the outside of the piston.

3. Assemble remaining rods to pistons.

    NOTE: The connecting rod should never be clamped in a bench vise when installing the piston on it as tightening the clamp screw will likely twist the rod.

Check Rod and Piston Alignment

1. Assemble the piston and connecting rod assembly to the alignment fixture (fig. 53) and check with the "V" block resting against the piston skirt to see that the rod and piston are in alignment. Both pins on the "V" block should rest against the face of the plate on the fixture. The piston should be in the same alignment as the connecting rod when this check is made.

2. A quick check of a piston and connecting rod assembly for both cock and twist can be made without disassembling the rod from the piston. This method saves considerable time on any repair operation that does not normally require the removal of the rod from the piston.

3. To make this check, the connecting rod and piston assembly is mounted on the alignment fixture and the piston is set in line with the connecting rod. Then place the "V" block on the piston skirt. If both pins on the block contact the face plate, the rod is not cocked (fig. 53).

4. Then, with the "V" block on the piston skirt and the pins against the face plate, tip the piston first in one direction and then in the other (fig. 54). If the pins on the block re-

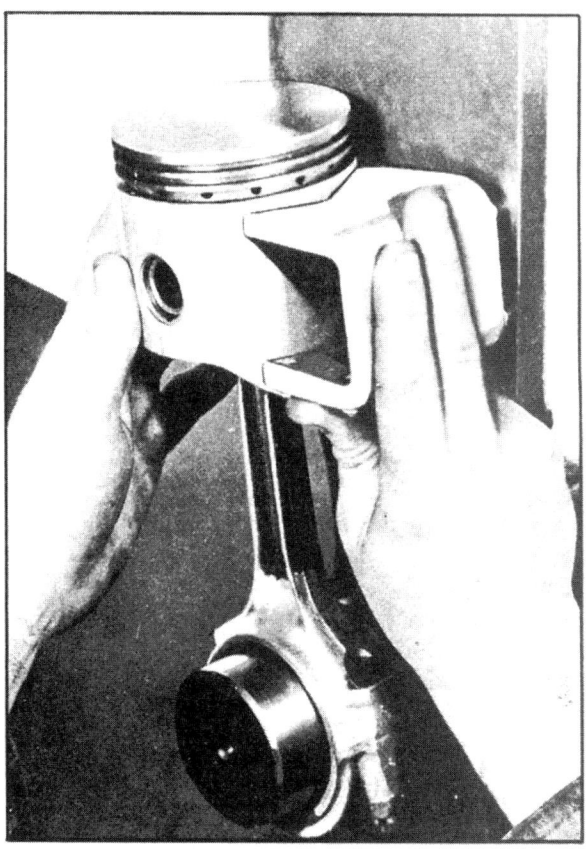

Fig. 53—Checking Piston and Connecting Rod Assembly

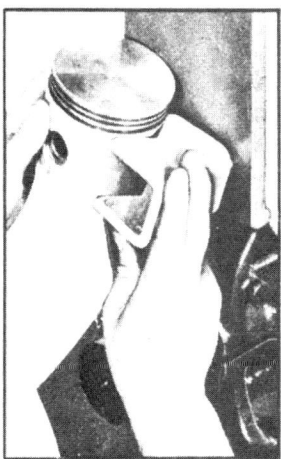

Fig. 54—Checking Piston and Connecting Rod Assembly for Twisted Connecting Rod

main against the face plate, there is no twist in the connecting rod.

5. If one pin leaves the face plate while the piston is being tipped in one direction and the other pin leaves the face plate while the piston is being tipped in the other direction, the connecting rod is twisted and should be straightened until both pins follow the face plate.

PISTON RING FITTING

Both compression rings in both the 216 and 235 engines, with the exception of the upper ring in the (1950-51) 235 engine, is of the taper-face type. The top ring in the (1950-51) 235 engine is a deep-section twist type, $3/32''$ wide.

The face of the taper-face type compression rings are tapered one thousandth of an inch, being wider at the bottom. With this design, the lower edge of the ring tends to scrape the excess oil from the cylinder wall and acts as an oil control ring until the regular oil control ring is seated (broken in) in the cylinder.

The deep-section twist type compression ring takes its name, twist type, from its installed position which is cocked or twisted (fig. 55). It

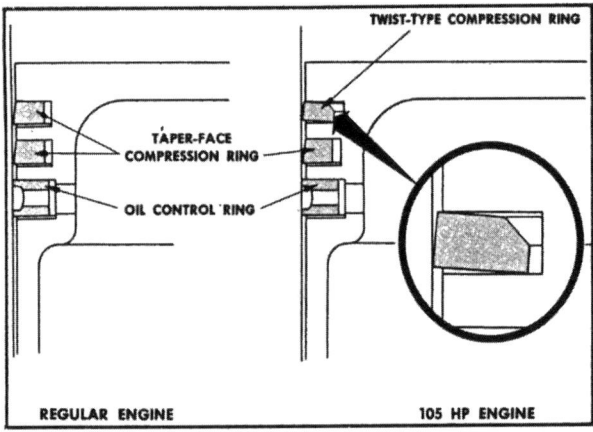

Fig. 55—Piston Ring Comparison

assumes and maintains this position for life because the upper edge of its inside diameter is chamfered, making the ring unbalanced in cross section.

All compression rings are marked with the word "TOP" cast in the upper side of the ring. When installing compression rings, make sure the side marked "TOP" is toward the top of the piston.

Chevrolet piston rings are furnished in standard sizes as well as .005", .020", .030" and .040" oversizes.

1. Select rings comparable in size to the pistons being used.
2. Slip the ring in the cylinder bore; then, using the head of a piston, press the ring down into the cylinder bore about two inches.
   NOTE: Using a piston in this way will place the ring square with the cylinder walls.
3. Check the space or gap between the ends of the ring with a feeler gauge. This gap should be from .005" to .015".
4. If the gap between the ends of the ring is less than .005", remove the ring and try another for fit, or the gap in the tight fitting ring may be enlarged as follows.
5. Remove the ring from the cylinder, then clamp a fine cut file in a vise and grasping each end of the ring firmly between the thumb and fingers, work the two ends of the ring across the surfaces of the file. Press the ring together at the gap lightly until the proper gap is obtained. Be careful not to distort the ring during this operation or it may bind in the ring groove of the piston. Fit each ring separately to the cylinder in which it is going to be used.
6. New pistons, rings and cylinder bores wear considerably during seating and gaps widen quickly; however, engine operation will not become seriously affected if ring gaps do not become greater than $1/32''$.
7. Carefully remove all particles of carbon from the ring grooves in the piston and inspect the grooves carefully for burrs or nicks that might cause the rings to hang up.
8. Slip the outer surface of the ring into the piston ring groove and roll the ring entirely around the groove to make sure that the ring is free and does not bind in the groove at any point (fig. 56). If binding occurs, the cause should be determined and removed by care-

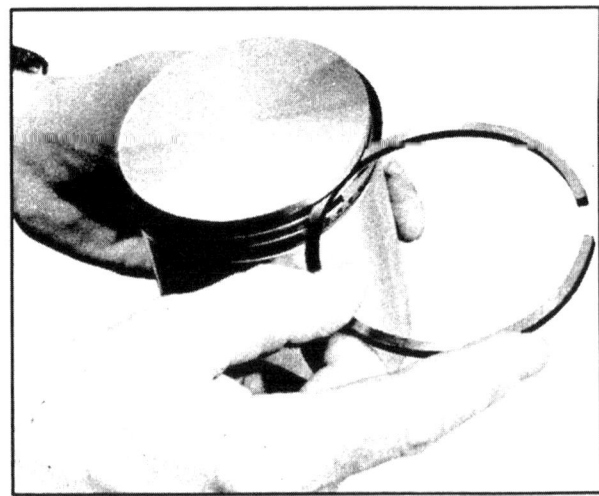

Fig. 56—Rolling Piston Ring in Ring Groove

fully dressing with a fine cut file. However, if the binding is caused by a distorted ring, install a new ring.

9. Proper clearance of the piston ring in its piston ring groove is very important in maintaining engine performance and in preventing excessive oil consumption. Therefore, when fitting new rings, the following clearances between the top and bottom surfaces of the ring grooves should be provided.
10. The compression rings should be fitted so

that a .0015" feeler gauge will be free, but a .003" feeler will cause a rather heavy drag.

11. At the bottom of oil control groove, a .002" feeler should be free, but a .0035" feeler should produce a heavy drag (fig. 57).

Fig. 57—Checking Piston Ring Clearance in Ring Groove

12. Assemble the rings to the pistons as they are fitted and make a final test of the ring fit in the grooves by repeating the fitting procedure given above.

NOTE: It is important that each ring be fitted to its individual cylinder for proper gap spacing and to its individual piston and groove for proper groove clearance.

ASSEMBLE PISTONS AND CONNECTING RODS TO ENGINE

When the rods are being reassembled, they should be installed in the same cylinder from which they were removed and with the stamped number on the camshaft side.

The condition of the crank pins on the crankshaft should be checked when installing new rods. Damaged crank pins can only be corrected by the installation of a new crankshaft, as it is impossible to insure connecting rod bearing life on a damaged crank pin.

1. Position piston rings in piston ring grooves so that gaps will be spaced 120° apart.

   CAUTION: Never install pistons with piston ring gaps in line as gaps in this position will allow gases to leak past the rings.

2. Lubricate pistons and cylinder bores, remove bearing caps and install piston and rod assemblies using piston inserter KMO-357 (fig. 58).

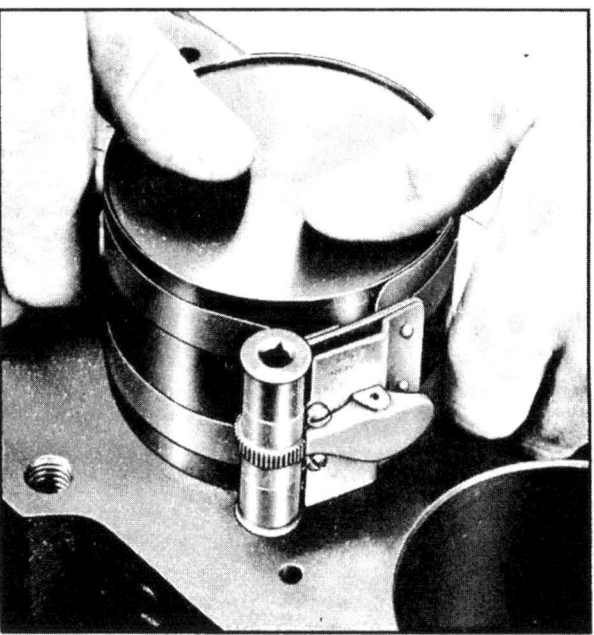

Fig. 58—Installing Piston in Cylinder Bore

NOTE: Piston and rods must be installed with the piston pin clamp on the camshaft side.

3. Lubricate crank pin and pull connecting rod down onto it, making sure the numbered side of the rod is toward the camshaft.

4. Install three .002" shims on each connecting rod bolt and then install the bearing cap with the numbered side toward the camshaft. Install the connecting rod oil dipper with its open side toward the camshaft. Assemble and tighten the bearing cap nuts to 40-50 ft. lbs. torque using a torque wrench.

5. Install remaining piston and connecting rod assemblies as described above.

6. Adjust connecting rod bearings as outlined under "Minor Service Operations, Connecting Rod Bearings—Adjust."

7. Install "pal" locking nuts with open side of nut toward end of bolt. Turn "pal" nut up finger tight and then ½ turn more.

CONNECTING ROD DIPPERS, OIL TROUGHS AND NOZZLES

Checking and adjusting connecting rod dippers, oil troughs and oil nozzles must be performed according to instructions given under "Minor Service Operations, Connecting Rod Bearing Lubrication."

OIL PUMP ASSEMBLY

If the inspection indicated excessive oil pump wear it is advisable to replace the entire oil pump. If the old pump is to be used it should be assembled as follows.

ENGINE ASSEMBLY 6-38

1. Place the drive gear and shaft in the pump body and install the idler gear so that the smooth side of gear will be toward the cover.
2. Install a new GENUINE Chevrolet gasket to assure correct end clearance of the gears.
3. Install the cover and attaching screws. Tighten screws securely and check to see that shaft turns freely.

CYLINDER HEAD

Condition the cylinder head and valves according to procedure given in "Minor Service Operations, Cylinder Head and Valve Conditioning."

ROCKER SHAFT OIL LINE PIPE

On the 216 engine and (1948-50) 235 engine, the pipe leading from the oil distributor to the rocker arm shaft passes directly through the water jacket of the cylinder block. If this pipe is removed for any reason, it must be replaced by a new pipe and nipple assembly, part number 609912, installed according to the following instructions.

1. Coat the threads of the nipple that is fastened to the pipe with white lead.
2. Thread the pipe through the block from push rod side and screw nipple securely in block.
3. Install nipple and sleeve nut at lower end of pipe on left side of block, coating threads of nipple with white lead and tighten securely.
4. Make a bend in lower end of pipe and connect to fitting at oil distributor location.
5. Bend pipe on right side of block to provide clearance when push rod cover is installed and so upper end of pipe extends straight up for cylinder head installation.

On the (1950-51) 235 engine, the rocker shaft oil line pipe extends forward in the push rod compartment from a fitting in the tappet ledge just above the rear camshaft bearing to the center and then upward to a fitting between the hollow rocker arm shafts. To replace this pipe, cut a new pipe to proper length, install new nipples at each end, and install pipe to cylinder block fitting. Then bend pipe to proper contour so that clearance is provided for the push rods and push rod cover and so that the end of the pipe extends straight up for cylinder head installation.

ENGINE ASSEMBLY

1. Place the oil pump in position in the block fitting. Install the oil pump retaining screw and tighten securely, being sure that the tapered end of screw draws down into the hole in pump body. Tighten lock nut securely.
2. Install the oil pump to block oil line and tighten the connector nuts securely. Install oil screen and body assembly and the oil pipe between screen and pump. The high side of the screen housing goes toward center of engine.
3. Check to see that the crankcase ventilator baffle (attached to block at oil filter hole) is not damaged and is securely bolted in place. Turn the crankshaft to see that the camshaft lobes clear the baffle.
4. Check to see that all connecting rod bolt nuts and main bearing bolts are properly tightened and locked. Check to see that the crankcase is clean.
5. Install new oil pan gaskets and end corks. Carefully place the oil pan in position and tighten pan bolts securely.
   NOTE: Tighten oil pan corner bolts to 12½-15 ft. lbs. Tighten oil pan flange bolts to 6-7½ ft. lbs.
6. Lubricate the clutch pilot bearing with a small amount of high melting point grease. Place the clutch disc and clutch cover assembly in position and install the pilot tool K-411.
7. Turn the clutch cover until the "X" on the cover lines up with the "X" on the flywheel. Install the attaching bolts loosely and then tighten them a turn at a time to take up the spring pressure evenly and prevent clutch distortion. Tighten bolts to 25-30 ft. lbs. torque and then remove pilot tool.
8. Pack the clutch fork ball seat with a small amount of high melting point grease and snap the fork onto the ball with the end extending through opening in clutch housing.
9. Turn engine assembly over in engine stand.
10. Place a new cylinder head gasket on the block following the installation instructions stamped on gasket. This assures alignment of water passages and bolt holes in head and block with openings in gasket. Install two guide pins to position gasket and pilot cylinder head.
11. Carefully place cylinder head in position over guide pins, pilot the rocker arm oil tube through opening in head and lower the head into position. Remove guide pins and install all cylinder head bolts and tighten them finger tight.
12. Tighten the cylinder head bolts a little at a time in the order shown (fig. 18). The final tightening should be 70-80 ft. lbs.
13. Install the twelve valve lifters in right side of block and on (1950-51) 235 engine, install rocker arm shaft oil line making connection at cylinder block.
14. Install push rod cover using a new gasket and tighten attaching screws evenly to 6-7½ ft. lbs. tension.
15. Install new manifold to cylinder head gaskets, manifold assembly and attaching parts. Tighten center clamp bolts to 15-20 ft. lbs.

torque and the two end clamp bolts to 25-30 ft. lbs. Check manifold heat control valve as instructed under "Minor Service Operations, Engine Tune-Up."

16. Place a new oil distributor to block gasket (No. 1, fig. 59) in position on left side of block. Place the oil distributor, distributor cover gasket (No. 2) and cover in position and install the retaining screws. Tighten to 6-7½ ft. lbs. tension.

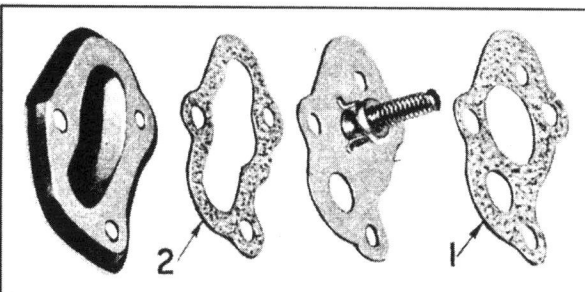

Fig. 59—Oil Distributor Cover and Gaskets

CAUTION: *The gasket marked "1" (fig. 59) must be placed between oil distributor and engine block, and the one marked "2" must be placed between distributor and cover.*

17. Install water pump using a new gasket and tighten attaching bolts to 25-30 ft. lbs. Install thermostat housing, place thermostat in housing, install new water outlet gasket and water outlet, and install attaching bolts. Tighten bolts securely.
18. Install carburetor and tighten nuts evenly. Place throttle rod in position and connect it to the bell crank and throttle shaft arm.
19. Install crankcase ventilator tube. Connect tube brace to oil pan flange. Install oil gauge rod.
20. Adjust spark plug gaps to .040" on (1948) models and to .035" on (1949-51) models. Using new gaskets install spark plugs and tighten to 12-15 ft. lbs. torque on (1948) models and to 20-25 ft. lbs. torque on (1949-51) models.
21. Install the fuel pump using a new gasket and tighten attaching bolts to 15-20 ft. lbs. Place the fuel pump to carburetor gas line and the vacuum spark control line in position and connect them to carburetor and clip at water outlet. Connect the gas line to the fuel pump.
22. Install ignition distributor following instructions in Section 12 of this manual and connect vacuum line to distributor spark control.
23. Lubricate the recess on the inside of clutch throwout bearing collar and coat the throwout fork grooves with a small amount of high melting point grease and place bearing assembly in position on the throwout fork.
24. Carefully clean the mating faces on clutch housing and transmission case. Pilot the clutch shaft of transmission through throwout bearing and into clutch disc and pilot bearing. Work the transmission up against the clutch housing until bearing retainer pilots into pilot hole in clutch housing. Install and tighten the transmission mounting bolts securely.

NOTE: *Properly support the transmission as it is being installed or the clutch disc may be damaged.*

25. Install the clutch housing underpan and retaining bolts.
26. Remove the fourth cylinder head bolt from the rear on the right side and third from the rear on the left side of the engine and using lift kit J-4536, install the proper lifting tool. Attach lifting attachments to suitable hoist, release engine from stand and lift engine with hoist.
27. Install starting motor and tighten attaching bolts securely.
28. Install generator loosely and attach slotted brace. Place fan belt over fan and around pump, generator and crankshaft pulleys. Shift the generator to properly align pulleys and tighten anchor bolts. Force the generator away from engine to tighten belt until it has ¾ inch free travel (fig. 60) midway between generator and pump pulleys. Tighten generator to brace bolt securely to secure generator in position.

Fig. 60—Fan Belt Adjustment

ENGINE INSTALLATION

1. Lower engine assembly into chassis as a unit.
2. Install rear engine mounting bolts and tighten securely.
3. Install front engine support making sure clearance between upper plate and retainer is correct. See "Minor Service Operations, Checking Clearance of Support." Remove lifting attachment and install cylinder head bolts and tighten to 70-80 ft. lbs.
4. Drop the twelve push rods down through openings in head and into position in the lifters. Figure 61 shows cross section of lifters and push rods.

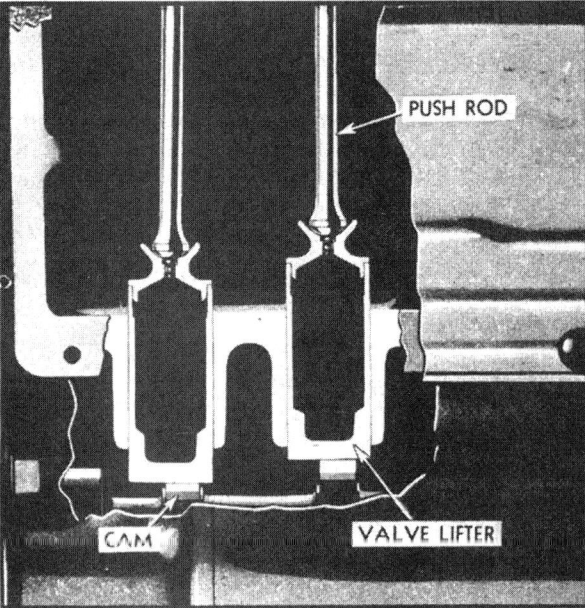

Fig. 61—Valve Lifters

5. Install and tighten securely, the two rocker arm cover studs in the cylinder head. Place the oil connector over open ends of the two rocker shaft assemblies and place this assembly on the cylinder head so that the studs will enter the center support on each shaft.

   NOTE: Make sure that the shafts are positioned with the large section of the two end support bolt holes up.

6. Install the two bolts and stud nut which retain each rocker arm shaft. Draw them down evenly and tighten to 25-30 ft. lbs. tension.
7. Connect rocker arm oil line to oil connector and tighten securely.
8. Adjust universal ball joint as outlined in Transmission Section.
9. On ½ ton:
   (a) Fasten trunnion bearings to front yoke and tighten cap screws securely. Use new lock plates under cap screws and bend tangs up to lock screws.
   (b) Slide ball collar forward on propeller shaft housing, assemble transmission support to frame cross member, install collar cap screws and tighten securely.
   (c) Remove speedometer drive gear and lubricate the universal by filling the housing with one pint of SAE 90 transmission lubricant.
10. On ¾ ton:
    (a) Slide splines of front propeller shaft into rear yoke of front universal joint.
    (b) Bolt support bracket to frame cross member securely.
    (c) Lubricate the universal ball and bolt ball collar to rear end of transmission housing.
    (d) Raise rear propeller shaft, seat trunnion bearings in front yoke of universal, install "U" clamps and tighten securely.
    (e) Lubricate universal joint with SAE 90 transmission lubricant and lubricate front universal by filling housing with one pint of SAE 90 transmission lubricant.
11. On all 1 ton and (1948-50) 1½ and 2 ton, seat trunnion bearings to front yoke of universal joint, install "U" clamps and tighten securely.
12. On (1951) 1½ and 2 ton:
    (a) Install front propeller shaft and bearing support assembly, positioning the front universal joint front yoke on the four flange bolts. Install and tighten securely the nuts attaching propeller shaft support bracket to frame cross member.
    (b) Install four universal joint flange lockwashers and nuts and tighten securely.
    (c) Raise front end of rear propeller shaft, align trunnion bearings with front yoke and install trunnion bearing "U" clamps and tighten securely.
13. Connect clutch pedal adjusting link to clutch fork and adjust to give ¾" to 1" free pedal travel.
14. Connect speedometer cable to transmission and replace starter pedal.
15. (a) On ½ and ¾ ton, connect the 1st and reverse control rod to the shifter lever on the left side of the transmission and the 2nd and 3rd control rod to the bell crank on the left side of the clutch housing.
    (b) On other models, make sure transmission is in neutral, then replace transmission cover with gear shift lever and parking lever attached, using a new cover gasket, and replace transmission hole cover. Fill transmission with SAE 90 transmission lubricant.

ENGINE ASSEMBLY 6-41

16. (a) On all 1 ton and (1948-50) 1½ and 2 ton, connect parking brake pull rod assembly to parking lever.
    (b) On (1951) 1½ and 2 ton, connect inner and outer levers to parking brake operating lever and connect brake lever return spring to brake operating lever.
17. Replace floor mat and accelerator pedal.
18. Replace exhaust pipe to manifold and tighten attaching bolts securely.
19. Connect vacuum lines.
20. Connect line to oil pressure gauge and install temperature element in cylinder head.
21. Connect choke and throttle control cables to carburetor.
    NOTE: If oil bath cleaner is used, disassemble, clean and refill before installing.
22. Connect horn wire to horn.
23. Connect generator and field wires to generator.
24. Attach gasoline line to fuel pump.
25. Mount coil in position and install coil mounting screws.
26. Attach coil wires to distributor.
27. Attach battery cable and ammeter wire to starting switch terminal and on vehicles equipped with push button starter, attach battery cable and ammeter wire to large terminal on solenoid and starter switch wire to small terminal.
28. Install radiator and radiator support to frame cross member bolts.
29. Install radiator support to fender brace bolts.
30. Refill radiator and crankcase.
31. Start engine and allow to run until properly normalized and adjust valves as outlined in "Minor Service Operations, Valve Adjustment."
32. Install rocker arm cover using a new gasket and check for leaks.
33. Replace hood assembly and connect hood hinges.

TROUBLES AND REMEDIES
ENGINE

Symptom and Probable Cause	Probable Remedy
LACK OF POWER	
1. Poor Compression	
a. Incorrect valve lash	a. Adjust valve lash according to instructions under "Valve Adjustment"
b. Leaky valves	b. Remove cylinder head and grind valves
c. Valve stems or lifters sticking	c. Free up or replace
d. Valve springs weak or broken	d. Replace springs
e. Valve timing incorrect	e. Correct valve timing
f. Leaking cylinder head gasket	f. Replace gasket
g. Piston rings broken	g. Replace rings
h. Poor fits between pistons, rings and cylinders	h. Overhaul engine
2. Ignition System Improperly Adjusted	
a. Ignition not properly timed	a. Set ignition according to instructions under "Engine Tune-Up"
b. Octane selector not adjusted for grade of fuel being used	b. Set octane selector. See "Engine Tune-Up"
c. Spark plugs faulty	c. Replace or clean, adjust and test spark plugs
d. Distributor points not set correctly	d. Set distributor points and time engine
3. Lack of Fuel	
a. Dirt or water in carburetor	a. Clean carburetor
b. Gas lines partly plugged	b. Clean gas lines
c. Dirt in gas tank	c. Clean gas tank
d. Air leaks in gas line	d. Tighten and check gas lines
e. Fuel pump not functioning properly	e. Replace or repair fuel pump
4. Carburetor Air Inlet Restricted	
a. Air cleaner dirty	a. Clean air cleaner
b. Carburetor choke partly closed	b. Adjust or replace choke mechanism

Symptom and Probable Cause

5. **Overheating**
   a. Lack of water
   b. Fan belt loose
   c. Fan belt worn or oil soaked
   d. Thermostat sticking closed
   e. Water pump inoperative
   f. Cooling system clogged
   g. Incorrect ignition or valve timing
   h. Brakes dragging
   i. Improper grade and viscosity oil being used
   j. Fuel mixture too lean
   k. Valves improperly adjusted
   l. Defective ignition system
   m. Exhaust system partly restricted
6. **Overcooling**
   a. Thermostat holding open

EXCESSIVE OIL CONSUMPTION

1. **Leaking Oil**
   a. Oil pan drain plug loose
   b. Oil pan retainer bolts loose
   c. Oil pan gaskets damaged.
   d. Timing gear cover loose or gasket damaged
   e. Oil return from timing gear case to block restricted, causing leak at crankshaft fan pulley hub
   f. Push rod or rocker arm cover gaskets damaged or covers loose
   g. Fuel pump loose or gasket damaged
   h. Rear main bearing leaking oil into clutch housing
2. **Burning Oil**
   a. Broken piston rings
   b. Rings not correctly seated to cylinder walls
   c. Piston rings worn excessively or stuck in ring grooves
   d. Piston ring oil return holes clogged with carbon
   e. Excessive clearance between piston and cylinder wall due to wear or improper fitting
   f. Cylinder walls scored, tapered or out-of-round

HARD STARTING

1. **Slow Cranking**
   a. Heavy engine oil
   b. Partially discharged battery
   c. Faulty or undercapacity battery
   d. Poor battery connections
   e. Faulty starter switch
   f. Faulty starting motor or drive
2. **Ignition Trouble**
   a. Distributor points burned or corroded
   b. Points improperly adjusted
   c. Spark plugs improperly gapped

Probable Remedy

a. Refill system
b. Adjust or replace
c. Replace belt
d. Replace thermostat
e. Replace water pump
f. Clean and reverse flush
g. Retime engine
h. Adjust brakes
i. Change to correct oil
j. Overhaul or adjust carburetor
k. Adjust valves
l. See "Engine Tune-Up"
m. Clean or replace

a. Replace thermostat

a. Tighten drain plug
b. Tighten oil pan bolts
c. Replace pan gaskets
d. Tighten cover bolts or **replace gasket**
e. Remove oil pan and **clean oil return passages**

f. Tighten covers or replace **gaskets**

g. Tighten fuel pump or **replace gasket**
h. Adjust or replace main **bearing or main bearing oil seal**

a. Replace rings
b. Give sufficient time for rings to seat. Replace if necessary
c. Replace rings

d. Replace rings

e. Fit new pistons

f. Recondition cylinders and fit new pistons

a. Change to lighter oil
b. Charge battery
c. Replace battery
d. Clean and tighten or replace connections
e. Replace switch
f. Overhaul starting motor

a. Clean or replace points
b. Readjust points to .018", adjust new points to .022".
c. Set plug gap at .040" (1948 models) or to .035" (1949-51 models).

ENGINE ASSEMBLY 6-43

Symptom and Probable Cause

    d. Spark plug wires loose and corroded in distributor cap
    e. Loose connections in primary circuit
    f. Series resistance in condenser circuit
    g. Low capacity condenser
3. **Engine Condition**
    a. Valves holding open
    b. Valves burned
    c. Leaking manifold gasket
    d. Loose carburetor mounting
    e. Faulty pistons, rings or cylinders
4. **Carburetion**
    a. Choke not operating properly
    b. Throttle not set properly
    c. Carburetor dirty and passages restricted

POPPING, SPITTING AND DETONATION
1. **Overheated Intake Manifold**
    a. Manifold heat control spring not properly installed
    b. Manifold heat control valve sticking
2. **Ignition Trouble**
    a. Loose wiring connections
    b. Faulty wiring
    c. Faulty spark plugs
3. **Carburetion**
    a. Lean combustion mixture
    b. Dirt in carburetor
    c. Restricted gas supply to carburetor
    d. Leaking carburetor or intake manifold gaskets
4. **Valves**
    a. Valves adjusted too tight
    b. Valves sticking

    c. Exhaust valves thin and heads overheating
    d. Weak valve springs
    e. Valves timed early
5. **Cylinder Head**
    a. Excessive carbon deposits in combustion chamber
    b. Cylinder head water passages partly clogged causing hot spot in combustion chamber
    c. Partly restricted exhaust ports in cylinder head
    d. Cylinder head gasket blown between cylinders
6. **Spark Plugs**
    a. Spark plugs glazed
    b. Wrong heat range plug being used
7. **Exhaust System**
    a. Exhaust manifold or muffler restricted causing back pressure

ROUGH ENGINE IDLE
1. **Carburetor**
    a. Improper idling adjustment
    b. Carburetor float needle valve not seating

Probable Remedy

    d. Clean wire and cap terminals

    e. Tighten all connections in primary circuit
    f. Clean all connections in condenser circuit
    g. Install proper condenser

    a. Adjust valves
    b. Grind valves
    c. Tighten manifold bolts or replace gasket
    d. Tighten carburetor
    e. See "Poor Compression"

    a. Adjust or repair choke mechanism
    b. Set throttle
    c. Overhaul carburetor

    a. Adjust according to instructions under "Engine Tune-Up"
    b. Free up heat control valve

    a. Tighten all wire connections
    b. Replace faulty wiring
    c. Clean or replace and adjust plugs

    a. Clean and adjust carburetor
    b. Clean carburetor
    c. Clean gas lines and check for restrictions
    d. Tighten carburetor to manifold and manifold to head bolts or replace gaskets

    a. Adjust valve lash
    b. Lubricate and free up. Grind valves if necessary
    c. Replace valves
    d. Replace valve springs
    e. Retime. See "Timing Gear Installation"

    a. Remove head and clean carbon

    b. Remove cylinder head and clean water passages
    c. Remove cylinder head and clean exhaust ports
    d. Replace cylinder head gasket

    a. Clean or replace spark plugs
    b. Change to correct spark plugs

    a. Clean or replace manifold and muffler

    a. Adjust according to instructions
    b. Clean or replace

ENGINE ASSEMBLY 6-44

Symptom and Probable Cause	Probable Remedy

2. Air Leaks
   a. Carburetor to manifold heat insulator leaks
   b. Manifold to head gasket leaks

   c. Air leaks in windshield wiper vacuum line
   d. Air leaks in hydrovac or two-speed axle vacuum cylinder lines

3. Valves
   a. Improper lash adjustment
   b. Valves not seating properly
   c. Valves loose in guides

4. Cylinder Head
   a. Cracks in exhaust ports
   b. Head gasket leaks

Remedies:
a. Tighten carburetor to manifold bolts or replace heat insulator
b. Tighten manifold to head bolts or replace gaskets
c. Check for leaks and repair
d. Check all lines and correct leaks

a. Check and adjust valves
b. Grind valves
c. Condition valves

a. Replace cylinder head
b. Replace cylinder head gasket

ENGINE MISSES ON ACCELERATION

1. Carburetion
   a. Accelerating pump jet plugged or vapor vent ball in pump plunger not working
   b. Lean fuel mixture

2. Ignition Trouble
   a. Faulty spark plugs
   b. Faulty ignition wiring
   c. Improperly adjusted or faulty distributor points
   d. Weak coil

3. Engine
   a. Burned or improperly adjusted valves
   b. Leaky manifold gaskets
   c. Poor compression due to cylinder, piston or ring condition
   d. Leaky cylinder head gasket

Remedies:
a. Overhaul carburetor
b. Overhaul carburetor

a. Clean, adjust or replace plugs
b. Replace faulty wiring
c. Adjust or replace distributor points
d. Replace coil

a. Adjust, replace or grind valves
b. Tighten manifold or replace gaskets
c. Overhaul engine
d. Replace gasket

ENGINE NOISE

1. Crankshaft Bearings Loose
   a. Bearings improperly fitted
   b. Crankshaft journals out-of-round
   c. Crankshaft journals rough
   d. Oil passages in block restricted
   e. Insufficient oil
   f. Improper grade and viscosity oil being used
   g. Oil pump failure
   h. Contaminated oil

Remedies:
a. Readjust main bearings
b. Replace or recondition crankshaft
c. Replace or recondition crankshaft
d. Clean passages
e. Adjust or replace bearings. Replenish oil
f. Adjust bearings and change to correct oil
g. Replace oil pump, adjust or replace bearings and other damaged parts
h. Wash motor thoroughly. Adjust or replace bearings and other damaged parts

2. Connecting Rod Bearings Loose
   a. Improperly adjusted bearings
   b. Crankpins rough
   c. Insufficient oil
   d. Oil pump failure
   e. Connecting rod dipper broken or damaged
   f. Oil troughs or lines not adjusted properly or restricted
   g. Improper grade and viscosity of oil used

Remedies:
a. Adjust bearings
b. Polish or replace shaft. Adjust or replace rods
c. Adjust or replace rods and replenish oil
d. Replace oil pump. Replace or adjust rod bearings
e. Adjust or replace rod and dipper
f. Clean, adjust or replace oil troughs and lines
g. Adjust or replace rod bearings and change to proper oil

Symptom and Probable Cause

3. Pistons or Pins Loose
  a. Excessive cylinder wear

  b. Improperly fitted pistons or pins
  c. Contaminated oil
  d. Faulty fuel or ignition system causing unburned fuel to flush the oil from cylinder walls
  e. Piston pin or bushing wear

4. Engine Noise — General
  a. Bent connecting rod
  b. Excessive end play in camshaft

  c. Excessive crankshaft end play
  d. Broken piston ring

  e. Loose timing gears
  f. Dry push rod sockets
  g. Bent oil gauge rod
  h. Improperly adjusted valve lash
  i. Sticking valves

Probable Remedy

  a. Hone cylinders and fit new pistons and rings. Make sure all abrasive that would cause cylinder wear is removed
  b. Replace pistons or pins
  c. Make necessary replacements, flush oiling system and use new oil
  d. Make necessary repairs to fuel or ignition system, replace worn parts and change oil

  e. Ream bushings and install oversize piston pins

  a. Replace rod
  b. Replace camshaft thrust plate, or correct end play by pressing gear on further
  c. Replace main bearings
  d. Replace broken ring and check condition of cylinder wall
  e. Replace timing gears
  f. Polish and lubricate push rod sockets
  g. Replace oil gauge rod
  h. Adjust valve lash
  i. Free or grind valves

ENGINE ASSEMBLY 6-46

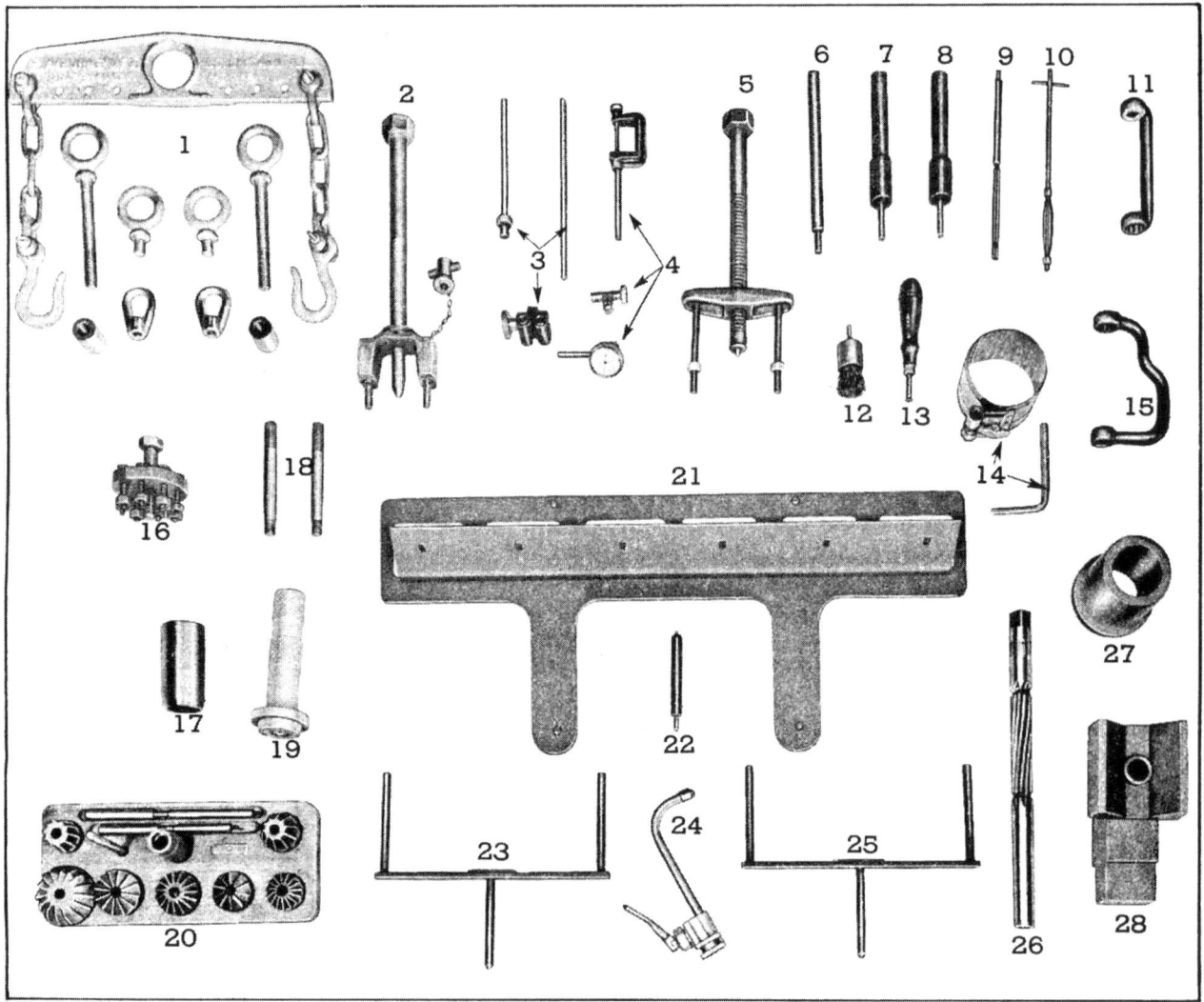

Fig. 62—Engine Special Tools

1. J-4536 — Lift Kit
2. J-1287 — Harmonic Balancer Puller and Replacer
3. J-4656 — Indicator Swivel Set
4. KMO-30 — Indicator Set
5. T-126-R — Crankshaft Gear Puller
6. J-267 — Valve Stem Guide Remover
7. J-1089 — Valve Guide Replacer (Intake)
8. J-1090 — Valve Guide Replacer (Exhaust)
9. .343" — Valve Guide Reamer (Finish)
10. KMO-122 — Valve Guide Cleaner
11. KMO-187-1 — Cylinder Head Wrench Attachment (Close Sweep)
12. KMO-7004 — Carbon Removing Brush
13. KMO-230 — Distributor Cap Terminal Brush
14. KMO-357 — Piston Ring Compressor
15. KMO-187-10 — Cylinder Head Wrench Attachment (Wide Sweep)
16. J-1226 — Water Pump Fan Pulley Puller
17. J-966 — Timing Gear Cover Centering Gauge
18. N-344 — Cylinder Head Guide Pins (2)
19. J-995 — Timing Gear Cover Oil Seal Replacer
20. KMO-105-B — Valve Reseater Set
21. J-969-1A — Oil Pan Target
22. J-793-5 — Nozzle Setting Tool
23. J-969-2A — Trough Depth Gauge
24. J-793-3 — Water Faucet Assembly
25. J-1541 — Trough Depth Gauge
26. J-965-3 — Piston Pin Bushing Expansion Reamer
27. J-971 — Camshaft Gear Remover and Replacer
28. J-965-A — Piston Reaming Fixture

ENGINE SPECIFICATIONS

Type   Valve-in-Head

Number of Cylinders.........6

Piston Displacement—
- 216 Engine.................216.5 cu. in.
- 235 Engine.................235.5 cu. in.

Bore—
- 216 Engine.................3½″
- 235 Engine.................3 9/16″

Stroke—
- 216 Engine.................3¾″
- 235 Engine.................3 15/16″

Compression Ratio—
- 216 Engine.................6.6:1
- 235 Engine.................6.7:1

Horsepower (S.A.E.)—
- 216 Engine.................29.4
- 235 Engine.................30.4

Firing Order.................1-5-3-6-2-4

Cylinder Block
- Bore Size—
  - 216 Engine.................3.4995″-3.5015″
  - 235 Engine.................3.5620″-3.5640″

Crankshaft—
- Number of Bearings.........4
- Bearing Journal Diameter—
  - Front.....................2.6835″-2.6845″
  - Front—Intermediate........2.7145″-2.7155″
  - Rear—Intermediate.........2.7455″-2.7465″
  - Rear......................2.7765″-2.7775″
- Thrust Taken..............Rear Intermediate
- End Clearance.............003″-.009″
- Connecting Rod Journal Diameter..........2.311″-2.312″
- Journal Out-of-Round......001″ Max.
- Runout—At Intermediate Journal............002″ Max.
- Crankshaft Main Bearing—
  - Bearing Clearance........Selective Fit
  - Undersize Bearings Available..........002″-.010″-.020″-.030″

Connecting Rod—
- Center to Center Length.....6 13/16″
- Upper Bearing..............Locked on Pin
- Lower Bearing..............Cast Babbitt
- Bearing Bore Diameter......2.3135″-2.3140″
- Connecting Rod Bearing—Lower Bearing Clearance......Selective Fit
- Clearance Rod to Crankpin checked at upper half of bearing.........004″-.012″
- Clearance Rod to Piston Pin Boss..............025″ Minimum

Piston—
- Diameter Clearance at Skirt—
  - Pass on...................0015″ Feeler
  - Hold on...................003″ Feeler
- Oversize Pistons Available....005″-.010″-.020″-.030″-.040″
- Piston Pin—
  - Diameter.................8645″-.8650″
  - Oversize.................003″-.005″-.010″
  - Piston Pin Fit............Thumb Push Fit
- Compression Ring—
  - Quantity.................2
  - Type: 216 Engine.........Both Taper-Face
  - (1948-49) 235 Engine.Both Taper-Face
  - (1950-51) 235 Engine. Upper, Twist-Type, Lower Taper-Face
  - Width: Taper-Face........1235″-.1240″
  -      Twist-Type........093″-.0935″
  - Gap......................005″-.015″
  - Ring and Groove Clearance..............0015″-.003″
- Oil Ring—
  - Quantity.................1
  - Type.....................Wide-Slot
  - Width....................1860″-.1865″
  - Gap......................005″-.015″
  - Ring and Groove Clearance...............002″-.0035″
- Ring Gap Spacing...........120°

Camshaft—
- Number of Bearings.......4
- Bearing Journal Diameter
  - Front....................2.0282″-2.0292″
  - Front—Intermediate....1.9657″-1.9667″
  - Rear—Intermediate.....1.9032″-1.9042″
  - Rear.....................1.8407″-1.8417″
- Runout at Intermediate Bearing..................002″ Max.
- Thrust Taken...............By Thrustplate
- Camshaft End Clearance....001″ to .005″
- Camshaft Bearings
  - Type.....................Steel Backed Babbitt Lined
  - Front....................2.0307″-2.0317″
  - Front—Intermediate.....1.9682″-1.9692″
  - Rear—Intermediate......1.9057″-1.9067″
  - Rear.....................1.8432″-1.8442″
- Bearing Clearance..........002″-.004″
- Camshaft End Plug Assemble in Crankcase....Flush to 1/32″ Deep

Intake Valve—
- Lash—Hot—
  - Normal Operation..........006″-.008″
  - Heavy Duty Operation.....010″
- Seat Angle.................30°
- Diameter—Head
  - 216 Engine...............1 41/64″
  - (1948-49) 235 Engine......1 41/64″
  - (1950-51) 235 Engine......1 5/16″

ENGINE ASSEMBLY 6-47

Length—Overall—
　216 Engine................6.260″-6.290″
　(1948-49) 235 Engine.....6.260″-6.290″
　(1950-51) 235 Engine.....6.364″-6.394″
Diameter—Stem.............3410″-.3417″
Guide Ream................3427″-.3437″
Stem to Guide Clearance.....001″-.003″
Intake Opens...............1° A.U.D.C.
Intake Closes..............39° A.L.D.C.
Intake Period..............218°
Width of Seat (in head)......3/64″-1/16″

Exhaust Valve—
　Lash—Hot—
　　Normal Operation.........013″-.015″
　　Heavy Duty Operation.....020″
　Seat Angle: (1948-49) Engines..30°
　　　　　　　(1950-51) Engines..45°
　Diameter—Head:
　　(1948-49) Engines........1 15/32″
　　(1950-51) Engines........1 1/2″
　Length—Overall:
　　(1948-49) Engines........4.839″-4.869″
　　(1950-51) Engines........4.902″-4.932″
　Diameter—Stem.............3400″-.3407″
　Guide Ream................3427″-.3437″
　Stem to Guide Clearance....002″ to .004″
　Exhaust Opens.............42° B.L.D.C.
　Exhaust Closes............9° A.U.D.C.
　Exhaust Period............231°
　Width of Seat (in head)...1/16″-3/32″

Valve Guide—
　Extend Above Head—　　Intake　Exhaust
　216 Engine..............1 1/16″　61/64″
　(1948-49) 235 Engine....1 1/16″　61/64″
　(1950-51) 235 Engine....1″　　　55/64″

Valve Lifter—
　Diameter..................989″-.990″
　Clearance Block to Lifter....Selective Fit

Valve Spring—
　Free Length...............2 1/8″
　Lbs. Pressure at 1 1/2″....124-140 lbs.

Valve Rocker—
　Rocker Shaft Diameter.....7910″-.7917″
　Rocker Arm Bore...........7922″-.7935″

Timing Gears—
　Backlash—
　　216 Engine (Bakelite)....003″-.005″
　　235 Engine (Aluminum)....004″-.006″

Crankshaft Gear—
　Material..................Steel
　Teeth.....................27
　Runout....................003″

Camshaft Gear—
　Material:
　　216 Engine..............Bakelite and Fabric with Steel Hub
　　(1948-50) 235 Engine....Aluminum with Steel Hub
　　(1951) 235 Engine.......Aluminum
　Teeth.....................54
　Runout....................004″

Oil Pump—
　Type and Drive............Driven by Tang on Distributor Shaft
　Lbs. Pressure at 2000 RPM..14 lbs.

Spark Plugs—
　Make, Model, Size:
　　(1948) Engines..........AC, 104, 10 mm.
　　(1949-51) Engines.......AC, 44-5 Com. 14 mm.
　Gap:
　　(1948) Engines..........040″
　　(1949-51) Engines.......035″

Front Engine Mounting—
　Support Clearance.........3/64″-5/64″

Distributor—
　Point Gap—
　　Readjust................018″
　　Adjust New Points.......022″
　Point Spring Tension......17-21 Ounces

Idling Speed.............450-500 RPM

Vacuum Reading at Idling Speed...........17-21 inches

Fan Belt Adjustment—
　Deflection Midway Between Pulleys...................3/4″

Clutch Housing Pilot Hole—
　Runout....................008″ Max.

Flywheel—
　Runout....................008″ Max.

TORQUE WRENCH SPECIFICATIONS
ENGINE BOLTS AND NUTS

Cylinder Head Bolts...........70-80 ft. lbs.
Valve Rocker Shaft Support
　Bolts and Stud Nuts........25-30 ft. lbs.
Manifold Center Clamp Bolts..15-20 ft. lbs.
Manifold End Clamp Bolts.....25-30 ft. lbs.
Connecting Rod Nuts
　(with oiled threads).......40-50 ft. lbs.
Main Bearing Cap Bolts
　(with oiled threads).......100-110 ft. lbs.
Crankcase Front End Plate
　Screws....................15-20 ft. lbs.
Timing Gear Cover Screws.....6-7 1/2 ft. lbs.
Clutch Housing Attaching Bolts.45-55 ft. lbs.
Flywheel Mounting Bolts......50-65 ft. lbs.
Oil Pan Flange Bolts.........6-7 1/2 ft. lbs.
Oil Pan Corner Bolts.........12 1/2-15 ft. lbs.
Clutch Cover to Flywheel Bolts.25-30 ft. lbs.
Push Rod Cover Screws........6-7 1/2 ft. lbs.
Oil Distributor Cover Screws..6-7 1/2 ft. lbs.
Water Pump Attaching Bolts...25-30 ft. lbs.
Fuel Pump Attaching Bolts....15-20 ft. lbs.
Spark Plugs: (1948) Engines...12-15 ft. lbs.
　　　　　　　(1949-51) Engines.20-25 ft. lbs.

FUEL SYSTEM

INDEX

	Page
Carter Downdraft Carburetor	6-49
Description and Operation	6-49
Minor Service Operations	6-53
Idle Mixture Adjustment	6-53
Idle Speed Adjustment	6-53
Float Level Adjustment	6-54
Metering Rod	6-54
Major Service Operations	6-55
Carburetor	6-55
Removal	6-55
Disassembly	6-55
Inspection	6-56
Repairs	6-56
Throttle Valve	6-56
Choke Valve	6-56
Assembly	6-57
Installation	6-58
GM Model "B" Downdraft Carburetor	6-58
Description and Operation	6-58
Minor Service Operations	6-60
Idle Mixture Adjustment	6-60
Idle Speed Adjustment	6-60
Float Level Adjustment	6-60
Major Service Operations	6-62
Carburetor	6-62
Removal	6-62
Disassembly	6-62
Inspection	6-62
Repairs	6-63
Choke Valve	6-63
Assembly	6-64
Installation	6-64
Carter Updraft Carburetor	6-65
Description and Operation	6-65
Minor Service Operations	6-67
Idle Adjustment	6-67

	Page
Accelerating Pump Stroke Adjustment	6-67
Major Service Operations	6-67
Carburetor	6-67
Removal	6-67
Disassembly	6-67
Inspection	6-68
Assembly	6-68
Installation	6-69
Fuel Pump	6-70
Description and Operation	6-70
Minor Service Operations	6-71
Major Service Operations	6-71
Removal and Disassembly	6-71
Inspection	6-71
Assembly	6-72
Fuel and Vacuum Pump	6-72
General Description and Operation	6-72
Minor Service Operations	6-73
Maintenance	6-73
Locating Pump Trouble	6-74
Locating Vacuum Section Trouble	6-74
Major Service Operations	6-74
Disassembly	6-74
Inspection	6-75
Assembly	6-75
Air Cleaner	6-76
Description and Operation	6-76
Service Operations	6-77
Standard Cleaner	6-77
Oil Bath Air Cleaner	6-77
Oil Bath Cleaner, C.O.E.	6-77
Governor	6-78
Description and Operation	6-78
Adjustment	6-78

FUEL SYSTEM

There are three types of balanced carburetors used on Chevrolet trucks (1948-51). The Carter downdraft carburetor is used on all conventional models for the years (1948-49); the GM Model "B" downdraft carburetor is used on all conventional models for the years (1950-51); and the Carter updraft type is used on all Forward Control and Cab-Over-Engine models, (1948-51) inclusive. Each carburetor contributes materially to the power, performance, economy and smooth operation of the Chevrolet engine to which it is attached, but since they differ in construction they will be treated separately in this section.

CARTER DOWNDRAFT CARBURETOR

GENERAL DESCRIPTION

The Carter downdraft carburetor is used on all (1948-49) conventional truck models.

This carburetor embodies a principle which employs three venturis, one located above and two below the level of the gasoline in the float chamber. This triple venturi has the effect of increasing the suction on the first or primary venturi, causing the nozzle to start delivering gasoline at a very low air speed. The nozzle enters the primary venturi at an angle, discharging upward against the air stream. This angle provides an even flow of correctly proportioned and finely atomized fuel.

The gasoline thus atomized in the primary venturi, is kept centrally located in the air stream by the surrounding blanket of air passing into the second venturi and this process is repeated by the air in the main venturi. By this means the fuel mixture is carried to the cylinders in a more perfectly atomized condition. This insulated atomization results in increased smoothness of operation at both low and high speeds.

The fuel mixture quality is controlled by a metering rod operating in the metering rod jet, and operated by the throttle lever. There are two steps of different diameters on this metering rod. The larger diameter, or economy step, is tapered and controls the gasoline flow to about seven-eighths throttle, at which time the smaller diameter, or power step, becomes effective, giving full power for either high speed or hard low speed pulling. By this means, both maximum power and greater economy are available without changing the carburetor adjustment. Figure 63 shows a diagramatic view of the downdraft carburetor with details of various passages, jets, etc. identified.

The air pressure in the carburetor float chamber is balanced with the pressure inside of the air horn by a system of passages in the carburetor. The air intake for the balance passage consists of a brass tube pressed into the wall of the air horn and extending to the center of the air horn. This tube connects with a passage in the side of the air horn (fig. 64). With this balanced pressure, the proportions of air and gasoline in the mixture delivered to the engine remain substantially the same at all times, even when the air cleaner is restricted by dirt.

The choke consists of a one-piece choke valve, fastened by means of two screws to the choke shaft which is offset to one side of the carburetor air horn. The valve is machined with an angle on each end to permit solid seating against the wall of the air horn. Due to the choke valve seating against the walls of the air horn, it cannot be damaged by backfire.

The inner choke lever is mounted on a boss on the air horn and is retained by a snap ring fitted into a groove in the boss.

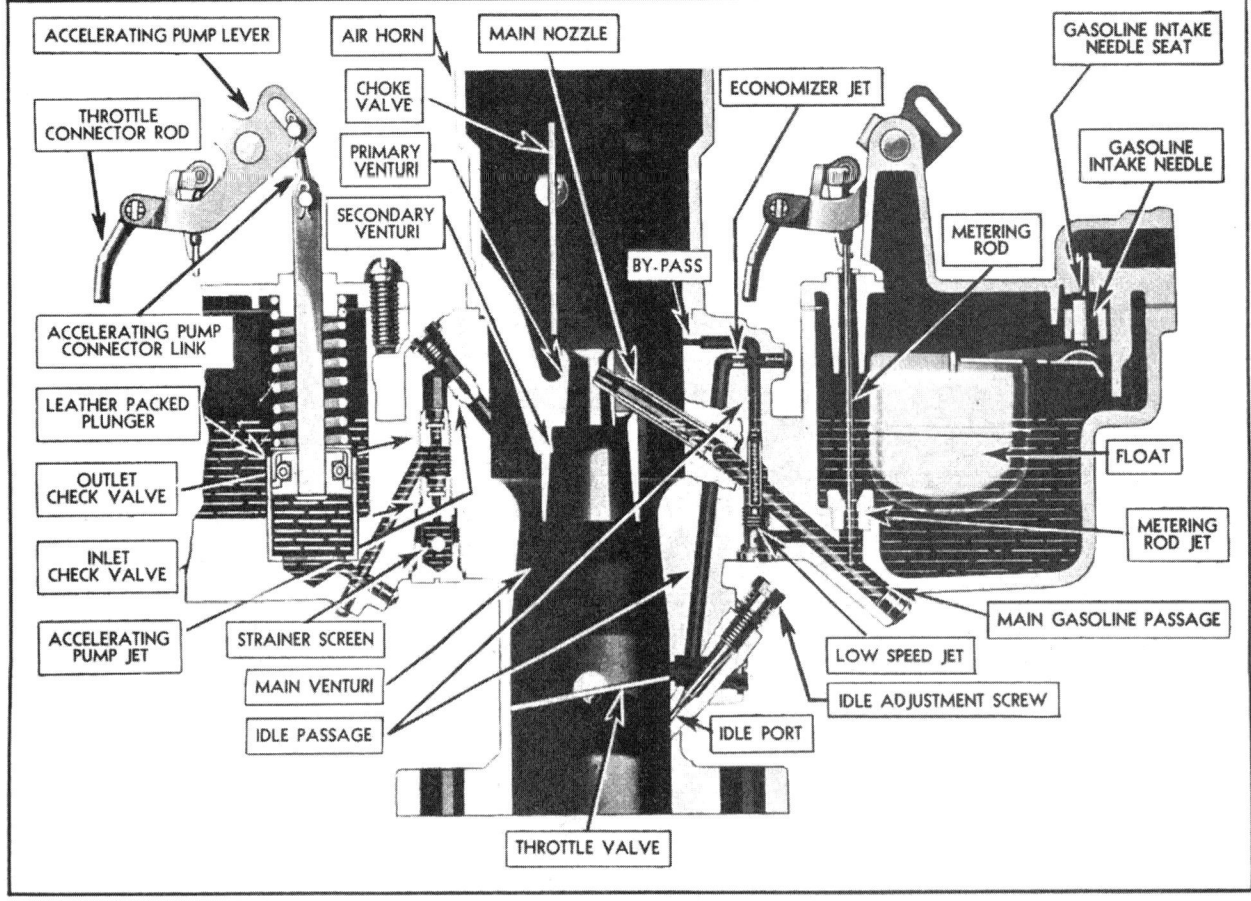

Fig. 63—Diagrammatic View of 1949 Downdraft Carburetor

Fig. 64—Carburetor Balance Passages

The outer choke lever is attached to the choke valve shaft and a light coil spring is used to connect the inner lever to the outer lever. In this way the outer choke lever and valve are operated by the inner choke lever through the spring. When the choke button on the instrument panel is pulled out, it causes the inner choke lever to rotate around the boss on which it is mounted. The light coil spring which is attached to it causes the outer choke lever to rotate, which rotates the choke valve shaft and closes the choke valve.

On 1949 models only, the inner choke lever also incorporates a pin which engages a slot in the fast idle link (fig. 65). This link is attached and pivots at its lower end on the throttle valve shaft. The throttle stop screw bears against this link. Thus, when the choke button on the instrument panel is pulled out and the inner choke lever rotates around the boss, the pin on the inner choke lever which is engaged in the slot in the fast idle link, causes the link to move. This movement is such that it causes an opening of the throttle through the throttle stop screw which bears against this link. This provides for a compensation in throttle opening with choke valve operation and prevents unnecessary flooding.

The accelerating pump consists of a cylinder with a plunger and two check valves, one on the inlet and one on the outlet side. The accelerating pump plunger, including the shaft, guide and leather is made as an assembly. The shaft is rectangular and bears in the bowl cover. The inlet check valve has a bakelite disc, while the outlet check valve has a brass disc. The brass disc aids fuel economy since its weight tends to keep it on its seat and prevents lifting from the seat due to air velocity in the carburetor.

The accelerating pump arrangement is slightly different between the 1948 and 1949 models. The plunger coil spring is located under the piston in 1948 and above the piston in 1949. This lowers the piston in the cylinder for 1949 models and permits it to be below the fluid level at all times. On 1949 models, a slot at the attaching point of the piston shaft and actuating link, allows the piston to move downward at its own rate. This rate being controlled by positive non-variable spring pressure.

Gasoline enters the low speed jet through a $3/64''$ hole drilled through the jet at the recess between the threaded section and the base of the jet, which coincides with the low speed well in the carburetor body (fig. 63). The metering hole is drilled vertically and is $.035''$ in diameter. This design prevents the possibility of the engine stalling due to gasoline surging away from this jet when the brakes are applied suddenly.

The main nozzle is of two-piece construction, with the inner nozzle pressed into the outer nozzle, thereby maintaining the proper relationship between the openings in the walls of the two nozzles. The nozzle assembly is held in place by a brass plug having a $.130''$-$.150''$ hole drilled through its center.

The throttle shaft end of the throttle connector rod fits through the throttle lever and is retained by a hairpin lock at this point. The pump arm end of the rod is flattened and has a small groove machined into it to receive a lock. When the connector rod is assembled to the pump arm, a small coil spring fits over the rod and is held in place by a stamped lock. This method of attachment provides a minimum of friction while still providing an anti-rattling device.

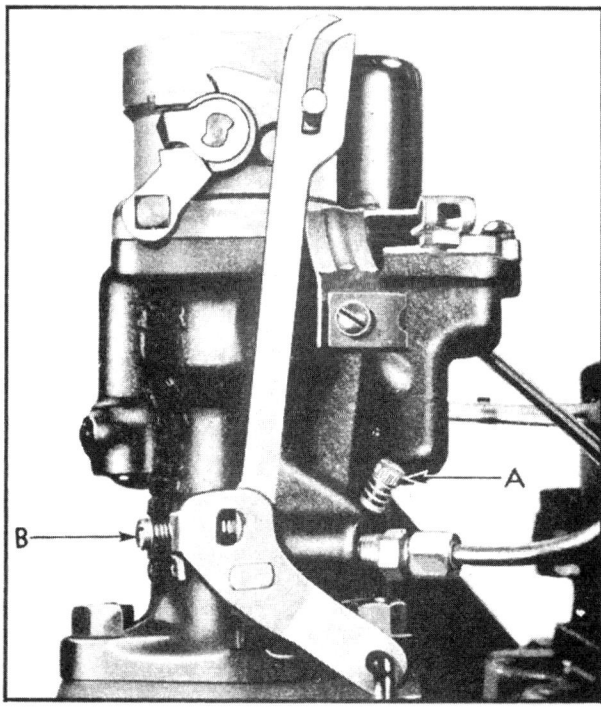

Fig. 65—Fast Idle Link

OPERATION

Accelerating Pump

The upward movement of the pump plunger, when the throttle is closed, draws a small quantity of gasoline into the bottom of the pump cylinder. The slightest opening of the throttle causes an immediate discharge through the pump jet into the main venturi (fig. 66).

Fig. 66—Carburetor Accelerator Pump Operation

Starting

With the choke valve in the closed position, as when starting a cold engine, suction from the down stroke of the engine piston draws a small amount of air past the choke valve (fig. 67). This air is then mixed with gasoline drawn from the main nozzle and forms a rich mixture for easy starting. When the engine starts, the incoming rush of air overcomes the choke shaft spring tension and opens the choke valve just the right amount to maintain a running mixture.

On 1949 models only, whenever the choke is used, the throttle is automatically opened far enough to keep the engine running. The throttle opening varies with choke position, and is approximately 12° on full choke.

Idling

At idling speed the throttle is almost completely closed. The suction from the down stroke of the engine piston is concentrated on the idling port below the throttle valve. This suction is applied to the low speed passage in the carburetor body and results in air being drawn in through the by-pass hole in the carburetor body. The air is then swept over the top of the low speed jet, causing gasoline to be lifted from the jet. The gasoline and air mixture then passes through the economizer and down the idle passage to the idling ports, where it mixes with air passing the throttle and is discharged into the throat of the carburetor (fig. 68). It is then carried on through the manifold to the cylinders.

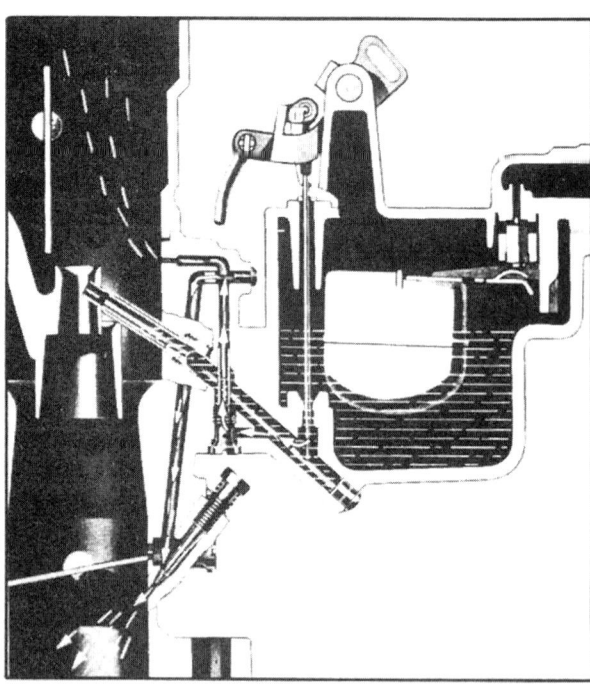

Fig. 68—Carburetor Operation During Idling

As the throttle valve is opened, the idling port above the throttle valve is uncovered and further increases the suction on the idling system, permitting it to furnish the necessary fuel mixture for the increase in engine speed.

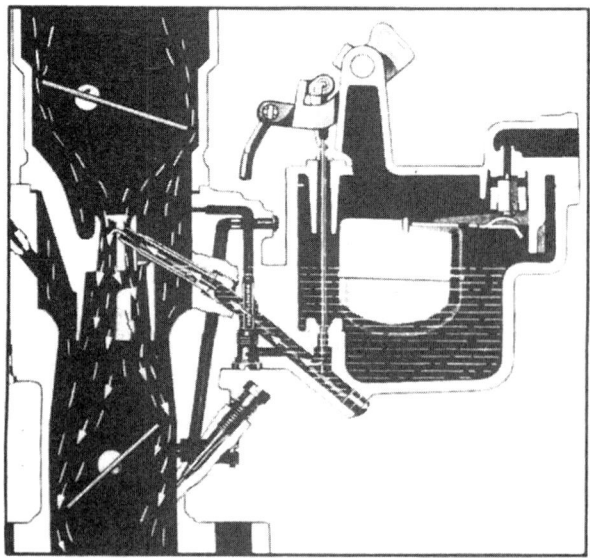

Fig. 67—Carburetor Operation When Starting Engine

Low Speed

At low speed the throttle is partly open and suction from the down stroke of the engine piston draws air in through the air horn. The air in passing through the main venturi increases in velocity with the result that the suction is increased over the secondary venturi. The increased air speed through the secondary venturi in turn steps up the suction on the primary venturi and thereby increases the air speed through the primary venturi. The air, passing through the primary venturi, draws gasoline from the main nozzle (fig. 69) where it is mixed with the air passing through the primary, secondary, and main venturi forming a finely atomized mixture which then passes on into the manifold and cylinders.

High Speed

The carburetor operation at higher speeds is similar to the low speed operation with the exception of raising the metering rod in the metering rod jet. This serves the same purpose as increasing the size of the jet and thereby furnishes the additional gasoline required for higher speeds and wide open throttle power operation.

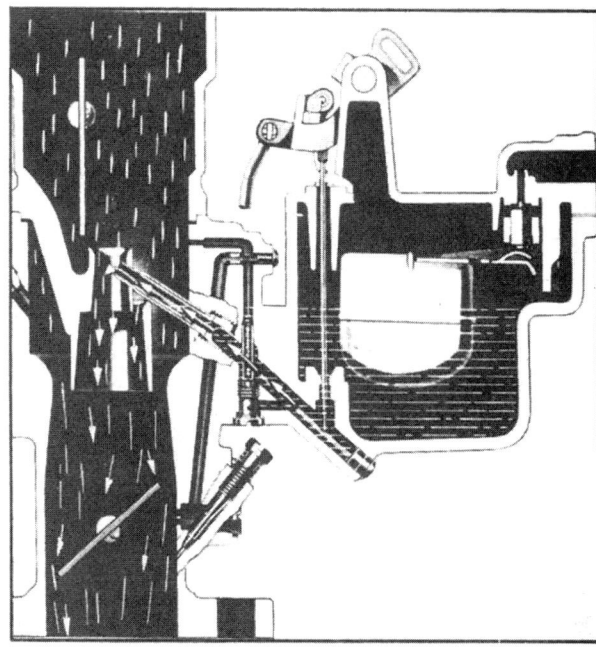

Fig. 69—Carburetor Low Speed Operation

MINOR SERVICE OPERATIONS

All carburetors are carefully tested and adjusted to the engine requirements before leaving the factory. Too often in servicing operations, adjustments are made on the carburetor, when in reality something else is causing uneven running, or the engine has not thoroughly warmed up.

Before making any carburetor adjustments, make sure that the carburetor to manifold and manifold to cylinder head bolts are tight, thus preventing air leaks and have the engine thoroughly warmed up to operating temperature.

There are four adjustments that can be made on the carburetor to improve performance when necessary; idling mixture and idling speed adjustments which should be made together and which are external adjustments, and float level and metering rod adjustments which are internal.

Idle Mixture Adjustment

1. Screw idle adjusting screw "A" (fig. 70) all the way in.
2. Back off idle adjusting screw "A" 1¾ turns.
3. Allow engine to idle.
4. Turn screw either way from this position until best idle point is reached.

   NOTE: If it is necessary to turn adjusting screw more than ½ turn in either direction to get a satisfactory idle, internal trouble is indicated.

Idle Speed Adjustment

1. Make sure hand throttle and hand choke on instrument panel are pushed all way in.
2. Adjust throttle lever stop screw "B" (fig. 70)

Fig. 70—Carburetor Idle Adjustment

so engine runs at approximately 450 to 500 revolutions per minute. (On 1948 models, the idle screw rests against a boss cast in the carburetor body, whereas on 1949 models, it seats on the lower end of the fast-idle link as shown in (fig. 70).

3. If engine runs too fast, back screw out. If engine runs too slow, turn screw in until proper speed is obtained.

4. Recheck idle mixture adjustment as indicated in number 4 above.

Float Level Adjustment

1. Remove carburetor air cleaner from air horn.
2. Remove dust cover from carburetor bowl.
3. With throttle valve in open position, remove stamped retainer from pump arm end of the throttle connector rod by pushing in on the retainer and turning it 90 degrees. Remove anti-rattle spring.
4. Disconnect metering rod spring and remove metering rod and metering rod disc, being careful not to bend the rod.
5. (a) On 1948 models, unhook pump connector link spring.
   (b) On 1949 models, remove hairpin lock from pump connector link and remove pump link.
6. Remove four bowl cover screws and remove bowl cover and float assembly.
7. Remove bowl cover gasket.
8. With bowl cover upside down, measure the distance from the top of the float to the machined under surface of the bowl cover (fig. 71).

   NOTE: This distance should be ½" and can be accurately checked with J-818-1 Float Level Gauge.

9. If float level must be reset, bend lip contacting intake needle up to lower the float and down to raise it.

   NOTE: Do not make this adjustment by pressing on the float. Bend the lip that contacts the needle.

10. Turn cover right side up and check the low position of the float by measuring from the under side of the cover to the top of the float at the outer end. This distance should be 1".

    NOTE: If adjustment is necessary, bend the two stops on the float with a small pair of pliers.

11. Replace bowl cover using a new gasket.
12. Connect carburetor pump lever to pump plunger by installing pump connector link spring (1948) or by installing pump connector link and hairpin lock (1949).
13. Replace metering rod disc and metering rod and connect metering rod spring.
14. Attach throttle connecting rod to pump lever and secure with anti-rattle spring and stamped retainer.
15. Replace carburetor bowl dust cover.
16. Install carburetor air cleaner on air horn.

Metering Rod

The metering rod controls the amount of gasoline that passes through the jet and may be changed to meet various climatic, gasoline or driving conditions.

There are three metering rods available which are marked as follows:

Standard	67-46
1 Step Lean	68-49
1 Step Rich	66-42

Whenever a new metering rod is to be installed or after the old metering rod has been removed, a metering rod gauge T-109-25 should be used to assure that the position of the throttle valve and the metering rod are in correct relation with each other.

The following procedure should be followed to synchronize the metering rod with the throttle valve.

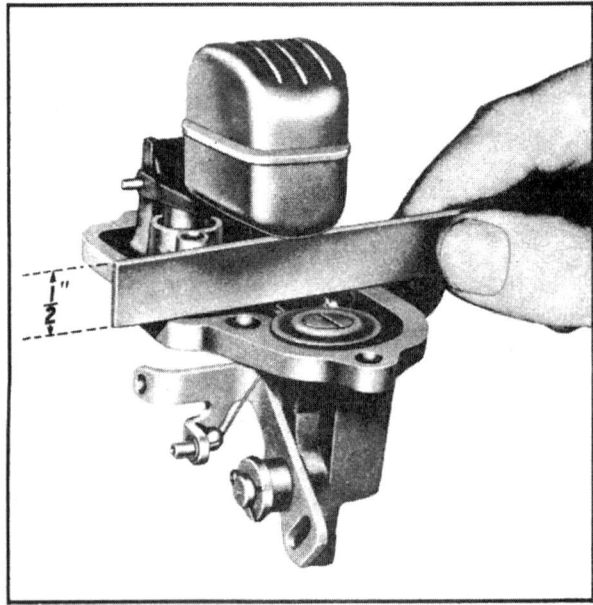

Fig. 71—Checking Carburetor Float Level

1. Remove carburetor air cleaner.
2. Remove dust cover from carburetor bowl.
3. Disconnect metering rod spring and remove metering rod.
4. Disconnect connector rod from throttle lever.
5. Make sure choke valve is fully open and back off throttle stop screw until throttle valve is closed tightly.
6. Install metering rod gauge T-109-25 by threading it through the bowl cover.

   NOTE: Make sure gauge seats in metering rod jet (fig. 72).

7. Press down on the pump arm until the pivot pin rests firmly on top of the gauge (fig. 72).
8. With pump arm in this position and the throttle valve fully closed, bend throttle connector rod at the throttle valve end so that connector rod will enter hole in throttle valve lever freely. Install hairpin lock.
9. Remove metering rod gauge, install metering disc and rod and connect metering rod spring.
10. Turn throttle stop screw in until throttle just starts to open.
11. Replace carburetor bowl dust cover.
12. Replace carburetor air cleaner.
13. Adjust idling speed and idling mixture.

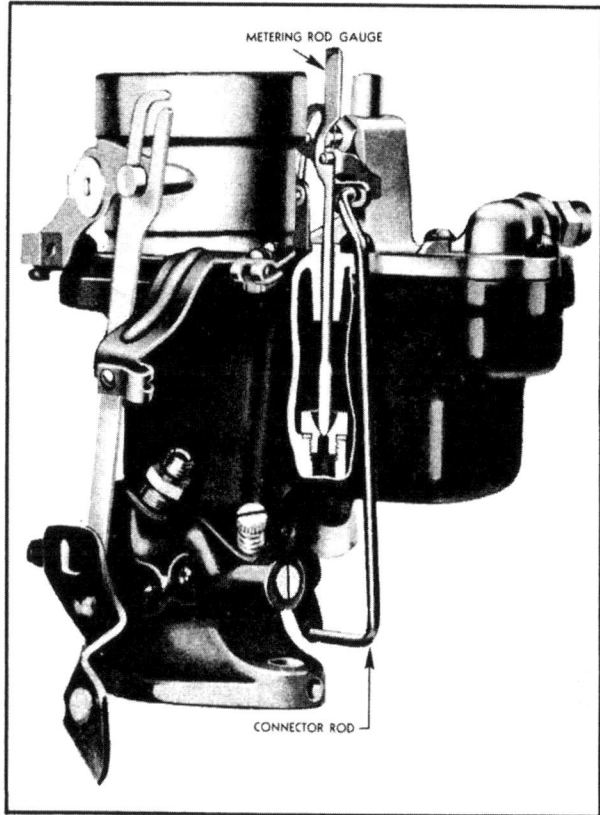

Fig. 72—Checking Throttle Connecting Rod with Metering Rod Gauge

MAJOR SERVICE OPERATIONS

The perfect carburetor delivers the proper gasoline and air ratios for all speeds of the particular motor for which it was designed. By completely overhauling at regular intervals, which will allow cleaning and replacing of all worn parts, the carburetor can be returned to its original condition and it will then deliver the proper ratios as it did when new.

CARBURETOR

Removal

1. Loosen air cleaner clamp bolt and remove air cleaner.
2. Disconnect fuel and vacuum lines from carburetor.
3. Release the choke and throttle cable clamps and lock screws and remove cables from carburetor.
4. Disconnect throttle rod from throttle shaft lever.
5. Remove the two carburetor flange to manifold stud nuts and lift carburetor off.

Disassembly

1. Remove dust cover from carburetor bowl.
2. With the throttle valve in the open position, remove stamped retainer and anti-rattle spring from pump arm end of throttle connector rod and hairpin lock from throttle lever end and remove connector rod.
3. Disconnect metering rod spring and remove metering rod and disc being careful not to bend rod.
4. Unhook pump connector link spring (1948) or remove hairpin lock from pump connector link and remove pump connector link (1949).
5. Remove four bowl cover screws and remove bowl cover and float assembly.
6. Remove float hinge pin and remove float and needle valve from cover.
7. Using tool J-816-4 remove needle valve seat from cover.
8. Remove accelerating pump plunger spring, pump plunger and metering rod jet from carburetor float bowl.

   NOTE: Use tool J-816-4 to remove metering rod jet.

9. Loosen three screws attaching air horn to carburetor body.
10. Remove main nozzle passage plug using tool J-816-7.

11. Remove main nozzle screw plug using tool J-816-2.
12. With a screwdriver, reach down through the air horn and press on the "D" section of the main nozzle to remove nozzle from primary venturi.

    NOTE: Do not press on end of the main nozzle.

13. Remove air horn screws and air horn.
14. Remove low speed jet using tool J-816-2.
15. Remove passage plug and screen for accelerating pump check valves using tool J-816-4.
16. Remove inlet and outlet check valves using tool J-816-2.
17. Remove passage plug for accelerating pump jet using tool J-816-2.
18. Remove accelerating pump jet using tool J-816-1.
19. Remove idle adjusting screw and idle port passage plug using tool J-816-7.
20. It will not be necessary to remove the choke or throttle valves unless the following inspections indicate that they require replacement.

Inspection

1. Wash all parts thoroughly in cleaning solvent.
2. Check the idle ports and first by-pass for carbon deposits.
3. Blow out all drilled passages with compressed air in the opposite direction to that of normal flow of air or gasoline.
4. Inspect the main nozzle for burrs at the venturi end.
5. Blow out the low speed jet and make sure the metering hole in jet is clean.
6. Check operation of inlet and outlet check valves.
7. Inspect accelerating pump jet to make sure it is clean.
8. Inspect accelerating pump plunger. If the leather or its expanding spring are damaged in any way the plunger assembly should be replaced.
9. Inspect the metering rod and metering rod jet for wear or damage and make sure correct metering rod is being used.
10. Check float for dents and wear on lip and float pin. Check bowl cover for warpage and wear in countershaft hole. If needle shows groove on seating surface replace both needle and seat.
11. Check throttle shaft arm for looseness on the shaft and for excessive wear at throttle rod connection.
12. Check throttle shaft for excessive looseness in the carburetor body.
13. Inspect throttle arm for wear.
14. Make sure choke valve opens and closes freely. Hold lever in closed position and push valve open to see that choke spring has normal tension.
15. Replace all worn or damaged parts. If throttle or choke valve parts require replacement they may be replaced according to the following procedure.

REPAIRS

Throttle Valve

1. File off upset ends of throttle valve to shaft screws, remove screws and throttle valve.
2. Loosen throttle arm lock screw and remove arm from shaft.
3. Remove shaft and lever assembly. Replace damaged parts.
4. Install throttle shaft and lever assembly.
5. Place throttle arm on end of shaft and tighten lock screw.

Fig. 73—Correct Assembly of Throttle Valve

6. Place throttle valve on shaft with the letter "C" stamped on valve toward the idle port (fig. 73). Install new valve to shaft screws, tighten securely and upset ends so they will not loosen.

Choke Valve

1. File off upset ends of choke valve to shaft screws, remove screws and choke valve.
2. Disconnect choke spring from outer choke lever and remove shaft assembly.
3. Remove snap ring holding inner choke lever on boss of air horn and remove lever and spring. Replace all damaged or worn parts.

4. Place spring and inner choke lever on air horn boss and install snap ring—on 1949 models while installing inner choke lever, engage lever pin in slot of fast-idle link.
5. Install choke shaft assembly and hook choke spring to outer choke lever.
6. Place choke valve in position with letter "C" on valve toward the top.
7. Install new valve to shaft screws, tighten securely and upset ends so they will not loosen.

ASSEMBLY

1. Install air horn to carburetor body making sure the small gasket is in place at the balance passage and that the control clip assembly is on the screw above the idling adjusting screw.
2. Assemble copper gasket (4) on main nozzle (5) (fig. 74). Hold carburetor with air horn down, line up "D" section on end of nozzle

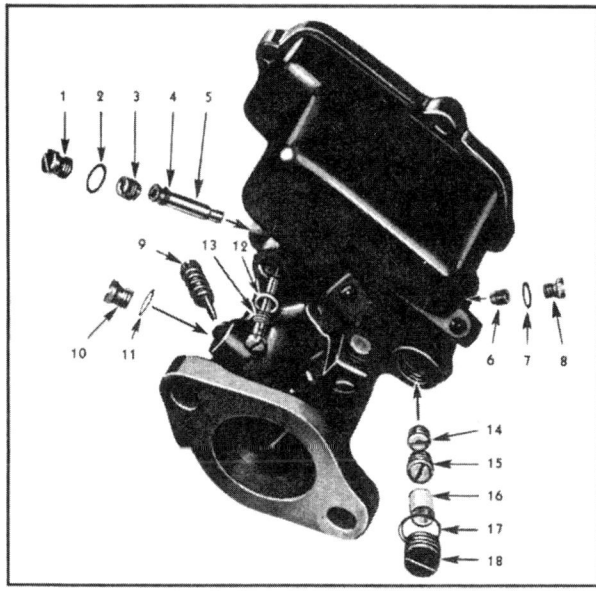

Fig. 74—Downdraft Carburetor Jets and Plugs

1. Passage Plug
2. Passage Plug Gasket
3. Nozzle Screw
4. Main Nozzle Gasket
5. Main Nozzle
6. Pump Jet
7. Passage Plug Gasket
8. Passage Plug
9. Idle Adjusting Screw and Tension Spring
10. Passage Plug
11. Passage Plug Gasket
12. Low Speed Jet Gasket
13. Low Speed Jet
14. Pump Outlet Check Valve
15. Pump Inlet Check Valve
16. Pump Strainer Screen
17. Passage Plug Gasket
18. Pump Screen Retainer and Passage Plug

with "D" opening in primary venturi and drop nozzle into the opening.
3. Install nozzle screw plug (3) and tighten it securely. Tighten the three air horn screws and then install main nozzle passage plug (1) using a new copper gasket (2) and tighten securely.

4. Install the low speed jet (13) and gasket (12) in carburetor body and tighten securely. Remove jet and check bearing at end. If there is a complete bearing around the end of the

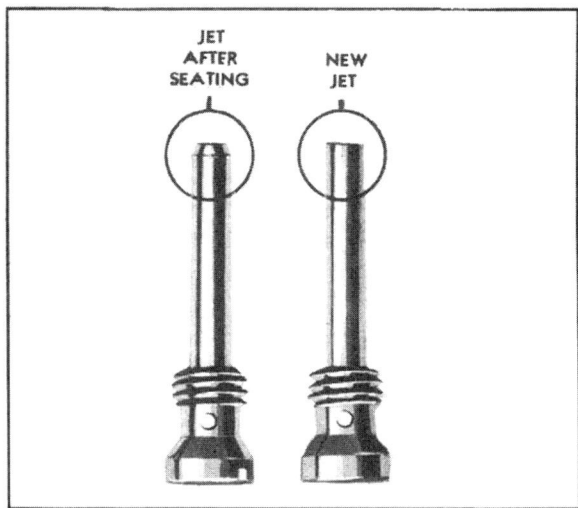

Fig. 75—Checking Seat on Low Speed Jet

jet as indicated in Figure 75 reinstall jet. If bearing is not complete, install a new jet.
5. Install the inlet (14) and outlet (15) check valves, tightening securely.
6. Install strainer screen (16) passage plug (18) and gasket (17) and tighten plug securely.
7. Install accelerating pump jet (6), plug (8) and gasket (7), tightening both jet and plug securely.
8. Install the metering rod jet and gasket and tighten securely.
9. Using sleeve J-507, install the accelerating pump plunger and plunger spring.

NOTE: On 1948 models, the plunger spring is placed in the pump cylinder first and the plunger is installed. On 1949 models, the pump plunger is installed first and then the plunger spring is slipped over the pump plunger shaft.

10. Install the float needle valve, seat and washer in the bowl cover, tightening seat securely.
11. Install float and float hinge pin.
12. With the cover turned upside down and gasket removed, check float level and adjust if necessary as outlined under "Float Level Adjustment."
13. On 1948 models, install a new accelerating pump cylinder cork gasket to the bowl cover.
14. Install a new bowl gasket and install cover to bowl and tighten securely.
15. Connect carburetor pump lever to pump plunger with connector link spring (1948) or with connector link and hairpin lock (1949).

ENGINE ASSEMBLY 6-58

16. Assemble throttle connector rod to the pump arm and install anti-rattle spring and retainer to rod end.
17. With choke valve fully open, back off throttle stop screw until throttle valve closes tightly.
18. Install metering rod gauge T-109-25 and synchronize metering rod with throttle lever as outlined under "Metering Rod."
19. Remove metering rod gauge and install proper metering rod with disc dropping it into position and hook eye over pivot pin. Hook metering rod spring to metering rod.
20. Turn throttle stop screw in with choke valve open until throttle starts to open and then ¾ turn more.
21. Install the idling adjusting screw and spring (9) (fig. 74). Turn screw in until it seats and then back off 1¾ turns.
22. Install idle port passage plug (10) and gasket (11) and tighten securely.
23. Lubricate pump arm felt wick with a few drops of engine oil and install dust cover and attaching screw.

INSTALLATION

1. Place carburetor in position on manifold studs and install retaining nuts. Tighten evenly and securely.
2. Connect fuel and vacuum lines to carburetor.
3. Push choke and throttle button in against instrument panel.
4. Install carburetor throttle rod to throttle lever.
5. Push hand throttle wire and conduit through clamp on carburetor and hole in end of throttle lever rod.
6. Tighten clamp and install wire guide leaving about ⅛ inch between guide and throttle lever rod with throttle valve closed.
7. Push choke wire and conduit through clamp on carburetor and enter wire in connector on choke lever.
8. Tighten clamp and wire retaining screw in connector.
9. Check choke and throttle operation by pulling choke and throttle button on dash all the way out. Throttle valve should be fully open and choke valve fully closed.
10. Push buttons all the way in. Throttle valve should be fully closed to stop screw and choke valve should be fully open.
11. Install air cleaner.
12. Start engine and after it has warmed to operating temperature make necessary idle mixture and idle speed adjustment as outlined under "Idle Mixture" and "Idle Speed Adjustment."

GM MODEL "B" DOWNDRAFT CARBURETOR

GENERAL DESCRIPTION

The GM Model "B" downdraft carburetor is used on all (1950-51) conventional truck models.

This carburetor presents several distinct features of importance to the truck owner and the mechanic. Foremost among these features are:

(a) Concentric fuel bowl—regardless of any shift of fuel level in the bowl, the main metering jet is at all times immersed in fuel.
(b) Centrally located main discharge nozzle—A shift in fuel level has little or no effect on the rate of discharge from the nozzle.
(c) The main well and support assembly, which contains the main metering jet and the power valve, is attached to the cover and suspended in the float bowl which provides ease in servicing.
(d) A fast idle mechanism, which is in linkage with the choke lever, is an aid to faster, more efficient cold weather starting and helps to prevent over-choking.

Although functionally the same, there are two model "B" carburetors used; one is for the 216 engine and the other for the 235 engine. The only differences between the two carburetors are the size of the carburetor throat diameter and the size of orifices in some of the carburetor jets.

	Size of I.D. of Main Venturi	Size of Throttle Bore
216 Engine	1.218"	1-1/2"
235 Engine	1.343"	1-9/16"

OPERATION

Idle System

At idling speed, the throttle is almost completely closed. The idle fuel first passes from the bowl through the calibrated main metering jet "A" (fig. 76) in the bottom of the main well support assembly "B."

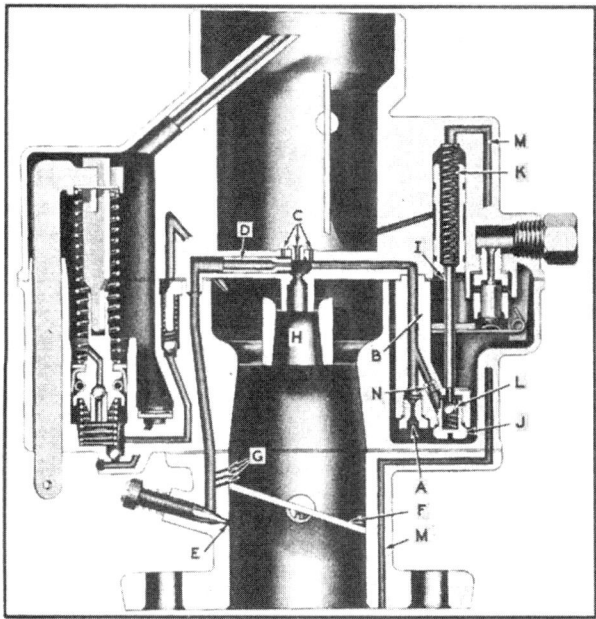

Fig. 76—Carburetor Cross Section

The fuel is then drawn up the main well by manifold vacuum (suction) to the crossbar of the air horn. Air joins the solid fuel through the three calibrated air bleeds "C" in the center of the crossbar. The fuel/air mixture is then calibrated by the idle tube "D" and passes down the passage in the float bowl to the throttle body.

The idle fuel is then metered to the engine by the idle adjusting needle hole "E" which is below the throttle valve "F." As the throttle valve is opened, the secondary idle holes "G" are exposed in turn to manifold vacuum and deliver additional fuel to meet the increased engine demand.

Part Throttle System

As the throttle valve "F" is opened to a greater degree, additional suction is applied to the main discharge nozzle "H" in the crossbar and suction is decreased at idle holes. As a consequence the fuel begins to pass from the main nozzle rather than through the idle system.

The calibration of the main metering jet "A" and the air bleeds "C" in the crossbar, control and maintain the economical fuel/air ratios throughout the driving range.

Power System

To provide for additional fuel for sustained high speed operation or increased road load power, the vacuum operated power system delivers such fuel readily and economically.

A direct manifold vacuum passage "M" within the carburetor which connects to the engine intake manifold, operates this system. At any manifold vacuum above 5″ of mercury, the power actuating piston "I" is held by suction in the "Up" position against the compression of the power spring "K." Consequently, no fuel passes through the ball type power valve "J." With any decrease in vacuum below 5″ mercury, the calibrated power spring "K" immediately forces the power piston down, which unseats the spring loaded ball "L" in the power valve "J." Fuel then passes readily around the ball into the base of the main well support assembly. The calibrated power restriction "N" meters the fuel prior to joining the fuel from the main metering jet "A," and is delivered to the engine. Conversely as the manifold vacuum rises above 5″ mercury, the power piston is drawn immediately to the "Up" position and the engine returns to the economical part throttle mixtures of the carburetor.

There is no adjustment required for either the part throttle or power systems.

Float System

The Model "B" carburetor is completely balanced. The balance tube connects the carburetor air intake and the float bowl (fig. 77), thereby

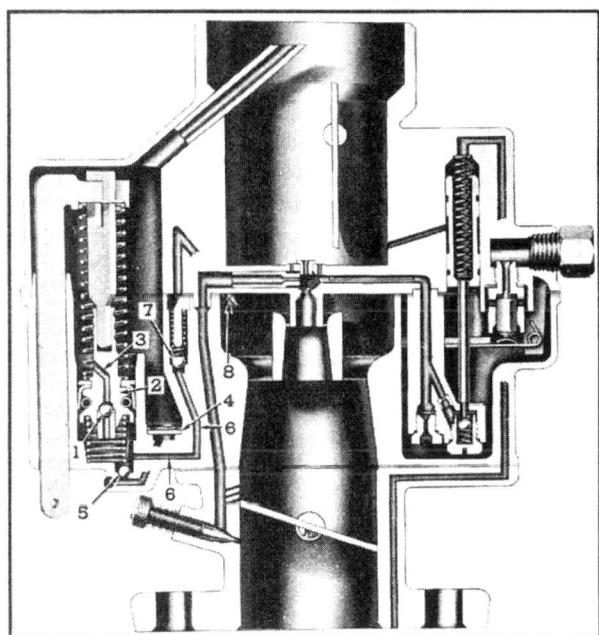

Fig. 77—Carburetor Cross Section

equalizing air pressures. In this manner, any accumulation of dirt in the air cleaner is compensated for and prevents any erratic richer mixtures.

To aid in maintaining the correct fuel level, under all conditions, the carburetor employs twin floats. It is of utmost importance that the floats be adjusted carefully and accurately.

ENGINE ASSEMBLY 6-60

Pump System

To provide for smooth, quick acceleration, a double spring pump plunger is used in the Model "B" carburetor. The rates of compression of the top spring versus the bottom spring is calibrated to insure a smooth, sustained charge of fuel for acceleration.

To exclude dirt, all fuel for the pump system first passes through the pump screen "4" (fig. 77) in the bottom of the float bowl. It is then drawn past the ball check "5" into the pump well on the intake stroke of the plunger "2." Upon acceleration, force of the pump plunger seats the ball check "5" and forces the fuel up passage "6." The pressure of the fuel lifts the pump outlet ball check "7" from its seat, overcoming the check ball spring pressure. The fuel is then sprayed on the bottom edge of the venturi by the pump jet "8" and delivered to the engine. Targeting of the pump jet is maintained at manufacture.

For greater driving ease, the plunger head is designed to eliminate fuel percolation in the pump system. This has been accomplished by designing a by-pass around a ball check "1" in the plunger head "2." When the engine is not operating, any build up of fuel vapors in the pump will by-pass this ball allowing the hot fuel and vapors to circulate up the passage "3" in the plunger head and return to the float bowl. Otherwise, any vapor pressure built up would evacuate the fuel in the pump system into the engine manifold, causing poor initial acceleration due to lack of fuel in the pump system when engine is hot.

MINOR SERVICE OPERATION

All carburetors are carefully calibrated to the engine requirements and then are tested and adjusted before leaving the factory. Too often, in servicing operations, adjustments are made on the carburetor, when in reality something else is causing uneven running or the engine has not thoroughly warmed up.

Before making any carburetor adjustments, make sure that the carburetor to manifold and manifold to cylinder head bolts are tight, thus preventing air leaks. Of equal importance is to have the engine thoroughly warmed up to operating temperature. On the G.M. Model "B" carburetor, there are only two external adjustments and one internal adjustment. The idle mixture and idle speed adjustments are external adjustments and should be made together. The only internal adjustment is the float level adjustment.

Idle Mixture Adjustment

1. Screw idle adjusting screw "A" (fig. 78) all the way in.
2. Back off idle adjusting screw "A" 1½ to 2½ turns.

   NOTE: Do not turn the adjusting screw in too tight or damage to the seat and needle may result.

3. Allow engine to idle.
4. Turn screw either way from this position until best idle is obtained.

Idle Speed Adjustment

1. Make sure hand throttle and hand choke buttons on instrument panel are pushed in all the way and that the accelerator and throttle linkage is free so that throttle stop screw "B" (fig. 78) is against the stop.
2. Turn screw "B" in or out to obtain an idling speed of 450 to 500 revolutions per minute.
3. Recheck idle mixture adjustment so that the idle mixture and idle speed adjustments, in combination with each other, produce a smooth idle at the required RPM's.

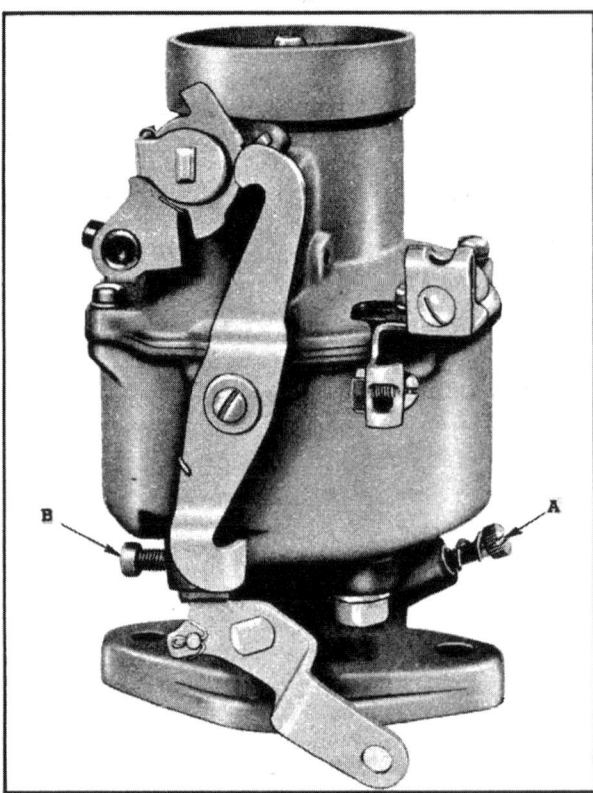

Fig. 78—Idle and Mixture Adjustment

Float Level Adjustment

1. Remove carburetor air cleaner from air horn.
2. Disconnect choke wire from connector on choke lever.
3. Disconnect fuel line at carburetor cover fitting.

ENGINE ASSEMBLY 6-61

4. Remove 4 cover attaching screws and choke bracket.
5. While holding throttle kick lever, lift cover straight up to prevent damage to floats.
6. With cover fully assembled and cover gasket in position, place assembly up-ended on a flat surface.
7. Place float level gauge, part number 3696192, into position (fig. 79) with tang at center of gauge located in main discharge nozzle of the cover.

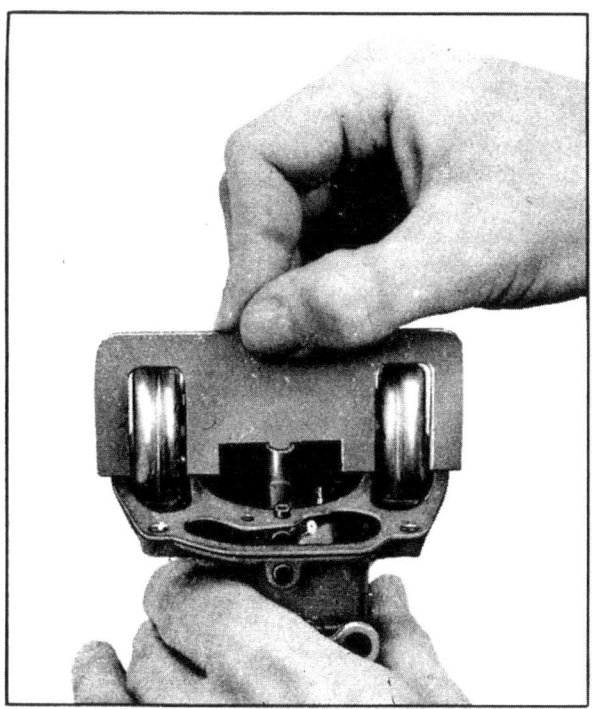

Fig. 79—Checking Float Level

8. Bend float arms vertically so that each float just touches top portion of gauge.
9. Carefully bend float arms horizontally so that each float is centered in the gauge. Tilt assemble 90° each side and check that floats do not touch gauge (fig. 80). This insures that floats will not rub inner sides of float bowl. Recheck level adjustment.

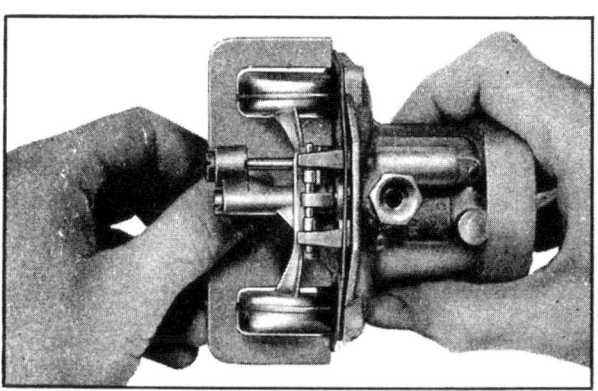

Fig. 80—Checking Float Clearance

Float Drop Adjustment

To insure sufficient entry of fuel under high speed operation, it is necessary to check and adjust the float drop.

1. With the cover assembly held right side up and floats suspended freely, carefully bend the float tang at rear of float assembly so that the bottom of the float is 1¾" below the gasket surface (fig. 81).

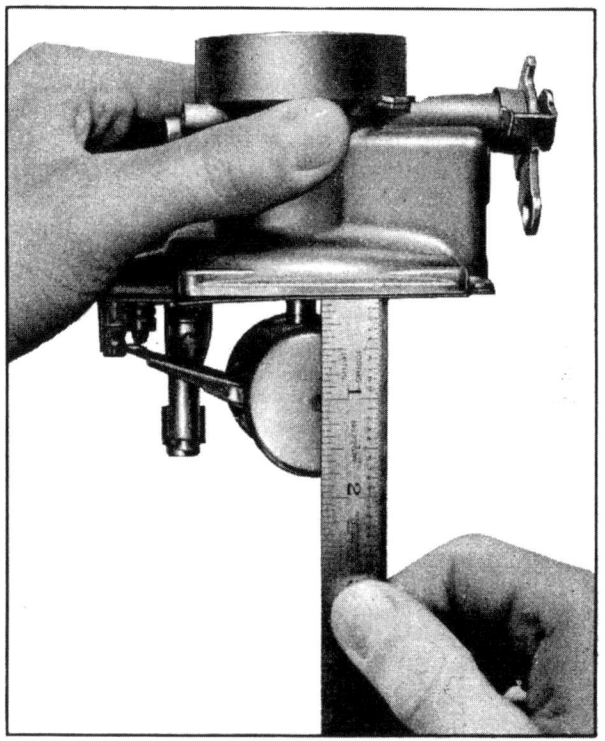

Fig. 81—Float Drop Adjustment

Fig. 82—Assembly Cover to Bowl

ENGINE ASSEMBLY 6-62

Air Horn Installation

1. Rotate throttle kick lever clockwise against tension of spring to a vertical position and carefully place cover assembly on bowl (fig. 82).
2. Install 4 attaching screws and choke bracket and tighten screws securely.
3. Connect fuel line to carburetor cover fitting.
4. Enter choke wire into connector on choke lever, check to see that choke button is pushed in against instrument panel and choke valve is fully open. Then tighten choke wire retaining screw in connector.
5. Replace carburetor air cleaner and check and adjust, if necessary, idle speed and idle mixture.

MAJOR SERVICE OPERATIONS

The perfect carburetor delivers the proper gasoline and air ratios for all speeds of the particular engine for which it was designed. By completely disassembling at regular intervals, which will allow cleaning of all parts and passages, the carburetor can be returned to its original condition and it will then deliver the proper ratios as it did when new.

Because of the simplicity of design of the Model "B" carburetor, few parts are used which will require replacement. Accurate calibration of passages and discharge holes, require that extreme care be taken in cleaning. Use only carburetor solvent and compressed air to clean all passages and passage discharge holes. Never use wire or other pointed instrument to clean as calibration of carburetor will be affected.

CARBURETOR

Removal

1. Loosen air cleaner clamp and remove air cleaner.
2. Disconnect fuel and vacuum lines from carburetor.
3. Release the choke and throttle cable clamps and lock screws and remove cables from carburetor.
4. Disconnect throttle rod from throttle shaft lever.
5. Remove the two carburetor flange to manifold stud nuts and lift carburetor off.

Disassembly

1. Remove 4 cover attaching screws and choke bracket.
2. While holding throttle kick lever, lift cover straight up to prevent damage to floats.
3. Place cover up-ended on flat surface and remove float hinge pin, floats and float needle.
4. Using screw driver of proper width, remove float needle seat and red fibre gasket.
5. Remove main metering jet and power valve assembly from main well support.

   NOTE: Use care when removing power valve not to lose small spring and ball.

6. Remove main well support attaching screw and remove support. Then, lift power piston and spring from cover.
7. Lift air horn gasket from cover.
8. Remove throttle kick lever and spring by removing retaining screw and washer.
9. Holding pump plunger all the way down, remove cotter pin or hairpin retainer from pump link and remove pump link from throttle lever and pump plunger. Pump plunger may now be lifted from bowl.
10. Lift pump spring from pump well and remove ball check from bottom of well.
11. With small screwdriver, rotate pump discharge guide until it can be removed. Pump discharge spring and ball check will fall from bowl when turned upside down.
12. Remove pump screen retainer and pump screen from bowl.
13. With bowl upside down, remove 2 throttle body attaching screws and remove throttle body assembly.
14. Remove idle adjusting needle and spring from throttle body.
15. Figure 83 illustrates carburetor completely disassembled.

Inspection

1. Wash all parts thoroughly in carburetor solvent and dry with compressed air.
2. Check all ports and passages for carbon deposits.
3. Blow out all drilled passages with compressed air and check with flashlight to make sure they are clean.

   NOTE: Do not, under any circumstances, use wire or other pointed instrument to clean drilled passages or calibrated holes in carburetor. Holes and passages are carefully calibrated and use of wire or other cleaning instrument will destroy calibration of carburetor.

4. Inspect pump plunger. If the leather or its expanding spring are damaged, in any way, the plunger assembly should be replaced.
5. Check floats for dents and wear on lip and hinge pin. Also check cover for wear in hinge pin holes.
6. Check float needle. If wear is noted on float needle, install new float needle assembly con-

ENGINE ASSEMBLY 6-63

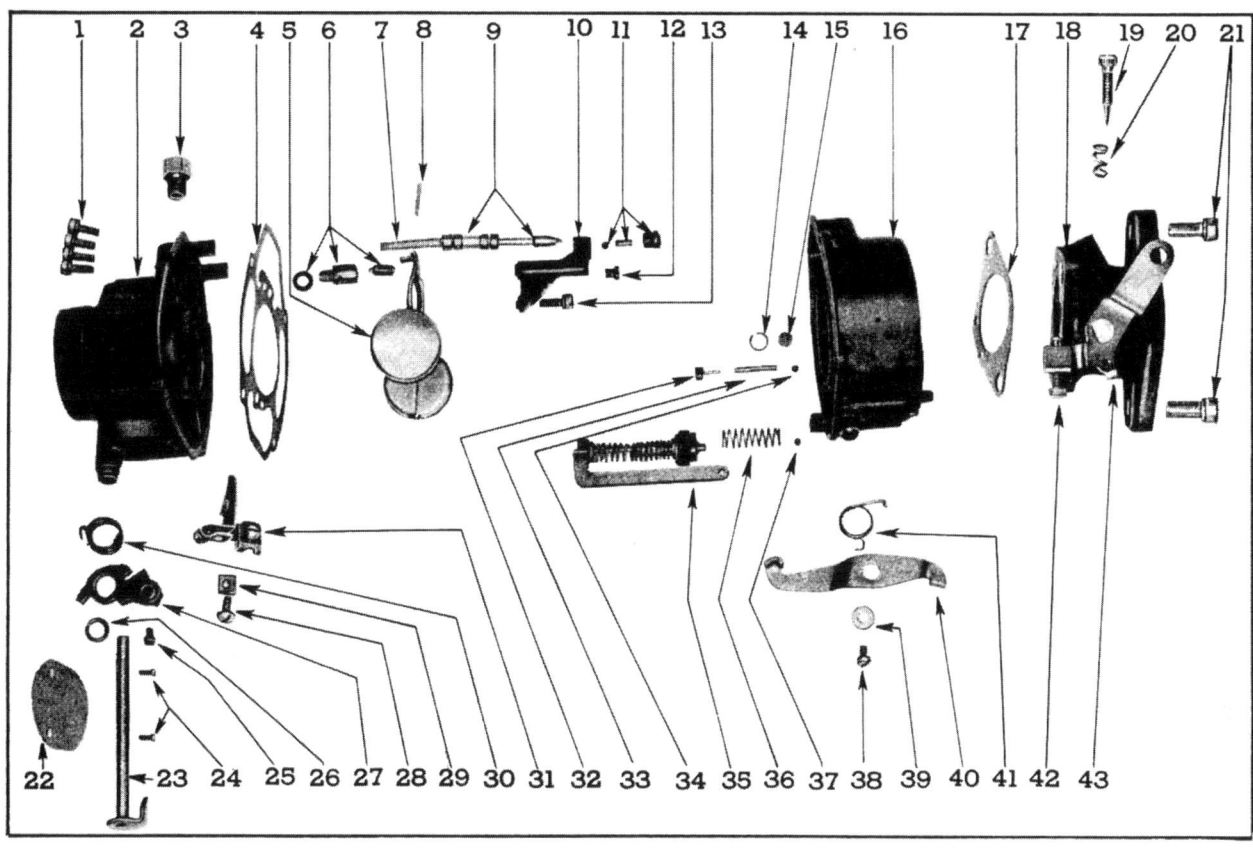

Fig. 83—Carburetor—Layout

1. Screw—Cover Attaching
2. Air Horn
3. Fuel Inlet Fitting
4. Gasket—Air Horn
5. Float
6. Float Needle, Seat, Gasket Assy.
7. Power Spring
8. Float Hinge Pin
9. Power Piston
10. Main Well Support
11. Power Valve Assembly
12. Main Metering Jet
13. Screw—Attaching
14. Retainer—Pump Screen
15. Pump Screen
16. Float Bowl
17. Gasket—Throttle Body
18. Throttle Body Assembly
19. Idle Adjusting Needle
20. Spring—Idle Needle
21. Screw—Throttle Body
22. Choke Valve
23. Choke Shaft
24. Screw—Choke Valve
25. Screw—Choke Lever
26. Retainer—Choke Lever
27. Choke Lever
28. Screw—Bracket
29. Nut—Bracket
30. Spring—Choke Shaft
31. Choke Bracket
32. Guide—Pump Discharge
33. Spring—Pump Discharge
34. Ball—Pump Discharge—3/16 Steel
35. Pump Plunger Assy.
36. Spring—Pump Return
37. Ball—Pump Check—5/32 Aluminum
38. Screw—Throttle Kicker
39. Washer—Throttle Kicker
40. Throttle Kicker
41. Spring—Throttle Kicker
42. Screw—Throttle Valve
43. Throttle Shaft

sisting of matched and tested needle and seat and new fibre washer.

7. Check power piston for burrs or other damage. Piston must move freely in cover bore.
8. Check pump screen—make sure it is clean.
9. Check throttle arm for looseness on the shaft and for excessive wear at throttle rod connection.
10. Check throttle shaft for excessive looseness in throttle body.

NOTE: Any damage or excessive wear in throttle arm or shaft necessitates replacement of the throttle body assembly. This is due to the close tolerance of throttle valve fit required and the fact that the idle discharge holes are drilled in relation to a proper fitting valve.

11. Make sure choke valve opens and closes freely. Hold lever in closed position and push

valve open to see that choke spring has normal tension.

REPAIRS

Choke Valve

1. Remove choke valve screws and choke valve.
2. Disconnect choke spring from outer choke lever and shaft assembly and remove choke shaft assembly.
3. Remove choke swivel retaining ring which retains swivel on boss of cover and remove swivel and spring.
4. Place choke spring on cover boss with extended hook end against cover.
5. Place choke swivel assembly on boss with lug and screw on the inside. Lock retaining ring into groove.
6. Slip choke shaft into air horn. Center choke valve and tighten screws. The letters "RP"

or "C" must face outward with choke valve closed (fig. 84).

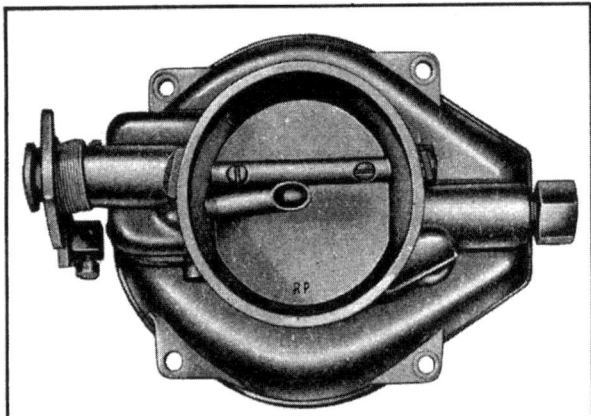

Fig. 84—Installation of Choke Valve

7. Turn choke spring clockwise until outside hooked end engages slot in bottom of choke swivel assembly. With small piece of wire, wind inside end of choke spring approximately ½ turn and hook over end of choke shaft assembly. Ascertain that choke assembly has free movement.

ASSEMBLY

1. Install idle needle and spring finger tight in throttle body. As a temporary idle adjustment, back needle out 1½ turns.
2. Using a new throttle body gasket, attach bowl to throttle body. Tighten screws evenly and securely.
3. Place clean pump screen in bottom of bowl and lock retainer into position.
4. Drop small aluminum ball in pump well.

NOTE: After installing ball ascertain that ball lifts freely from its seat.

5. Place pump return spring into pump well and center it by depressing with finger.
6. Install pump plunger and connect pump link to throttle lever and pump rod. Install cotter pin or hairpin retainers at both upper and lower ends.
7. Drop large steel ball into pump discharge cavity of bowl and place bronze color spring on top of ball.
8. Index end of pump discharge guide into bronze color spring and press down until guide is flush with bowl surface.
9. Place throttle kick lever spring on bowl boss with smaller hooked end against bowl. Rotate clockwise until small end engages lower boss.
10. Attach throttle kick lever with screw and washer. Flat portion of lever must be against idle screw.
11. Place new air horn gasket, part 7002799, on air horn.
12. Place power piston spring and power piston in air horn cavity and attach main well support to air horn.
13. Install main metering jet and tighten securely.
14. Hold power piston stem down and install power ball, spring and plug and tighten securely.
15. Install float needle seat using new fibre washer and install float needle.
16. Attach float with hinge pin.

NOTE: Float tang must face cover.

17. Adjust float setting as outlined under, "Minor Service Operations, Float Level Adjustment."
18. Rotate throttle kick lever clockwise until extended hooked end engages lower half of lever. Turn lever to vertical position against tension of spring. Cam portion of lever will now be in position to engage cam portion of choke swivel.
19. Holding throttle kick lever as described, place cover assembly on bowl (fig. 82). Install attaching screws and choke bracket and tighten screws securely.

INSTALLATION

1. Place carburetor in position on manifold studs and install retaining nuts. Tighten evenly and securely.
2. Connect fuel and vacuum lines to carburetor.
3. Connect throttle rod to throttle shaft lever.
4. Push hand throttle wire and conduit through bracket on carburetor and wire through hole in end of throttle lever rod.
5. Tighten clamp and making sure throttle button is pushed in against dash, install wire guide on end of throttle wire leaving about ⅛" between guide and throttle lever rod with throttle valve closed.
6. Push choke wire and conduit through bracket on carburetor and enter wire in connector on choke lever.
7. Make sure choke button is pushed in against dash, then tighten bracket clamp and wire retaining screw in connector.
8. Check choke and throttle operation by pulling choke and throttle buttons on dash all the way out. Throttle valve should be fully open and choke valve fully closed.
9. Push buttons all the way in. Throttle valve should be fully closed to stop screw and choke valve should be fully open.
10. Install air cleaner, start engine and warm to operating temperature. Make necessary idle mixture and idle speed adjustments as outlined under "Minor Service Operations, Idle Mixture and Idle Speed Adjustments."

CARTER UPDRAFT CARBURETOR

GENERAL DESCRIPTION

Due to the construction of the Forward Control and Cab-Over-Engine trucks, a downdraft carburetor cannot be used; therefore, the manifolds are designed for mounting a carburetor directly below the center of the manifolds.

This updraft carburetor is balanced so that the pressure on the inside of the air horn and in the float chamber remains constant. This type carburetor also embodies an accelerating pump, a vacuum controlled power jet and a spring mounted auxiliary air valve in the choke valve. Figure 85 shows the carburetor in cross section.

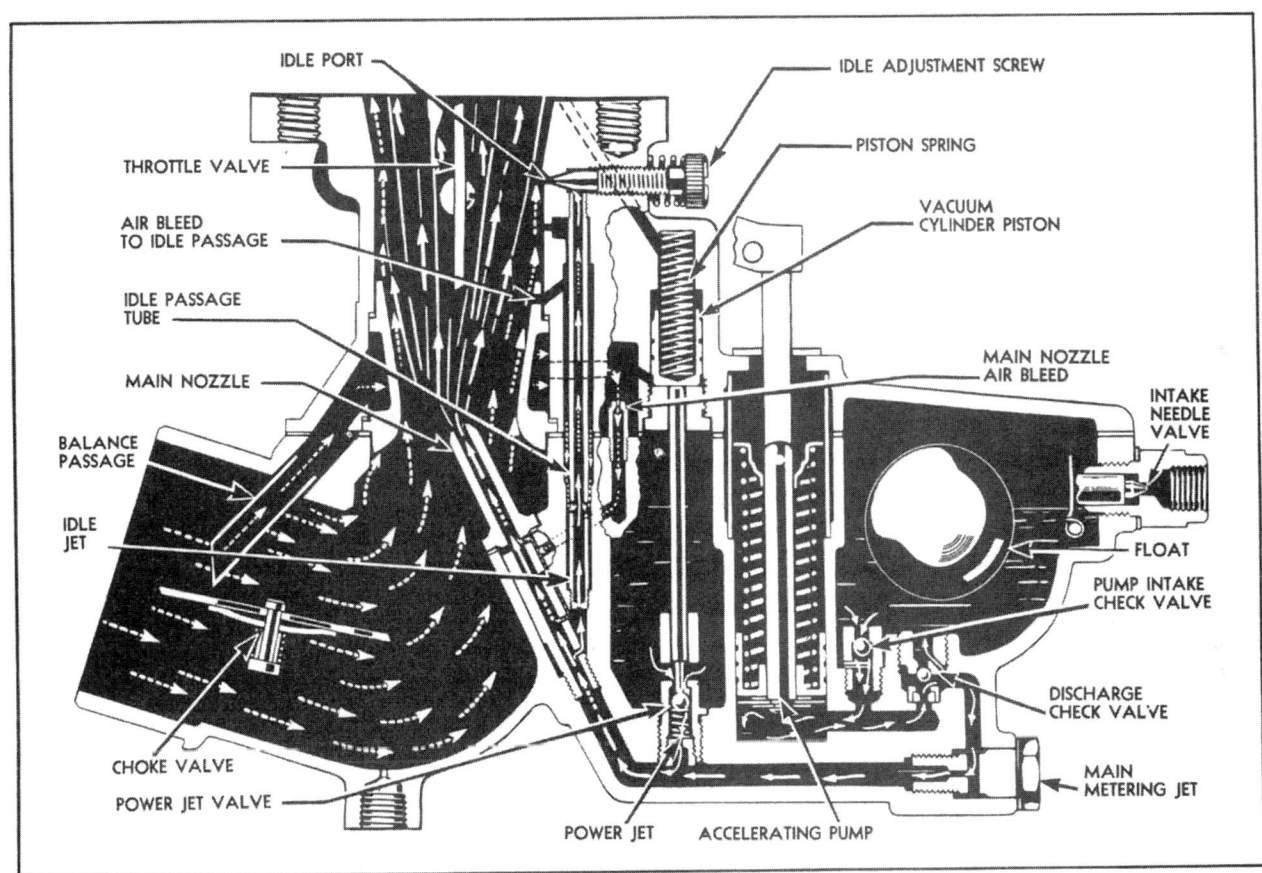

Fig. 85—Diagrammatic View of Updraft Carburetor

OPERATION

Starting

With the choke valve in "closed" position when starting, air is drawn in through the bleeder hole in the choke valve and mixed with gasoline drawn from the main nozzle, forming a rich mixture for easy starting. When the engine starts, the auxiliary air valve located at the center of the choke valve opens, admitting additional air and prevents overchoking (fig. 86).

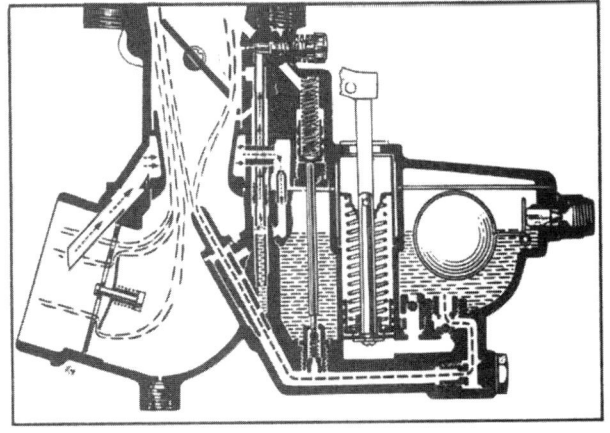

Fig. 86—Choke Valve Position When Starting

Idling

At idling speed, air is drawn in through the air bleed to idle passage and passes between the idle passage tube and the carburetor casting to the lower end of the tube. Here it passes over the idle jet drawing gasoline from it. The gasoline and air are mixed while passing up the idle passage tube and discharged into the manifold through the idle port (fig. 87).

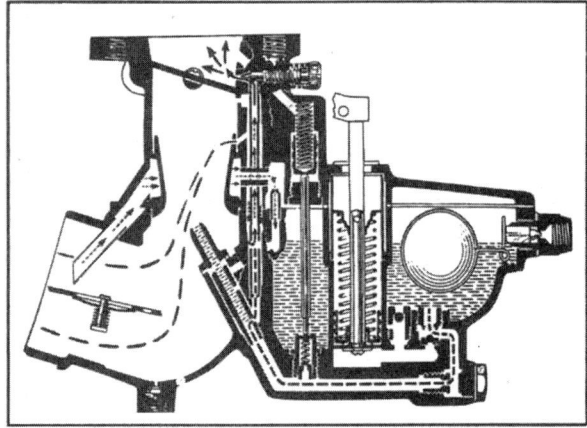

Fig. 87—Air Drawing Gas from Idle Jet

Accelerating Pump

As the throttle is closed, the accelerating pump piston is drawn upward, compressing the spring. This results in gasoline flowing from the float chamber through the intake check valve into the pump cylinder.

When the throttle is opened quickly, the piston rod and plate are forced down the cylinder, allowing the spring tension on the piston to force the gasoline out of the cylinder, closing the intake check valve and opening the discharge valve. The pump discharge then passes into the venturi through the main nozzle (fig. 88).

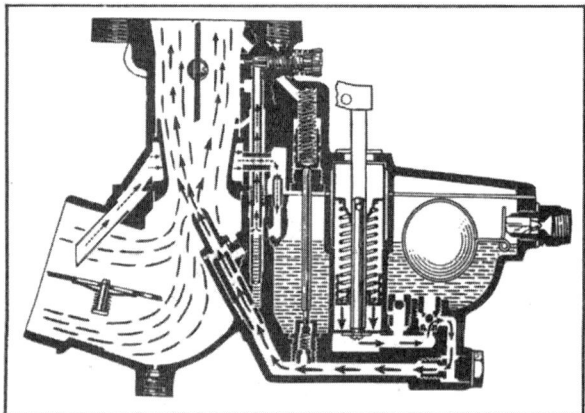

Fig. 88—Accelerator Pump Action

Low Speed

At low speed, the gasoline flows from the float chamber through the discharge check valve, through the main metering jet to the main nozzle (fig. 89). Suction on the down stroke of the engine piston draws air through the air intake. This air passing over the main nozzle raises gasoline from the nozzle. The gasoline and air are then mixed in the venturi and pass through the throat of the carburetor to the manifold and cylinders.

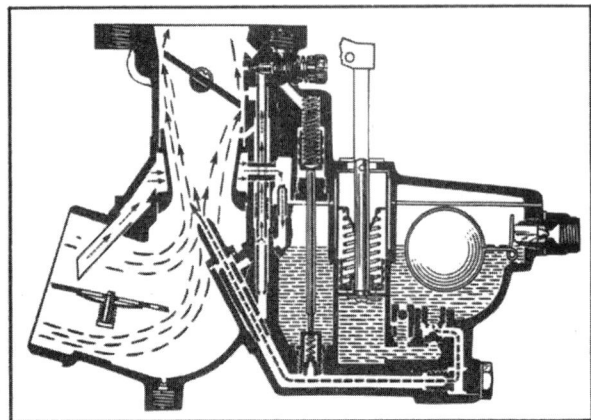

Fig. 89—Main Jet Operation at Idle

At intermediate speeds, air enters the well surrounding the main nozzle through the main nozzle air bleed. This aids in lifting the gasoline as the gasoline in the main nozzle starts to lower with the increase in speed.

During the operations described above, the high manifold vacuum impressed on the vacuum cylinder draws the piston upward, allowing the spring in the power jet to close the valve in the power jet.

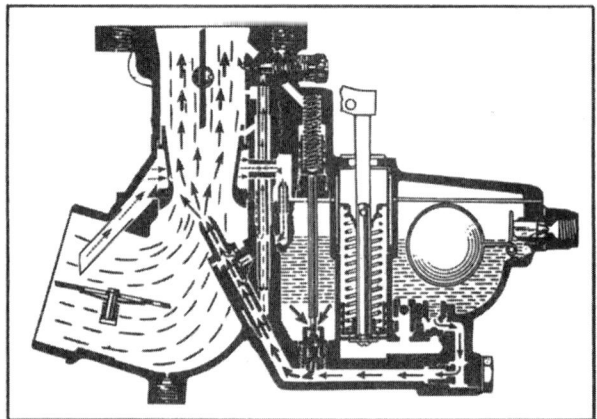

Fig. 90—Main Jet Operation at Higher Speeds

Full Throttle

At the higher speeds, or full throttle operation, the manifold vacuum is reduced allowing the spring in the vacuum cylinder to force the vacuum piston downward, causing the push rod to open the valve in the power jet. This permits gasoline to flow from the power jet into the passage leading to the main nozzle, increasing the flow of gasoline over that passing through the main metering jet (fig. 90).

MINOR SERVICE OPERATIONS

Before making any carburetor adjustments, make sure that the carburetor and manifold flange bolts are tight, the air cleaner to carburetor pipe and hose connections are tight, carburetor air cleaner is clean and that correct carburetor to manifold gasket is used.

These precautions or pre-service checks are always advisable, as any one will cause improper carburetor operation. The engine should always be brought to operating temperature before any adjustment is made.

Idle Adjustment

1. Make sure engine is at operating temperature and that choke valve is in a fully released position.
2. Adjust throttle stop screw "B" (fig. 91) to allow the engine to run at approximately 450 to 500 revolutions per minute.
3. Turn idle adjusting screw "A" (fig. 91) to provide a smooth idle and correct combustion mixture which will usually place screw from ½ to 1½ turns open.

Accelerating Pump Stroke Adjustment

Two connector holes are provided in the carburetor pump plunger shaft and throttle arm, which allow for two adjustments of pump stroke. With holes used which are closest to the throttle valve shaft, a short pump stroke is obtainable.

Fig. 91—Carburetor Adjustment

This position would normally be used for summer operation. By using the holes which are the farthest from the throttle valve shaft, a long pump stroke is obtained which should be used for winter operation.

MAJOR SERVICE OPERATIONS

CARBURETOR

Removal

1. (a) C.O.E. Models.
   Remove rear half of left fender skirt.
   (b) Forward Control models.
   Remove the toe-pan attaching screws, disconnect the wiring to the stop light switch, disconnect accelerator pedal rod from the throttle control rod and remove the toe-pan.
2. (a) On C.O.E. models, disconnect air cleaner pipe from air horn.
   (b) On Forward Control models, disconnect air cleaner from air horn and remove air cleaner.
3. Disconnect fuel and vacuum lines.
4. Release choke and throttle clamps and lock screws and remove cables from carburetor.
5. Disconnect throttle rod from throttle shaft lever.
6. Remove two carburetor-to-manifold stud nuts and remove carburetor.

Disassembly

1. Remove six screws attaching upper to lower body.

   NOTE: The upper body should be removed from lower body with the accelerating pump parts attached (fig. 92).

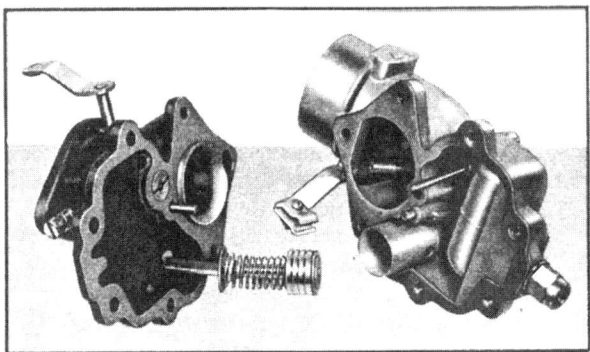

Fig. 92—Bowl Cover Assembly

2. Compress the accelerating pump piston spring and remove connector pin. Remove

the spring retainer, spring, piston and fibre washer from the pump rod and plate assembly.
3. Remove venturi from upper carburetor body.
4. Remove accelerating pump packing retainer, disconnect pump shaft from throttle arm and remove shaft and packing.
5. Remove plug from vacuum power cylinder using tool J-816-4 and remove the piston and spring.
6. Remove the idle passage tube, idle adjusting screw and idle hole plug from carburetor upper body.
7. Remove accelerating pump sleeve, power jet push rod, float lever hinge pin, float and needle valve from carburetor lower body.
8. Remove accelerating pump intake check valve, discharge check valve and power jet using tool J-816-7.
9. Remove main nozzle air bleed, idle jet, main nozzle and main metering jet from carburetor lower body, using tool J-816-1.

Inspection

1. Wash all parts in cleaning solvent.
2. Blow out all drilled passages in the carburetor upper and lower body with compressed air.

   NOTE: Blow through passages in direction opposite to normal air or gasoline flow.

3. Inspect idling ports, idle air bleed passage, balance passage and vacuum spark advance port making sure they are free from carbon deposits or dirt.
4. Check vacuum power jet piston in its cylinder to make sure it is free.

   NOTE: Should the piston stick, the vacuum power jet may be in operation at all speeds, resulting in poor gasoline economy.

5. Disassemble the power jet using tool J-816-2. Care must be taken not to lose jet spring or ball in disassembly.

   NOTE: The power jet must be cleaned thoroughly as any dirt in this jet may either stop the flow of gasoline at high speeds and result in poor performance, or cause the valve to be held off its seat, allowing jet to be in operation at all speeds resulting in poor economy.

6. Inspect accelerating pump intake and discharge check valves to make sure balls are free and seating properly.

7. Inspect needle valve and seat, low speed jet, main nozzle air bleed and main metering jet to make sure they are not damaged and are thoroughly clean.
8. Make sure float does not leak.
9. Replace all gaskets and all worn or damaged parts.

Assembly

1. If choke valve has been removed, it must be reassembled so that flutter valve is on opposite side of valve from inlet and small bleed hole is toward balance vent when valve is closed.
2. Install main metering jet with new gasket in carburetor lower body and tighten securely.
3. Install main nozzle with new gasket, idle jet and main nozzle air bleed in carburetor lower body and tighten securely.
4. Install the accelerating pump intake and discharge check valves and vacuum power jet in carburetor lower body and tighten securely (fig. 93).

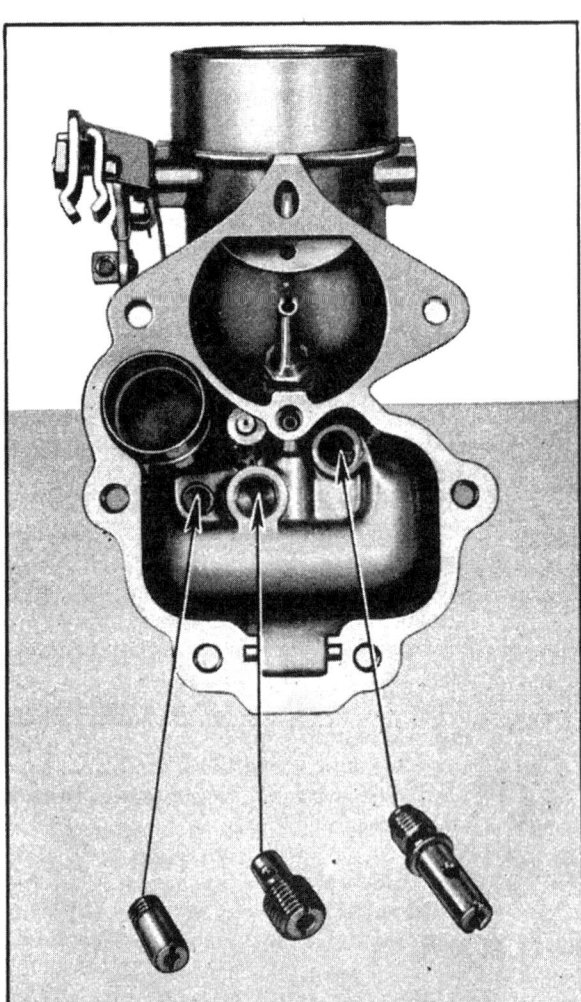

Fig. 93—Carburetor Jet Installation

5. Install needle valve and float, assemble float hinge pin and plug assembly.
6. Check float level using tool J-818-13A. Proper float level should be from 0 to 1/32 of an inch below the top of the float chamber.

   NOTE: Gauge should be placed across the machined surface of the float chamber, with gasket removed, and lip of float lever held firmly against end of seated needle valve as shown in Figure 94.

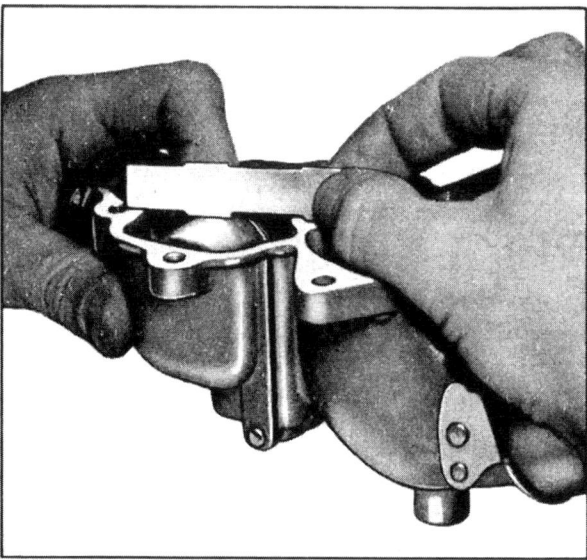

Fig. 94—Checking Float Level

7. Place small end of vacuum power jet push rod in jet.
8. Assemble accelerating pump sleeve in lower body pump cylinder with holes in sleeve down.
9. If throttle valve has been removed from upper body, it must be reassembled with the notch on the valve lined up with port for vacuum line in body.

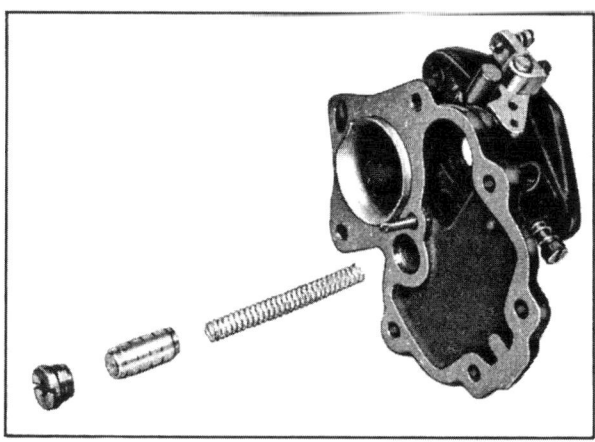

Fig. 95—Vacuum Spring, Piston and Plug Assembly

10. Assemble the piston, spring and plug in the vacuum power cylinder in the carburetor upper body (fig. 95) and tighten plug securely.
11. Install idle passage tube, idle hole plug and idle adjusting screw in carburetor upper body.
12. Turn adjusting screw all the way in and then back off one complete turn.
13. Place accelerating pump plunger shaft link packing between the two plates and place assembly over link and connect link to throttle arm using holes as described under "Accelerating Pump Stroke Adjustment."
14. Install packing retainer and attaching screw.
15. Assemble fibre washer, piston, spring and spring retainer on accelerating pump rod and plate assembly. Compress spring and connect rod to plunger shaft by installing the brass pin (fig. 96).

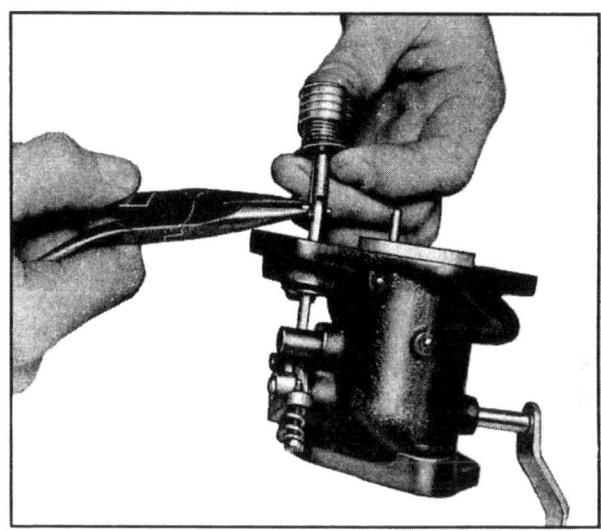

Fig. 96—Accelerating Pump Assembly

16. Place new gasket on venturi and install venturi in carburetor upper body making sure hole in lower flange of venturi aligns with air bleed to idle passage hole in carburetor upper body.
17. Place a new body gasket on carburetor lower body and assemble upper body to lower body.

    NOTE: Care must be taken to properly enter the accelerating pump piston and the vacuum power push rod during this operation.

18. Install and tighten the carburetor body screws.

Installation

1. Install special gasket on carburetor (fig. 97) making sure port for vacuum cylinder is

ENGINE ASSEMBLY 6-70

open. Then install carburetor to manifold and tighten stud nuts securely.

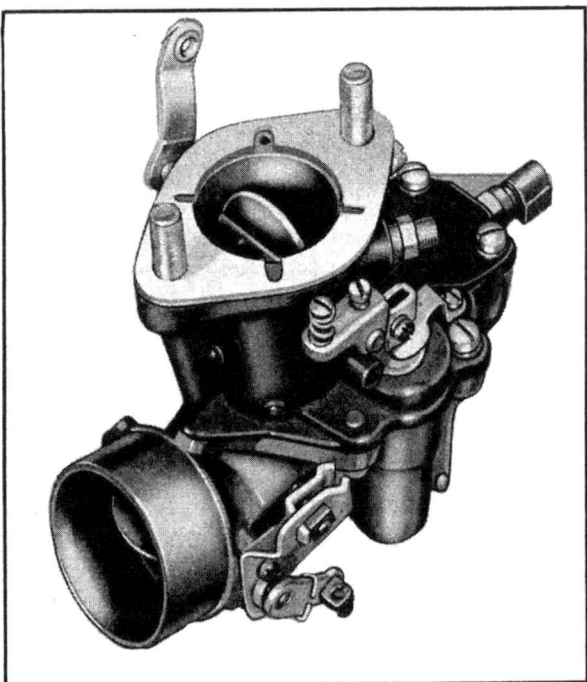

Fig. 97—Vacuum Pump Cylinder Port

2. Connect throttle rod to throttle shaft lever.
3. Connect fuel and vacuum lines.
4. Make sure choke and throttle buttons are in against instrument panel, then push hand throttle wire and conduit through clamp on carburetor and hole in end of throttle to lever rod.
5. Tighten clamp and install wire guide leaving about ⅛" between guide and throttle to lever rod.
6. Push choke wire and conduit through clamp on carburetor and enter wire in connector on choke lever. Tighten clamp and wire retaining screw.
7. Check choke and throttle operation. With knobs all the way out, choke valve should be fully closed and throttle valve fully open.
8. With knobs all the way in, choke valve should be fully open and throttle valve fully closed to the stop screw.
9. (a) On C.O.E. models, connect air cleaner pipe to air horn on carburetor.
   (b) On Forward Control models, replace air cleaner on carburetor air horn and tighten securely.
10. Start engine and after it has warmed up, make necessary idle mixture and idle speed adjustment as outlined under "Idle Mixture and Idle Speed Adjustment."
11. (a) On C.O.E. models, replace rear half of left fender skirt.
    (b) On Forward Control models, replace toe-pan, connect accelerator pedal rod to throttle control rod, connect stop light and replace the toe-pan attaching screws.

FUEL PUMP

GENERAL DESCRIPTION

The diaphragm type fuel pump (fig. 98) used on all truck models, mounts on the right side of the crankcase near the front of the engine. It is operated by a rocker arm that reaches through the side of the crankcase and rides on a special cam on the engine camshaft.

The fuel pump consists of a body, rocker arm and link assembly, diaphragm, diaphragm spring, oil seal, seal spring, cover, inlet and outlet valves, strainer, bowl and bowl retainer. The diaphragm consists of several layers of specially treated cloth, which are not affected by gasoline or benzol, held together by two metal discs and a push rod. An oil seal assembly fits around the push rod and is held down on the pump body by the seal spring.

The glass bowl must seal fuel and air tight to provide the vacuum necessary to draw fuel from the fuel tank. The bowl provides an area for sediment and water to settle before the fuel is filtered through the fine screen at the top and taken into the pump. A large surge chamber in the outlet side of the pump provides an air space to cushion the discharge impulses of the pump. The inlet and outlet valve assemblies are interchangeable.

OPERATION

In operation, the diaphragm is pulled down against the tension of the diaphragm spring by the action of the cam and rocker arm. This causes a partial vacuum in the pump chamber which opens the inlet valve and applies this vacuum to the bowl chamber and inlet line from the fuel tank. Further movement of the camshaft releases the rocker arm and the diaphragm spring pushes the diaphragm up, the intake valve closes and the outlet valve is forced open, permitting the fuel to be forced into the outlet line and up to the carburetor. Each revolution of the camshaft repeats this operation bringing additional fuel in through the inlet, up into the bowl, through the filter

ENGINE ASSEMBLY 6-71

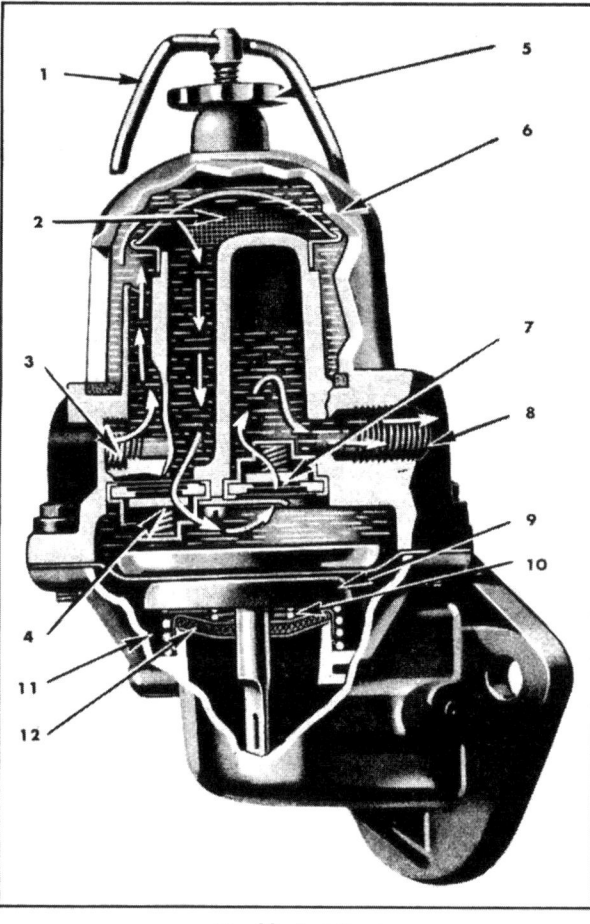

Fig. 98—Fuel Pump

1. Bowl Retainer
2. Filter Screen
3. Inlet
4. Inlet Valve
5. Bowl Retainer Nut
6. Sediment Bowl
7. Outlet Valve
8. Outlet
9. Diaphragm
10. Oil Seal Spring
11. Diaphragm Spring
12. Oil Seal

screen, through the inlet and outlet valves and up to the carburetor.

When the fuel in the carburetor bowl raises the float to where it closes the needle valve, the fuel pump diaphragm spring is not strong enough to force the needle valve off its seat; therefore, the diaphragm stays near the bottom of the stroke. The fuel pump rocker arm idles on the cam and only moves the diaphragm a few thousandths of an inch to replace the fuel that entered the carburetor between fuel pump strokes. A constant pressure, equal to the tension of the diaphragm spring, is maintained on the fuel in the line to the carburetor.

MINOR SERVICE OPERATIONS

The fuel pump should be checked regularly to make sure that the mounting bolts, cover to body bolts, bowl retaining nut and inlet and outlet connections are tight. The sediment bowl should be checked and cleaned regularly.

The glass bowl permits visual inspection to determine the amount of sediment or water in the fuel pump. When sediment or water is visible proceed as follows:

1. Loosen the bowl retaining nut, remove bowl and clean.
2. Remove gasket and clean all dirt and water from the top of fuel pump.
3. Install a new gasket and the bowl.
4. Tighten retaining nut to create a little tension and turn bowl slightly to make sure it seats. Tighten retaining nut securely.
5. Start engine and check to see that fuel pump fills with fuel and that there is no indication of leaks.

MAJOR SERVICE OPERATIONS

Removal and Disassembly

1. Disconnect fuel inlet and outlet lines from the fuel pump.
2. Remove the two attaching screws and remove pump and gasket.
3. Loosen bowl retaining nut and remove bowl and filter bowl screen.
4. Remove top cover screws and top cover assembly.
5. Raise edge of diaphragm and with a thin bladed screwdriver lift the spring and oil seal over edge of boss in the fuel pump body.
6. Unhook diaphragm from the link by pressing down and away from the rocker arm side.
7. Remove oil seal and retainer from diaphragm.
8. Remove valve assembly retainer screws and remove valve retainer.
9. Remove valve assemblies and gaskets, noting that the inlet valve is assembled in the cover so that the valve opens downward, the valve spring being visible at the bottom of the valve cage. The outlet valve is assembled in the cover so this valve opens upward, the valve spring not being visible when the valve is assembled in the cover in this position.

Inspection

1. Wash all parts thoroughly in cleaning solvent.
2. Inspect the rocker arm and link for excessive wear and for loose hinge pin.
3. Inspect body and cover for cracks or damaged flanges.
4. Inspect diaphragm for cracks or wear that would cause leaks.
5. Inspect oil seal and retainer for damage.
6. Make sure the valves are clean and that they seat properly under normal spring tension.
7. Check the bowl for chips around the rim that would make a good seal difficult.
8. Inspect the filter screen for rust or restriction.

Assembly

1. Install the oil seal to the diaphragm push rod in the following manner. Assemble oil seal spring, upper retainer, two leather seals and lower retainer with convex side out. This is extremely important in order to seal the fuel pump from any oil that might come up from the crankcase.
2. Raise the fuel pump link with a screwdriver (fig. 99), install the diaphragm spring and hook the diaphragm pull rod over the end of the link.
3. Install valve assemblies and paper gaskets making sure to install the inlet valve with the spring down and the outlet valve with the spring up.

   NOTE: The inlet valve is assembled in the cover next to the tapped passage marked "INT."

4. Install the valve retainer with the convex side up and secure in place with two retainer screws.
5. Assemble the top cover assembly to the fuel pump body and tighten the cover screws alternately and securely.
6. Assemble the filter screen on the cover and assemble the glass filter bowl to the cover making sure the cork gasket is in good condition and that the bowl nut is tight to prevent air leaks.
7. Test fuel pump operation by connecting a piece of gas line to the pump inlet, dipping end of line in container of gas and pumping rocker arm a few strokes.
8. Place a new gasket between pump and engine and install the attaching screws, connect fuel lines to pump, start engine and check pump operation.

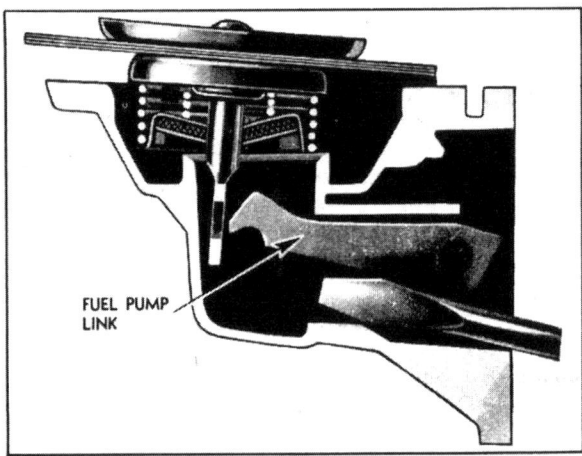

Fig. 99—Method of Assembling Fuel Pump Diaphragm to Link

FUEL AND VACUUM PUMP

GENERAL DESCRIPTION

The AC combination fuel and vacuum pump is used extensively as optional equipment on all truck models. This pump assembly, which is mounted on the right side of the engine crankcase at the front, is operated by an eccentric on the engine camshaft which actuates the pump rocker arm. The single rocker arm actuates both the fuel and vacuum sections of the pump through separate links which permits each section to function independently of the other section (fig. 100).

The fuel and vacuum sections form two separate, independently operating diaphragm type pumps. They are combined in one assembly for compactness and to permit operation from one eccentric on the camshaft.

A fuel filter, consisting of a bowl and fine mesh screen is incorporated in the fuel section of the pump. Fuel from the gasoline tank first enters the bowl then flows through the screen into the fuel pump. The bowl provides a settling chamber for water and dirt which cannot pass the screen. The bowl and screen should be cleaned periodically.

OPERATION

Fuel Pump

Downward movement of the pump diaphragm, or the suction stroke, is caused by the rotation of an eccentric on the camshaft actuating the pump rocker arm. Through a connecting link the diaphragm is moved downward against the pressure of the diaphragm spring, producing a vacuum in the fuel chamber. Atmospheric pressure then pushes fuel from the tank, through the fuel line, bowl, strainer and into the fuel chamber above the diaphragm.

On the return stroke of the rocker arm, the diaphragm spring forces the diaphragm up, the inlet valve closes, and the outlet valve is forced open, allowing fuel to flow through the outlet to the carburetor.

The link is hinged to the rocker arm so that the link and the connected diaphragm can be moved down, but not up, by the rocker arm. The link and the diaphragm are moved upward only by the diaphragm spring. The pump, therefore, delivers fuel

ENGINE ASSEMBLY 6-73

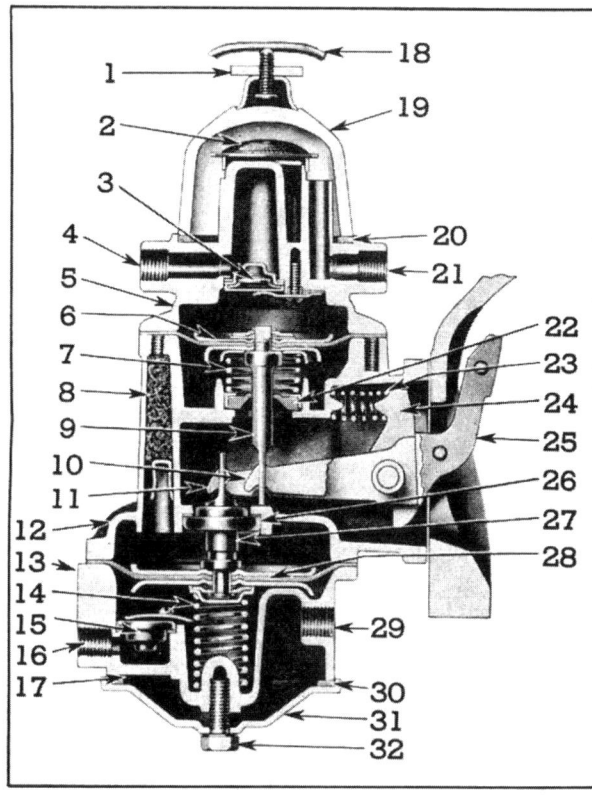

Fig. 100—Fuel and Vacuum Pump

1. Bowl Retainer Nut
2. Fuel Filter Screen
3. Outlet Valve
4. Outlet Port
5. Fuel Pump Cover
6. Fuel Pump Diaphragm
7. Diaphragm Spring
8. Air Filter
9. Pull Rod
10. Fuel Link
11. Vacuum Link
12. Pump Body
13. Vacuum Cover
14. Diaphragm Spring
15. Outlet Valve
16. Outlet Port
17. Screen
18. Bail Assembly
19. Sediment Bowl
20. Bowl Gasket
21. Inlet Port
22. Oil Seal
23. Rocker Arm Spring
24. Link Spacer
25. Rocker Arm
26. Oil Seal
27. Pull Rod
28. Vacuum Diaphragm
29. Inlet Port
30. Cover Plate Gasket
31. Cover Plate
32. Capscrew Gasket

to the carburetor only when the fuel pressure in the outlet line is less than the pressure maintained by the diaphragm spring. This condition arises when the float needle valve is not seated and the fuel passage from the pump into the carburetor float chamber is open. When the needle valve in the carburetor float chamber is closed and held in place by the pressure of the fuel on the float, the pump builds up pressure until it overcomes the resistance of the diaphragm spring. The pressure moves the diaphragm and link down until the rocker arm barely contacts the link and results in almost complete stoppage of diaphragm movement until more fuel is needed. The only function of the rocker arm spring is to make the rocker arm follow the camshaft eccentric.

The inbuilt airdome provides a pocket in which fuel under pressure can compress a certain volume of air. When the pressure is relieved (pump on vacuum stroke) the pocket of compressed air pushes the fuel on to its destination. The airdome minimizes flow variations experienced with two-cycle pump stroke and gives increased fuel flow characteristics.

Fuel Pump Vacuum Section

The vacuum suction acts as a booster to the intake manifold suction thus providing uniform operation of the windshield wiper at all engine speed and loads. Both sections of the combination pump are actuated by a single rocker arm. Rocker arm movement, through the link and pull rod, pushes the diaphragm into the air chamber against spring pressure. Pressure created by the diaphragm movement expels air through the outlet port and into the manifold. The return stroke (low point of cam) releases the compressed diaphragm spring, creating a vacuum and pulling air through the inlet valve from the windshield wiper.

When manifold vacuum is greater than that created by the pump, the stronger manifold vacuum pulls the diaphragm into the air chamber against spring pressure thus moving the links out of engagement with the rocker arm. Under this condition the rocker arm continues to move with the cam, but produces only a fluttering effect on the diaphragm. The windshield wiper then operates on manifold vacuum without assistance from the pump. When intake manifold vacuum is low, as on acceleration or at high speed, the vacuum created by the pump will assure adequate operation of the wiper.

Service Pumps by Following Methods

1. Complete replacement with a NEW pump. Part No. 5591547.
2. Diaphragm repair with DIAPHRAGM kit.
    Fuel Type, Part No. 5591843.
    Vacuum Type, Part No. 5591738.

MINOR SERVICE OPERATIONS

Maintenance

Sediment and water sometimes become trapped within the fuel pump filtering bowl, causing difficult engine operation. Difficulty because of moisture is more likely to occur at low winter temperatures. To avoid this trouble, remove and clean the filter bowl and screen at least twice a year, preferably in the spring and fall. The fuel pump must also be checked regularly to make sure that the mounting bolts, cover to body screws, bowl retaining nut and fuel line connections are tight.

ENGINE ASSEMBLY 6-74

Locating Pump Trouble

Always check while the pump is installed on the engine. Do not take it off to check it.

1. Be sure there is gas in the tank.
2. Disconnect pump to carburetor line at the carburetor. Use a fuel analyzer gauge to check for idle pressure of 3 to 4 pounds. Minimum bleed (capacity) at idle, is one pint of fuel in one minute. If pump is not up to the foregoing specifications, first check below items "a" thru "f." If pump does not then meet specifications, it should be removed for overhaul or replacement.

    If fuel pump analyzer gauge is not available, a simple test can be made by disconnecting pump to carburetor line at the carburetor. With the ignition switch off, use the starting motor to turn the engine over a few times. If gas spurts from the pump (or open end of the line), the pump, gas line and tank are O.K., and trouble is in the carburetor, ignition or engine. If no gas flows, or if only a little gas flows, do the following:

    (a) Fuel bowl gasket worn or damaged. REPLACE GASKET.
    (b) Fuel bowl screen or strainer clogged or corroded. CLEAN THE SCREEN OR REPLACE.
    (c) Fuel line connections loose or cracked. TIGHTEN OR REPLACE FUEL LINE FITTINGS.
    (d) Fuel line clogged. BLOW OUT WITH COMPRESSED AIR.
    (e) Diaphragm flange screws loose. TIGHTEN FLANGE SCREWS.
    (f) Flexible inlet line broken or porous. REPLACE FLEXIBLE LINE.

3. If correction of the above six items does not place the pump in operating condition, it should be removed for replacement or overhaul.

Locating Vacuum Section Trouble

1. Disconnect outlet (manifold) line from pump.
2. Open vacuum valve to windshield wiper and operate engine from idle, through slow acceleration to about 40 MPH.
3. The wiper should start operating on only pump vacuum at about 15 MPH engine speed and reach full speed at about 40 MPH and thus indicate that the vacuum section is operating correctly.
4. If the wiper does not operate, then also detach windshield wiper line at pump and join it to the already detached outlet line with a piece of rubber hose.
5. SLOWLY operate engine from idle to about 25 MPH, and the wiper should run at full speed, operating on the engine vacuum only. If it does not, it can be assumed that the wiper motor or tubing is defective.
6. The pump vacuum section is inoperative if the windshield wiper operates on engine vacuum, but not on pump vacuum.
7. The pump vacuum section, when disconnected from intake manifold, should produce 8-10 inches of vacuum at about 25 MPH engine speed.

MAJOR SERVICE OPERATIONS

Disassembly

NOTE: Before proceeding with the following operation, wash the outside of the unit with cleaning solvent and blow off with compressed air to remove loose grit and grease.

1. Mark edges of fuel and vacuum cover and body diaphragm flanges with a file. The parts may then be reassembled in the same relative position. Note that the fuel diaphragm flange is symmetrical, and the vacuum diaphragm flange has bulges where the screw holes occur.
2. Remove fuel cover screws and lockwashers. Separate cover from body by jarring cover loose with a screwdriver handle.
3. Remove fuel valve and cage retainer screw and lift out retainer, two valve and cage assemblies and two gaskets.
4. Loosen bail thumb nut, swing bail to the side and remove from cover. Remove bowl, screen and bowl gasket.
5. Remove only two cover screws from opposite sides of the vacuum cover, and substitute for them two No. 10-32x1½ inch fillister head screws. Turn the two long screws all the way down, and then remove the balance of the regular cover screws. Alternately back off the two long screws, a few turns at a time, until the force of the heavy vacuum diaphragm spring is no longer effective. Rap the cover with a screwdriver handle if the flanges stick together. Remove the two long screws, the cover assembly and diaphragm spring.
6. Remove vacuum valve and cage retainer screw and lift out retainer, two valve and cage assemblies and two gaskets.
7. Remove vacuum cover plate screw and gasket. Lift off the cover plate, cover gasket, screen retainer, and screen.
8. File riveted end of rocker arm pin flush with

steel washer, or cut off end with ⅜" drill. Drive out rocker arm pin with a drift punch and hammer. Wiggle rocker arm until links unhook from both diaphragms. Then remove rocker arm spring, rocker arm, and link assembly.

9. Remove bushing from rocker arm to disassemble rocker arm, two vacuum links, one fuel link, link spacer, and link washers (there may be one or two link washers).
10. Lift vacuum diaphragm straight out of body to avoid damage to staked-in oil seal.
11. Remove fuel diaphragm by pulling straight out to aviod damage to oil seal. Lift diaphragm spring and spring retainer from pump body.

Inspection

1. Blow out all passages with compressed air.
2. Check parts of fuel pump as follows:
   (a) Top cover and pump body—Make visual check for cracks and breakage. Inspect for diaphragm flange warpage by testing on a smooth flat surface. Examine all threaded holes for stripped or crossed threads. Broken, damaged, or severely warped castings must be replaced.
   (b) Valves, valve and cage assemblies—Replace. Extent of wear cannot be determined visually.
   (c) Screen—Inspect for damage to edges and wire spacing. Replace if damaged or corroded.
   (d) Rocker Arm—Inspect for wear or scores at camshaft pad, at point of contact with link and pull rod.
   (e) Rocker Arm Pin and Washer—Replace.
   (f) Link—Replace link because amount of wear cannot be determined visually.
   (g) Rocker Arm Spring—Replace. Spring may be weak from distortion or corrosion.
   (h) Diaphragm Spring—Replace. Spring may be weak from distortion or corrosion.
   (i) Diaphragm—Always replace.
   (j) Gaskets—Always replace gaskets to assure tight seals.

Assembly

NOTE: Soak new diaphragm assembly in clean kerosene while performing the following steps. Fuel oil or gasoline may be used.

1. Assemble link spacer (spacer also retains rocker arm spring) over fuel link. Place one vacuum link on each side of the fuel link. The hook ends of the vacuum links should come together so that they surround the fuel link. All link hooks should point in the same direction. Place assembly of links and spacer between lobes of rocker arm with one spacer washer on the outer side of each vacuum link. Slide rocker arm bushing through holes in rocker arm, spacer washers, and links.
2. Stand the pump body on the bench, fuel flange down. Set rocker arm spring in position with one end over cone cast into the body. Slide rocker arm and link assembly into body. Outer end of rocker arm spring slips over projection on link spacer, and the open end of all link hooks must point toward vacuum flange. Temporarily retain rocker arm and link assembly with small end of tool PT-6.
3. Turn the pump body over so the fuel diaphragm flange is up. Set the diaphragm spring on the staked-in oil seal, and the retainer on top of the spring. Push diaphragm pull rod through retainer, spring and oil seal. Flat of pull rod must be at right angles to link. Hook diaphragm pull rod to fuel link.

NOTE: Fuel link is the short, center link.

4. Drive tool PT-6 out with permanent rocker arm pin. Place washer over small end of pin and spread pin end.
5. Place valve and cage gaskets in recesses provided in fuel cover. Place valve and cages on top of gaskets. Inlet valve must have 3-legged spider facing out of cover, and outlet valve must have 3-legged spider facing into cover. Secure valve assemblies with retainer and screw.
6. Install fuel screen, bowl gasket and bowl. Retain bowl with bail assembly, turning thumb nut only finger tight.
7. Push on rocker arm until diaphragm is flat across body flange and install fuel cover on body, making sure that file marks on cover and body line up. While holding diaphragm flat, install cover screws and lockwashers loosely until screws just engage lockwashers. Pump the rocker arm three or four full strokes and tighten cover screws securely.
8. Diaphragm must be flexed by several full strokes of rocker arm before tightening cover screws, or pump will deliver too much pressure.
9. Place valve and cage gaskets in recesses provided in vacuum cover. Place valve and cages on top of gaskets. Inlet valve must have 3-legged spider facing out of cover, and outlet valve must have 3-legged spider facing into cover. Secure valve assemblies with retainer and screw.
10. Turn vacuum cover over, and install screen, one screen retainer, and gasket. Position cover plate and retain with cover screws and gasket.

11. Clamp pump body in vise by one of mounting flange ears. Insert vacuum diaphragm pull rod straight through oil seal.

    CAUTION: *Do not tilt diaphragm pull rod excessively as this may damage the oil seal. Push rocker arm toward pump to raise vacuum links and hook them to link slot in pull rod.*

12. The vacuum diaphragm must be held level with body flange during the following operations. The diaphragm is held level by inserting a 3/32 inch piece of metal between rocker arm stop and body. This spacer can be made from a piece of steel, 3/16 inch x 3/32 inch x 8 inches. Bend one end to form a right angle hook, 3/8 inch from bend to end. This tool is also available from your AC jobber as Type PT-8.

13. Place vacuum spring over location on upper diaphragm protector. Place vacuum cover over spring, and align the file marks.

14. Insert two No. 10-32 x 1½ inch screws in two opposite holes in cover flange. Turn these long screws down, alternating a few turns on each. Insert regular screws with lockwashers, and tighten until screws just engage lockwashers. Replace two long screws with regular screws and lockwashers.

15. Remove 3/32 inch spacer from rocker arm position. This allows the heavy vacuum spring to push diaphragm into a flexed position. Tighten all cover screws securely.

16. Combination fuel and vacuum pump cannot be bench tested because of the heavy vacuum section spring. The only adequate test for this type pump is with a low-pressure gauge when the pump is mounted on the engine.

AIR CLEANER

GENERAL DESCRIPTION

Air cleaners on all truck models operate primarily to remove dust and dirt from the air that is taken into the carburetor and engine. All air cleaners used incorporate flame arresters.

The standard cleaner used on all ½, ¾, 1 and 1½ ton conventional trucks has an element (fig. 101) consisting of a copper gauze filter that is saturated in heavy oil. As air filters through this element, dirt and dust are deposited on the oily surfaces of the gauze.

This gauze also quenches any flame that may be caused by engine backfire through the carburetor.

A heavy duty, oil bath type cleaner, used as standard equipment on 2-ton conventional is also available on all other vehicles when vehicles are to be used in unusually dusty areas. This cleaner is interchangeable with the standard air cleaner and will not affect power or economy in any way. Air entering this cleaner must go directly down in a narrow space around the cleaner to the oil level in the cleaner body. The air must then turn and go up through the copper gauze and back down into the carburetor. As the direction of air flow is reversed, heavy particles in the air are thrown into the oil in the cleaner body, greatly reducing the amount of dirt to be deposited in the copper gauze.

The air cleaner used on all C.O.E. models is the oil bath type, but due to vehicle construction it is mounted on a bracket at the right rear of the sub-frame and connected to the carburetor by means of hoses and tubing. Operation is very similar to the oil bath cleaner as used on 2-ton conventional with air being drawn into cleaner through a series of holes. The air then passes down through a narrow space around the cleaner to the oil level in the cleaner body; *here it reverses direction and*

Fig. 101—Standard Air Cleaner

passes over the oil surface depositing dirt and dust into the oil and then flows up through a gauze filter, which further cleans the air and into the flexible tubing leading to the carburetor intake.

The air cleaner used on all Forward Control models is a specially shaped flame arrester type, which is of one piece construction incorporating a steel mesh filter element and eight rows of eight louvers equally spaced around the body to admit air. Except for washing, there are no service operations other than replacement.

SERVICE OPERATIONS

STANDARD CLEANER

1. Remove cover wing nut, cover and filter element.
2. Wash filter element thoroughly in cleaning solvent.
3. Let element dry and dip in engine oil. Drain surplus oil from element.
4. Install element and cover, and secure with wing nut.

OIL BATH AIR CLEANER

1. Loosen clamp screw and remove cleaner assembly.
2. Remove cover wing nut, cover and filter element (fig. 102).

Fig. 102—Oil Bath Air Cleaner

NOTE: Do not pry the filter element loose if it sticks. It must be removed by hand, otherwise damage to the filter element flange may result. This flange must lie flat against the body to insure a tight seat at this point to prevent air leaks when the cover is assembled.

3. Empty oil out of cleaner and clean out all oil and accumulated dirt.
4. Wash body with cleaning solvent and wipe dry.
5. Wash filter element by slushing up and down in cleaning solvent.
6. Dry filter unit with an air hose or let stand until dry.
7. Fill body of cleaner with one pint of SAE 50 engine oil in summer and lighter in winter.
8. Assemble filter element to body of cleaner, being sure that the flange rests against the top flange of the body.
9. Install cover making sure gasket is clean and in good condition over its entire surface so a tight seat is obtained and install cover wing nut.
10. Assemble cleaner to carburetor making sure it fits tight and is set down securely so that the felt pad rests against the carburetor to assure a good seat at this point. Tighten clamp.

OIL BATH CLEANER—C.O.E.

Cleaner is serviced in the same manner as the regular oil bath cleaner, but does not have to be removed completely.

1. From underneath cab unhook lower portion or oil reservoir from cleaner. Remove, drain oil and clean in cleaning solvent.
2. Filter element can be removed by pulling straight down to remove from cleaner housing.
3. Wash filter unit by slushing up and down in cleaning solvent; then drain and allow to dry.
4. Fill body of cleaner with SAE 50 engine oil in summer and lighter in winter.
5. Install filter element in cleaner housing making sure it seats properly.
6. Install body of cleaner clamping in place with two clamps.
7. Check all hose and pipe connections to air cleaner to make sure that they are tight.

ENGINE GOVERNOR

GENERAL DESCRIPTION

A Handy Vari-Speed governor is used as standard equipment on the 1½ and 2 ton school bus.

In addition to the above model usage, the governor is also available as an R.P.O. on all other truck models with the exception of the ¾ and 1 Ton Forward Control. The governor is mounted between the carburetor and the intake manifold and automatically governs the maximum speed at which the truck engine may be operated, which in turn limits the maximum speed at which the vehicle may be operated.

OPERATION

The governor (fig. 103) is operated by the vacuum existing in the intake manifold under varying conditions of engine operation and the flow of air past the governor valve. A shaft carried on a needle type roller bearing extends through the body of the governor and this shaft is offset from the center line of the throat. On the shaft is mounted a throttle plate or throttle valve. The valve is slightly offset on the shaft and in its wide open position is about 10 degrees from vertical (fig. 103).

mum engine speed of the model vehicle for which it is intended. However, there will be occasions when minor adjustments are required to satisfy local conditions where the truck is operating.

To adjust a governor for higher speed, turn the adjusting cap "C" (fig. 104) counter-clockwise or to the left; for lower speeds turn adjusting cap "C" clockwise or to the right. One turn on the adjusting screw will change the speed approximately 300-400 R.P.M. or 4-5 M.P.H.

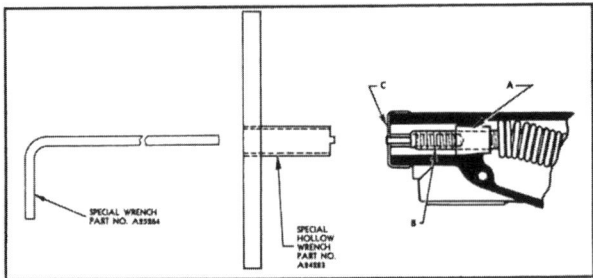

Fig. 104—Governor Adjustment

When a more sensitive regulation is desired or if the governor is too sensitive and inclined to surge, correct the adjustment as follows by means of the calibrating nut shown at "A."

Too Sensitive

1. If a governor is too sensitive or on the point of surging, remove adjusting cap and hexagonal shaft assembly and place special hollow wrench A-24283 in position on nut "A." Insert special adjusting wrench A-25264 through this wrench and turn main adjusting screw "B" to the right one turn.

    NOTE: Special wrenches A-24283 and A-25264 are available at King-Seeley Distributors.

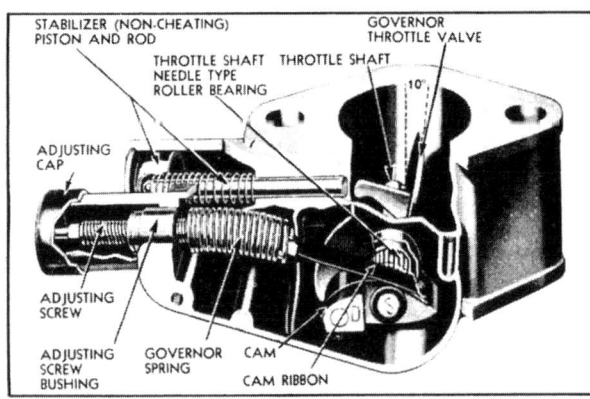

Fig. 103—Diagrammatic View of Governor

The gas mixture rushing from the carburetor through the governor throat strikes the offset throttle valve and tends to draw it closed. This action is opposed by a governor spring which is attached to the valve shaft through a cam ribbon and cam. By adjusting the pull of this spring, the governor valve can be made to remain open, and then closed at a predetermined engine speed. Adjustment of the spring pull is accomplished by changing the number of spring coils operating.

ADJUSTMENT

All governors are calibrated and adjusted in assembly to insure accurate control of the maxi-

2. With hollow wrench in slot of nut "A," turn this nut to the right about ¼ turn using the special wrench A-25264. The main adjusting screw "B" must be kept from turning while nut "A" is adjusted.

Not Stable

1. If a more sensitive governor is desired, adjust main screw "B" to the left one turn and while holding this screw in new position, turn nut "A" to the left ¼ turn at a time until desired regulation is obtained.

2. When adjustment is completed, tap lightly on end of hollow wrench so that nut "A" will seat properly.

TROUBLES AND REMEDIES

FUEL SYSTEM

Symptom and Probable Causes

Excessive Fuel Consumption
  a. Improper adjustment
  b. Improper float level adjustment
  c. Vacuum power piston sticking or improperly seating or loose power jet valve
  d. Dirty air cleaner
  e. Fuel leaks

  f. Sticking controls

  g. Improper engine temperature
  h. Engine improperly tuned
  i. Dragging brakes
  j. Tires underinflated
  k. Vehicle overloaded

Fast Idle
  a. Improper adjustment
  b. Controls sticking

Will Not Idle Properly
  a. Improper adjustment
  b. Restricted passages in carburetor body
  c. Air leaking into intake manifold

  d. Engine improperly tuned

Engine Misses on Acceleration
  a. Accelerating pump valves not seating or pump inoperative
  b. Improper spark plug adjustment
  c. Improper valve adjustment
  d. Sticking or burnt valves

Probable Remedy

  a. Adjust idle mixture and throttle stop screws
  b. Check and adjust float level
  c. Overhaul carburetor replacing faulty parts

  d. Clean air cleaner
  e. Check carburetor, fuel pump, fuel tank and all lines and connections for leaks
  f. Check choke and throttle valve and manifold spring for proper operation
  g. Refer to "Cooling Section"
  h. Tune engine—see "Engine Section"
  i. Refer to "Brake Section"
  j. Inflate to recommended pressure
  k. Load only to rated capacity

  a. Adjust idle mixture and throttle stop screws
  b. Free-up controls and lubricate linkage

  a. Adjust idle mixture and throttle stop screws
  b. Overhaul carburetor
  c. Check for leaks at carburetor flange, at intake manifold to cylinder head gaskets, at windshield wiper vacuum line and vacuum brake and vacuum booster lines (when used)
  d. Tune engine—see "Engine Section"

  a. Overhaul carburetor

  b. See "Spark Plugs—Engine Section"
  c. Adjust valves—see "Engine Section"
  d. Free-up with kerosene and oil or grind valves

FUEL SYSTEM SPECIFICATIONS

Air Cleaner
  Make..AC
  Type: ½, ¾, 1 and 1½ Ton..................................Standard
        2 Ton Conventional and C.O.E......................Oil Bath

Carburetor
  Make and Type
    1948-49 Conventional Trucks.........................Carter Downdraft
    1948-51 C.O.E. and Forward Control..................Carter Updraft
    1950-51 Conventional Trucks.........................GM Model "B" Downdraft

Fuel Pump
  Make, Model..AC, model AF
  Pressure...4 lbs. Max.

ENGINE ASSEMBLY 6-80

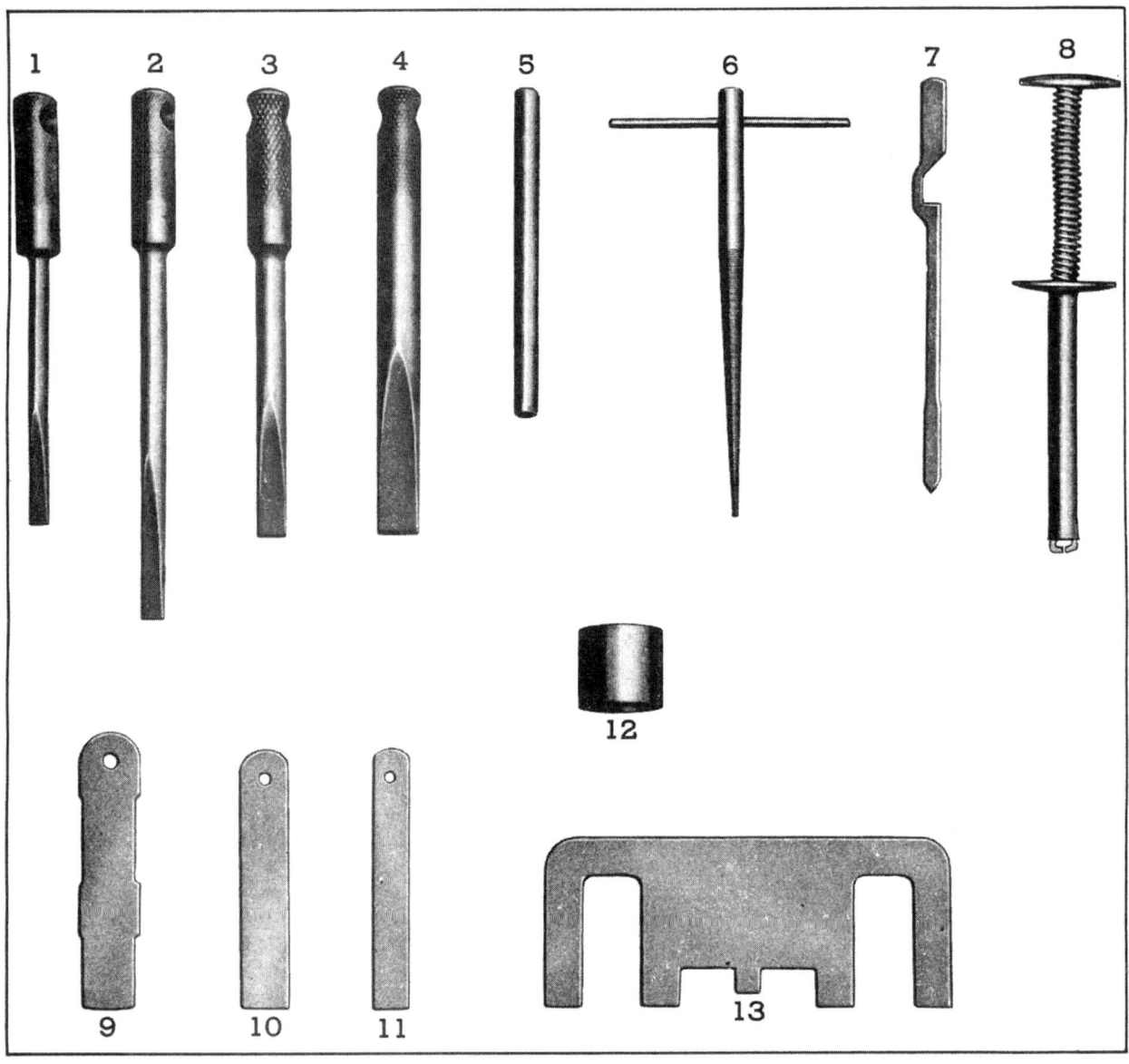

Fig. 105—Carburetor Special Tools

NOTE: Tools 1-12 make up Tool Set KMO-268
1. J-816-1   Jet Wrench 3/16"
2. J-816-2   Jet Wrench 1/4"
3. J-816-7   Jet Wrench 5/16"
4. J-816-4   Jet Wrench 7/16"
5. J-816-5   Jet Wrench Handle
6. J-508   Nozzle Puller and Handle
7. T-109-25   Metering Rod Gauge
8. KMO-65-4   Butterfly Valve Screw Holder
9. J-818-13A Float Level Gauge (C.O.E. and Forward Control)
10. J-818-1   Float Level Gauge 1/2"
11. J-818-2   Float Level Gauge 3/8"
12. J-507   Loading Cylinder 3/4"
13. Pt. No. 3696192 Float Level Gauge

G. M. MODEL "B" CARBURETOR SPECIFICATIONS

	216 Engine 7002050	235 Engine 7002051
Air Horn Assembly		
Part Number	7002053	7002048
Identification (stamped on air horn)	50	51
Air Horn Gasket		
Part Number	7002799	7002799
Main Well and Power Valve Support		
Part Number	7002061	7002158
Identification (stamped on support)	50	51

ENGINE ASSEMBLY 6-81

Float Bowl
- Part Number.. 7002889 / 7002890
- Identification Number (embossed on bottom of bowl)........... 7002089 / 7002046
- I. D. Main Venturi.. 1.218" / 1.343"
- I. D. Primary Venturi..................................... .562" / .593"

Throttle Body Assembly
- Part Number.. 7002104 / 7002110
- Identification (cast in manifold bolting flange)........... 7002105 / 7002128
- Flange bolt centers....................................... 2¹¹⁄₁₆" / 2¹⁵⁄₁₆"

Float Needle Valve and Seat
- Unit Part Number... 7002358 / 7002359
- Seat Size.. .076" / .091"
- Identification (one groove on O.D. of .076" seat, two grooves on O.D. of .091" seat) (Needle valve the same for both carburetors.)

Main Metering Jet
- Standard
  - Part Number... 7002651 / 7002658
  - Size.. .051" / .058"
- One Step Lean
  - Part Number... 7002650 / 7002657
  - Size.. .050" / .057"
- One Step Rich
  - Part Number... 7002652 / 7002659
  - Size.. .052" / .059"

  (Jets are stamped with size number for identification 51, 58, etc.)

Power Valve Piston Spring
- Part Number.. 7002071 / 7002366
- Identification (7002366 has copper flash)
- Free Length.. 2³⁄₁₆" / 2¹⁷⁄₆₄"

Accelerator Pump Link
- Part Number.. 7002820 / 7002820

COOLING SYSTEM

INDEX

	Page		Page
General Description	6-81	Reverse Flushing	6-84
Minor Service Operations	6-82	Major Service Operations	6-84
Antifreeze	6-82	Water Pump	6-84
Fan Belt Adjustment	6-83	Disassembly	6-84
Thermostat	6-83	Inspection	6-85
Cleaning and Reverse Flushing	6-83	Assembly	6-85
Cleaning	6-84	Radiator—Replacement	6-86

GENERAL DESCRIPTION

The cooling system of all truck models is designed with two purposes in mind; first, to carry off a certain amount of the heat created in the engine so it will not operate at too high a temperature; and second, to maintain the engine heat at the temperature which will produce the most efficient and economical operation of the engine.

Fig. 106 shows a cross section view of the cooling system.

The water pump (fig. 107) is the ball bearing type and requires no care other than to make certain the air vent at the top of the housing and the drain holes in the bottom do not become plugged with dirt or grease.

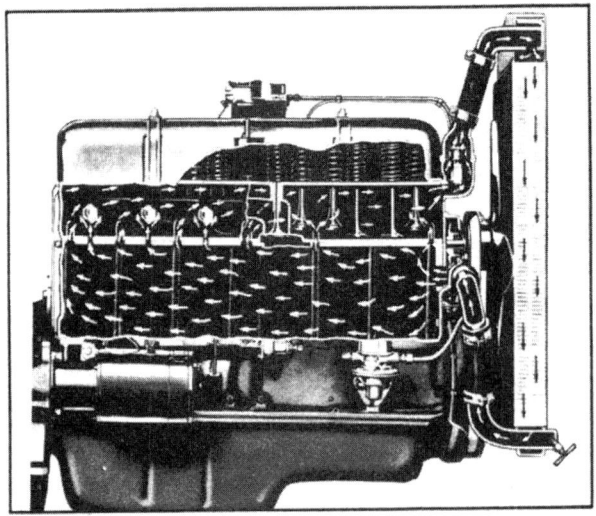

Fig. 106—Cross Section of Cooling System

The thermostat, mounted in the cylinder head water outlet, restricts the flow of water to the radiator until a predetermined temperature is reached, thus minimizing the length of time required to reach efficient operating temperature.

A pressure cooling system is provided for only on Cab-Over-Engine models by their being equipped with a pressure type radiator cap. This type cap incorporates a valve which acts to seal the cooling system so that it operates under 3½ to 4½ pounds per square inch pressure. By operating under this pressure, the boiling point of coolant in the system is raised approximately 10 degrees.

Since the action of the cooling system controls the operating temperature of the engine, it is essential that systematic inspection of units in the system be made periodically to maintain the efficiency of the system.

The shaft and the double row ball bearing are integral. The bearing is packed with a special high melting point grease at the time of manufacture and requires no further lubrication. The ends of the bearing are sealed to retain the lubricant and prevent dust and dirt from entering.

The shaft and bearing are retained in the housing by a metal cap, which is a press fit on the housing. The thrust washer has two lugs, which fit into two slots in the end of the rotor. One side of the thrust washer bears against the ground thrust surface of the pump housing and the other against the seal. The rubber seal bears against the machined surface on the inside of the rotor and also against the thrust washer. A coil spring mounted inside, and an integral part of the seal, maintains a constant pressure against the thrust washer and rotor, assuring a positive seat. An air vent in the top of the housing and drain holes in the bottom, prevent any water seepage past the thrust washer from entering the bearing.

All fans are of the four blade type with blades spaced so as to dampen out vibrations and of a size to provide adequate cooling. The fan blades are bolted directly to the water pump pulley, which is driven from the crankshaft pulley by means of a "V" type endless fan belt.

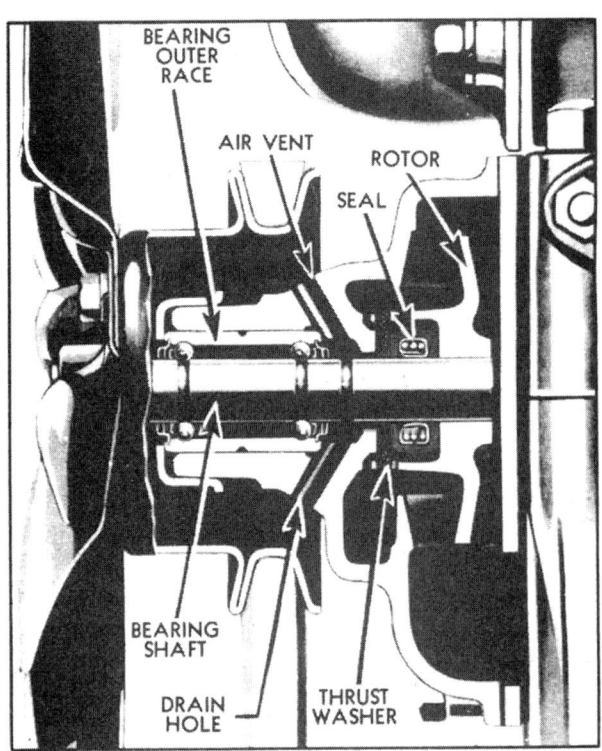

Fig. 107—Cross Section of Ball Bearing Water Pump

MINOR SERVICE OPERATIONS

ANTIFREEZE

In selecting an antifreeze solution for winter operation, the local conditions and the type of service must be considered. In any event, it is very essential to make certain checks and do certain things to at least insure the antifreeze remaining in the cooling system. To be certain that the solution will not leak out and be lost entirely, resulting in little or no protection against freezing, or seep into the working parts of the engine, the following procedure should be followed in conditioning the system.

1. Drain the entire cooling system including the cylinder block.

   NOTE: If considerable rust, scale, oil or grease is present in the water drained out, it is advisable to flush and clean the system.

2. Tighten all cylinder head bolts in sequence as shown in Figure 18 of "Engine Section."
3. Check the water pump for leaks, excessive end play or looseness of the shaft in the pump.

   NOTE: Should the water pump leak or indicate that leakage would occur with antifreeze in the system, it should be repaired, see "Major Service Operations, Water Pump."

4. Inspect fan belt. Replace if badly worn. Adjust belt to proper tension; allow ¾" deflection of belt when a light pressure is applied to belt at a point midway between pulleys (fig. 60).
5. Inspect all radiator and heater hoses. If hoses are collapsed, cracked or in any way indicate a rotted condition on the inside, replacement should be made. Carefully check and tighten all hose clamps.
6. Check the thermostat. Make sure it does not stick open or closed.

   NOTE: Standard thermostats are rated at 143°. A 160° or 180° thermostat should be installed when permanent antifreeze is used.

7. Fill the cooling system with the proper quantity of antifreeze and water according to instructions of manufacturer of antifreeze.

   NOTE: Be sure to allow for additional amount of antifreeze solution when truck is equipped with a hot water heater.

8. Warm up engine and recheck radiator, water pump and all hose connections for leaks with ENGINE HOT.
9. Check and adjust valves when necessary. See "Engine Section."

   NOTE: Tightening of cylinder head bolts will affect valve clearance adjustment.

FAN BELT ADJUSTMENT

1. Loosen bolt at generator slotted bracket.
2. Pull generator away from engine until desired belt tension is obtained.

   NOTE: With correct adjustment, a light pressure on the belt at a point midway between pulleys should cause ¾" deflection (fig. 60).

3. Tighten all generator bolts securely.

THERMOSTAT

The thermostat consists of a restriction valve actuated by a thermostatic element. This unit is mounted in the housing at the cylinder head water outlet above the water pump.

Thermostats are designed to open and close at predetermined temperatures and if not operating properly should be removed and tested.

1. Remove radiator to water outlet hose and remove gas line clip from water outlet.
2. Remove water outlet to thermostat housing bolts and remove water outlet, gasket and thermostat.
3. Inspect thermostat bellows and valve to make sure they are in good condition.
4. Place thermostat in hot water 25° above the temperature stamped on the thermostat valve.
5. Submerge the bellows completely and agitate the water thoroughly. Under this condition the valve should open fully.
6. Remove the thermostat and place in water 10° below temperature indicated on the valve.
7. With bellows completely submerged and water agitated thoroughly, the valve should close completely.
8. If thermostat checks satisfactorily, replace using a new housing gasket.

CLEANING AND REVERSE FLUSHING

Unless water in the cooling system is treated with a corrosion preventive, rust and scale may eventually clog water passages in the radiator and water jackets. This rust accumulation (fig. 108) will result in inefficient operation of the cool-

Fig. 108—Cross Section Showing Rust Accumulation in Water Passages

ing system, vitally affecting engine performance and economy of operation.

Two common causes of corrosion are: (1) air suction—air may be drawn into the system due to low liquid level in the radiator, leaky water pump or loose hose connections; (2) exhaust gas leakage—exhaust gas may be blown into the cooling system past the cylinder head gasket or through cracks in the cylinder head and block.

Periodic service must be performed to the engine cooling system to keep it in efficient operating condition. These services should include a complete cleaning and reverse flushing as well as a reconditioning service as explained under "Antifreeze."

Cleaning

A good cleaning solution should be used to loosen the rust and scale before reverse flushing the cooling system. There are a number of cleaning solutions available and the manufacturer's instructions with the particular cleaner being used should always be followed.

An excellent preparation to use for this purpose is G. M. Cooling System Cleaner. The following directions for cleaning the system applies only when this type cleaner is used.

1. Drain the cooling system including the cylinder block and then close both drain cocks.
2. Remove thermostat and replace thermostat housing.
3. Add the liquid portion (No. 1) of the cooling system cleaner.
4. Fill the cooling system with water to a level of about 3 inches below the top of the overflow pipe.
5. Cover the radiator and run the engine at moderate speed until the heat indicator reaches 180 degrees.
6. Remove cover from radiator and continue to run the engine for 20 minutes. AVOID BOILING.
7. While the engine is still running, add the powder portion (No. 2) of the cooling system cleaner and continue to run the engine for 10 minutes.
8. At the end of this time, stop the engine, wait a few minutes and then open the drain cocks and lower hose connection.

   CAUTION: Be careful not to scald your hands.

Reverse Flushing

Reverse flushing should always be accomplished after the system is thoroughly cleaned as outlined above. Flushing is accomplished through the system in a direction opposite to the normal flow. This action causes the water to get behind the corrosion deposits and force them out.

Radiator

1. Remove the upper and lower radiator hoses and replace the radiator cap.
2. Attach a lead-away hose at the top of the radiator.
3. Attach a new piece of hose to the radiator outlet connection and insert the flushing gun in this hose.
4. Connect the water hose of the flushing gun to a water outlet and the air hose to an air line.
5. Turn on the water and when the radiator is full, turn on the air in short blasts, allowing the radiator to fill between blasts of air.

   CAUTION: Apply air gradually as a clogged radiator will stand only a limited pressure.

6. Continue this flushing until the water from the lead-away hose runs clear.

Cylinder Block and Cylinder Head

1. With thermostat removed, attach a lead-away hose to the water pump inlet and a length of new hose to the water outlet connection at the top of the engine.
2. Insert the flushing gun in the new hose.
3. Turn on the water and when the engine water jacket is full, turn on the air in short blasts.
4. Continue this flushing until the water from the lead-away hose runs clear.

Hot Water Heater

1. Remove water outlet hose from heater core pipe.
2. Remove inlet hose from engine connection.
3. Insert flushing gun and flush heater core. Care must be taken when applying air pressure to prevent damage to the core.

After cooling system has been cleaned and reverse flushed, the system should be thoroughly reconditioned. Procedure for reconditioning as outlined under "Antifreeze" in this section should be followed.

Dirt and bugs may be cleaned out of the radiator air passages by blowing out with air pressure from the back of the core.

MAJOR SERVICE OPERATIONS

WATER PUMP

To facilitate water pump repair in case of leakage, tool J-1226 has been developed for use in removing the water pump pulley. Repairs to replace the water pump seal and/or thrust washer should be performed in the following manner using repair kit No. 3690932.

Disassembly

1. Place pump assembly in vise and remove pump plate attaching screws. Remove pump from vise and remove plate and plate gasket.
2. Assemble water pump puller J-1226 to pulley.
   CAUTION: Make sure tool is installed with puller plate square with pulley face.

ENGINE ASSEMBLY 6-85

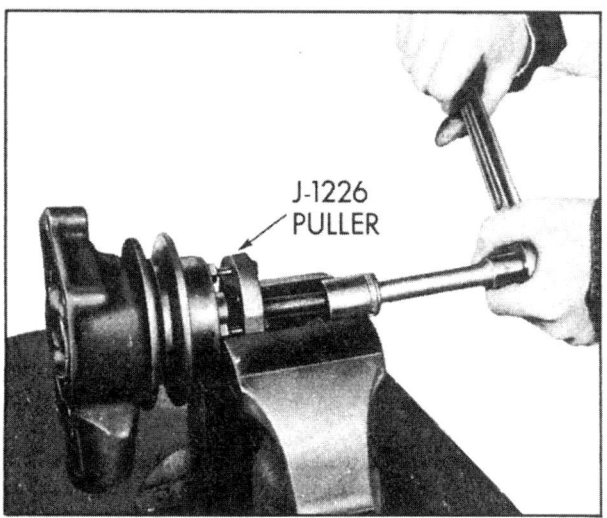

Fig. 109—Removing Water Pump Pulley

3. Place puller plate in vise (fig. 109) and tighten puller screw to remove pulley. Remove tool from pulley.
4. Place pump body in vise and with a long drift punch, remove bearing retainer from pump body.
5. Support pump on milled shoulder of body in a hand arbor press or on press plate J-1453 in arbor press and press shaft and bearing assembly out of pump body and rotor (fig. 110).

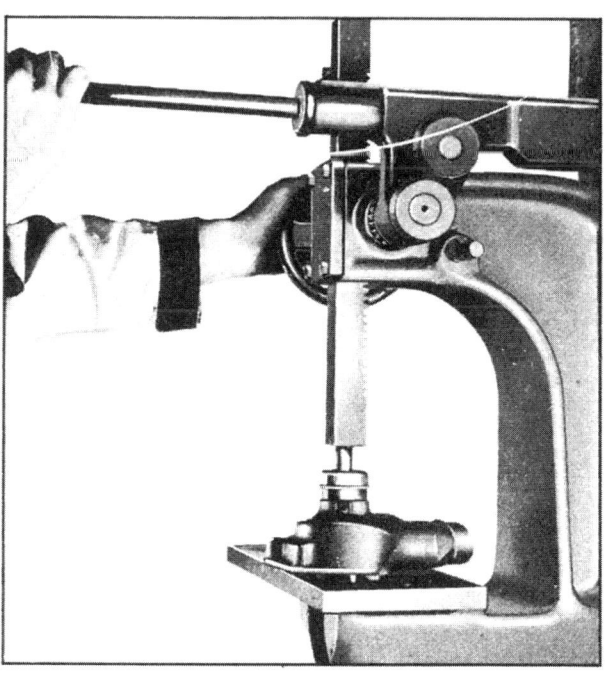

Fig. 110—Removing Shaft and Bearing Assembly

6. Remove thrust washer and seal assembly from rotor and discard.

Inspection

1. Wash all parts except pump shaft bearing in cleaning solvent.

   NOTE: Pump shaft bearing is a permanently sealed and lubricated bearing and should not be washed in cleaning solvent.

2. Inspect shaft and bearing assembly for roughness or excessive end play. Remove any rust or scale from shaft with fine emery cloth. The bearing should be wrapped in cloth while this operation is performed to prevent emery dust from entering bearing.
3. Inspect seat for thrust washer in pump body for pit marks or scoring. If seat for thrust washer is scored or pitted, the water pump should be replaced.

Assembly

1. Install pump shaft and bearing assembly into pump body bearing bore applying pressure to outer race until it bottoms.
2. Press shaft and bearing retainer onto pump body using a short piece of 1½" I.D. pipe or pilot of J-2671 transmission third speed bushing installer (fig. 111).

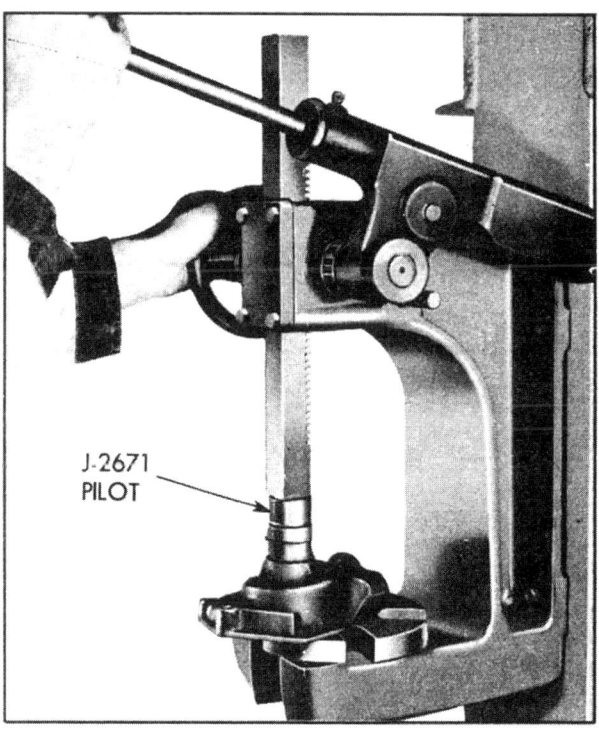

Fig. 111—Installing Shaft and Bearing Retainer

3. Coat end of the rubber seal opposite to the end having the three projections with sealer, then place seal into rotor bore with the sealer coated end down.

ENGINE ASSEMBLY 6-86

4. Coat both sides of thrust washer with a small amount of water pump grease and install washer on top of seal assembly so that two lugs index with slots in the rotor.
5. Lay the rotor and seal assembly on a flat surface on an arbor press and carefully press the shaft and housing assembly into the rotor (fig. 112).

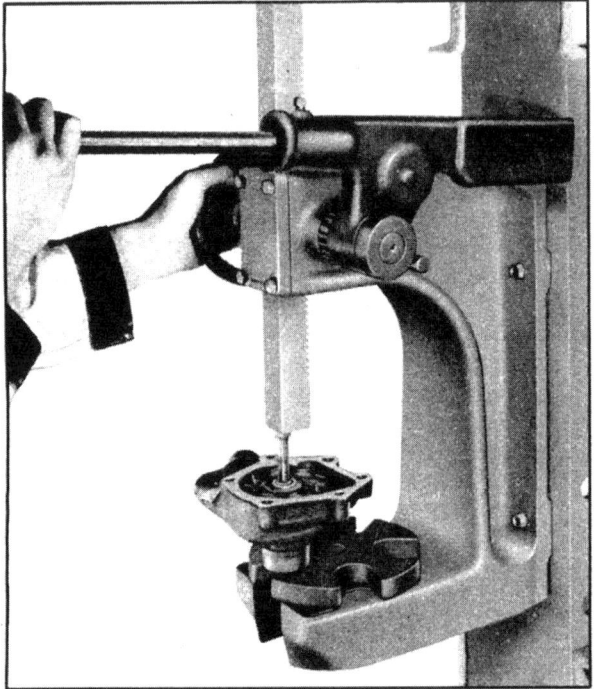

Fig. 112 Installing Shaft and Housing into Rotor

6. Check clearance between face of rotor and pump body (fig. 113). This clearance should be .010" to .035".

Fig. 113—Checking Clearance Between Face of Rotor and Pump Body

7. Place pump in arbor press with end of pump shaft supported on a small flat plate and press pump pulley onto shaft (fig. 114) until pulley is flush with end of shaft.

Fig. 114—Installing Pump Pulley

8. Install pump plate to pump body using a new gasket, install screws, tighten securely and stake in place.

RADIATOR REPLACEMENT

Conventional Models

1. Remove drain plug and drain radiator.
2. Raise hood and block in open position.
3. Remove radiator to water outlet hose.
4. Remove radiator to inlet pipe hose.
5. Remove radiator core to radiator support bolts and lift radiator core straight up to remove.

   NOTE: On models that use a shroud, the shroud may be pushed back and allowed to drop in back of fan blades.

6. Slide radiator core into position with radiator flange in back of radiator support flanges.
7. On models with shroud, lift shroud into position and install radiator core to radiator support bolts.
8. Install radiator hoses and replace radiator drain plug.
9. Fill cooling system and check for leaks and lower hood.

C.O.E. Models

Radiator replacement on C.O.E. models is accomplished in the same manner except the hood must be removed.

ENGINE ASSEMBLY 6-87

Forward Control Models
1. Remove radiator grille.
2. Open drain plug and drain radiator.
3. Disconnect windshield wiper hose and the compartment light wire.
4. Disconnect horn wires at horn and tape.
5. Remove horn and horn bracket.
6. Remove upper, lower and both side radiator baffles.
7. Remove radiator filler pipe hose and radiator overflow extension pipe hose.
8. Raise engine cover and prop open.
9. Disconnect radiator hoses.
10. Disconnect radiator support from frame cross member.
11. Disconnect radiator support from upper attaching brackets.
12. Remove radiator and radiator support from vehicle.
13. Disconnect radiator core from radiator support and remove.
14. Replace radiator core in radiator support, replacing wiring harness clips and connect.
15. Replace radiator and radiator support in vehicle and connect to upper attaching brackets.
16. Connect radiator support to frame cross member, installing cushions and spacer plate.
17. Install radiator hoses.
18. Install radiator baffles.
19. Install horn and horn bracket and connect horn wires.
20. Connect windshield wiper and compartment light wire.
21. Close radiator drain and replace grille.
22. Fill cooling system and check for leaks.
23. Close engine cover and lock.

TROUBLES AND REMEDIES
COOLING SYSTEM

Symptom and Probable Cause — **Probable Remedy**

Overheating
a. Lack of coolant
b. Fan belt loose
c. Fan belt oil soaked
d. Thermostat sticks closed
e. Water pump inoperative
f. Cooling system clogged
g. Incorrect ignition timing
h. Brakes dragging
i. Manifold heat valve thermostatic spring damaged
j. Manifold heat valve stuck due to seized shaft

a. Refill system and check for leaks
b. Adjust
c. Replace fan belt
d. Replace thermostat
e. Replace water pump
f. Clean entire system and reverse flush
g. Retime engine
h. Adjust brakes
i. Replace spring
j. Free manifold heat valve shaft

Overcooling
a. Thermostat remains open
b. Extremely cold climate

a. Replace thermostat
b. Cover part of radiator area

Loss of Coolant
a. Leaking radiator
b. Loose or damaged hose connection
c. Leaking water pump
d. Loose or damaged heater hose
e. Leaking heater unit
f. Leak at cylinder head gasket
g. Cracked cylinder head
h. Cracked cylinder or block expansion plug loose
i. Engine operating at too high temperature

a. Replace or repair
b. Tighten or replace hose connections
c. Replace water pump
d. Tighten or replace hose
e. Replace or repair heater core
f. Replace gasket and tighten bolts securely and evenly
g. Replace cylinder head
h. Make necessary repairs or replacements
i. See overheating causes

Circulation System Noisy
a. Pump bearings rough
b. Fan blades loose or bent
c. Fan belt noisy in pulley
d. Fan belt inner plies loose

a. Replace pump
b. Tighten or replace fan blades
c. Dress belt with belt dressing or soap and adjust
d. Replace fan belt

ENGINE ASSEMBLY 6-88

COOLING SYSTEM SPECIFICATIONS

Cooling Capacity
½, ¾, 1 and 1½ Ton..15 quarts
2 Ton................17 quarts

Water Pump
Type and drive.......Centrifugal by fan belt
Location............Front of cylinder block
Capacity............47 gal. per minute at 4000 engine RPM
Impeller location....Pump body
Bearings............Permanently sealed and lubricated ball
Seal................Molded rubber automatically adjusted by spring tension

Fan
Diameter............18″
Number of blades....4

Fan Belt
Deflection..........¾″
Adjustment..........By moving generator

Thermostat

	Stamped	Starts to Open at	Fully Opened
Regular............	143	140°—147°	170°
Accessory types			
For Alcohol Antifreeze.........	151	148°—156°	176°
For Permanent Antifreeze......	160	157°—165°	185°
	180	175°—184°	204°

Radiator Core
Make and type......Harrison, ribbed cellular
Frontal area........407 sq. inches

CLUTCH

INDEX

	Page
General Description..................6-88
Operation.........................6-89
Minor Service Operations.............6-90
Free Pedal Travel—Adjust...........6-90
Clutch Retracting Springs—Replace....6-90
Major Service Operations.............6-90
Clutch.........................6-90
Removal.....................6-90
Disassembly..................6-91
Inspection...................6-91
Repairs.....................6-92

	Page
Pilot Bearing....................6-92
Assembly......................6-92
Clutch and Brake Pedal..............6-92
Disassembly..................6-93
Inspection...................6-93
Repairs.....................6-93
Clutch and Brake Pedal Hub Bushings 6-93
Pedal Shaft..................6-93
Assembly....................6-93
Clutch and/or Brake Pedal Lever Rods—Forward Control..................6-93

GENERAL DESCRIPTION

The clutch used on all trucks is a single plate dry disc type consisting of two basic assemblies, the driven disc and facing assembly and the cover, pressure plate and diaphragm spring assembly. See Figure 115 for layout of clutch parts.

The entire clutch assembly is mounted on a splined transmission clutch gear and bolted to the flywheel through the clutch cover. The driven disc assembly, which includes a hub and torsional springs, has conventional clutch facing riveted on both sides of the disc.

The pressure plate and diaphragm spring are assembled in the clutch cover and mounted to the flywheel over the driven disc assembly. The diaphragm spring is dished to maintain a constant pressure on the pressure plate which in turn holds the driven disc in contact with the flywheel face. This spring has eighteen tapered fingers pointing inward and is made from very high quality steel, carefully heat treated and shot blasted to secure long life. The action of this diaphragm spring can be compared to the flexing action of the bottom of an ordinary oil can. By depressing the clutch pedal, the throw-out bearing is forced against the diaphragm spring fingers causing the diaphragm spring to pivot on pivot rings (fig. 116).

An oil impregnated type pilot bearing is installed in the end of the crankshaft and serves as a pilot for the transmission clutch gear. The re-

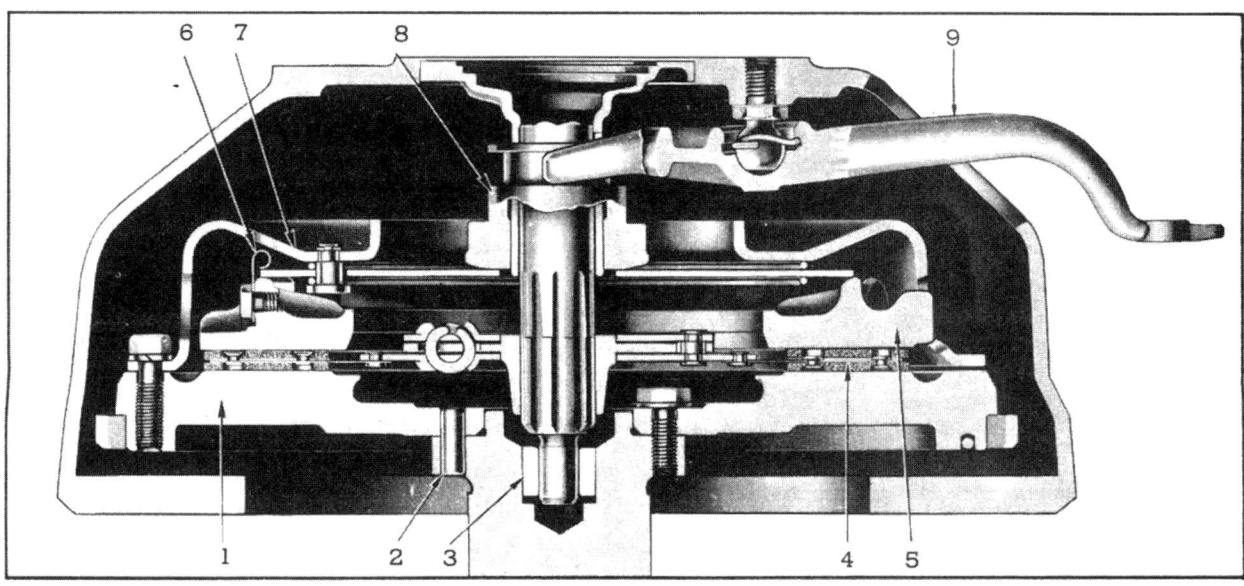

Fig. 115—Clutch Cross Section

1. Flywheel
2. Dowel
3. Bushing
4. Driven Disc
5. Pressure Plate
6. Spring
7. Cover
8. Throwout Bearing
9. Fork

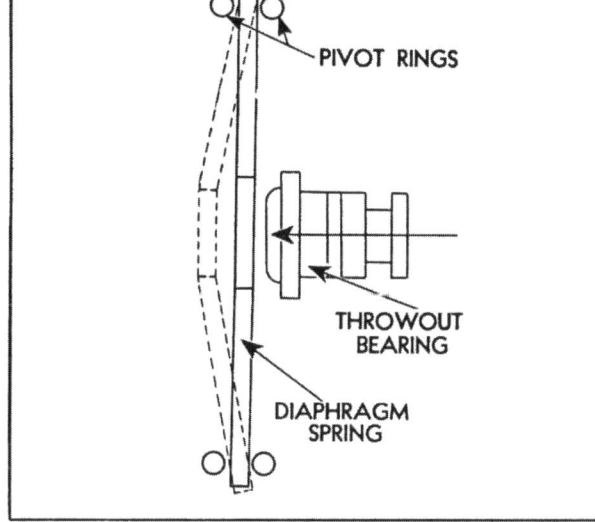

Fig. 116—Action of Diaphragm Spring

lease bearing which is a part of the clutch release collar and bearing assembly is a sealed ball type. The release fork is ball stud mounted in the clutch housing, the inner end of the fork engaging the grooves in the release collar for actuating the collar and bearing.

OPERATION

The clutch is always engaged unless purposely disengaged by the driver by depressing the foot pedal. In the engaged position, the diaphragm spring fingers are flat and the entire rim of the spring exerts pressure against the pressure plate (fig. 117).

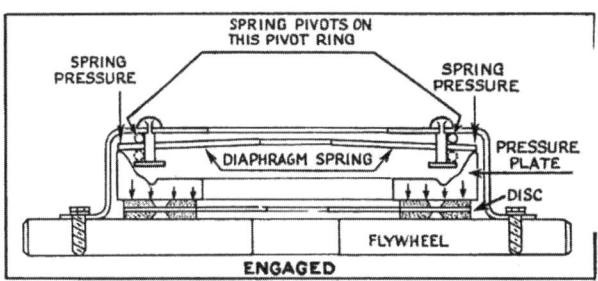

Fig. 117—Engaged Position of Diaphragm Spring

When the clutch pedal is depressed, pressure of the throwout bearing on the inner ends of the diaphragm fingers causes a diaphragm action and the outer ends of the fingers, near the rim, pivot on the inner pivot ring. This action causes the rim of the diaphragm spring and the pressure plate to move away from the clutch disc disengaging the clutch (fig. 118). When the clutch pedal is released and the throwout bearing no longer contacts the fingers, the spring in the diaphragm causes the fingers to pivot about the rear pivot ring and the rim to bear against the pressure plate.

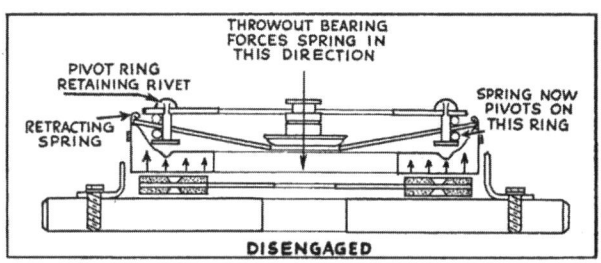

Fig. 118—Disengaged Position of Diaphragm Spring

MINOR SERVICE OPERATIONS

The dry disc type clutch requires very little care during its life. Only one simple adjustment is necessary to maintain clutch efficiency and assure long life. This adjustment is for the amount of free clutch pedal travel before the throwout bearing contacts the clutch fingers (fig. 119). As clutch facings wear, the amount of free pedal travel is reduced and in time this will result in the clutch pedal being held tight against the pedal stop on toe board resulting in clutch slippage. Therefore, it is necessary to adjust pedal at periodic intervals to provide sufficient free pedal travel ¾" - 1" to permit full engagement of the clutch.

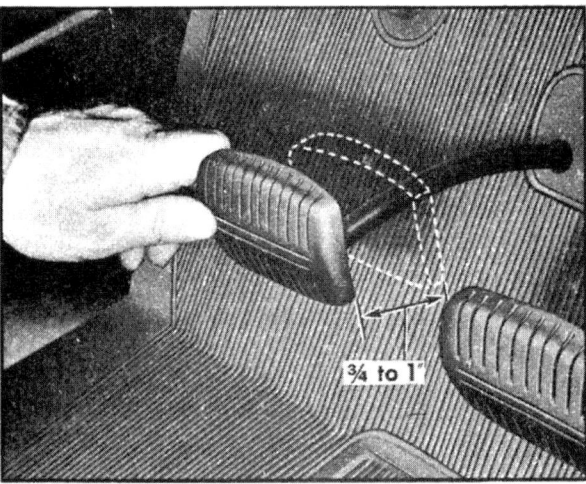

Fig 119—Clutch Pedal Free Travel

ADJUSTMENT—FREE PEDAL TRAVEL

1. Loosen check nut "A" (fig. 120).
2. Turn adjusting nut "B" until free pedal travel is ¾" to 1".

NOTE: Check this free travel with one finger on the pedal and not with the foot as the adjustment is sensitive.

3. Tighten check nut "A."

CLUTCH RETRACTING SPRINGS

A rattle in the clutch assembly at idling speeds with the clutch released may be caused by insufficient tension on the pressure plate retracting springs. This noise can easily be remedied by replacing the springs, as follows:

1. Remove the clutch housing underpan.
2. Hand crank the engine until one retracting spring attaching bolt is at the bottom. Remove the bolt and retracting spring and install a new spring.
3. Replace the other retracting springs in the same manner.
4. Replace clutch housing underpan.

If replacing the retracting springs does not correct the rattle condition, the clearance between the drive lugs on the pressure plate and the slots in the cover should be checked. If this clearance exceeds .008", the pressure plate and/or cover assembly should be replaced to obtain proper clearance.

Fig. 120—Clutch Pedal Free Travel Adjustment

MAJOR SERVICE OPERATIONS

There are many things which affect good clutch operation. Therefore, it is necessary, before performing any major clutch operations, to make certain preliminary inspections to determine whether or not the trouble is actually in the clutch.

1. Check the clutch pedal and make sure that the pedal has ¾" to 1" free travel before the clutch starts to disengage.
2. Check the clutch pedal bushing for wear and for sticking on the shaft or loose mountings.
3. Lubricate the pedal linkage.
4. Tighten all front and rear engine mounting bolts. Should the mountings be oil soaked, it will be necessary to replace them.
5. Check spring shackle bushings and pins.

CLUTCH

Removal

1. Remove transmission as outlined in "Transmission Section."
2. Remove clutch throwout bearing from the fork.
3. Remove lock nut from adjusting link and remove clutch fork by pressing it away from its ball mounting with a screwdriver, until the fork snaps loose from the ball.

ENGINE ASSEMBLY 6-91

NOTE: The retainer may be removed from the fork by prying out with a small screwdriver.

4. Install clutch pilot tool K-411 to support the clutch assembly during removal.
5. Loosen the clutch attaching bolts one turn at a time to prevent distortion of clutch cover until diaphragm spring is released.
6. Remove clutch pilot tool and remove clutch assembly from vehicle.

Disassembly

1. Remove the three clutch pressure plate retracting springs (fig. 121) and remove pressure plate from clutch cover.

Fig. 121—Removing or Replacing Pressure Plate Retracting Springs

NOTE: When disassembling, note position of "O" marks on pressure plate and cover. These marks must be aligned in assembly to maintain balance.

2. The clutch diaphragm spring and two pivot rings are riveted to the clutch cover (fig. 117). Spring, ring and cover should be inspected for excessive wear or damage and if there is a defect, it is necessary to replace the complete cover assembly.

Inspection

1. Wash all parts, except throwout bearing in cleaning solvent.

NOTE: The throwout bearing is permanently packed with lubricant and should not be soaked in cleaning solvent as this may dissolve the lubricant.

2. Inspect pressure plate and flywheel for scores on the contact surfaces.
3. Check pressure plate drive lugs for burrs. These lugs must move freely in the cover.
4. Check clearance between lugs and cover. This clearance should be .002"-.008".
5. Check throwout bearing for roughness and free fit on the sleeve of the transmission clutch gear bearing retainer.
6. Check runout of transmission pilot hole in clutch housing by removing flywheel stud and installing an indicator (fig. 50). The runout should be within .008" indicator reading.
7. Check fit of ball in clutch fork (fig. 122). This fit should be snug without end play.

Fig. 122—Checking Free Fit of Fork Ball in Clutch

8. Inspect clutch disc for worn, loose or oil soaked facings, broken springs, loose rivets or riding.
9. Examine splines in hub and make sure they slide freely on splines of transmission clutch shaft. If splines are worn, the clutch should be replaced.

Fig. 123—Clutch Pilot Bearing Remover

ENGINE ASSEMBLY 6-92

REPAIRS

Pilot Bearing

The clutch pilot bearing is an oil impregnated type bearing pressed into the crankshaft. This bearing requires attention only when the clutch is removed from the vehicle, at which time it should be cleaned and inspected for excessive wear or damage and should be replaced if necessary. To remove, install pilot bearing puller J-1448 and remove bearing from crankshaft (fig. 123). In replacing this bearing, use clutch pilot bearing driver J-1522. Place bearing on pilot of tool with radius in bore of bearing next to shoulder of tool and drive into crankshaft.

ASSEMBLY

1. Install the pressure plate in the cover assembly lining up the "O" mark on pressure plate driving lug with "O" mark on flange of cover (fig. 121).
2. Install the three pressure plate retracting springs (fig. 121). The clutch is now ready to be installed.
3. Hand crank the engine until "X" mark on flywheel is at the bottom.
4. Install clutch disc, pressure plate and cover assembly and support them with clutch pilot tool K-411.
5. Turn clutch assembly until "X" mark on clutch cover flange lines up with "X" mark on flywheel.
6. Install attaching bolts and tighten each one a turn at a time to prevent distorting the cover as the spring pressure is taken up.
7. Remove clutch pilot K-411.
8. Pack clutch fork ball seat with a small amount of high melting point grease and install a new retainer in the groove of the clutch fork if the old retainer is worn or damaged.

   NOTE: Install retainer with high side up, away from bottom of the ball socket and with open end of retainer on the horizontal.

9. Replace clutch fork on the clutch fork ball in clutch housing by snapping it onto the ball.
10. Lubricate the recess on the inside of the throwout bearing collar and coat the throwout fork groove with a small amount of high melting point grease (fig. 124).

    CAUTION: Be careful not to use too much lubricant.

11. Install throwout bearing assembly to the throwout fork.
12. Assemble transmission as outlined in Transmission Section.

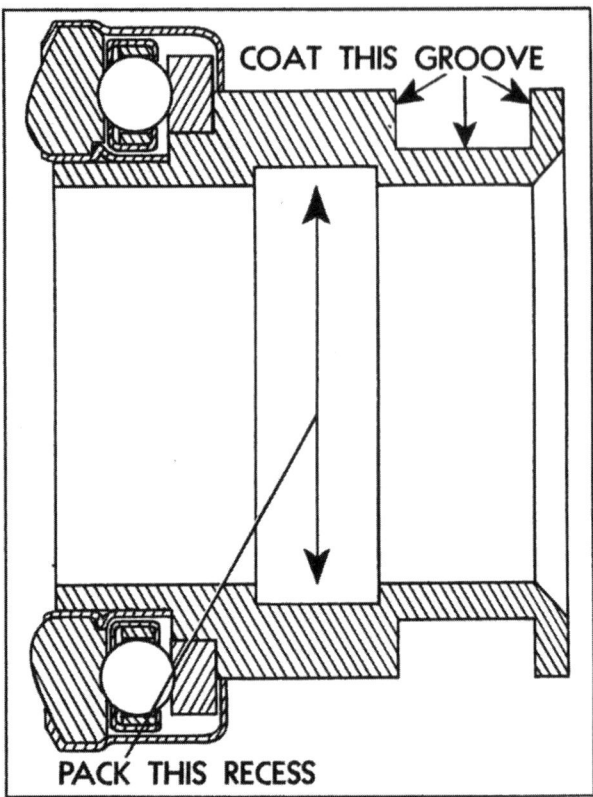

Fig. 124—Lubrication Points on Clutch Throwout Bearing Collar

CLUTCH AND BRAKE PEDAL

The pedals and main cylinder are mounted on a common bracket on all except the C.O.E. and Forward Control models. The pedal shaft is common to both clutch and brake pedal being retained to the frame side rail with a nut and lockwasher and supported in the mounting bracket. Pedals are separated by a pedal hub spacer and the shaft is so grooved that lubrication is accomplished through one lubricating fitting located in the brake pedal hub. Both pedal hubs are bushed and pedals are retained on the pedal shaft by a special shaft spring, an inner and outer spring retainer and a lock ring.

The Forward Control pedals are mounted on a common shaft supported in a bracket on top of the side rail. Pedals are separated by a pedal hub spacer and held tightly together with spring and retainer between the bracket and the clutch pedal. The shaft is attached to the bracket by a nut and lockwasher. The clutch pedal and brake pedal are connected to an idler shaft by means of rods. This idler shaft is mounted the same as the pedals on the regular truck.

The C.O.E. pedals are mounted on the left side member of the subframe. The pedals are not mounted on a common shaft but the shafts are supported by a common bracket. The clutch pedal is linked to an idler shaft mounted in a bracket supported on the bottom flange of left side member of the frame. Each pedal is equipped with a lubrication fitting.

Disassembly (Conventional)

1. Disconnect upper brake and clutch pedals from lower halves by removing connecting bolt.
2. Disconnect main cylinder link from brake pedal.
3. Disconnect clutch pedal link from clutch pedal.
4. Disconnect spring extension from brake pedal.
5. Remove lock ring, outer retainer, spring, inner retainer and spacer from pedal shaft.
6. Slide brake pedal from pedal shaft.
7. Remove spacer from pedal shaft turning spacer to index with groove on shaft.
8. Remove clevis from master cylinder link.
9. Slide clutch pedal from pedal shaft.

Inspection

1. Clean all parts in cleaning solvent.
2. Inspect pedal hub bushings for excessive wear or scoring.
3. Inspect pedal shaft for scoring on bearing surfaces.

REPAIRS

Clutch and Brake Pedal Hub Bushing

1. Remove old bushings from pedal hub.
2. Install new bushings and press into position in an arbor press using a flat plate to drive bushing.

   NOTE: Be sure bushings do not extend outside either face of pedal hubs.

Pedal Shaft

1. Remove retaining nut and lockwasher from outside of frame side member.
2. With punch drive shaft out of pedal bracket and frame side member toward center of vehicle.
3. Install new pedal shaft through pedal bracket and into frame side member and install retaining nut and lockwasher and tighten securely.

Assembly (Conventional)

1. Install clutch pedal on pedal shaft.
2. Install pedal hub spacer.
3. Install brake pedal on pedal shaft.
4. Install hub spacer, spring inner retainer, spring, spring outer retainer and secure in place with lock ring in ring groove of pedal shaft.
5. Install clevis to main cylinder link.
6. Connect main cylinder link to brake pedal.
7. Assemble upper brake and clutch pedals to lower pedals and secure with bolts, nuts and lockwashers.
8. Connect spring extension to brake pedal and adjust pedal toe board clearance. See "Brake Section."
9. Connect clutch pedal link to clutch pedal and check and adjust free pedal travel, if necessary.
10. Lubricate pedal shaft.

CLUTCH AND/OR BRAKE PEDAL LEVER RODS (Forward Control Models)

Removal

1. Remove front floor pan.
2. Remove cotter pin and clevis pin from upper end of clutch and/or brake pedal lever rods.
3. Remove cotter pin and clevis pin from lower end of clutch and/or brake pedal lever rods.
4. Remove clevis and lock nut from upper end of rod or rods and remove rods.

Installation

1. Install lock nut and clevis on the clutch pedal rod. The smaller diameter rod is the clutch pedal lever rod.
2. Install lower end of rod to clutch lever, inserting clevis pin and cotter pin.
3. With pedal in rest position, adjust clevis to allow ¾" to 1" free pedal travel and lock with lock nut.
4. Install lock nut and clevis on the brake lever rod.
5. Install lower end of rod to brake lever.
6. Adjust brake rod clevis to give 1" pedal to floor board clearance and install upper end to brake pedal, inserting clevis pin and cotter pin.
7. Replace front floor pan.

TROUBLES AND REMEDIES

CLUTCH

Symptom and Probable Cause	Probable Remedy
Slipping	
a. Improper adjustment	a. Adjust pedal travel
b. Oil soaked	b. Install new disc

Symptom and Probable Cause
c. Sticking pressure plate

d. Worn splines on clutch gear
e. Lining torn loose from disc

Grabbing
a. Oil on lining
b. Worn splines on clutch gear
c. Sticking pressure plate
d. Worn shackles
e. Loose engine mountings

Rattling
a. Weak retracting springs
b. Excessive clearance at driving lugs
c. Throwout fork loose on ball stud

Probable Remedy
c. Check fit of drive lugs on pressure plate in slots of cover. If necessary, replace pressure plate or cover.
d. Replace transmission clutch gear
e. Install new disc

a. Install new disc
b. Replace transmission clutch gear
c. Check fit of drive lugs in cover
d. Replace shackle bushings and pins
e. Tighten or replace mountings

a. Replace springs
b. Replace pressure plate or cover
c. Check ball stud and retaining spring and replace if necessary

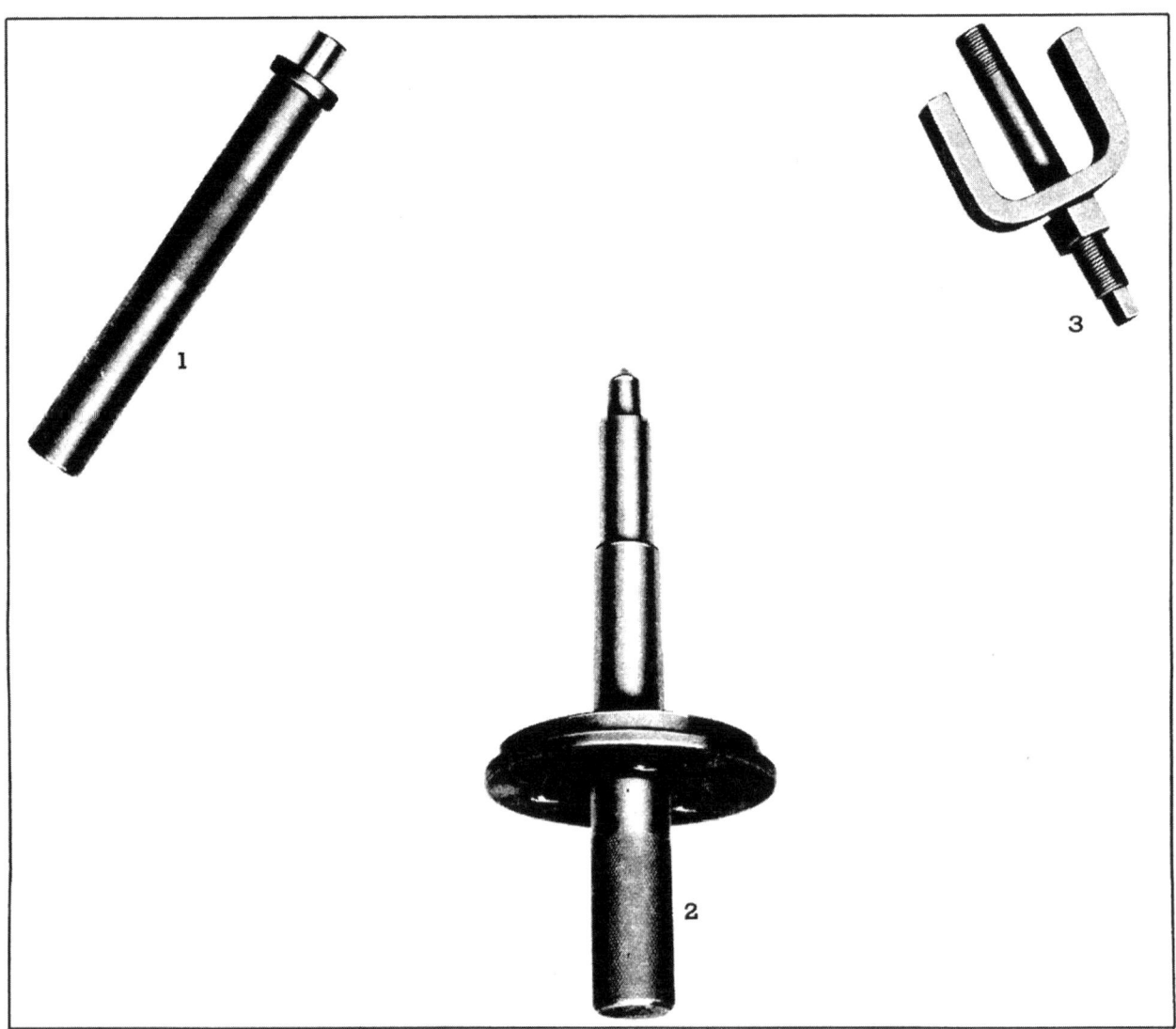

Fig. 125—Clutch Special Tools

1. J-1522 Clutch Pilot Bearing Driver
2. K-411   Clutch Pilot Tool
3. J-1448 Clutch Pilot Bearing Puller

CLUTCH SPECIFICATIONS

Type .... Single Plate Dry Disc
Disc Diameter .... ½ Ton - 9⅛"
All others - 10¾"
Clutch Pressure Spring
Type .... Diaphragm
Diameter .... 9"
Clutch Release Bearing
Type .... Sealed
Make .... New Departure

Clutch Pilot Bearing
Type .... Oil Impregnated Bushing
Clearance between—
Pressure Plate Drive
Lugs and Cover .... .002" - .008"
Transmission Pilot Hole
Runout not to exceed.... .008"
Clutch Pedal
Free Pedal Travel ..... ¾" to 1"

SERVICE NEWS REFERENCE

Month	Page No.	Subject

SECTION 7
TRANSMISSION

CONTENTS OF THIS SECTION

	Page
Three-Speed Transmission	7- 1
Four-Speed Transmission	7-13
Troubles and Remedies	7-31
Transmission Special Tools	7-32
Service News Reference	7-34

3-SPEED TRANSMISSION

INDEX

	Page		Page
General Description	7- 1	Synchronizer Energizing Springs	7- 9
Minor Service Operations	7- 2	Reverse Idler Gear Bushings	7- 9
Steering Column Gearshift Adjustment	7- 2	Countergear Needle Bearings	7- 9
Rear Bearing Support and/or Speedometer Drive Gear	7- 3	Transmission Assembly	7- 9
		Reverse Idler Gear	7- 9
Side Cover Assembly	7- 4	Countergear	7-10
Major Service Operations	7- 4	Rear Bearing	7-10
Transmission Removal	7- 4	Synchronizer Clutch Sleeve	7-11
Transmission Disassembly	7- 5	Mainshaft	7-11
Cleaning and Inspection	7- 6	Universal Joint	7-11
Repairs	7- 8	Side Cover Assembly	7-11
Clutch Gear Bearing	7- 8	Universal Joint Ball Adjustment	7-11
Clutch Sleeve	7- 8	Transmission Installation	7-12
Synchronizer Rings	7- 8	Specifications	7-13

GENERAL DESCRIPTION

A three-speed synchromesh transmission (fig. (fig. 1) is used as standard equipment on the commercial ½ and ¾ ton trucks. The transmission incorporates all helical gears which are machined from drop forged steel gear blanks, heat treated for strength and long life. The shafts are machined from high grade steel, heat treated and ground to close limits.

The rear end of the clutch gear is supported by a heavy duty ball bearing at the front end of the transmission case and is piloted at its front end in an oil impregnated bushing mounted in the engine crankshaft. The front end of the mainshaft is piloted in roller bearings set into the hollow end of the clutch gear and the rear end is carried by a ball bearing mounted in the rear of the transmission case.

The countergear is carried on roller bearings at both ends while thrust is taken on thrust washers located between ends of gear and front and rear of the case.

The reverse idler gear is carried on ball-indented bronze bushings while thrust is taken on thrust washers located between ends of gear and front and rear of the case.

A speedometer gear is mounted to the rear of

TRANSMISSION 7-2

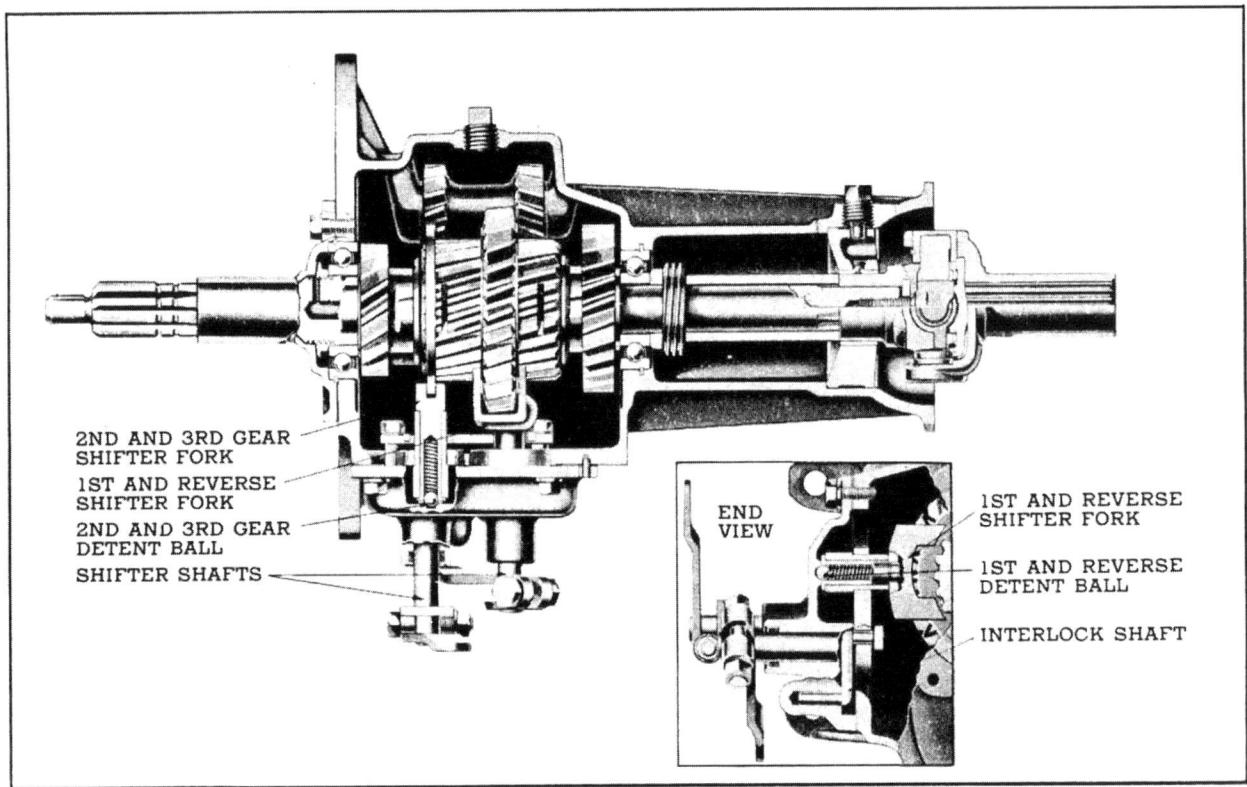

Fig. 1—Cross Section—3-Speed Transmission

the mainshaft rear bearing and located between a speedometer gear spacer and universal joint spacer. The universal joint front yoke is supported in a rear bearing support assembly located at the rear end of the transmission housing. This bearing support is located and held in position in the housing by means of a special square head pipe plug.

Gearshifting is manual through steering column gearshift mechanism (fig. 2) to the transmission cover located on the side of the transmission. Shifting is accomplished by two rotating cranks which directly engage the gears to be shifted, thus affording a highly efficient mechanical action. The shifter gate for selection between first and reverse and second and high is contained in the shifter housing mounted on the lower portion of the steering column mast jacket. Two shifter control rods connect the shifter levers on the transmission to the outer shifter levers on this housing.

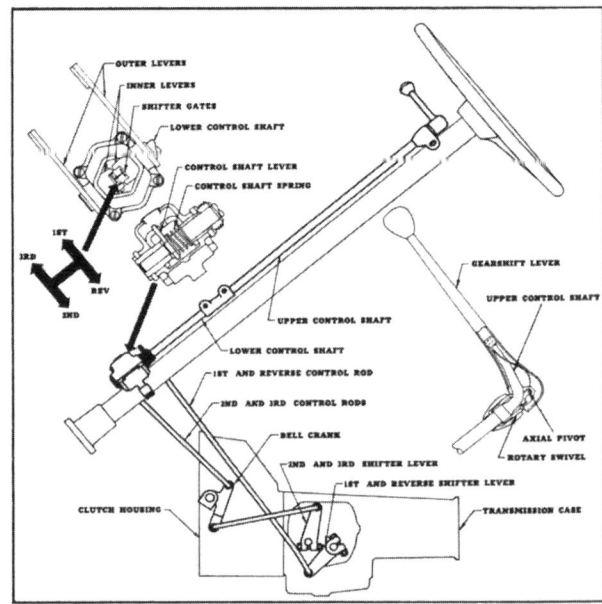

Fig. 2—Steering Column Gearshift

MINOR SERVICE OPERATIONS

STEERING COLUMN GEARSHIFT—ADJUST

In cases where insufficient clearance is encountered between the gearshift lever and the steering wheel or when the gearshift linkage has been disconnected or removed for steering gear overhaul, proper adjustment sequence is important.

1. Check clearance between gearshift lever and gearshift control upper support "B" (fig. 3).

This clearance, as measured from the lower edge of gearshift lever to the top of upper support, should be 3/32" to 1/8".

2. To correct this clearance remove upper bolt from upper and lower control shaft clamp and remove two screws holding upper support to steering gear housing and remove upper control shaft assembly.

3. Screw upper support up or down to get necessary 3/32" to 1/8" clearance and replace upper control shaft, tighten clamp bolt and replace upper support screws.

4. Check clearance between end of gearshift lever and lower edge of steering wheel rim "A" (fig. 3). This clearance should be $2\tfrac{9}{16}" \pm \tfrac{1}{8}"$ on all 1948 models and $2\tfrac{13}{16}" \pm \tfrac{1}{8}"$ on all 1949-51 models.

5. To correct this clearance loosen two gearshift control shaft and housing assembly clamp bolts and move housing assembly with upper and lower control shafts and gearshift lever up or down to obtain necessary clearance. With proper clearance obtained, tighten housing assembly clamp bolts.

6. With transmission in neutral, gearshift lever should be horizontal. To move gearshift lever to horizontal position; on 1948 models, disconnect 2nd and 3rd speed control rod swivel from housing outer lever and adjust swivel to bring gearshift lever in a horizontal plane. On 1949-51 models, loosen 2nd and 3rd speed control rod swivel clamp at housing outer lever and adjust swivel to bring gearshift lever into a horizontal plane.

7. Remove housing cover and check to make sure that shifter gates in inner levers are aligned. If alignment is off; on 1948 models, disconnect 1st and reverse speed control rod swivel from housing outer lever and adjust swivel until shifter gates are aligned. On 1949-51 models; loosen 1st and reverse speed control rod swivel clamp at housing outer lever and adjust swivel until shifter gates are aligned.

REAR BEARING SUPPORT AND/OR SPEEDOMETER DRIVE GEAR

The transmission bearing support (fig. 1) is serviced as an assembly in order to assure proper transmission alignment. Should the bushing in this assembly become worn, it will be necessary to replace the assembly. Also, if replacement of speedometer drive gear is required, the bearing support must be removed.

Removal

1. Remove capscrews holding universal joint ball collar to transmission rear face.
2. On ½ ton:
   a. Remove bolts which retain transmission support to frame cross member.
   b. Slide universal joint ball and collar back on torque tube, remove capscrews which retain front trunnion bearings to front yoke and split joint.
   c. Raise front end of torque tube for clearance.
3. On ¾ ton:
   a. Disconnect the intermediate universal joint by removing the two trunnion bearing "U" clamps, split joint and lower front end of rear propeller shaft to floor.
   b. Remove nuts attaching propeller shaft bearing support bracket to frame cross member and remove shaft assembly from vehicle.
4. Remove universal joint or yoke capscrew and slide the universal joint (¾ ton) or yoke (½ ton) off the mainshaft.
5. Remove square head pipe plug from top rear of transmission housing and using a hook puller, pull transmission rear bearing support assembly out of rear of transmission housing.
6. Disconnect speedometer cable from speedometer driven gear and remove speedometer driven gear, universal joint spacer, speedometer drive gear and drive gear spacer.

Installation

1. Install speedometer drive gear spacer, drive gear, driven gear and universal joint spacer. Connect speedometer cable to speedometer driven gear.
2. Install rear bearing support assembly, indexing the 3/8" diameter hole in support with tapped hole in case. Install special square head pipe plug.

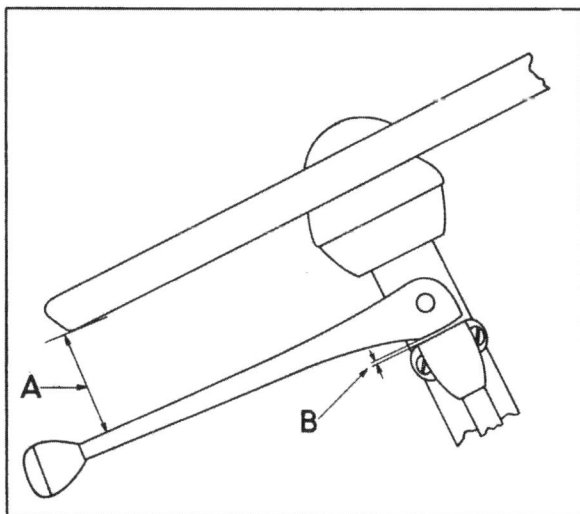

Fig. 3—Gearshift Lever Clearances

3. Install universal joint (¾ ton) or front yoke (½ ton); install retaining capscrew and tighten to 15-20 ft. lbs.
4. On ½ ton:
   a. Lower front end of propeller shaft and connect universal joint, tighten capscrews securely and bend lock plate tangs into locking position.
   b. Slide universal joint ball and collar forward on torque tube, install capscrews and tighten to 8-12 ft. lbs. Install transmission support to frame cross member bolts and tighten securely.
5. On ¾ ton:
   a. Slide the propeller shaft assembly onto transmission universal joint and install nuts attaching propeller shaft bearing support bracket to frame cross member.
   b. Slide the ball collar forward, position the gaskets and install the four retaining capscrews. Tighten the capscrews to 8-12 ft. lbs. torque.
   c. Raise front end of rear propeller shaft, align rear joint and intermediate joint for proper balance and install two trunnion bearing "U" clamps to intermediate universal joint and tighten securely.
6. Remove the pipe plug, lubricate the universal joint bearings through the pipe plug opening, and replace the plug.

SIDE COVER ASSEMBLY

On any replacement of parts in the side cover assembly it is necessary to remove cover from transmission case.
1. Drain transmission and disconnect shifter levers from shifter shafts by removing lock bolts and then pulling levers from shafts.
2. To replace shifter shaft and fork assembly, interlock or poppets and springs, remove cover assembly from transmission case.
3. Remove capscrews and remove shifter interlock retainer. This will allow removal of shifter shaft and fork assembly, poppets and springs or interlock from cover.
4. Replace necessary parts and install shifter interlock retainer.
5. With transmission gears in neutral and shifter forks in neutral position, install cover to transmission using a new gasket and tighten retaining capscrews securely.

NOTE: Hump on first and reverse shifter fork (fig. 4) must be toward rear of transmission.

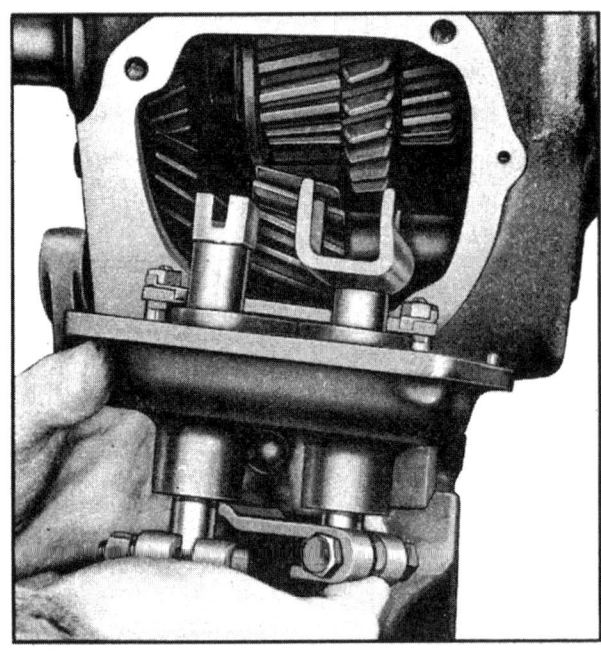

Fig. 4—Cover Assembly Installation

6. Attach shifter levers to shifter shafts and install lock bolts, tightening securely.
7. Fill transmission with 1½ pints of SAE 90 transmission lubricant.

MAJOR SERVICE OPERATIONS

REMOVAL

1. Remove accelerator pedal, floor mat and transmission cover from the body floor.
2. Disconnect the speedometer cable from speedometer driven gear on transmission housing. Disconnect shift control rods from the shifter levers at the transmission.
3. Drain lubricant from transmission.
4. On ½ ton:
   a. Remove the 4 capscrews holding the universal joint ball collar to transmission rear face and remove bolts which retain transmission support to frame cross member.
   b. Remove battery and place jack under propeller shaft to hold in position.
   c. Slide the universal ball and collar back on the propeller shaft housing and remove the capscrews which retain front trunnion bearings to the front yoke and split joint.
   d. Raise front end of propeller shaft as high as it will go with jack to provide clearance.

5. On ¾ ton:
   a. Disconnect the intermediate universal joint by removing the two trunnion bearing "U" clamps, split joint and lower front end of rear propeller shaft to floor.
   b. Remove the 4 capscrews attaching the universal joint ball collar to the rear face of transmission case and slip ball collar back on housing.
   c. Remove nuts attaching propeller shaft bearing support bracket to frame cross member and remove shaft assembly from vehicle.
6. Remove the 2 top transmission to clutch housing capscrews and insert 2 transmission guide pins, J-1116 in these holes.
7. Remove the flywheel underpan and remove the 2 lower transmission to clutch housing capscrews.
8. Slide the transmission straight back on guide pins until the clutch gear shaft is free of splines in the clutch disc.

   NOTE: The use of the 2 guide pins during this operation will support the transmission and prevent damage to the clutch disc through springing.
9. Remove transmission through the opening in the body floor.

DISASSEMBLY

1. Mount the transmission in the transmission holding fixture J-934.
2. Remove the four capscrews which fasten the shifter cover to the left side of the transmission. Remove the cover and the shifter assembly.

   NOTE: Under ordinary circumstances it is not necessary to remove the shifter assembly from the shifter cover. Service of the above is covered under "Minor Service Operations."
3. Place the transmission in two gears at once to lock the mainshaft, and remove the universal joint or yoke retaining capscrew and lockwasher. Slide the yoke off the mainshaft.

   CAUTION: Care should be used when shifting the gears into second or third to prevent damage to the wedge angles.
4. Remove the four clutch gear bearing retainer screws and shakeproof washers. Remove the retainer. Note the screw holes in the retainer are unevenly spaced so that the retainer may only be assembled to the case in one position, matching up the oil return slot with the hole in the case.

5. Install the special clutch gear and bearing puller J-937 by screwing the threaded sleeve (left handed thread) on to the clutch gear shaft. Turning the puller handle will remove the gear and bearing without damage to mainshaft pilot bearing (fig. 5).
6. Remove the 14 roller bearings from inside the clutch gear.

Fig. 5—Removing Clutch Gear and Bearing

7. Remove the square head pipe plug from the top of the bearing retainer and using a hook puller, pull transmission rear bearing support assembly out of the rear of the transmission housing.
8. Remove universal joint spacer, speedometer drive gear and drive gear spacer.
9. Turn the yoke of the mainshaft removing and replacing tool J-938 back on the threads and screw adapter J-938-7 on to puller shaft, then install puller shaft into the threaded end of the mainshaft. Bolt the yoke of the tool to the rear face of the transmission case.

   IMPORTANT: Turn the front synchronizer ring so that the lugs line up with the slots in the main shaft helical spline (fig. 6).
10. While holding puller shaft handle, turn the puller handle clockwise to force the mainshaft out of the rear bearing (fig. 7). Disassemble the puller from mainshaft and the transmission case and remove the mainshaft from transmission through the front of the case.
11. Shift the second speed gear into the clutch sleeve. Remove the clutch sleeve assembly, first and reverse sliding gear and second

TRANSMISSION 7-6

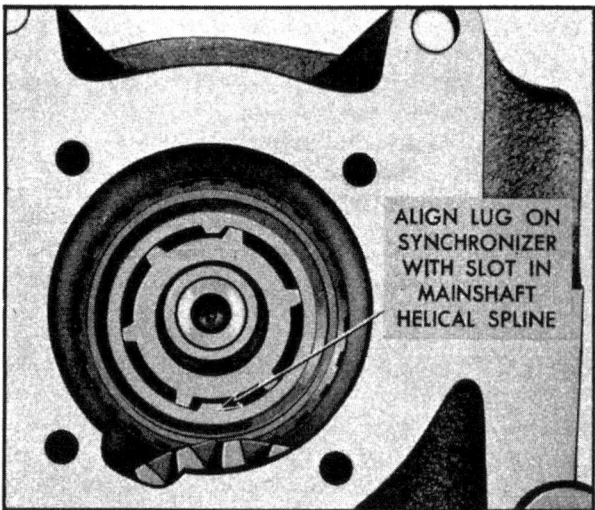

Fig. 6—Synchronizer Alignment

speed gear from the case as a unit. Remove the second speed gear thrustwasher from the case.

Fig 7—Removing Mainshaft

12. Expand the rear bearing lock ring into the case (fig. 8) with the special expanding tool J-3185. This raises the lock ring from the groove in the bearing and the bearing may be removed by lightly tapping the outer race toward the inside of the case. It is necessary to remove the rear bearing before attempting to remove the countergear.

13. Remove the countershaft by driving it from the rear to the front of the case, using a brass drift. Remove the countergear, and the front and rear thrustwashers and needle bearings from bottom of case.

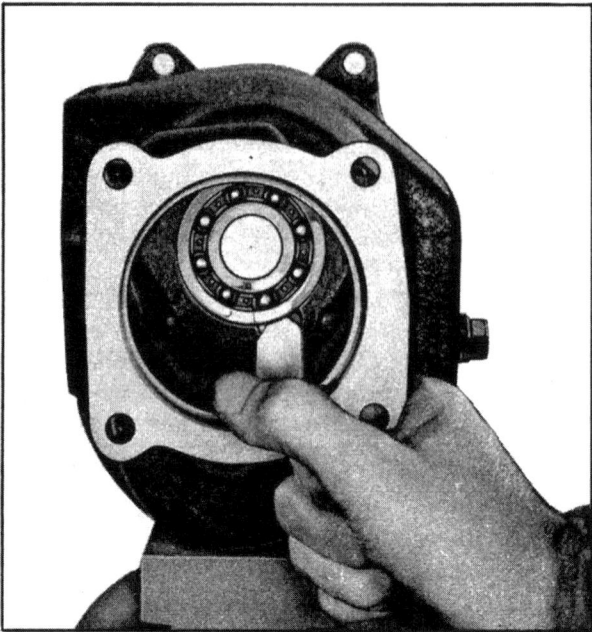

Fig. 8—Removing Rear Bearing

NOTE: It is necessary to remove the countergear before removing the reverse idler shaft, otherwise the idler shaft will strike the countergear.

14. Drive out the reverse idler shaft expanding plug from inside of the case. A hook-nosed punch or drift will be found most suitable for this job.

15. Drive the idler shaft lock pin into the shaft. This pin is shorter in length than the diameter of the shaft so that the shaft may be slipped out when the pin is driven in. Do not turn the shaft while removing as the lock pin may drop down between the idler shaft bushings.

16. Remove reverse idler shaft and thrustwashers. Layout of the three speed transmission parts is shown in Figure 9.

CLEANING AND INSPECTION

Bearings

1. Wash the bearings thoroughly in a cleaning solvent.
2. Blow out the bearings with compressed air.

   CAUTION: Do not allow the bearings to spin but turn them slowly by hand. Spinning bearings will damage the race and balls.

3. After making sure the bearings are clean, lubricate them with light engine oil and check them for roughness. Roughness may be determined by slowly turning the outer race by hand.

TRANSMISSION 7-7

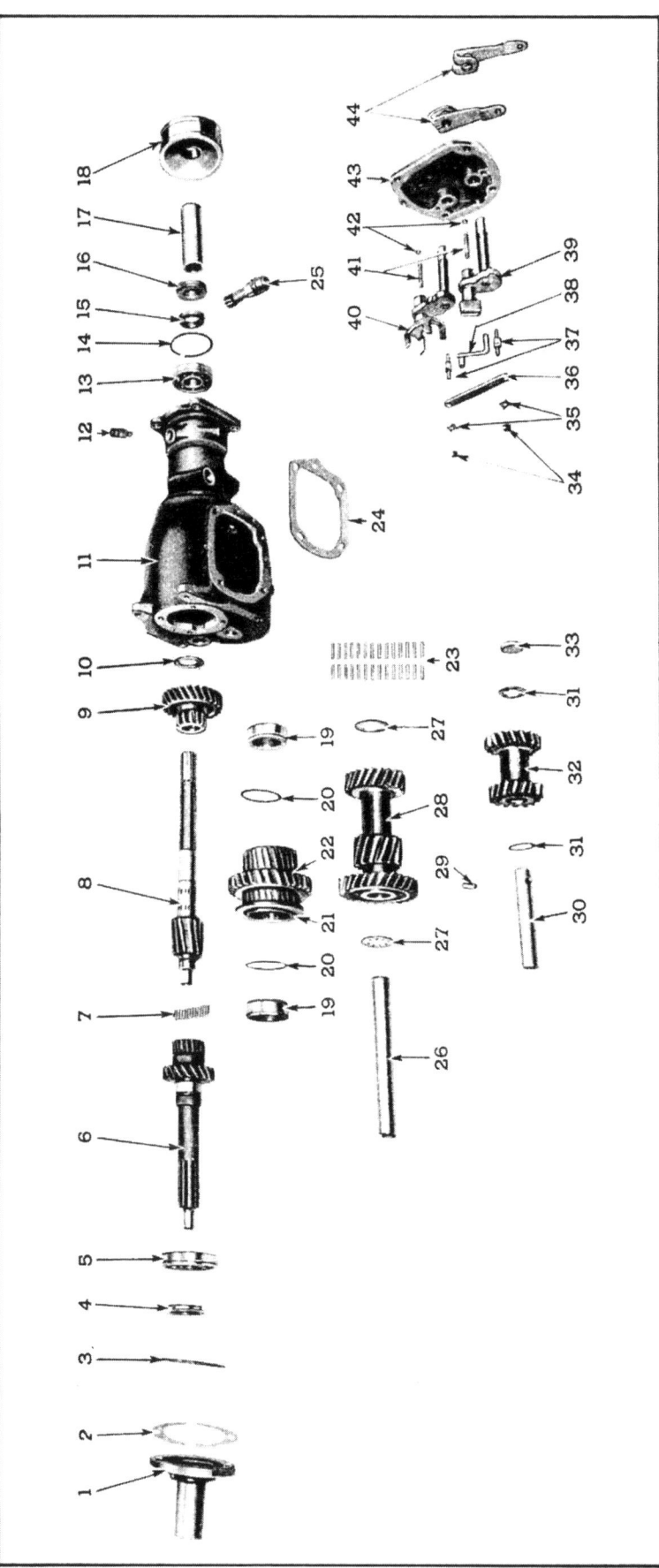

Fig. 9—Layout of Transmission Parts

1. Clutch Gear Bearing Retainer
2. Clutch Gear Bearing Retainer Gasket
3. Clutch Gear Bearing Snap Ring
4. Clutch Gear Bearing Nut and Oil Slinger
5. Clutch Gear Bearing
6. Clutch Gear
7. Main Shaft Pilot Needle Bearings
8. Main Shaft
9. Second Speed Gear
10. Second Speed Gear Thrust Washer
11. Transmission Case
12. Bearing Support Retainer Plug
13. Main Shaft Rear Bearing
14. Main Shaft Rear Bearing Snap Ring
15. Speedometer Drive Gear Spacer
16. Speedometer Drive Gear
17. Universal Joint Spacer
18. Rear Bearing Support
19. Synchronizer Ring
20. Synchronizer Ring Snap Ring
21. Synchronizer Drum
22. First and Reverse Gear
23. Countershaft Needle Bearings
24. Transmission Cover Gasket
25. Speedometer Driven Gear
26. Countershaft
27. Counter Gear Thrust Washer
28. Counter Gear Assembly
29. Reverse Idler Shaft Lock Pin
30. Reverse Idler Shaft
31. Reverse Idler Gear Thrust Washer
32. Reverse Idler Gear
33. Expansion Plug
34. Shifter Interlock Retainer Stud Nut
35. Shifter Interlock Retainer Stud Nut Lock
36. Shifter Interlock Retainer
37. Shifter Interlock Retainer Stud
38. Shifter Interlock Shaft
39. Second and Third Shifter Fork
40. First and Reverse Shifter Fork
41. Shifter Fork Detent Spring
42. Shifter Fork Detent Ball
43. Transmission Cover
44. Shifter Shaft Lever

TRANSMISSION 7-8

Transmission Case

Wash the transmission case inside and outside with a cleaning solvent and inspect for cracks. Inspect the front face which fits against clutch housing for burrs and if any are present, dress them off with a fine cut mill file.

Gears

1. Inspect all gears and, if necessary, replace any that are worn or damaged.
2. Check the first and reverse sliding gear to make sure it slides freely on clutch sleeve.
3. Check the clutch sleeve to see that it slides freely on mainshaft.

REPAIRS

Clutch Gear Bearing—Removal

1. Place the clutch gear in a vise and remove the bearing retainer nut and oil slinger, using the special wrench J-933 (fig. 10). The retaining nut and oil slinger is a one piece steel casting machined with a left handed thread and is locked in place on the clutch gearshaft by being staked into a hole provided for that purpose.
2. To remove the clutch gear bearing place the special press plate J-936 over the gear and against the bearing. Using an arbor press, press the shaft out of the bearing (fig. 11).

CAUTION: *Do not attempt to drive the shaft out of the bearing or the bearing will be seriously damaged.*

Clutch Gear Bearing—Replace

1. Using an arbor press, press the clutch gear bearing on to the clutch gear with the locating ring toward the front of the gearshaft so that the bearing will enter the case to the maximum possible depth.

Fig. 10—Retaining Nut and Oil Slinger Remover Tool

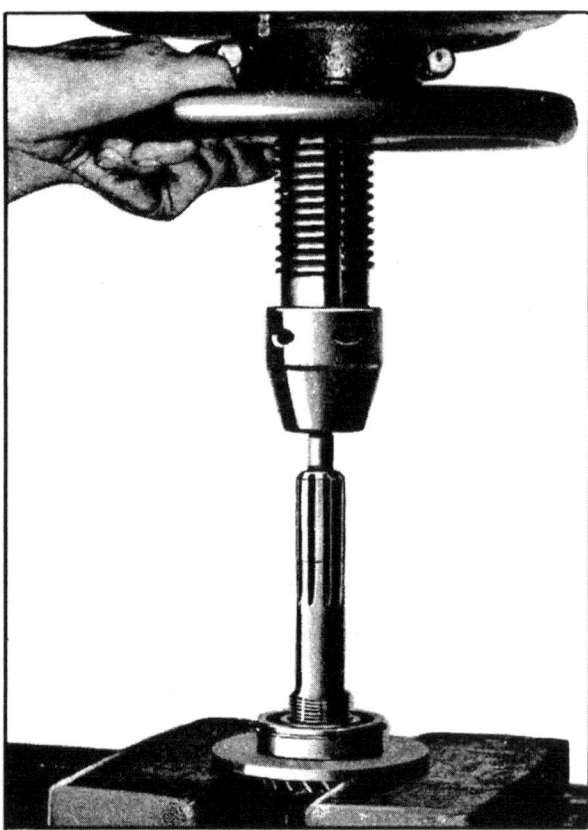

Fig. 11—Removing Clutch Gear Bearing

2. Install the combination clutch bearing retaining nut and oil slinger on the clutch gearshaft and draw it up tight, using special wrench J-933.
3. Lock the retaining nut oil slinger in place by staking it into the hole with a center punch. Care must be used not to damage the threads on the shaft.

Clutch Sleeve—Disassembly

1. Remove the second speed gear.
2. Remove the first and reverse sliding gear.
3. Turn the synchronizer ring in the clutch sleeve until the ends of the synchonizer ring retainer can be seen through the slot in the clutch sleeve.
4. Using special pliers J-932 expand the retainer into the counterbore in clutch sleeve, this raises the retainer from the grooves in the ring and may be easily slipped out (fig. 12).
5. Check the synchronizing cones for wear or for being loose in the clutch sleeve. If cones are damaged in any way, it will be necessary to replace the clutch sleeve assembly and both synchronizer rings.

Synchronizer Rings

1. Inspect the synchronizer rings for smoothness.

TRANSMISSION 7-9

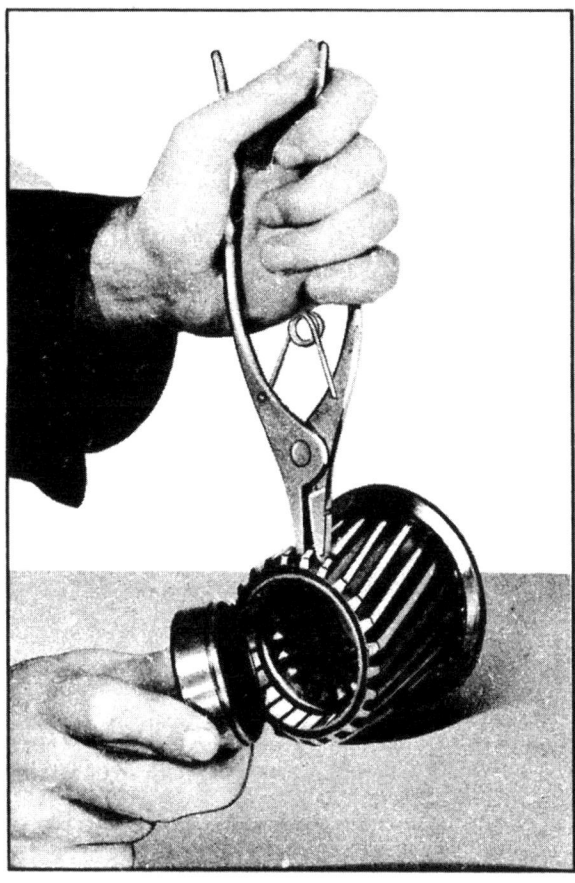

Fig. 12—Removing Synchronizer Ring

2. Place the synchronizer rings in the synchronizing cones and check with thumbs to see that rings do not rock. Excessive rocking indicates a poor fit between the rings and cone, which will not permit proper synchronizing of gears during shifting.

Synchronizer Energizing Spring

1. It will be noticed upon examining these springs that one of the ends is slightly offset. Each spring must be assembled in its groove in the clutch gear and the second speed gear with the offset or locking end between the third and fourth teeth of either of the two banks of teeth on these gears, thus keeping the spring from turning in its groove (fig. 13).

2. Under normal operation it should never be necessary to replace the energizing springs; however, should an energizing spring be removed for any reason, a new spring should be installed. The spring may be removed by slipping a thin blade under the spring and raising it sufficiently to slide it off over the clutch gear teeth.

Fig. 13—Correct Position of Energizing Spring

CAUTION: In replacing either energizing spring, be very careful not to distort the spring when expanding it over the clutch teeth.

Reverse Idler Gear Bushings

1. The bushings used in the idler gear are pressed into the gear then peened into holes in the bores to lock them into place, and are accurately bored with special diamond boring tools. This insures the positive alignment of the bushings and their shafts, as well as proper meshing of the gears. Because of the high degree of accuracy to which these parts are machined, the bushings are not serviced separately.

2. Check bushings for excessive wear by using a narrow feeler gauge between the shaft and the bushing. The proper clearance is from .002" to .004".

Countergear Needle Bearings

1. All countergear needle bearings should be inspected closely and if excessive wear shows they should all be replaced as well as the shaft.

TRANSMISSION ASSEMBLY

Reverse Idler Gear

1. Lubricate the reverse idler thrustwashers and install the gear and thrustwashers in the transmission case with the gear having the chamfered teeth to the rear of the case.

2. Install the idler shaft, making sure that the lock pin hole in the shaft lines up with the hole in the case at the same angle (fig. 14).

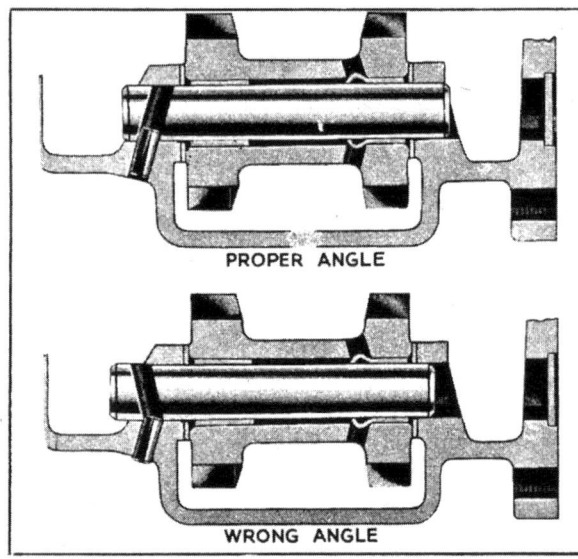

Fig. 14—Reverse Idler Gear Shaft and Lock Pin

3. Use a new idler shaft lock pin, coat the pin with Permatex and drive it in approximately $\frac{1}{16}$" beyond flush with case; peen the hole slightly. This lock pin must be a tight fit in the case to prevent oil leaks.
4. Install the idler shaft expansion plug in the case. A new plug should always be used whenever possible.

Countergear

1. Place some cup grease in the roller bearing area of each end of the countergear and install the 25 rollers in each end. The grease will hold the rollers in place while placing the gear into case and installing the countershaft (fig. 15).
2. Install the countergear in the case; lubricate the forward thrustwasher, and install it between the countergear and case.
3. Feed the assembly tool J-1617 (fig. 16) in from the front, tapered end first, picking up

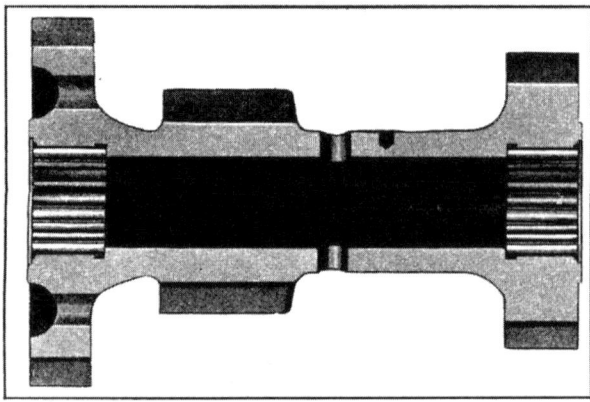

Fig. 15—Roller Bearing Countergear

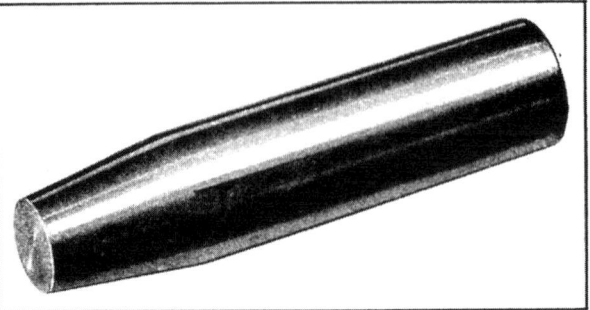

Fig. 16—Countershaft Assembly Tool

the forward thrustwasher and the countergear being careful to keep the roller bearings in place.
4. Lubricate the countershaft and install it in from the front, pushing the assembly tool ahead of it (fig. 17).
5. Lubricate the rear thrustwasher and slip it between the countergear and case, picking it up with the assembly tool as it is pushed through by the shaft.

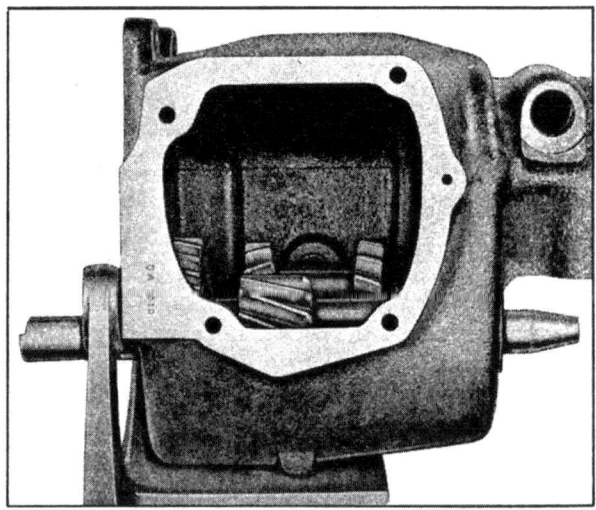

Fig. 17—Assembly of Countershaft

6. The flat on the forward end of the shaft engages the clutch housing when transmission is installed in chassis, and keeps the countershaft from turning. This flat must be horizontal and at the top, or the transmission cannot be assembled to clutch housing.

Rear Bearing

1. Install the rear bearing lock ring in the case. Start the bearing in from the rear making sure the wide side is to the front of case and use the lock ring expanding tool J-3185, to expand the ring in the case.
2. Using a brass drift, tap the bearing on the outer race until it passes inside the lock ring;

then remove the lock ring expanding tool and continue to tap the bearing until the lock ring seats in the groove in the bearing.

Synchronizing Clutch Sleeve
1. Install the synchronizer rings and retainers in the counterbores in the ends of the clutch sleeve.

   NOTE: Make sure retainers seat in groove all the way around the rings.

2. Install the first and reverse sliding gear on the second and third speed clutch. Mesh the clutch teeth of the second speed gear with the internal splines of the second and third speed clutch.
3. Coat the grooved side of the thrustwasher with grease and place the washer on the back face of the second speed gear.
4. Install the second and third speed clutch assembly in the transmission case. Insert finger through the rear bearing to line up the thrustwasher and second speed gear with the bearing.

Mainshaft
1. For initial lubrication, place transmission lubricant on second speed bearing area of the mainshaft. When installing the mainshaft, the lugs on the front synchronizer must slide through the slots in the mainshaft spline. Push the shaft into the clutch sleeve as far as possible by hand, picking up the second speed gear and thrustwasher.
2. Turn the yoke of the Mainshaft Removing and Replacing Tool J-938, down on the threads and screw adapter J-938-7, onto puller shaft, then install the tool shaft into the threaded end of the mainshaft. Bolt the yoke of the tool to the rear face of the transmission case.
3. Turn the tool handle counterclockwise until the main shaft is seated in the rear bearing. The proper seating of the shaft may be determined by checking the end play of the second speed gear which should be approximately .010".
4. Remove the tool from the rear face of transmission case.

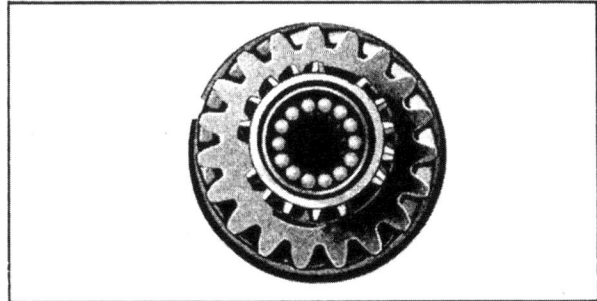

Fig. 18—Main Shaft Pilot Bearing Rollers in Clutch Gear

5. Place some cup grease in the mainshaft pilot hole in the clutch gear and install the 14 roller bearings (fig. 18). After being assembled in the pilot hole, these bearings will lock themselves in place and cannot fall out. Install the clutch gear in the transmission case.
6. Using a brass drift, tap the clutch gear bearing on the outer race until the bearing locating ring seats against the case, being careful to drive the assembly straight to prevent damage to the mainshaft pilot and pilot bearing.

   CAUTION: During this operation make sure that the synchronizer ring lugs line up with the slots between the clutch teeth on the clutch gear.

7. Install the clutch gear bearing retainer and gasket, making sure that the oil slot in the retainer lines up with the oil slot in the front face of the transmission case. Do not allow the gasket to protrude beyond the edge of the retainer.
8. Install the retainer screws, using the special shakeproof washers. Tighten the retaining capscrews to 10-12 ft. lbs. torque.

Universal Joint
1. Install the spacer, speedometer drive gear and universal joint spacer on mainshaft. Install the speedometer driven gear in the housing.
2. Install bearing support, indexing the ⅜" diameter hole in support assembly with the tapped hole in the case. Install special square head pipe plug.
3. Slide the universal joint front yoke on main shaft, install washer and capscrew, tighten to 15-20 ft. lbs.

Side Cover Assembly
1. With transmission gears in neutral and shifter forks in neutral position, install cover to transmission using a new gasket and tighten retaining capscrews securely.

   NOTE: Hump on first and reverse shifter fork must be toward rear of transmission (fig. 4).

2. Carefully note that locating pin hole in cover flange is indexed with locating pin in case and install retaining capscrews; tighten to 10-12 ft. lbs. torque.

UNIVERSAL JOINT BALL ADJUSTMENT

Due to construction of the universal ball joint on the ½ and ¾ ton trucks it is important that proper adjustment be made at this point.

This type joint, if improperly adjusted, may

result in oil leakage if too loose, or a complaint of transmission noise if too tight.

Whenever the universal joint is broken for any service operation, or should a leak at this point be experienced, the adjustment should be performed with the ball joint collar oil seal (cork) removed. Attempted adjustment with this cork seal in place, whether it be a new or old seal, will give a false adjustment.

The following procedure should be followed in making this adjustment:

1. On ½ ton models, remove universal joint ball from torque tube and on ¾ ton models, remove intermediate universal joint yoke and dust shield and then remove bearing support bracket and rubber cushion from propeller shaft housing.
2. Wash the universal ball (½ ton) or ball end of propeller shaft housing (¾ ton) thoroughly in cleaning solvent, then inspect it for roughness. If ball is rough, smooth up with fine emery paper or if deeply scored, replace.
3. Using four new universal ball collar shims as a starting point, install universal ball and collar on ½ ton, or housing and collar on ¾ ton. Tighten attaching bolts to 8-12 ft. lbs. torque.

   NOTE: Do not install ball joint collar oil seal (cork) at this time.

4. With attaching bolts tight, place both hands on the universal ball or on the housing assembly close to the ball (fig. 19). If the as-

Fig. 19—Checking Ball Adjustment

sembly can be moved and is a snug fit, the torque ball is properly adjusted.

NOTE: If the ball or housing assembly cannot be moved by hand or is too loose, remove the ball collar attaching bolts and remove shims to tighten or add shims to loosen until proper adjustment is secured.

5. Remove universal ball or housing assembly noting number of shims used for later assembly.

TRANSMISSION INSTALLATION

1. Install transmission through opening in floor.
2. Place the transmission on guide pins and start mainshaft in clutch disc and slide forward making sure the step at the end of the countershaft is flush with the face of the transmission and engages properly with the clutch housing. This keeps the shaft from turning as well as helps align transmission properly.
3. Install the two lower transmission mounting bolts and lockwashers and tighten securely. Remove the two upper guide pins and install the top mounting bolts and lockwashers and tighten securely.
4. Install flywheel underpan.
5. On ½ ton:
   a. Install a new ball collar oil seal (cork) in ball collar, after first lubricating it with a graphite grease for lubrication. Then assemble collar with number of shims determined at adjustment and the universal ball on the torque tube.
   b. Lower the propeller shaft into position and align yokes together. With the lock plates in position, install and tighten securely, the capscrews which retain front trunnion bearings to front yoke. Bend up the tangs on the lock plates.
   c. Slide the universal ball and collar forward, position the gaskets and install the capscrews which attach the universal ball collar to the rear face of transmission case. Tighten capscrews to 8-12 ft. lbs. torque.
   d. Install the capscrews which attach the transmission support to frame cross member and tighten securely.
   e. Install the battery.
6. On ¾ ton:
   a. Install a new ball collar oil seal (cork) in ball collar, after first lubricating it with a graphite grease and assemble the number of shims determined at adjustment on the propeller shaft forward of the collar.
   b. Assemble rubber cushion to housing and assemble support bracket over cushion.
   c. Install bearing dust shield and universal joint front yoke. Install nut and tighten securely. Lock nut with cotter pin.
   d. Slide the propeller shaft assembly onto transmission universal joint assembly and install nuts attaching propeller shaft bearing support bracket to frame cross member.

e. Slide the ball collar forward, position the gaskets and install the four retaining capscrews. Tighten the capscrews to 8-12 ft. lbs. torque.
f. Raise front end of rear propeller shaft, align rear joint and intermediate joint for proper balance and install two trunnion bearing "U" clamps to intermediate universal joint and tighten securely.
7. Attach speedometer cable to speedometer driven gear.
8. Connect the shifter control rods to shifter levers at the transmission (fig. 2).
9. Install the transmission cover, floor mat, and the accelerator pedal.
10. Remove the square head pipe plug, lubricate the universal joint bearings through the opening, and replace the pipe plug.
11. Fill the transmission with 1½ pints of transmission lubricant.
12. Road test for transmission operation in all speeds.

TRANSMISSION SPECIFICATIONS

Type
Selective Syncromesh

Speeds
Three forward—one reverse

Mounting
Unit power plant

Gears
Helical

Bearings
Clutch Gear ....ND 954388
Mainshaft Pilot...14 Rollers...$\frac{3}{16}$" Dia. x $\frac{33}{64}$"
Mainshaft Rear ....ND 954168
Countershaft—Chevrolet 591211—⅛" Dia. x ¾"
Reverse ....Bronze
Transmission Rear ....Bronze

Gear Ratio
First 2.94-1
Second 1.68-1
Third 1-1
Reverse 2.94-1

Service Data—Mainshaft and Gears
Mainshaft Run Out ....Not Over 004"

Shifting
Remote........Mounted on Steering Column
Yoke Lock ....Ball

Lubricant
Capacity ....1½ pts.
Type ....SAE 90

TORQUE SPECIFICATIONS
3-SPEED TRANSMISSION

Clutch Gear Bearing Retainer Bolts 10-12 ft. lbs.
Transmission Cover Bolts ....10-12 ft. lbs.

Universal Joint Retainer Bolt.......15-20 ft. lbs.

FOUR-SPEED TRANSMISSION

INDEX

	Page
General Description	7-14
Minor Service Operations	7-18
Remote Control Gearshift Lever— Cab-Over-Engine	7-18
Gearshift Lever—Conventional and Forward Control	7-18
Transmission Cover—Conventional and Forward Control	7-18
Rear Bearing Retainer Oil Seal and/or Speedometer Gears	7-19
Major Service Operations	7-21
Transmission Removal	7-21
Transmission Disassembly	7-21
Repairs	7-22
Clutch Gear and Shaft	7-22
Mainshaft Assembly	7-23
Countershaft	7-27
Reverse Idler Gear Bushings	7-27
Countershaft Front Bearing	7-28
Transmission Assembly	7-28
Final Inspection	7-29
Transmission Installation	7-30
Specifications	7-30

GENERAL DESCRIPTION

The four speed transmission is a heavy duty type, designed to give efficient service in every type of truck operation. The transmission incorporates synchromesh action in second, third and fourth gears. All gears are helical except first and reverse.

The transmission case is made of cast iron, accurately machined to give the proper alignment of the gears and their shafts. All gears are machined from drop forged steel gear blanks, heat treated for strength and long life. The shafts are machined from high grade steel, heat treated and ground to close limits.

The clutch gear is supported by a heavy-duty ball bearing. The forward end of the mainshaft is supported by a loose roller type bearing inside the clutch gear, while the rear end receives its support from a ball bearing in the transmission case.

The countershaft is supported at the rear by a single row ball bearing which takes the thrust load, and by a roller bearing at the front.

The idler gear bearings are steel-backed, bronze bushings, staked in the gear hub. The idler shaft has oil pockets for improved lubrication. Figure 20 shows the cross section of this transmission

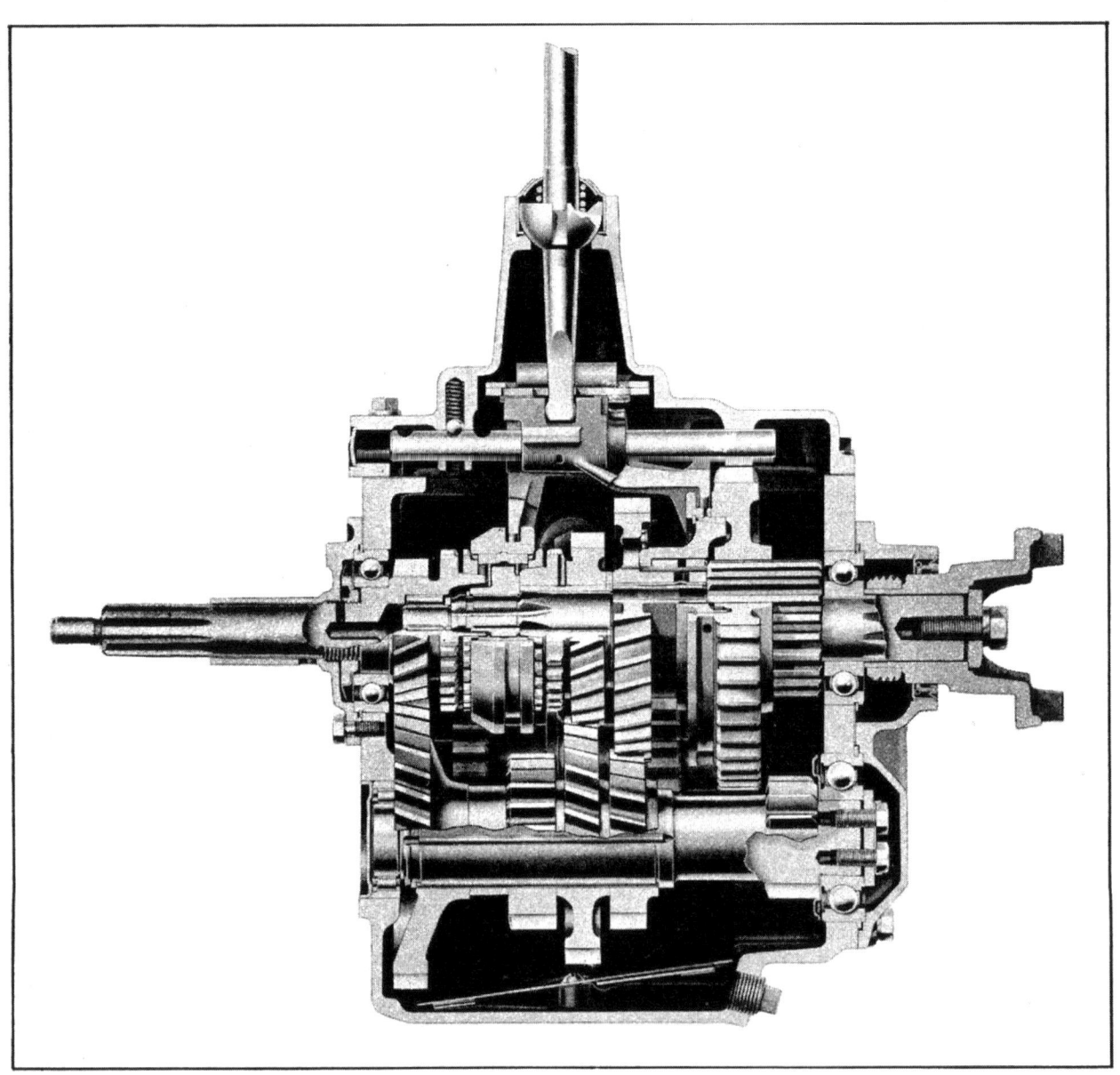

Fig. 20—Cross Section Four-Speed Transmission

and the relative position of all of the parts.

All illustrations are of the 1948 and early 1949 transmissions. During 1949 a change was made in the mainshaft and first and reverse sliding gear incorporating a method of spline attachment known as the skip tooth design (fig. 21). This

Fig. 21—Skip Tooth Design Mainshaft

change provides for a closer fit between the gear and mainshaft at the spline location.

Also at this same time, a change was made in the third and fourth speed clutch hub. In this later design (fig. 22) the key slots in the clutch

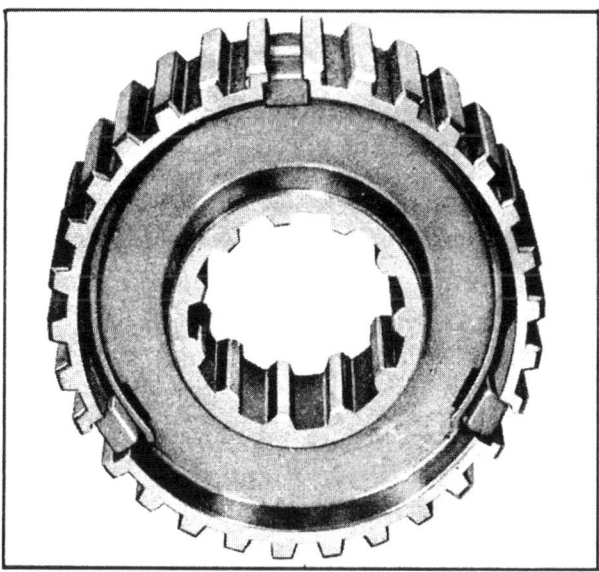

Fig. 22—Clutch Hub Key Slots

hub are machined at the outer edges to provide shoulders for retaining the clutch keys in their proper position. Neither of these changes affect overhaul procedure and these parts may be used in 1948 and early 1949 models.

Operation

Synchronization is obtained in all forward speeds except first. The second speed synchronizer cone is located in the first and reverse gear as as illustrated in Figure 23. The second speed syn-

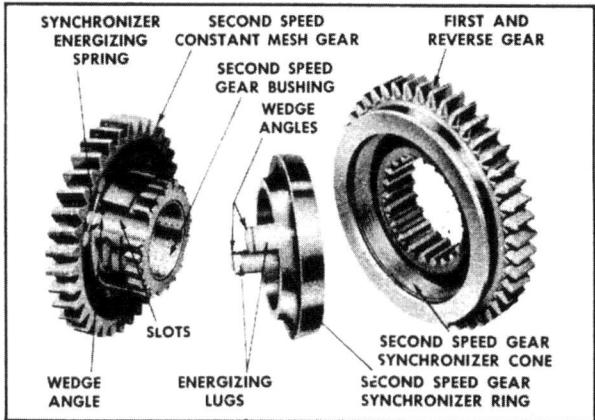

Fig. 23—Second Speed Synchronizer Parts

chronizer ring is also located in the first and reverse gear and is retained in position by a retainer ring. The energizing lugs are part of the synchronizer ring and the two synchronizer energizing springs are located on the second speed gear which is a constant mesh gear.

The first and reverse gear is splined to the mainshaft and rotates at propeller shaft speed. The second speed gear is free of the mainshaft, but is in constant mesh with the second speed gear on the countershaft and its speed is controlled by the engine. The second speed gear therefore must be synchronized to first and reverse gear speed before a shift into second speed may be accomplished.

When the shift lever is moved toward the second speed position, it operates the shifter fork which in turn slides the first and reverse gear forward on the mainshaft splines.

The second speed synchronizer ring moves with the first and reverse gear and as it moves forward the two energizing lugs contact the energizing springs on the second speed gear. This initial contact causes a friction pick up between the synchronizer ring and the second speed synchronizer cone which is transmitted through the driving lugs to the second speed gear. Further forward movement of the first and reverse gear causes the wedge angle on the driving lugs of the synchronizer ring to contact the wedge angle in the second speed gear. This action increases the braking friction between the second and first speed gears which brings them to the same speed. When they have reached the same speed the pressure on the wedge angles and synchronizer is relieved, permitting the clutch teeth on the second speed gear to engage the internal splines of the first and reverse sliding gear, thereby completing the shift.

Synchronization of third and fourth speeds is accomplished through the use of a clutch hub splined to the mainshaft. This hub has external teeth on which a clutch sleeve is splined. A detent around the inside diameter of the clutch sleeve allows for positioning of three clutch keys which are held out in engagement with this detent by two clutch key springs one on each side of the clutch hub. The clutch keys in turn are engaged with slots in two synchronizer cones mounted one on each side of the hub. This entire assembly rotates at propeller shaft speed and is used to synchronize the gear speeds when shifting into either third or fourth gear. Both clutch gear and third speed gear are constant mesh gears and their speed is controlled by the engine. Parts making up the shifting unit, with exception of the clutch hub, are shown in Figure 24.

The synchronization of the third speed gear is accomplished in the following manner. When the shifter lever is moved toward the third speed position it operates the shifter fork which in turn slides the clutch sleeve on the clutch hub toward the third speed gear. The clutch keys which are held in the detent on the inside diameter of the sleeve by the two clutch key springs move with the sleeve. As the clutch keys move they push the bronze third speed synchronizer cone into contact with the steel cone on the third speed gear and start the synchronization of the third speed gear. Further movement of the clutch sleeve causes the wedge angles of the clutch sleeve internal teeth to apply additional pressure to the wedge angles on the bronze synchronizer cone. This additional pressure on the synchronizer cone brings about the full synchronization of the clutch and third speed gear. At this instant, pressure is relieved from the synchronizer cone allowing final engagement of internal teeth of clutch sleeve and external drive teeth of third speed gear.

During all of this, the clutch gear synchronizer cone is inoperative. The action while shifting into fourth speed is identical with that described above except that shifting movements are in the opposite direction and obviously the third speed synchonizer cone remains inoperative. Figure 25 shows exploded view of transmission assembly.

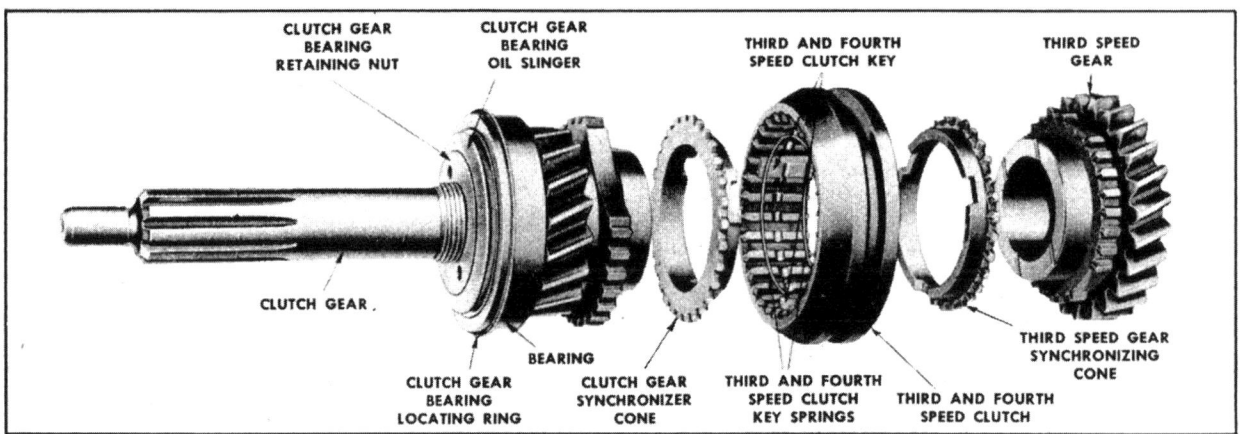

Fig. 24—Layout of Shifting Unit Parts

TRANSMISSION 7-17

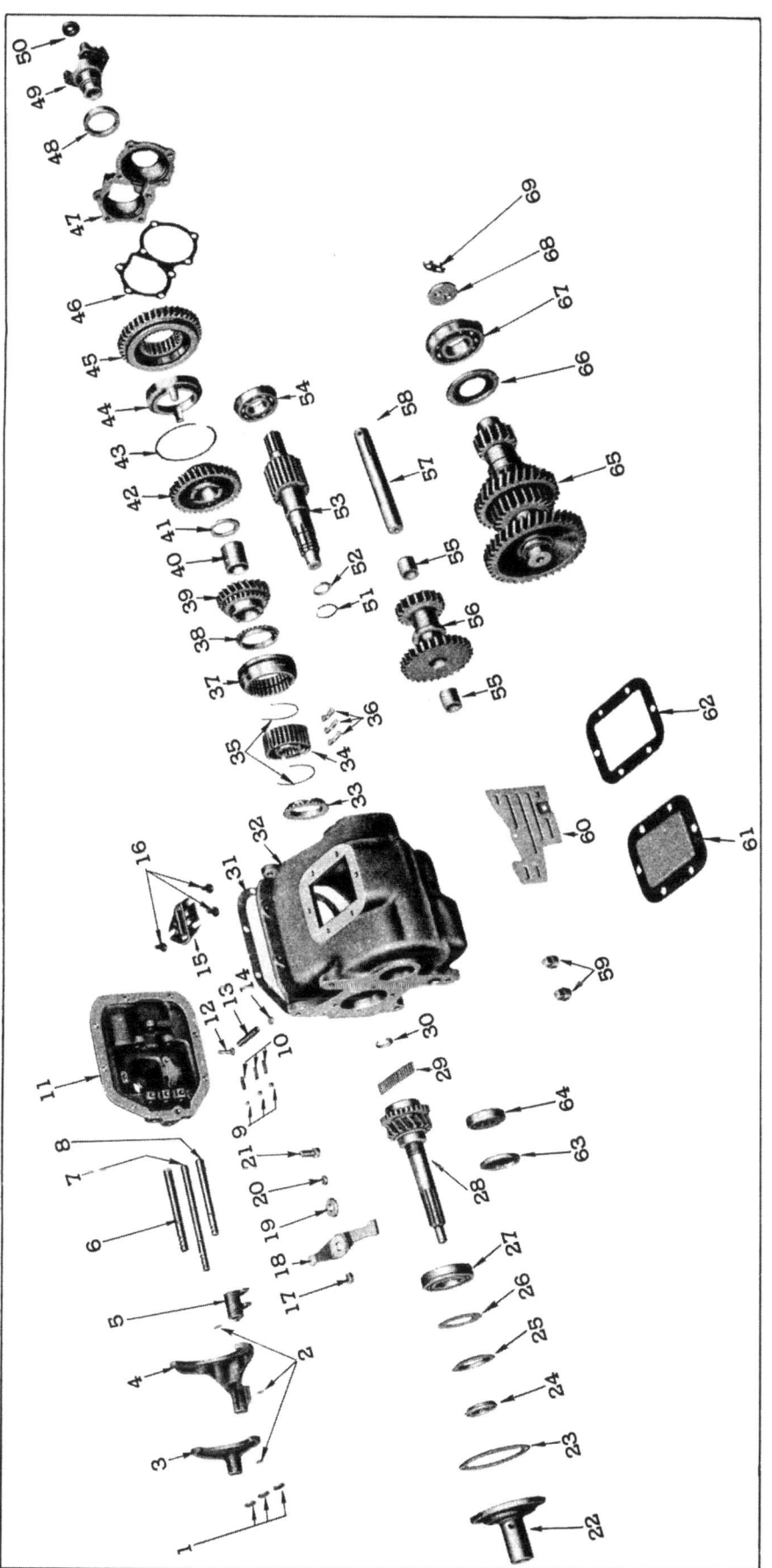

Fig. 25—Layout of 4-Speed Transmission Parts

1. Expansion Plug
2. Taper Pin
3. Third and Fourth Speed Shifter Yoke
4. First and Second Speed Shifter Yoke
5. Reverse Shifter Head
6. Third and Fourth Speed Shifter Shaft
7. First and Second Speed Shifter Shaft
8. Reverse Shifter Shaft
9. Yoke Lock Ball
10. Yoke Lock Ball Spring
11. Transmission Cover
12. Reverse Shifter Compression Pin
13. Reverse Shifter Compression Pin Spring
14. Expansion Plug
15. Shifter Interlock Assembly
16. Shifter Interlock Pin
17. Hexagon Nut
18. Reverse Shifter Lever
19. Flat Washer
20. Reverse Shifter Lever Spacer
21. Hexagon Head Bolt
22. Clutch Gear Bearing Retainer
23. Clutch Gear Bearing Retainer Gasket
24. Clutch Gear Bearing Retainer Nut
25. Clutch Gear Bearing Oil Slinger
26. Clutch Gear Bearing Deflector
27. Clutch Gear Bearing
28. Clutch Gear
29. Transmission Mainshaft Pilot Roller Bearings
30. Transmission Mainshaft Pilot Roller Bearing Retainer
31. Transmission Cover Gasket
32. Transmission Case
33. Clutch Gear Synchronizer Cone
34. Third and Fourth Speed Clutch Hub
35. Third and Fourth Speed Clutch Key Spring Ring
36. Third and Fourth Speed Clutch Key
37. Third and Fourth Speed Clutch Sleeve
38. Third Speed Gear Synchronizer Cone
39. Third Speed Gear
40. Third Speed Gear Mainshaft Bushing
41. Second Speed Gear Thrust Washer
42. Second Speed Constant Mesh Gear
43. Second Speed Gear Synchronizing Ring Retainer
44. Second Speed Gear Synchronizing Ring
45. First and Reverse Gear
46. Transmission Rear Bearing Retainer Gasket
47. Transmission Rear Bearing Retainer
48. Oil Seal
49. Universal Joint Front Flange
50. Flat Washer
51. Third and Fourth Speed Clutch Hub Retainer Ring
52. Transmission Mainshaft Pilot Roller Bearing Spacer
53. Transmission Mainshaft
54. Transmission Mainshaft Bearing
55. Reverse Idler Bushing
56. Reverse Idler Gear
57. Reverse Idler Gear Shaft
58. Taper Pin
59. Drain and Filler Plugs
60. Chip Collector
61. Power Take Off Cover
62. Power Take Off Cover Gasket
63. Countershaft Front Bearing Spacer
64. Countershaft Front Roller Bearing
65. Countershaft Assembly
66. Countershaft Rear Bearing Oil Deflector
67. Countershaft Rear Bearing
68. Countershaft Rear Bearing Retainer
69. Lock Plate

MINOR SERVICE OPERATIONS

REMOTE CONTROL GEARSHIFT LEVER— C.O.E.

Removal

1. Disconnect the gearshift lever from top of engine cover.
2. Lower cloth boot wire and raise boot above transmission cover tower.
3. Remove the nut from the stub gearshift lever and raise the gearshift lever link assembly from the top of the lever.
4. Remove gearshift lever assembly with tool K-353.

Installation

1. Install the gearshift lever link assembly to the top of the stub gearshift lever. Replace the nut and tighten.
2. Install the boot and cloth boot wire over the transmission cover tower.
3. Replace the remote control gearshift lever on top of engine cover.

TRANSMISSION GEARSHIFT LEVER— ALL MODELS EXCEPT C. O. E.

Removal

1. Slide the open side of K-353 Gearshift Lever Remover and Replacer over the lever, engage the lugs of the tool in the open slot of the retainer (fig. 26), then press down on the

Fig. 26—Removing Gearshift Lever

tool and turn it to the left to disengage the lugs on the retainer.
2. Lift the lever out of the cover.

Installation

1. Place the gearshift lever in position in transmission cover.
2. Slide the open end of K-353 Gearshift Lever Remover and Replacer over the lever, engage the lugs of the tool in the open slot of the retainer, then press down on the tool and turn to the right to engage the lugs on the retainer.

TRANSMISSION COVER— ALL MODELS EXCEPT C. O. E.

Removal

1. Remove accelerator pedal, floor mat and transmission cover from body floor on conventional models. On Forward Control models, remove the front floor pan.
2. Remove gearshift lever from transmission cover, using the K-353 Gearshift Remover and Replacer.
3. Remove capscrews attaching transmission cover to transmission case and remove cover.

CAUTION: Place a piece of cardboard over transmission cover opening, using two of the cover attaching screws to hold it in place. This will keep anything from falling into the transmission case.

Disassembly

1. With a small punch drive out pins that retain shifter yokes and reverse shifter head to shifter shafts.

   NOTE: Pin holding reverse shifter head to shifter shaft must be removed and shifter head removed from cover before first and second speed shifter yoke retainer pin can be removed.

2. Turn shifter shafts one-half turn to raise yoke lock balls out of the notches in the shifter shafts and drive shafts out of cover and shifter yokes. Shifter shafts will push expansion plugs out ahead of them.

   CAUTION: Care should be exercised so that yoke lock balls and springs which are located in the cover are not lost as the shifter shafts are removed.

3. Should it be necessary to remove the shifter interlock assembly, cut the ends from the three shifter interlock pins and drive pins out of cover to remove assembly. If interlock assembly is removed, new shifter interlock pins must be used and properly supported when re-riveting.
4. Should it be necessary to replace reverse shifter compression pin or spring, the reverse shifter compression pin spring expansion plug must be removed from the cover. Extreme care must be used in removing this expansion plug as it is under spring tension.

5. In replacing reverse shifter compression pin or spring, support cover in a vise and apply pressure to hold expansion plug in place while staking in position (fig. 27).

Fig. 27—Staking Expansion Plug

Assembly

1. In reassembling the transmission cover, care must be used in installing the shifter shafts. They should be installed in the order shown in Figure 28, namely: reverse speed, low speed and high speed.

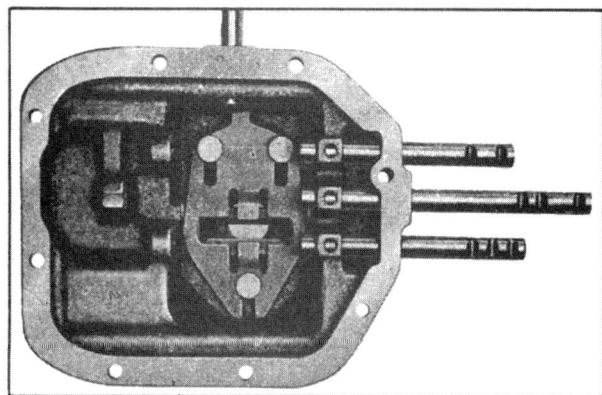

Fig. 28—Order of Shifter Shaft Assembly

2. Place yoke lock ball springs and yoke lock balls in position in holes in cover.
3. Start shifter shafts into cover, depress yoke lock balls with small punch and push shafts on over balls. Hold shifter yokes and reverse shifter head in position and push shafts on through yokes and reverse shifter head, until retainer pin holes in yokes and reverse shifter head align with holes in shafts. Then install tapered grooved retainer pins.
4. Install shifter shaft hole expansion plugs and stake them in place.

Installation

1. Remove cardboard covering from transmission case.
2. Make sure all transmission gears are in neutral and install cover assembly with new gasket to transmission case, making sure shifting yokes slide over their proper gears and that reverse shifter lever properly engages reverse shifter head.
3. Install transmission cover attaching bolts and tighten to 20-25 ft. lbs.
4. Using K-353 Gearshift Lever Remover and Replacer, replace gearshift lever and check operation by shifting into all gears.
5. On conventional models, replace transmission cover to body floor, install floor mat and replace accelerator pedal. On Forward Control models replace front floor pan.

REAR BEARING RETAINER OIL SEAL AND/OR SPEEDOMETER GEARS

Removal and Installation—1 Ton and (1948-50) 1½ and 2 Ton

1. Break universal joint at transmission universal joint flange by removing two trunnion bearing "U" clamps and tape bearings.
2. Remove speedometer driven gear from bearing retainer.
3. Remove universal joint flange retaining bolt, lockwasher and flat washer and remove yoke and speedometer drive gear from mainshaft.
4. To replace rear bearing retainer oil seal:
    a. Drain lubricant from transmission and remove rear bearing retainer and gasket.
    b. Drive old seal out of bearing retainer.
    c. Lightly coat the outer diameter of the new oil seal with Permatex and install it in retainer using J-1488 Differential Side Bearing Replacer (fig. 29).

Fig. 29—Installing Oil Seal

TRANSMISSION 7-20

    d. Install bearing retainer to transmission case using a new gasket. Place Permatex or other suitable sealing compound on bolt threads and tighten to 20-25 ft. lbs. torque.

5. To replace speedometer gears, press speedometer drive gear off hub of universal joint flange and press new gear into position using K-343 Speedometer Replacer.

NOTE: The drive gear must be pressed onto the front yoke with the chamfer on the O.D. of the gear away from the universal joint.

6. Install universal joint flange and speedometer gear assembly and install universal joint flange flat washer, lockwasher and retainer bolt. Tighten bolt to 60-65 ft. lbs.

7. Replace speedometer driven gear.

8. Connect the universal joint to the universal joint flange.

9. If the transmission was drained, refill with 5½ pts. of S. A. E. 90 gear lubricant.

Removal and Installation (1951) 1½ and 2 Ton

1. Disconnect the intermediate universal joint by removing the two trunnion bearing "U" clamps, split joint and lower front end of rear propeller shaft to floor.

2. Remove the four universal joint flange nuts.

3. Remove nuts attaching propeller shaft bearing support bracket to frame cross member and remove front propeller shaft and bearing support assembly.

4. Disconnect the end of brake shoe lever from brake shoe operating link by removing adjusting nut, lever, lever spring and flat washer.

5. Remove anchor pin lock at upper end of outer brake shoe.

6. Disconnect outer shoe spring, loosen outer shoe adjusting bolt lock nut and back off the adjusting bolt until there is sufficient clearance for the outer shoe flange.

7. Slide the brake shoes and lever assembly straight back and remove from vehicle.

8. Remove speedometer driven gear from bearing retainer.

9. Remove universal joint flange retaining bolt, lockwasher and flat washer and remove parking brake drum and universal joint flange assembly from mainshaft.

10. To replace rear bearing retainer oil seal:
    a. Drain lubricant from transmission and remove rear bearing retainer and gasket.

    b. Drive old seal out of bearing retainer.

    c. Lightly coat the outer diameter of the new oil seal with Permatex and install it in retainer using J-1488 Differential Side Bearing Replacer (fig. 29).

    d. Install bearing retainer to transmission case using a new gasket. Place Permatex, or other suitable sealing compound, on bolt threads and tighten to 20-25 ft. lbs. torque.

11. To replace speedometer gears, press speedometer drive gear off hub of universal joint flange and press new gear into position using K-343 Speedometer Replacer.

NOTE: The drive gear must be pressed onto the front yoke with the chamfer on the O.D. of the gear away from the universal joint.

12. Install parking brake drum and universal joint flange assembly and install universal joint flange flat washer, lockwasher and retainer bolt. Tighten bolt to 60-65 ft. lbs. torque.

13. Replace speedometer driven gear.

14. Install the parking brake shoes and lever assembly, positioning the shoes on both sides of the parking brake drum while sliding the upper end of the outer shoe on the anchor pin.

15. Install anchor pin lock at upper end of outer shoe.

16. Install outer shoe spring and run adjusting bolt up to approximate position.

17. Connect the end of the brake shoe lever to the operating link by installing flat washer, spring, lever and adjusting nut on end of operating link.

18. Adjust the parking brake as outlined in Brake Section under "Minor Service Operations."

19. Install front propeller shaft and bearing support assembly positioning the universal joint front yoke on the 4 flange bolts. Install and tighten securely the nuts attaching propeller shaft support bracket to frame cross member.

20. Install four universal joint flange lockwashers and nuts and tighten securely.

21. Raise front end of rear propeller shaft, align trunnion bearings with front yoke and install two trunnion bearing "U" clamps and tighten securely.

MAJOR SERVICE OPERATIONS

TRANSMISSION

Removal

1. Remove screws which fasten steering jacket grommet to floor and slide grommet up jacket out of the way.
2. Remove accelerator pedal and floor mat.
3. Remove the sheet metal screws attaching transmission cover to body floor and remove cover. On Forward Control models, remove both the front and rear floor pans.
4. Remove speedometer cable from transmission rear bearing retainer.
5. On 1 ton and (1948-50) 1½ and 2 ton remove cotter key and pin attaching parking brake pull rod assembly to parking lever.
6. On (1951) 1½ and 2 ton, disconnect parking brake lever return spring from parking brake operating lever and remove cotter key and pin attaching inner and outer levers to parking brake operating lever.
7. Remove parking brake lever lock, flat washer and spring and remove parking brake lever.
8. Drain the lubricant from the transmission.
9. On 1 ton and (1948-50) 1½ and 2 ton break the universal joint at transmission universal joint flange and tape bearings in the trunnions.
10. On (1951) 1½ and 2 ton:
    a. Disconnect the intermediate universal joint by removing the two trunnion bearing "U" clamps, split joint and lower front end of rear propeller shaft to floor.
    b. Remove the four universal joint flange nuts.
    c. Remove nuts attaching propeller shaft bearing support bracket to frame cross member and remove front propeller shaft and bearing assembly.
11. Remove the two top capscrews attaching the transmission to clutch housing and insert the two transmission Guide Pins J-1126 in these holes.
12. Remove the flywheel underpan and remove the two lower transmission to clutch housing capscrews.
13. Slide the transmission straight back on the guide pins until the clutch gear is free of the splines in the clutch disc. The guide pins in the top holes support the transmission during this operation and prevent damage to the clutch disc.
14. Remove transmission from vehicle.

Disassembly

1. Remove transmission cover assembly by lifting straight up from transmission.
2. Remove reverse shifter lever bolt nut, screw bolt out of case and remove reverse shifter lever, bolt spacer and large flat washer.
3. Remove clutch gear bearing retainer and gasket and remove clutch gear from case using J-2669 Clutch Gear Remover (fig. 30).

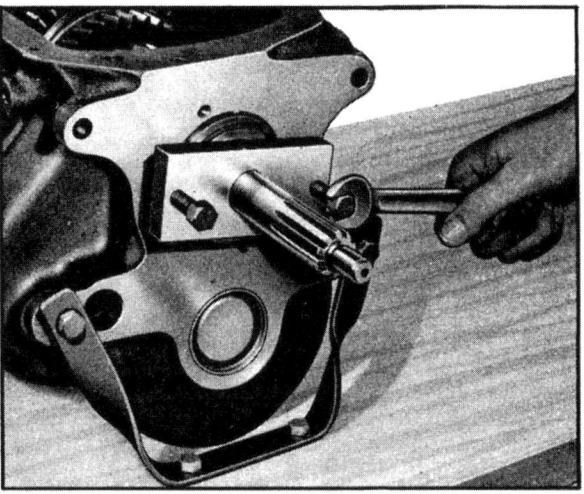

Fig. 30—Removing Clutch Gear

CAUTION: Index cut out section of clutch gear with countershaft driven gear to obtain clearance in removing clutch gear and shaft.

4. Remove clutch gear synchronizer cone and transmission mainshaft pilot bearing roller spacer from end of mainshaft.
5. Remove speedometer driven gear from rear bearing retainer.
6. On 1 ton and (1948-50) 1½ and 2 ton place transmission in two gears at once to lock gears and remove universal joint flange retaining bolt, lockwasher, plain washer and universal joint from flange.
7. On (1951) 1½ and 2 ton:
    a. Disconnect the end of the brake shoe lever from brake shoe operating link by removing adjusting nut, lever, lever spring and flat washer.
    b. Remove anchor pin lock at upper end of outer brake shoe.
    c. Disconnect outer shoe spring and remove outer shoe adjusting bolt plate.
    d. Slide the brake shoes and lever assembly straight back and remove from the vehicle.
    e. Remove the parking brake operating lever lock bolt and remove the operating lever and operating link.
    f. Remove the universal joint flange retaining bolt, lockwasher and flat washer and

remove parking brake drum and universal joint flange assembly from mainshaft.
8. Remove rear bearing retainer and gasket.
9. To remove the mainshaft assembly the entire assembly must be pulled back to remove rear mainshaft bearing from the case. Install J-2667 Mainshaft and Bearing Assembly Remover and Replacer to rear face of transmission case and pull shaft and bearing assembly out of bearing pilot hole in case (fig. 31).

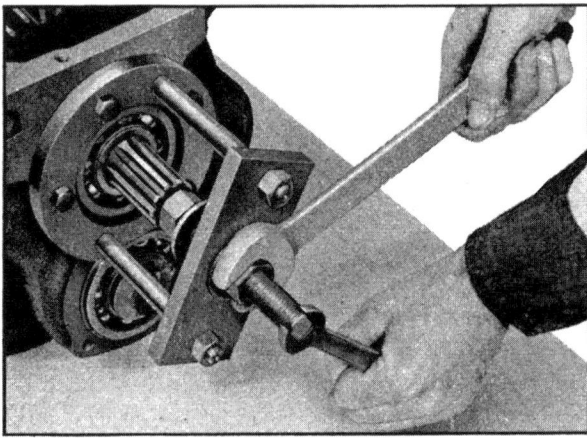

Fig. 31—Removing Mainshaft

10. Remove J-2667 from back of transmission case and then move mainshaft assembly back as far as it will go.
11. To remove mainshaft rear bearing install J-1619 Propeller Shaft Bearing Remover and remove bearing from shaft (fig. 32).

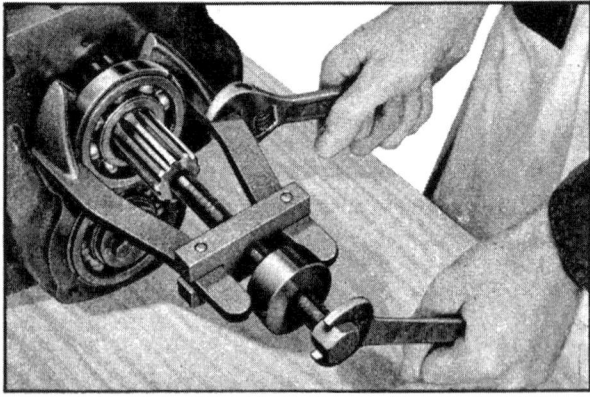

Fig. 32—Removing Mainshaft Rear Bearing

12. With first and second speed sliding gear forward, raise front end of mainshaft up and lift mainshaft assembly out of case.
13. To remove reverse idler gear drive out reverse gear shaft retaining pin using a small punch. This pin is driven into the shaft after which the shaft may be driven out of the case from front to rear using a brass drift. With shaft removed, remove reverse idler gear from case.
14. To remove countershaft assembly, drive a punch through the countershaft front bearing spacer and pry spacer out.
15. Drive countershaft with rear bearing to the rear of case using a brass drift on front end of shaft until rear bearing is driven out of the case.
16. Remove rear bearing retainer bolt lock plate, retainer bolts and retainer.
17. Using TR-278-R Differential Side Bearing puller, remove rear bearing and oil deflector from rear end of countershaft (fig. 33).

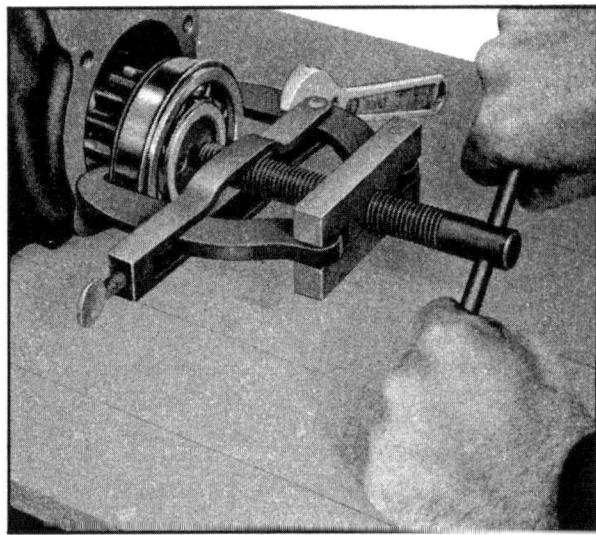

Fig. 33—Removing Countershaft Rear Bearing

18. Raise front end of countershaft assembly and lift from case.
19. Remove transmission chip collector from bottom of transmission case.

REPAIRS

Clutch Gear and Shaft—Disassembly

1. Remove transmission mainshaft pilot bearing rollers (18) from clutch gear if not already removed and remove transmission mainshaft pilot bearing roller retainer from recess in shaft.
2. Place clutch shaft in a vise and using J-2670 Spanner Wrench, remove clutch gear bearing retaining nut (fig. 34), oil slinger and oil deflector.
3. To remove bearing, place clutch gear and bearing assembly in an arbor press and using J-2228 Press Plate mounted in press plate holder, press gear and shaft out of bearing (fig. 35).

TRANSMISSION 7-23

Fig. 34—Removing Clutch Gear Bearing Retainer Nut

Inspection

1. Wash all parts in cleaning solvent.
2. Inspect roller bearings for pits or galling.
3. Inspect bearing diameter in shaft recess for galling.
4. Inspect gear teeth for excessive wear.
5. Inspect clutch shaft pilot for excessive wear.
6. Rotate clutch gear bearing slowly by hand and check for roughness.

Assembly

1. Install bearing on shaft and using J-1453 Press Plate press bearing into position (fig. 36).

Fig. 35—Removing Clutch Gear Bearing

2. Install oil deflector, oil slinger and retainer nut. Note that nut is designed to fit contour of oil slinger.

   CAUTION: *When installing the above parts make sure the oil deflector centers around retainer nut hub.*

3. Place clutch shaft in vise and with Spanner Wrench J-2670 tighten retainer nut securely and stake in place.
4. Apply a small amount of grease to bearing surface in shaft recess, install (18) transmission mainshaft pilot roller bearings and install roller bearing retainer.

   NOTE: *This roller bearing retainer holds bearings in position (fig. 37) and in final transmission assembly is pushed forward into recess by mainshaft pilot.*

Fig. 36—Replacing Clutch Gear Bearing

Mainshaft Assembly—Disassembly

1. Remove third and fourth speed clutch hub retainer ring from pilot end of mainshaft.
2. Support assembly on first and reverse sliding gear in arbor press (fig. 38) and press mainshaft out of gear cluster.
3. Remove third and fourth speed clutch key springs from 3rd and 4th speed clutch hub and remove clutch sleeve from clutch hub.

   NOTE: *Exercise care not to lose (3) clutch keys.*

4. Remove third speed gear synchronizer cone from 3rd speed gear.
5. Remove third speed gear mainshaft bushing from 3rd speed gear.
6. Remove 3rd speed gear.

Fig. 37—Roller Bearing Retainer

NOTE: Second speed thrust washer goes between 3rd speed gear and 2nd speed gear.

7. Remove 2nd speed gear from 2nd speed synchronizing ring lugs.
8. Remove 2nd speed gear synchronizing ring retainer and remove second speed gear synchronizing ring from 1st speed gear.

Inspection

1. Wash all parts in cleaning solvent.
2. Inspect mainshaft for scoring or excessive wear at thrust surfaces or splines.
3. Inspect clutch hub and clutch sleeve for excessive wear and make sure sleeve slides freely on clutch hub. Also check fit of clutch hub on mainshaft splines.

   NOTE: Third and fourth speed clutch sleeve should slide freely on third and fourth speed clutch hub but clutch hub should be snug fit on shaft splines.

4. Inspect 3rd speed gear thrust surfaces for excessive scoring and inspect third speed gear mainshaft bushing for excessive wear.

   NOTE: 3rd speed gear must be a running fit on mainshaft bushing and mainshaft bushing should be press fit on shaft.

5. Check second speed thrust washer for excessive scoring.
6. Inspect 2nd speed gear for excessive wear at thrust surface or in bronze bushing. Check synchronizer springs for looseness or breakage. Synchronizer springs may be replaced by removing the rivets and installing a new spring with new special rivets.

   NOTE: If bushing is worn excessively the gear assembly must be replaced.

7. Inspect second speed gear synchronizing ring for excessive wear.
8. Inspect bronze synchronizer cone in 1st speed gear for excessive wear or damage. Also inspect clutch gear synchronizer cone and third speed gear synchronizer cone for excessive wear or damage.

   NOTE: First and reverse sliding gear must be sliding fit on mainshaft splines and must not have excessive radial or circumferential play.

9. Inspect all gear teeth for excessive wear.

Assembly

1. Install 2nd speed gear synchronizing ring into 1st and reverse sliding gear and install the second speed gear synchronizing ring retainer.

   CAUTION: Make sure synchronizing ring retainer is seated fully in snap ring groove of 1st speed gear.

2. Install universal joint yoke on mainshaft and tighten attaching bolt.

Fig. 38—Disassembly of Mainshaft

3. Place yoke in vise with shaft in a vertical position.
4. Slide the 1st and reverse sliding gear on the mainshaft splines with synchronizing ring toward front of shaft. Select a fit of the gear on the shaft by turning it about to several different spline positions to obtain the best possible fit (fig. 39).
5. Slide the gear onto the shaft to approximately the first gear position making sure that the energizing lugs are not touching the mainshaft.
6. Place a block of wood under one edge of the gear which will allow the opposite unsupported edge of the gear to drop downward.
7. Place a dial indicator so it rests against the top side of the unsupported edge of the gear at the shifter yoke groove.
8. Holding the supported side of the gear tightly against the block, lift gear at dial indicator position as far as possible (fig. 40). The amount of movement should not exceed .015" max. at the first gear position.

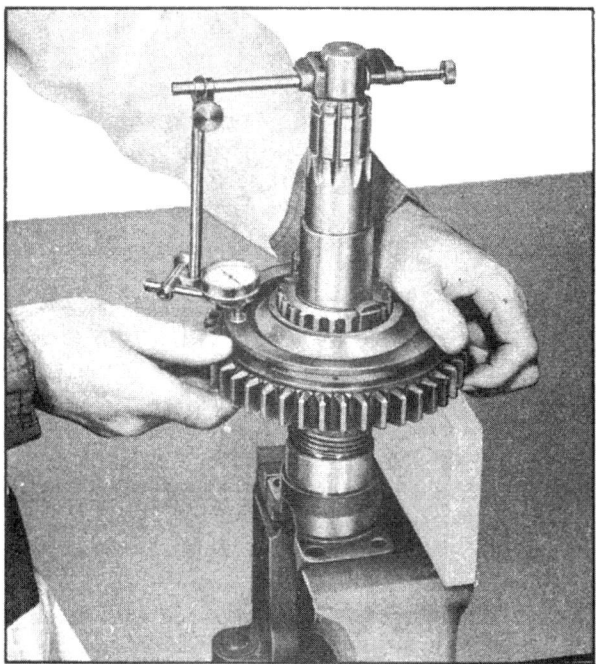

Fig. 40—Checking Spline Fit

11. Install 2nd speed gear on shaft with synchronizer springs toward synchronizing ring in 1st speed gear.

NOTE: Position gear so two cut-out sec-

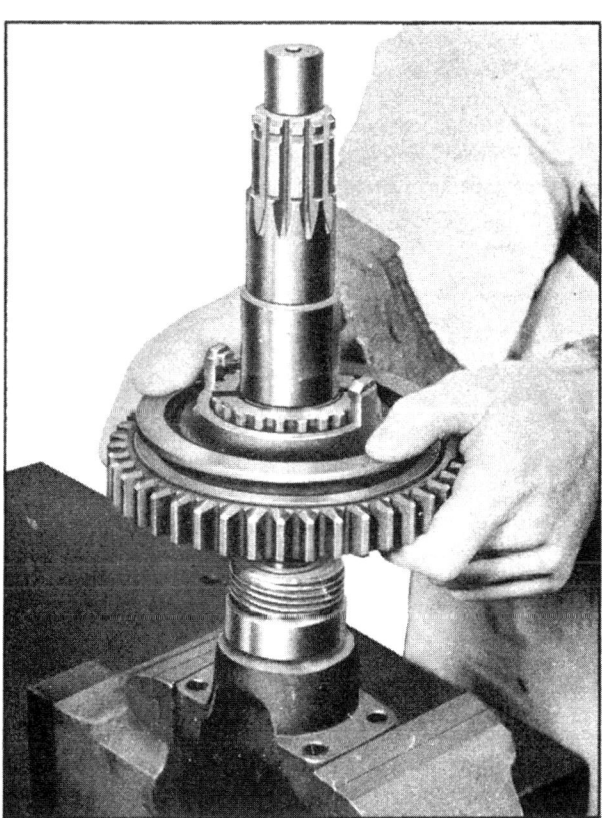

Fig. 39—Selecting Spline Fit

9. When the proper fit has been obtained, mark the matching splines on both gear and shaft so as to assure assembly of parts in the transmission in the same position (fig. 41).
10. Remove universal joint yoke attaching nut and universal joint yoke.

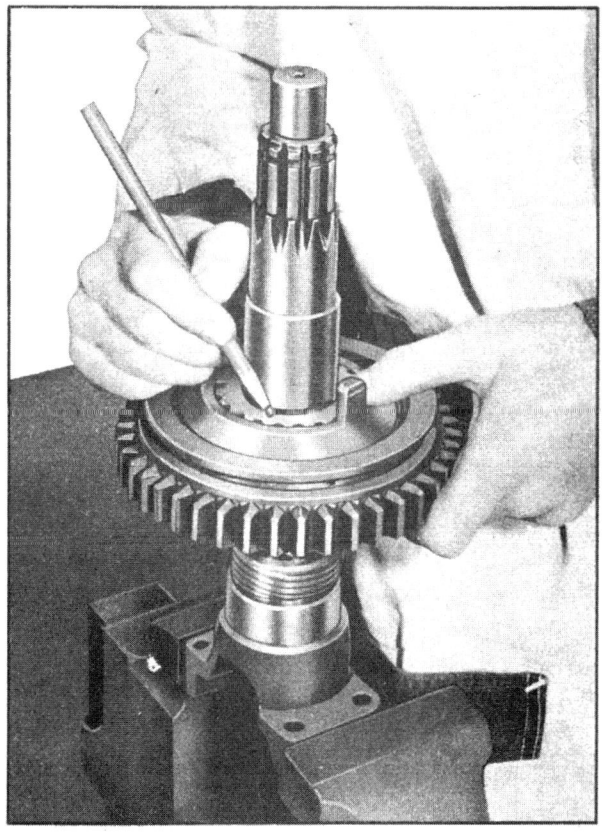

Fig. 41—Marking Best Fit Position

tions index with prongs on synchronizing ring in 1st speed gear.

12. Install second speed thrust washer.

13. Install 3rd speed gear mainshaft bushing on mainshaft using J-2671 Bushing Installer and press down onto shaft (fig. 42) until it bottoms on second speed thrust washer.

14. Check endplay of 2nd speed gear. This endplay should be .012" ± .003".

15. Install 3rd speed gear over mainshaft bushing and install third speed synchronizer cone on taper of 3rd speed gear.

16. Install clutch sleeve over clutch hub with taper toward long shoulder on hub and drop (3) clutch keys into position. Install clutch key springs, one on each side of clutch hub making sure springs fit under (3) clutch keys to hold them out against clutch sleeve.

NOTE: Both clutch key springs must be installed in the same relative position to provide even tension on (3) clutch keys (fig. 43).

Fig. 42—Installing Third Speed Gear Bushing

17. Support mainshaft assembly in arbor press, install clutch hub assembly with taper on clutch sleeve and long shoulder of clutch hub toward pilot on mainshaft and press clutch hub assembly onto shaft until it bottoms (fig. 44).

CAUTION: Exercise extreme care that slots in third speed gear synchronizer cone index with (3) clutch keys in clutch hub assembly.

18. Check endplay of 3rd speed gear. This endplay should be .012" ± .002".

19. Install clutch hub retainer ring.

Fig. 43—Clutch Key Spring Position

NOTE: The retainer ring is a selective lock ring and should be checked carefully for proper thickness at assembly. There are four thickness rings available, therefore, be sure to select the proper ring that will assemble with .007" maximum end clearance (fig. 45).

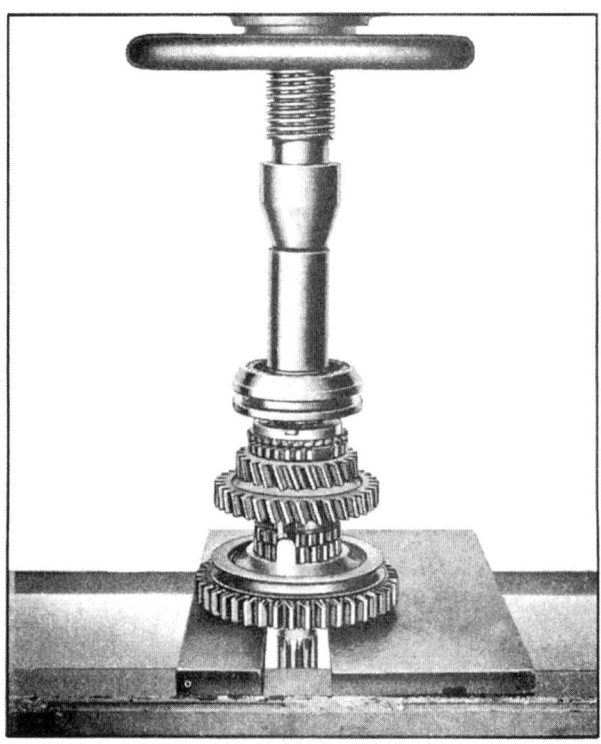

Fig. 44—Installing Clutch Hub

Countershaft

Should it be necessary to replace any of the countershaft gears, the lock ring on front end of shaft should first be removed and then the assembly supported in an arbor press and the shaft pressed out of the train of gears.

When reassembling the new gears to the countershaft, care must be taken to place gears in correct position on shaft. The radius end of the second speed gear faces the first speed gear. The third speed gear is installed next and inasmuch as both sides of this gear are identical it may be installed either way. The reverse speed gear is installed on the shaft next and must be installed so that the chamfered end of the teeth will face the counter driven gear. Only one spacer is used and that is installed between the reverse gear and the counter driven gear. The counter driven gear is installed last. Figure 46 shows correct relations of gears when installed on the countershaft.

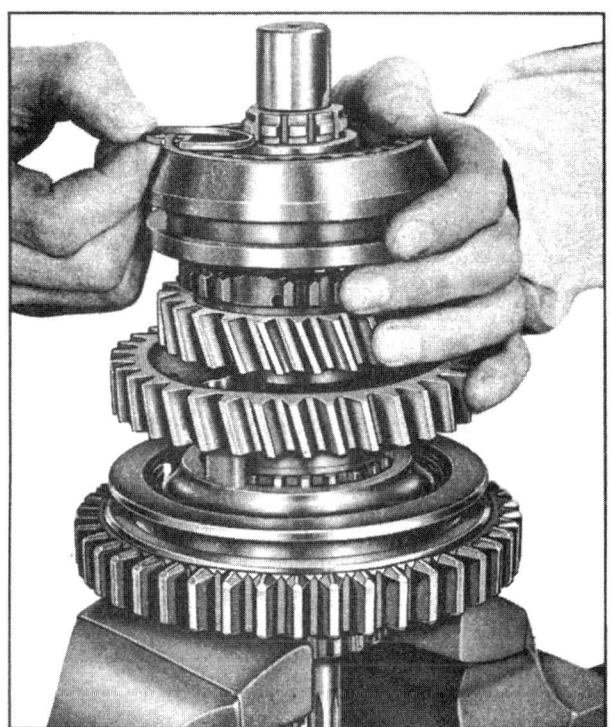

Fig. 45—Selecting Proper Retainer Ring

When pressing the gears on the countershaft, new countershaft drive pins should be used and after all gears are pressed into position, the round pins should be driven 1/32" below flush with shoulder on counter driven gear hub. The snap ring installed as gear retainer, on front end of countershaft, is a selective lock ring and should be checked carefully for proper thickness at assembly.

Reverse Idler Gear Bushings

If the reverse idler gear bushings show signs of wear, they should be removed with J-1614 Pitman Shaft Bushing Remover. This same tool may be used to replace these bushings in the gear (fig. 47).

Press bushings into gear from each end until flush with ends of gear and then stake in position using J-2680 Reverse Idler Gear Bushing Staker (fig. 48).

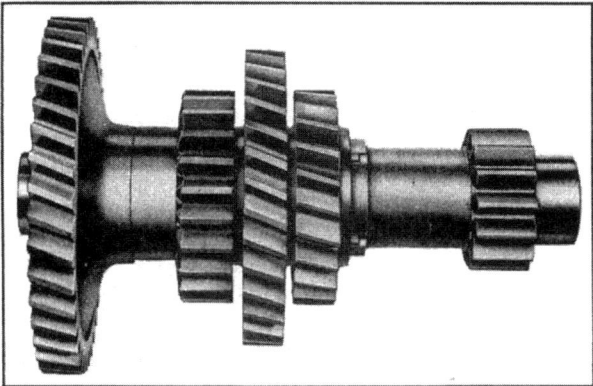

Fig. 46—Correct Countershaft Gear Position

CAUTION: *It is important that these bushings be properly staked as they are split bushings and may have a tendency to creep if not properly staked.*

After the new bushings are installed and staked in position they must be line reamed to size using

Fig. 47—Replacing Reverse Idler Gear Bushing

J-2668 Reverse Idler Gear Bushing Reamer (fig. 49).

Countershaft Front Bearing

The countershaft front roller bearing is a press fit in the case. If, upon inspection it is found

Fig. 48—Staking Reverse Idler Gear Bushings

that this bearing needs replacement, it may be driven through and into the case using J-994 Differential Side Bearing Replacer. The same tool may be used to install bearing in case. When installing, drive bearing in until it is flush with inside face of case.

TRANSMISSION ASSEMBLY

1. Install chip collector in bottom of transmission case and tighten attaching screws securely.
2. Assemble the countergear front bearing spacer into the case. The open side of the spacer should be toward the outside and its edge flush with the transmission case.

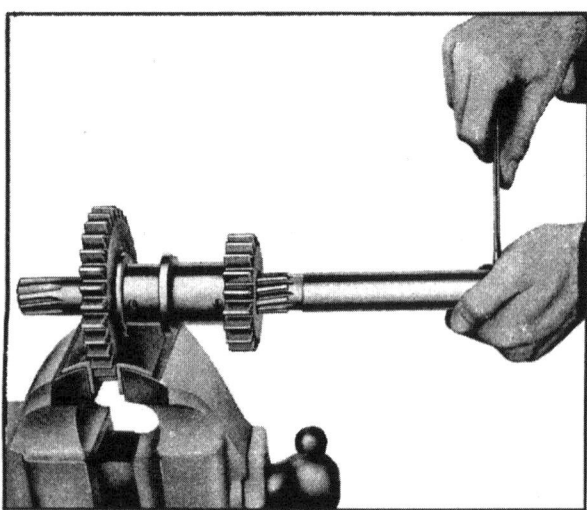

Fig. 49—Reaming Reverse Idler Gear Bushings

3. Install countershaft assembly in the transmission with rear bearing hub extending through rear bearing hole in case.
4. Install rear bearing oil deflector and rear bearing on countershaft assembly using bearing retainer to press bearing onto shaft (fig. 50). Lock bolts by bending tangs on bolt lock plate.

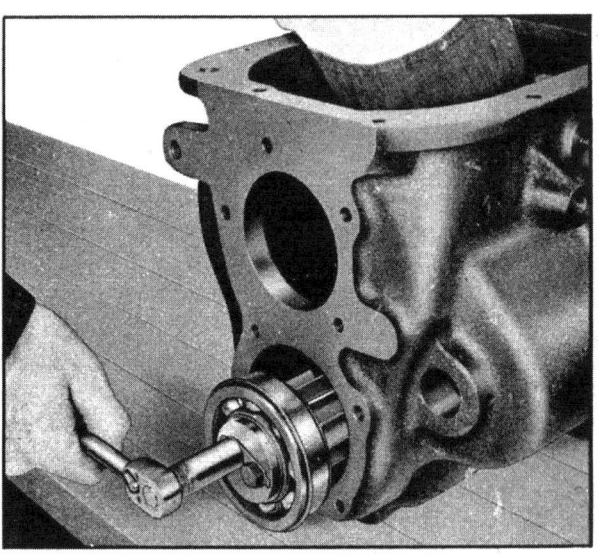

Fig. 50—Installing Rear Bearing on Countershaft

5. Move countershaft assembly forward and position in case. Rear bearing outer snap ring limits forward movement of countershaft.
6. Place reverse idler gear in transmission case and install idler gear shaft from rear to front being careful to have slot in end of shaft in a horizontal position.
7. Drive idler gear shaft in until hole in shaft aligns with lock pin hole in case and install lock pin.
8. Install mainshaft assembly into case with rear of shaft protruding out of rear bearing hole in case.
9. Install mainshaft rear bearing onto shaft using J-2667 Bearing Installer (fig. 51).
10. Install transmission mainshaft pilot bearing roller spacer to pilot end of mainshaft, install clutch gear synchronizer cone to pilot end of mainshaft and move mainshaft forward until clutch sleeve clears third speed gear on countershaft assembly.
11. Index cut out portion of clutch gear teeth to obtain clearance over countershaft driven gear and install clutch gear assembly into case.
12. Install clutch gear bearing retainer using a new gasket. Apply Permatex or other suitable sealing compound to bearing or retainer bolt threads, install bolts and tighten to 15-18 ft. lbs.

13. Raise front end of mainshaft and enter pilot into transmission mainshaft pilot bearing rollers in clutch gear.
14. Install J-2667 Mainshaft and Bearing Installer to back of transmission case and press mainshaft and bearing assembly into case (fig. 52).

Fig. 51—Installing Rear Bearing on Mainshaft

CAUTION: *Make sure three cut-out sections of 4th speed synchronizer cone align with three clutch keys in clutch assembly.*

15. Install rear bearing retainer using a new gasket. Apply Permatex or other suitable sealer to rear bearing retainer bolt threads, install bolts and tighten to 20-25 ft. lbs.
16. Place reverse shifter lever into position and thread shifter lever bolt with bolt sleeve and flat washer through lever and into case from inside out. Tighten bolt fingertight and install shifter lever bolt nut and tighten to 40-45 ft. lbs. Stake bolt securely to nut at one place.

NOTE: *Reverse shifter lever bolt is a standard bolt and the sleeve is used under the head of bolt to act as shoulder for shifter lever to pivot on.*

17. On 1 ton and (1948-50) 1½ and 2 ton, install universal joint front flange with speedometer drive gear in place onto transmission mainshaft. Lock transmission in two gears and tighten yoke retaining bolt to 60-65 ft. lbs.
18. On (1951) 1½ and 2 ton:
    a. Install parking brake drum and universal joint flange assembly, and install universal joint flange flat washer, lockwasher and retainer bolt. Tighten bolt to 60-65 ft. lbs.
    b. Install the parking brake shoe and lever assembly, positioning the shoes on both sides of the parking brake drum while sliding the upper end of the outer shoe on the anchor pin.
    c. Install the anchor pin lock at upper end of outer shoe.
    d. Install outer shoe adjusting bolt plate and install outer shoe spring.
    e. Install the parking brake operating lever and operating link and install lockwasher and lock bolt for operating lever shaft.
    f. Connect the end of the brake shoe lever to the operating link by installing flat washer, spring, lever and adjusting nut on end of operating link.
19. Install speedometer driven gear in rear bearing retainer and tighten securely.
20. Make sure all transmission gears are in neutral and using a new gasket, install cover assembly making sure shifting yokes slide over their proper gears and that reverse shifter lever properly engages reverse shifter head. Install transmission cover attaching bolts and tighten to 20-25 ft. lbs.
21. Check operation of transmission by shifting into all gears and making sure there is no binding in any position.

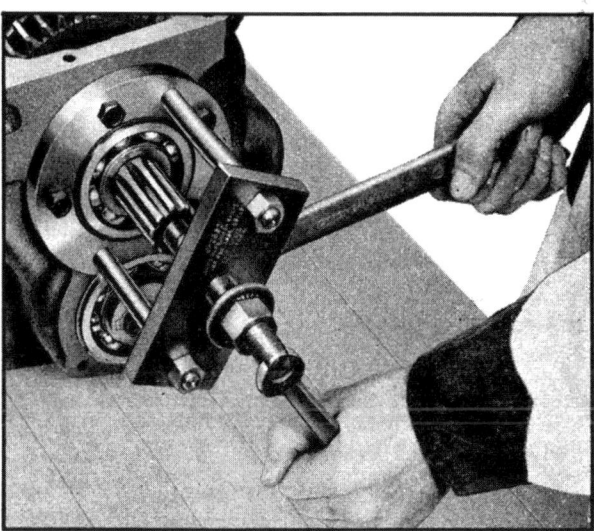

Fig. 52—Installing Mainshaft Into Case

Final Inspection

Recheck the power take off cover making sure it is tightened to 20-25 ft. lbs. Install the transmission filler and drain plugs loosely. Do not fill transmission at this time as lubricant will run out the two lower mounting bolt holes.

Due to construction of universal ball joints on the ½ and ¾ ton trucks, it is important that proper adjustment be made at this point.

This type joint, if improperly adjusted, may result in oil leakage if too loose, or a complaint of transmission noise if too tight. Therefore, when ever this joint is broken, its adjustment must be checked when reassembling. Refer to page 7-11 for "Universal Joint Ball Adjustment."

TRANSMISSION INSTALLATION

1. Install transmission through opening in floor.
2. Place the transmission on guide pins and start mainshaft in clutch disc and slide forward.
3. Install the lower transmission mounting bolts, remove the upper guide pins and install the top mounting bolts.
4. Install the flywheel underpan.
5. On 1 ton and (1948-50) 1½ and 2 ton, position the propeller shaft and trunnion bearings in place and install the "U" bolts and hex nuts and tighten securely.
6. On (1951) 1½ and 2 ton:
   a. Install front propeller shaft and bearing support assembly, positioning the universal joint front yoke on the four flange bolts. Install and tighten securely the nuts attaching propeller shaft support bracket to frame cross member.
   b. Install four universal joint flange lockwashers and nuts and tighten securely.
   c. Raise front end of rear propeller shaft, align trunnnion bearings with front yoke and install two trunnion bearing "U" clamps and tighten securely.
7. Install parking brake lever and install spring, flat washer and parking brake lever lock.
8. On 1 ton and (1948-50) 1½ and 2 ton, connect parking brake pull rod assembly to parking lever.
9. On (1951) 1½ and 2 ton, connect inner and outer levers to parking brake operating lever and connect brake lever return spring to brake operating lever.
10. On (1951) 1½ and 2 ton, adjust parking brake as outlined in Brake Section under "Minor Service Operations."
11. Install the speedometer cable in the rear bearing retainer.
12. Fill the transmission with 6 pts. of S.A.E. 90 gear lubricant and tighten drain and filler plugs to 30-35 ft. lbs.
13. Install the transmission floor cover to body floor. On Forward Control models, install front and rear floor pans.
14. Install the floor mat and connect up the foot accelerator pedal.
15. Slide the mast jacket grommet in position and install the retainer screws.
16. Road test the vehicle for operation of transmission in all speeds.

TRANSMISSION SPECIFICATIONS

Type
  Selective Synchromesh—second, third, fourth
Speeds
  Four forward—one reverse
Mounting
  Unit power plant
Gears
  Spur—first and reverse
  Helical—Second, third and fourth
Bearings
  Clutch shaft pilot in crankshaft...Oil—impregnated bronze bushing
  Clutch gear—S. R. Ball .... N.D. 954358
  Mainshaft—pilot—18 Rollers .... CH 7450010
  Mainshaft—rear—S. R. Ball .... N.D. 954127
  Countershaft—rear—S. R. Ball .... N.D. 954164
  Countershaft—front—Roller .... Hy 142260
  Reverse gears—Steel backed bronze, ball indented
Gear Ratio
  First .... 7.06 to 1
  Second .... 3.58 to 1
  Third .... 1.71 to 1
  Fourth .... Direct
  Reverse .... 6.78 to 1
Service Data—Mainshaft and Gears
  Mainshaft—Run Out .... Not Over .004"
  Rock of 1st and reverse sliding gear
    on main shaft splines .... .015" max.
  Endplay of 2nd speed gear......... .009"-.015"
  Endplay of 3rd speed gear .... .010"-.014"
  Clearance between Shifting Fork
    and Sliding Gears .... .009"-.019"
Shifting
  Yoke Lock .... Ball
  Spring Free Length .... 1 1/32"
  Closed Length .... 19/32"
Reverse Gear
  Reverse Idler Shaft Diameter .. 1.1267"-1.1277"
  Reverse Idler Gear Bushings ... 1.1272"-1.1282"
                                      in gear
Lubricant
  Capacity .... 6 pints
  Type .... SAE 90

TORQUE SPECIFICATIONS—4-SPEED TRANSMISSION

Rear Bearing Retainer Bolts...... 20-25 ft. lbs.
Power Take-Off Cover Bolts....... 20-25 ft. lbs.
Transmission Cover Bolts .... 20-25 ft. lbs.
Universal Joint Yoke Attaching
  Bolt .... 15-20 ft. lbs.
Clutch Gear Bearing Retainer Bolts 10-12 ft. lbs.
Transmission Filler and Drain Plugs 30-35 ft. lbs.
Countergear Rear Bearing Retainer
  Bolts .... 15-20 ft. lbs.
Universal Joint Flange Bolt .... 60-65 ft. lbs.

TROUBLES AND REMEDIES

TRANSMISSION

SYMPTOM AND PROBABLE CAUSE

PROBABLE REMEDY

Slips Out of High Gear

a. Transmission loose on clutch housing.
b. Misalignment between the transmission and engine (3-speed transmission).

c. Shifter detent spring weak or broken.
d. Bent shifter fork.
e. Damaged mainshaft pilot bearing.

f. Excessive clearance between shifter collar and synchronizer hub splines.

a. Tighten transmission on clutch housing.
b. Check and correct the alignment of crankshaft pilot, clutch housing bore and transmission assembly.
c. Replace spring.
d. Replace shifter fork.
e. Replace mainshaft pilot bearing (check bore in clutch gear and pilot end of mainshaft for wear or damage).
f. Check for excessive clearance.

Slips Out of Low Gear

a. Shifter detent spring weak or broken.
b. Bent shifter fork.
c. Worn low speed gears.

d. Excessive clearance between 1st speed gear splines and mainshaft splines.

a. Replace spring.
b. Replace shifter fork.
c. Replace low speed sliding gear and countergear. Low speed countershaft gear only on 4-speed transmission.
d. Check for excessive clearance. See Mainshaft—Assembly.

Slips Out of Second Gear

a. Loose spline fit between first and reverse sliding gear and mainshaft.
b. Worn or bell mouthed bushing in second speed mainshaft gear.

a. Check for excessive clearance. See Mainshaft—Assembly.
b. Check for excessive clearance. See Mainshaft—Assembly.

Slips Out of Reverse Gear

a. Excessive clearance between first speed gear splines and mainshaft splines.

a. Check for excessive clearance. See Mainshaft—Assembly.

Noisy in Reverse

a. Worn reverse idler gear bushings.

a. Replace idler gear. Bushings only on 4-speed transmissions.

Difficulty in Shifting into Low Gear

a. Worn reverse latch on lower end of gearshift lever.
b. Worn gearshift interlock guide plate.

a. Replace reverse latch.

b. Replace gearshift interlock guide plate.

Lubricant Leak in Clutch Housing

a. Transmission case overfilled with lubricant.

b. Clutch gear retainer loose.

a. Lower lubricant to proper level (See Lubrication section).
b. Remove transmission, replace gasket and tighten clutch gear bearing retainer.

Noisy in High Gear

a. Excessive clearance between first speed gear splines and mainshaft splines.

a. Check for excessive clearance. See Mainshaft—Assembly.

TRANSMISSION 7-32

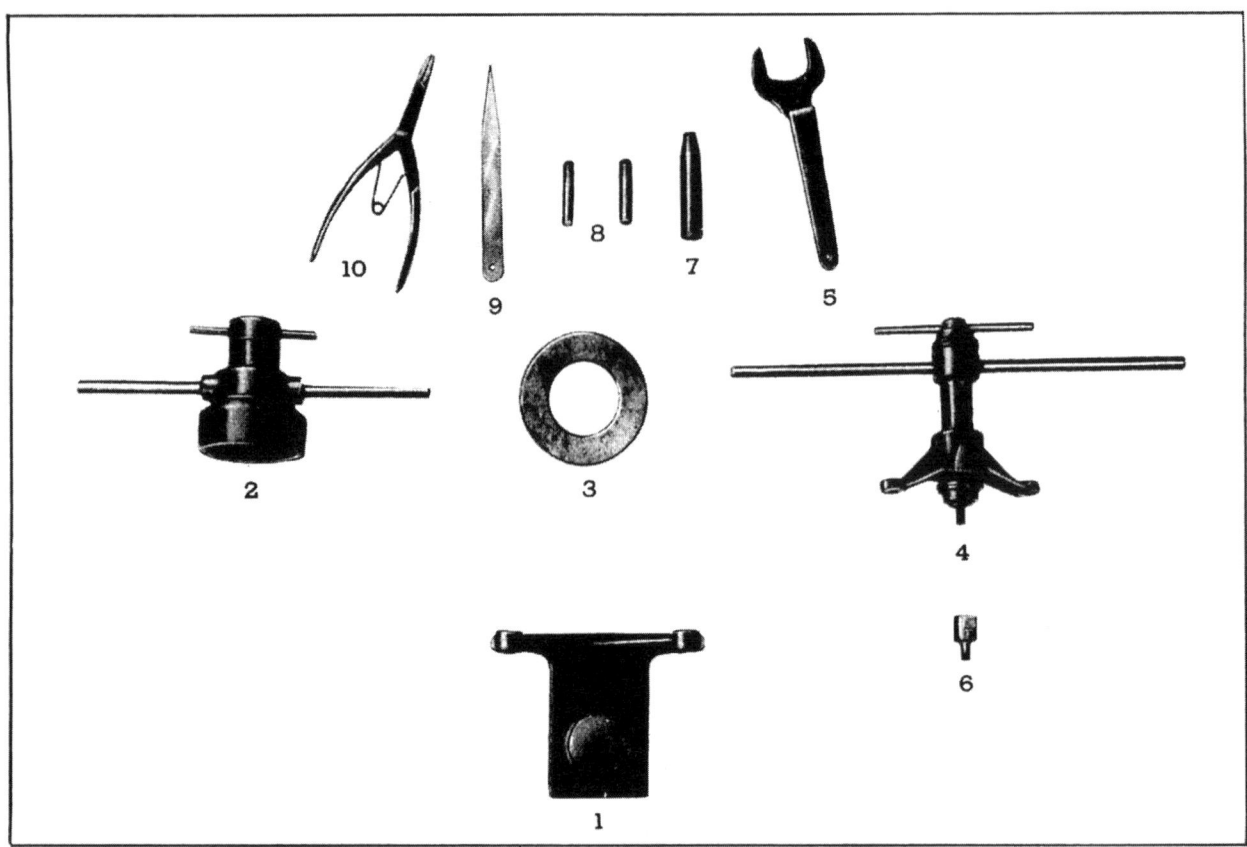

Fig. 53—Transmission Special Tools (3 Speed)

1. J-934 Transmission Assembly Holding Stand
2. J-937 Clutch Gear and Bearing Puller
3. J-936 Clutch Gear Bearing Remover
4. J-938 Transmission Main Shaft Remover and Replacer
5. J-933 Clutch Gear Bearing Retainer Wrench
6. J-938-7 Mainshaft Remover and Replacer Adapter
7. J-1617 Countershaft Assembly Tool
8. J-1126 Transmission Guide Pins
9. J-3185 Rear Bearing Snap Ring Remover and Replacer
10. J-932 Synchronizing Ring Retainer, Remover and Replacer

TRANSMISSION 7-33

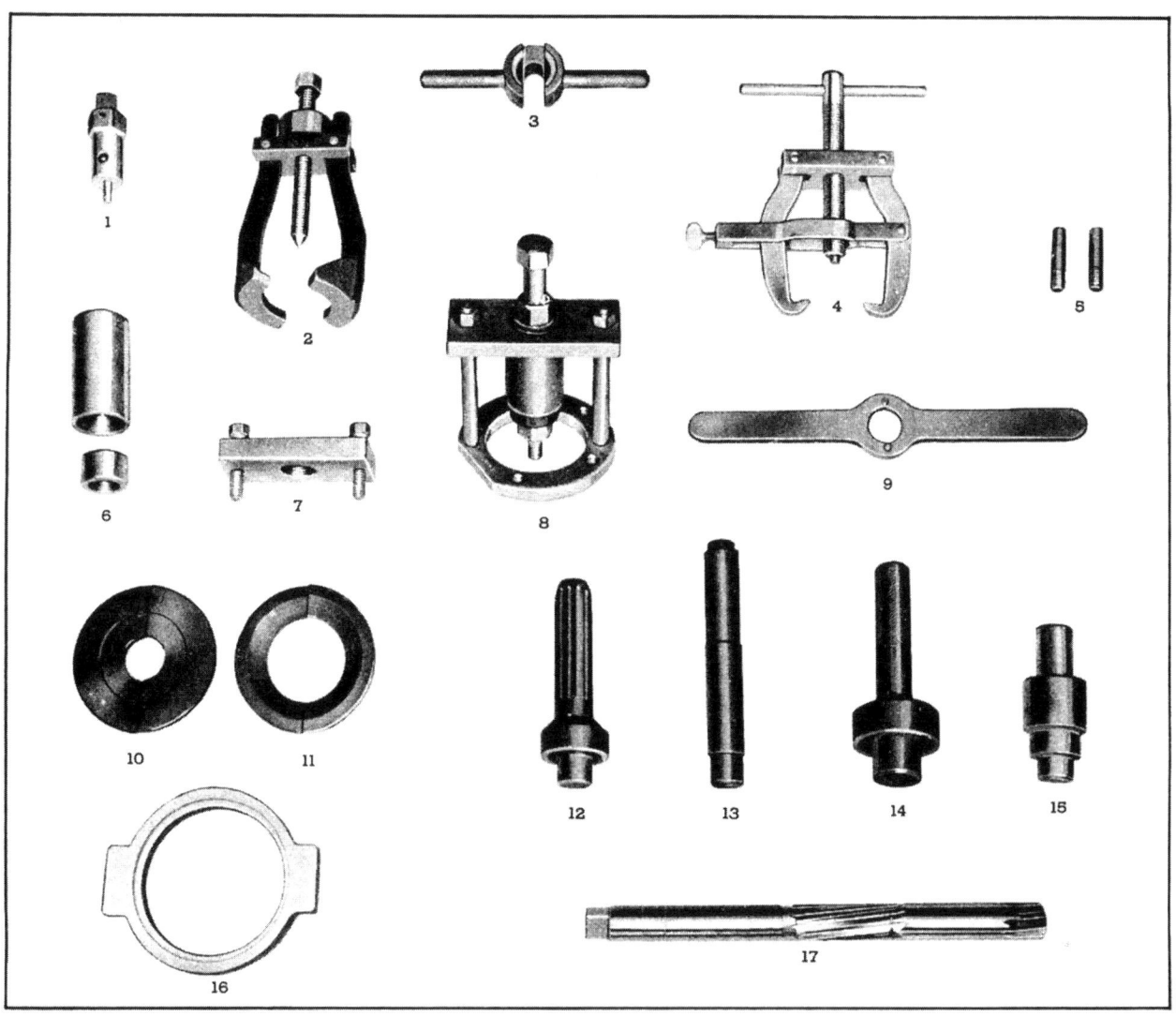

Fig. 54—Four Speed Transmission Special Tools

1. J-2680 Reverse Idler Gear Bushing Staking Tool
2. J-1619 Transmission Mainshaft Bearing Puller
3. K-353 Gear Shift Lever Remover and Replacer
4. TR-278-R Countershaft Rear Bearing Remover
5. J-1126 Transmission Guide Pin Set (2)
6. J-2671 Third Speed Gear Bushing Installer
7. J-2669 Clutch Gear Remover
8. J-2667 Mainshaft and Bearing Assembly, Remover and Replacer
9. J-2670 Clutch Gear Bearing Retainer Nut Spanner Wrench
10. J-1453 Clutch Gear Bearing Replacer
11. J-2228 Clutch Gear Bearing Remover Plate
12. J-994 Countershaft Front Bearing Remover and Replacer
13. J-1614 Reverse Idler Gear Bushing Remover and Replacer
14. J-1488 Rear Bearing Retainer Oil Seal Driver
15. K-343 Speedometer Gear Replacer
16. J-358-1 Press Plate Holder
17. J-2668 Reverse Idler Gear Bushing Reamer (1.128")

SERVICE NEWS REFERENCE

Month	Page No.	Subject

SECTION 8

FUEL AND EXHAUST

CONTENTS OF THIS SECTION

	Page
Fuel Tanks	8-1
Exhaust System	8-2

INDEX

	Page		Page
Fuel Tanks	8-1	Chassis and Single Unit Bodies	8-2
General Description	8-1	Capacities	8-2
Service Operations	8-2	Exhaust System	8-2
Removal and Installation	8-2	General Description	8-2
All Cab Models	8-2		

FUEL TANKS

GENERAL DESCRIPTION

All 1949-51 cab model trucks of all series have the gasoline tank behind the seat. The tank is of 17½ gallon capacity made with two steel sections, seam welded together. The filler neck comes through the right side of the cab, at a convenient height from the ground. Exceptional stiffness is secured by the combination of the welded flanges and depressed ribs in both the front and rear halves. The tank is mounted on two tank supports which are welded to the floor panel and is securely held in place by two adjustable steel straps attached to the tank supports (fig. 1). Metal to metal contact between the tank and supports and the tank and straps is prevented by the use of anti-squeak material.

Gasoline tanks on all 1948 models and all other 1949-51 truck models are mounted on the frame side rail between the cab location and the rear axle. The tanks on these truck models consist of an upper and lower half, each with a wide flange and baffles which are welded into the tank halves. The two tank sections are seam welded at the flange around the entire tank to assure leakproof construction. Exceptional stiffness is secured by the combination of the welded flanges and depressed ribs in both upper and lower tank sections. Baffle plates are incorporated to provide additional stiffness and to prevent the surging of gasoline within the tank.

The gasoline tank used on the 1½ and 2 ton school busses is of 3-piece constuction with the top, bottom and sides of one piece while the ends are separate pieces. The tank joints and end joints are made with lock seams at the metal edges and then soldered.

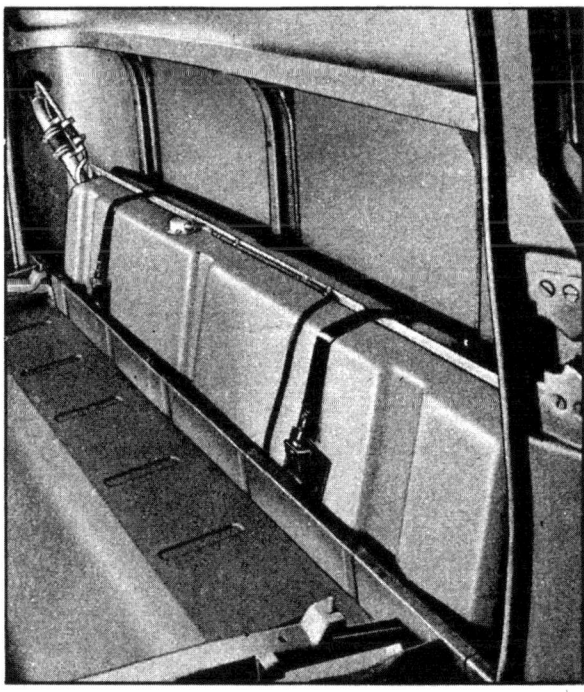

Fig. 1—Cab Mounted Tank

Upper and lower filler necks vary as to size, length and shape depending on model requirements. These necks are all treated so that rust will not form and get into the fuel system. Lower filler necks are bolted to the tank and then sweat soldered in place to eliminate any possibility of leakage at this point.

All frame mounted tanks are located on the right side of the chassis and lay lengthwise and just inside the frame side rail on ½, ¾ and 1 ton models, except Forward Control units, and just outside the frame side rail on Forward Control and 1½ and 2 Ton models. A strong mounting of two metal straps anchor these tanks to gas tank mounting brackets which are bolted to the frame side member. Metal-to-metal contact between tank and brackets is prevented by the use of anti-squeak material.

SERVICE OPERATIONS

REMOVAL AND INSTALLATION

All Cab Models (1949-51)

1. Drain tank.
2. Remove seat back. See Section 1 for details.
3. Disconnect filler neck hose connection and vent pipe hose connection at lower clamp.
4. Disconnect gasoline line from the tank. Be sure ignition switch is in the "Off" position.
5. Disconnect gauge wire from the float unit.
6. Remove tank support straps and then remove tank from the cab.

Chassis and Single Unit Bodies

1. Drain tank.
2. Disconnect filler neck hose connection at lower clamp.
3. Disconnect gasoline line from tank. Be sure ignition switch is in "Off" position.
4. Disconnect gauge wire from float unit.

   NOTE: On models where top of tank is not readily accessible, loosen tank support straps enough to disconnect gauge wire on float unit.

5. Remove tank support straps and lower tank to floor.

Installation is performed by reversing the above operations.

GASOLINE TANK CAPACITIES

Cab Models .... 17½ gal.
Chassis and Single unit Bodies:
    ½ ton, ¾ ton and Forward Control ...... 16 gal.
    All school bus chassis .... 30 gal.
    All others except school bus .... 18 gal.

EXHAUST SYSTEM

GENERAL DESCRIPTION

The exhaust system on all models consists of an exhaust pipe, muffler and a tail pipe.

The muffler used on all 1948-49 models is of the "reverse flow" type utilizing reverse flow and diffusion principle for quiet operation (fig. 2), and

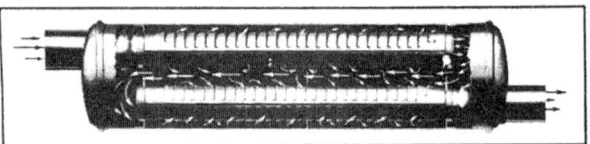

Fig. 2—Muffler Cross Section

a large diameter tail pipe to reduce back pressure. The tail pipe extends back of the rear axle discharging exhaust gases at a point that prevents fumes from entering the driver compartment.

The gas flow from the engine, considerably straightened out by its passage through the long exhaust pipe, reaches the muffler through the inlet tube, reverses at the rear end and flows into the outlet tube and to the outlet (fig. 2). The flow, however, is not restricted to the tubes, since the gases pour out in jets from each perforation, mingling with the gases from the adjoining tube. The resulting mixing and baffling, with the velocity changes and reversals in direction of flow, aids in silencing.

The muffler end of the exhaust pipe slides into the muffler inlet and is held in place by a clamp. Small projections on the end of the exhaust pipe properly locate this pipe to proper depth in the muffler.

The muffler end of the tail pipe slides over the outlet pipe of the muffler and is held in place by a clamp. The back end of this tail pipe is supported by a clamp around the pipe which attaches to the frame side rail.

A bracket, extending from the frame and with the underside conforming to the curvature of the muffler, supports the muffler by a detachable strap around the muffler body.

The muffler used on all 1950-51 models (fig. 3), is of the "straight through" construction in which there is a straight path for exhaust gases from the

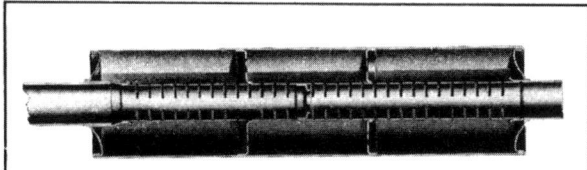

Fig. 3—Muffler Cross Section

exhaust pipe to the tail pipe. It consists of a 1¾ inch diameter central tube with narrow circumferential slots and a shell surrounding this tube. Located midway in this central tube is a baffle with a one-inch diameter restriction. The shell, surrounding the central tube, is divided into three resonance chambers by a front and rear baffle each of which is perforated with six holes.

In its exit from the manifold, exhaust gas must be allowed to expand gradually and to cool, thereby reducing the pressure which is the cause of noise when the gas is discharged directly into the atmosphere. The straight through muffler construction maintains a low exhaust back pressure while maintaining satisfactory sound absorption qualities. Some of the exhaust gases enter the resonance chambers through the slots while the remainder continues through the central baffle tube. The sound is diffused in the resonance chambers.

The exhaust pipe and muffler joint is electrically welded making it a unified structure, and if the muffler need be replaced at any time, the exhaust pipe is sawed through as close to the muffler inlet as possible. This will allow a new muffler to be slipped over the end of the exhaust pipe as replacement mufflers are attached with clamps. If the exhaust pipe requires replacement, it will be necessary to replace both the exhaust pipe and muffler with service replacement parts.

The muffler end of the tail pipe slides over the outlet pipe of the muffler and is held in place by a clamp. The back end of this tail pipe on ½ and ¾ ton models is supported by a clamp around the pipe which attaches to the frame side rail.

A bracket, extending from the frame and with the underside conforming to the curvature of the muffler, supports the muffler by a detachable strap around the muffler body.

When installing a new exhaust pipe, exhaust pipe and muffler assembly, or a new tail pipe, on any model (1948-51), care should be taken to have the proper relationship of each part to the other. Incorrectly assembled parts of the exhaust system are frequently the cause of annoying rattles due to incorrect clearances, or unusual noises difficult to locate, due to changes or obstructions to the normal flow of exhaust gases. Leave all clamp bolts and muffler strap bolts loose until all parts are in proper relation to each other. Slight rotation of the muffler may be necessary to line up the inlet and outlet pipes. After all parts are correctly aligned, tighten the front muffler and exhaust pipe clamp before tightening the rear clamp and strap bolt.

SERVICE NEWS REFERENCE

Month	Page No.	Subject

SECTION 9

STEERING GEAR ASSEMBLY

CONTENTS OF THIS SECTION

	Page
Steering Gear Assembly	9- 1
Troubles and Remedies	9-11
Specifications	9-11
Special Tools	9-12
Service News Reference	9-13

INDEX

	Page		Page
General Description	9-1	Repairs	9- 7
Minor Service Operations	9-3	Sector Shaft Bushing and Packing Replacement	9- 7
Adjustments	9-3	Sector Shaft Packing Replacement	9- 7
Steering Column Gearshift Linkage	9-4	Assembly	9- 8
Mast Jacket Upper Bearing Replacement	9-4	Assembly of Ball Nut	9- 8
Major Service Operations	9-4	Assembly of Steering Gear	9- 9
Removal—All Except C.O.E.	9-4	Adjustment—On Bench	9- 9
Removal—C.O.E.	9-5	Installation—All Except C.O.E.	9-10
Disassembly	9-5	Installation—C.O.E.	9-10
Disassembly of Ball Nut	9-6		
Inspection	9-6		

GENERAL DESCRIPTION

The steering gear (fig. 1) used on all truck models is of the recirculating ball type. This type steering gear provides for ease of handling by having a roller contact between the worm and the gear.

The principal working arrangement of the recirculating ball type steering gear consists of a "ball nut" connected to the steering worm and in mesh with the sector gear. Precision finished helical grooves inside the ball nut match helical grooves in the worm, and it is in these grooves that ball bearings roll around as the steering wheel is turned. There are two complete ball circuits within the ball nut. To keep the balls from running out of the end of either circuit, the nut is equipped with two tubular ball guides, each of which deflects the balls away from their helical

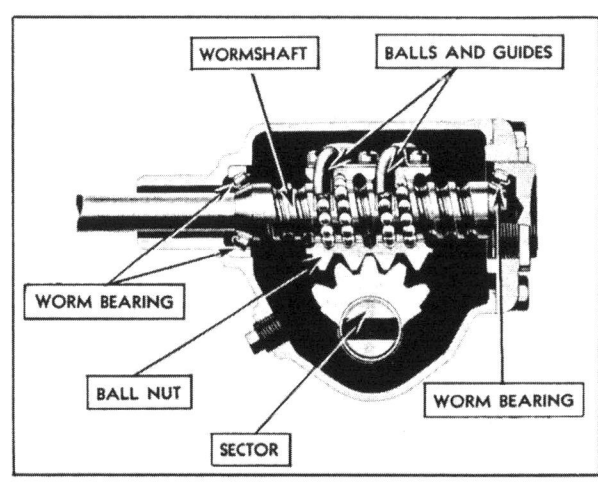

Fig. 1—Steering Gear Worm, Nut and Ball Circuits

STEERING GEAR ASSEMBLY 9-2

path at one end of their travel, guides them diagonally across the back of the nut, and returns them to their helical path between the ball nut and the worm at the other end of their travel.

The balls within the helical path constitute a thread between the worm and ball nut, so that when the worm is turned, the nut moves along the worm as with the ordinary screw thread. At the same time, the balls roll freely between the worm and the ball nut, circulating within their closed circuits so that screw motion is obtained with rolling instead of sliding contact between the parts.

Rugged rack teeth in that portion of the ball nut that faces the sector and the sector gear teeth, are cut so as to provide true gear action between the sector and ball nut when the ball nut is located at a slight angle. This type of construction provides a means for backlash adjustment between the ball nut and the sector in that all that is required is to shift the sector shaft slightly along its own axis. This is accomplished by means of a convenient thrust screw, known as a lash adjuster.

The sector teeth are also cut so that when the sector is adjusted to take out all backlash at the center of travel or straight ahead position, there will be slight backlash at each end of travel, thus snugness of the sector in the rack teeth in a straight ahead position can be obtained without sacrifice of perfect freedom at extreme positions, right or left, of the front wheels.

The sector shaft is straddle mounted in antifriction bushings and a grease seal is provided at the outer end of the shaft.

The worm is integrally welded to the main shaft and is mounted between two barrel roller bearings. The lower of these bearings is adjustable toward the upper for taking out end play in the worm shaft and for obtaining proper worm bearing load.

The horn wire is soldered to a contact ring, pressed into the mast jacket and insulated from the worm shaft (fig. 2). A spring loaded contact horn button is in the steering wheel and when depressed, the horn button contacts the contact ring. The wire from the horn is attached to a connector terminal at the mast jacket cover plate.

Steering gear ratio on all ½, ¾, 1, and 1½ ton models, except the Forward Control and the 1½ ton school bus, is 26.24 to 1. On Forward Control models the ratio is 19.8 to 1 and on the 1½ ton school bus and on all 2 ton models, conventional and C.O.E., the ratio is 27.76 to 1.

The steering gear used on the 1½ ton school bus and all 2 ton models is heavier and of slightly different construction than the steering gear used on ½, ¾, 1 and 1½ ton conventional models. In this heavier steering gear, the steering mast jacket is pressed directly into the housing instead of into a housing cover and 100 balls of 9/32" diameter (50 in each circuit) are used instead of 60 as in the smaller models. Because of this greater number of balls, the worm, ball nut, worm bearings, etc., are all correspondingly larger.

The steering gear assembly used on the ¾ and 1 ton Forward Control models is similar to the steering gear used on the 1½ ton school bus and 2 ton models insofar as having the mast jacket pressed directly into the housing. Consequently, the procedure for repairs will be the same on Forward Control models as it is on the heavier models. The sector shaft bushings on Forward Control models are of different dimensions, however, and there are 60 balls (30 in each circuit) as there are in the steering gear used in ½, ¾, 1 and 1½ ton conventional models.

All Cab-Over-Engine trucks are equipped with a special lubricant filler pipe (fig. 3) to bring the lubricant to the proper level due to the extreme angle at which the steering assembly is mounted. It is very important that this lubricant filler pipe be used as failure to do so will result in low lubricant level and seizure in the steering assembly.

Fig. 3—C.O.E. Steering Gear Oiler

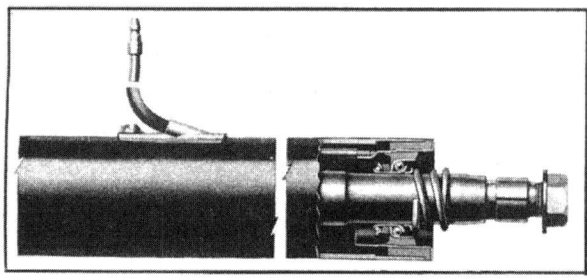

Fig. 2—Mast Jacket Bearing

MINOR SERVICE OPERATIONS

ADJUSTMENTS

Correct adjustment of steering gear is very important. While there are but two adjustments to be made, the following procedure must be followed step-by-step in order given.

1. Disconnect the steering connecting rod from the pitman arm, taking care to note relative positions of steering connecting rod parts before disturbing them.

2. Loosen the lock nut "B" (fig. 4) and turn the lash adjuster "A" a few turns in a counter-clockwise direction. This removes from the worm bearings the load imposed by close

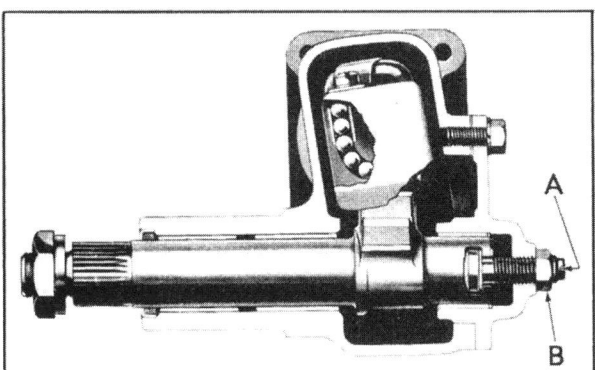

Fig. 4—Sector Adjustment Points

meshing of rack and sector teeth. Turn steering wheel gently in one direction until stopped by gear, then back away about one turn.

CAUTION: Do not turn steering wheel hard against stops when steering connecting rod is disconnected as damage to ball guides may result.

3. Using J-544-A Steering Gear Checking Scale, measure the pull at the rim of the wheel which is required to keep the wheel in motion. This should be between 1 and 1½ pounds. (fig. 5).

    NOTE: When making this check, it is important that the line of the scale be kept tangent to the rim of the wheel.

    If the pull necessary to move the wheel does not lie between the limits given above, adjustment of worm bearings is necessary.

4. To adjust the worm bearing, loosen lock nut "C" (fig. 6) and turn worm bearing thrust screw "D" until there is no perceptible end play in worm. Check pull at wheel rim as outlined above, readjusting if necessary, to obtain proper pull. Tighten lock nut "C" and

Fig. 5—Checking Load on Steering Gear

recheck pull as it must lie between the limits specified after the lock nut is tightened. If the gear feels "lumpy" after adjustment of worm bearings, there is probably damage in the bearings due to severe impact or to improper adjustment and the assembly must be disassembled for replacement of damaged parts. For instructions on removing and disassembly refer to "Major Service Operations."

5. After proper adjustment of worm is obtained, and all mounting bolts securely tightened, adjust lash adjuster "A" (fig. 4). First turn the steering wheel gently from one stop all

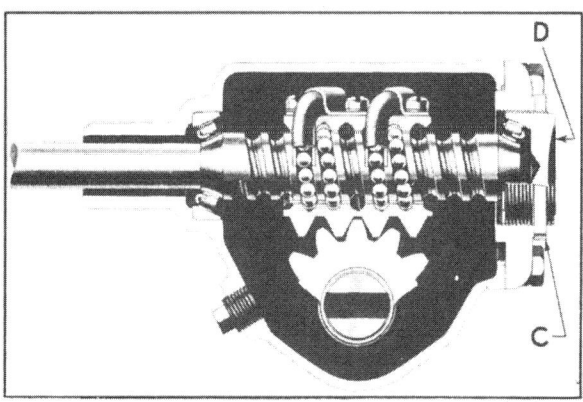

Fig. 6—Worm Bearing Adjustment Points

the way to the other, carefully counting the total number of turns. Then turn wheel back exactly half way, to center position. Mark wheel at top or bottom center with a piece of tape. Turn lash adjuster "A" (fig. 4) clockwise to take out all lash in gear teeth, and tighten lock nut "B". Check pull at wheel rim with checking scale as before, taking the highest reading of checking scale as the wheel is turned through center position. This should be between 2 and 2½ pounds. Readjust, if necessary, to obtain proper pull. Tighten lock nut "B" and recheck pull, as it must lie between the specified limits after lock is tightened.

6. Reassemble steering connecting rod to pitman arm.

Steering Column Gearshift Linkage—Adjust

In cases where insufficient clearance is encountered, on models with steering column gearshift, between the gearshift lever and the steering wheel, or whenever the gearshift linkage has been removed or disconnected, as on a steering gear overhaul, proper adjustment sequence is important. Adjustment should be made as outlined in Section 7.

MAST JACKET UPPER BEARING REPLACEMENT

1. Disconnect horn wire at connector.

2. Remove horn button, then remove steering wheel using J-2927-A puller.

3. Remove cover plate from mast jacket. Attach a piece of tie wire to the end of horn wire which enters the mast jacket.

4. Screw bearing puller J-2565 into top of bearing. Tightening the center screw in the puller removes the bearing from the mast jacket (fig. 7).

5. Transfer tie wire to end of wire attached to new bearing assembly. Start bearing into mast jacket and drive it into place with special driver J-2565 (fig. 8).

6. Pull wire through opening in mast jacket and install the cover plate.

7. Install the steering shaft upper bearing spring seat (with flared end up) and spring. Install steering wheel and insert horn button insulator, contact and spring assembly in opening provided in steering wheel hub, making sure the contact brush (solid end) is in the downward position. Install contact cup, positioning the tang on the lower side in the opening provided in the steering wheel hub.

8. Install steering wheel washer and nut and tighten. Install horn button, connect horn wire at mast jacket and test operation of horn.

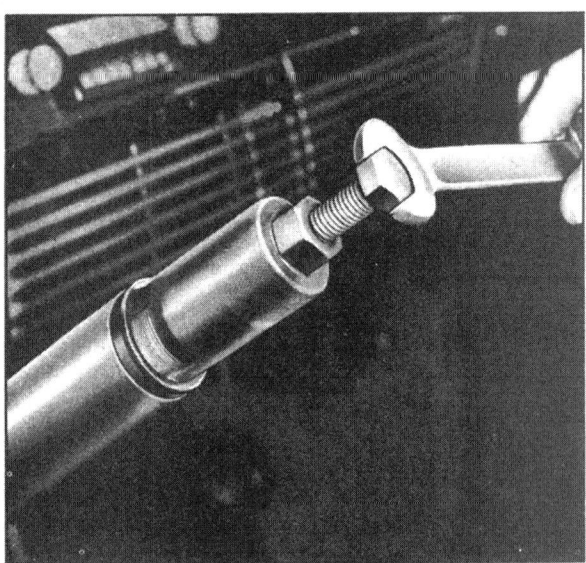

Fig. 7—Removing Mast Jacket Upper Bearing

Fig. 8—Replacing Mast Jacket Upper Bearing

MAJOR SERVICE OPERATIONS

STEERING GEAR

Removal—All Except C.O.E.

1. Disconnect horn wire and remove wire retainer from steering mast jacket.

2. Remove horn button and steering wheel using J-2927-A puller.

3. Remove seat cushion except on Forward Control models.

STEERING GEAR ASSEMBLY 9-5

4. Remove steering mast jacket to instrument panel bolts, bracket and grommet.
5. On ½ and ¾ ton:
   a. Disconnect gearshift upper control shaft support from the mast jacket.
   b. Separate upper steering control shaft from lower shaft by removing lower bolt from upper and lower shaft clamp.
6. Remove sheet metal screws attaching steering mast jacket toe-board grommet and seal to toe-board plate. Slide toe-board grommet and seal up mast jacket and remove toe-board plate.
7. On Forward Control models, hoist front end of vehicle and remove mast jacket opening cover located underneath vehicle.
8. On ½ and ¾ ton, remove bolts and clamp attaching the gearshift control housing to the steering column mast jacket.
9. Disconnect pitman arm using J-1025 puller.
10. Remove all steering gear housing to frame mounting bolts.
11. On Forward Control models, steering gear assembly can now be moved forward, down and out of vehicle.
12. On all other models:
    a. From inside cab remove three bolts attaching the rear of left front fender skirt to toe-board.
    b. Remove the six bolts attaching fender skirt to fender ledge.
    c. Remove fender to dash brace rod and disconnect horn wire from horn.
    d. Working under fender pry rear of fender skirt forward and outward until it rests on the outside toe-board flange.
    e. Working over fender pry fender skirt outward along frame at steering gear housing to provide proper clearance between frame and opening in fender skirt.
    f. Slide steering gear assembly slightly upward toward toe-board, then rotate until attaching flange is up. Raise slightly and slide forward removing assembly over front of front fender.

Removal—C.O.E.

1. Remove steering wheel using J-2927-A puller and disconnect dash mounting bracket.
2. Remove left hand floor pan and steering column grommet.
3. Disconnect horn wire.
4. Remove fender skirt bolts and remove skirt.
5. Remove pitman arm using tool J-1025.
6. Remove steering gear to frame mounting bolts.

7. Move gear back to clear radiator grille side baffle assembly. It will then be possible to drop the gear down through the fender skirt opening pulling the steering column through opening in floor.

Disassembly

As with any ball or roller bearing unit the steering gear parts must be kept free of dirt. Clean paper or rags should be spread on the bench before starting disassembly of the steering gear.

1. Loosen the lock nut "B" on the end of the sector shaft (fig. 4); then turn the lash adjuster "A" a few turns counterclockwise. This will remove the load from the worm bearings caused by the close meshing of the rack and sector teeth.
2. Loosen the lock nut "C" (fig. 6) on the worm bearing thrust screw and turn the thrust screw "D" counterclockwise a few turns.
3. Place a pan under the assembly to catch the lubricant and remove the bolts attaching the side cover to the housing.
4. Pull the side cover with the sector and shaft from the housing.

NOTE: If sector does not clear the opening in the housing easily, turn the worm shaft by hand until the sector will pass through the opening in the housing.

5. On ½, ¾, 1 and 1½ ton conventional models:
   a. Remove steering gear upper housing cover assembly with steering mast jacket from steering gear housing and worm shaft by sliding it up and off worm shaft.
   b. Remove worm shaft and nut assembly from steering housing by lifting out of steering housing.

CAUTION: Use care that the ball nut does not run down to either end of the worm. Damage will be done to the ends of the ball guides if the nut is allowed to rotate until stopped at the end of the worm.

   c. Remove lower worm bearing lock nut adjuster and bearing.
6. On Forward Control, and 1½ ton School Bus, and all 2 ton models:
   a. Place the steering housing in a bench vise and remove the housing end cover and lower worm bearing.

NOTE: Do not clamp the housing too tightly in vise as damage may result from excessive pressure.

STEERING GEAR ASSEMBLY 9-6

b. Draw the worm shaft and nut assembly from the housing. Lay this assembly flat on the bench so that the ball nut will not thread down to either end. Damage will be done to the ends of the ball guides if the nut is allowed to rotate until stopped at the end of the worm.

7. Remove the lock nut from the lash adjuster and unscrew the lash adjuster from the side cover. Slide the lash adjuster out of slot in the end of the sector shaft.

Disassembly of Ball Bearing Nut

As a rule, disassembly of the ball bearing nut will not be necessary, if it is perfectly free with no indication of binding or tightness when rotated on the worm. However, if there is any indication of binding or tightness, the unit should be disassembled, cleaned and inspected.

1. Remove the screws and clamp retaining the ball guides in the nut. Draw the guides out of the nut.
2. Turn the nut upside down and rotate the worm shaft back and forth until all the balls have dropped out of the nut into a clean pan.

With the balls removed the nut can be pulled endwise off the worm.

Inspection

With the steering gear completely disassembled (figs. 9 and 10) wash all parts in cleaning solvent. Dry them thoroughly with clean rags. With a magnifying glass inspect the roller bearings, cones, worms and nut grooves and the surface of all balls for signs of indentation. Also check for any signs of chipping or breakdown of the surface.

Any parts that show signs of damage should be replaced. Balls must be replaced with genuine Chevrolet parts made according to special specifications for this steering gear. No non-genuine balls should be used regardless of grade or quality.

Inspect the sector shaft for wear and check the fit of the shaft in the housing bushing.

Inspect the fit of the pilot on the end of the sector shaft in its bushing in the side cover. If this bushing is worn a new side cover and bushing assembly should be installed as it is impractical to replace this bushing in the service department.

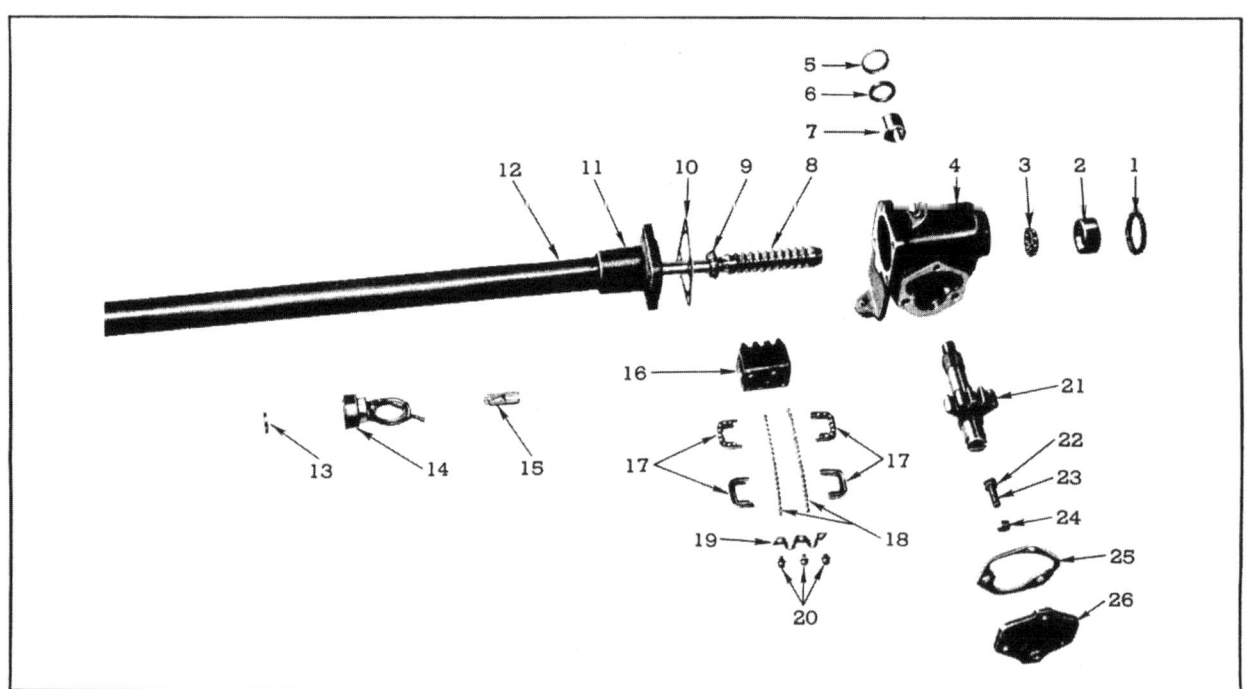

Fig. 9—Layout of ½, ¾, 1, 1½ Ton Steering Gear Parts Except Forward Control and 1½ Ton School Bus

1. Worm Bearing Adjuster Lock Nut
2. Worm Bearing Adjuster
3. Lower Worm Shaft Roller Bearing
4. Housing
5. Sector Shaft Packing
6. Sector Shaft Packing Retainer
7. Sector Shaft Bushing
8. Worm Shaft Assembly
9. Upper Worm Shaft Roller Bearing
10. Housing End Cover Gasket
11. Housing End Cover
12. Mast Jacket
13. Upper Bearing Spring Seat
14. Mast Jacket Bearing Assembly
15. Horn Wire Retainer
16. Ball Nut
17. Ball Guides
18. Balls
19. Ball Guide Clamp
20. Bolt with Internal Tooth Lockwasher
21. Sector and Shaft
22. Lash Adjuster Shim
23. Lash Adjuster
24. Check Nut
25. Housing Side Cover Gasket
26. Housing Side Cover and Bushing Assembly

STEERING GEAR ASSEMBLY 9-7

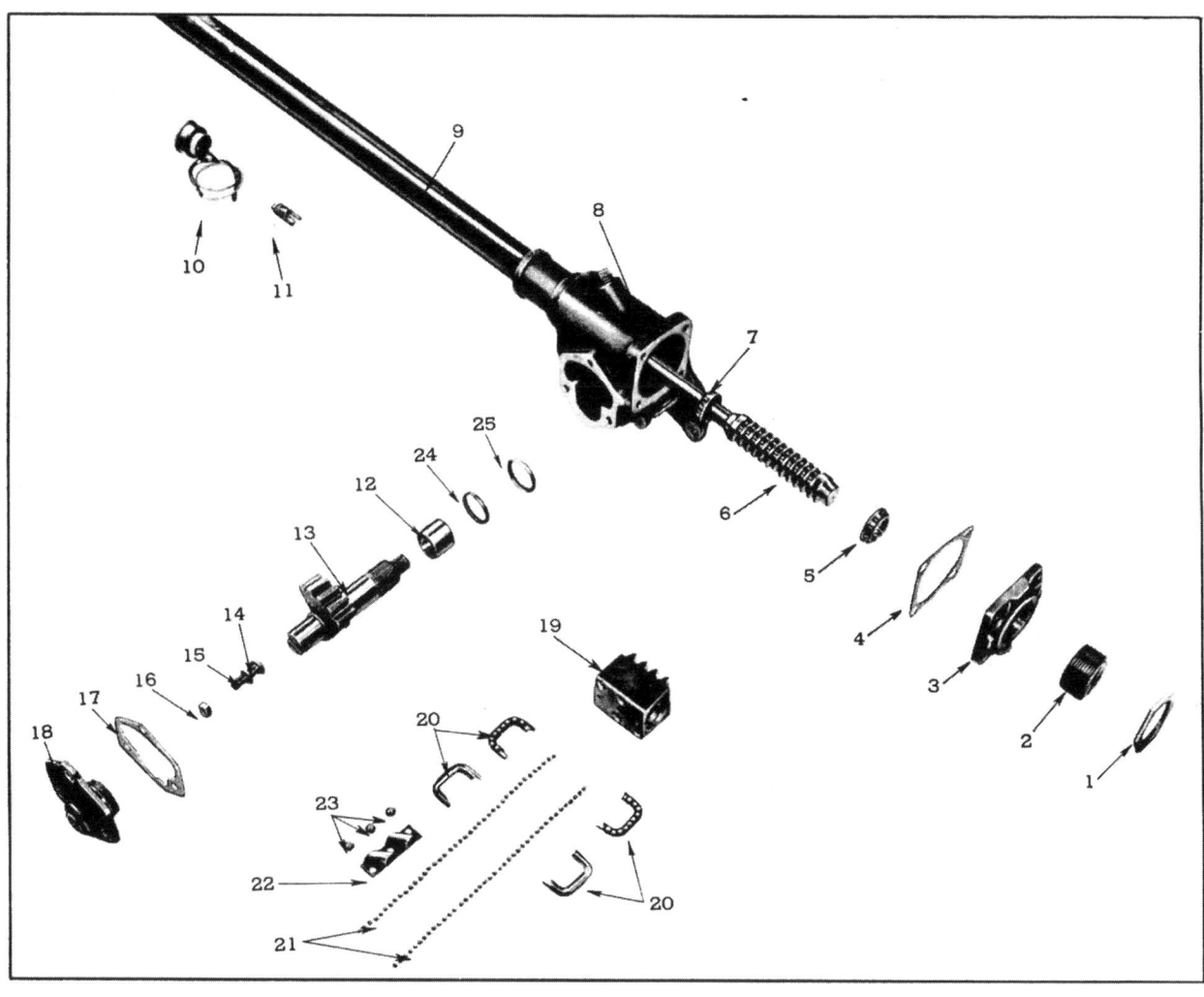

Fig. 10—Steering Gear ¾ and 1 Ton Forward Control, 1½ Ton School Bus and all 2 Ton

1. Worm Bearing Adjuster Lock Nut
2. Worm Bearing Adjuster
3. Housing End Cover
4. End Cover Gasket
5. Lower Worm Shaft Roller Bearing
6. Worm Shaft Assembly
7. Upper Worm Shaft Roller Bearing
8. Housing
9. Mast Jacket
10. Mast Jacket Bearing Assembly
11. Horn Wire Retainer
12. Sector Shaft Bushing
13. Sector and Shaft
14. Lash Adjuster
15. Lash Adjuster Shim
16. Check Nut
17. Housing Side Cover Gasket
18. Housing Side Cover and Bushing Assembly
19. Ball Nut
20. Ball Guides
21. Balls
22. Ball Guide Clamp
23. Bolt With Internal Tooth Lockwasher
24. Sector Shaft Packing
25. Sector Shaft Packing Retainer

Check the ball guides for any damage at the ends where they deflect or pick the balls from their helical path. Any damaged guides should be replaced.

REPAIRS

Sector Shaft Bushing and Packing Replacement

1. Support steering gear housing in an arbor press and press sector shaft bushing, packing and packing retainer from housing (fig. 11). Use Sector Shaft Bushing Driver J-1614 for ½, ¾, 1 and 1½ ton models, except the 1½ ton school bus, and use driver J-1615 on the 1½ ton school bus and all 2 ton models.

2. Press new bushing into position using the same sector shaft bushing driver as used for removal.

   NOTE: Bushings are diamond bored to size and require no further reaming.

3. Press new packing and retainer into housing.

Sector Shaft Packing Replacement

1. Pry packing retainer out of housing and remove packing.
2. Soak new packing in engine oil to lubricate it; then, install it in a new packing retainer.
3. Press packing retainer and packing into housing.

STEERING GEAR ASSEMBLY 9-8

Fig. 11—Replacing Sector Shaft Bushings

ASSEMBLY

Ball Nut

1. Place the worm shaft flat on the bench and slip the nut over the worm with the ball guide holes up and the shallow end of the rack teeth to the left from the steering wheel position. Align the grooves in the worm and nut by sighting through the ball guide holes.

2. On ½, ¾, 1 and 1½ ton models, count 30 balls (50 on the 1½ ton School Bus and all 2 ton models) into a suitable container. This is the proper number of balls for one circuit. Drop the counted balls from the container into one of the guide holes while turning the worm gradually away from that hole. Continue until the ball circuit is full from the bottom of one guide hole to the bottom of the other or until stopped by reaching the end of the worm.

   NOTE: In cases where the balls are stopped by the end of the worm, hold down those balls already dropped into the nut with the blunt end of a clean rod or punch (fig. 12) and turn the worm in the reverse direction a few turns. The filling of the circuit can then be continued. It may be necessary to work the worm back and forth, holding the balls down first in one hole then the other, to close up the spaces between the balls and fill the circuit completely and solidly.

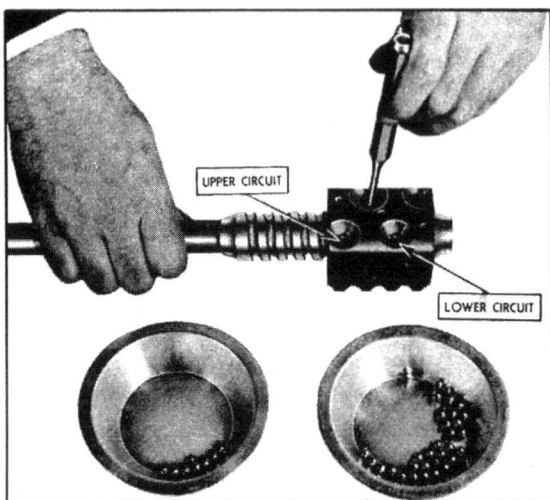

Fig. 12—Filling Ball Circuits in Nut

3. Lay one-half of the ball guide, groove up, on the bench and place the remaining balls from the count container in it (fig. 13). The number of the balls remaining should just fill the guide.

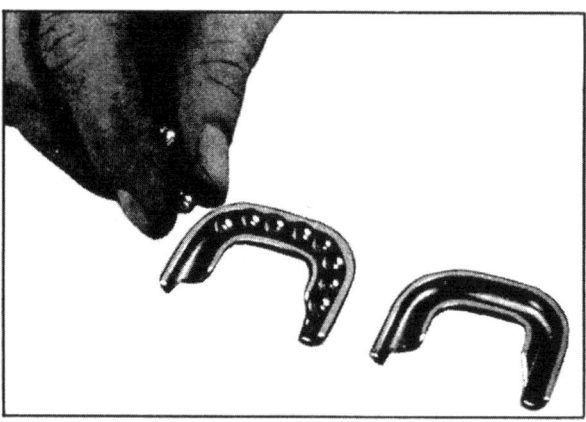

Fig. 13—Filling Ball Guides

4. Close this half of guide with the other half. Hold the two halves together and plug each open end with vaseline so balls will not drop out while installing guide.

5. Push the guide into the guide holes of the nut (fig. 14). This completes one circuit of balls. If the guide does not push all the way down easily, tap it lightly into place with the wooden handle of a screwdriver.

6. Fill the second ball circuit in the same manner as described.

7. Assemble the ball guide clamp to the nut, being sure to use lockwashers under the clamp screws, then tighten the screws securely.

Check the assembly by rotating the nut on the worm to see that it moves *freely. Do not rotate*

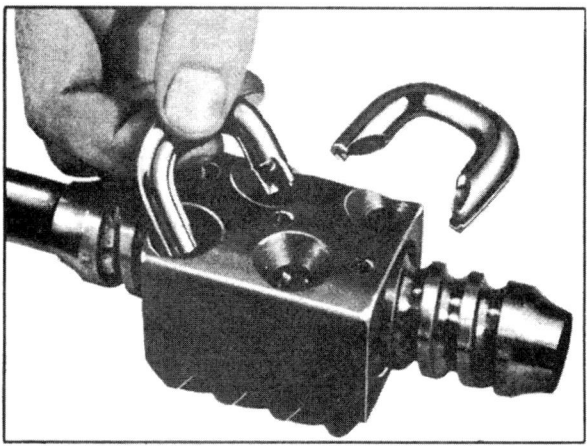

Fig. 14—Removing or Replacing Ball Guides

the nut to the end of the worm threads as this may damage the ball guides. If there is any "stickiness" in the motion of the nut, some slight damage to the ends of the ball guides may have been overlooked.

Assembly of Steering Gear

After a major service overhaul where all of the original factory installed lubricant has been washed out of the steering gear assembly; the threads of the adjuster cup, side cover bolts and lash adjuster should be coated with a suitable non-drying, oil-resistant sealing compound such as Permatex No. 2. This is to prevent leakage of gear lubricant from the steering gear assembly. The compound should not be applied to female threads and extreme care should be exercised in applying this compound to the bearing adjuster cup, as the compound must be kept away from the bearing race.

1. On ½, ¾, 1 and 1½ ton conventional models:
   a. Place the worm shaft and nut assembly into the housing and place the upper roller bearing over the worm shaft.
   b. Place a new housing end cover gasket over the end of the worm shaft, make sure the horn wire is through the opening in the mast jacket, and then slide the housing end cover with mast jacket over the worm shaft and assemble it to the housing.
   c. Install lower roller bearing, worm bearing adjuster and lock nut in lower end of housing.
2. On Forward Control, 1½ ton school bus, and all 2 ton models:
   a. Place the upper roller bearing over the end of the worm shaft; then, after making sure the end of the horn wire is through its opening in the housing, place the worm shaft and nut assembly into the housing.
   b. Back the worm bearing adjuster out of the housing end cover a few turns. Install the lower roller bearing and assemble the lower end cover to the housing using a new gasket.
3. Assemble the lash adjuster with shim in the slot in the end of sector shaft. Check the end clearance which should not be greater than .002" (fig. 15). For the purpose of adjusting this end clearance, a steering gear lash adjuster shim unit Part Number 605142 is available. It contains four shims—.063", .065", .067" and .069" thick.

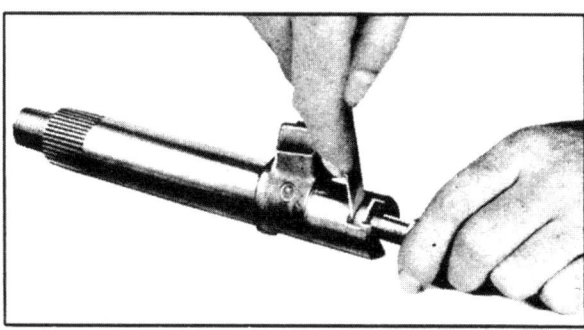

Fig. 15—Checking Sector Shaft Lash Adjuster End Clearance

4. After the lash adjuster end clearance has been adjusted, start the sector shaft pilot into the bushing in the side cover. Then, using a screwdriver through the hole in the cover, turn the lash adjuster in a counterclockwise direction to pull the sector shaft pilot into its bushing as far as it will go.
5. Rotate the worm shaft by hand until the ball nut is about in the center of travel. This is to make sure that the rack and sector will engage properly, with the center tooth of the sector entering the center tooth space of the nut.
6. Place a new gasket on side cover, then push the side cover assembly including sector shaft into place. After making sure there is some lash between the rack and sector teeth, assemble and tighten the side cover bolts.

Adjustment—On Bench

1. Tighten the worm bearing adjuster until all worm shaft end play has been removed. Then tighten the lock nut.
2. Install the steering wheel on the worm shaft temporarily. Carefully turn the steering wheel all the way in one direction and then turn back about one turn.
3. Using a J-544-A Steering Gear Checking Scale, at right angles to one spoke at wheel rim, measure the pull required to keep the

wheel in motion. This should be between 1 and 1½ pounds. If necessary, adjust the worm bearing adjuster until proper pull is obtained.

4. Turn the steering wheel from one stop all the way to the other, counting the number of turns. Then turn the wheel back exactly half the number of turns to the center position and mark the wheel at the top or bottom with a piece of tape.

5. Turn the sector lash adjuster screw clockwise to remove all lash between rack and sector teeth. Tighten the lock nut.

   NOTE: Be sure adjustment is not changed while tightening the lock nut.

6. Using the J-544-A Steering Gear Checking Scale, check the pull at the rim of the steering wheel. Take the highest reading on the scale as the wheel is pulled through the center position. This should be between 2 and 2½ pounds.

7. If necessary, readjust the lash adjuster screw to obtain the proper pull. Tighten the lock nut to 10-15 ft. lbs. torque and again check the pull.

8. Fill the assembly with steering gear lubricant to the level of the filler plug hole and replace filler plug. On Cab-Over-Engine models fill assembly through the lubricant filler pipe to approximately ½ inch from top.

INSTALLATION—ALL EXCEPT C.O.E.

1. Place the steering assembly back in the vehicle and align housing and bracket to frame. Install all mounting bolts and draw up snug, but do not tighten.

2. On conventional models, push fenders skirt in place and start all bolts in position (do not tighten as leaving them loose helps in aligning holes and fender brace). After all bolts are in place, start tightening bolts from front to rear.

3. Assemble pitman arm, lockwasher and nut and tighten to 90-100 ft. lbs. torque. Do not pound on pitman arm as this may cause internal damage.

4. On ½ and ¾ ton, install the gearshift control housing on the mast jacket using caution to locate dowel on housing in elongated slot of mast jacket. Do not tighten clamp bolts.

5. On Forward Control models, install mast jacket opening cover.

6. Install toe-board plate. Attach a piece of tie wire to the end of the horn wire that enters the mast jacket, then push the horn wire inside the opening in the mast jacket. Slide mast jacket toe-board seal and grommet over mast jacket. Place floor mat in position, making sure edge of opening for mast jacket is between grommet and seal. Assemble to toe-board plate.

7. Pull horn wire through opening in mast jacket and install wire retainer.
   a. On ½ and ¾ ton, check clearance between gearshift lever and gearshift upper control shaft support as instructed in Section 7 under "Steering Column Gearshift—Adjustment."
   b. Replace upper control shaft. Tighten clamp bolt and replace upper support screws.

8. Install mast jacket to instrument panel grommet, bracket and spacers, if any. Install bracket bolts and tighten securely. Then, tighten housing to frame side rail bolts to 40-50 ft. lbs. torque.

9. Install seat cushion on conventional models.

10. Install steering shaft upper bearing spring seat (with the flared end up) and spring. Install steering wheel and insert horn button insulator, contact and spring assembly in opening provided in steering wheel hub, making sure the contact brush (solid end) is in the downward position. Install contact cup, positioning the tang on the lower side in the opening provided in the steering wheel hub.

11. Install steering wheel washer and nut and tighten to 35-40 ft. lbs. torque. Install horn button. Connect horn wire at mast jacket. Test operation of horn.

    NOTE: On models where it was necessary to remove clamp holding vacuum lines, align the vacuum lines to their proper position and install clamp.

12. Check clearance between end of gearshift lever and lower edge of steering wheel rim as instructed in Section 7 under "Steering Column Gearshift—Adjustment."

INSTALLATION—C.O.E.

1. Place steering assembly back in vehicle and align housing and bracket to frame. Start all mounting bolts and draw up snug, but do not tighten.

2. Replace fender skirt.

3. Assemble pitman arm, lockwasher and nut and tighten to 90-100 ft. lbs. torque.

STEERING GEAR ASSEMBLY 9-11

4. Install mast jacket to instrument panel clamp making sure it is not necessary to force mast jacket in place to install clamp. If necessary, adjust dash mounting bracket to fit and then tighten. Tighten housing to frame bolts to 40-50 ft. lbs. torque.

5. Replace left hand floor pan and steering column grommet.
6. Install steering wheel, horn contact and retaining nut and tighten to 35-40 ft. lbs. torque; then, install horn button cap and connect horn wire.

TROUBLES AND REMEDIES
STEERING GEAR

| Symptom and Probable Cause | Probable Remedy |

Hard Steering

a. Lack of lubrication.

b. Tie rod ends too tight.
c. Underinflated tires.
d. Improper adjustment.

a. Lubricate steering gear, tie rod ends and steering connecting rod ball joints.
b. Readjust tie rod ends.
c. Inflate tires to recommended pressure.
d. Adjust according to instructions.

Loose Steering

a. Improper adjustments.
b. Loose ball joints.
c. Worn steering knuckle bushings.
d. Worn sector shaft bushings.

a. Adjust according to instructions.
b. Adjust ball joints.
c. Replace steering knuckle bushings.
d. Replace bushings.

STEERING GEAR SPECIFICATIONS

Gear Ratio

½, ¾, 1 and 1½ Ton Conventional Models..26.24 to 1
¾ and 1 Ton Forward Control Models..19.8 to 1
1½ Ton School Bus and all 2 Ton Models..27.76 to 1
Type ....Recirculating Ball
Number. Balls Used
  ½, ¾, 1 and 1½ Ton Conventional Models and Forward Control 60
  1½ Ton School Bus, and all 2 Ton Models... 100
End Clearance—Lash Adjuster to Sector Slot.. .002" Max.
Worm Bearing Adjustment....................................1 to 1½ lbs. to keep wheel in motion
Lash Adjustment or High point..2 to 2½ pounds

TORQUE SPECIFICATIONS
STEERING GEAR

Steering Gear to Frame Bolt Nuts...40-50 ft. lbs.
Pitman Arm Nut ....90-100 ft. lbs.
Steering Wheel Nut..30-40 ft. lbs.
Lash Adjuster Lock Nut..10-15 ft. lbs.

STEERING GEAR ASSEMBLY 9-12

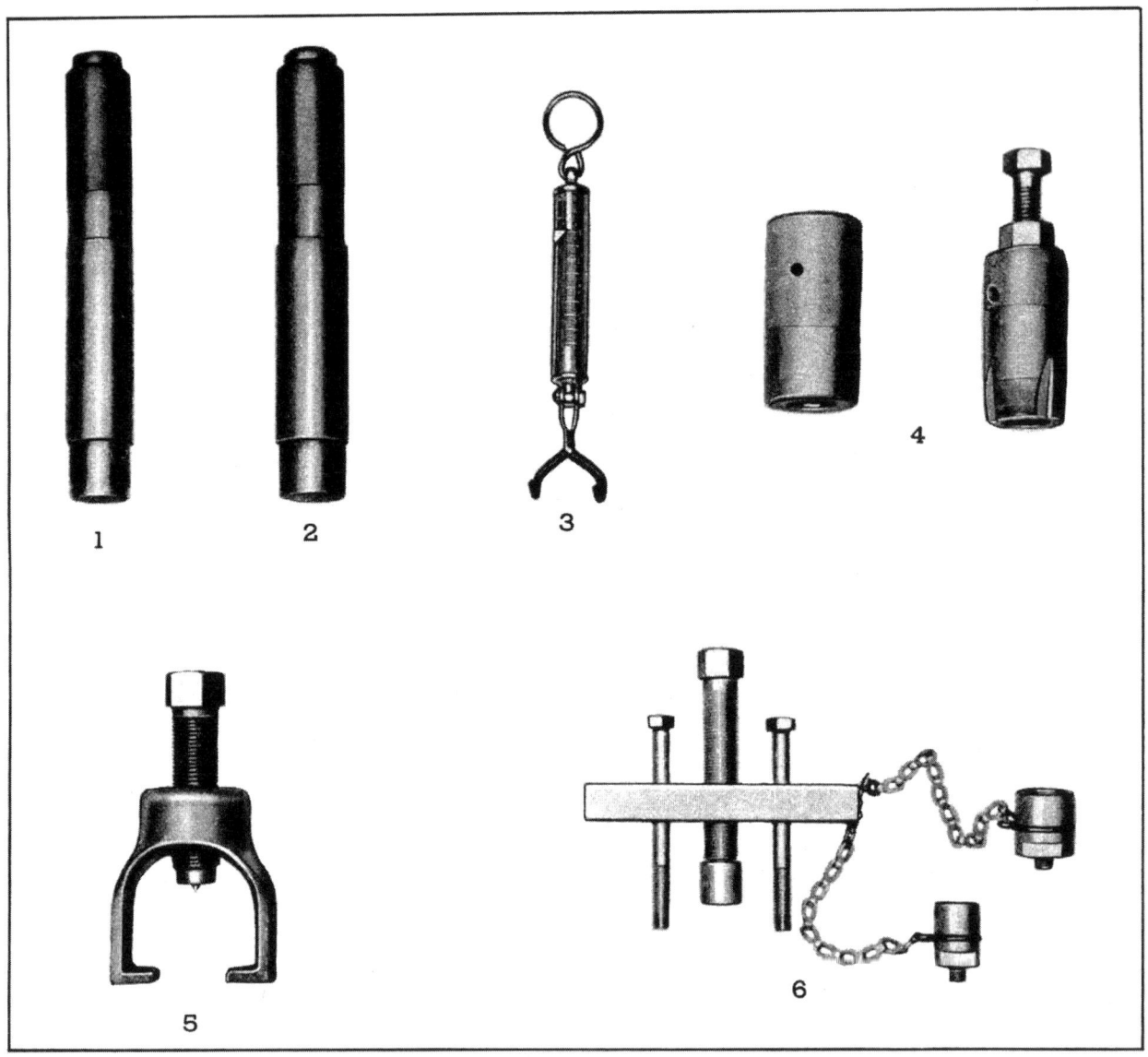

Fig. 16—Steering Gear Special Tools

1. J-1614 Pitman Shaft Bushing Driver
2. J-1615 Pitman Shaft Bushing Driver
3. J-544-A Steering Wheel Checking Scale
4. J-2565 Mast Jacket Bearing Remover and Replacer
5. J-1025 Pitman Arm Puller
6. J-2927-A Steering Wheel Puller

SECTION 10

WHEELS AND TIRES

CONTENTS OF THIS SECTION

	Page
Wheels and Tires	10-1
Troubles and Remedies	10-8
Service News Reference	10-8

INDEX

	Page		Page
General Description	10-1	1, 1½ and 2 Ton (3 Section Rim)	10-3
Tire Inflation Table	10-1	1½ Ton Special, 2 Ton and C.O.E. (2 Section Rim)	10-5
Maintenance	10-2		
Mounting Synthetic Tubes	10-2	Balancing	10-7
Tire Changing	10-2	Wheel and Tire Balance	10-7
½ Ton	10-2	Static Balance	10-7
¾ Ton	10-2	Dynamic Balance	10-7

GENERAL DESCRIPTION

There are four types of steel disc wheels used on Chevrolet trucks. The ½ ton models are equipped with drop center rim wheels, ¾ ton models are equipped with two-piece rims, 1, 1½ and 2 ton models are equipped with a three section rim, but a two section rim is optional on 1½ ton special, 2 ton and C.O.E.

Chevrolet commercial vehicles are equipped with part synthetic rubber tires and all synthetic tubes. Vehicles should be equipped with tires having a rated capacity to handle the anticipated loads as overloading tires seriously affects their life. The recommended size tires for the various vehicles is given in the Load Capacity Chart, Section O.

Maintaining the correct tire pressure is one of the most important elements in tire maintenance. The following table gives the proper inflation pressure for the various size tires used on Chevrolet trucks.

INFLATION TABLE

6.00-16- 6 ply rating	front 30 p.s.i., rear 36 p.s.i.
6.50-16- 6 ply rating	front 26 p.s.i., rear 36 p.s.i.
6.50-20- 6 ply rating	front 40 p.s.i., rear 50 p.s.i.
6.70-15- 6 ply rating	front 26 p.s.i., rear 30 p.s.i.
7.00-17- 6 ply rating	front 40 p.s.i., rear 45 p.s.i.
7.00-17- 8 ply rating	front 40 p.s.i., rear 55 p.s.i.
7.00-18- 8 ply rating	front 40 p.s.i., rear 55 p.s.i.
7.00-20- 8 ply rating	front 40 p.s.i., rear 55 p.s.i.
7.00-20-10 ply rating	front 45 p.s.i., rear 70 p.s.i.
7.50-17- 8 ply rating	front 40 p.s.i., rear 60 p.s.i.
7.50-17-10 ply rating	front 40 p.s.i., rear 75 p.s.i.
7.50-20- 8 ply rating	front 40 p.s.i., rear 60 p.s.i.
7.50-20-10 ply rating	front 45 p.s.i., rear 75 p.s.i.
8.25-20-10 ply rating	front 40 p.s.i., rear 65 p.s.i.
8.25-20-12 ply rating	front 60 p.s.i., rear 75 p.s.i.
9.00-20-10 ply rating	rear 65 p.s.i.

LIGHT TRUCK 15 INCH TIRE

Ply Rating	Load per Tire (Pounds)	Tire Pressure (Pounds)
6 (1948-51)	1410	36
	1500	40
8 (1948-50)	1410	36
	1500	40
	1590	44
	1670	48

MAINTENANCE

MOUNTING SYNTHETIC TUBES

1. Before installing tube in tire, clean inside of casing thoroughly.
2. Insert tube in tire and inflate until it is nearly rounded out.
3. Inspect rim for rust scale and bent flanges—clean rust scale and straighten flanges where necessary.
4. Using a brush or cloth swab, apply a solution of neutral vegetable oil soap to the inside and outside of tire beads and also to the rim side of the tube. Do not allow soap solution to run down into tire.
5. When mounting tire and tube on a drop center rim, follow the standard procedure. Be sure tire is centered on rim so that beads are out of rim well before inflating. Do not allow tire to hang loosely on wheel while inflating.
6. Center valve and pull it firmly against the rim. Hold in this position and inflate until tire beads are firmly seated on rim against flanges.
7. Completely deflate tire by removing valve core.
8. Reinflate tire to recommended pressure.

CAUTION: When tube and flap are not properly lubricated and mounted, they will stretch thin in the tire bead and rim region. This will cause premature failure.

TIRE CHANGING
½-TON—DROP CENTER RIMS

Mounting Tire

1. Examine the inside of the casing and remove all dirt or foreign matter. An air hose equipped with a dusting nozzle and valve does a quick, efficient job of removing loose dirt. In the case of mounting a new or repaired tire, it may be necessary to brush out scale and dirt, or to wipe out with a dry sponge about the size of the casing.
2. Insert deflated tube in tire with valve at the location of the balance mark on the outside of the casing. Inflate the tube until it is barely rounded out, not stretched.
3. Wet a small cloth about 8 inches square with Ru-Glyde or similar rubber lubricant and wipe both inside walls of the tire, wetting only the area of the shoulder of the bead and about 2 inches of the side wall. Also wet the exposed area of the tube.
4. Apply one tire bead by pushing portion of bead into bottom of well; then force remaining portion over flange with tire mounting tool.
5. Spread tire and put valve stem through rim hole. A valve extension, or a valve fishing tool, may be found helpful for this operation.
6. Apply second bead, starting opposite the valve by forcing bead down into rim well, and then continue to work remainder of bead over the flange using a tire mounting tool.
7. With the tire flat on floor, with valve up, check to be sure that tire is in center of wheel. Pull out valve stem so that its base seats firmly on inner surface of the rim, at the same time centering the valve. Hold in this position and slowly inflate until both beads are properly seated.
8. Check to be sure centering ribs show evenly all around and above rim flange. Then, deflate tire completely by either removing the valve core or by using a deflating cap.
9. The assembly is now ready for inflation to recommended pressure.

¾ TON—TWO PIECE RIMS

Demounting Tire

1. Completely deflate tire by removing valve core.
2. Support wheel disc (retaining ring side up) on three or four wood blocks (2" x 4" block 3" or 4" long) to keep tire off the floor.
3. Loosen the tire bead from its seat in the rim by driving the flat end of the tire iron between the bead and the rim. Hold the iron down on the side wall to avoid cutting the bead, and make sure the iron is driven in until it strikes the rim. Apply downward pressure on the tire iron to force the bead away from the retaining ring. Continue around the tire until it is loosened all the way around and the retaining ring can be moved from its support on the gutter diameter and into the gutter well.
4. Insert curved end of tire iron in the square notch in the retaining ring and pry out and

up while holding the ring down into the gutter at the opposite side (fig. 1). Continue this operation until the cutaway portion of the retaining ring nearest the tire iron spans the outside diameter of the rim gutter.

Fig. 1—¾ Ton Tire Removal

5. Continue to pry the remainder of this half of the retaining ring from the gutter by moving progressively toward the other cutaway portion in the ring.
6. The remainder of the retaining ring can now be pried out of the gutter and the ring removed.
7. Turn the wheel over and place it on the blocks with the ring side down; then force tire from wheel rim. Remove tire flap and tube from tire.

Mounting Tire

1. Remove all rust scale from the rim and retainer ring.
2. Insert tube in tire and inflate until tube is nearly rounded out.
3. Lubricate tire beads, rim sides of tube and both sides of flap with a solution of neutral vegetable oil soap or Ru-Glyde or similar rubber lubricant. Insert flap in tire.
4. Place the wheel (rim flange down) on three or four small blocks.
5. Place tire on rim with the valve in line with the valve hole in the rim. Insert valve through hole, then work the tire onto the rim until the outer bead clears the rim gutter.
6. Place the retainer ring on the wheel rim and start the side of the ring opposite the square notch into the rim gutter at "C" (fig. 2) making sure the two cutaway portions of the ring rest on the sides of the wheel at "A" (fig. 2). Hold the first portion of the ring in the rim gutter and pry the remaining portion over the wheel rim. To pry the last portion into place, insert the tire iron in the notch, "B" (fig. 2) thus putting tension on the ring, and tap the ring with a hammer until it drops into place.
7. Inflate slowly to not more than 10 pounds. See that the retainer ring is properly seated on its support in the rim gutter (tapping lightly with a hammer will help seat it firmly), and make sure that the tire bead rests evenly against the rim.

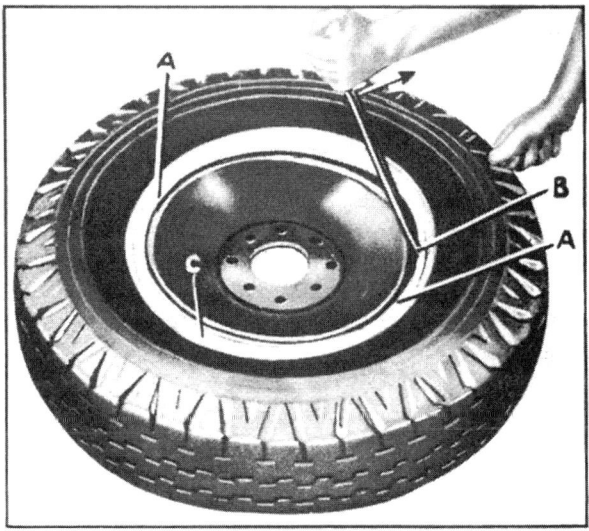

Fig. 2—¾ Ton Tire Installation

8. Turn the tire and wheel over with the ring down, or lean it against a wall with the ring side in. Completely deflate tire by removing valve core and then reinflate to recommended pressure.

1, 1½ AND 2 TON— WITH THREE SECTION RIMS

Demounting Tire

1. Completely deflate tire by removing the valve core.
2. Using a hammer, tap around the side ring progressively to move it in toward the center of the rim until it clears the clamp ring (fig. 3).

3. Starting at the split in the clamp ring, raise its end out of the rim gutter using a screwdriver and the tire iron (fig. 4). Then remove the clamp ring by prying it out of the gutter with the tire iron, moving progressively around the rim (fig. 5).
4. Drive the curved end of the tire iron in between the side ring and the tire bead (fig. 6). Then pry down on the opposite end of tire iron to move the tire bead away from the side ring flange (fig. 7). Continue the foregoing operation progressively around the tire until the side ring is removed. In some cases it may be necessary to work around the tire more than once.

NOTE: The tire bead seat on the side ring is slightly tapered; this design makes removal of ring much easier.

5. Push the valve stem up inside the tire to

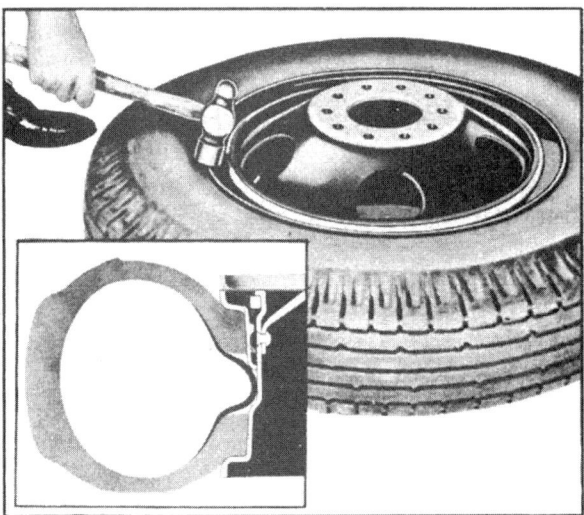

Fig. 3—Releasing Tire Clamp Ring

Fig. 4—Raising End of Clamp Ring

Fig. 5—Removing Tire Clamp Ring

Fig. 6—Starting Side Ring Removal

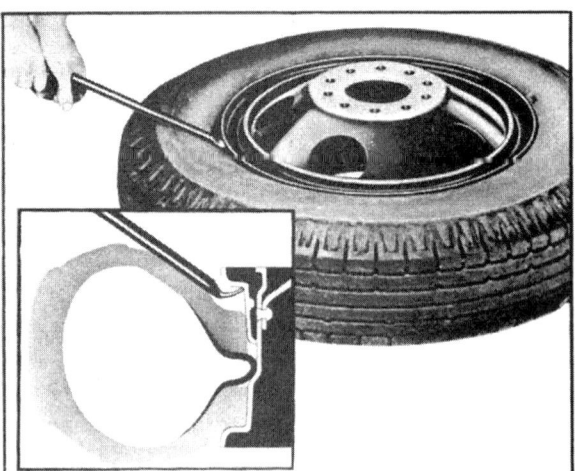

Fig. 7—Removing Side Ring

prevent damage while removing the tire. The tire may be removed from the rim by turning it over and following the procedure described in step 4.

Mounting Tire

1. Remove all rust scale from the rim, side ring and clamp ring.
2. Insert tube in tire and inflate until tube is nearly rounded out.
3. Lubricate tire beads, rim sides of tube, and

both sides of flap with a solution of neutral vegetable oil soap or Ru-Glyde or similar rubber lubricant. Insert flap in tire.

4. Place tire on rim with valve in line with the valve hole in rim. Insert valve through hole; then work tire onto rim.

5. Place side ring into position on tire and rim; then press the side ring into tire and onto the rim using the tapered end of tire iron until the clamp ring gutter is exposed. Insert end of clamp ring in gutter and work progressively around the tire until the clamp ring is seated in the gutter (fig. 8).

Fig. 8—Replacing Clamp Ring

6. Inflate tire slowly while checking to see that the side ring moves out over the clamp ring locking it into the gutter. Completely deflate the tire and then reinflate to recommended pressures.

1½ TON SPECIAL AND 2 TON WITH 2 SECTION RIMS

To facilitate assembly and removal, two cutaway sections "A" (fig. 9) and an operating notch "B" are incorporated in the locking flange of the side ring.

In separating the side ring from the wheel rim of the spare or new wheel for tire installation, stand the wheel up with the operating notch in the side ring at the top. The straight end of a tire iron is inserted and driven into the operating notch (fig. 10). The tool is moved as a lever to lift the side ring away from the rim. After the side ring has passed over the rim gutter at the operating notch work progressively around entire rim until side ring is separated from wheel rim.

Demounting Tire

1. Completely deflate tire by removing the valve core.

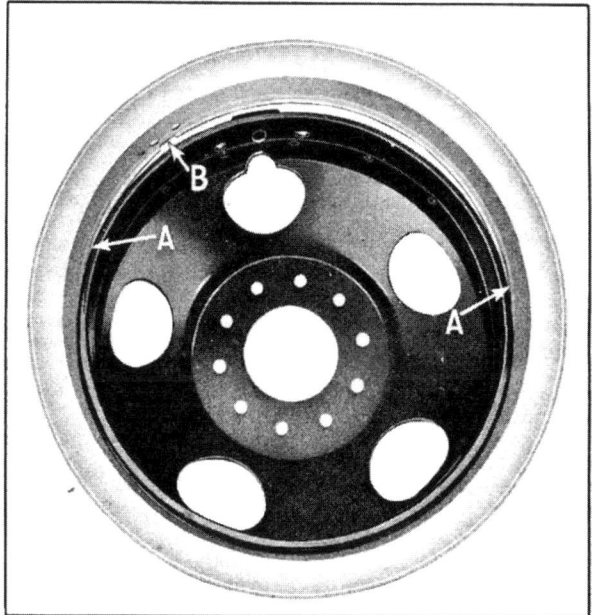

Fig. 9—Side Ring Assembly Points

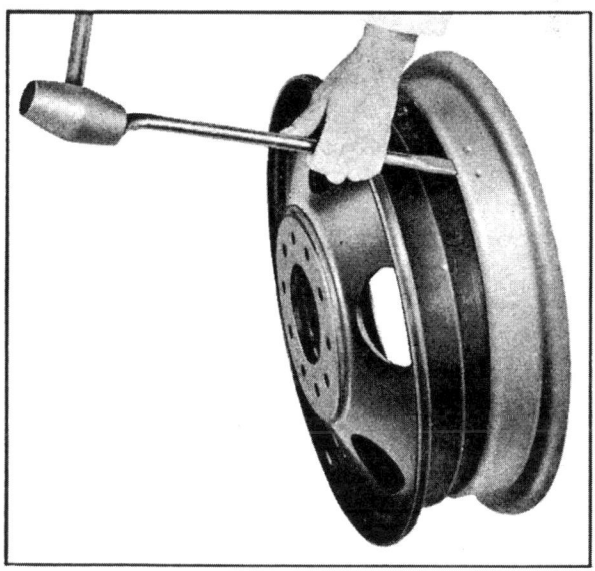

Fig. 10—Iron in Operating Notch

2. Loosen the tire bead from its seat in the side ring by driving the bead loosening end of a tire iron between the tire bead and the side ring (fig. 11). Repeat this operation progressively around the side ring prying until bead is loose.

3. Insert straight end of tire iron into operating notch located at double pimples "B" (fig. 12).

4. Push side ring down at point opposite operating notch and force tire iron handle down causing side ring to disengage from rim gutter. Repeat progressively around side ring prying ring from rim gutter until free.

5. To free opposite tire bead from wheel rim,

WHEELS AND TIRES 10-6

turn tire over and repeat bead loosening operation (fig. 13).

NOTE: It is not necessary to remove side ring from tire bead if tire is to be removed for tube repair only. Simply loosen tire bead from wheel rim as in Figure 13. Then turn assembly over and remove ring with tire attached as in Figure 12.

Mounting the Tire

1. Remove all rust scale from wheel rim and side ring.
2. Insert tube in tire and inflate until tube is nearly rounded out.
3. Lubricate tire beads, rim sides of tube and both sides of flap with a solution of neutral vegetable soap or Ru-Glyde or similar rubber lubricant. Insert flap in tire.

Fig. 13—Loosening Tire Bead

Fig. 11—Loosening Tire Bead

Fig. 12—Disengaging Side Ring from Rim Gutter

4. Place disc portion of wheel on floor with rim gutter up and install tire and tube assembly indexing tube valve stem with stem support in wheel rim and with valve stem pointing in desired direction.
5. Place side ring in position with operating notch "B" (fig. 14) approximately three inches from valve on either side.

Fig. 14—Positioning Side Ring

6. The two cutaway sections opposite each other "A" (fig. 15) on inner diameter of side ring are positioned so as to span the rim gutter.
7. At point "C" (fig. 15), opposite valve, force ring into rim gutter as far as possible.
8. Insert straight end of tire iron into operating notch "B" (fig. 16). Then pull in direction indicated.
9. Retain pressure with tool and strike side ring downward at a point between operating notch and cutaway section, thereby engaging side ring over rim gutter at these points.
10. Remove tool and strike additional blows pro-

Fig. 15—Positioning Rim into Rim Gutter

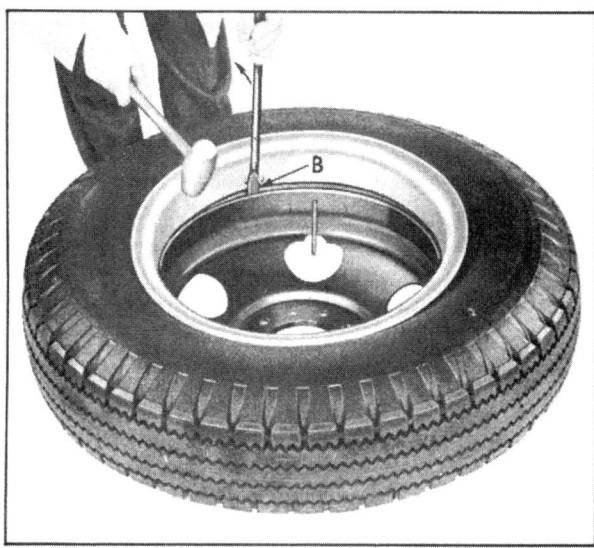

Fig. 16—Engaging Side Ring over Rim Gutter

Fig. 17—Checking Side Ring for Bind on Rim

gressively toward other cutaway section until entire toe of side ring has passed over the rim gutter.

11. While the side ring is being applied to the wheel rim, it is tight and requires force or hammer blows to complete the application. When the side ring is completely installed on the rim, it is no longer tight and can be depressed or will yield to a light hammer blow. Precaution should be taken to see that the side ring is not binding on the rim and can be freely depressed (fig. 17) before inflating the tire.

BALANCING

Original equipment tires and tubes (15" and 16" only) are marked by the tire manufacturer so that the light portion of the casing is counterbalanced by the heavy portion of the tube.

Due to irregularities in tread wear, caused by sudden brake applications, misalignment, low inflation pressure, or tube and casing repairs, a casing and tube assembly can lose its original balance. If a disturbance is felt in the steering wheel due to the action of the front wheels, the first items to check are pressures and the balance of the tire and wheel assembly.

WHEEL AND TIRE BALANCE

Wheel balance is the equal distribution of the weight of the wheel and tire assembly around the axis of rotation. There are two ways in which every wheel must be balanced—statically and dynamically.

Static Balance

Static balance (sometimes called still balance) is the equal distribution of weight of the wheel and tire assembly about the axis of rotation in such a manner that the assembly has no tendency to rotate by itself, regardless of its position. For example: A wheel with a chunk of dirt on the rim will always rotate by itself until the heavy side is at the bottom. Any wheel with a heavy side like this is statically out of balance. Static unbalance of a wheel causes a hopping or pounding action (up and down) which frequently leads to wheel "flutter" and quite often to wheel "tramp."

Dynamic Balance

Dynamic balance (sometimes called running balance) means that the wheel must be in static balance, and also run smoothly at all speeds on an axis which runs through the center line of the wheel and tire and is perpendicular to the axis of rotation.

Wheels must be both statically and dynamically

balanced to give maximum steering ease and stability at speeds where unbalance becomes noticeable. The wheels must be statically balanced before they can be balanced dynamically.

Before the wheel assembly is balanced, the wheel and tire must be clean and free from all foreign matter. The tires should be in good condition and properly mounted with the balance mark on the tire lined up with the valve stem in the tube. Bent wheels that have runout over $1/16''$ on $1/2$, $3/4$ and 1 ton or $1/8''$ on $1\frac{1}{2}$ and 2 ton should either be replaced or straightened before being balanced.

When balancing wheels and tires, it is recommended that the instructions covering the operation of the wheel balancer being used are closely followed, so that proper balancing of wheels and tires is obtained.

TROUBLES AND REMEDIES
WHEELS AND TIRES

Symptom and Probable Cause	Probable Remedy
Front Wheel Shimmy	
a. Loose wheel lugs	a. Tighten lugs
b. Loose or broken wheel bearing	b. Tighten or replace bearing and adjust according to instructions
c. Bent wheel	c. Replace or straighten wheel
d. Improper alignment	d. Correct alignment as per specifications
e. Wheel out of balance	e. Balance wheel
f. Loose tie rod ends	f. Replace tie rod ends
Hard Steering	
a. Low air pressure in tires	a. Inflate tire to recommended pressure per load
b. Lack of lubrication	b. Lubricate according to instructions
c. Improper wheel alignment	c. Front alignment correction
d. Sagging front or rear spring	d. Replace springs as required
e. Bent wheel or spindle	e. Straighten or replace wheel or replace spindle
f. Broken wheel bearings	f. Replace necessary bearings
Improper Tire Wear	
a. Improper air pressures per load carried on vehicles	a. Inflate to recommended pressure
b. Not rotating tires as required	b. Rotate tires according to instructions
c. Improper acting brakes	c. Correct brakes as required
d. Improper camber	d. Align front end as per specifications
e. High speed driving on turns	e. Take turns more slowly
f. Bent axle	f. Straighten or replace axle
g. Rapid stopping	g. Apply brakes slowly as approaching stop
Noise in Front or Rear Wheels	
a. Loose wheel lugs	a. Tighten wheel lugs
b. Broken or rough wheel bearings	b. Replace bearings according to instructions
c. Scored drums	c. Replace brake lining and remachine drums
d. Lack of lubrication	d. Lubricate as per instructions

SERVICE NEWS REFERENCE

Month	Page No.	Subject

SECTION 11

CHASSIS SHEET METAL

CONTENTS OF THIS SECTION

	Page
Hood	11- 1
Radiator Grille and Baffles	11- 7
Front End Sheet Metal	11-10
Rear Fender	11-11
Running Board	11-11
C.O.E. Sheet Metal	11-12
Service News Reference	11-13

HOOD ASSEMBLY

INDEX

	Page		Page
General Description	11-1	Hood Support Arms	11-4
Minor Service Operations	11-2	Lower Catch Plate	11-4
Front Name Plate	11-2	Major Service Operations	11-4
Center Moulding	11-2	Hood Assembly	11-4
Side Name or Series Plate	11-3	Removal	11-4
Upper Catch Plate Bolt	11-3	Installation	11-4
Replace	11-3	Alignment	11-4
Adjust	11-3	Hood Half	11-6
Upper Catch Plate	11-3	Removal	11-6
Hood Hinge	11-3	Installation	11-6

GENERAL DESCRIPTION

The hood is an alligator jaw type, opening at the front and operated by a counter-balancing device comprised of a spring loaded support arm on each side of cowl, and so designed that the spring tension holds the hood in the open position.

The hood, comprised of two panels, right and left, when opened, provides access to the engine compartment (fig. 1). The opening line along the sides is at the juncture of the hood panels and the front fender ledge.

The hood lock is located below the upper grille bar, in line with the left end of name plate, and can be released by pulling the lever forward (fig. 2). The safety catch can then be released by reaching under the nose of hood and pulling forward and up on the catch release (fig. 3).

To close hood, lower it to the safety latch position and then push down on nose of hood to lock it.

The hinge arrangement is designed to permit proper hood opening without interference.

Each hood hinge comprises a pressed steel plate with two hinge support arms securely pinned by heavy rivets to bosses in the plate. Heavy bracing,

Fig. 1—Engine Compartment Accessibility

Fig. 2—Hood Lock Release

welded to the hood panels, provides the rigid mounting point for hood ends of the hinge arms, which are attached by bolts to the hood panels.

Each hinge plate is rigidly attached to the side of the cowl by three bolts, two of which are $3/8''$ hex head and extend through the cowl from inside into square nuts permanently staked in place on the outside of the hinge plate (fig. 4). The lower ($5/16''$ hex head) bolt, extends from the outside through the plate and cowl into an anchor nut permanently located in place on the inside of the cowl.

The holes through the cowl and hinge plate are elongated horizontally as well as being considerably wider than the bolt diameters to provide for shifting either hinge plate in any direction necessary for proper hood adjustment and replacement.

Fig. 3—Hood Safety Catch Release

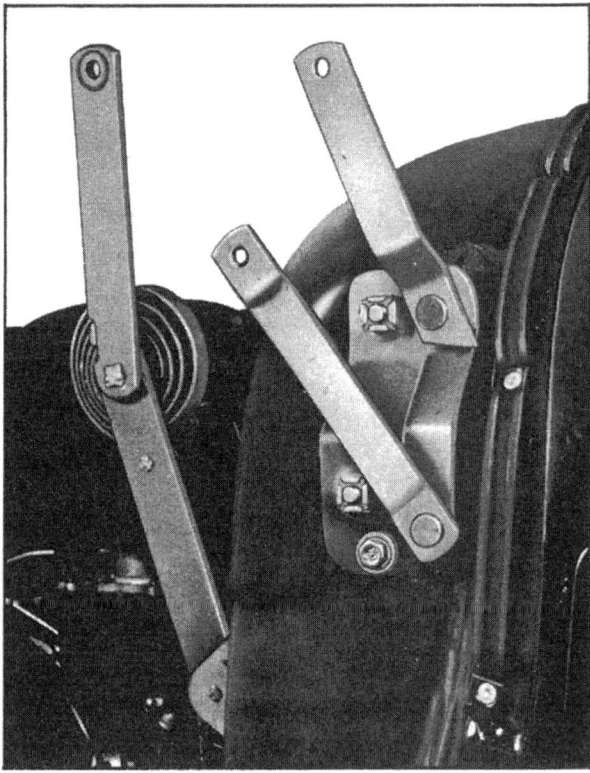

Fig. 4—Hood Hinge Plate and Support Arm

MINOR SERVICE OPERATIONS

FRONT NAME PLATE

Replacement

1. Open hood and working from underside of hood remove the bolts and washers attaching name plate to hood. Then remove name plate.
2. Place new hood front name plate in position and install the bolts and washers attaching it to hood.

CENTER MOULDING

Replacement

1. Open hood and remove hood front name plate as explained above.
2. Working from underside of hood, bend the metal tangs in a straight vertical position and remove center moulding.
3. Place new hood top center moulding in position on hood, making sure the metal tangs are through hood properly, and that moulding is flush and centered on hood.
4. Working from underside of hood, twist the metal tangs into a locked position.

CAUTION: Care must be used when bending moulding retainer tangs as excessive bending will cause them to break off.

5. Install hood front name plate and close hood.

SIDE NAME OR SERIES PLATE

Replacement

1. Open hood and remove the metal retainers attaching name or series plate to hood and remove plate.
2. Place new side name or series plate in position on hood and install the metal retainers attaching plate on hood securely.

UPPER CATCH PLATE BOLT

Replacement

1. Open hood, loosen lock nut on catch bolt and remove nut.
2. Remove catch bolt, spring and spring retainer from upper catch plate.
3. Place spring retainer and spring over catch bolt and install in upper catch plate.
4. Install lock nut, leaving loose, and adjust hood lock as outlined under adjustment.
5. Holding catch bolt, tighten lock nut and close hood.

Adjustment

1. The closing or locking tension of the lock bolt in the lock plate may be adjusted by loosening the lock nut on the bolt and turning the bolt in the retaining plate (fig. 5) clockwise to increase the tension or counterclockwise to reduce it.

   NOTE: This adjustment also changes the spacing between the underside of the hood and top of grille. Proper spacing at this point is 1/16" which should produce approximately 1/32" compression of the rubber bumpers on the top grille baffle.

2. Lock the lock nut and close hood.

UPPER CATCH PLATE

Replacement

1. Open hood and remove the screws and lockwashers attaching the upper hood catch plate to hood. Also, remove attaching parts of hood brace rods at hood catch end. Loosen attaching parts at hood end and swing out of way.
2. Remove catch plate from hood and remove catch bolt lock nut, bolt, spring and spring retainer.

   NOTE: The safety latch is part of the upper catch plate and is not serviced separately.

3. Install the catch plate bolt, spring, spring retainer and lock nut to new catch plate.
4. Place upper hood catch plate in position on hood and install the screws tying upper hood catch plate to corners of hood and to hood panel brace rods.
5. Install screws attaching upper catch plate to hood.
6. Adjust hood lock and close hood.

HOOD HINGE

Removal

1. Open hood and prop in an upright position.
2. Remove the 2 hex head shoulder bolts attaching hood hinge support arms to hood.
3. From inside of cowl, remove the 2 hinge to cowl bolts. From outside, at cowl hood hinge, remove 1 hex head bolt and washer attaching hood hinge to cowl and remove hinge.

   NOTE: The reason for working from inside to outside at this point is to prevent hinge from falling and causing any damage.

Installation

1. Place hood hinge in position on cowl, align all bolt holes and start the hex head bolt and washer, attaching hood hinge to cowl loosely.
2. Working from inside, install the 2 hinge to cowl bolts loosely.
3. Adjust hood as outlined in steps 7, 8 and 9 under "Hood Alignment."
4. After hood has been positioned, tighten the 2 hinge to cowl bolts from under the cab.
5. Open hood and tighten the outer hinge to cowl bolt securely.

Fig. 5—Hood Lock Bolt and Safety Latch

SUPPORT ARMS

Removal

1. Open hood and prop in upright position.
2. Remove the hex head shoulder bolt attaching hood support arm to hood side.
3. Remove the hex head bolts attaching hood support arm bracket to dash and remove hood support arm.

Installation

1. Place hood support arm in position and install the hex head shoulder bolt attaching it to hood side and tighten securely.
2. Swing lower support arm toward dash panel, placing the bracket in a normal position. Install bolts and washers and tighten securely.

LOWER CATCH PLATE

Replacement

1. Open hood and remove the bolts attaching lower catch plate to radiator grille upper baffle (fig. 6). Then remove catch plate.
2. Place the lower hood catch plate in position on radiator grille upper baffle and start the bolts attaching it to baffle, loosely.
3. Follow operations 2, 3 and 4 under adjustment.

Adjustment

1. Open hood and loosen the bolts attaching lock plate to radiator upper baffle. Snug screws up.
2. Drop hood to closed position and lock. This will center hood lock plate.

   NOTE: If the lock plate is not centered and the screws are tightened with the plate positioned all the way forward, closing the hood will allow the lock bolt to force the latch back and catch under the plate making it impossible to open hood.

3. Raise the hood, move lock plate forward $1/32''$ and tighten the lock plate screws securely.
4. Adjust hood lock stud as necessary to allow hood to close when slammed.

Fig. 6—Hood Lock Plate on Top Radiator Baffle

MAJOR SERVICE OPERATIONS

HOOD ASSEMBLY

Removal

1. Lay a fender cover along cowl top to prevent hood from scratching cowl top.
2. Open hood and prop in full upright position.
3. Remove the hex head shoulder bolts on each side attaching hood hinge arms to hood.
4. Remove the hex head shoulder bolts on each side attaching spring loaded hood support to hood.

   CAUTION: When bolts are removed from Support arms, the hood if not held, will fall down and damage hood as well as fender tops. Care must be used at all times.

5. Remove hood from vehicle.

Installation

1. Lay a fender cover along cowl top to prevent hood from scratching cowl top.
2. Place the hood in position and prop in full upright position.
3. Starting on one side, connect the hood hinge arms to hood with the shoulder bolts; then, install the hex head shoulder bolt attaching the spring loaded hood support to hood and tighten all securely.
4. Remove the fender cover from cowl and close hood. Check hood fit and if necessary, adjust as described under "Hood Alignment" in this section.

Alignment

The following procedure may be used to correct improperly fitted hoods. Use all or any part of this procedure as necessary to obtain proper appearance and operation.

1. Loosen fender and skirt attaching bolts to body. Loosen radiator support bolts. Push fenders down to provide clearance for hood adjustment.
2. Check and adjust fender skirt to dash brace rods. Measurements should be taken from center of bolt head to edge of bracket (fig. 7).

	L	R
½ and ¾ ton	27¼"	27"
1, 1½ and 2 ton	27½"	27¼"

Fig. 7—Fender Skirt to Dash Brace Rods

3. Loosen outer hood hinge bolts completely, both sides.
4. Disconnect hood supports from hood and swing hood supports down out of the way. Loosen bolts attaching hood supports to body, both sides. This will permit vertical adjustment of hood supports after hood alignment is completed.
5. Loosen two inner hood hinge bolts, both sides. (Leave these bolts just snug so that hinge can just be moved by jarring or exerting pressure on the hood.)
6. Remove hood lock plate.
7. Adjust hood fore and aft to obtain ⅛" to ¼" gap between rear edge of hood and cowl ledge.

NOTE: If the gap is not even, tight at sides and open at top center or vice versa, add or remove shims between the radiator support and frame cross member, as necessary, to obtain even hood gap at hood ledge, both at center and sides, and tighten radiator support bolts to 5 ft. lbs.

8. Lift front of hood and place 4" block under hood nose to hold it up.
9. Force rear end of hood down tightly on hood ledge anti-squeak. Hood should be down very tight against the anti-squeak to compensate for upward push of hood supports after they are connected. Supports will push the hood up as far as the play in the hinge rivets will allow. Center hood as necessary without disturbing fore and aft position and tighten two inner hood hinge bolts on each side while hood is held down.

NOTE: If hood hinges bottom on uneven surface "A" (fig. 8) on the step at cowl sides before hood is down to position described above, it may be necessary to remove hinges and smooth or hammer the step to remove bumps to permit lowering of hinges. If the hood is still not down far enough, it may be necessary to enlarge and elongate the holes "B" (fig. 8) in the cowl with a rat tail file. This will permit the hinge attaching bolts to rotate in the slotted holes in the cowl when the hood is pushed down, and due to the position of the hinge arms on the hinges, may allow additional downward movement of the hood.

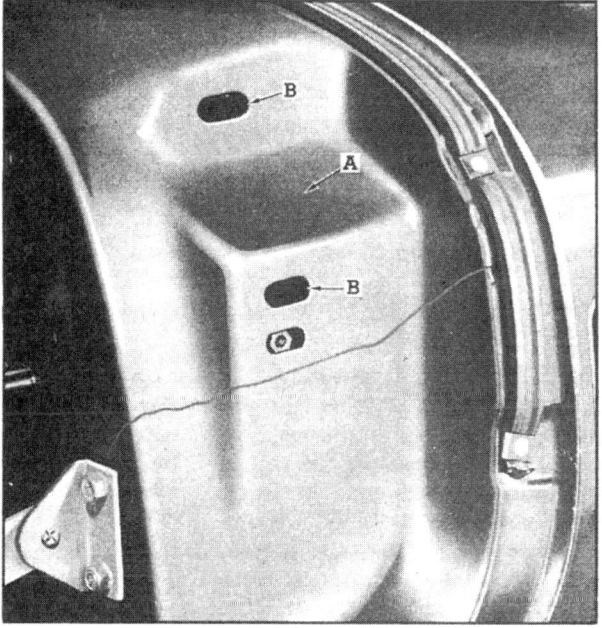

Fig. 8—Hood Hinge Plate Mounting Surface

10. Remove 4" block, lower hood and check hood fit at cowl.

Hood should be very tight against the anti-squeak across top of cowl.

If the hood touches the anti-squeak tightly at the sides but bows up in the center, adjust as follows:

a. Remove two outer screws on each side holding center bracket to hood reinforcement at rear of hood.
b. Loosen two inner screws in bracket.

c. Pry outer ends of bracket away from reinforcement and place flat washers as necessary between outer ends of bracket and reinforcement on both sides (fig. 9).

d. Reinstall outer screws through the flat washers and tighten all bracket to reinforcement attaching screws securely.

This will bring center of hood down and reduce the possibility of flutter at the center of hood. If hood still does not touch anti-squeak tightly after the above operations, it will be necessary to shim under anti-squeak to prevent hood flutter, as it is not possible to lower hood further.

Fig. 9—Adjusting Hood Tension Against Anti-Squeak

11. Tighten outer hood hinge bolts, both sides.

12. Reassemble hood supports to hood, both sides. With hood in raised position and resting on hood supports, tighten bolts attaching hood supports to dash, both sides. These were originally loosened at the dash to permit vertical adjustment of the hood support after the hood had been adjusted to its new position. This readjustment is necessary to prevent the possibility of one hood support being fully locked in the open position and the other being partially open.

13. Replace hood lock plate, tightening plate attaching screws just snug, and push hood lock plate to the rear as far as the clearance in the screw holes will allow. Drop hood to closed position and lock, this will center hood lock plate. Then raise hood, move lock plate forward 1/32" and tighten lock plate screws.

14. Adjust lock stud to proper length as necessary to hold hood closed.

The lock stud may appear to be too short to get proper adjustment. This will usually be due to a bent hood lock plate or bent upper catch plate, these plates being bent by slamming the hood shut while improperly adjusted. It will be necessary to straighten the bent plates if this condition exists, to bring the lock stud to proper position to hold hood closed.

15. Lower hood to locked position and raise rear end of fenders to fit lower edge of hood and tighten fender and skirt to body attaching parts.

HOOD HALF

Removal

1. Lay a fender cover along cowl top to prevent hood from scratching cowl top.
2. Open hood and prop in full upright position.
3. Remove hood and stand in an upright vertical position on fender cover on floor.
4. Remove the hood upper catch plate.
5. Remove front hood name plate.
6. Remove hood top center moulding.
7. Remove hood side name and series plate (on side to be replaced only).
8. From underside of hood remove 3 of the 6 round slotted head bolts (on side to be replaced only) from the hood top rear reinforcement tie plate.

NOTE: The above procedure is for either the right or left hood half depending on hood half to be replaced.

9. Lay hood down on fender cover to prevent it from being scratched and using a sharp chisel cut the 12 rivet heads, starting from front to rear attaching the hood halves together in center.

NOTE: After rivets have been cut it is sometimes necessary to use a small drift or punch to remove rivets.

10. Remove the 3 rubber hood bumpers from hood bottom ledge which is going to be replaced.

Installation

1. Align the two hood halves together and install the 3 round slotted head bolts in the rear reinforcement tie plate and tighten securely.
2. Using the hood upper catch plate as a brace only while riveting is in process, install it to hood using 2 of the slotted head bolts.
3. Stand the hood up in a vertical position and start riveting 10 rivets, working from bottom to top. After this riveting is done, remove hood upper catch plate from hood and proceed in riveting the remaining 2 rivets.

CHASSIS SHEET METAL 11-7

CAUTION: Before attempting any additional work, check outside top center of hood and make sure it is a flush fit so hood top center moulding lays flat on hood top.

4. Install hood top center moulding.
5. Install hood front name plate.
6. Install hood upper catch plate.
7. Install hood side name and series plate.
8. Install the 3 rubber grommets to hood ledge.
9. Lay fender cover along cowl top and install hood.
10. Check hood fit and alignment and adjust if necessary.

RADIATOR GRILLE AND BAFFLES

INDEX

	Page
General Description	11-7
Service Operations	11-7
Radiator Grille Upper Baffle	11-7
Front Bumper Filler Panel	11-7
Radiator Grille Assembly	11-8
Radiator Grille Lower Baffle	11-8
Radiator Core Support	11-9

GENERAL DESCRIPTION

The radiator grille is serviced in the field as a complete assembly. The extent to which the grille may be disassembled consists only of removing the radiator grille upper bar which is the only part of the grille assembly that may be serviced and only when grille assembly is removed from vehicle.

Parking lights are incorporated, in between the grille bars on the right and left side, and are attached by 2 hex head nuts making them easily serviced as a unit. By removing the outer lens retainer and lens, held in place by 2 screws, the bulbs are exposed and easily serviced.

SERVICE OPERATIONS

RADIATOR GRILLE UPPER BAFFLE

Removal

1. Open hood and remove lower catch plate from baffle.
2. Remove wiring harness from retainer clips along radiator core support.
3. Remove bolts tying radiator grille upper baffle to radiator core support.
4. Remove sheet metal screw tying radiator grille upper baffle to front fender ledge (both sides).
5. Remove the hex head bolts and the sheet metal screws attaching radiator grille upper baffle to the top radiator grille moulding.
6. Remove the hex head bolt attaching the radiator grille upper baffle to the radiator grille vertical brace. Remove baffle from vehicle.

Installation

1. Place the radiator grille upper baffle in position and install the hex head bolt attaching the baffle to the radiator grille vertical brace.
2. Install the hex head bolts and the sheet metal screws attaching radiator grille upper baffle to the top radiator grille moulding.
3. Install the sheet metal screws attaching radiator grille upper baffle to front fender ledges (both sides).
4. Install the bolts and wire retainers attaching grille upper baffle to radiator core support.

   NOTE: The metal wire retainers go on the top attaching bolts only, as the bolts on the side require no retainers.

5. Install the wiring harness in the retainers across the top of the radiator core support.
6. Install the lower catch but do not tighten the bolts securely until it is adjusted according to instructions under "Hood Alignment" in this section.

FRONT BUMPER FILLER PANEL

Removal—½ Ton

1. Remove the hex head nuts which attach the bumper face bar to support arms.

2. Remove bolts from face bar and remove face bar and apron.
3. Where apron is going to be replaced, remove the hex head bolts attaching license plate holder to apron and remove license plate holder.

Installation

1. Lay the bumper filler panel on top of the support arms. Place the bumper face bar in position and install the round head bolts in through face bar filler apron and support arms.
2. Install the hex head nuts and tighten securely.
3. In cases where the license plate bracket has been removed, install it with the hex head bolts and tighten securely.

Replacement—All Except ½ Ton

1. Remove bolts attaching filler panel to frame extensions and remove panel.
2. Install new panel and tighten attaching bolts securely being sure to install the reinforcement under the filler panel on 1 and 1½ ton models.

RADIATOR GRILLE ASSEMBLY

Removal

1. Open hood and remove radiator grille upper baffle.
2. Remove sheet metal screws (on each side) attaching upper grille bar to front fender inner corners.
3. Disconnect parking light wires from junction block. Remove wires from retainers and pull them out through grille bars (both sides).
4. Working under vehicle, remove the hex head bolts attaching radiator grille to forward part of fender skirt (each side).
5. Remove the sheet metal screws and hex head bolt attaching radiator grille to radiator grille lower baffle.
6. Remove the hex head bolts attaching the radiator grille lower baffle and the radiator grille front vertical brace to the radiator core support rods and move rods to one side.
7. Remove the hex head bolts attaching the radiator grille lower baffle to the radiator grille side vertical braces. Remove radiator grille from vehicle.
8. Remove sheet metal screws attaching grille upper bar to grille side braces and remove upper front grille bar.
9. Remove the hex head nuts attaching parking lights to grille bars (each side) and remove parking lights from grille.

NOTE: When the top grille bar is being replaced, remove the 2 metal screw retainers and install on new part.

Installation

1. Install the parking lights in grille assembly.
2. Place the grille upper bar in position and install the sheet metal screws attaching it to side braces.
3. Place the grille assembly in position on vehicle.

NOTE: It is sometimes necessary to spring the grille side vertical braces in positioning the grille in place.

4. Install the hex head bolts attaching the radiator grille lower baffle and the radiator grille front vertical brace to the radiator core support rods.
5. Install the hex head bolts attaching the radiator grille lower baffle to the radiator grille side vertical braces.
6. Install the sheet metal screws and the hex head bolt attaching radiator grille to radiator grille lower baffle.
7. Install the hex head bolts (each side) attaching radiator grille to forward part of fender skirt.
8. Feed the parking light wires in through grille bars and snap in wire retainers. Then, connect light leads to junction block terminals.
9. Install sheet metal screws (on each side) attaching upper grille bar to front fender inner corners.
10. Install radiator grille upper baffle.

CAUTION: Do not attempt to close hood if the lower catch plate has in any way had adjustment changed until this adjustment has been corrected as outlined under "Hood Lower Catch Plate Adjustment."

RADIATOR GRILLE LOWER BAFFLE

Removal—½ and ¾ Ton

1. Remove the hex head bolts (each side) attaching bumper support arms to frame and remove bumper as an assembly.
2. Remove the sheet metal screws and hex head capscrew attaching radiator grille lower baffle to radiator grille.
3. Remove the hex head bolts attaching the radiator grille lower baffle and the radiator grille front vertical brace to the radiator core support rods.
4. Remove the hex head capscrews attaching

the radiator grille lower baffle to the radiator grille side vertical braces.
5. Remove the sheet metal screws (each side) attaching radiator grille lower baffle to fender skirt.
6. Remove the hex head capscrews (each side) attaching radiator grille lower baffle to radiator core support.
7. Remove radiator grille lower baffle from vehicle.

Installation

1. Place radiator grille lower baffle on vehicle making sure the metal braces are in between radiator core support and fender skirt.

   NOTE: By using a screwdriver in between the two mentioned parts it will provide enough clearance to slide the braces up in place.

2. Install the hex head capscrews (each side) loosely, attaching radiator grille lower baffle to radiator core support.
3. Install the hex head bolts attaching the radiator grille lower baffle and the radiator grille front vertical brace to the radiator core support rods.
4. Install the sheet metal screws and the hex head capscrew attaching radiator grille lower baffle to radiator grille.
5. Install the sheet metal screws (each side) attaching radiator grille lower baffle to fender skirt.
6. Install the hex head capscrews attaching the radiator grille lower baffle to the radiator grille side vertical braces.
7. Tighten the hex head capscrews (each side) attaching radiator grille lower baffle to radiator core support. See step 2.
8. Place the front bumper in position and install the hex head bolts (each side) attaching bumper support arms to frame.

Removal—1, 1½ and 2 Ton

1. Remove radiator grille as outlined under grille replacement.
2. Remove sheet metal screws attaching baffle to fender skirt.
3. Remove hex head capscrews attaching baffle to radiator core support. Remove radiator grille lower baffle.

Installation

1. Place radiator grille lower baffle in position making sure the metal braces are in between the radiator core support and fender skirt.
2. Replace screws attaching baffle to radiator core support.
3. Replace screws attaching baffle to fender skirt.
4. Replace radiator grille as outlined under "Grille Replacement."

RADIATOR CORE SUPPORT

Removal

1. Open hood and drain radiator.
2. Disconnect headlamp wiring harness from fender skirt wire retainers (each side) and across the top of radiator grille upper baffle and pull wire back to one side.
3. Remove the radiator grille upper baffle.
4. Remove the hex head bolts (each side) attaching radiator core support side bracket to front fender ledge and front fender skirt.
5. Remove hex head capscrew (each side) attaching front end sheet metal support rods to radiator core support.
6. Disconnect upper and lower radiator hoses.
7. Working under front fender remove the capscrews (each side) attaching front fender brace and fender skirt to radiator core support.
8. Remove the hex head capscrews, retainer plate and anti-squeak attaching radiator core support to front frame cross member.
9. Lift radiator core support from vehicle.

   NOTE: Radiator core may be removed from radiator core support by removing hex head capscrews (each side) attaching radiator core to radiator core support.

Installation

1. Making sure the anti-squeak spacers are in position on frame cross member, place radiator core support in position on vehicle.
2. Install the anti-squeak, retainer plate and hex head capscrews attaching radiator core support to frame cross member.
3. Install the hex head capscrews attaching the front sheet metal support rods to radiator core support.
4. Working under front fender, install the capscrews (each side) attaching fender brace and fender skirt to radiator core support and radiator grille lower baffle.
5. From above, install the hex head bolts (each side) attaching radiator core support side braces to front fender ledge and fender skirt.
6. Install radiator grille upper baffle.
7. Connect upper and lower radiator hoses.
8. Refill radiator and check hose connections.

CAUTION: If hood lower catch plate has for any reason had the adjustment changed it is important that it be adjusted as outlined under "Hood Lower Catch Plate Adjustment" in this section.

FRONT END SHEET METAL

INDEX

	Page		Page
Front End Sheet Metal	11-10	Front Fender	11-10
Removal as an Assembly	11-10	Rear Fender	11-11
Installation as an Assembly	11-10	Running Board	11-11

FRONT END SHEET METAL

Removal as an Assembly

1. Drain radiator and remove hood assembly.
2. Remove all radiator hoses.
3. Disconnect electrical wiring from junction blocks on both fender skirts and disconnect horn wires.
4. Remove wiring harness from retainer clips located on both front fender skirts and across radiator core support.
5. Release the tension on fender brace rods by backing off the front hex nut as many threads as necessary (each rod).
6. Remove the hex head capscrews (each side) attaching brace rods to dash and remove rods.
7. Remove the hex head capscrews, plate, and spacer attaching radiator core support to front cross member.
8. Remove slotted head screws (each side) attaching rear of fender skirt to toe board.
9. From under vehicle remove hex head bolts (each side) attaching rear of front fenders to cowl.
10. Raise the front sheet metal assembly enough to clear the front bumper face bar and radiator grille filler panel and lift assembly from chassis.

Installation as an Assembly

1. Pull the spring loaded hood support arms up out of the way.
2. Place the sheet metal assembly in position on vehicle.
3. Install the anti-squeak spacers under radiator core support, then install the anti-squeak and steel retainer and bolts loosely in core support.

   NOTE: The above is to help align the sheet metal and keeps the front end centered while working on the rear of sheet metal installation.

4. Align fenders to cowl and from inside of cab, install the slotted head screws (each side) attaching rear of front fender skirts to toe board.
5. Working under vehicle, install the hex head bolts (each side) attaching rear of front fenders to cowl.
6. Tighten the hex capscrews attaching radiator core support to frame front cross member securely.
7. From above, connect the fender braces to dash panel, then adjust the brace rod adjusting nut and lock securely.
8. Connect headlamp wiring (both lights) to junction block and snap wiring harness in retainers on fenders and radiator core support.
9. Connect horn wires.
10. Connect upper and lower radiator hoses and refill radiator.
11. Install hood assembly.
12. Close hood. Recheck work and if necessary, adjust headlamp aim.

FRONT FENDER

Removal

1. Open hood and remove radiator grille upper baffle.
2. Remove sheet metal screws (from fender to be replaced) attaching radiator grille top moulding to inner corner of front fender in back of grille moulding.
3. Remove the hex head bolts attaching radiator core support top side bracket to front fender ledge, skirt and fender brace.
4. Working under front fender, remove the capscrews attaching front fender brace and fender skirt to radiator core support.
5. Remove the hex head bolts attaching front fender skirt and front fender to radiator grille side.
6. Remove the sheet metal screws attaching front fender skirt to radiator grille lower baffle.
7. Remove the hex head bolts attaching rear of front fender to cowl.

CHASSIS SHEET METAL 11-11

8. From inside cab under floor mat, remove the round slotted head bolts attaching rear of front fender skirt to toe pan.
9. At junction block, disconnect headlamp wiring and remove harness from retainers on fender skirt.
10. Remove hex head nut from fender support rod, then lift fender and fender skirt off vehicle as a unit.

Disassembly

When front fender is being replaced it is necessary to remove fender skirt and headlamp from fender. Proceed as follows:

1. Disconnect the headlamp ground wire from fender skirt, remove rubber grommet and pull harness through skirt.
2. Remove headlamp as an assembly.
3. Remove the hex head capscrews attaching front fender to fender skirt and remove fender.

NOTE: Where front fender skirt is being replaced, transfer wire retainers to new skirt.

Assembly

1. Making sure the anti-squeak is in position, place the fender ledge over the fender skirt, then install the hex head capscrews attaching front fender to fender skirt and tighten securely.
2. Install headlamp and connect ground wire to fender skirt with metal screw.
3. Thread the headlamp harness through the fender skirt, then install the rubber grommet in skirt around wiring harness.

Installation

1. Place front fender in position on vehicle and install the hex head bolts attaching rear of front fender to cowl.
2. From under cab, install the round slotted head bolts attaching rear of front fender skirt to toe pan.
3. Working under front fender, install the capscrews attaching front fender brace, fender skirt and radiator grille lower baffle to radiator core support.
4. Install the sheet metal screws attaching front fender skirt to radiator grille lower baffle.
5. Install the hex head bolts attaching front fender skirt and front fender to radiator grille side.
6. Working above, install the sheet metal screws attaching radiator grille top moulding to inner corner of front fender in back of grille moulding.
7. Install the hex head bolts attaching radiator core support top side bracket to front fender ledge, skirt and fender brace.
8. Install hex head nut on fender support rod. Adjust and lock securely.
9. Install radiator grille upper baffle.
10. At junction block, connect headlamp wiring and snap harness in retainers on fender skirt.
11. Close hood and recheck work and if necessary, adjust headlamp aim.

REAR FENDER

Removal—½ Ton

1. Remove fender to running board attaching bolts.
2. Remove fender to splash apron attaching bolts.
3. Remove bolts attaching fender to pick-up box or body.
4. Remove frame to fender brace rod bolt.
5. Remove fender.

Installation

1. Place rear fender in position and install fender to pick-up box or body bolts.
2. Install fender to splash apron attaching bolts.
3. Install fender to running board attaching bolts.
4. Replace fender to frame brace rod attaching bolt.

RUNNING BOARD

Removal

1. Remove bolts attaching running board to running board support arms.
2. On vehicles with rear fenders, remove running board to fender attaching bolts.
3. On vehicles with splash apron, remove running board to apron and apron support to running board attaching bolts.
4. Remove running board.

Installation

1. Position running board on support arms and install running board to support arm attaching bolts.
2. On vehicles with rear fender, install running board to rear fender attaching bolts.
3. On vehicles with splash apron, install running board to splash apron and apron support to running board attaching bolts.

C.O.E. SHEET METAL

INDEX

	Page		Page
General Description	11-12	Lower Step Plate	11-12
Service Operations	11-12	Step Riser	11-12
Hood Replacement	11-12	Body Extension	11-13
Fender Replacement	11-12	Step Riser Support	11-13
Upper Step Plate	11-12	Step Riser Support Cross Bar	11-13

GENERAL DESCRIPTION

The majority of the features of the Cab-Over-Engine trucks are the same or very much like those of the conventional trucks.

The hood is the alligator jaw opening type with two chrome-plated external hinges at the rear and is held in the open position by a centrally mounted telescope type support. In structure, it is a rigid one piece metal panel with a shallow but wide longitudinal moulding effect at its center. Catches are located at the front corners of the hood. These are unlocked by pulling them upward against the force of over-center springs. When unlatched, they serve as convenient handles for lifting the hood.

The following operations cover only those things that are not common to all other models.

SERVICE OPERATIONS

HOOD REPLACEMENT

1. Open hood, block in open position and disconnect hood arm support at cowl.
2. Place fender cover over cowl to protect finish and remove hinge to hood bolts and lift off hood assembly.
3. Replace hood and install hinge to hood attaching bolts.
4. Connect hood arm support to cowl.
5. Lower hood and check alignment.
6. If alignment is incorrect, loosen hinge to cowl and hinge to hood bolts and align hood.

FENDER REPLACEMENT

1. Open hood and remove radiator upper baffle to fender bolt.
2. Remove fender to grille bolts.
3. Remove fender to cowl bolts.
4. Remove fender to step riser bolts.
5. Remove step plate riser support brace to cowl bolt.
6. Remove fender assembly.
7. Place fender in position and install fender to cowl bolts.
8. Install fender to grille bolts.
9. Install fender to step riser bolts.
10. Install step plate riser support brace to cowl bolt.
11. Replace radiator upper baffle to fender bolt.

STEP PLATE—UPPER—REPLACEMENT

1. Remove step plate to fender flange screws.
2. Remove step plate to step riser flange screws.
3. Remove step plate to body extension flange screws.
4. Remove step plate.
5. Install new step plate and attaching screws.

STEP PLATE—LOWER—REPLACEMENT

1. Remove step plate to step riser flange screws.
2. Remove step plate to step riser support screws.
3. Remove step plate to body extension flange screws.
4. Remove step plate.
5. Install new step plate and attaching screws.

STEP RISER—REPLACEMENT

1. Remove step plate—upper.
2. Remove lower step plate to riser screws.
3. Remove step riser to body extension screws.
4. Remove step riser to fender flange screws.

5. Remove step riser to step riser support screws.
6. Remove step riser.
7. Install new step riser and attaching screws.

BODY EXTENSION—REPLACEMENT

1. Remove body extension to body sill bolts.
2. Remove body extension to fender splash guard bolts.
3. Remove body extension to step riser bolts.
4. Remove body extension to step riser support bolts.
5. Remove body extension.
6. Replace body extension and attaching screws.

STEP RISER SUPPORT—REPLACEMENT

1. Remove lower step plate.
2. Remove step riser support to step riser bolts.
3. Remove step riser support to body extension bolts.
4. Remove step riser support to step riser support cross bar bolts.
5. Remove step riser support.
6. Replace step riser support and attaching bolts.

STEP RISER SUPPORT CROSS BAR—REPLACEMENT

1. Remove step riser support cross bar to step riser support bolts and remove cross bar.
2. Replace cross bar and attaching bolts.

SERVICE NEWS REFERENCE

Month	Page No.	Subject

SERVICE NEWS REFERENCE

Month	Page No.	Subject

SECTION 12

ELECTRICAL SYSTEM

CONTENTS OF THIS SECTION

	Page
Electrical System	12-1
Generating System	12-5
Starting System	12-18
Ignition System	12-24
Instruments and Gauges	12-30
Lighting System	12-33
Troubles and Remedies	12-38
Specifications	12-41
Service News Reference	12-42

ELECTRICAL SYSTEM

INDEX

	Page		Page
Wiring	12-1	Filling	12-4
Battery	12-1	Trucks in Stock	12-4
Charging	12-4	Batteries in Stock	12-4

WIRING

The wiring diagrams (figs. 1 and 2) show all the electrical units and circuits in the 1948 to 1951 truck models. The positions of the electrical units are shown diagrammatically and the wiring harness loom is indicated by the cross-hatched sections.

The insulation of each wire is distinctly patterned and colored to assist in tracing circuits and making the right connections. The identifying color and pattern of each wire is shown on the wiring diagrams.

In the wiring harness, protection is provided for all wiring leading from the light switch by a thermal circuit breaker. This circuit breaker is located right in the light switch and consists of a bi-metal thermostatic element, which when overheated by a current flow of more than 30 amperes on 1948-49 models and 42 amperes on 1950-51 models, opens all circuits leading out of the switch. Then, when the bi-metal element has cooled sufficiently, electrical contact is restored. Protection against destruction of the wiring is thereby provided.

A fuse box on 1948-49 models (fig. 3), is mounted on the engine side of the dash and contains fuses for the five lighting circuits headlamp upper and lower beams, parking lamps, tail lamp and stop lamp. These circuits are individually fused so that failure of one circuit will not prevent operation of another. Thus a short circuit, caused by external damage, in any of these circuits can blow only the fuse protecting that circuit.

The fuse box on 1950-51 models contains fuses only for the tail and stop lamps and is mounted on the engine side of the dash on all models except Forward Control. The fuse box contains the fuses for these two circuits plus a spare fuse, which is mounted on the inside of the cover. The fuse box on Forward Control models is located under the instrument panel.

BATTERY

The battery, popularly referred to as "storage battery" is in reality an electro-chemical apparatus so constructed to change the energy put into it by the generator to chemical energy or "charged" as we now say. This chemical energy can then be converted into electrical energy by making a continuous uninterrupted circuit between the positive and negative terminals of the battery, through the wiring system and electrical circuits of the vehicle.

The battery consists of three acid proof compartments or cells. Within each cell are two elements, one positive and one negative. Each element consists of a number of plates called "grids," the openings of which are filled with a lead paste. Each group of plates is connected together and

"Portions of materials contained herein have been reprinted with permission of General Motors Corporation, Service Technology Group."

ELECTRICAL SYSTEM 12-2

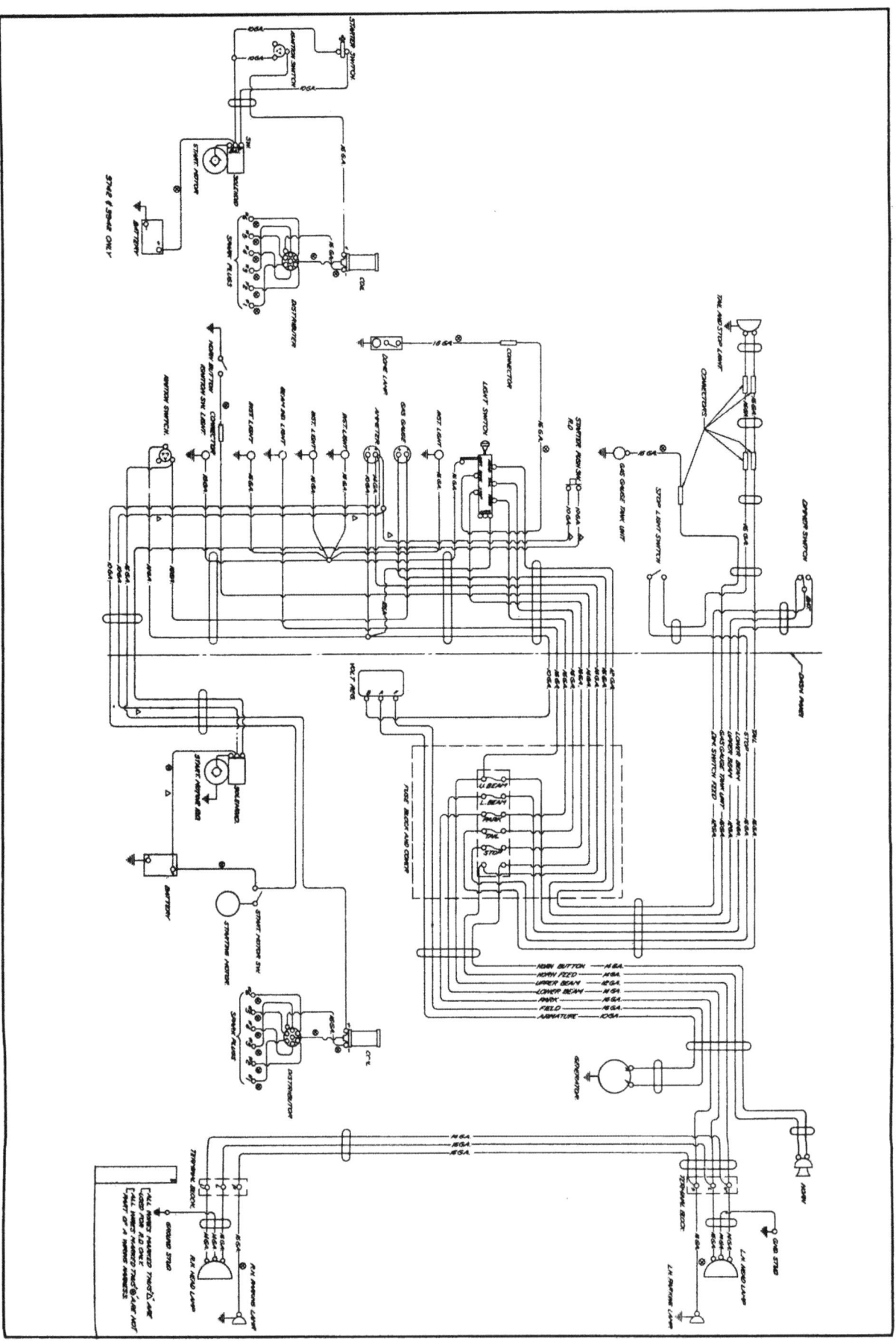

Fig. 1—(1948-49) Wiring Diagram

ELECTRICAL SYSTEM 12-3

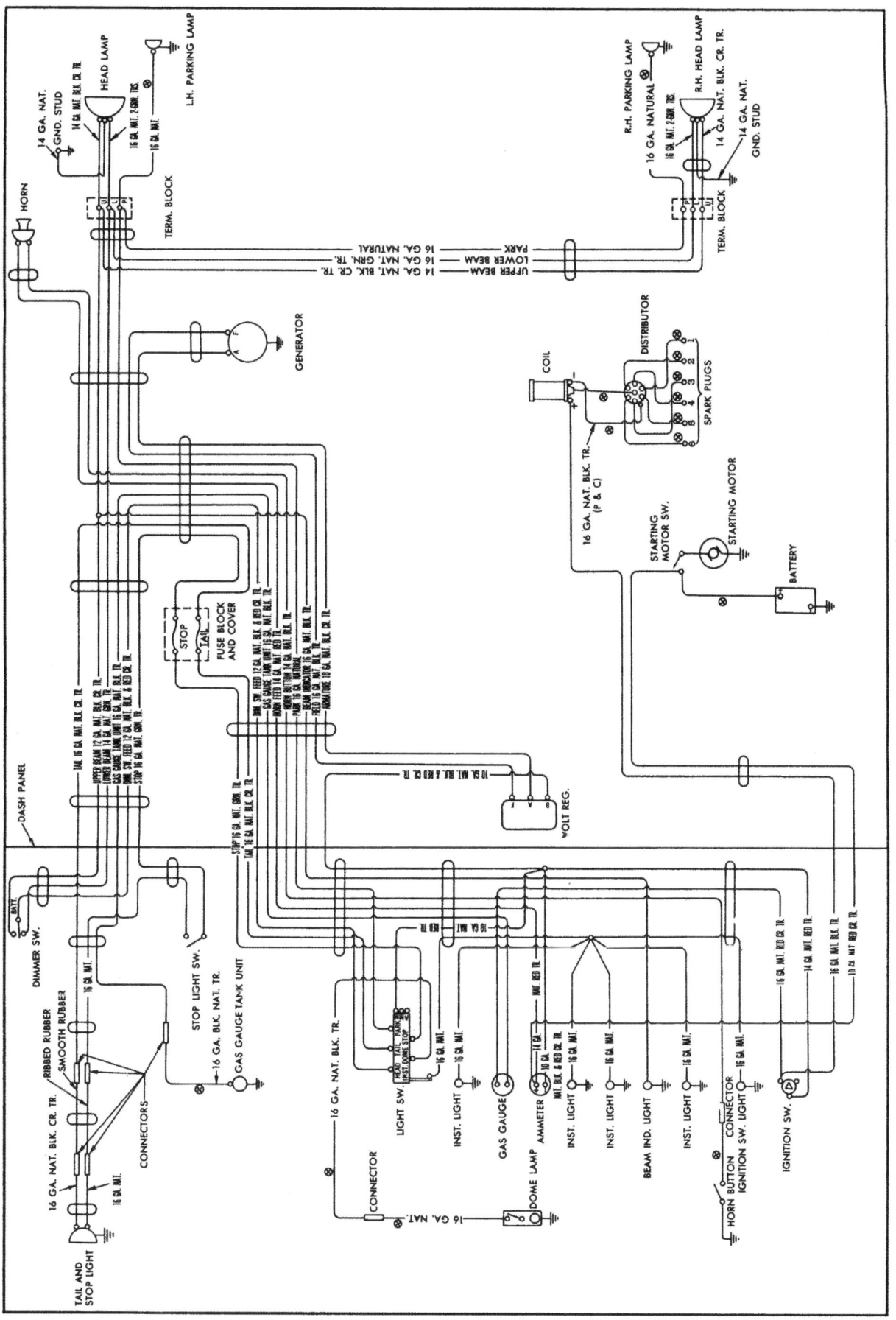

Fig. 2—(1950-51) Wiring Diagram

ELECTRICAL SYSTEM 12-4

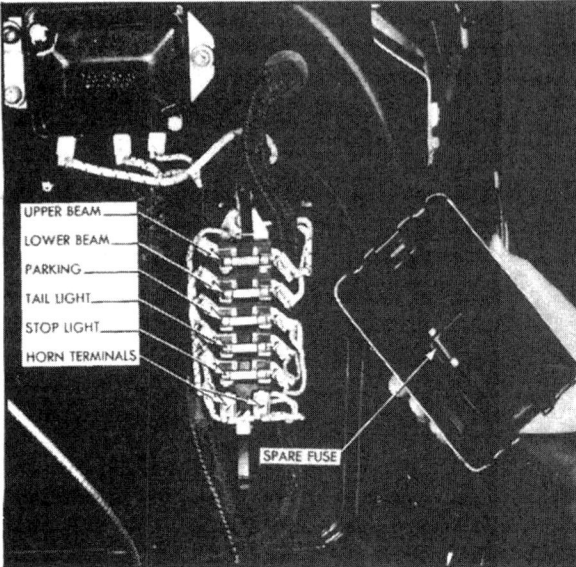

Fig. 3—Fuse Box

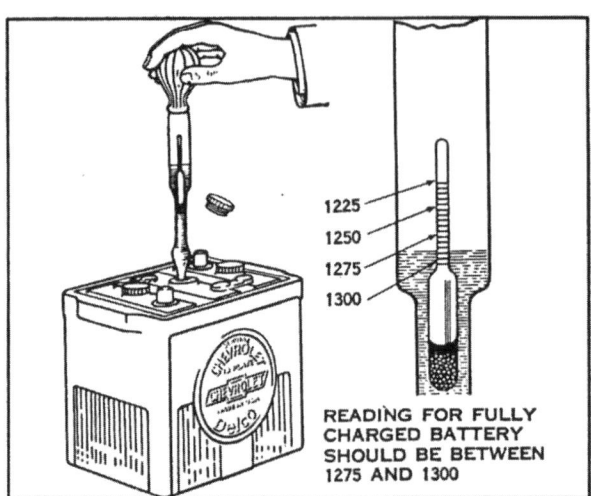

Fig. 4—Testing Specific Gravity of Battery

the positive are separated from the negative by porous separators between each plate.

The liquid in which these plates are immersed is called electrolyte (sulphuric acid and water). When the battery is receiving electrical energy from the generator, acid is driven from the composition of the plates and causes the battery to be in a state of charge. When current is drawn from the battery, the acid combines with the lead paste of the plates forming a chemical compound. As the sulphuric acid reacts to combine with the lead paste, the electrolyte solution becomes practically all distilled water and when this condition exists, the battery is said to be in a state of discharge.

The efficiency of a battery, therefore, is in direct proportion to its state of charge. To obtain the maximum efficiency, whatever amount of current is withdrawn from or generated by the battery must be compensated for by running the generator long enough to restore the battery to the condition known as "charged."

The generator is designed to restore battery energy consumed in starting and then to assume the burden of supplying complete electrical load. If the generator fails in its duty and the battery becomes run down or in a state of discharge, charging from an outside source is necessary.

Charging

Charging a battery by causing an electric current to flow through it sets up a certain electro-chemical action between the positive and negative plates in the presence of the electrolyte. This reaction results in a condition called "gassing." The cover on each cell has a vent or opening so that the gas produced may be vented to atmosphere. The filler caps should be removed when charging.

To check the battery for its state of charge, a hydrometer should be used (fig. 4). In order to obtain an accurate check the battery must be disconnected from the charger before testing. A fully charged battery should have a specific gravity of 1.275 to 1.300 while a fully discharged battery will have a specific gravity of approximately 1.150.

Filling

Batteries should be filled with sufficient quantity of distilled water to bring the electrolyte up to level of split ring (approx. $17/_{32}''$ above the top of plates) in each cell.

New Trucks in Stock

1. Check battery electrolyte on each new truck received; add sufficient distilled water to bring the electrolyte up to level of split ring (approx. $17/_{32}''$ above the top of plates) in each cell.
2. Check electrolyte and add distilled water, as necessary, at weekly or semi-monthly intervals, depending upon the weather; warm weather causes greater water loss.
3. If the specific gravity of the battery is below 1.225, remove it and place on the charging line. Charge the battery until the specific gravity reaches 1.275 to 1.300.

Before a new truck is delivered to a customer, make sure the specific gravity of the battery electrolyte measures at least 1.260—preferably higher. Under no circumstances should acid be added to a new battery to increase the specific gravity of the electrolyte.

New Batteries in Parts Stock

1. Batteries in stock should be checked for solution level and specific gravity in accordance with the procedure listed above.
2. Batteries on display should be rotated periodically with those in stock to avoid possibility of old batteries remaining in stock.

GENERATING SYSTEM

INDEX

	Page		Page
General Description	12-5	Circuit Breaker	12-9
Generator	12-6	Voltage Regulator	12-10
Circuit Breaker	12-6	Current Regulator	12-11
Voltage Regulator	12-6	Battery Charging Rate	12-12
Current Regulator	12-6	Repairs	12-13
Operation	12-6	Cleaning Regulator Contact Points	12-13
Circuit Breaker	12-6	Replacing Contact Support Brackets	12-13
Voltage Regulator	12-7	Installing New Springs	12-13
Temperature Compensation	12-7	Repolarizing Generators	12-13
Current Regulator	12-7	Regulator Replacement	12-14
Resistances	12-7	Generator Overhaul	12-15
Regulator Polarity	12-7	Removal	12-15
Quick Checks of Generating System	12-8	Disassembly	12-15
Regulator Maintenance	12-9	Testing Generator Parts	12-15
General Instructions	12-9	Assembly	12-17
Checks and Adjustments	12-9	Installation	12-17

GENERAL DESCRIPTION

The generating system consists of a belt driven generator mounted on the left side of engine, a voltage and current regulator mounted on the left fender skirt on 1948-49 models and on the left side of the cowl of all 1950-51 models except Forward Control, and the necessary wiring to properly connect the two units and the battery. On Forward Control models, the current and voltage regulator is mounted under the instrument panel. The purpose of this system is to convert just enough mechanical energy from the engine into electrical energy to supply all electrically operated accessories and keep the battery fully charged.

The generator is a two-brush shunt wound unit. The combined voltage and current regulator keeps the voltage and amperage within safe operating limits under the most adverse conditions and increases or decreases the amperage output to meet the varying requirements of the battery and electrical accessories.

The voltage and current regulator assembly actually consists of three units—the voltage regulator, the current regulator and the circuit breaker (fig. 5).

The voltage regulator controls the maximum voltage of the generator and keeps it from exceeding a predetermined value fixed by the regulator setting. This prevents excessive voltage at the lamp bulbs, ignition points and radio, thereby prolonging their life and also prevents battery overcharge. The actual charging rate to the battery at a given

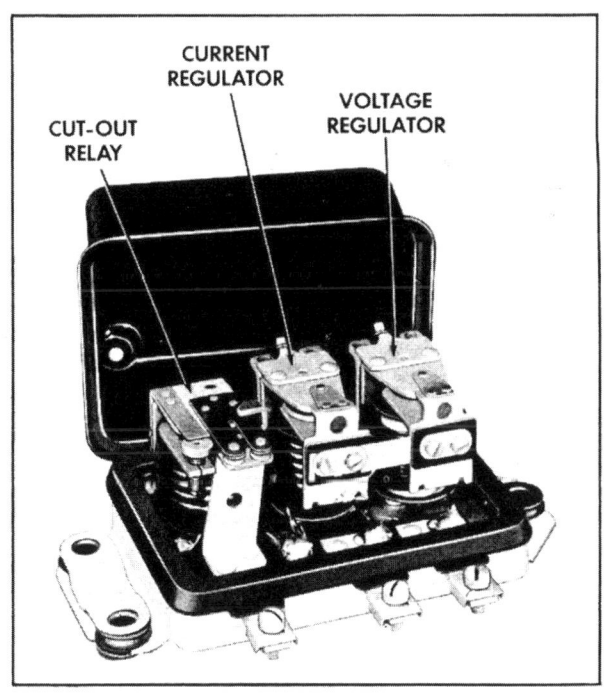

Fig. 5—Voltage and Current Regulator

generator voltage depends upon the state of charge (counter voltage) of the battery.

The current regulator controls the maximum amperage output of the generator, thereby preventing damage to the generator due to overload.

The circuit breaker (cut-out relay) unit of the

regulator is an automatic switch in the charging circuit, between the generator and the battery. When the generator voltage exceeds the voltage for which the circuit breaker is set, (slightly above battery voltage) the circuit breaker points close and the generator begins to supply electrical energy to operate electrical units and charge the battery. When the generator voltage drops below that of the battery, the current starts to flow from the battery to the generator which opens the circuit breaker points and breaks the circuit.

Generator

The generator housing (field frame) has the two pole shoes attached to it 180° apart. The field coils are around the pole shoes. The armature is centered between the pole shoes and is held in place by bearings in the frames (end plates). The end plates have openings for circulation of air for cooling. Air is circulated through the generator by the combined pulley and fan that are mounted on the front end of armature shaft. The commutator end frame (end plate) is fitted with the brush holders that hold the brushes in correct position under spring tension against the armature commutator. One brush is grounded to the frame while the other is insulated from the frame.

The insulated (positive) brush is connected to the positive "A" terminal of the generator and to one terminal of the field coils. The other end of the field coils is connected to the insulated field "F" terminal of the generator.

Circuit Breaker (Cutout Relay)

The cutout relay (fig. 6) has two windings assembled on one core, a series winding of a few

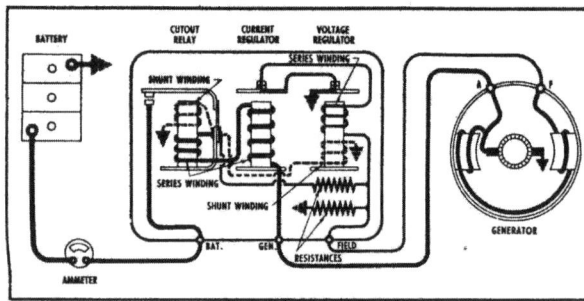

Fig. 6—Circuit Diagram

turns of heavy wire (solid line) and a shunt winding of many turns of fine wire (dashed line). The shunt winding is shunted across the generator so that the generator voltage is impressed upon it at all times. The series winding is connected in series with the charging circuit so that the generator output passes through it.

The relay core and windings are assembled into a frame. A flat steel armature is attached to the frame by a flexible hinge so that it is centered just above the end of the core. The armature has two contact points which are located just above a similar number of stationary contact points. When the generator is not operating, the armature contact points are held away from the stationary points by the tension of a flat spring riveted on the side of the armature.

Voltage Regulator

The voltage regulator (fig. 6) has two windings assembled on a single core, a shunt winding consisting of many turns of fine wire (dashed line) which is shunted across the generator; and a series winding of a few turns of relatively heavy wire (solid line) which is connected in series with the generator field circuit when the regulator contact points are closed.

The windings and core are assembled into a frame. A flat steel armature is attached to the frame by a flexible hinge so that it is just above the end of the core. The armature contains a contact point which is just beneath a stationary contact point. When the voltage regulator is not operating, the tension of a spiral spring holds the armature away from the core so that the points are in contact and the generator field circuit is completed to ground through them.

Current Regulator

The current regulator (fig. 6) has a series winding of a few turns of heavy wire (solid line) which carries all generator output. The winding core is assembled into a frame. A flat steel armature is attached to the frame by a flexible hinge so that it is just above the core. The armature has a contact point which is just below a stationary contact point. When the current regulator is not operating, the tension of a spiral spring holds the armature away from the core so that the points are in contact. In this position, the generator field circuit is completed to ground through the current regulator contact points in series with the voltage regulator contact points.

OPERATION

In order for the generating system to operate, the positive wire from the generator must be connected to the generator (GEN) terminal of the regulator, the wire from the field terminal of the generator connected to the field (F) terminal of the regulator and the wire from the battery through the ammeter to the battery (BAT) terminal of the regulator.

Circuit Breaker (Cutout Relay)

When the generator voltage builds up to a value great enough to charge the battery, the magnetism induced by the current flowing through the shunt winding is sufficient to overcome the armature spring tension and pull the armature toward the core so that the contact points close. This completes the circuit between the generator and battery. The current which flows from the generator to the battery passes through the series winding in the proper direction to add to the magnetism holding the armature down and the points closed.

When the generator slows down or stops, current begins to flow from the battery to the generator. This reverses the direction that the current flows through the series winding, thus causing a reversal of the series winding magnetic field. The magnetic field of the shunt winding does not reverse. Therefore, instead of helping each other, the two windings now magnetically oppose each other so that the resultant magnetic field becomes insufficient to hold the armature down. The flat spring pulls the armature away from the core so that the points separate; this opens the circuit between the generator and battery.

Voltage Regulator

When the generator voltage reaches the value for which the voltage regulator is adjusted, the magnetic field produced by the two windings (shunt and series) overcomes the armature spring tension and pulls the armature down so that the contact points separate. This inserts resistance into the generator field circuit so that the generator field current and voltage are reduced. Reduction of the generator voltage reduces the magnetic field of the regulator shunt winding. Also, opening the regulator points opens the regulator series winding circuit so that its magnetic field collapses completely. This results in the magnetic field reducing sufficiently to allow the spiral spring to pull the armature away from the core so that the contact points again close. This directly grounds the generator field circuit so that the generator voltage and output increase. The above cycle of action again takes place and the cycle continues at a rate of 150 to 250 times a second, regulating the voltage to a constant value. By thus maintaining a constant voltage, the generator supplies varying amounts of current to meet the varying states of battery charge and electrical load.

Temperature Compensation

The voltage regulator is compensated for temperature by means of a bi-metal thermostatic hinge on the armature. This causes the regulator to regulate for a higher voltage when cold which partly compensates for the fact that a higher voltage is required to charge a cold battery.

Current Regulator

When the load demands are heavy, as for example when electrical devices are turned on and the battery is in a discharged condition, the voltage may not increase to a value sufficient to cause the voltage regulator to operate. Consequently, generator output will continue to increase until the generator reaches its rated maximum output. This is the current value for which the current regulator is set. Therefore, when the generator reaches its rated output, this output flowing through the current regulator winding creates sufficient magnetism to pull the current regulator armature down and open the contact points. With the points open, resistance is inserted into the generator field circuit and the generator output is reduced.

As soon as the generator output starts to fall off, the magnetic field of the current regulator winding is reduced and the spiral spring tension pulls the armature up. This closes the contact points, thereby removing the resistance from the field circuit, output increases and the above cycle is repeated. The cycle continues to take place while the current regulator is in operation 150 to 250 times a second, preventing the generator from exceeding its rated maximum.

When the electrical load is reduced, electrical devices turned off or battery comes up to charge, the voltage increases until the voltage regulator begins to operate and tapers the generator output down. This prevents the current regulator from operating. Either the voltage regulator or the current regulator controls the generator at any one time—the two never operate at the same time.

Resistances

The current and voltage regulator circuits use a common resistance (fig. 6) which is inserted in the field circuit when either the current or voltage regulator operates. A second resistance (fig. 6) is connected between the regulator field terminal and the relay frame, which places it in parallel with the generator field coils. The sudden reduction in field current, occurring when either the current or voltage regulator contact points open, is accompanied by a surge of induced voltage in the field coils as the strength of the magnetic field changes. These surges are partially dissipated by the second resistance, thus preventing excessive arcing at the contact points.

Regulator Polarity

Some regulators are designed for use with negative grounded batteries while others are designed for use with positive grounded batteries. Using the wrong polarity regulator on an installation will cause the regulator contact points to pit badly and give very short life. As a safeguard against installation of the wrong polarity regulator, regulators designed for positive grounded systems have copper plated current and voltage regulator armatures while regulators for negative grounded systems have cadmium plated armatures.

ELECTRICAL SYSTEM 12-8

QUICK CHECKS OF GENERATING SYSTEM

The following checks can be made to determine whether or not the units are operating normally. If not, the checks will indicate whether the generator or regulator is at fault so that proper corrective steps may be taken.

1. **A Fully Charged Battery and a Low Charging Rate** indicates normal voltage regulator operation. To check the current regulator, remove the battery wire from the battery (BAT) terminal of the regulator. Connect the positive lead of an ammeter to the battery terminal of the regulator and the negative lead to the battery wire. With the ignition switch in the "Off" position, depress the starting switch and crank the engine for about fifteen seconds. Then start the engine and, with it running at medium speed, turn on lights, radio and other electrical accessories and note quickly the generator output. This should be the value for which the current regulator is set (32 to 40 amperes).

    Now turn off the lights, radio and other accessories and allow the engine to continue running. As soon as the generator has replaced in the battery the current used in cranking, the voltage regulator, if operating properly, will taper the output down to a few amperes.

2. **A Fully Charged Battery and a High Charging Rate.**
    (a) With ammeter hooked up as in previous check, start engine and run it at medium speed. Disconnect the field wire from the field circuit and the output should immediately drop to zero. If it does not, the generator field circuit is grounded either inside the generator or in the wiring harness. If the output drops off to "zero" with the field lead disconnected, the trouble has been isolated in the regulator. Reconnect the field lead on the field terminal of the regulator.
    (b) Remove the regulator cover and depress the voltage regulator armature manually to open the points. If the output now drops off, the voltage regulator unit has been failing to reduce the output as the battery came up to charge and voltage regulator adjustment is indicated. (Instructions for adjusting the regulator are covered under the heading "Checks and Adjustments.")
    (c) If separating the voltage regulator contact points does not cause the output to drop off, the field circuit within the regulator is shorted and the regulator should be replaced.

3. **With a Low Battery and a Low or No Charging Rate** check the entire charging connections; corroded battery terminals, loose or corroded ground strap, and frayed or damaged wires. The high resistance resulting from these conditions will prevent normal charge from reaching the battery. If the entire charging circuit is in good condition, then either the regulator or generator is at fault.

    (a) With a jumper wire, ground the field terminal of the regulator to the engine block or other good ground. This completes the generator field circuit without its having to pass through the regulator. Increase the generator speed to determine which unit needs attention. Use care to avoid excessive speed, since under these conditions, the generator may produce a dangerously high output.

    (b) If the output increases, the regulator needs attention. Check for dirty or oxidized contact points or a low voltage setting.

    (c) If the generator output remains at a few amperes with the field terminal grounded, the generator is at fault and should be checked further.

    (d) If the generator does not show any output at all, either with or without the field terminal grounded, very quickly disconnect the generator lead from the generator (GEN) terminal of the regulator and strike it against a convenient ground with the generator operating at a medium speed. If a spark does not occur, the trouble has now been definitely isolated in the generator and it should be removed and repaired.

    If a spark does occur, likely the generator can build up but the circuit breaker is not operating to permit the current to flow to the battery due to burnt points, points not closing, open voltage winding in circuit breaker, grounded circuit breaker, or too high closing voltage setting.

CAUTION: Do not operate the generator with the generator lead disconnected for any length of time since this is open circuit operation and the units will be damaged. A burned regulator resistance unit, regulator winding, or fused contacts can result only from an open circuit operation or extreme resistance in the charging circuit. With these conditions check wiring before reinstalling regulator.

REGULATOR MAINTENANCE

GENERAL INSTRUCTIONS

1. Mechanical checks and adjustments (air gaps, point opening) must be made with the battery disconnected and the regulator preferably off the vehicle.

   CAUTION: The cutout relay contact points must never be closed by hand with the battery connected to the regulator. This would cause a high current to flow through the units which would seriously damage them.

2. Electrical checks and adjustments may be made either on or off the vehicle.
3. The regulator must always be operated with the type generator for which it is designed.
4. The regulator must be mounted in the operating position when electrical settings are checked and adjusted, and it must be at operating temperature.
5. If regulator is replaced, adjustment is made on bench, or a new or rebuilt generator is installed, the generator should be repolarized (page 13) after the leads are connected and before engine is started.

CHECKS AND ADJUSTMENTS

When checking and adjusting current and voltage regulator units, it is essential that reliable instruments be used. A volt-ammeter with ¼ ohm variable resistance in series with the ammeter is required for checking and adjusting voltage regulators.

Before making any checks or adjustments, the regulator must be at operating temperature. Operating temperature shall be assumed to exist after not less than 15 minutes of continuous operation with a charging rate of 8-10 amperes.

CIRCUIT BREAKER (CUTOUT RELAY)

The cutout relay requires three checks and adjustments; air gap, point opening and closing voltage. All mechanical adjustments should be made with the battery wire disconnected from the regulator terminal to prevent accidental short circuits.

Closing Voltage

1. Disconnect battery wire from the battery terminal (BAT) of the regulator.
2. Connect positive lead of voltmeter to generator terminal of regulator and negative lead to ground.
3. Connect positive lead of ammeter to battery terminal of regulator and negative lead to the battery wire (fig. 7).
4. Slowly increase engine speed and note voltage at which circuit breaker points close.

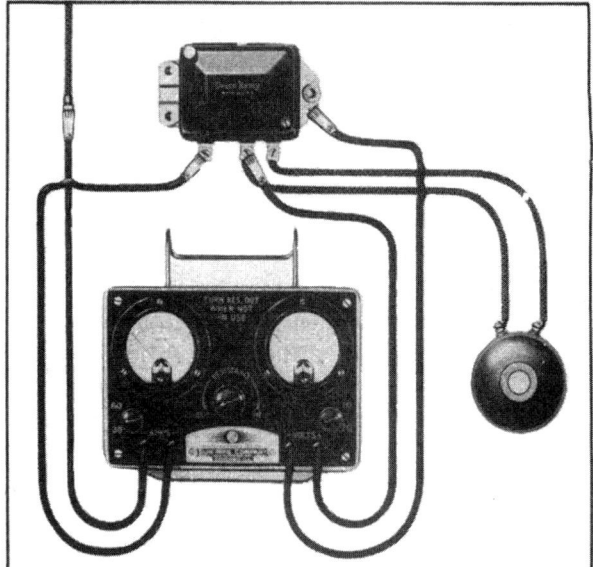

Fig. 7—Volt-Ammeter Connections for Checking Circuit Breaker

NOTE: Closing voltage should be from 5.9 to 6.8 volts. Preferred 6.4 volts.

5. When necessary to make a correction, adjust closing voltage by turning adjusting screw (fig. 8) until the preferred setting of 6.4 volts is obtained. Turn screw clockwise to increase spring tension and closing voltage, counterclockwise to decrease spring tension and closing voltage.

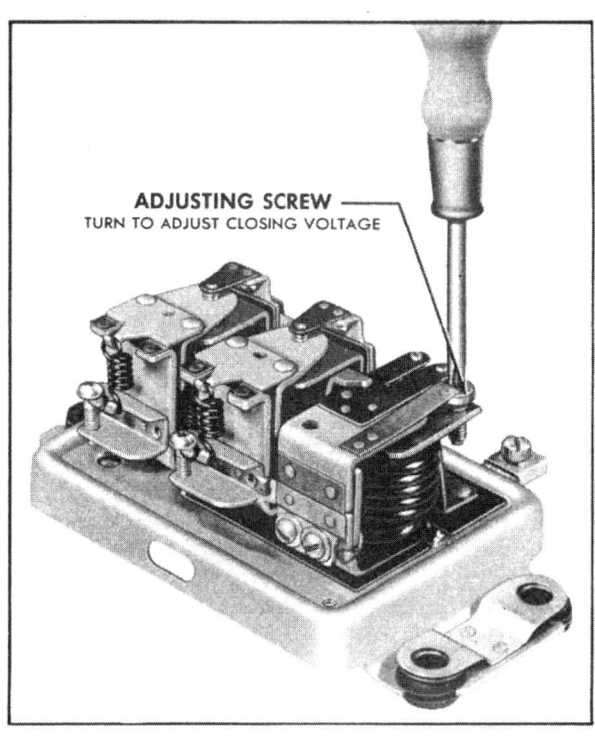

Fig. 8—Closing Voltage Adjusting Screws

ELECTRICAL SYSTEM 12-10

6. With closing voltage adjusted, increase engine speed to close points, then slowly decrease engine speed and note discharge current necessary to open circuit breaker points.

   NOTE: This current should be 0 to 4 amperes. If the reverse (discharge) current necessary to open the points is not within the 0 to 4 ampere limit, the air gap and point opening should be checked and adjusted.

Air Gap

1. Place finger on armature directly above core and move armature down until points just close.
2. Measure the air gap between the armature and center of core (fig. 9). This gap should be .020".

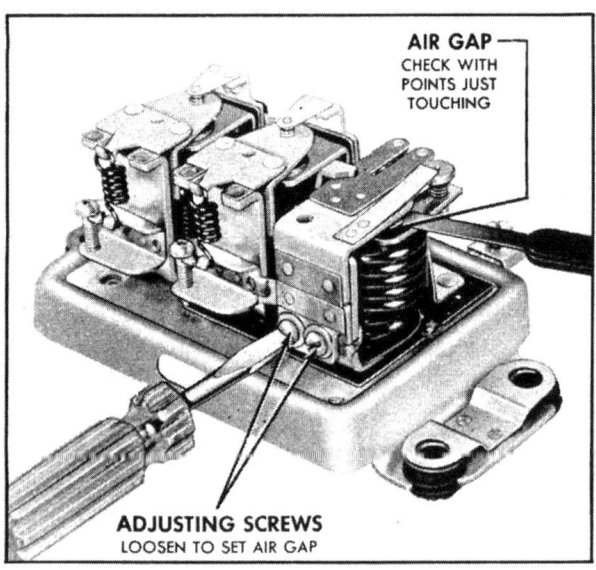

Fig. 9—Air Gap Adjusting Screws

3. If both sets of points do not close simultaneously, bend spring fingers so they do.
4. To adjust air gap, loosen two screws at the back of relay (fig. 9) and raise or lower the armature as required. Tighten screws securely after adjustment.

Point Opening

1. Check point opening. This opening should be .020" and may be adjusted by bending the upper armature stop (fig. 10).

   After making air gap or point opening adjustments, recheck closing voltage and opening amperage and make any necessary readjustments.

VOLTAGE REGULATOR

Two checks and adjustments are required on the voltage regulator; air gap and voltage setting.

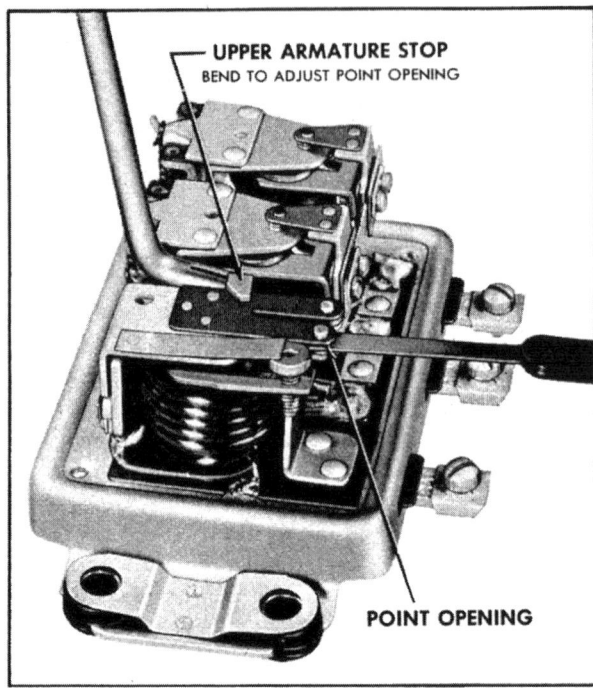

Fig. 10—Adjusting Point Opening

To check and adjust the voltage setting, connect the volt-ammeter tester to the regulator as follows:

1. Remove the battery wire from the battery terminal of the regulator and connect the positive lead of the ammeter to the battery terminal and the negative lead to the battery wire.
2. Connect the positive lead of the voltmeter to the battery terminal of the regulator and the negative lead to a good ground (fig. 11).
3. Start the engine and run it at a speed equivalent to approximately 30 M.P.H.

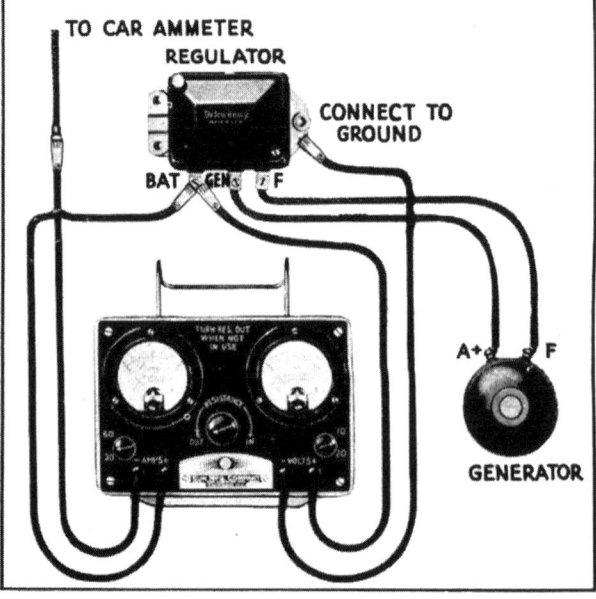

Fig. 11—Volt-Ammeter Connections for Checking Voltage Regulator

4. If the output is less than 8 amperes, turn on lights to permit increased generator output, then cut in the resistance on the volt-ampere tester by turning the resistance knob to the right until the output is reduced to 8-10 amperes.
5. Operate the generator at this speed for at least 15 minutes to bring the regulator up to operating temperature.
6. Retard the generator speed until the circuit breaker points open, then bring generator back to speed and note voltage setting, which should be from 7.0 to 7.7 volts. Preferred 7.4 volts.

   NOTE: When checking voltage regulator setting the regulator cover must be in place.

7. To adjust voltage setting, remove regulator cover and turn adjusting screw (fig. 12) clockwise to increase voltage setting or counterclockwise to decrease voltage setting.

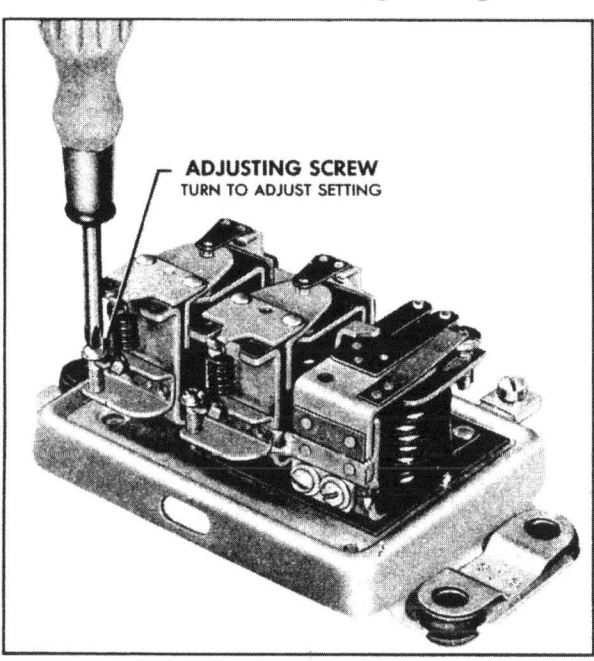

Fig. 12—Voltage Regulator Adjusting Screw

CAUTION: If adjusting screw is turned down (clockwise) beyond the normal range required for adjustment, the spring support may be bent beyond its elastic limit and fail to return when pressure is relieved. In such a case, turn the screw counterclockwise until sufficient clearance develops between the screw head and the spring support, then bend spring support up carefully with small pliers until contact is made with the screw head. The final setting of the unit should always be approached by increasing the spring tension, never by reducing it. In other words, if the setting is found to be too high, the unit should be adjusted below the required value and then raised to the exact setting by increasing the spring tension.

8. After each adjustment and before taking voltage reading, replace the regulator cover, reduce the engine speed until the relay points open and then slowly increase the engine speed again.

Air Gap

1. Place fingers on armature directly above core and move armature down to the core and release it until the contact points just touch.
2. Measure the air gap between the armature and the center of core (fig. 13). This gap should be .075"-.085"

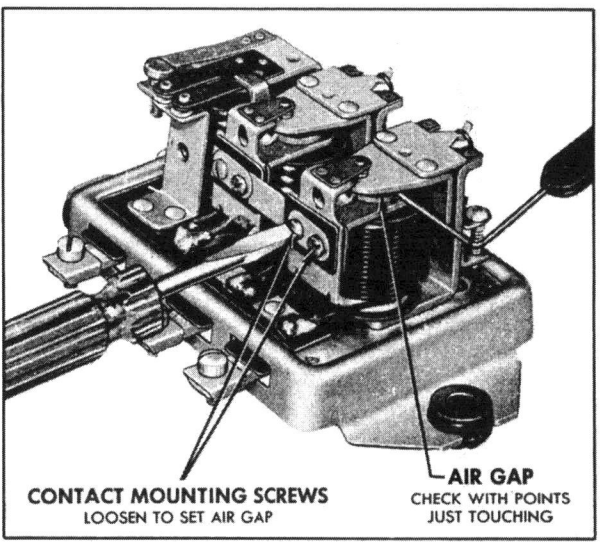

Fig. 13—Checking and Adjusting Air Gap

3. To adjust air gap, loosen the contact mounting screws and raise or lower the contact bracket as required.
4. Tighten contact bracket mounting screws securely making sure points are lined up.
5. After making air gap adjustment, recheck voltage setting and make any necessary readjustments.

CURRENT REGULATOR

Two checks and adjustments are required on the current regulator; air gap and current setting. The air gap on the current regulator is checked and adjusted in exactly the same manner as on the voltage regulator already described.

Current Setting

To check the current setting adjustment:

1. Remove the regulator cover and connect a

jumper lead from the voltage regulator upper point support bracket to the armature.

NOTE: This shorts the voltage regulator points and prevents them from operating while the current regulator is being checked (fig. 14).

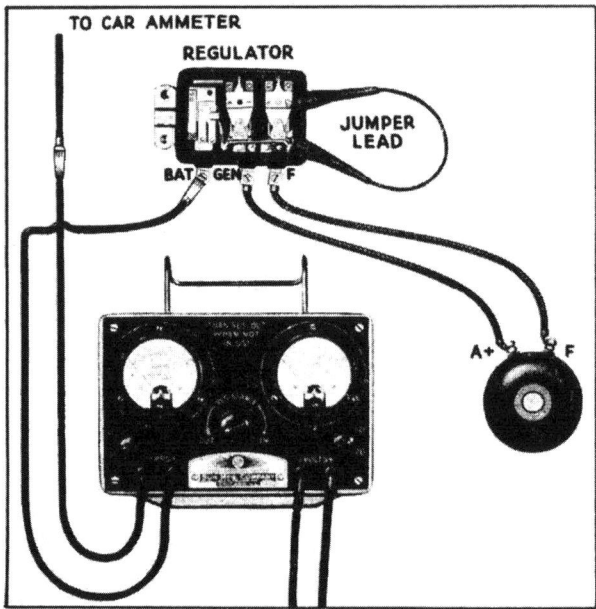

Fig. 14—Volt-Ammeter Connections for Checking Current Regulator

2. Remove the battery wire from the battery terminal of the regulator and connect the positive lead of the ammeter to the battery terminal of the regulator and the negative lead to the battery wire.

3. Make sure that the ammeter resistance knob is turned to the out position, turn on lights, radio, and other electrical accessories to create the necessary amperage load.

4. Increase the engine speed until output remains constant. The current setting with the unit at operating temperature should be from 32 to 40 amperes. Preferred 36 amperes.

NOTE: The engine should be run at medium speed at least 15 minutes before making checks or adjustments on the regulator. This is necessary to bring the regulator up to operating temperature.

5. To adjust the current setting, turn adjusting screw clockwise to increase the current setting or counterclockwise to decrease the setting. See "Caution Note" under voltage setting of voltage regulator.

BATTERY CHARGING RATE

The shunt wound generator, controlled by current and voltage regulation, is an ideal generating unit since it has the capacity to supply the necessary current for lights and accessories in addition to charging the battery.

At normal operating speed, the battery charging rate is controlled by the regulator voltage setting, the counter voltage (state of charge) of the battery, and resistance in the charging circuit. Figure 15 gives the battery charging curves up to 20 amperes and the generator voltage necessary with different specific gravity readings (state of charge) of the battery.

It will be noted by referring to Figure 15 that when the battery is in a discharged condition, 1.160 specific gravity, slightly more than 7 volts generator pressure will produce 20 amperes charging rate. It will also be noted that it would take 7.8 volts generator pressure to produce 20 amperes at 1.250 specific gravity and over 8.3 volts to produce 20 amperes charging rate with the battery specific gravity at 1.280.

We have already stated that the voltage control unit should be set to control the generator voltage at between 7.0 and 7.7 volts. Assuming that it is set at 7.3 volts, we will be unable to produce the battery charging rate shown by the curves above the heavy line at 7.3 volts (fig. 15). Therefore, if

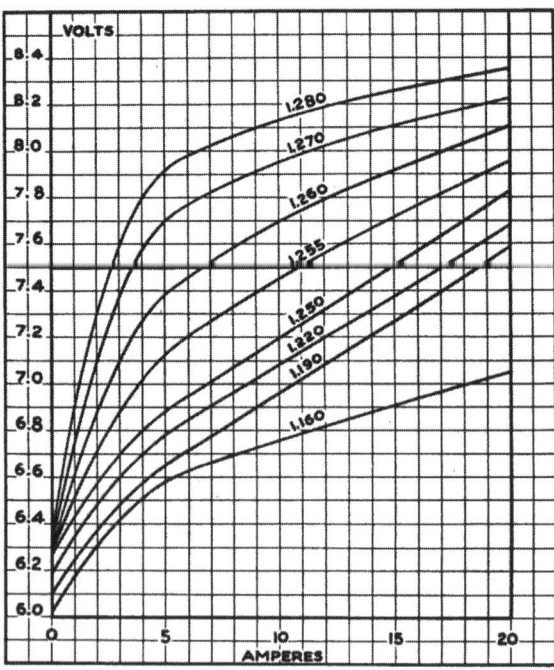

Fig. 15—Battery Charging Curve

the battery is fully charged—1.280, we will have a maximum battery charging rate of 2 amperes. If the battery specific gravity is 1.250, the maximum charging rate will be 12 amperes. As the battery specific gravity rises, the charging rate tapers off. This is known as the "Constant Potential System" and is considered the ideal way of charging a battery.

When lights or electrical accessories are turned

on, the electrical energy to operate them is taken from the charging circuit and the generator output will increase to supply these accessories and still maintain about the same charging rate to the battery. This is true providing the accessory load plus the charging rate, as required by the state of charge of the battery, does not exceed 32 to 40 amperes. In that case the current regulator will hold the total output at 32 to 40 amperes.

REPAIRS

Cleaning Regulator Contact Points

Cleaning the contact points of the current and voltage regulator properly is one of the most important operations the service man will be called upon to perform. Dirty or oxidized contact points arc and burn, cause reduced generator output, and run down batteries. If the points are properly cleaned the regulator will be restored to normal operation. If improperly cleaned, improvement in performance will be small and only temporary.

1. Loosen the upper contact bracket mounting screws, so that the bracket may be tilted to one side (fig. 16).

    NOTE: Never use sandpaper or emery cloth to clean the contact points because particles of embedded grit in the regulator points will cause them to corrode.

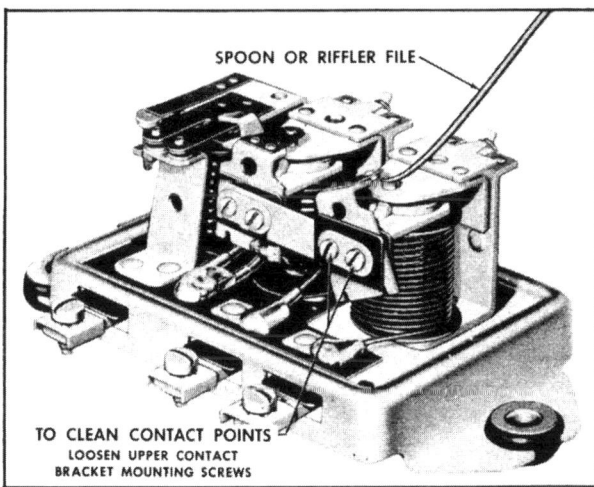

Fig. 16—Cleaning Contact Points

2. Use a thin, fine-cut ignition point file and file each point separately.

    NOTE: Do not use the file excessively on the rounded (smaller) point.

3. If a cavity is found in the flat point, clean it out with a spoon or riffler file (fig. 17).

4. Make sure the cavity is actually cleaned out, so good clean contact is made between the points.

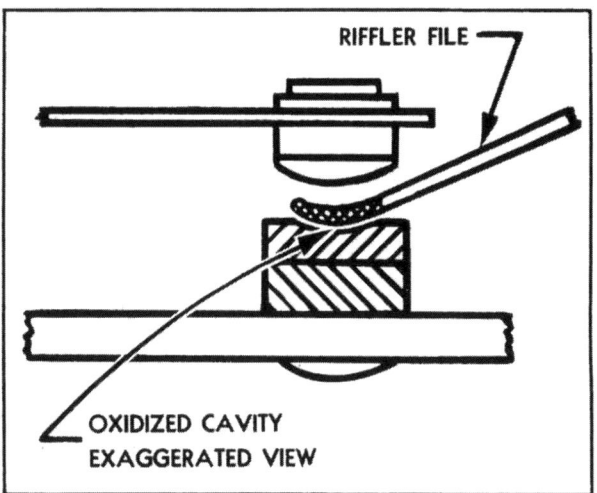

Fig. 17—Cleaning Flat Regulator Point

5. Rotate upper contact bracket into position, tighten mounting screws and adjust the air gap.

Replacing Contact Support Brackets

Voltage or current regulator contact support brackets can be replaced by carefully noting the relationship of the parts as they are removed. Note particularly that the connector strap is insulated from the voltage regulator contact mounting screws while it is connected to the current regulator contact mounting screws. New bushings should always be used when installing a contact support bracket since the old bushings may be distorted or damaged.

Installing New Springs

If it becomes necessary to replace the spring on either the current or voltage regulator unit, the new spring should first be hooked on the lower spring support and then stretched up until it can be hooked at the upper end. Stretch the spring only by means of a screwdriver blade inserted between the turns—do not pry the spring into place as this is likely to bend the spring supports.

Repolarizing Generators

If the polarity of the generator is reversed, the circuit breaker contact points will vibrate and burn. To make sure the generator has the correct polarity after connecting it with the regulator, momentarily connect a jumper lead between the generator (GEN) terminal and the battery (BAT) terminal of the regulator before starting the engine. The momentary surge of battery current to the generator will correctly polarize the generator.

The installation of radio by-press condensers of too high capacity on the field terminal of the regulator or generator will cause the current and voltage regulator contact points to oxidize. Oxidized points cause a high resistance and may result in a low charging rate and a discharged battery. **Do not connect radio by-pass condensers to the field terminal of the regulator or generator.**

If a condenser has been installed to the field terminal, disconnect condenser and clean the contact points of both the current and voltage regulator as explained under the heading "Cleaning Contact Points."

Regulator Replacement

1. Disconnect the battery wire from the battery terminal of the regulator and the generator to regulator wires from the generator and field terminals of the regulator.
2. Remove the screws attaching the regulator to cowl and remove old regulator.
3. Make sure the cowl is clean so the new regulator will ground properly. Place the regulator in position and install the attaching screws.
4. Connect the wire leading from the field terminal of the generator to the field (F) terminal of the regulator. This is the natural wire with single black tracer.
5. Connect the positive wire from the generator to the generator (GEN) terminal of the regulator. This is the natural wire with black cross tracer.
6. Connect the battery wire from the ammeter to the battery (BAT) terminal of the regulator.
7. Start engine and check regulator operation. If necessary adjust regulator as outlined under "Checks and Adjustments."

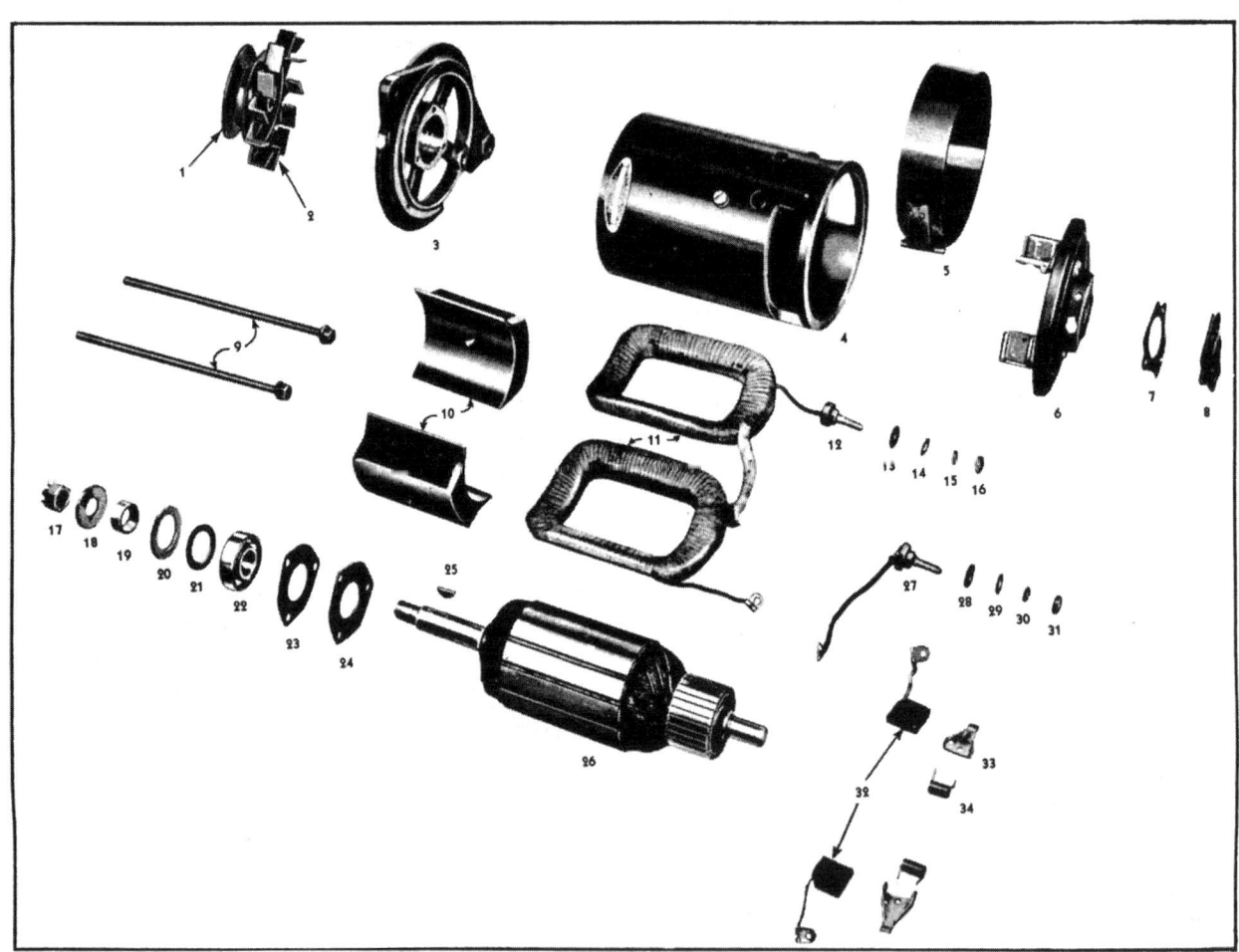

Fig. 18—Generator Parts Layout

1. Pulley
2. Fan (part of pulley)
3. Frame Drive End
4. Field Frame
5. Band
6. Frame with Pins, Commutator End
7. End Frame Cover Gasket
8. Commutator End Frame Cover
9. Through Bolts
10. Pole Shoes
11. Field Coils
12. Stud
13. Insulation Washer
14. Flat Washer
15. Lockwasher
16. Nut
17. Nut
18. Washer
19. Spacer Collar
20. Retainer
21. Felt Washer
22. Bearing
23. Retainer Plate Gasket
24. Retainer Plate
25. Key
26. Armature
27. Terminal Stud and Lead
28. Insulation Washer
29. Flat Washer
30. Lockwasher
31. Nut
32. Brushes
33. Brush Arm
34. Brush Spring

ELECTRICAL SYSTEM 12-15

GENERATOR OVERHAUL

Removal

1. Disconnect the field and positive wires from the generator.
2. Remove the generator brace nut, fan belt and bracket bolts.
3. Remove the generator from the engine.

Disassembly

1. Place the generator in a bench vise, use the vise as a holding fixture only, being careful not to pinch the generator frame.
2. Remove the generator pulley and key.
3. Remove the commutator cover band, brush lead machine screws, through-bolts and commutator end frame assembly from the generator.
4. Remove the drive end frame and armature assembly.
5. Remove the drive end bearing retainer plate screws, drive end bearing outside spacer collar and end frame from the armature shaft.

   NOTE: The drive end bearing retainer gasket, retainer and spacer washer should then be removed from the end of the armature shaft.

6. Remove the drive end bearing inside spacer washers and felt washer.

With the generator completely disassembled (fig. 18) wash all parts in cleaning solvent.

TESTING GENERATOR PARTS

Field Coil Test for Continuous Circuit

1. Place the test prods on the field coil leads (fig. 19).

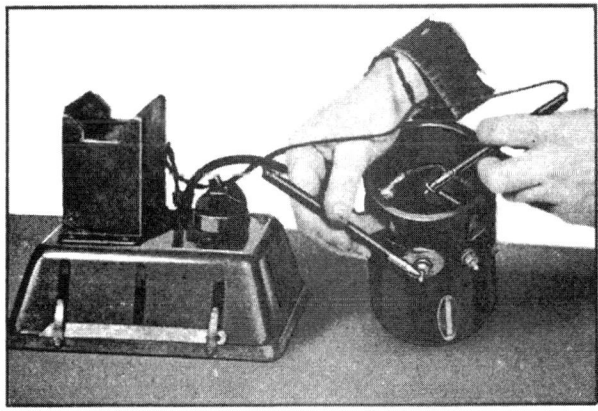

Fig. 19—Field Coil Test for Continuous Circuit

2. If the test lamp lights, the field coils are not open circuited.
3. If the test lamp does not light, the field coils are open circuited and should be replaced.

Field Coil Test for Ground

1. Place test prod leads, one to the ground and the other to field coil terminal (fig. 20).

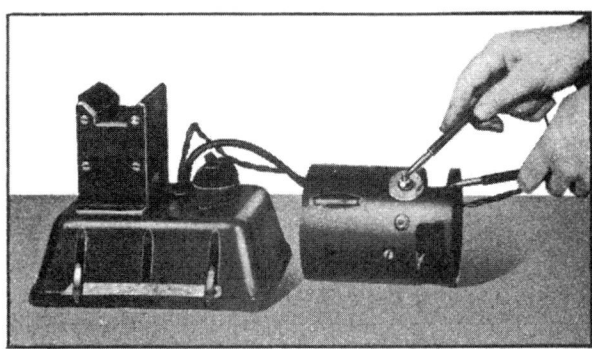

Fig. 20—Field Coil Test for Ground

2. If the test lamp lights, field coils are grounded and should be replaced.
3. If the test lamp does not light, field coils are not grounded.

Field Coil Balancing Test

1. Slide the insulation off the soldered connection between the two field coils.

   NOTE: This test is made with a battery, an ammeter and two leads.

2. Place one test lead on the soldered connection and the other one on end of the field coil (fig. 21).

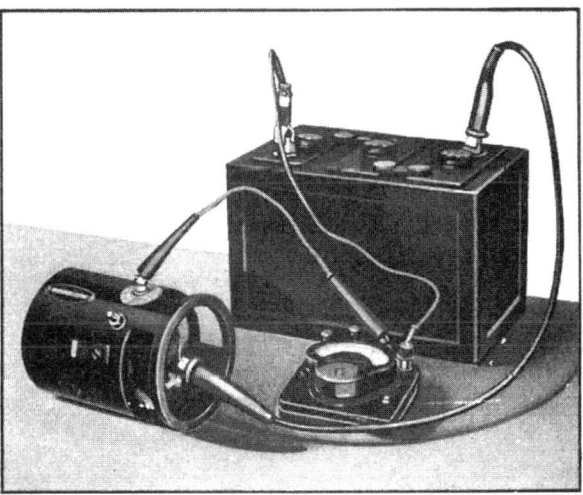

Fig. 21—Field Coil Balancing Test

3. Take a reading on the ammeter.
4. Remove the lead from the end of the field coil and place it on the end of the other field coil and take a reading.
5. If one field coil draws more current than the other, there is an internal short in the field coil and the coil that draws the most current should be replaced.

ELECTRICAL SYSTEM 12-16

Brush Lead to Generator Positive Terminal Test for Continuous Circuit

1. Place test prods, one on end of wire and the other on the terminal (fig. 22).

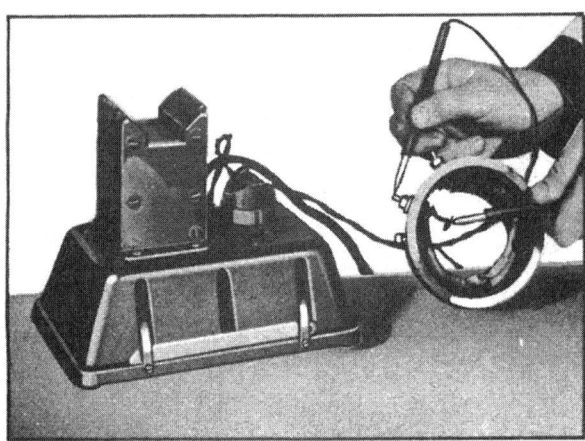

Fig. 22—Brush Lead to Positive Terminal Test for Continuous Circuit

2. If the test lamp lights, the wire is not open circuited.
3. If test lamp does not light, the wire is open circuited and should be replaced.

Generator Positive Terminal Test for Ground

1. Place one test prod on the terminal and the other on the generator frame (fig. 23).

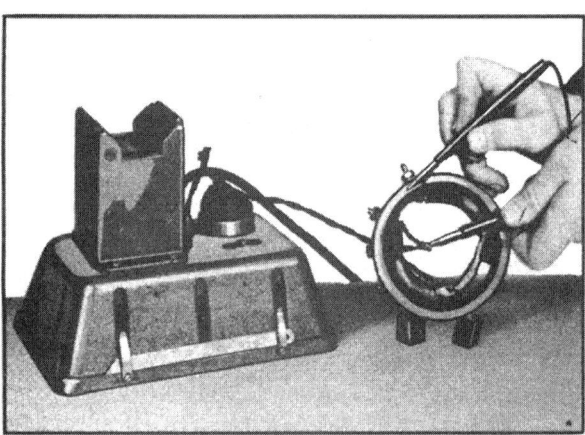

Fig. 23—Positive Terminal Test for Ground

2. If the test lamp lights, the terminal insulation is broken down and should be replaced.
3. If the lamp does not light, the insulation is OK.

Positive Brush Test for Ground

1. Place test prod leads, one on the positive brush and the other on the end frame (fig. 24).

Fig. 24—Positive Brush Holder Test for Ground

2. If the test lamp lights, the positive brush holder is grounded and it should be replaced.
3. If the test lamp does not light, the brush holder is not grounded.

Brush Holder Spring Tension

Check to see that the brush holder springs have enough tension to hold the brushes snugly against the commutator. Proper spring tension is from 24 to 28 ounces. Check brushes for wear and condition. Replace if necessary.

Fig. 25—Armature Test for Ground

ELECTRICAL SYSTEM 12-17

Front Bushing Fit

Check the fit of the armature shaft in the front bushing and if this bushing is worn, replace it with a new one.

Armature Test for Ground

1. Place the test prod leads, one to the armature core and the other to the commutator bars (fig. 25).
2. If the test lamp lights, the armature is grounded and should be replaced.
3. If the test lamp does not light, the armature is not grounded.

Armature Test for Short

1. Place the armature on the growler, and with a hack saw blade over the armature core, rotate the armature and test (fig. 26).

Fig. 26—Armature Test for Short

2. If the saw blade does not vibrate, the armature is not short circuited.
3. If the saw blade vibrates, the armature is short circuited.
4. To determine whether the armature or the commutator is shorted, clean out between the commutator bars and recheck the armature.
5. If the saw blade still vibrates, the armature is short circuited and should be replaced.

Armature to Commutator Leads

Check to see that the armature to commutator leads are properly soldered to the commutator.

Commutator

Check the commutator for roughness, and if rough, turn down on a lathe until it is thoroughly cleaned up, after which sand off with 00 sandpaper. Undercut the mica and again check the armature on the growler.

REASSEMBLE, TEST AND INSTALL GENERATOR

After all parts have been thoroughly tested and inspected, and worn or damaged parts replaced the generator should be reassembled.

1. Place the steel spacer washer, retainer plate, plate gasket and bearing in position on the drive end of armature shaft.
2. Place the felt washer in position in the drive end frame, place the felt retainer washer against felt and place frame over armature shaft. Install retainer plate to frame screws.
3. Install spacer collar, pulley, flat washer, nut and cotter pin.
4. Place the armature and frame assembly in the field frame.
5. Place new brushes in the brush holders so that the center of contact end of brush can rest against commutator when in position. Pull the brushes back against spring tension and slide the end frame into position over armature shaft and up against frame. Install the two long through bolts and tighten securely.

NOTE: New brushes should not be sanded in to fit the contour of the commutator. The brushes will seat in about ten hours of operation.

6. Connect the negative brush lead to the brush holder. Connect the positive brush lead, the field coil lead and the generator positive lead wire to the insulated positive brush holder.
7. Motor the generator by grounding the field terminal to generator frame, connecting the generator positive terminal to positive terminal of battery with a good ammeter in the circuit and connecting the battery negative lead to generator frame. The generator should run as a motor and draw from 4 to 6 amperes.

NOTE: When connecting the generator to battery to run it as a motor make sure the positive of battery is connected to positive of generator, otherwise the residual magnetism of generator will be reversed, thereby reversing the polarity of generator.

8. Place generator in position, install the generator to bracket bolts, tighten snugly and

ELECTRICAL SYSTEM 12-18

install cotter pins. Place the fan belt in position on pulley, install generator brace bolt, adjust fan belt by forcing generator away from engine until the belt has ¾" deflection midway between generator and fan, tighten generator brace bolt.

9. Connect the wire with single black tracer leading from field terminal of regulator to field terminal (closest to engine block) of generator. Connect the wire with black cross tracer to positive terminal of generator.

NOTE: It is good practice, after installing a new or rebuilt generator on a vehicle, to use a jumper lead to momentarily connect the battery terminal of the regulator with the generator terminal. This sends a current through the generator windings, assuring that the generator will build up with proper polarity.

10. Check the voltage setting and generator output (amperage) as described under "Care and Adjustment."

STARTING SYSTEM

INDEX

	Page		Page
Description and Operation	12-18	Starting Motor	12-21
Repairs	12-19	Removal	12-21
Starter Switch Replacement	12-19	Disassembly	12-21
Solenoid Replacement (Forward Control)	12-19	Testing Starting Motor Parts	12-21
Solenoid Adjustment (Forward Control)	12-20	Assembly	12-23
Solenoid Contacts—Replace (Forward Control)	12-20	Installation	12-23

DESCRIPTION AND OPERATION

The starting system has only one function to perform—to crank the engine. In the starting system, there are three units; the battery, the starting switch and the starting motor.

There are two types of starter switches used on truck models. All models except the Forward Control use the regular foot operated, direct contact type. The Forward Control models use the solenoid type.

The battery supplies the energy, the switch completes the circuit, allowing this energy to flow to the starting motor. The motor then delivers mechanical energy and does the actual work of cranking the engine. The starting equipment is used for a short time only and then remains idle until it is again needed to start the engine. The battery, however, performs other functions.

It should be noted that the starting motor draws a large amount of current for a short period of time, whereas the generator replaces this current by charging the battery at a lower rate for a much longer period of time.

The starting motor for either the regular or Forward Control model trucks is the same. The only difference is in the method of engaging the starter pinion and the flywheel teeth. The one type is actuated manually with the foot pedal, the other is actuated magnetically with the solenoid. In each case, positive engagement is assured until

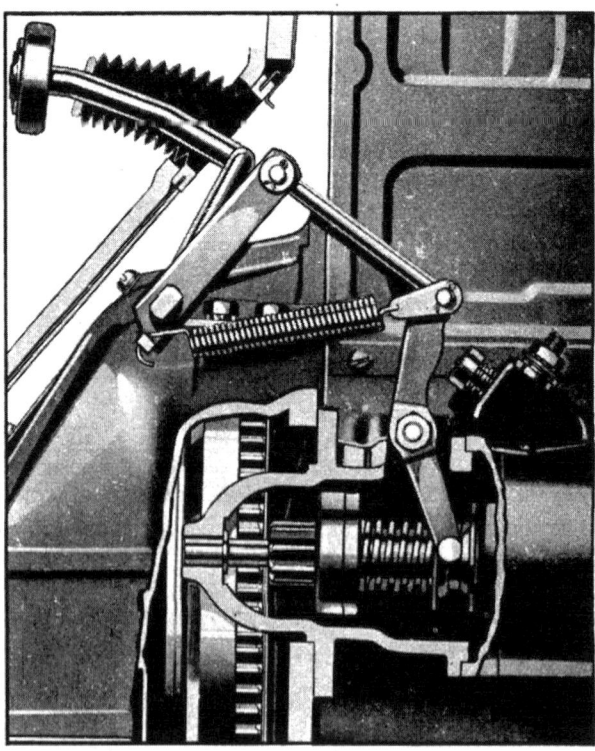

Fig. 27—Cut-Away View of Starting Motor Drive

the engine is started or the switch released.

In this design, the starter pinion in conjunction

ELECTRICAL SYSTEM 12-19

with an over-running clutch (or roller clutch), a compression spring and pulley-like sheave are mounted as an assembly on the splined part of the armature shaft. The sheave and spring are mounted to rotate freely on the outer diameter of the tube portion of the assembly (fig. 27).

A multiple spring and roller over-running mechanism (fig. 28), similar to that of a bicycle coaster brake, is located between the outer part of the clutch, which is attached to the pinion, and the inner part splined to the armature shaft.

A shift lever, bolted at its fulcrum to the starter motor housing has a yoke at its lower end which straddles the sheave; integral bosses on its inner end engage the sheave grooves. Its upper end connects to the starter pedal through linkage or to the solenoid plunger link.

On the models using the foot pedal to actuate the starting motor, depressing the foot pedal causes the lever to shift the pinion into mesh with the flywheel teeth. Further pedal movement brings an offset portion of the lever into contact with the button on the starter switch, thereby closing the switch contacts.

On Forward Control models, depressing the starter button on the instrument panel causes the "pull-in" and the "hold-in" coil of the solenoid to become energized. When these are energized it causes the heavy plunger inside the solenoid body to move forward, and through linkage causes the starting motor pinion to shift into mesh with the flywheel gear teeth. As the plunger is moved forward, a contact plate is also moved forward forming a direct circuit from the battery to the starting motor and shorting out the "pull-in" coil.

In either method, in case the teeth on the pinion butt against the flywheel ring gear and prevent engagement, the compression spring allows the sheave to move along the sleeve, permitting the starter contacts to close. The instant the armature starts to rotate, the compression spring pushes the pinion into full mesh with the flywheel immediately.

After the engine fires, and before the pinion can be withdrawn from the flywheel teeth, the over-running clutch allows the pinion to spin freely or over run on the armature shaft. The tension of the starter pedal return spring or solenoid plunger spring holds the pinion out of mesh with the flywheel while the engine is operating.

REPAIRS

Before removing a starting motor from an engine, certain tests should be made to be sure that the starting motor is in need of repair.

1. Check the battery. If the specific gravity is below 1.175, the battery is discharged and should be recharged.
2. Check the battery ground connection at the frame and clean and tighten if necessary.
3. Check the battery terminals. Dirty terminals result in poor connection between the battery and the electrical units. They should be cleaned regularly and the battery washed off with a solution of bicarbonate of soda and water.
4. Remove the starting motor switch or solenoid and check the contacts to be sure that they are clean and not burned or corroded.

If, after making the foregoing inspections the starting motor still does not function, it should be removed and disassembled.

Starter Switch Replacement

1. Disconnect the battery ground strap from battery negative post.
2. Disconnect the positive cable and ammeter wire from starter switch and remove switch to starter screws.
3. Remove switch assembly and inspect it for damaged or faulty terminals.
4. Make sure the side insulators are in position in the switch, place switch in position on the starter and install the attaching screws.
5. Connect the positive cable and ammeter wire to starter switch and tighten nut securely.
6. Place ground strap on negative battery post and tighten securely. Check starter operation.

Solenoid Replacement (Forward Control)

1. Disconnect the battery ground strap from battery negative post.
2. Disconnect solenoid plunger from starter shifter lever.

Fig. 28—Starter Drive Over-Running Clutch

ELECTRICAL SYSTEM 12-20

3. Disconnect the positive cable, ammeter wire, starter switch wire and connector strap from solenoid; remove solenoid to starter bolts and remove solenoid assembly.
4. Place new solenoid in position on the starter and install the attaching bolts.
5. Connect solenoid plunger to starter shifter lever and adjust as instructed under "Solenoid Adjustment."
6. Connect the positive cable, ammeter wire, starter switch wire and connector strap to starter solenoid and tighten nuts securely.
7. Place ground strap on negative battery post and tighten securely. Check starter operation.

Solenoid Adjustment (Forward Control)

1. Connect the battery ground strap to the battery negative post.
2. Connect positive battery cable or jumper lead from the postive battery post to the starter switch terminal (small) on the solenoid. **Make no other connections.**
3. Push in the solenoid plunger by hand. The plunger will remain in as long as the battery is connected in this manner.
4. Remove flywheel underpan.
5. Check for 3/16" clearance between starter pinion and starter housing (fig. 29) with a piece of 3/16" stock.

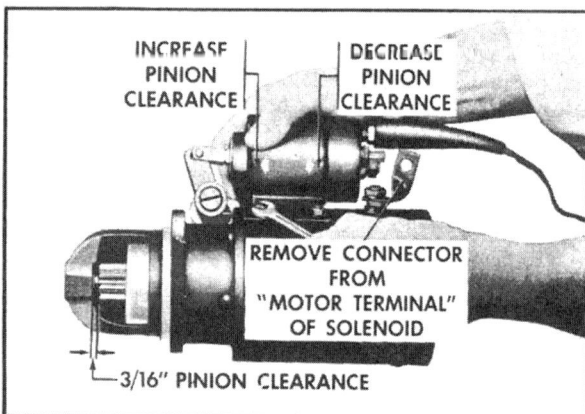

Fig. 29—Adjustment of Solenoid for Pinion Clearance

6. Adjust this clearance by loosening the solenoid to starter housing attaching bolts and moving the solenoid backward or forward on the starter housing. When the proper adjustment is obtained, tighten solenoid attaching bolts.
7. Replace flywheel underpan.
8. Remove the jumper lead from starter switch terminal and ground strap from negative battery post.

Solenoid Contacts—Replace (Forward Control)

1. Remove solenoid from starting motor and remove solenoid plunger from solenoid body.
2. Remove cover retaining screws and remove cover.
3. Remove nuts, lockwashers, flatwashers and insulating washers from terminal studs.
4. Remove nut, lockwasher, flat washer, and two insulating washers from starter switch lead screw.
5. Remove two terminal stud support plate to solenoid housing screws and remove support plate, insulating plate, one terminal stud, starter switch lead stud.
6. Remove outer spring retainer and spring from solenoid plunger contact ring.
7. Compress solenoid plunger contact ring spring, remove retainer, insulating washer, and contact ring from plunger and remove plunger from solenoid body.
8. Unsolder remaining terminal stud from solenoid lead coil.
9. Place new contact ring and insulating washer on plunger, compress spring and install retainer with open side of retainer up.

NOTE: Make sure the three lugs on bottom of contact ring index with slots in lower insulating washer.

10. Install solenoid plunger assembly into solenoid body. Carefully solder new terminal stud to solenoid lead.
11. Place solenoid plunger spring and outer spring retainer in position over end of solenoid plunger.
12. Place terminal support insulator plate and terminal support plate over terminal stud soldered to solenoid lead. Make sure lugs in terminal support plate fit into holes in insulator.
13. Place starter switch lead stud up through terminal insulator plate and terminal support being careful to index lugs on stud with slots in insulator plate. Snap stud into position.
14. Insert other terminal stud up through support insulator plate and terminal support; then install terminal support plate to solenoid housing screws and lockwashers and tighten securely.
15. Install two insulating washers, flat washers, lockwasher and nut to starter switch lead stud and tighten securely.
16. Install insulating washer, flat washer, lockwasher and nut on solenoid terminal studs and tighten securely.
17. Install cover and cover attaching screw and tighten securely.

18. Test solenoid for proper operation and install to starting motor. Adjust as outlined under "Solenoid Adjustment."

STARTING MOTOR

Removal

1. Disconnect battery ground strap from negative battery post.
2. Disconnect wires from starter switch or starter solenoid.
3. Disconnect starter pedal shaft and spring from starter shift lever.
4. Remove the two starter drive housing to clutch housing bolts, pull starter assembly forward to clear the clutch housing and remove starter.

Disassembly

1. Remove starter switch or solenoid from starting motor.
2. Remove commutator cover band, through bolts and rear housing.
3. Remove the field coil to brush lead machine screws and the commutator end frame assembly. Remove armature assembly.
4. Remove the shift lever to drive housing bolt and remove the shift lever. Remove drive mechanism.
5. With starter completely disassembled, EXCEPT FOR STARTER DRIVE OVER-RUNNING CLUTCH, wash all parts in cleaning solvent.

The illustration (fig. 30) shows an exploded view of the starter parts.

TESTS

Field Coil Circuit Test

1. Place the test prods on the field coil leads (fig. 31).
2. If test lamp lights, the field coils are OK as far as continuous circuit.
3. If test lamp does not light, there is an open circuit and replacement or repairs must be made.

Field Coil Ground Test

1. Place one test prod on frame and the other on field coil lead (fig. 32).
2. If test lamp does not light, the coils are not grounded.

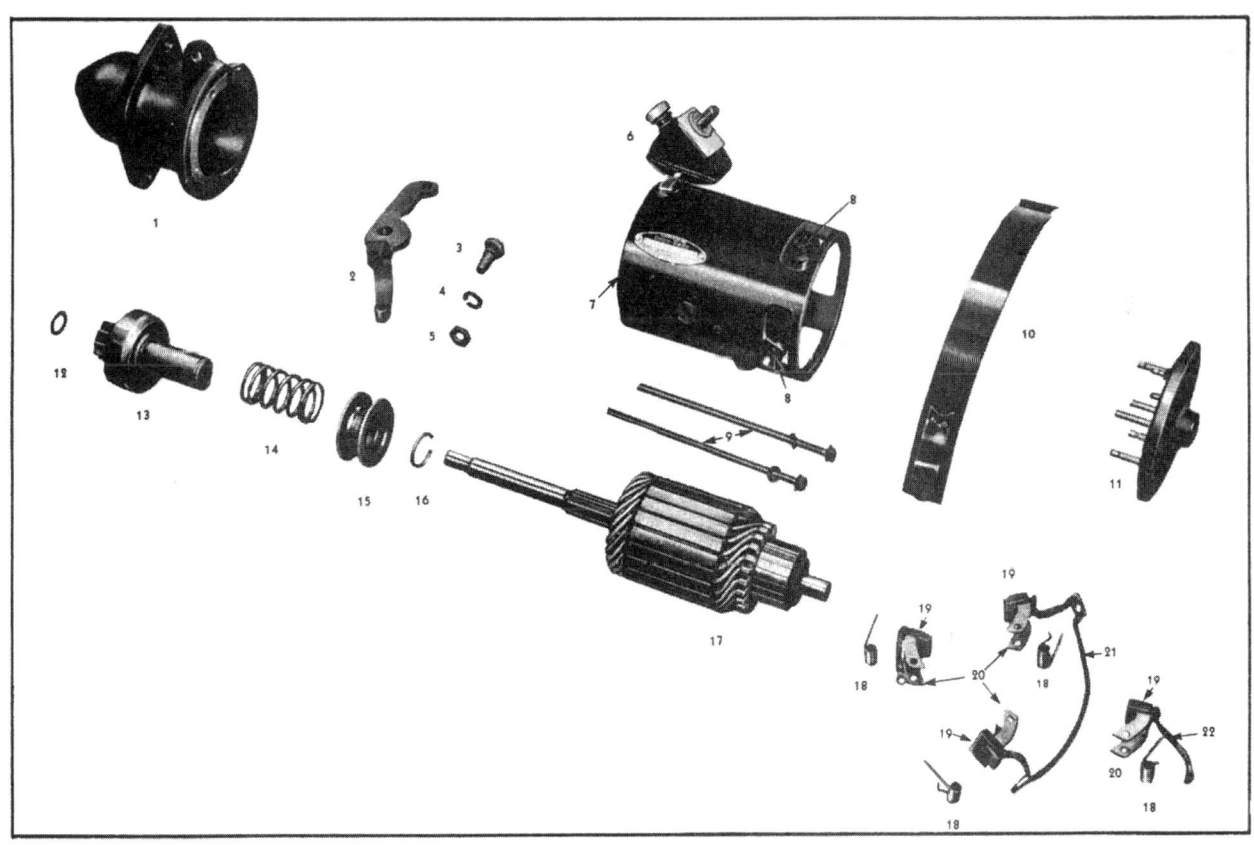

Fig. 30—Starting Motor Parts Layout

1. Drive Housing
2. Shift Lever
3. Bolt (shift lever)
4. Lockwasher
5. Nut
6. Switch
7. Field Frame
8. Field Coils
9. Through Bolts
10. Band
11. Brush Holder Frame with Pins
12. End Spacer
13. Starter Drive Shaft and Pinion
14. Spring
15. Sheave
16. Snap Ring
17. Armature
18. Brush Springs
19. Brushes
20. Brush Holders
21. Brush Field Lead
22. Brush to Ground Lead

ELECTRICAL SYSTEM 12-22

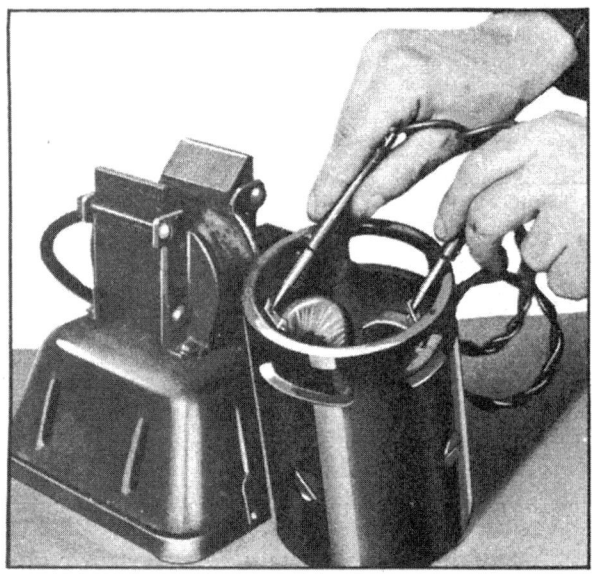

Fig. 31—Field Coil Test for Continuous Circuit

3. If test lamp lights, one or both field coils are grounded.

   NOTE: If test lamp lights, break solder connection between the two coils and test each one separately. Replace the grounded coil.

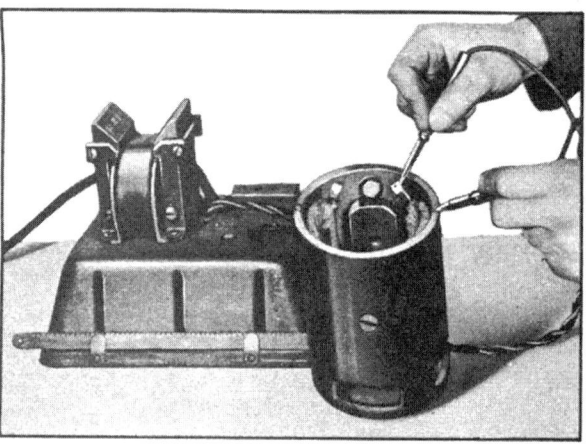

Fig. 32—Field Coil Test for Ground

4. Inspect the field coil connections to switch terminal for good connections and proper insulation.

Armature Test

1. Place one test prod on the armature and the other on the commutator (fig. 33).
2. If the test lamp lights, the armature is grounded and should be replaced.
3. Place the armature on the growler and with a saw blade over the armature core, rotate the armature and test (fig. 34).

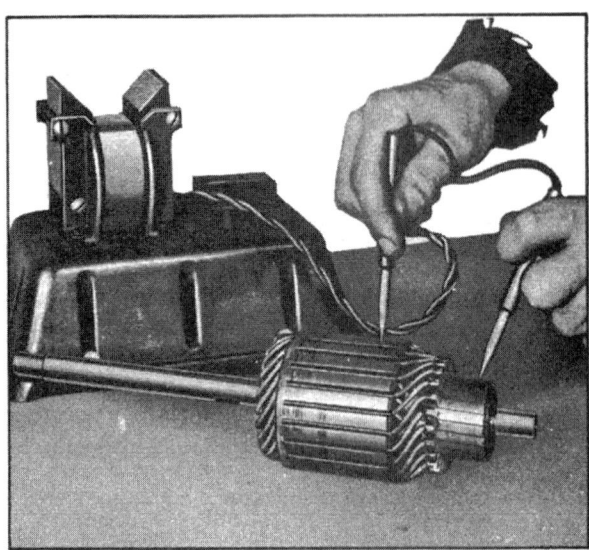

Fig. 33—Armature Test for Ground

4. If the saw blade does not vibrate, the armature is not shorted.
5. If the saw blade vibrates, the armature is short circuited and should be replaced.

Fig. 34—Armature Test for Short

Commutator

Inspect the commutator for roughness. If it is rough, turn down on a lathe until it is thoroughly cleaned up, then sand off the commutator with 00 sandpaper.

Insulated Brush Holder Test

1. Place one test prod lead to the cover and the other to the brush holder (fig. 35).
2. If the test lamp lights, brush holder is grounded and should be replaced.
3. If the test lamp does not light, the brush holder is not grounded.

ELECTRICAL SYSTEM 12-23

Fig. 35—Insulated Brush Holder Test for Ground

Brushes and Leads

1. Check the condition of the brushes and if they are pitted or worn, they should be replaced.
2. Check the tension of the brush holder springs; they should have enough tension to hold the brushes snugly against the commutator.
3. Disconnect the brush ground leads from the end frame and clean all terminals and replace.
4. Check the insulation of the brush to field coil leads. The insulation should not be broken.

Drive Housing Bushing

Check the condition of the drive housing bushing. The armature shaft should fit snugly in this bushing; if it is worn it should be replaced.

Commutator End Frame Bushing

Check condition of bushing in the end frame. If the bushing is damaged or worn excessively, the commutator end frame assembly must be replaced.

Starter Switch

1. Inspect the switch contacts for excessive pitting or roughness that would cause high resistance.
2. Check the switch shaft for proper insulation.

Starter Drive

1. Check the over-running clutch for free reverse action and looseness.
2. Check the spring for normal tension and the sheave for wear.
3. Inspect the gear for wear or damage; replace the assembly if damaged.
4. If necessary the spring or sheave can be replaced by forcing the sheave toward the clutch and removing lock ring from end of tube (fig. 36).

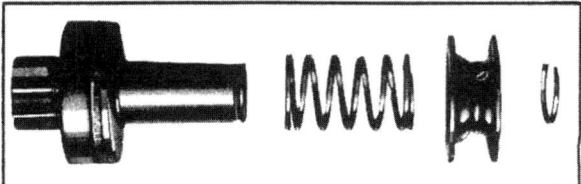

Fig. 36—Starting Motor Drive Mechanism

5. Thread the shift lever through the slot in the drive housing, while at the same time engaging the bosses on the inner end of the lever in the sheave grooves on the drive mechanism, then slide the lever and the drive into the housing together.
6. Assemble the pivot bolt through the shift lever to the housing.

ASSEMBLY

1. Assemble commutator end washer and commutator end frame assembly to the armature.
2. Assemble the armature and commutator end frame assembly to the starting motor housing.
3. Thread the armature shaft through the drive mechanism, making sure to install the thrust washer between the drive and the drive housing bushing.
4. Install the through bolts and tighten them securely.
5. Assemble the field coil to brush lead machine screws.
6. Connect the starting motor to a battery and operate for running test.
7. Assemble commutator cover band.
8. (a) On manually operated starters install the starting switch insulators in the switch and assemble the switch to the motor.
   (b) On Forward Control models, install the solenoid to the starting motor. Adjust as instructed under "Solenoid Adjustment." Test operation of starting motor and solenoid.

INSTALLATION

1. Place starter in position, install and tighten the attaching bolts.
2. Connect all wires to the starter switch or solenoid.
3. Connect battery ground strap to the battery negative post.

ELECTRICAL SYSTEM 12-24

IGNITION SYSTEM

INDEX

	Page		Page
General Description	12-24	Spark Plug Wires and/or Distributor Cap Replacement	12-27
Automatic Spark Control	12-26	Distributor Overhaul	12-28
Care and Adjustments	12-26	Removal	12-28
Repairs	12-26	Disassembly	12-28
Ignition Switch Replacement	12-26	Cleaning and Inspection	12-28
Ignition Coil Replacement	12-27	Assembly	12-28
Distributor Point Replacement	12-27	Installation	12-29
Distributor Condenser Replacement	12-27	Spark Plug Service	12-29

GENERAL DESCRIPTION

The ignition system consists of the ignition switch, coil, distributor, spark plugs, vacuum spark control, the necessary wiring and connections to properly connect the various units, as well as the battery and ammeter which are covered

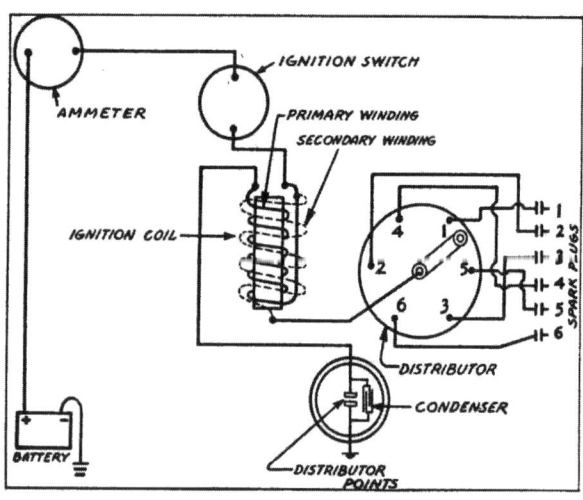

Fig. 37—Ignition Circuit

elsewhere in this section. Figure 37 shows a diagrammatic view of the ignition system.

The ignition switch, located in the low tension circuit between the battery and coil, is used to make or break the ignition circuit when starting or stopping the engine.

The ignition coil transforms the battery current to high-tension current necessary to jump the gap at the spark plugs.

The distributor is mounted on the right side of engine. It incorporates the distributor points which open and close to make and break the primary circuit, the condenser which prevents arcing at the points and aids in breaking down the magnetic field in the coil, the mechanical spark advance mechanism which advances and retards the spark with changes in engine speed, the distributor cap which has the terminals for high tension current distribution to the spark plugs and the rotor which distributes the high tension current to the terminals in the cap.

The spark plugs, which are AC-14 millimeter, are positioned in each combusion chamber to provide for the spark which ignites the combustion mixture.

The vacuum spark control is attached to the distributor bracket and connects to the distributor. The diaphragm chamber is connected to the carburetor so that engine vacuum can advance the spark and so that it will retard slightly when engine vacuum decreases on acceleration.

The coil consists of a soft laminated core over which is placed the low tension (primary) winding and the high tension (secondary) winding. This assembly is carefully insulated and placed in a metal container, the necessary connections are made, the assembly is then filled with transformer oil and hermetically sealed to prevent the entrance of moisture. A large insulator is used at the secondary terminal to provide effective insulation.

The distributor housing is designed to pilot down into the right side of cylinder block which supports the distributor and provides a bearing for the distributor shaft. A drive gear is located near the lower end of shaft and meshes with a gear on the engine camshaft to drive the distributor shaft at camshaft speed. A plate fitted with pivot pins for the governor weights is attached near the top of the shaft. The weights are placed on the pivots, the cam assembly is placed over the top of shaft and the springs are installed. The weight cover and stop plate is placed over the governor and adjusted to obtain the desired maximum governor spark advance. Figure 38 shows construction details.

ELECTRICAL SYSTEM 12-25

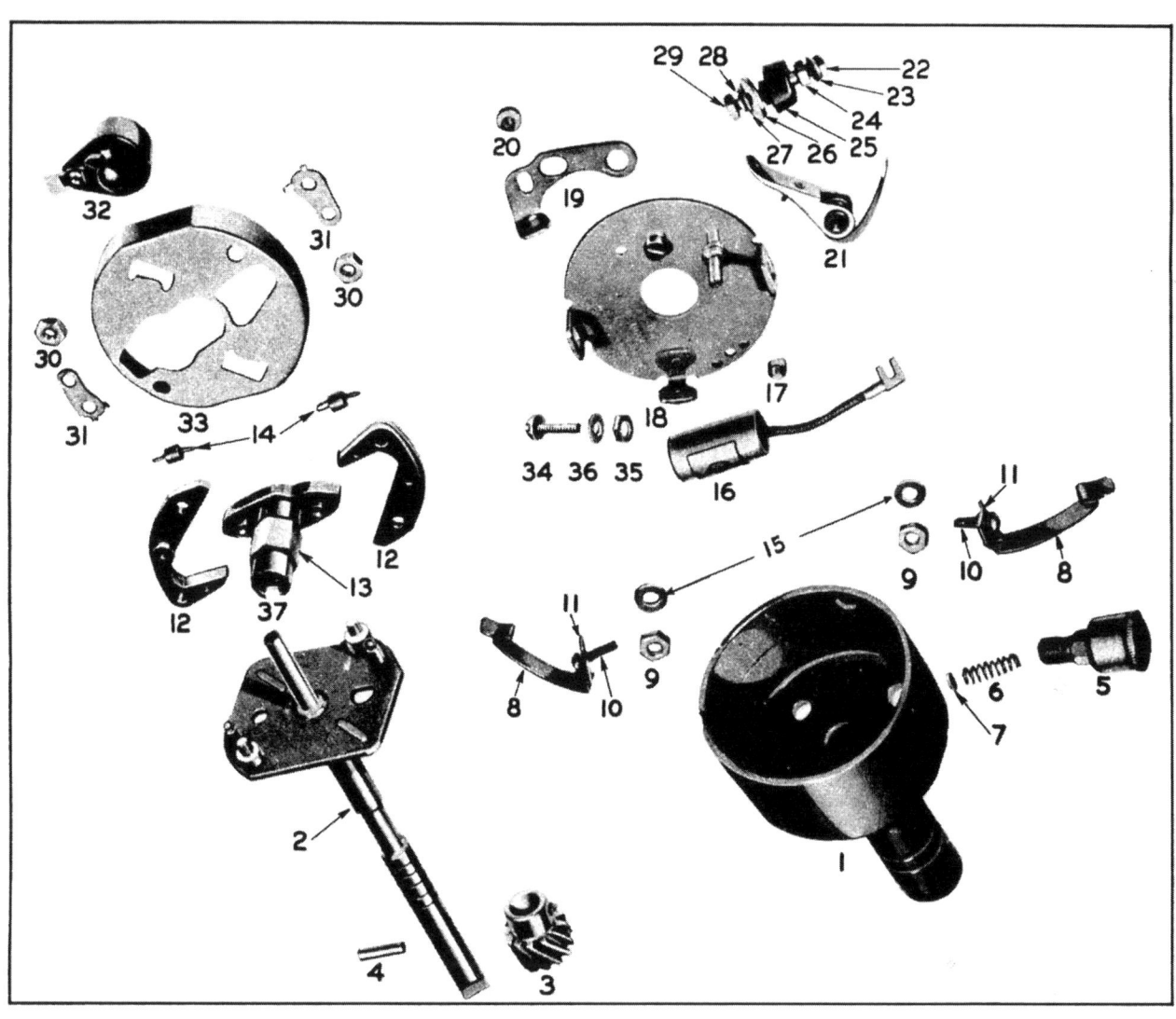

Fig. 38—Layout of Distributor Parts

1. Housing
2. Mainshaft and Weight Plate
3. Gear
4. Gear Pin
5. Grease Cup
6. Plug Spring
7. Bakelite Plug
8. Cap Springs
9. Retaining Nuts
10. Retaining Screws
11. Cap Spring Supports
12. Governor Weights
13. Cam Assembly
14. Weight Springs
15. Flate Washers
16. Condenser
17. Condenser Attaching Screw
18. Breaker Plate
19. Contact Point and Support
20. Contact Adjusting Screw
21. Breaker Arm
22. Terminal Stud Plain Nut (Inside)
23. Terminal Stud Plain Washer (Inside)
24. Terminal Stud
25. Terminal Stud Insulating Bushing (Inside)
26. Terminal Stud Insulating Washer (Outside)
27. Terminal Stud Plain Washer (Outside)
28. Terminal Stud Lockwasher (Outside)
29. Terminal Stud Nut
30. Weight Plate Nuts
31. Weight Plate Nut Lockwasher
32. Rotor
33. Weight Cover and Stop Plate
34. Attaching Screw
35. Nut
36. Lockwasher
37. Shaft Felt Wick (in Cam)

The breaker plate, which is internally grounded, sets directly above the governor mechanism and is attached to the distributor housing. One distributor point and support sets over the pivot pin on the breaker plate and is held in place by a lock screw. The location of this point can be moved for point gap adjustment by loosening the lock screw and turning the eccentric adjusting screw as desired. The other point and arm assembly is fitted with an insulating bushing which pilots over the pivot pin. The breaker arm is fitted with a fibre block which extends out toward the cam; as the cam turns the lobes contact the fibre block and cause the points to open (fig. 39).

The condenser is attached to the breaker plate and the lead connected to the insulated terminal at the point where the breaker arm connects. This places the condenser across the breaker points. The rotor attaches to the top of the cam and turns at camshaft speed. The distributor cap sets on top of the housing with a positioning lug engaging a groove in the housing. Clamps hold the cap in

ELECTRICAL SYSTEM 12-26

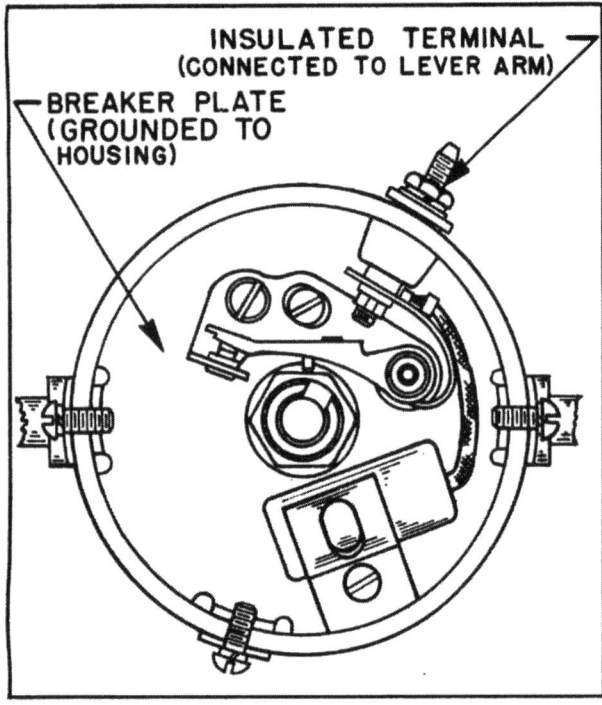

Fig. 39—Distributor Connections

position. The center terminal of the cap engages the spring contact of the rotor to transmit high tension current from the coil to the rotor; as the rotor turns the current can be transmitted to the different spark plug wire terminals.

AUTOMATIC SPARK CONTROL

To get the best performance and economy from an engine at all speeds and under all load conditions, it is necessary to change the ignition timing with variations in speed and load conditions. This is done automatically by two methods.

When the engine is idling below 600 R.P.M. the spark will occur according to the timing setting (5° before top center). As the engine speed is increased, the governor weights in the distributor start to swing outward advancing the spark. This spark advance increases as the speed increases until the maximum governor advance is reached, as in the right hand sketch (fig. 40). This maximum advance is 32.5° to 39.5° at 3450 R.P.M. of the 216 engine and 29° to 33° at 3700 R.P.M. of the 235 engine. Then, as the speed decreases, the springs

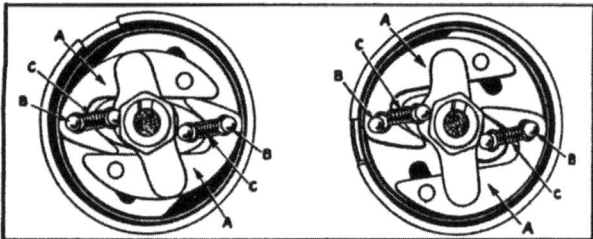

Fig. 40—Mechanical Breaker Advance Mechanism
A—Governor Weight   B—Weight Spring Pin   C—Weight Spring

pull the weights inward as in the left hand sketch (fig. 40), retarding the spark to maintain governor advance in direct relation to engine speed.

The vacuum spark advance operates entirely independent of the governor advance. As the carburetor throttle is opened slightly from the idling position, manifold vacuum is applied to the vacuum spark control passage in the carburetor which causes the vacuum spark control diaphragm to compress the spring and advance the spark. This advances the spark a maximum of 20° but only with comparatively high manifold vacuum. Each time the throttle is opened wider for acceleration, the manifold vacuum momentarily decreases, retarding the spark to prevent excessive detonation. At high vehicle speed with nearly wide open throttle, the vacuum is low; therefore, the vacuum spark advance is not in operation. However, under this condition maximum governor advance is in use.

Care and Adjustment

Normal care consists of maintaining tight, corrosion free connections in the entire circuit, making sure the wires are properly insulated and protected against possible shorts, keeping the vacuum spark control line connections tight, keeping excessive grease and oil from the distributor, coil, spark plugs and wires. Place a drop or two of oil on the felt wick in the distributor cam, tighten the grease cup a turn every 1000 miles and keep the points clean and properly adjusted.

Instructions covering distributor point adjustment and ignition timing will be found under "Engine Tune-up," in Section 6.

REPAIRS

Ignition Switch Replacement

1. Raise floor mat, remove battery cover and disconnect positive battery cable from battery.
2. Remove lock cylinder.

   NOTE: To remove lock cylinder, insert key in lock and turn clockwise until stop is reached. Insert a stiff wire in small hole on lock face, depress tumbler and continue to turn key clockwise until cylinder can be removed.

3. Disconnect wires from ignition switch.

   NOTE: Identify wires as removed for easy installation.

4. Loosen two screws retaining switch to ignition lock light plate—rotate counterclockwise and remove.
5. Install new switch and tighten retaining screws securely.
6. Connect wires to switch.

ELECTRICAL SYSTEM 12-27

7. Replace lock cylinder.
8. Replace battery cable to battery, battery cover and floor mat.

Ignition Coil Replacement

1. Disconnect the distributor and ignition switch leads from terminals on coil and pull the high tension wire from terminal at bottom of coil. Remove coil to cylinder head attaching screws.
2. Place new coil in position and install attaching screws.
3. Place high tension lead securely in terminal at bottom of coil, and connect distributor and ignition leads to terminals on coil. Start engine to test coil operation.

Distributor Point Replacement

1. Remove wires from numbers 1, 2 and 3 spark plugs, release the distributor cap clamps, remove cap and pull it back out of the way.
2. Remove rotor.
3. Loosen the insulated terminal inside nut, unhook the breaker arm spring from terminal and remove arm assembly.
4. Remove the contact point support lock screw and remove contact point and support assembly.
5. Carefully wipe the protective film of oil from the contact points of the new set.
6. Place the contact point and support assembly in position over the pivot pin and adjusting screw and install the lock screw loosely.
7. Place the breaker arm over pivot pin and hook the arm spring over the terminal stud. Tighten terminal stud nut securely.
8. Crank the engine until the distributor point cam follower is on the extreme peak of a lobe on the cam which will provide maximum breaker point opening. Turn the eccentric adjusting screw (fig. 41) to right or left to obtain a point opening of .022".

NOTE: The standard point setting is .018". When new points are installed adjust points to .022" as the rubbing block will wear down slightly while seating to the cam.

9. Tighten the point support lock screw and recheck point opening. Install rotor.
10. Place cap in position and hook the clamps. Install numbers 1, 2 and 3 spark plug wires.
11. Check and set ignition timing with a timing light (See Engine Tune-Up, Section 6).

Distributor Condenser Replacement

1. Remove the distributor cap and lift off the rotor.
2. Loosen the terminal inside nut and remove condenser lead from terminal.
3. Remove the screw that attaches condenser tab to distributor plate and remove condenser.
4. Place the new condenser in position and install the condenser tab to breaker plate screw.
5. Place the condenser lead in position on the terminal and tighten the nut securely.
6. Install rotor and distributor cap.

Spark Plug Wires and/or Distributor Cap Replacement

1. Disconnect all wires from the spark plugs and the high tension wire from bottom of coil.
2. Remove distributor cap and remove all wires from cap.
3. Inspect the wires for damaged insulation and loose or damaged terminals.
4. Inspect the cap for cracks and damaged terminals. If the cap is suitable for additional service, clean the contacts on the inside of cap and the terminals on the top of cap.
5. Replace all damaged parts.
6. If new wires are being installed or the old wires were removed from the old rubber support, place one long and two short wires through each of the supports.
7. Place the vinylite nipples on the distributor end of all wires.

Fig. 41—Adjusting Distributor Points

ELECTRICAL SYSTEM 12-28

8. Attach the two sets of wires to the spark plugs with the two long wires attached to numbers 1 and 6 plugs.
9. Place the coil to distributor wire securely in the terminal of coil and the center terminal of distributor.
10. Install the cap and hook the retainers.
11. Place the long wire attached to number 1 spark plug securely in the cap terminal farthest from engine block and install the remaining wires in a clockwise direction from number 1 according to the firing order of 1-5-3-6-2-4.
12. Start engine and test operation.

DISTRIBUTOR OVERHAUL

Removal

1. Disconnect the low tension wire from terminal on distributor.
2. Remove distributor cap and hand crank the engine until the rotor points directly away from engine (at 90° to block); scratch a mark on outside of distributor in line with rotor.
3. Loosen the distributor clamp screw and work the distributor up out of cylinder block.

Disassembly

1. Remove rotor, loosen insulated terminal inside nut and remove breaker arm.
2. Remove contact point support lock screw and remove contact point and support.
3. Remove attaching screw and remove condenser.
4. Remove the insulated terminal stud and bushings.
5. Remove breaker plate to distributor housing screws and cap clamps.
6. Lift out the breaker plate.
7. Remove the lubrication cup, spring and bakelite shaft contact plug.
8. Drive out the distributor gear to shaft pin, remove gear from shaft and shaft with advance mechanism from body.
9. Remove the governor weight springs, release the lock plate tangs, remove the nuts and governor weight cover and stop plate.
10. Remove the cam and governor weights.

Cleaning and Inspection

1. Wash all parts in cleaning solvent.
2. Inspect the shaft for wear, and check its fit in the bearings in the distributor body. If the shaft or bearings are worn, the shaft and distributor body should be replaced.
3. Mount the shaft in "V" blocks and check the shaft alignment with a dial gauge. The runout should not exceed .002".
4. Inspect the governor weights for wear or burrs and free fit on their pins.
5. Inspect the cam for wear or roughness. Then check its fit on the end of the shaft. It should be absolutely free, without any looseness.
6. Inspect the condition of the distributor points—dirty points should be cleaned and badly pitted points should be replaced.
7. Test the condenser for series resistance, microfarad capacity (.18 to .23) and insulation breakdown, following the instructions given by the manufacturer of the test equipment used.
8. Inspect the distributor cap and spark plug wires for damage. See "Spark Plug Wires and/or Distributor Cap Replacement" if replacement is necessary.

Assembly

1. Assemble the governor weights over their pivot pins. Lubricate the top end of the shaft with light engine oil and install the cam.
2. Install the weight cover and stop plate, the lock plates and nuts. Tighten nuts securely and lock them by bending up the lock plate tangs. Install the two weight springs.
3. Lubricate the shaft and install it in the distributor housing.
4. Install the drive gear and retainer pin. Check to see that the shaft turns freely.
5. Place the breaker plate in the distributor body and install breaker plate to distributor housing screws. Place the distributor cap springs and screws in position and securely tighten.
6. Install the insulated primary terminal insulating bushings, terminal stud, lock clip and nut on the outer end, and washer and nut on inner end.
7. Clean the condenser mounting tab, place the condenser in position and install the attaching screw. Connect the lead to the insulated terminal.
8. Clean all oil carefully from contact points, place the contact point and support assembly in position over the pivot pin and install the lock screw securely.
9. Place the breaker arm over the pivot pin and hook the arm spring over the terminal stud. Tighten terminal stud nut securely.
10. Turn the distributor shaft until the breaker arm rubbing block is on the extreme top of a lobe of the cam which will provide maximum breaker point opening.
11. Turn the eccentric adjusting screw (fig. 41) to the right or left to obtain .018" point opening (.022" if new points are being used).

ELECTRICAL SYSTEM 12-29

12. Tighten point support lock screw and recheck point opening.
13. Install the bakelite shaft contact plug, spring and grease cup properly filled with chassis lubricant and install rotor on top of cam.

Installation

1. Turn the rotor about ¼" in a clockwise direction past the mark previously placed on distributor housing.
2. Start the distributor down into block with the mark previously placed on distributor housing at 90° to engine block and then push distributor down into position.

   NOTE: It may be necessary to move rotor slightly to start gear into mesh with camshaft gear, but rotor should line up with the mark when distributor is down in place.

3. Tighten the distributor clamp enough to hold the distributor in place and connect low tension wire to distributor terminal.
4. Time the ignition according to instructions under "Engine Tune-Up," Section 6.

Installation.

(When engine has been turned or if distributor was not properly marked when removed)

1. Remove valve rocker arm cover.
2. Hand crank the engine until number 1 intake valve (second valve from front of head) closes and continue to crank it slowly about ⅓ turn until number 1 piston is at top of cylinder.

   NOTE: This can be determined by watching at the timing indicator opening on clutch housing above starter mounting, until U/C marking on flywheel lines up with pointer.

3. Start the distributor down into right side of engine block with the distributor cap spring clips parallel with engine block, turn rotor slightly clockwise from 90° to engine block and push distributor down into position.

   NOTE: In some cases it may be necessary to remove distributor and turn oil pump shaft with a long screwdriver so that the slot in oil pump shaft will line up with tang on distributor shaft.

4. Turn distributor body slightly until points are just slightly open and tighten distributor clamp screw.

5. Place distributor cap in position and check to see that rotor lines up with terminal for number 1 spark plug.
6. Install distributor cap, check all high tension wire connections and connect spark plug wires if they have been disconnected or removed.
7. Connect the low tension wire to distributor terminal.
8. Start engine and set timing according to instructions under "Engine Tune-Up," Section 6.

SPARK PLUG SERVICE

1. Disconnect the spark plug wires from plugs and carefully remove the spark plugs.
2. Inspect the plugs for cracked porcelain both above and below the body. If porcelain is cracked the plug or plugs must be replaced. It is advisable to replace the plugs in sets. If only part of the set is to be replaced, be sure to use plugs of the same make and heat range.
3. Inspect the electrodes for excessive wear or damage, inspect the insulators for heavy blisters near the inner ends. If the electrodes are badly worn or damaged or if the porcelains are badly blistered the plugs should be replaced.
4. If the spark plugs are to be kept in service they should be thoroughly cleaned with an abrasive, air-blast type cleaner to remove the oxide from the insulator. This oxide coating will probably be in powder form if the plug has had but 3000 or 4000 miles of service since cleaning; however, it eventually melts and forms a glazed surface which is very difficult to remove even with a sand-blast cleaner. This fused oxide coating is very de-

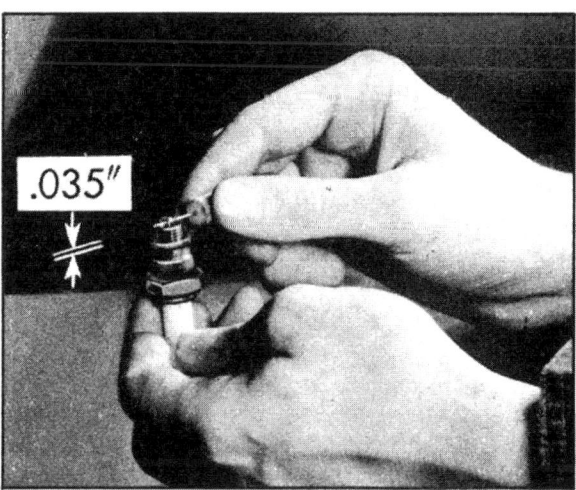

Fig. 42—Setting Spark Plug Gap

ELECTRICAL SYSTEM 12-30

ceiving; after cleaning the plug it will look clean, but there will still be an invisible layer of the glazed oxide which may cause a miss at high speed. Plugs in this condition should be thoroughly recleaned to remove this coating.

5. After cleaning the plugs inspect them again for damage that was not visible before cleaning. Set the electrode gaps to .035" using a round feeler gauge (fig. 42).

NOTE: Never bend the center electrode as this will probably crack the porcelain insulator. Make all adjustments with the side electrode.

6. Place new gaskets on the spark plugs and tighten the plugs into the head with a torque wrench to 20-25 ft.-lbs. tension.

7. If a torque wrench is not available, tighten the plugs "finger tight" plus ½ turn.

8. Connect the wires to their respective spark plugs according to the firing order of 1-5-3-6-2-4.

INSTRUMENTS AND GAUGES

INDEX

	Page		Page
Description and Operation	12-30	Temperature Indicator Replacement	12-32
Service Operations	12-31	Oil Pressure Gauge	12-33
Ammeter	12-31	Speedometer Service	12-33
Fuel Gauge	12-31	Head Replacement	12-33
Testing	12-31	Horn Adjustment	12-33
Tank Unit Replacement	12-32	Horn Replacement	12-33

DESCRIPTION AND OPERATION

The ammeter, fuel gauge, temperature indicator, oil pressure gauge and speedometer come under the classification of instruments and gauges.

Ammeter

The ammeter is a current operated electro-magnetic instrument, used to measure the approximate flow of current in the circuit. It is placed in the main circuit between the battery and the generator. The flow of current from the generator to battery or from battery to most electrical equipment is indicated by this instrument. Exceptions to this rule include the starting motor, horns, cigarette lighter and some electrical accessories that might be attached to the battery side of ammeter.

Fuel Gauge

The fuel gauge consists of a dash or indicating unit and a tank unit plus the necessary wiring (fig. 43). The circuit is connected to the dead side of the ignition switch; therefore, it registers only when the ignition switch is "on." The dash unit operates on the electro-magnetic principle, counteracted by a counterweight on the indicator hand. When the current is "off," the counterweight returns the hand to the "empty" position. When the switch is "on," current flows from the ignition switch to the fuel gauge dash unit small terminal, through the choke or limiting coil to the common connection between the two coils. From this point, current can travel through the operating coil of the dash unit to ground and also over the wire to the tank unit and through this unit to ground. When the tank is empty, the float will be near the bottom of tank and the contact finger cuts out the resistance of the tank unit so that most of the

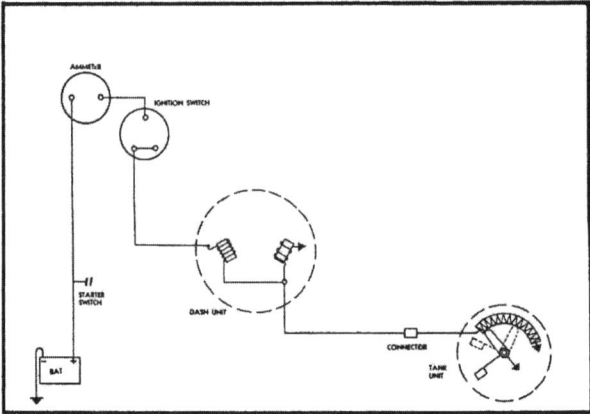

Fig. 43—Gasoline Gauge Circuits

current passes to the tank unit and directly to ground and very little current passes through the dash unit operating coil; therefore, the gauge shows empty. As more fuel is placed in the tank, the float is raised causing the contact finger of tank unit to move across the resistance unit, inserting more coils of resistance in the tank circuit (fig. 43). This additional resistance, forces more current through the dash unit operating coil which moves the indicating hand over toward the "full" side of scale.

Temperature Indicator

The temperature indicator consists of an indicating unit on the dash, an ether filled bulb in the cylinder head and a small tube forming an air tight connection between the two units. As the water in the cylinder head warms up, the ether expands causing the hand on the dash unit to move toward the right, indicating the water temperature.

Oil Pressure Gauge

The oil pressure gauge mounts in the instrument cluster and is connected to the engine pressure oil system by a small pipe. The oil pressure created by the oil pump, causes the gauge hand to move to the right recording the pressure.

Speedometer

The speedometer, mounted to the right of the instrument group, is driven by a cable and gears from the transmission mainshaft. This unit incorporates two devices—the speedometer to indicate rate of speed and the odometer to record the distance traveled.

SERVICE OPERATIONS

Ammeter, gas gauge, oil gauge, and temperature gauge are all contained in a single unit mounting plate which is enclosed by a bezel and glass with the entire cluster fastened to the dash panel with four attaching nuts. To replace any of the gauges, it is necessary to remove the entire cluster and remove the bezel and glass for unit replacements. The following procedure covers removal of any of the above instruments from the cluster.

1. Raise floor mat, remove battery cover and disconnect positive battery terminal from battery.
2. Remove light sockets from instrument cluster.
3. Disconnect oil pressure line from oil pressure gauge.
4. Disconnect wiring from ammeter and gas gauge.

   NOTE: Identify wires as removed for easy installation.

5. Remove four nuts retaining instrument cluster to dash panel and remove instrument cluster.

   CAUTION: If temperature gauge is not going to be replaced exercise care that heat indicator line is not damaged.

6. Bend tangs which retain chrome bezel to cluster housing and remove bezel, glass and cluster face.
7. Remove cluster instrument retainers and remove instrument to be replaced.
8. Install new instrument, instrument retainers and replace cluster face, glass and bezel.
9. Bend edge of bezel to retain it to housing and install cluster assembly to dash with four retaining nuts.
10. Connect wires to ammeter and gas gauge, connect oil pressure line to oil pressure gauge and install light sockets.
11. Connect battery cable, install battery cover and replace floor mat.

AMMETER

The ammeter requires very little service other than keeping the terminal nuts clean and tight.

FUEL GAUGE

The most common cause of fuel gauge trouble is high resistance in the circuit. Make sure all connections are tight and free from dirt, paint or corrosion.

Since the fuel gauge consists of two remotely located units and the connecting wires, it is sometimes difficult to determine which unit is at fault. A gas gauge tester KMO-204 (fig. 44) is available for testing the units. If a unit is proved to be faulty it should be replaced.

Testing Fuel Gauge

A—1. With ignition switch "OFF," disconnect tank wire from back of dash unit. (This is the larger terminal.)
2. Attach the red wire of the tester to this terminal and black wire to a good ground.
3. Turn ignition switch "ON"—move tester arm up and down, dash unit should register "FULL" and "EMPTY" if it is OK. If so, turn ignition switch "OFF" and reconnect tank wire.
4. If dash unit does not register at all on above test—before replacing it, make certain that it is getting current from the ignition switch. This can be quickly tested by

ELECTRICAL SYSTEM 12-32

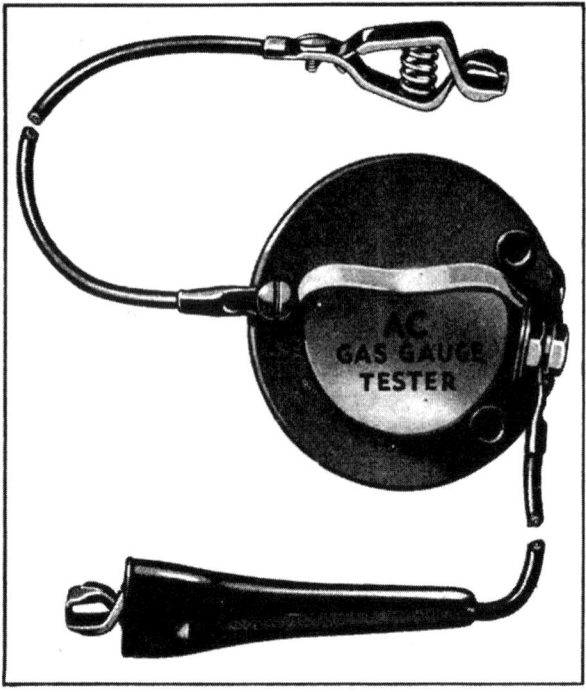

Fig. 44—Gasoline Gauge Tester

connecting a 6-volt lamp from ignition terminal (left hand terminal on back of dash unit) to ground.

B— If dash unit is OK, next check the wiring between dash and tank units as follows:

1. Disconnect tank unit wire near the gas tank at the connector or terminal junction block.
2. Attach the red wire of the tester to the connection running to the dash and the black wire to ground.
3. If on this test dash unit reads "EMPTY" at all times or the reading is noticeably lower than during the check at the dash unit, look for shorts or leaks in the wiring between dash and tank. Leaks are most likely to occur at terminal junctions. If dash unit reads above "FULL" at all times or if it reads higher at "EMPTY" and "FULL" than readings obtained when checking at the dash, look for poor connection or break in the wiring. Be sure contacts in connectors are clean.

C—1. If dash unit and wiring check OK, remove tank unit. Clean away all dirt that has collected around tank unit terminal as road dirt, particularly calcium chloride, causes an electrical leak that will cause an error in reading.

2. After cleaning thoroughly, connect tank unit to the wire leading to dash, grounding the tank unit with a short piece of wire from the outer edge to any part of the car. Turn ignition switch "ON" and move the float arm up and down. If this unit is OK, the dash unit will give corresponding "EMPTY" and "FULL" readings.

3. If tank unit is OK reinstall in the tank—if not, replace with a new tank unit but first repeat above test before installing in the tank.

NOTE: Always check tank units for freedom of movement of the float arm by raising it to various positions and observing that it will fall to "EMPTY" position in every instance.

Tank Unit Replacement

1. (a) Trucks with tank in cab.
   Move seat assembly forward and disconnect tank unit at connector.

   (b) Trucks with tank inside frame.
   Disconnect tank unit at connector and disconnect fuel line from tank. Drain fuel from tank until the tank can be conveniently handled. Release tank support straps and remove tank.

2. Remove tank gauge unit attaching screws and gauge unit. Make necessary tests as explained under "Testing Fuel Gauge."

3. Thoroughly clean the flanges of the new gauge, place a new gasket on tank and securely attach gauge to tank. Attach wire to terminal.

4. (a) Trucks with tank in cab.
   Connect fuel gauge wire to connector and reposition seat.

   (b) Trucks with tank inside frame.
   Place tank in position and tighten tank support straps. Connect fuel line to tank and fuel gauge wire to connector. Place any fuel removed back in tank.

TEMPERATURE INDICATOR

The temperature indicator requires very little attention other than avoiding damage to the line between the indicator and the bulb. If this unit fails to register at all, look for leaks or restricted line. If the hand stays in the "hot" range it likely was caused by an overheated engine. The only remedy is replacement of the entire unit.

Replacement

1. Drain the cooling system until the coolant level is below the top of cylinder head. Remove fitting nut from left rear corner of cylinder head and remove indicator bulb.

2. Remove grommet from cowl so that bulb can be pulled through. Remove dash unit as outlined under "Service Operations."

ELECTRICAL SYSTEM 12-33

3. Work bulb of new unit through opening in dash being careful not to bend pipe excessively. Connect indicator securely to instrument panel and work the surplus pipe through dash. Install grommet, make necessary coil or long bends in pipe to take up slack, place bulb in fitting on cylinder head and tighten securely. Refill cooling system.

OIL PRESSURE GAUGE

The oil pressure gauge requires very little attention. If the control line should become restricted it should be blown out or replaced.

SPEEDOMETER SERVICE

The speedometer head requires comparatively little service, and as special equipment is required to render this service, most automobile dealers send the speedometer to an authorized AC speedometer service station.

Cable Replacement or Lubrication

1. Disconnect the speedometer cable from the speedometer head and fitting at the transmission. Remove the old cable by pulling it out from speedometer end of conduit.

   NOTE: If old cable is broken, it may be necessary to remove lower piece from transmission end of conduit.

2. Lubricate the lower ¾ of cable with AC speedometer cable lubricant and push the cable into conduit. Connect lower end to fitting on transmission and upper end to speedometer head. Road test vehicle for speedometer operation.

Head Replacement

1. Disconnect light sockets from speedometer cluster housing.
2. Disconnect speedometer cable from head.
3. Remove nuts attaching speedometer housing cluster to dash and remove speedometer cluster.
4. Bend tangs which retain chrome bezel to housing and remove bezel and glass.
5. Remove two screws which retain speedometer head to housing and remove head.
6. Install new speedometer head and retaining screws.
7. Replace glass and bezel and bend edge of bezel to retain it to housing.
8. Install speedometer cluster with retaining nuts and connect speedometer cable to head.
9. Replace light sockets.

HORN ADJUSTMENT

Horn adjustment is accomplished by the adjusting screw located on the back of the horn body.

HORN REPLACEMENT

1. Disconnect wires to horn.
2. Remove two nuts and lockwashers retaining horn to mounting bracket on intake manifold.
3. Install new horn and fasten securely to mounting bracket.
4. Replace wires to horn connections.
5. Test for operation and adjust if necessary.

LIGHTING SYSTEM

INDEX

	Page		Page
Description and Operation	12-33	Sealed Beam Headlamp—Overhaul	12-36
Care and Adjustment	12-35	Lighting Switch—Replacement	12-36
Headlamp Beam	12-35	Stoplight Switch—Replacement	12-37
Service Operations	12-36	Dimmer Switch—Replacement	12-37
Sealed Beam Unit Replacement	12-36	Parking Light Service	12-37
		Tail and Stop Light Service	12-37

DESCRIPTION AND OPERATION

The lighting and wiring units include the lighting switch, stop light switch, dimmer switch, dome light switch, head and parking lights, tail and stop lights, instrument lights, the wiring harness and other wiring except that covered under other circuits.

The lighting switch is mounted near the left end of the instrument panel. All current entering the lighting switch passes through a 30 ampere thermal circuit breaker on (1948-49) models and 42 ampere on (1950-51) models. If all lights fail to operate, look for trouble at this circuit breaker, the light switch or the wiring between the battery and the light switch.

When the switch control button is pulled out to the first position, an internal circuit is established to the switch terminals for the parking lamps, instrument lights, and tail lamps. When the switch is pulled out to the last position, an internal circuit is established to the switch terminals for the headlamps, instrument lights and tail lamps. The current for the instrument lights passes through a rheostat which is regulated by the light switch knob. By turning the switch knob, the instrument lights can be dimmed or turned completely off.

The mechanically operated stop light switch is attached to the underside of the toe pan between the clutch and brake pedals. The actuating lever or arm of the switch extends out to the right between the brake pedal and toe pan. When the brake pedal is released it holds the switch arm in the "off" position (fig. 45), but when the brake pedal is pushed down, a spring within the switch causes the switch arm to follow the pedal, closing the circuit within the switch and lighting the stop lights.

Fig. 45—Stoplight Switch-Off Position

The dimmer switch is located on the toe pan to the left of the clutch pedal. When the headlights are on, this switch is used to change the lights from high to low beam or from low beam to high beam. Each time the switch button is depressed and released, the lights are switched from one beam to another.

The dome lamp switch is located at the left end of the dome lamp assembly, directly above the rear window. Moving this switch backwards turns the light on and moving it forward turns the light off.

All trucks are equipped with "Sealed Beam" headlight units in which the light source, the reflector, lens and gasket are all assembled in a securely sealed unit. Figure 46 shows the component parts of the light. This sealed construction prevents tarnished reflectors and keeps dirt and moisture from the reflector and inside of the lens. This assures maximum lighting efficiency throughout the life of the unit.

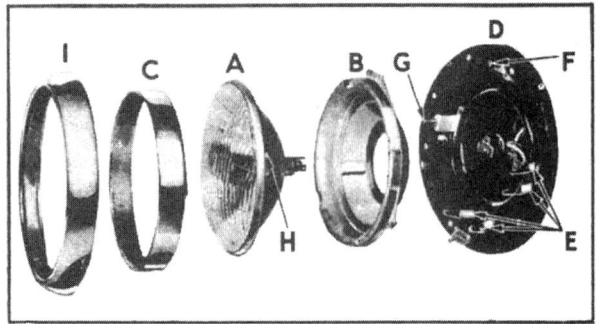

Fig. 46—Sealed Beam Headlamp Parts

The "Sealed Beam" units have two separate filaments located in the unit in positions to produce an upper (country) light beam and a lower (traffic) light beam. The upper beam is designed to illuminate the road evenly for considerable distance ahead of the vehicle and should only be used on the open highway when no other vehicles are approaching. The lower beam is adjusted to illuminate the right side of the road a reasonable distance ahead but to prevent glare in the eyes of oncoming drivers.

When the upper beams are in use a red pilot light will be seen through a small opening at the bottom of the speedometer dial. The dimmer switch is used to switch from one beam to the other.

Parking lamps are mounted between the two upper grille bars at their outer ends. A three candle power bulb is used in each parking lamp.

Combination stop and tail lamps are used. On all models except the Panels, two bulbs are used; one having 21 candle power for the stop light and one having 3 candle power for the tail light. The Panel models use a double filament bulb having 21 candle power for the stop light and 3 candle power for the tail lights. The stop light is controlled by the stop light switch, actuated by the brake pedal, independent of the other light circuit while the tail light, is turned on by the lighting switch.

The instruments are indirectly illuminated by a series of small bulbs back of the instrument panel. Each individual light socket is fitted with a spring clip so that it can be pushed into an opening in the instrument carrier and will be held in place by the clip. These lights are turned on by the regular light switch and can be dimmed by the light switch rheostat.

CARE AND ADJUSTMENT

In general, care of the lighting units and wiring system consists of an occasional check to see that all wiring connections are tight, that the lighting units are tightly mounted to provide a good ground and that the wiring is not pinched or worn to a point that a short circuit might result. All lights should be checked regularly to see that they light correctly and do not flicker.

HEADLAMP BEAM ADJUSTMENT

To obtain the maximum results in road illumination and the safety that has been built into the headlighting equipment, the headlamps must be properly aimed.

1. Make a headlamp aiming screen (fig. 47). A vertical line must be drawn to represent the center of the chart and will be used in positioning the screen. Horizontal line "A" must be drawn across the screen. Vertical lines "B" and "C" must be placed on each side of the center line according to model of truck.

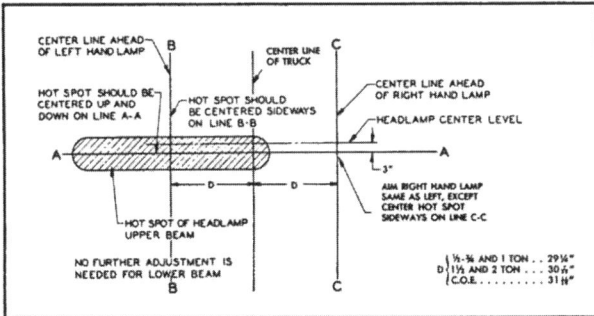

Fig. 47—Headlamp Aiming Screen

2. Place the car on a level floor 25' from a wall or object that will act as a support for the screen. Sight from the center of rear window past the windshield division channel on each side and place the screen center line midway between these two points.

3. Raise or lower the screen until the horizontal line "A" is 3" below the center of headlamps.

   NOTE: If State Laws require a loading allowance when adjusting headlamps, place the line as much below the headlamp center as the particular State requires.

4. Turn on the headlights and place the dimmer switch in the position to produce the upper (bright) beam. Remove the headlamp rims and cover one headlamp.

5. Check the position of the light beam on the screen. If the hot spot of the light beam does not center on intersection of line "A" and the vertical line directly in front of the light (fig. 47), adjustment is necessary.

6. Turning the vertical adjusting screw "In" or "Out" will raise or lower the light beam as desired. Turning the horizontal adjusting screw (fig. 48) "In" or "Out" will center the beam on the vertical line "B" or "C."

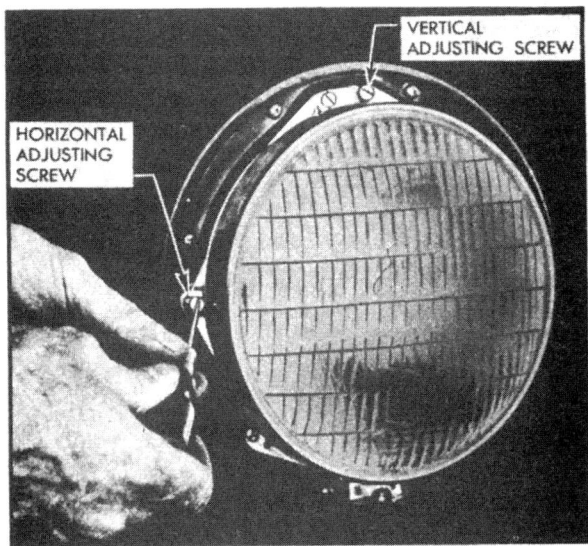

Fig. 48—Headlamp Adjusting Screws

7. Install headlamp rim and adjust the opposite light in the same manner. Figure 49 illustrates a headlamp correctly aimed. It is not necessary to adjust the headlamp for the lower beam.

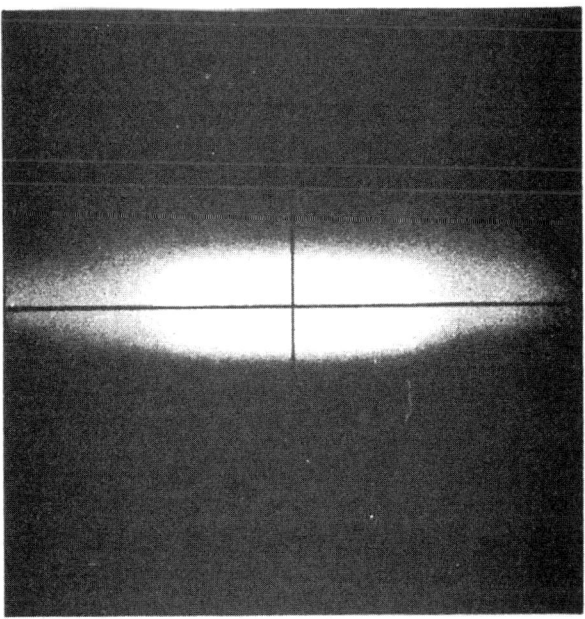

Fig. 49—Properly Aimed Headlamp Beam

SERVICE OPERATIONS

SEALED BEAM UNIT REPLACEMENT

1. Loosen clamp screw and remove headlamp door rim by pulling it out at the bottom and unhooking the top (fig. 50).

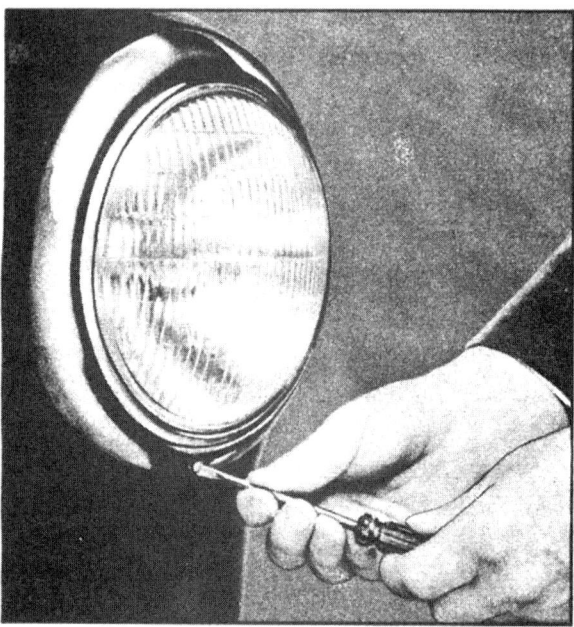

Fig. 50—Removing Headlamp Rim

2. Remove the three screws attaching retaining ring (fig. 51). DO NOT DISTURB THE AIMING SCREWS.

Fig. 51—Removing Sealed Beam Retaining Ring Screws

3. Rotate retainer ring counterclockwise and remove ring. Pull sealed beam unit forward and disconnect connector plug from unit.

4. Connect plug to new sealed beam unit, place unit in position and install retaining ring. Tighten retaining screws securely.
5. Hook the headlamp rim at the top and pull it down into place. Install and tighten the clamp screw.

SEALED BEAM HEADLAMP OVERHAUL

1. Remove rim, retaining ring and sealed beam unit as instructed above.
2. Remove the vertical and horizontal adjusting screws and unhook the four coil springs attaching the sub-body. Remove sub-body assembly.
3. Remove the screws attaching the lamp housing to fender and remove lamp housing.
4. Disconnect the light socket wires from the junction block and ground. Work wire through grommet and remove socket and wire assembly. Replace all damaged parts.
5. Work the light socket wires through grommet and connect them to their respective terminals.
6. Place lamp housing in position and install the attaching screw. Place sub-body in position and hook up the springs. Install the two adjusting screws and tighten to approximately their original adjustment.
7. Connect sealed beam unit to lamp socket and install sealed beam unit, retaining ring and attaching screws.
8. Focus the headlamp beam according to instructions under "Headlamp Beam Adjustment."

LIGHTING SWITCH REPLACEMENT

1. Disconnect all wires from the lighting switch and either tag them for correct installation or make sure you can properly connect them by reference to Figure 52.

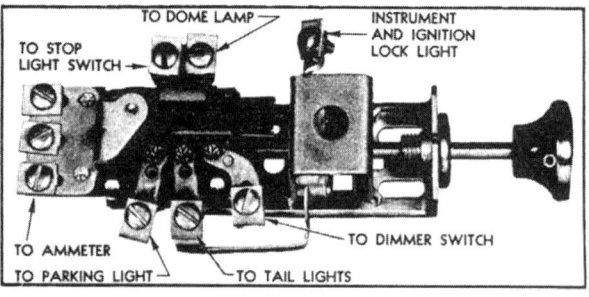

Fig. 52—Light Switch Wiring Identification

2. Depress the switch shaft retainer, (fig. 53) and remove the knob and shaft.
3. Remove the switch retaining nut and the switch assembly.

ELECTRICAL SYSTEM 12-37

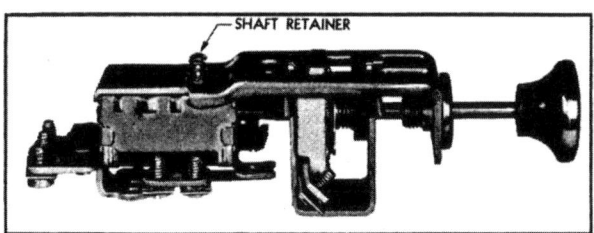

Fig. 53—Light Switch Shaft Retainer

4. Place the new switch in position and install the retaining nut.

5. Push the switch knob and shaft assembly into position so that the retainer seats in the groove.

   CAUTION: Do not depress retainer button during this operation.

6. Connect all wires to the lighting switch terminals according to the notations made when disconnecting or according to connections shown in Figure 52.

7. Check operation of all lights.

STOPLIGHT SWITCH REPLACEMENT

1. Disconnect the wires from the two terminals at top of switch.
2. Remove screws attaching switch to underside of toe pan and remove switch.
3. Place new switch in position and install the attaching screws.
4. Connect the wires to switch terminals and test stoplight operation.

DIMMER SWITCH REPLACEMENT

1. Disconnect the three wires from the switch noting the wire removed from each terminal.
2. Remove the screws that attach the switch to cowl brace and remove switch.
3. Place new switch in position and install the attaching screws securely.
4. Connect the wires to their respective switch terminals and test the switch operation.

PARKING LIGHT SERVICE

1. Remove the two screws attaching the parking lamp door with lens and remove the door assembly.
2. Remove bulb assembly.
3. To remove parking light body, remove the attaching stud nuts from under fender and disconnect wire from junction block.
4. Place lamp body in position and install attaching stud nuts. Run the wire through cut-outs in radiator side baffle and connect to junction block.
5. Install bulb, place lamp door with lens in position and install the attaching screws. Test light operation.

TAIL AND STOP LIGHT SERVICE

The tail and stop lamp bulbs may be changed by removing the lamp door attaching screws and lamp door.

TROUBLES AND REMEDIES
ELECTRICAL
BATTERY AND STARTING SYSTEM

Symptom and Probable Cause	Probable Remedy
Slow Engine Cranking Speed	
Partially discharged battery	Charge or change battery and determine cause of battery condition
Low capacity battery	Cycle battery to improve capacity or replace it
Faulty battery cell	Replace battery
Loose or corroded terminals	Clean and tighten terminal
Under capacity cables	Replace battery cables
Burned starter switch contacts	Replace switch
Internal starting motor trouble	Overhaul starting motor
Heavy oil or other engine trouble causing undue load	Make necessary repairs to engine
Starter Engages but Will Not Crank Engine	
Partially discharged battery	Charge or change battery
Faulty battery cells	Replace battery
Bent armature shaft or damaged drive mechanism	Overhaul starter
Faulty armature or fields	Overhaul starter
Faulty starter switch	Replace switch
Starter Will Not Run	
Battery fully discharged	Replace or charge battery
Disconnected battery cables	Replace faulty cables
Shorted or open starter circuit	Make necessary repairs

GENERATING SYSTEM

Symptom and Probable Cause	Probable Remedy
Low Charging Rate	
Fully charged battery and low charging rate	This is a normal condition with a fully charged battery
Fan belt slipping	Replace or adjust belt
Generator commutator dirty	Clean commutator
High resistance in charging circuit	Check charging circuit progressively and make necessary repairs to remove high resistance
Too low voltage setting of voltage regulator unit	Adjust voltage regulator
Oxidized voltage regulator points	Clean and adjust points
Partially shorted field coils	Overhaul generator
High Charging Rate with Fully Charged Battery	
Voltage regulator setting too high	Adjust voltage regulator
Voltage regulator points stuck	Clean and adjust points and readjust regulator
Regulator unit improperly grounded	Remove regulator and clean connections. Readjust regulator
Generator field circuit to regulator short circuited	Test to locate short circuit and make necessary repairs
Shunt field circuit short circuited within regulator	Replace regulator
Low Battery and No Charging Rate	
Fan belt broken or loose	Replace or tighten fan belt
Charging circuit open between regulator and battery	Locate open circuit and make necessary repairs
Cut-out voltage winding open circuited	Replace regulator unit
Corroded points in current and voltage regulator	Clean points and readjust regulator
Open circuit between generator and regulator	Locate open circuit and make necessary repairs to wiring
Internal trouble in generator	Overhaul generator

ELECTRICAL SYSTEM 12-39

Symptom and Probable Cause   **Probable Remedy**

IGNITION SYSTEM

Engine Will Not Start
(See Starting and Fuel System Troubles)

Symptom and Probable Cause	Probable Remedy
Ignition switch not turned on	Turn switch on
Weak battery	Charge battery
Excessive moisture on high tension wiring or spark plugs	Dry parts, coat with PIB
Cracked distributor cap	Replace cap
Faulty coil or condenser	Replace faulty unit
Coil to distributor high tension wire not in place	Properly install wire
Loose connections or broken wire in low tension circuit	Tighten or replace wires
Improperly adjusted or faulty distributor points	Clean and adjust or replace points

Hard Starting
(See Starting and Fuel System Troubles)

Symptom and Probable Cause	Probable Remedy
Faulty or improperly set spark plugs	Clean and adjust or replace spark plugs
Improperly adjusted or faulty distributor points	Clean or replace and adjust points
Loose connections in primary circuit	Tighten loose connections
Worn or oil soaked high tension wires	Replace high tension wires
Low capacity condenser	Replace condenser
Low capacity coil	Replace coil
Faulty distributor cap or rotor	Replace faulty part

Engine Misfires

Symptom and Probable Cause	Probable Remedy
Dirty or worn spark plugs	Clean or replace plugs
Damaged insulation on high tension wires or wires disconnected	Connect or replace wires
Distributor cap cracked	Replace cap
Poor cylinder compression	See Engine Troubles
Improper distributor point adjustment	Adjust distributor points

LIGHTING CIRCUITS

Sympton and Probable Cause   **Probable Remedy**

Headlights Dim (Engine idling or shut off)

Symptom and Probable Cause	Probable Remedy
Partly discharged battery	Charge battery
Defective cells in battery	Replace battery
High resistance in light circuit	Check headlight circuit including ground connections. Make necessary repairs.
Faulty sealed beam units	Replace defective units

Headlights Dim (engine running above idle)

Symptom and Probable Cause	Probable Remedy
High resistance in light circuit	Check lighting circuit including ground connections. Make necessary repairs.
Faulty sealed beam units	Replace defective units
Faulty voltage control unit	Test voltage control and generator. Make necessary repairs

Lights Flicker

Symptom and Probable Cause	Probable Remedy
Loose connections or damaged wires in lighting circuit	Tighten connections and check for damaged wiring
Light wiring insulation damaged producing momentary short	Check light wiring and replace or tape damaged wires

All Lights Operate Intermittently

Symptom and Probable Cause	Probable Remedy
Overload or short circuit in the lighting circuit	Check wiring in all circuits in use at the time for short circuits Make necessary corrections.

Symptom and Probable Cause	Probable Remedy
Tail and/or Stoplight Will Not Light	
Fuse burned out	Check for short and replace fuse
Burned out bulb	Replace bulb
Wires broken, disconnected or loose, or poorly grounded lamp body	Make necessary repairs and tighten all connections
All Lights—Will Not Light	
Discharged battery	Recharge battery and correct cause
Loose connection between battery and light switch	Tighten connections
Defective circuit breaker or light switch	Replace light switch

GASOLINE GAUGE

Symptom and Probable Cause	Probable Remedy
Gauge Shows Empty at All Times	
Tank unit shorted	Replace unit
Wire from dash unit to tank unit shorted	Replace wire or repair short
Float stuck in empty position	Replace tank unit
Dash unit improperly grounded on instrument panel	Properly ground dash unit
Gauge Shows Full at All Times	
Tank unit burned out	Replace tank unit
Wire between units disconnected or broken	Connect or replace wire
High resistance in wire between units	Clean connections and terminals
Float stuck in full position	Replace tank unit
Gauge Does Not Register Accurately (within normal limits)	
Bent hand on dash unit	Replace unit or straighten hand
High resistance in circuit	Check and correct circuit
Partial short in circuit	Correct cause of short
Loose electrical connections	Tighten connections at dash unit, tank unit and connector

HORNS

Symptom and Probable Cause	Probable Remedy
Will Not Blow	
Loose connections or broken wire	Tighten loose connection or replace broken wire
Horn button not making contact	Adjust horn button contact
Horn improperly adjusted or faulty	Adjust or replace horn
Horn Tone Poor	
Horn improperly adjusted	Adjust horn

SPECIFICATIONS

Battery
Make — Delco-Remy
Plates per cell
  School Bus — 19
  All Others — 15
Ampere hour capacity (at 20 hour rate)
  School Bus — 125
  All others — 100
Voltage — 6
Specific gravity (fully charged) — 1.275 to 1.300
Specific gravity (fully discharged) — 1.150

Starting Motor
Make — Delco-Remy
Brush spring tension — 24 to 28 ounces

Generator
Make — Delco-Remy
Brush spring tension — 24 to 28 ounces

Regulator
Make — Delco-Remy
Voltage regulator armature air gap — .075" to .085"
Voltage regulator voltage setting — 7.0 to 7.7 volts, 7.4 volts preferred
Current regulator amperage setting — 32 to 40 amperes, 36 amperes preferred
Current regulator armature air gap — .075" to .085"
Cut-out relay points close (hot) — 5.9 to 6.8 volts, 6.4 volts preferred
Cut-out relay points open (reverse flow) — 0 to 4 amperes
Cut-out relay armature air gap — .020"
Cut-out relay point opening — .020"

Distributor
Make — Delco-Remy
Type of advance — Centrifugal
Firing order — 1-5-3-6-2-4
Breaker point gap — New 018"-.024", Old .015"-.022"
Breaker arm spring tension — 17-21 oz.
Ignition timing — 5° B.U.D.C.

Condenser
Capacity — .2 microfarad

Spark Plugs
Make — AC
Type — AC-44-5 COM
Size — 14 mm
Plug gap — .035"
Recommended torque — 20 to 25 ft. lb.

Ignition Coil
Make — Delco-Remy

Lamp Bulb Data

Location	Candle Power	Bulb No.
Headlamp (sealed beam)	45-35 watts	Sealed Beam
Parking Lamp	3	63
Tail Lamp	3	63
Stop Lamp	21	1129
Panel Models (tail and stop lamp)	21-3	1154
Ignition Lock Lamp	2	55
Headlamp Beam Indicator	1	51
Instrument Cluster	2	55
Dome Lamp	15	87

SERVICE NEWS REFERENCE

Month	Page No.	Subject

1952 SUPPLEMENT

1952 SUPPLEMENT

to the

1948-51 CHEVROLET TRUCK SHOP MANUAL

FOREWORD

This supplement has been prepared for use with the 1948-51 Truck Shop Manual and covers major changes for the 1952 product along with recent changes that affect the servicing of models prior to 1952.

Unless otherwise stated within the Supplement, the information in the 1948-51 Truck Shop Manual that applies to 1951 models, will also apply to 1952 models.

CHEVROLET MOTOR DIVISION
GENERAL MOTORS CORPORATION
DETROIT, MICHIGAN

Copyright—1952
Chevrolet Motor Division
General Motors Corporation

Printed U.S.A.

SECTION INDEX

Section	NAME	Page
0	LUBRICATION	3
1	CAB AND BODY	3
4	REAR AXLE	6
5	BRAKES	9
6	ENGINE ASSEMBLY	12
7	TRANSMISSION	15

Reprinted with Permission of General Motors Corp

1952
LOAD CAPACITY CHART

TYPE	MODEL SERIES	MODEL WHEEL-BASE	NOMINAL RATING	GROSS VEHICLE WEIGHT	MINIMUM TIRES AND EQUIPMENT TIRE SIZE AND PLY RATING FRONT	MINIMUM TIRES AND EQUIPMENT TIRE SIZE AND PLY RATING REAR	EQUIPMENT
SEDAN DELIVERY	1508 KJ	115		§ 4000	6.70-15-4	6.70-15-4	
				4100	6.70-15-6	6.70-15-6	
LIGHT DUTY	3100 KP	116	½ Ton	§ 4200	6.00-16-6	6.00-16-6	
				* 4800	6.00-16-6	6.50-16-6	
MEDIUM DUTY	3600 KR	125¼	¾ Ton	§ 5400	15-6	15-6	
				* 5800	7.00-17-6	7.00-17-8	2-stage, 8-leaf rear spring
	3742 KT	125¼	¾ Ton	§ 6200	15-6	15-6	
				6600	7.00-17-6	7.00-17-6	
				* 7000	7.00-17-6	7.00-17-8	
	3800 KS	137	1 Ton	§ 6200	7.00-17-6	7.00-17-8	
				7000	7.00-17-6	7.50-17-8	
				* 8800	7.00-18-8	7.00-18-8 Dual	2-stage, 8-leaf rear spring and auxiliary, and hydrovac
	3942 KU	137	1 Ton	§ 6700	7.00-17-6	7.00-17-6	
				7100	7.00-17-6	7.00-17-8	Double acting rear shock absorbers
				7500	7.00-17-6	7.50-17-8	Above plus stabilizer
				*10000	7.00-18-8	7.00-18-8 Dual	Above plus 2-stage, 8-leaf rear spring and auxiliary, and hydrovac
HEAVY DUTY	4100 VJ	137	1½ Ton	§10000	6.50-20-6	6.50-20-6 Dual	
				11000	6.50-20-6	7.00-20-8 Dual	
	4400 VK	161		12500	6.50-20-6	7.00-20-10 Dual	11-leaf rear spring & aux., hydrovac, and on 4100, heavy duty frame
				*14000	7.00-20-8	7.50-20-8 Dual	Above plus 8-leaf front spring
	5100S VPS / 5400S VRS / 5700S VSS	110 / 134 / 158	1½ Ton Special Cab-Over-Engine	§14000	7.50-20-8	7.50-20-8 Dual	
	6100S VVS / 6400S VWS / 6500S VYS	137 / 161 / 179	1½ Ton Special Conventional	*15000	7.50-20-8	8.25-20-10 Dual	
	5100 VP / 5400 VR / 5700 VS	110 / 134 / 158	2 Ton Cab-Over-Engine	§14000	7.50-20-8	7.50-20-8 Dual	
	6100 VV / 6400 VW / 6500 VY	137 / 161 / 179	2 Ton Conventional	*16000	7.50-20-8	8.25-20-10 Dual	
SCHOOL BUS CHASSIS	3802 Plus RPO 329 KS	137	16 Pupils	*§7600	7.50-17-8	7.50-17-10	9-leaf rear spring & hydrovac
	4502 VL	161	30 Pupils	§10500	6.50-20-6	6.50-20-6 Dual	
			36 Pupils	*12000	6.50-20-6	7.00-20-8 Dual	
	6702 VX	199	42 Pupils	§13500	7.50-20-8	7.50-20-8 Dual	
			48-54 Pupils	*16000	7.50-20-8	8.25-20-10 Dual	

*A plate is supplied with each vehicle showing chassis number and maximum Gross Vehicle Weight (GVW). The maximum GVW rating includes the truck chassis with lubricants, water and full tank or tanks of fuel, plus the weight of the cab or driver's compartment, body, and special chassis and body equipment, and payload. These GVW ratings are reduced per above table when tires and/or equipment of lesser capacity are used. Series KJ plate shows no GVW.

§Base trucks, tires shown included in base price.

Extra ply rating and/or oversize tires and equipment are available with no increase in gross vehicle weight rating.

SECTION 0

GENERAL LUBRICATION

FRONT WHEELS

Front wheels of ½, ¾ and 1 ton trucks are equipped with ball bearings. Front wheels of the 1½ and 2 ton trucks are equipped with barrel type roller bearings.

Lubrication of both types should be with a high melting point front wheel bearing lubricant.

CAUTION: Long fibrous or viscous type lubricants must not be used to lubricate front wheel bearings

STARTING MOTOR

Starting motor end frames are equipped with oil-less bearings and do not require lubrication.

HYDROVAC

The Hydrovac unit is equipped with a lubrication plug in the closed end of the shell approximately ½" from the bottom of the cylinder. One ounce of Bendix Vacuum Cylinder Oil or Delco Shock Absorber Fluid should be added at 10,000 mile intervals or each six month period, especially prior to the start of cold weather.

SECTION 1

CAB AND BODY

DOOR VENTILATOR ASSEMBLY

The door ventilator assembly should be removed from the truck door if it is necessary to replace the frame assembly with division channel, the ventilator frame weatherstrip, or the ventilator glass channel.

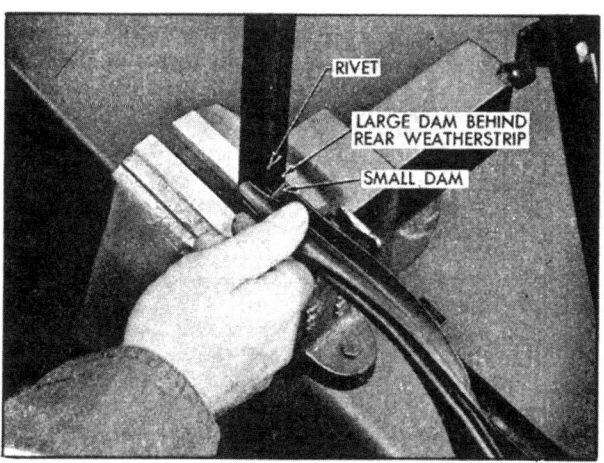

Figure 1

Disassembly

1. Drill out the ventilator hinge pivot rivet (use a ⅛" diameter drill).
2. Remove the hexagon nut, spring, and washers from "T" shaft of ventilator glass assembly.
3. Remove the ventilator glass assembly from ventilator frame.
4. Drill out the lower rivet (fig. 1) attaching the ventilator glass rear weatherstrip assembly to the division channel (use a ⅛" drill).
5. Remove the frame weatherstrip from "clinched" channel of ventilator frame.

Assembly

1. Lubricate bottom section of frame weatherstrip with soap or rubber lubricant and then proceed as follows:
    a. At the lower end, rotate the ventilator frame weatherstrip into the "clinched" channel of the frame as shown in Figure 1. Carefully place the larger of the two rubber dams on the end of the weather-

3

strip behind the rear weatherstrip assembly. The small dam goes in front.

> CAUTION: The ventilator glass rear weatherstrip assembly is a metal and rubber molded assembly and care must be taken so as not to bend this weatherstrip.

    b. Correctly position the frame weatherstrip at its lower end and then proceed to install the complete weatherstrip around the ventilator frame.
2. Install a new tubular rivet, Part No. 443587, attaching the rear weatherstrip to the division channel.
3. Apply a seal of 3-M Weatherstrip Adhesive between the rear weatherstrip assembly and the frame weatherstrip ends both top and bottom. Any openings between the two weatherstrips are to be filled with Weatherstrip Adhesive to be effective against the entrance of water at top and bottom.
4. Replace the ventilator glass assembly in ventilator frame as follows:
    a. Install the ventilator glass assembly and replace washers, spring and hexagon nut on "T" shaft.
    b. Install a new ventilator hinge pivot rivet, Part No. 3695553.
    c. Check operation of ventilator and adjust hexagon nut to obtain proper tension of spring on ventilator "T" shaft.
5. Install ventilator assembly in door.

DOOR HANDLES AND LOCKS

The 1952 Chevrolet trucks are equipped with stationary type door handles with a push button type latch control in each handle (fig. 2). The outside key lock is in the right hand push button.

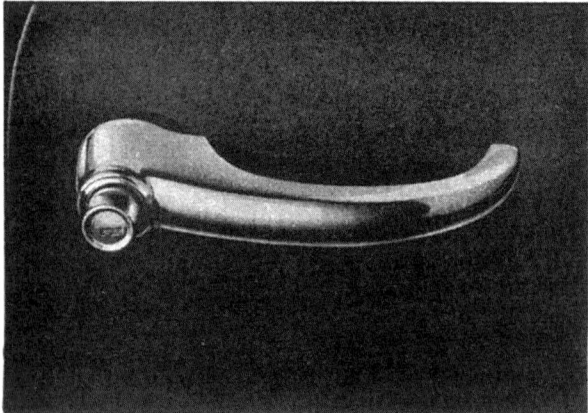

Figure 2

Outside Handles—Replace

1. Remove the inner door and window regulator handles and fiber washers.

NOTE: These handles are retained to the shafts by set screws over which a finish head screw is installed.

2. Remove the trim panel and sponge spacer washers.
3. Raise the window and then working through the access hole in door inner panel, remove two screws and lock washers attaching door handle to door outer panel.
4. Remove door handle with push button latch control and door handle front and rear gaskets.
5. To install, place door handle with push button latch control and front and rear gaskets in position, then install attaching screws.
6. Replace trim panel and inner door and window regulator handles.

Lock Cylinder—Replace

1. Remove the door outside handle.
2. Remove the lock retaining snap ring, then remove stop washer, spring and spring seat, noting relative positions of the stop washer and spring seat.
3. Remove the lock cylinder and push button shaft assembly.

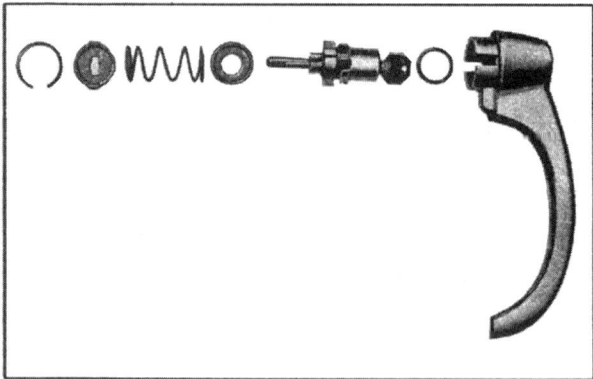

Figure 3

4. Remove the handle sealing ring. Figure 3 shows the handle disassembled.
5. If necessary, the lock cylinder, lock cylinder housing and push button shaft may be disassembled as follows:

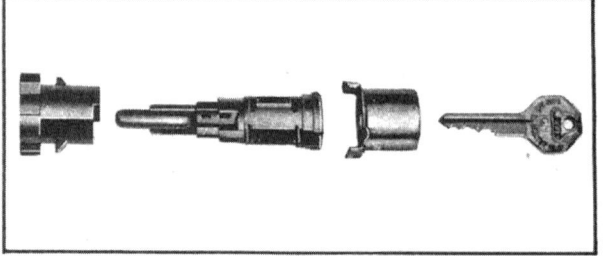

Figure 4

a. Bend the ears of the push button cap sufficiently to disengage cap from cylinder housing. Disassemble cap, cylinder housing and lock cylinder. Figure 4 shows the lock disassembled.

b. Repair or replace the lock cylinder.

c. Assemble lock cylinder into housing and replace the push button cap, rebending ears to original position.

6. Install handle sealing ring, lock cylinder and push button shaft assembly, spring seat, spring, stop washer and retainer.

7. Assemble door outside handle to door.

Lock Assembly—Replace

1. Remove inside control handles, trim panel and garnish molding.

2. Remove the door glass upper run channel and raise door window to closed position.

3. Remove screws which secure the run channel guide to the door pillar and lift out the guide.

4. Remove screws attaching remote control to door inner panel and swing the remote control downward to free the connecting link from rectangular tang of door lock.

Figure 5

5. Remove the three screws "A" attaching the lock assembly to the door pillar facing (fig. 5) and remove the lock assembly through the access hole in door inner panel.

6. The door lock spring (fig. 6) is the only component part of the lock assembly that is serviceable. It may be removed by lifting the spring off the lower anchor and then working the spring off the upper anchor a coil at a time. Replace with a new spring, working it into position.

7. Make sure the door lock that is to be installed is lubricated properly with Lubriplate or equivalent. Install the lock in the door, install and tighten attaching screws securely.

8. Connect the remote control connecting link to the door lock, place the remote control in position on the door and install three attach-

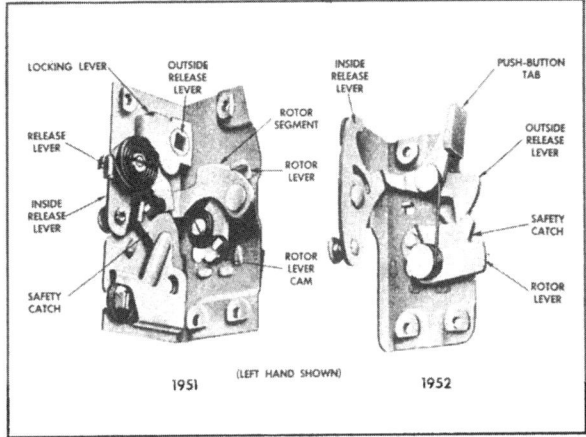

Figure 6

ing screws loosely, adjust the remote control to provide full travel, then tighten screws securely.

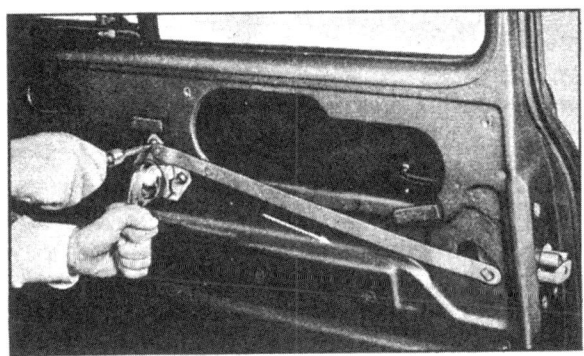

Figure 7

NOTE: To adjust remote control to provide full travel; place remote control handle in the fully locked position, then move remote control toward lock (fig. 7) to remove all play and tighten screws securely.

9. Replace run channel guide and then the door glass upper run channel making sure to engage spring clip.

10. Install trim panel, inside control handles and garnish molding.

DOOR STRIKER PLATE

Raised beads on the back of the striker plate and on the pillar facing and serrations on both the front and back of the striker plate spacers, coupled with movable anchor plates in the pillar, allow for "in and out" or "up and down" adjustment for a close fit of the door on the lock side.

The striker plate spacer must be assembled so that the vertical serrations on the spacer are toward the lock pillar and mate with the vertical bead on the pillar facing (fig. 8). Likewise, the horizontal serrations must be toward the front so that they match the horizontal bead of the striker plate.

Adjustment

The striker should be positioned so that the bottom of rotor housing just makes contact with the corresponding surface on the striker without lifting the door and so that the door outer panel is flush with the cab outer panel.

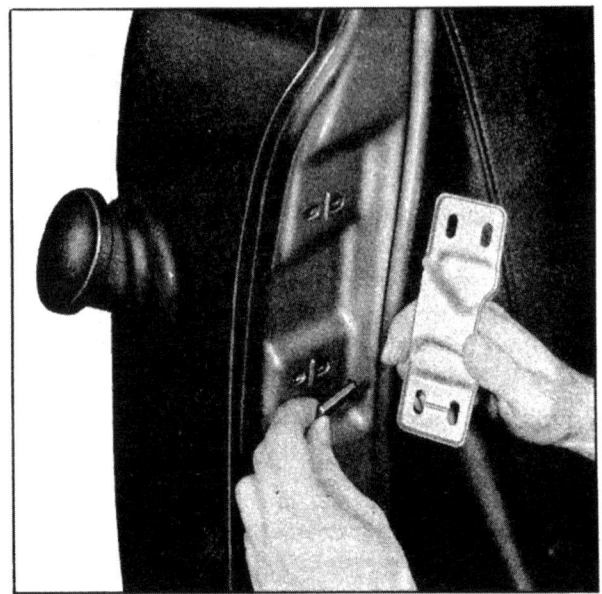

Figure 8

SECTION 4

REAR AXLE

DIFFERENTIAL CARRIER AND TORQUE TUBE ASSEMBLY

The depth of the bore in the differential carrier against which the pinion double row bearing seats has been reduced .015" on ½ ton truck models. This necessitates a change in the shim set-up for adjusting the pinion depth in ring gear. Although the same number and thickness shims are available, (namely .012", .015", .018" and .021"), only one shim is used between the double row bearing and the bottom of the bore in the carrier instead of the two shims which were formerly used.

When installing a new ring gear and pinion in an axle equipped with the new differential carrier and torque tube assembly, one .018" shim should be used as a starting point. Checking the tooth pattern according to instructions under, "Adjusting Ring Gear and Pinion," will establish any changes in the shimming that may be necessary to procure proper pinion depth adjustment.

The new differential carrier and torque tube assemblies went into production as a mid-season change in 1951 starting with rear axle serial number JE608. New service assemblies carry a different part number and are identified by a band of yellow paint around the torque tube. Mechanics should remember that only one shim is to be used when assembling the pinion and propeller shaft in a differential carrier assembly of serial number JE608 or later, or in an assembly identified by a band of yellow paint.

ADJUSTING RING GEAR AND PINION

Proper ring gear and pinion adjustment is important if the rear axle assembly is to provide quiet and trouble-free operation. The following procedure is recommended for checking gear tooth bearing, either before disassembly to determine whether improper adjustment is the cause of noisy operation, or following the installation of a new gear set.

Complaints of rear axle noise, which can nearly always be contributed to improper adjustment, can be placed in three general classifications:

1. DRIVE NOISE which is most pronounced on constant acceleration through the speed range of 15 to 45 M.P.H.

2. COAST NOISE which is most pronounced when the truck is allowed to coast through the speed range from 45 to 15 M.P.H. with the clutch engaged and throttle closed.

3. FLOAT NOISE which is most pronounced while holding the truck speed constant at intervals between 15 and 45 M.P.H.

Drive, coast and float noises will be very rough and irregular if the differential or pinion shaft bearings are rough, worn or loose.

Service personnel should refer to Figure 9 to familiarize themselves with the terms used in referring to the different parts of the gear tooth. The large end of the tooth is called the "heel" and the small end the "toe." Also, the top of the tooth, which is the part above the pitch line, is called the "face," while the part below the pitch line is called the "flank." The space between the meshed teeth is referred to as "backlash."

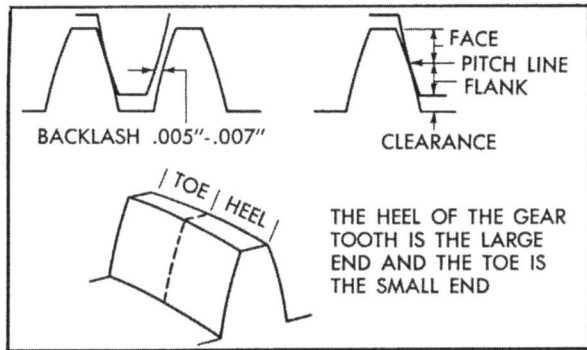

Figure 9

Adjustment

1. Raise rear of truck and place on stand jacks. Then, drain and flush rear axle housing and leave housing cover off.
2. Wipe ring gear and pinion dry with a clean cloth. Paint ring gear teeth lightly and evenly with red lead of suitable consistency.
3. Raise rear of truck and place on stand jacks. Then, apply parking brake to provide a heavy drag at the rear wheels.
4. Run engine slowly with transmission in first gear and then in reverse for a few seconds.
5. Stop the engine and compare the marks produced on the gear teeth with the marks shown in Figure 10. Tooth pattern "A" provides the ideal bearing for quietness and long life.
6. If the pattern shows a toe contact "B," it indicates not enough backlash. To correct, move the ring gear away from the pinion by loosening left-hand differential adjusting nut and tightening right-hand adjusting nut.

NOTE: Make adjustment one notch at a time, repeat check with red lead and continue adjustment until tooth contact appears as in "A."

7. If the pattern shows a heel contact "C," it indicates too much backlash. Make correction as in step No. 6, however, loosen right hand differential adjusting nut and tighten left hand adjusting nut to move ring gear toward pinion.
8. If the pattern shows a high face contact "D," it indicates that the pinion is too far out, that is, too far toward the front of the car. To correct, remove the differential carrier assembly and place in a vise or on a bench. Remove differential bearing caps and remove differential assembly. Remove three tapered bearing retainer screws and tap splined end of propeller shaft allowing pinion shaft to slide out. Be careful in removing the shaft that the metal shim or shims between ball bearing and carrier are not lost. Use a pair of micrometers to determine shim thickness.

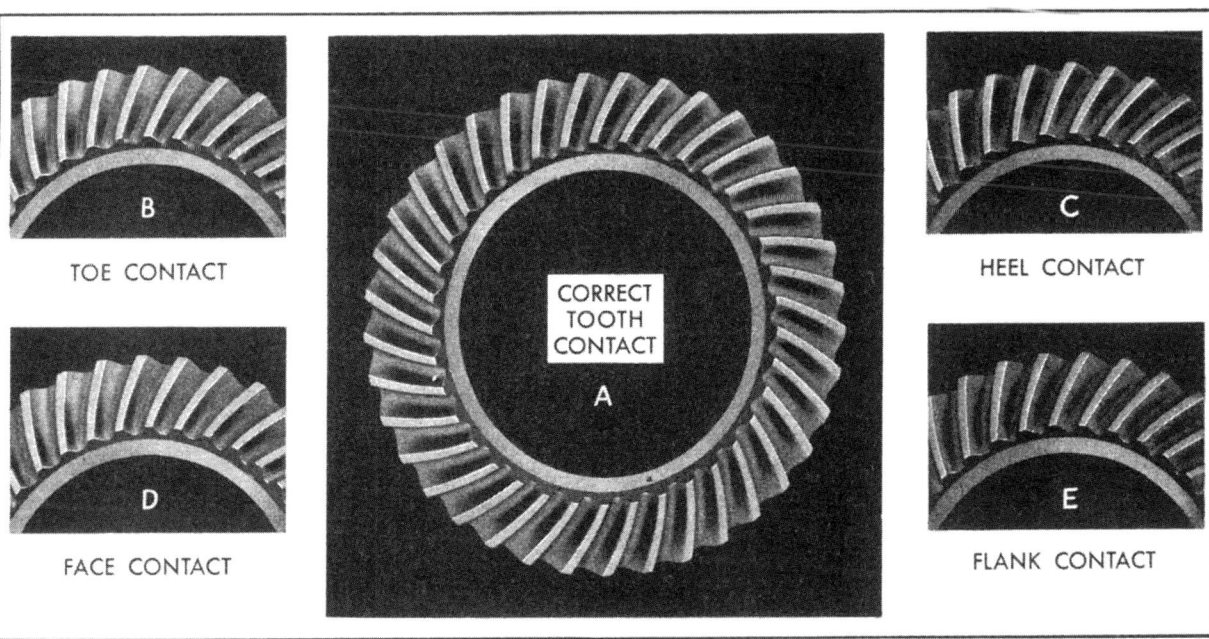

Figure 10

NOTE: Late model 1951 and all 1952 models have a shallower bore into which the pinion double row bearing seats. These models, therefore, use only one shim between the bearing and the bottom of the bore in the carrier, whereas the 1949-50 and early 1951 models used two shims.

Then, use a new shim or combination of shims to provide .006" increase in shim thickness. Reassemble and repeat check with red lead and continue adjustment until tooth contact appears as in "A."

NOTE: As a means of adjusting pinion depth, shims are available in thicknesses of .012", .015", .018" and .021".

9. If the pattern shows a flank contact "E," it indicates that the pinion is in too far. To correct, proceed as outlined in step No. 8 and select a new shim or shim combination to provide .006" reduction in shim thickness. Reassemble and repeat check with red lead and continue adjustment until tooth contact appears as in "A."
10. In making pinion adjustments, be sure backlash is correct before retesting with red lead for tooth pattern. Moving the pinion in reduces backlash and moving it out increases it.
11. When proper tooth contact is obtained, wipe red lead from gears and carrier with cloth moistened with clean gasoline or kerosene. Wipe out housing with clean cloth.
12. Pour a liberal quantity of rear axle lubricant on gears and bearings and turn rear wheels to work lubricant onto all surfaces.
13. Install housing cover using a new gasket, coating bolt threads with Permatex to avoid oil leaks.
14. Remove truck from stand jacks and fill differential carrier with proper quantity of S.A.E. 90 "Multi-Purpose" gear lubricant.

DIFFERENTIAL SIDE AND PINION GEARS

Starting with 1952, a change is being made in the method of cutting differential side and pinion gear teeth used in the 2-ton truck rear axles. The new gears are known as revacycle type and are of the same type as used on Chevrolet passenger cars and in the 2-speed rear axle since 1946. The gears used in all 2 ton truck axles prior to this change and still in effect on ½, ¾, 1 and 1½ ton trucks, are of the involute type.

When making repairs on truck rear axles, it is important that Dealers' parts and service personnel should be able to identify the proper differential gears for the rear axle involved.

By following the instructions given below, the gears may be easily identified:

Differential Side Gear

The differential side gears may be easily distinguished by noting the number of splines in the gear. The revacycle type gear, Part No. 3697746, has 27 splines while the involute type gear, Part No. 3661874, has 16 splines (fig. 11). Both the revacycle type and involute type side gears have 18 teeth.

The revacycle type differential side gear is sufficiently thinner than the involute type to compensate for a .060" thrust washer that is used with it.

NOTE: The revacycle type side gear, Part No. 3697746, for the 2-ton standard rear axle, should not be confused with the revacycle type side gear, Part No. 3698942, used in the late 1951 and 1952, 2-speed rear axle. Although both have 27 splines and fit the same axle shaft, the revacycle side gear, Part No. 3698942, used in the 2-speed axle, has 16 teeth (instead of 18) and is considerably thicker (½ inch).

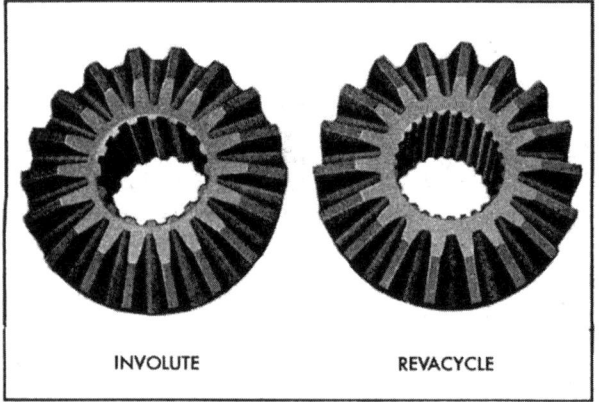

Figure 11

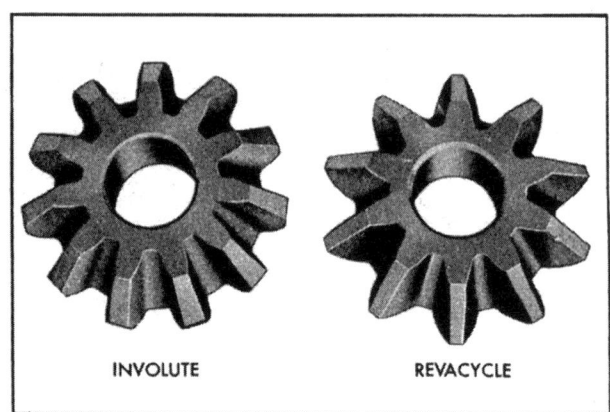

Figure 12

Differential Pinion Gear

The differential pinion gears may be easily distinguished by counting the number of gear teeth. The revacycle type gear, Part No. 3697745, has 10 teeth while the involute type gear, Part No. 370446, has 11 teeth (fig. 12).

The revacycle type pinion gear, like the revacycle side gear, is sufficiently thinner than the involute type to compensate for a .060" thrust washer that is used with it.

NOTE: The revacycle type pinion gear, Part No. 3697745, for the 2-ton standard rear axle should not be confused with the revacycle type pinion gear used in 1946-52, 2-speed rear axle. Pinion gear, Part No. 3682492, used in the 2-speed rear axle, has 9 teeth (instead of 10), is approximately 3/16" thicker, and is equipped with a bronze bushing.

AXLE SHAFT

Due to the change in the number of splines in the differential side gears (27 splines on 1952 models), a new axle shaft is required on 1952, 2-ton trucks and trucks equipped with 2-speed rear axle. These axle shafts are easily identified by the number of splines.

SECTION 5
BRAKES

PARKING BRAKE—1 TON

The pedal operated parking brake (fig. 13) used on 1952, 1 ton truck models is similar to the pedal operated parking brake used since 1948 on ½ and ¾ ton trucks and the adjustment is accomplished in the same manner as for the ¾ ton.

HYDRAULIC BRAKE ADJUSTMENT— ½ TON

The feeler gauge slot formerly incorporated in the brake drum of ½ ton models has been removed. This necessitates a revision in the procedure for major brake adjustment.

Heretofore, when performing a major brake adjustment, the feeler gauge slot was used when making the anchor pin adjustment to assure that proper clearance was obtained between brake drum and top and bottom of brake shoe assemblies. With the elimination of the feeler gauge slot it now becomes increasingly important that the adjustment of this anchor be carefully performed in order to obtain the necessary clearance between shoes and drum.

Adjustment—Front and Rear—Major

The major brake adjustment is intended for use when braking action is unequal, severe or otherwise unsatisfactory. This major adjustment must also be performed after new brake shoes have been installed or when the car has been driven sufficient mileage to warrant thorough inspection and cleaning of the brake assemblies and drums.

1. Raise vehicle and place on stand jacks.
2. Check fluid in master cylinder reservoir and add fluid if necessary.
3. Check brake pedal for free action, proper return to stop and proper clearance at toe board.

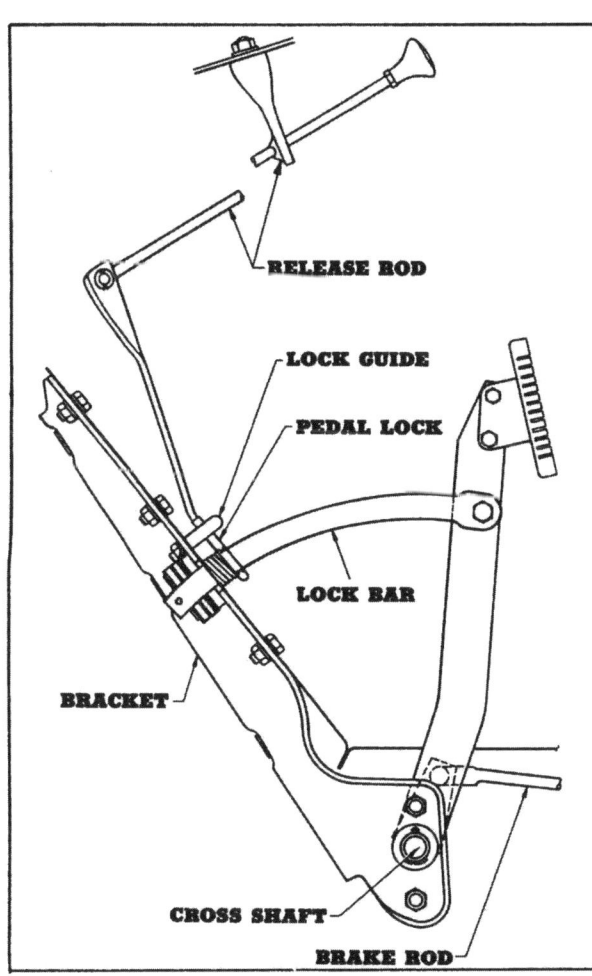

Figure 13

4. Check for proper release of master cylinder or leakage within cylinder by action of brake pedal. If improper release or leakage is found, overhaul master cylinder.

5. Inspect all brake hoses, pipes and connections for evidence of fluid leakage. Tighten any leaking connection, apply heavy pressure to brake pedal to build up pressure in system and recheck connections.

6. Remove all wheels, rear brake drums and front hub and drum assemblies.

    NOTE: Since stops are located on brake backing plates to prevent pistons from leaving wheel cylinders, it is not necessary to install wheel cylinder clamps when drums are removed; however, brake pedal must not be depressed while drums are removed.

7. Clean all dirt out of brake drums being careful not to get dirt in front wheel bearings. Inspect drums and replace or recondition if required.

8. Inspect front wheel bearings and oil seal and, if damaged, replace.

9. Blow all dirt from brake assemblies. Inspect brake linings for excessive wear, oil soaking and embedded foreign particles. If linings are worn excessively or are oil soaked, replace shoes.

10. Carefully pull lower edges of wheel cylinder boots away from cylinders and note whether interior is wet excessively with brake fluid. Excessive fluid at this point indicates leakage past the piston cup, requiring overhaul of wheel cylinder.

    NOTE: A slight amount of fluid is nearly always present and acts as lubricant for the piston.

11. Inspect rear brake flange plates for oil leaks past axle shaft oil seal. If leakage is evident, replace seal.

12. Tighten brake flange plate attaching bolts.

13. Disconnect parking brake cables from cross shaft outer levers.

14. If shoes are not removed for additional work, pry shoes away from brake flange plates and clean all rust and dirt from contact surfaces on shoe and flange plates, using fine emery cloth. Lubricate contact surfaces sparingly with Bendix or Delco brake lubricant or Lubriplate. On rear brakes, sparingly apply the same lubricant to parking brake strut and flange plate boss under the brake cable.

15. Lubricate front wheel bearings, install hub and drum assemblies, adjust wheel bearings and install front wheel and tire assemblies.

16. Install rear brake drums and drum retaining (stamped) nuts and install wheel and tire assemblies. Remove adjusting hole covers from all brake flange plates.

17. At each wheel:

    a. Loosen anchor pin nut just enough so that pin can shift in slotted hole in backing plate.

    NOTE: If nut is loosened too much, the anchor pin will tilt due to pull of brake shoe pull back springs.

    b. Using tool J-4707, turn brake adjusting screw to expand brake shoes until a heavy drag is felt on drum.

    c. Tap anchor pin and backing plate lightly to allow shoes to center in drum. If drag on drum changes, tighten adjusting screw a few more notches and again tap anchor pin and backing plate. Repeat this operation until drag remains constant. Then tighten anchor nut to 60-80 ft.-lbs. torque.

    d. Back off adjusting screw 14 notches and check wheel for freedom from drag, if drag is experienced, repeat operation No. 17. Replace adjusting hole covers.

18. Adjust the parking brakes as outlined under, "Brake Adjustment" on page 5-13, operations 22-28 in the 1948-51 Truck Shop Manual.

BRAKE SHOE PULL BACK SPRINGS—1½ AND 2 TON

The identification and proper installation of the brake shoe pull back springs on the rear brakes of 1951-52, 1½ and 2 ton trucks is of utmost importance for proper operation of these brakes.

Two different springs are used and due to a difference in weight characteristic, it is of prime importance that they be installed in the proper position to eliminate shoe drag (fig. 14). Comparison of the springs will indicate that two are black and two have a green identification. The springs with the green identification are installed with the small hooked end in the large hole in the shoe web, adjacent to each shoe adjusting wheel. Inspection of the two remaining black springs will show a decided difference in the looped ends of the spring. The large loop of the black spring is installed in the small hole in the shoe web at the sliding pivot anchor end. It is imperative that these springs be identified as prescribed and installed carefully using Brake Spring Remover and Replacer KMO 526. Over stressing or stretching of the black spring by installing in any other position than indicated above or installing of the green spring at the anchor pivot ends may result in uneven brake shoe wear due to dragging, and unsatisfactory brake operation.

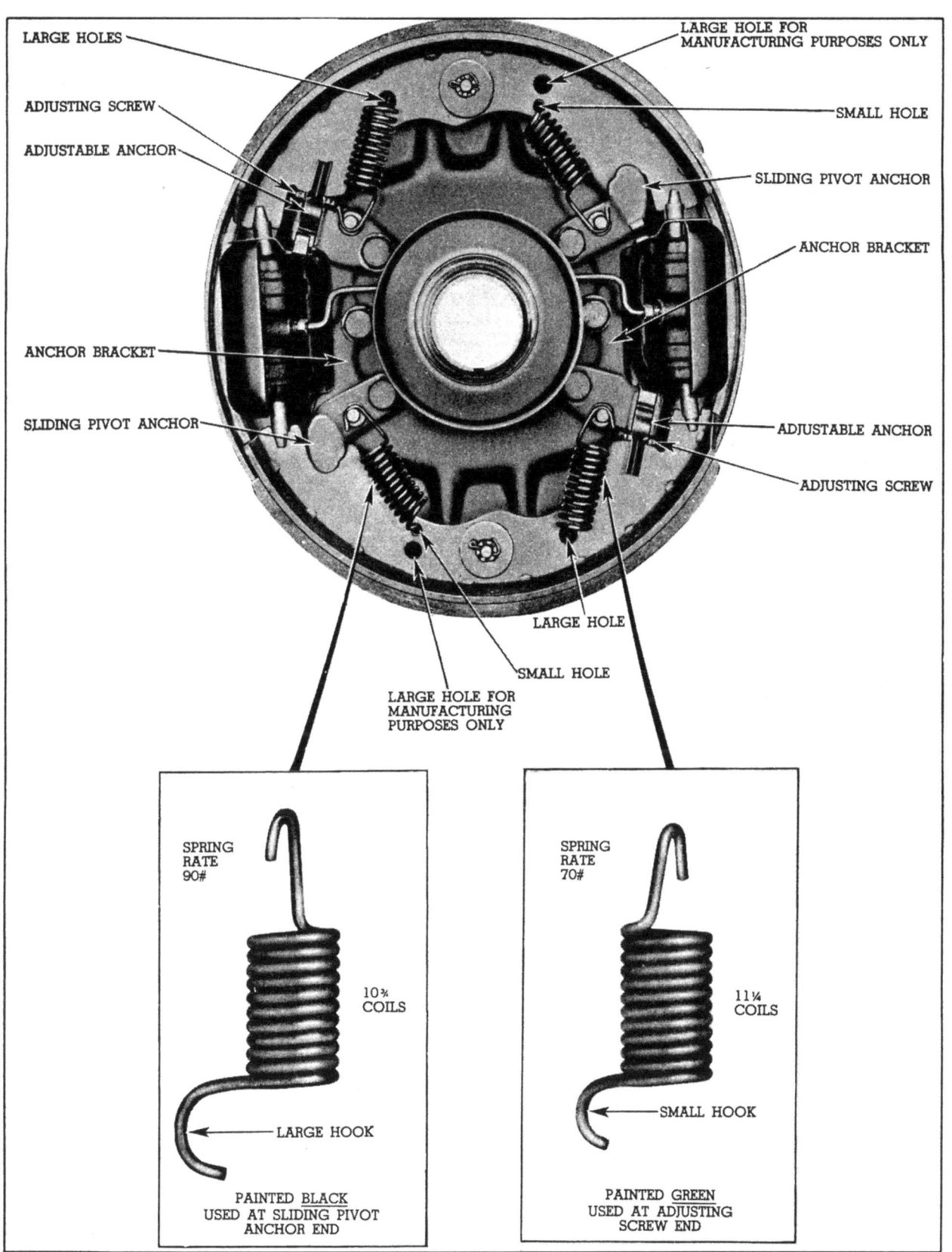

Figure 14

SECTION 6

ENGINE ASSEMBLY

POSITIVE CRANKCASE VENTILATION

Positive crankcase ventilation is used as regular equipment on Forward Control Models and a service unit is available for use on all other truck models 1949-52.

This unit is recommended for all types of operations which are particularly conducive to sludging of the engine, especially with regards to the slow speed multiple stop delivery service or where units are running almost continuously under dust conditions.

When the positive crankcase ventilation system is installed on a Chevrolet engine, an extra quantity of air is permitted to enter the intake manifold below the carburetor. This may in some instances result in a leaner air fuel ratio in the engine than is desirable.

On 1949 models equipped with Carter Carburetors, it is recommended that the one step rich metering rod be installed to enrich the mixture.

On 1950-52 models equipped with GM Model "B" Carburetors, no change in carburetion should be made unless definite evidence of lean mixture is experienced. If this condition is experienced, a one step rich main metering jet may then be installed.

Maintenance

Due to the nature of the materials carried by the system, the valve and pipe are subject to fouling due to sludge and carbon formations. At regular intervals of 10,000 miles or less, depending on operating conditions, the ventilation valve and the tube running from valve to oil filler pipe should be removed, disassembled and cleaned thoroughly.

> NOTE: Under cold weather operating conditions, when vehicles are operated at slow speeds with low engine temperatures, more rapid accumulations of harmful fumes may be present in the engine. Under these conditions of operation, the valve and tube must be cleaned more frequently than specified above.

1. Disassemble the valve (fig. 15) and clean the valve parts with any good cleaning solvent and then blow dry with compressed air. The wiggle pin, which floats loose in the center orifice of the valve, should be snapped out of position by pressing on the end of the pin so that the center orifice of the valve may be cleaned. The pin may then be snapped back into position.

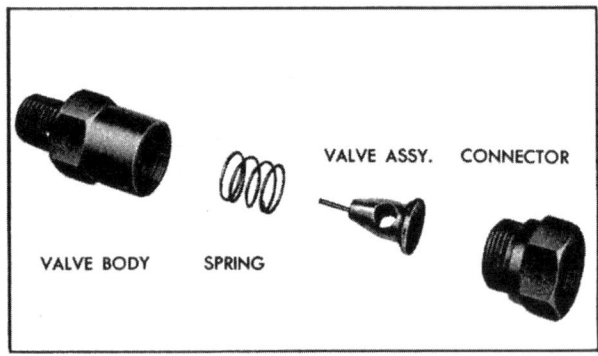

Figure 15

2. Check valve spring for free length which should be approximately $9/16''$. If improper action of the spring is suspected due to spring being distorted, bent, or etched from corrosive action, the valve assembly should be replaced.

3. When reassembling the valve parts, be sure to attach spring on valve by pushing the end coil over ridge and into groove machined just under head of valve. This is important for unless the spring is properly assembled, the valve will not contact the seat squarely and will not close properly. This would cause an improper idle due to the entrance of too much air into the intake manifold.

4. Check valve after assembly to make sure valve does not stick in valve body.

5. Clean the steel ventilator connecting tube and the intake manifold connection with solvent and blow dry with compressed air.

6. Inspect inside of oil filler pipe for sludge accumulations. If necessary, remove oil filler pipe and burn clean.

7. Check the crankcase oil level to insure that it is correctly maintained and not overfilled.

8. Remove oil filler tube and inspect for sludge accumulation, if necessary, burn clean; make sure all holes in baffle inside of oil filler tube are open. Inspect oil filler cap and gasket for sealing, if necessary replace gasket as ventilating system efficiency depends on a sealed cap at this point.

9. Inspect for and correct any air leaks at valve rocker cover, push rod cover, oil filler pipe or ventilator connecting tube and fittings.

CARBURETOR

New, revised GM Model "B" Carburetors have been released for 1952 production and for service use on 1932 to 51 Chevrolet trucks with the exception of C.O.E. and Forward Control models.

The new units released, model usage and parts included in each unit package are listed below in addition to the carburetor units that they supersede.

Part Number (Unit)	Supersedes (Unit)	Truck Model Usage	Parts Included in Kit
7004600	7004039	1932-36, 216 Engine 1941-52, 216 Engine 1941-49, 235 Engine	7004475 Carburetor 3692797 Insulator 839632 Gasket
7004040	7002540	1937-40, 216 Engine	7003966 Carburetor 3692797 Insulator
7004476	7003864	1950-52, 235 Engine	7004476 Carburetor

Unit Part Number 7004600 includes a flange gasket and a heat insulator. When installing this carburetor on past models for which the carburetor is adapted, either the flange gasket or the heat insulator as specified in the instruction leaflet included in the package, must be used to insure proper operation of the carburetor. Both the flange gasket and the insulator provide cutouts in the surface which is placed next to the carburetor flange to provide a vacuum opening for the operation of the power jet in the carburetor.

The flange gasket is a double thickness gasket with the two thicknesses stapled together. This gasket is to be used for replacement when the carburetor is installed on 1932 through 1936 trucks. These models were originally built with a flange gasket and do not use a heat insulator.

The heat insulator is used when the carburetor is installed on 1941 through 1949 trucks with either 216 or 235 engines and on 1950-51 models with 216 engine only.

When installing the carburetor on these models, the old heat insulator together with the inner metal sleeve in the insulator must be removed and replaced by the new heat insulator. The new heat insulator must be installed on the intake manifold so that the two vacuum ports are up and located next to the carburetor flange. The inner metal sleeve that was part of the old insulator is not used with the new insulator.

The flange gasket is not used on those models where the heat insulator is used and conversely the insulator is not used where the flange gasket is used.

Unit Part Number 7004040 which may be installed on all 1937 through 1940 trucks with 216 engine, includes a heat insulator which is used to replace the old heat insulator and inner metal sleeve. Here too, the new insulator must be installed on the intake manifold so that the two vacuum ports are up and located next to the carburetor flange.

Unit Part Number 7004476 is used only on 1950-51 trucks having a 235 engine. This is a stock carburetor, same as production, and the unit package consists only of the carburetor inasmuch as the heat insulator on the job may be reused. If the heat insulator is damaged, a new insulator may be ordered under Part Number 3692799.

Failure to follow the instructions for usage and assembly of the flange gasket or heat insulator as outlined above will result in the power jet being in operation at all times. This will materially enrich the carburetor mixture and result in very poor gasoline economy.

IDENTIFICATION

Inasmuch as the carburetors are similar in exterior appearance, each carburetor will be furnished with a brass tag carrying an embossed part number. This tag will be attached under one of the air horn attaching screws. In addition, each carburetor will have the last two digits of the part number stamped on the air horn, either on the inlet fitting boss or on the dome over the accelerating pump plunger, for identification in case the brass tag is lost.

OPERATION

These new carburetors (fig. 16) are functionally the same as far as operating principles are concerned. For a detailed description of operation of the GM Model "B" Carburetor, refer to the 1948-51 Truck Shop Manual.

Current production carburetors have float bowls and covers of heavier construction than the carburetors used on previous models. In addition, the carburetors incorporate a revised idle system and accelerating pump system. In the new idle system only two calibrated holes are drilled through the cross bar of the air horn. An addi-

"Portions of materials contained herein have been reprinted with permission of General Motors Corporation, Service Technology Group."

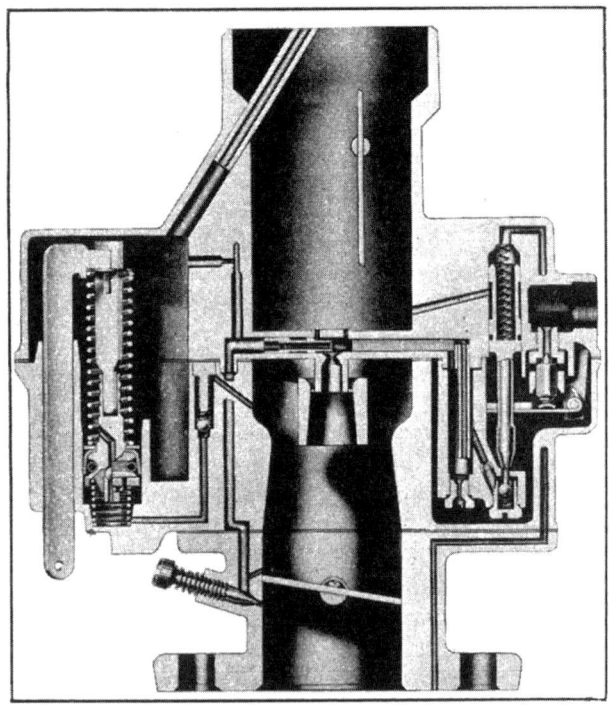

Figure 16

tional cored and drilled passage has been added to the air horn which connects to the present idle passage at one end and vents into the float chamber at the other end. This construction, tends to relieve more rapidly any build up of gasoline vapor in the cross bar and idle passages after a hot engine is shut off. In addition, this passage bleeds air into the mixture allowing for more thorough mixing of fuel and air and resulting in better atomization of fuel.

The accelerating pump system is revised in that the accelerator pump passage up into the cover and the pump jet are discontinued. The new construction consists simply of a metered hole drilled directly between the pump discharge passage and the main venturi section of the carburetor. This construction places the metered discharge hole just slightly above the fuel level in the float chamber and eliminates any lag of fuel injection during quick acceleration. In addition, the accelerator pump inlet ball, screen and passage have been eliminated. The accelerator pump plunger vapor vent now acts as an inlet passage as well as a vapor vent.

SERVICE OPERATIONS

The service operations remain the same as those outlined in the 1948-51 Truck Shop Manual.

COOLING SYSTEM

THERMOSTAT

Two thermostats are now being serviced; they are rated 151° and 181°.

The 151° thermostat is standard and should be used with alcohol antifreeze. The 181° thermostat should be installed when permanent antifreeze is used.

> NOTE: When checking spring dampened thermostats, removed from the car, for opening temperature, a slight chattering of the valve during opening and closing is satisfactory. Under actual operating conditions, the normal engine vibration smooths out the opening and closing action.

RADIATOR CAP

A pressure type radiator cap which regulates cooling system pressure at 3½ to 4½ p.s.i. is now installed on all truck models with the exception of Forward Control.

SECTION 7

TRANSMISSION

SPEEDOMETER DRIVE GEAR—REPLACE

A new service tool for use in removing and replacing the speedometer drive gear on the universal joint flange is now available.

Tool J-4869, Speedometer Gear Remover and Replacer (fig. 17) is for use on all 1948-52 truck models equipped with the 4-speed synchromesh transmission.

The speedometer gear remover and replacer tool should be used as shown in Figure 18 to press the speedometer drive gear off the universal joint flange. Usage of the replacer tool to press the new drive gear into position on universal joint flange is shown in Figure 19.

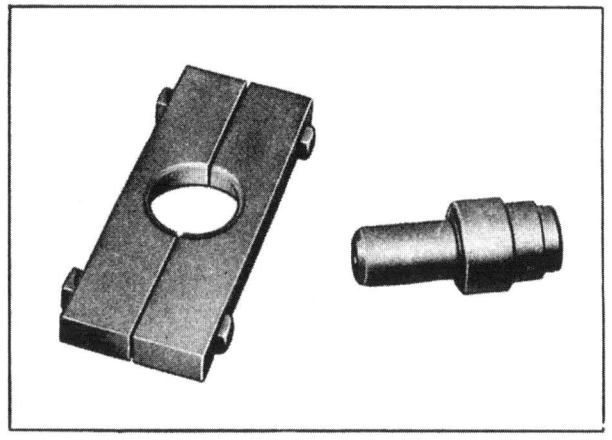

Figure 17

Figure 18

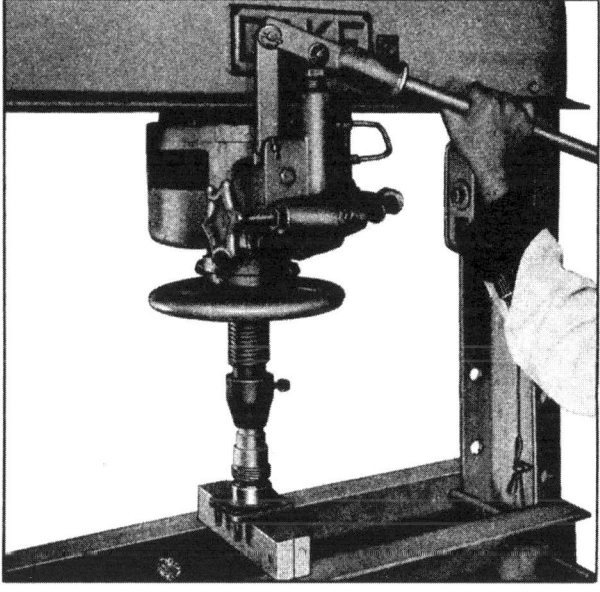

Figure 19